Reading Academic Hebrew

Reading Academic Hebrew

An Advanced Learner's Handbook

Nitza Krohn

BRILL

LEIDEN • BOSTON
2011

This book is printed on acid-free paper.

Library of Congress Cataloging-in-Publication Data

Krohn, Nitza.
  Reading academic Hebrew: an advanced learner's handbook / by Nitza Krohn.
    p. cm.
  Includes bibliographical references and index.
  ISBN 978-90-04-19618-6 (pbk. : alk. paper)
  1. Hebrew language—Readers. 2. Hebrew language—Textbooks for foreign speakers—English. I. Title.

PJ4575.E54.K76 2011
492.4'86—dc22

                                                                              2010053578

ISBN 978 90 04 19618 6

CONTENTS

Part Two: Answers to exercises

Part Three: Texts for reading and translation practice

Appendixes

ACKNOWLEDGEMENTS

I am deeply indebted to my husband, who patiently and meticulously read four successive drafts of the book, asked questions, offered comments, and made many necessary corrections, and to my friend and colleague Ms. Sima Ḥaruv whose trained linguistic eye caught errors and inaccuracies in her careful reading of the final draft. I am also grateful for the advice I have received along the way from my colleague at the Jewish Theological Seminary, Professor Edna Nahshon and from Dr. Emanuel Allon of Beit Berl College in Israel, as well as for the helpful suggestions of the anonymous reviewers. I also wish to thank sincerely the Lucius N. Littauer Foundation for the generous and timely grant that helped defray editing costs. Thanks also go to Karen Cullen, Brill's production team leader. And last, but not least, many thanks to my tireless and dedicated copy editor, Ms. Orna Goldman, for her expert help. Any errors and omissions that may still remain in the book are entirely mine.

LIST OF CHARTS, TABLES AND CHAPTER APPENDIXES

INTRODUCTION

The book has evolved from a graduate level course that I have been teaching at the Jewish Theological Seminary of America for the past fifteen years. It is aimed at students and researchers in various fields of Jewish studies who wish to access seminal and recent Hebrew language scholarship in their area of expertise, as well as those who are preparing to pass the qualifying translation exam mandated by their program.

"Reading Academic Hebrew" can be used as a course textbook, a self-study manual and a reference source for Hebrew teachers. Its purpose is to articulate for the advanced learner of Hebrew the grammatical and semantic knowledge that native Hebrew readers bring to the task of reading complex academic prose. This is accomplished via straightforward exposition of rules and modeling of strategies for solving reading comprehension problems. The linguistic explanations are illustrated with numerous examples from articles and books in the field of Jewish studies and from encyclopedia entries. Occasionally, citations from classical Hebrew sources are also included as illustrative of a given linguistic phenomenon. While some examples have been shortened (to better highlight the rule under the discussion), most are given "as is," that is, no attempt has been made to change or amend their original style. The original spelling (for the most part, plene) has also been retained, but for ease of reading, partial pointing has been added. Each citation is translated into English and many are accompanied by additional explanatory notes.

The Arrangement of the Book

Grammar and Lexis
The main body of the book includes 11 chapters. The first chapter is an overview of word order and sentence structure. Chapters 2 through 6 and Chapter 8 discuss the parts of speech (nouns, pronouns, adjectives, adverbs, verbs and prepositions). Chapter 7 and 9 treat verbless (nominal) sentences and "be" and "have" sentences, respectively. Chapter 10 reviews discontinuous sentence connectors. Chapter 11 focuses on various lexical matters, including foreign (loan) words.

At the beginning of each chapter there is a list of the covered topics and the expected competencies to be acquired; some chapters are introduced by a brief overview.

A "Confusables" section at the end of most chapters is designed to draw attention to distinctions among "look-alikes," namely, similar words and forms that non-native readers often fail to differentiate.

Grammar Practice
Each chapter is accompanied by practice exercises geared for comprehension (rather than production), requiring selection, identification, matching or categorization; some also call for translation.

Each exercise provides the section number for the rule(s) to be reviewed before answering, and the instructions are accompanied by a sample answer. Since the exercise material—like the examples in the main body of the book—is drawn from authentic scholarly texts, glossaries are provided for most exercises. In this way, the learner need not constantly refer to the dictionary and can focus on the grammatical point at issue. Solutions to all exercises are found in the Answers section (Part II of the book).

Practice Texts
Part III of the book contains fifteen sample texts for reading comprehension and translation practice. The texts—arranged by length—have been selected on the basis of their topic (relevance to students majoring in Jewish studies), their (relatively) non-technical content, and their level of difficulty (medium).

The vocabulary support for each text includes translation of the terminology specific to it, of foreign (loan) words, idiomatic expressions and other—"miscellaneous"—lexical items. There is also a cumulative alphabetical glossary of nouns and adjectives; the verbs can be looked up in Appendix II.

Within each text, various grammatical phenomena that might cause comprehension difficulties have been annotated and indexed to the relevant discussion in the book. Items selected for explication are bolded and a superscript number directs the reader to the side bar on the left, where a translation, a brief grammatical explanation and a reference to the relevant chapter and subsection in the book are provided. Items that share the same linguistic features have the same reference number (for example, once a double construct phrase has been flagged within a given text, all subsequent phrases of this nature in the text are similarly numbered). An additional feature is the shading of clauses whose verb precedes the subject. The texts are accompanied by English translations, allowing the learners to verify their understanding and assess their translation proficiency. The translations do not aspire to stylistic elegance; the goal is rather to model a translation that displays the reader's thorough comprehension of the Hebrew text and that would be acceptable to an examiner in a Hebrew-to-English translation exam.

Appendixes

The book contains the following appendixes:

- A list of time expressions by category at the end of Chapter 5 (Adverbs).
- A list of less-common prepositions at the end of Chapter 8 (Prepositions).
- Appendix I provides the numerical values of the letters of the Hebrew alphabet and explains how to convert Hebrew dates (years) to the Gregorian calendar.
- Appendix II is a glossary of verbs commonly used in academic writing.

Indexes

The English index is a subject index; the Hebrew index is a lexical index which provides a translation and a reference for close to 500 items appearing in the Grammar and Lexis section of the book.

Visual organizers for the presentation of the material

Various graphic devices were employed to make the information visually salient:

- Sample sentences from (modern) scholarly sources are framed and appear in a different (larger) font than the one used in the explanatory section of the book; examples from non-modern sources are enclosed in frames with a broken line.
- Shading, bolding and/or framing of individual linguistic items within the sample sentences draw attention to the grammatical point under discussion.
- Shading directs the reader from an item discussed in the main body of the text to a nearby text box that has additional or ancillary information.
- Scroll-shaped text boxes contain definitions of general grammatical terms.
- English translations of Hebrew words occurring within the text appear in italics (e.g., שנה *year*).

- a warning sign ⚠ alerts the reader to potential ambiguities or difficulties in comprehension.

- a weight-lifter icon with a number (e.g., 🏋#1) refers the reader to an exercise in the practice section after the chapter. Some sections may share an exercise (and therefore have the same number); in other cases, more than one exercise provides practice for the same structure (e.g., 🏋#1 & #2).

Abbreviations and conventions

f.   feminine

m.   masculine

sing.   singular

pl.   plural

* indicates a form that is incorrect or does not exist.

( ) within a word indicates an optional item (e.g.: ‏בל‎(מ)‏ ‏בלי‎ : may appear with the additional preposition ‏מ‎-).

[ ] within a translation indicate a reconstructed word or phrase that is not in the original

/ / indicate phonetic rendering of a letter or word (e.g. ‏עניו‎ /onyo/).

Hebrew words rendered in English letters are italicized in a slightly larger font (e.g., *sheva*); an inverted comma within such words indicates a separation between the syllables (e.g., *pi'el*).

The terms "pointed" and "unpointed" are used throughout the book to refer, respectively, to voweled and unvoweled Hebrew words.

Following the transliteration practices of Hebrew names and terms in the Jewish Encyclopedia, the letter ‏ח‎ is rendered as ḥ, and ‏כ‎ as kh.

Readers are invited to send comments and queries to the author at readingacademichebrew@gmail.com.

PART ONE

GRAMMAR AND LEXIS

1. WORD ORDER AND SENTENCE STRUCTURE
סדר המילים ומבנה המשפט

This chapter discusses:

- Departures from the subject-verb-object word order: verb before subject (section 1.1), object at the beginning of the sentence (section 1.2)

- Topicalization (section 2)

- Distance between sentence components (section 3)

- Verbless (nominal) sentences (section 4)

- Subjectless (impersonal) sentences (section 5)

- Multi-clause sentences: coordination (section 6.1) and subordination (section 6.2)

- Lexical repetition (section 7)

- Apposition (section 8)

- Ellipsis (section 9)

- Confusables: אשר ;ה"א at the beginning of the word; אך ;כי

This chapter will help the reader to:

- Identify the subject of the clause when the SVO word order is inverted

- Analyze and understand sentences in which the main sentence components appear in unexpected order or are at a distance from each other

- Translate topicalized sentences

- Recognize and translate verbless and subject-less sentences

- Analyze multi-clause sentences strategically

- Use lexical and orthographic clues to identify appositives

- Reconstruct the non-repeated element in elliptical sentences

A. Word order: an overview

Departures from the subject-verb-object (SVO) word order that is expected by readers of English are common in Hebrew. In the absence of a fixed word order, readers must rely on other clues, both grammatical and contextual, for sentence comprehension. Sections 1.1 and 1.2 below provide guidance in identifying, understanding and translating sentences in which the verb precedes the subject. Sections 2 and 3 discuss other departures from the expected word order.

1. Departures from the subject-verb-object word order

#1   1.1 Adverbial-verb-subject word order

בְּרֵאשִׁית בָּרָא אֱלֹהִים אֵת הַשָּׁמַיִם וְאֵת הָאָרֶץ (בראשית א א)
In the beginning God created the heavens and the earth (Genesis 1.1)

As illustrated by the first verse of Genesis, when the sentence begins with an adverbial, the verb is often placed <u>before</u> the subject.

The resulting word order is adverb-verb-subject. In this way, the verb can remain next to the adverb that describes it (examples 1–4).

An adverbial is a word, phrase or clause that answers such questions as "where," "when," "how" or "why". Question words (e.g., כֵּיצַד *how*) are also considered adverbials.

As a rule, however, there is no subject verb inversion when the subject is a personal pronoun or when the verb is in the present tense.

In translation into English, the adverb-verb-subject word order need not, and often cannot, be preserved.

The adverbial is shaded, the verb is bolded and the subject is framed:

---

(1) בְּתוֹךְ זְמַן קָצָר **רָכַשׁ** רש"י עָמְדָה חֲשׁוּבָה בַּקְּהִילוֹת צָרְפַת הַצְּפוֹנִית.
Within a short time, Rashi acquired an important position in the communities of northern France.

The sentence begins with a time adverbial.

(2) בְּאַשְׁכְּנַז וּבְצָרְפַת לֹא **קִיבְּלוּ** חֲכָמִים מַשְׂכּוֹרֶת עַל הוֹרָאָתָם בַּיְשִׁיבָה.
In Germany and France, the sages did not receive a salary for teaching at the yeshiva.

This sentence begins with an adverbial of place.

---

(3) בתלמוד הירושלמי לא נמצא למנהג זה כל זֵכֶר.
No trace of this custom is found in the Jerusalem Talmud.

The subject appears at the end of the sentence and is separated from the preceding verb. Note the use of כל after לא to intensify the negation.

(4) בתקופת הגאונים פותחו סוגות ספרותיות חדשות, שוכללה ההֲלָכָה, והֲהָגות היהודית פרחה בַּעֲקבות מִפגָשָה עם ההגות המוסלְמית.
During the period of the Geonim, new literary genres were developed, the Halakhah (Jewish law) was perfected, and Jewish philosophy flourished as a result of its encounter with Islamic philosophy.

Following the time adverbial בתקופת הגאונים, the verbs פותחו and שוכללה precede their respective subjects, סוגות and הלכה. The third verb – פרחה – follows its subject since the adverbial phrase בעקבות מפגשה עם ההגות המוסלמית appears at the end, rather than the beginning, of the clause.

(5) המחקר יבדוק כיצד הסתגלו העולים לחברה הישראלית וכיצד היא קלטה אותם.
The study will examine how the Olim (immigrants to Israel) adjusted to the Israeli society and how it absorbed them.

After the question word, the verb הסתגלו precedes the subject (העולים), but when the subject is a pronoun (היא), there is no subject-verb inversion.

1.1.1 A passive verb (i.e., a verb in the *binyanim nif'al, pu'al* and *huf'al*) may precede the subject even when no adverbial is present.

(6) נוצר סולם מעמדות, שבו בני חכמים תפסו מקום בראש.
A class system (literally: ladder) was created in which sons of sages occupied the top position.

The passive verb נוצר (in *nif'al*) precedes the subject. Note that the verb agrees with סולם, the first component of the construct (סמיכות) phrase סולם מעמדות.

1.1.2 The verb may also appear before the subject in certain set expressions (collocations). For example, פרצה מלחמה *a war broke out*, נפלה טעות *an error occurred*, התרחש נס *a miracle happened*, נשאלת השאלה *the question is asked*, ניטש פולמוס *a controversy took place*.

✗#1   1.2 Object-verb-subject word order

The object usually appears after the verb that it complements (example 7). However, for reasons of text cohesion or emphasis, writers sometimes pre-pose the object, that is, place it at the beginning of the sentence. The verb then appears <u>before</u> the subject. The resulting word order is object-verb-subject (OVS).

An object is defined as a sentence part (word, phrase or clause) that complements, and is required by, the verb. Objects are classified as direct or indirect.

The preposition את marks a **definite direct object** (but is not required before an **in**definite one); all other prepositions (e.g., ב, ל, מ, על, אל, עם) signal an **indirect object**.

Note that a noun is considered grammatically definite (specific) when (a) it is preceded by the definite article -ה (e.g., הספר *the book*), (b) it is a proper noun (i.e., a name), or (c) it has a possessive suffix (e.g., ספרי *my book*). When none of these conditions obtains, the noun is considered indefinite.

The object is shaded, the verb is bolded and the subject is framed:

(7) הדיון **יבדוק** את יחס המשכילים אל האישה היהודייה המודרנית.
The discussion will examine the attitude of the Maskilim to the modern Jewish woman.

In this example, the word order is SVO: the direct object יחס follows the verb. The translation follows the Hebrew word order.

(8) את הדימוי הזה של היהודי **קיבלה** הציונות מתנועת ההשׂכָּלָה.
Zionism received this image of the Jew from the Enlightenment movement.

The definite direct object הדימוי appears at the beginning of the sentence. Therefore, the verb קיבלה precedes the subject הציונות. The translation does not follow the Hebrew word order.

(9) אל חַכְמֵי שירה ולשון **הופנו** שאלות בענייני לשון השירה, כְּשֵׁם שהופנו אל חַכְמֵי הֲלָכָה **שאלות** בענייני הֲלָכָה.
Questions regarding the language of poetry were addressed to those knowledgeable in the language of poetry, just as questions in matters of Halakhah (Jewish law) were addressed to those knowledgeable in matters of Halakhah.

In both clauses, the verb precedes the subject, but for different reasons.
In the first clause, the verb is before the subject because the clause begins with an indirect object, אל חכמי שירה ולשון.
In the second clause, the verb appears before the subject because the clause begins with an adverbial, כשם ש.

1.2.1 Verb before subject in relative clauses

The verb may also precede the subject in relative clauses that begin with an inflected preposition (namely, a preposition with a personal pronoun suffix, such as בו, עליה, איתם).

A relative clause provides additional information about a noun or a noun phrase. Relative clauses in English begin with *who, which, whom, whose* or *that*.

The inflected preposition is shaded, the verb is bolded and the subject is framed:

---

(10) לֶחֶם זֶה שֶׁעָלָיו נֶאֱמֶרֶת הַבְּרָכָה אוכלים בִּתְחִילַת הָאֲרוּחה.
This bread, on which the blessing is said, is eaten at the start of the meal.

After the suffixed preposition עליו, which introduces the clause, the verb precedes the subject.

(11) מיסים שונים הוטלו על הקהילה, כְּגוֹן מַס שֶׁאוֹתוֹ שִׁילֵם כל יהודי אשר קנה מִצְרָכים כְּשֵׁרים.
Various taxes were imposed on the congregation, such as a tax which every Jew who bought kosher provisions paid.

(12) חג הסוכות נֶחֱשָׁב במסורת לזמן שֶׁבּוֹ נִקְבַּע גוֹרָלָהּ של השנה מִבְּחִינַת הַגְּשָׁמים.
The holiday of Sukkoth (Feast of Tabernacles) is considered in the tradition as the time at which the fate of the year is determined with respect to rainfall.

1.2.2 Translating object-verb-subject sentences into English

To conform to English word order conventions, the object-verb-subject (OVS) Hebrew word order is changed in translation to subject-verb-object (SVO) order.

Alternatively, the sentence can be translated in the passive mode. In this way, the object – now the subject of the passive sentence – remains in focus, at the beginning of the sentence.

The object is shaded, the verb is bolded and the subject is framed:

---

(13) אֶת הַפֶּרֶק הָראשון בתולְדוֹתָיו של חֵקֶר הַלָשׁוֹן העברית פָּתַח רס"ג.

Rasag (Rabbi Sa'adyah Gaon) opened the first chapter in the history of the research of the Hebrew language.
OR: The first chapter in the history of the research of the Hebrew language was opened by Rasag.

1.2.3 Distinguishing between a subject and a pre-posed object

As demonstrated above, given the flexibility of the word order in Hebrew, readers should not assume that the first noun of the sentence is necessarily the subject; the noun may be either the subject or the object. To determine the grammatical status of the noun, consider the following:

- **The first noun is the subject if** (a) it agrees with the verb in number (singular-plural) and gender (feminine-masculine), and (b) it is not preceded by a preposition.
- Conversely, **the first noun is the object if** (a) it does not agree with the verb, and (b) it is preceded by a preposition.

    However, an <u>indefinite direct object</u> can be identified as such on the basis of one clue only, namely, its lack of agreement with the verb (but see 1.2.3.2 below). This is because an indefinite direct object – unlike a <u>definite</u> direct object – is not introduced by את (examples 14–17).

1.2.3.1 A definite noun that appears in non-initial position in the sentence and is not preceded by את must be identified as the subject. (In example 13 the subject is רס"ג, in example 14 – התימנים, in example 15 – המשל, in example 16 – הקורא.)

The object is shaded, the verb is bolded and the subject is framed:

---

(14) **שִׁיטַת אִרְגּוּן** יְעִילה זו של הקהילה **לָמדוּ** הַתֵּימָנִים ממגורשי פורְטוּגל וּסְפָרד.
The Yemenites learned this efficient method of organization of the congregation from the Spanish and Portuguese exiles.

The indefinite construct phrase שיטת ארגון is not introduced by a preposition. Yet, since it does not agree with the verb, למדו, it must be ruled out as the subject of the sentence and identified as the direct object. An alternative phrasing (that is line with English word order) would be:

התימנים למדו שיטת ארגון יעילה זו של הקהילה ממגורשי פורטוגל וספרד.

(15) **תְּכוּנה זו שׁוֹאֵל** הַמָּשָׁל הפתוח מן המשל הסָגור ומן הָאַלֶּגוֹרְיָה.
The open fable borrows this feature from the closed fable and from allegory.
OR: This feature is borrowed by the open fable from the closed fable and from allegory.

Again, since the first noun, תכונה, does not agree with the verb, שואל, it is readily identified as the (pre-posed) object. An alternative phrasing would be:

המשל הפתוח שואל תכונה זו מן המשל הסגור ומן האלגוריה.

---

(16) **דַּיָּן** מעמיק **ימצא** הַקּוֹרֵא בספר בסוגיית התשובות.

The reader will find in the book a profound discussion of the issue of the responsa.

Both nouns – דַּיָּן and קוֹרֵא – agree with the verb יִמצא and neither is preceded by a preposition. Since הקורא is a definite noun not preceded by the preposition אֶת, it must be ruled out as the object and is identified as the subject of the sentence. An alternative phrasing (following the SVO word order) would be:

הקורא ימצא בספר דיון מעמיק בסוגיית התשובות.

(17) **חֶרֶךְ** שניתן להָצִיץ דַּרְכּוֹ אל עולם התַרגוּם, אל יַחסָם של חז"ל אליו ואל עולם בית הכנסת בִּכְלָל **מושיטים** לנו אותם קִטְעֵי מִקְרָא שעליהם נִקבע בספרות חז"ל כי הם נקראים בציבור אך אינם מיתרְגמים.

Those sections in the Bible that in the literature of Ḥazal it was determined are to be read in public, but not translated, offer us (literally: hand us) an aperture through which it is possible to peer into the world of the Targum (the Aramaic version of the Scriptures), (into) the attitude of Ḥazal to it, and (into) the universe of the synagogue in general.

We determine that the first (singular) noun, חרך *aperture*, is <u>not</u> the subject of the main clause – חרך מושיטים לנו אותם קטעי מקרא – because it does not agree with the plural verb, מושיטים. Since this verb agrees with the first noun of the construct phrase קטעי מקרא, we identify it as the subject of the main clause. Sequenced in SVO order the clause would read: אותם קטעי מקרא מושיטים לנו חרך.
Note that here אותם is a pronoun (*those*), NOT the inflected form of the preposition אֶת.[1]

1.2.3.2 On rare occasions, neither the agreement of the noun with the verb nor a preposition before the noun is available as a clue to determine the syntactic status (subject or object) of the noun. This could happen when an indefinite direct object happens to have the same number and gender as the subject and, therefore, it (too) agrees with the verb. The reader must then rely on semantic and context clues for sentence comprehension.

An often cited example of such grammatical ambiguity is the biblical verse from Job 14. 19:

אֲבָנִים שָׁחֲקוּ מַיִם (איוב יד יט)
Water wears away stones (Job 14.19)
In this verse, both nouns are indefinite, are plural and agree with the verb שחקו. There is no preposition to mark the object and thus distinguish it from the subject. The reader determines that the second noun, מים, is the subject solely on the basis of the context (in this case, the extra-linguistic knowledge that water can erode stone, not vice versa).

---

[1] See Chapter 3, 3.2.

Two modern examples in which the context helps determine the grammatical status of the noun (that is, subject or object) are given below.

The object is shaded, the verb is bolded and the subject is framed:

---

(18) סיבות רבות **מנו** פילוסופים, אנתרופולוגים וסוציולוגים למשבר הערכים בחברה.
Philosophers, anthropologists and sociologists enumerated many reasons for the crisis of values in society.

סיבות as well as פילוסופים, אנתרופולוגים וסוציולוגים agree with the verb מנו, are indefinite and are not introduced by a preposition. The reader determines the meaning on the basis of the semantic context: people can enumerate reasons, reasons cannot enumerate people. An alternative phrasing in SVO order would be:
פילוסופים, אנתרופולוגים וסוציולוגים מנו סיבות רבות למשבר הערכים בחברה.

(19) חֲזוּת הכל **רואה** המהר"ל בַּסֵּדֶר.
The Maharal (Rabbi Yehuda Löw of Prague) considers order the most important thing.
OR: Order is considered by the Maharal the most important thing.

As per 1.2.3.1 above, המהר"ל must be identified as the subject:
המהר"ל רואה בסדר (את) חזות הכל.
Note that (uncharacteristically) the definite object – the construct phrase חֲזוּת **הכל** – is not introduced by the preposition את. (This could be in imitation of biblical style, where the direct object marker is often dispensed with, or perhaps because the definite article – appearing, as it should, before the second noun of the construct phrase – is not salient). Without את, the syntactic role of חזות הכל as a direct object is not immediately apparent. Since the subject is המהר"ל, the verb רואה is read רוֹאֶה rather than רוֹאָה, the reading if חזות הכל were the subject (most nouns ending with -וּת are feminine singular[2]).

The rules for determining the role of the noun – object or subject – are summarized in the flow chart below. Note that the chart does not take into account the unusual occurrence (in modern non-literary texts) of a definite direct object <u>not</u> introduced by the preposition את (as seen in example 19 above).

---

[2] See Chapter 2, 6.1.

Flowchart for distinguishing subject and object in noun-verb-noun sentences

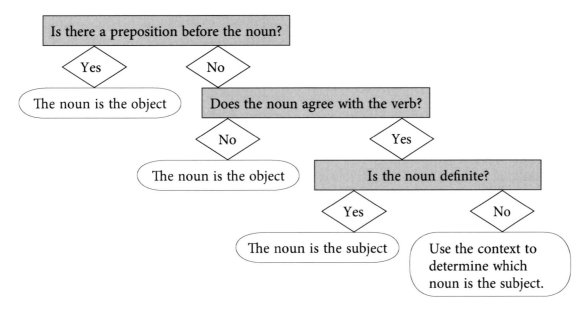

⚡#2 2. Topicalized sentences[3] משפטי ייחוד

הֶחָכָם עֵינָיו בְּרֹאשׁו (קהלת ב יד)
The wise man's eyes [are] in his head (Ecclesiastes 2.14)
(Literally: a wise man, his eyes are in his head)

יְרוּשָׁלַיִם הָרִים סָבִיב לָהּ (תהלים קכה ב)
Mountains [are] around Jerusalem (Psalms 125.2)
(Literally: Jerusalem, mountains around it)

נָשִׁים דַּעְתָּן קַלָּה (שבת)
Women [are] fickle-minded (Sabbath)
(Literally: women their mind is light)

Topicalization – also called "topic dislocation" – is an information focusing device already found in the Bible.

In topicalized sentences, the topic is put at the beginning of the sentence and the grammatical subject follows it.

Topicalized sentences have the following structure:

(a) A noun (or a noun phrase) is extracted from the sentence (or clause) and placed at its beginning, where it can receive more attention. From a syntactic viewpoint, however, this

---

[3] Also known as "casus pendens".

noun is not the subject of the sentence. In the above examples the topicalized (that is, extracted and pre-posed) nouns are החכם, ירושלים and נשים.

(b) The topicalized noun is referred to later in the sentence by means of a pronoun suffix (in the above examples, the pronoun suffix in עיניו refers to חכם, לה refers to ירושלים and דעתן refers to נשים). In this way, the pre-posing of the noun does not render the sentence ungrammatical. The suffix may be attached to a noun (examples 20–21), a preposition (examples 22–23) or a verb (example 24).

(c) The topicalized noun (or noun phrase) may be separated from the rest of the sentence with a dash (example 22) or a comma (example 24).

(d) Often, the topicalized noun is the second noun (סומך) in a construct phrase that serves as the subject in the undelrlying sentence (examples 20–21). Sentences in the "to be" and "to have" patterns particularly lend themselves to topicalization (examples 20 and 22).

2.1 Translating topicalized sentences

In translation into English, topicalized sentences are usually re-ordered to better conform to English word order conventions.

The topicalized element and the pronoun suffix that refers to it are shaded; a rephrased (non-topicalized) version of the sentence is given in brackets below the original sentence:

---

(20) הַסִּיפור מקורו באגדה עתיקה.
[המקור של הסיפור (הוא) באגדה עתיקה]
The origin of the story is an ancient legend.

(21) הַשְׁקָפה זו עבר זְמַנָהּ.
[הזמן של השקפה זו עבר]
This view is obsolete (literally: this view, its time has passed).

(22) הַיְצירה העיונית – לה היה קיום, אבל השירה נשתתקה.
[ליצירה העיונית היה קיום אבל השירה נשתתקה]
Theoretical work continued to exist (literally: had existence) but poetry became silent.

(23) לוח הלבנה שאומץ על ידי ישראל מצאו לו חז"ל סימוכין במקראות.
[חז"ל מצאו סימוכין ללוח הלבנה שאומץ על ידי ישראל במקראות]
Hazal found support in biblical sources for the lunar calendar adopted by the Israelites.

(24) הַיְחָסים המִשְׁפָטיים בין יהודים החיים בקהילות שונות, לא היה שום מוֹסָד בַּעַל-סַמְכָא יכול להַסְדירָם.
[שום מוסד בעל-סמכא לא היה יכול להסדיר את היחסים המשפטיים בין יהודים החיים בקהילות שונות]
There was no authoritative institution that could regulate the legal relations among Jews living in different communities.
OR: The legal relations among Jews living in different communities could not be regulated by any authoritative institution.

The direct object suffix that is attached to the verb (להסדירם=להסדיר אותם) refers to יחסים, the head noun of the topicalized phrase.

🏋#3   3. Distance between sentence components

In the long sentences that are characteristic of written scholarly discourse, the main constituents – subject, verb and object – may be separated by several intervening words. Readers are therefore advised to scan the entire sentence before attempting to identify its components.

3.1 A verb at a distance from the subject
The subject and the verb may not be contiguous, whether the verb precedes the subject (examples 25–26) or follows it (example 27).

The verb is bolded and the subject is framed:

---

(25) לְפִי דַעַת רַבִּי עֲקִיבָא כבר **נִיתְנָה** לְאָדָם הראשון – וּלְיָמִים לכל אדם – הַבְּרֵירה לִבְחוֹר בְּאַחַת משתי דרכים.

According to the opinion of Rabbi Akiva, the option to select one of two paths was already given to Adam (literally: the first man), and subsequently to each and every man.

The verb (נִיתְנָה) is separated from its subject (הברירה) by the indirect object (לאדם הראשון) and a parenthetical remark enclosed in dashes.

(26) כַּיָּאֶה לעבודתו של ביבליוֹגְרָף ראשון בְּמַעֲלָה **מוּבֵאת** כאן, בְּתַמְצִיתִיּוּת, ההיסטוריה של המקורות עצמם.

As befits the work of a first rate bibliographer, the history of the sources themselves is succinctly given here.

Two adverbials (כאן, בתמציתיות) separate the verb and the subject.

(27) נִיתוּחַ מַעֲמִיק יותר של המְקוֹרוֹת, בְּנוֹסָף לעֵדִיּוֹת הארכאולוגיות, **מַצְבִּיע** על כיוון אַחֵר.

A deeper analysis of the sources, in addition to the archeological evidence, points in another direction.

The word order is SVO, but the verb appears at a considerable distance from the subject.

3.2 An object at a distance from the verb (a split predicate phrase)
In the examples below, several words separate the verb from its object; this may occur even when the verb and its object form an idiomatic phrase. In translation, the verb and its object would follow each other directly.

> The predicate is the part of the sentence that says something about the subject. The predicate is composed of a verb (or a verb substitute) and its complements (object and/or adverb).

The verb and its object complement are bolded and the subject is framed:

(28) בשנות ה-80 של המאה ה-19 **העלו** ההגירה ההמונית של יהודים ממזרח אירופה
והשינויים המתחוללים בסביבה הפוליטית והכלכלית של אמריקה **סוגיות חברתיות
חדשות** אל מרכז הבימה של הפילנתרופיה היהודית האמריקנית.
In the 1880's, the mass immigration of Jews from Eastern Europe and the changes
occurring in the political and economic environment of America raised new social
issues to the center stage of American Jewish philanthropy.

(29) בְּאֶמְצָעוּת מְסָרִים אלה **לוֹבְשׁוֹת** תַּדְמִיּוֹת קוֹלֶקְטִיווִיּוֹת בישראל של יָמֵינוּ **צוּרָה.**
Through these messages, collective images in contemporary Israel take (literally:
wear) shape.

In this example, the components of the idiomatic predicate phrase לובשות צורה are separated by the subject.

(30) **אֶת מְקוֹמָהּ** של העברית כְּשְׂפַת דיבור **תָּפְסָה** בתקופת חז"ל השָּׂפָה הָאֲרָמִית.
Aramaic replaced (literally: took the place of) Hebrew as a spoken language in the
period of Ḥazal.
OR: In the period of Ḥazal, Hebrew as a spoken language was replaced by Aramaic.

The verb תפסה is separated from the (pre-posed) direct object מקום even though together
they form an idiomatic expression.

(31) בְּאָבִיב 1893 **רָקַם** העיתונאי הצעיר תֵּיאוֹדוֹר הֶרְצֶל, שְׁלִיחַ העיתון הווינָאִי היוּקְרָתִי
"נוֹיֶה פרִיֶה פרֶסֶה" בְּפָּרִיס, **תָּכְנִית,** שמַטָּרָתָהּ היְיתָה לִגְרוֹם לזַעֲזוּעַ עָמוֹק בְּדַעַת הַקָּהָל
העוֹלָמִית.
In the spring of 1893, the young journalist Theodore Herzl, the Paris correspondent
of the prestigious Viennese newspaper "The New Free Press," contrived a plan
whose objective was to deeply shock (literally: to cause a profound shock in) world
public opinion.

Despite the idiomatic nature of the phrase רקם תכנית *contrived a plan*, the direct object
תכנית is separated from the verb רקם by the subject, which in turn is amplified by a lengthy
appositive (appositives are discussed in section 8 below).

3.3 A split verb phrase
In the examples below, following an adverbial, the two-part verb phrase straddles the subject.
In translation, the entire verb phrase should appear after the subject.

In examples 32–33 the verb phrase consists of the verb "to be" in the past tense (היה, הייתה)
and a predicative adjective (an adjective that functions as a verb).

In examples 34–36, a past tense verb (ניסו, נטתה, ביקשו, נצטוו) is followed – at some
distance – by an infinitive, the two verbs forming one semantic unit.

Some other verbs that can be similarly complemented by a verb in the infinitive are: הצליח *succeeded*, התחיל *began*, התכונן *prepared*, סיים *finished*, המשיך *continued*, נהג *was accustomed*.

The split verb phrase is bolded and the subject is framed:

---

(32) מאז ומתמיד **הייתה** החקלאות בארץ ישראל **תלויה** בגשמים.
Agriculture in the Land of Israel has always been dependent on rainfall.

The two elements of the verb phrase הייתה תלויה straddle the subject.

(33) הֵן בְּגֶרְמַנְיָה וְהֵן בְּרוּסְיָה **הָיָה** חֶלְקָם שֶׁל הַמַּשְׂכִּילִים הַיְּהוּדִיִּים בִּצְמִיחָתָהּ שֶׁל הָאִשָּׁה הַמּוֹדֶרְנִית **קָטָן** יַחֲסִית.
In both Germany and Russia, the role of the Jewish Maskilim in the emergence of the modern woman was relatively small.

The verb phrase היה קטן straddles the subject חלקם.

(34) גם בפְרָעוֹת שׁל שׁנת 1096 **ניסו**, בְּדֶרֶךְ כְּלָל, פְּקִידָיו שֶׁל הַיִּנְרִיךְ הָרְבִיעִי **לְהָגֵן** על היהודים.
Even in the pogroms of the year 1096, the administrators of King Heinrich the Fourth generally tried to defend the Jews.

The two verbs in the verb phrase ניסו להגן are separated by the adverb בדרך כלל and then the subject, פקידיו של היינריך הרביעי

(35) מִצַּד אחד, **נָטְתָה** הַנְהָגַת החכמים **לְהִתְגַּבֵּשׁ** לְמֵעֵין מַעֲמָד סָגוּר, ומצד שני, **בִּיקְשׁוּ** החכמים עצמם **לִשְׁמוֹר** על עֲמָמִיּוּתָם.
On the one hand, the rabbinic leadership tended to consolidate into a kind of a closed class; on the other hand, the rabbis themselves wished to preserve their populism.

Both verb phrases ביקשו לשמור and נטתה להתגבש are split up and straddle their subjects.

(36) בפּולחָן **שׁנּצְטַווּ** בני ישראל **לקַיֵּים** במשכָּן במִדְבָּר **מִמַלֵּא** הלֶחֶם בצורותיו השונות כמה וכמה **תפקידים** מרכזיים .
In the ritual that the Israelites were commanded to observe in the tabernacle in the desert, bread in its various forms fulfilled several major roles.

The verb phrase נצטוו לקיים in the subordinate clause is split, straddling the subject, בני ישראל. In the main clause, the verb ממלא and its object תפקיד are separated and straddle the subject even though together they form the idiomatic expression ממלא תפקיד *fulfills a role.*

B. Sentence structure: an overview

This section introduces two sentence types that are peculiar to Hebrew – verbless sentences (section 4) and subject-less sentences (section 5). Sections 6 through 9 discuss syntactic phenomena that are also found in English, including multi-clause sentences, lexical repetition, apposition and ellipsis.

4. Verbless (nominal) sentences מִשְׁפָּטִים שֵׁמָנִיִּים

> בֵּן חָכָם יְשַׂמַּח אָב וּבֵן כְּסִיל תּוּגַת אִמּוֹ (משלי י א)
> *A wise son brings joy to his father and a dull son [is] his mother's sorrow*
> (Proverbs 10.1)

Since Hebrew does not have present tense forms for the verb "to be," some present tense sentences are verbless. In the example above, the first clause has a verb (יִשְׂמַח), while the second clause is verbless.

As seen in example 37, in the absence of a verb, there is no indication where the subject ends and the predicate begins.

> (37) רֵאשִׁיתָהּ שֶׁל הַסְּפָרַדִּית-הַיְּהוּדִית בִּימֵי הַבֵּינַיִים בִּסְפָרַד.
> The beginning of Judeo-Spanish [is] in the Middle Ages in Spain B.C.E.

To compensate for the "missing" verb, the third person pronouns הוּא, הִיא, הֵם, הֵן may be inserted. In this role, הוּא and הִיא are translated as *is* (rather than *he, she* or *it*); הֵם and הֵן are translated as *are* (rather than *they*). In this function, the third person pronoun is called copula (אוֹגֵד). Like any other verb, the copula is required to agree with the subject in gender and number.[4]

In most cases the copula is not obligatory: it need not be used when the predicate is an adjective, an adverb or a prepositional phrase (although after a long subject phrase there is a preference for using it). When the predicate is a noun, however, the copula is usually obligatory (example 38–40).

In the past and the future the copula is unnecessary, as the past and future forms of the verb "to be" are used: הָיָה/הָיְתָה/הָיִיתָ/הָיוּ and יִהְיֶה/תִּהְיֶה/יִהְיוּ, respectively.

> The biblical form תִּהְיֶינָה (feminine plural) is rare in modern Hebrew; יִהְיוּ is preferred for both הֵם and הֵן (but see example 46 below).

---

[4] See Chapter 7 for detailed discussion of copulas.

The copula is bolded, and the subject is framed:

(38) הַלּוּחַ הָעִבְרִי **הוא** לוח שמשי-יְרֵחִי.
The Hebrew calendar <u>is</u> a solar-lunar calendar.

(39) מִכֵּיוָן שֶׁהמשפחה **היא** הַמִּסְגֶּרֶת הַחֶבְרָתִית הַבְּסִיסִית בְּיוֹתֵר, הֲבָנָתָהּ **היא** חֵלֶק חשוב בכל ניתוח וְהֲבָנָה של חֶבְרָה כָּלְשֶׁהִי.
Since the family <u>is</u> the most basic social framework, its understanding <u>is</u> an important part of the analysis and understanding of any society.

The copula היא is used twice; in each case it agrees with the preceding subject.

(40) עֶרְכּוֹ של הספר **הוא** בתיאור הַחֵלֶק הַצַּבָרִי של האדם הָאֶרֶץ-ישראלי, ו**חולשתו** בְּהֶעָדְרוֹ של החלק הָאַחֵר.
The value of the book <u>is</u> in the description of the "Sabra" component of the Israeli, and its weakness <u>is</u> the absence of the other component [from the description of his personality].

In the first clause, the copula הוא links the subject phrase ערכו של הספר to the predicate. The second clause is also verbless, but without a copula; had a copula been inserted, it would have been היא (in agreement with the subject חולשה *weakness*), as follows:
וחולשתו היא בהיעדרו של החלק האחר.

4.1 Verbless sentences are also created through the omission of יש.[5]

(41) לקיבוצים הדתיים אוֹרַח חיים מיוחד.
[לקיבוצים הדתיים יש אורח חיים מיוחד]
Religious kibbutzim [have] a special way of life.

♱#4 5. Subjectless (impersonal) sentences משפטים סְתָמִיים

In subjectless sentences the "doer" of the action is not specified. Therefore, these sentences are considered impersonal. The identity of the subject, the "doer" – whether an individual or a group – may be unknown, unimportant, or generic, or it can be inferred from the immediate context.

Below are listed four types of impersonal sentences and their translation options.

(a) **Impersonal sentences type one: a plural masculine verb**

אומרים יֶשְׁנָהּ אֶרֶץ (טשרניחובסקי)
They say (OR: *it is said*) *there is a land* (Tchernichowsky)

---

[5] See Chapter 9, 2.2.

The verb – which may be in any tense – belongs to one of the active *binyanim* (e.g., *pa'al* in examples 43 and 45, *pi'el* in example 47, *hif'il*, in examples 42, 44, 46 and 48). Sentences of this type can be translated into English by adding a generic subject, such as *people, we, they* or *one*, or through conversion into the passive (examples 44–46 and 10 above).

The verb is shaded:

---

(42) בְּדִבְרֵי יְמֵי הלוח העברי **מבחינים** בין שתֵי תקופות.
In the history of the Hebrew calendar, <u>we</u> distinguish between two periods.

(43) בתקופת בית שני **היו קובעים** את ראשי החודָשים על פי עֵדים שראו את הירח.
In the period of the Second Temple, <u>they</u> used to determine the beginning of the months according to witnesses who saw the moon.

The use of the verb להיות in the past tense in conjunction with another (main) verb in the present tense serves to indicate a customary action in the past.[6]

(44) **מַעֲרִיכים** את האוכלוסייה בירושלים בראשית המֵאָה ה-19 ב-10,000 תושבים.
The population of Jerusalem at the beginning of the 19th century <u>is estimated</u> at 10,000 residents.

(45) לְתַקָנות אלה **קראו** גם הַסְכָּמות.
These ordinances <u>were</u> also <u>called</u> "agreements".

(46) בצְפון צָרפת **התירו** לצייר דְמויות אֱנושיות בְּתנָאי שלא תהיינה שְלֵמות.
In Northern France the drawing of human figures <u>was permitted</u> (OR: it was permitted to draw human figures) on condition that they would not be complete.

To limit the generality of the statement to a certain group of people, the verb is introduced by ה- יש in the present (e.g., יש האומרים *there are those who say*) or, in the past, by ש- היו (example 47).

Another possibility is to repeat the verb in the singular (e.g., אמר מי שאמר *someone said*) or in the plural (example 48).

---

(47) **היו שזיהו** את עֲמָלֵק עם ההיקסוס, שֶשָלטו באַכזריות בעולם העתיק במשך מאות שנים.
<u>There were those who</u> identified Amalek with the Hyksos, who ruled the ancient world cruelly for hundreds of years.

In the present tense this sentence would read: יש המזהים את עמלק עם ההיקסוס

(48) עם הזמן **הרחיבו מי שהרחיבו** את דברי התַנָא בשתי תוספות.
With time, <u>there were those</u> who expanded the words of the Tanna with two additions.

---

[6] See Chapter 6, 3.3.

(b) **Impersonal sentences type two: a singular masculine verb** (in any tense) **in a passive pattern** (*pa'ul, nif'al, pu'al* and *huf'al*)

A verb of saying or knowing is often involved (e.g., נֶאֱמַר ש/כי *it was said that,* /ש נראה *it appears that,* ידוע ש/כי *it is known that,* נמצא ש/כי *it was found that,* נקבע ש/כי *it was determined that*). Sentences of this type are translated into English with an empty (dummy) "it" subject.

> Note also עולה ש/כי *it can be concluded that, it is revealed that* (literally: *it arises that*), where the verb is not in a passive pattern (example 54).

---

(49) יָדוּעַ כי האדם שׂיחק במשׂחקים עוד בתקופה הפרֶה-היסטורית.
It is known that man played games already in the pre-historic era.

(50) ללחם מעמד מיוחד במנהג ובפולקלור היהודי: מְקוּבָּל לנהוג בו בכבוד מיוחד.
Bread has a special status in Jewish custom and folklore: it is customary to treat it with special respect.

⚠ Make sure to distinguish between this meaning of מקובל and another meaning, *a kabbalist.*

(51) יְצוּיַן שהשֵׁם "פְּרוֹזְדוֹר" אף הוא מִלה שׁאוּלה בעברית.
It should be noted that the noun "prozdor" (corridor) too is a borrowed word in Hebrew.

Note the use of the future tense here to convey necessity or obligation.

(52) במקרה זה הוּחלט לסטות מן הנוֹהַג המקוּבל.
In this case, it was decided to depart from the customary procedure.

(53) כבר בכתבֵי היד של הפיוטים נִיכָּר שניסו לדלֵג על המַחֲרוֹזוֹת המְפָרְטוֹת את חֲטאֵי אבות האומה.
Already in the manuscripts of the Piyyutim, it is apparent that they tried [OR: an attempt was made] to skip over strophes that itemize the sins of the patriarchs.

In this example there are two subject-less verbs: ניכר (*it is apparent*), and ניסו (*[they] tried*).

(54) מן האמור לעֵיל עולה כי ביטוּל הבחינה הפסיכוֹמֶטרית עלוּל לפגוע במועמדים מתאימים.
From what is said above it can be concluded that the abolition of the psychometric exam is liable to harm suitable candidates.

⚠️ Note that the impersonal expression ‎מְדוּבָּר בּ- (or ‎מדובר על) may be translated as *it is a matter of, it is a question of, it concerns, it is referred to* or *the discussion is about*... (rather than literally: *it is talked about*). Alternative expressions are ‎הַדְּבָר(ים) אֲמוּר(ים) בּ- and ‎הַכַּוָונָה ‎לְ- *the meaning is..., meaning that...*

---

(55) ‎אין **מדובר** במזל טוב אֶלָא בסיוּע אֱלוֹהי.
This is not a matter of good luck, but rather of divine assistance.

(56) ‎לא נמְסְרו פְּרָטים מְזַהים על חַיָה זו במְקְרָא (אם אָכֵן **מדובר בחיה**).
No identifying details were given in the Bible about this animal (if indeed an animal is referred to).

(c) **Impersonal sentences type three: a modal expression** (e.g., ‎רצוי *desirable*, ‎ראוי *appropriate, fitting*, ‎(אי)אפשר *(im)possible*, ‎כדאי *worthwhile*, ‎צריך *necessary*) **or an "affective" adjective** (e.g., ‎קשה *difficult*, ‎טוב *good*) **followed by a verb in the infinitive**
These sentences too are translated into English with an empty "it".

📜 Modal expressions indicate the attitude of the speaker toward the event, in terms of possibility, probability, necessity, expectation or desirability.

---

(57) ‎**רָאוי וניתָן לשפֵּר** את תְרומת הבּחינה הפְּסיכומֶטרית לאֵיכות הקַבָּלָה באוניברסיטאות.
It is worthwhile and possible to improve the contribution of the psychometric exam to the quality of admission into the universities.

Note that ‎ניתן+infinitive verb expresses possibility.[7]

(58) ‎**רָצוי להימָנַע** מהשימוש בּמוּנָח "רוֹע" בדיונים פּוליטיים.
It is desirable to avoid the use of the term "evil" in political discussions.

---

[7] See Chapter 11, 3.

(d) **Impersonal sentences type four: a present tense (singular or plural) masculine verb introduced by ה- or מי שֶ-**

אֵיזֶהוּ חָכָם? **הַלּוֹמֵד** מִכָּל אָדָם (אבות ד א)
Who is wise? He who learns from everyone (Mishnah Aboth 4.1)

הַזּׂרְעִים בְּדִמְעָה – בְּרִנָּה יִקְצֹרוּ (תהלים קכו ה)
They that sow in tears shall reap in joy (Psalms 126.5)

In translation, the unspecified subject may be rendered as *the person who, he who, (any)one who, whoever,* or *those who*.

---

(59) **המסיימים** את לימודיהם התקבלו לעבודה בשירות הממלכה.
<u>Those who</u> finished their studies were accepted to work in the service of the empire.

(60) בדור שֶלאחר הרמב"ם היו חכמים שאמרו: כל **המבקש** את האמונה בסִפְרֵי הפילוסופיה הוא כמי **שמבקש** את החיים בבית הקְבָרוֹת.
In the generation after Maimonedes, there were sages who said: <u>whoever</u> seeks faith in books of philosophy is like <u>one who</u> seeks life in the cemetery.

(61) **מי שיחפשׂוּ** בסיפורים עוֹמֶק צפויים לאַכְזָבָה.
<u>Those who</u> look for depth in the stories (should) expect disappointment.

---

6. Multi-clause sentences: coordination and subordination

Long sentences created through coordination and subordination of clauses are common in academic writing, reflecting its intricate processes of reasoning and argumentation.

6.1 Coordinate sentences מִשְׁפָּטִים מְחוּבָּרִים

הַיּוֹם קָצָר וְהַמְּלָאכָה מְרֻבָּה (אבות ב כ)
The day is short and the task is great (Mishnah Aboth 2.20)

Coordinate sentences are created through joining two or more clauses of equal grammatical and informational importance via conjunctions of:

(a) addition (-וְ *and,* גַּם, לֹא רַק . . . אֶלָּא *not only . . . but also*),

(b) contrast (אֲבָל, אַך, אוּלָם *but,* וְאִילּוּ *whereas,* אֶלָּא *rather*),

(c) alternative (אוֹ *or*),

(d) result (לָכֵן, לְפִיכָך, עַל כֵּן *therefore*), and

(e) reason or conclusion (שֶׁהֲרֵי, שֶׁכֵּן *since*).

The pronunciation of the וי״ו varies with the phonetic environment: it is usually pronounced with a *sheva*, וְ, but may be also pronounced (in careful speech) /vi/, /va/, /ve/ or /u/. These pronunciation rules are beyond the scope of this book.

אוּלָם may be preceded by -ו, usually at the beginning of the sentence. In translation, the וי״ו is disregarded (וְאוּלָם *but, however*). אוּלָם and אַך are more formal alternatives to אֲבָל *but*.

The initial וי״ו in וְאִילוּ *whereas* is an integral part of the word (in other words, it does not mean *and*; see examples 103–104 below). It is distinguishable from אִילוּ *if* (see Chapter 6, Confusables, 2).

---

(62) בְּאֵירוֹפָּה קַיָּמוֹת שִׁיטוֹת שׁוֹנוֹת שֶׁל "קַבָּלָה פְּתוּחָה" לְלֹא מִבְחָן פְּסִיכוֹמֶטְרִי, אַך אִי-שְׂבִיעוּת הָרָצוֹן מִשִּׁיטוֹת אֵלֶּה מִתְפַּשֶּׁטֶת וּבְבְּרִיטַנְיָה מוּכְנָסִים בְּהַדְרָגָה כְּלֵי מִיּוּן דּוֹמִים לַפְּסִיכוֹמֶטְרִי.

In Europe, various systems of "open admissions" without a psychometric exam exist, <u>but</u> the dissatisfaction from these methods is spreading <u>and</u> in Britain placement instruments similar to the psychometric exam are gradually being introduced.

The sentence contains three coordinate clauses; the conjunctions used are אַך (for contrast) and -ו (for addition).

#5   6.2 Complex sentences מִשְׁפָּטִים מוּרְכָּבִים

Complex sentences are hierarchical – rather than symmetrical – in nature. They are made up of a main (independent) clause (simple or coordinate) and at least one subordinate (dependent) clause. The independent clause usually contains the main idea of the sentence (but see 6.3.1(c) below). The subordinate clause may itself be coordinate or complex, that is, may embed within it another dependent clause, which in turn could embed yet another clause.

The clauses of the complex sentence do not appear in any fixed order: subordinate clauses may appear before, after or within the main clause.

In example 63 below, the interrupted main clause (a) is expanded via three subordinate clauses (b), (c) and (d); clauses (c) and (d) are coordinate, connected by -ו *and*. Clause (d) is verbless (the copula הוּא is used). The subordinate clauses (b) and (d) are embedded within the main clause by means of the subordinator -שֶׁ. The subordinator for clause (c), which begins with a present tense verb, is -הַ.

The subordinating particles are bolded, the main clause is shaded:

---

(63) (a) **רָאשׁוֹנֵי** הַסוֹפרים **הַהֶלֶנִיסְטִיים**, (b) **שֶׁבָּאוּ** בְּמַגָּע עם היהודים והיהדות,
(a) מתארים את היהודים כְּאוּמָה של פילוסופים, (c) **הַנִּשְׁלֶטֶת** בידי הכוהנים, (d) **וּשֶׁמֶרְכָּזָהּ**
הוא הַמִּקְדָּשׁ וּפוּלְחָנוֹ המיוּחד.

The first Hellenistic writers, who came into contact with Jews and Judaism, describe the Jews as a nation of philosophers, governed by the priests, and whose center is the temple and its special ritual.

Note that the copula הוּא in clause (d) agrees with the masculine noun מרכז (the final ה is a possessive suffix referring to אומה in the main clause).

6.3 Recognizing dependent clauses

A dependent clause can be recognized by the subordinator that embeds it within another clause (but see 6.3.2). The four subordinators – שֶׁ-, אשר, ה-, כי – are discussed below.

In addition, the dependent clause may be set off from the main clause by commas (examples 64–65) or, occasionally, by a dash. However, the punctuation rules have undergone changes over the years and are not consistently observed.

6.3.1 The subordinating particles: שֶׁ-, אשר, ה-, כי

(a) The subordinator -שֶׁ, and its (now) more formal variant
אֲשֶׁר, may be translated as *which, that, who, whom,* or *whose.*

> Historically, -שֶׁ is Mishnaic, אשר is biblical.

⚠ Note that -שֶׁ is a non-translated component in expressions that introduce adverbial clauses (e.g., -שֶׁ אחרי *after,* -שֶׁ מִשׁוּם *because,* -שֶׁ אַף עַל פִּי *even though*).

The subordinate clause is in brackets, the subordinating particle is bolded and the main (independent) clause is shaded:

---

(64) ההפרש בין שנת הירח לשנת השמש עלול לשבש את הקשר בין התאריך, **שֶׁ**[נקבע
לפי החודש והירח], ובין העונה החקלאית, **שֶׁ**[נקבעת לפי השמש].
The difference between a lunar year and a solar year is liable to disrupt the connection between the date, <u>which</u> is determined according to the month and the moon, and the agricultural season, <u>which</u> is determined according to the sun.

The subject of the verb נקבע is the immediately preceding תאריך; the subject of נקבעת is the preceding העונה החקלאית.

---

(65) הַגָּדַת פְּרַאג, **אשר** [נוֹצְרָה בּ-1526], הָיְתָה לְאַבְּטִיפּוֹס לְהַגָּדוֹת רַבּוֹת.
The Prague Haggadah, <u>which</u> was created in 1526, has become the prototype for many Haggadahs.

The main clause is interrupted by the dependent clause. The two verbs in the sentence, היתה and נוצרה share the subject, הגדת פראג.
Note the meaning of היתה ל- *became* (as distinct from היתה *was*).[8] This is also seen in example 68. Note also that the preferred spelling of היתה (when unpointed) is הייתה.

(66) הַמִּנְהָג **שׁ**[הִתְחִיל בְּבָבֶל] עָבַר מִשָּׁם לִסְפָרַד, לְצָרְפַת וְלְאַשְׁכְּנַז, וּמִשָּׁם לְכָל תְּפוּצוֹת יִשְׂרָאֵל.
The custom <u>that</u> began in Babylon moved from there to Spain, France and Germany and from there to all the countries of the Diaspora.

(67) הַמִּקְרָא מְסַפֵּר עַל אברהם אבינו **שׁ**[נֶאֱלַץ לָרֶדֶת לְמִצְרַיִם בִּגְלַל הָרָעָב בְּאֶרֶץ כְּנַעַן], וְכֵן גַּם עַל נֶכְדּוֹ יעקב, **שׁ**[יָרַד עִם כָּל בָּנָיו לְמִצְרַיִם מֵאוֹתָהּ סִיבָּה].
The Bible tells about Abraham the Patriarch <u>who</u> was forced to go down to Egypt because of the famine in the land of Canaan and also about his grandson Jacob <u>who</u> went down to Egypt with all his sons for the same reason.

(68) שַׁיְילוֹק, הַמַּלְוֶוה בְּרִיבִּית הַיְּהוּדִי, **שׁ**[תְּבִיעָתוֹ לְלִיטְרָה מִבְּשָׂרוֹ שֶׁל הַסּוֹחֵר הַנּוֹצְרִי רְווּיָה בְּאַסּוֹצִיאַצִיוֹת שֶׁל עֲלִילוֹת דָּם וְרֶצַח אֵל], הָיָה לִדְמוּת אִיקוֹנִית בְּשִׂיחַ בְּנוֹשֵׂא הַיְּהוּדִים וּמַעֲמָדָם.
Shylock, the Jewish moneylender, <u>whose</u> demand for a pound of the flesh of the Christian merchant is saturated with associations of blood libels and deicide, became an iconic figure in the discourse on the subject of the Jews and their status.

(69) בְּאוֹתָהּ שָׁנָה הוּא פִּרְסֵם סֵפֶר שִׁירָה **שׁ**[אוֹתוֹ הִקְדִּישׁ לְאִשְׁתּוֹ], **שׁ**[אוֹתָהּ הִכִּיר בּ-1914].
In that year, he published a book of poetry, <u>which</u> he dedicated to his wife, <u>whom</u> he met in 1914.

(b) The subordinator -הָ is used before a present tense verb that agrees with the antecedent noun. It is translated as *which, who* or *that*. Although the use of -ה rather than -שׁ as a subordinator before a present tense verb is considered preferable, it is an option that is not always exercised (see examples 64 above and 84 below).

⚠ Make sure to distinguish between the function of the initial ה"א as a definite article before nouns and adjectives and its function as a subordinator before a verb.

---

[8] See Chapter 7, 5.3.

(70) בעיית המים היא בעייה עתיקת יומין ה[מלַוֶוה את החיים בארץ ישראל מֵאָז תקופת
האָבות].

The problem of water is an ancient problem <u>that</u> has accompanied life in the Land of Israel since the period of the Patriarchs.

If the verb were in the past (or future) tense, the subordinator – -שׁ (or אשׁר) would be used:

בעיית המים היא בעייה עתיקת יומין **שׁ**ליוותה את החיים בארץ ישראל מאז תקופת האבות.

(71) היהדות דוגלת באמונה באל אחד ה[מנהיג את עולמו לבדו בהתאם לעקרונות
רציונליים של שכר ועונש] ה[מותאמים למעשיו של אדם].

Judaism espouses the belief in one God <u>who</u> rules his universe alone according to rational principles of reward and punishment <u>that</u> are tailored to man's deeds.

(72) בְּצַד הכהנים ה[מסבירים לעם את דְּבֵרי התורה] ובצד הנביאים **אשׁר** [הוכיחו את
העם על חטאיהם], מִתפתח בתקופת המלוכה גם מַעֲמָד של "חכמים".

Side by side with the priests, <u>who</u> explain the Torah to the people, and the prophets, <u>who</u> reproached the people for their sins, a class of "sages" also develops during the period of the monarchy.

In this example, the subordinator -ה is used before the present tense verb מסבירים, while אשׁר is used before the past tense verb הוכיחו.

(c) The subordinator **כי,** translated as *that*, can only be used before content clauses (instead of -שׁ).

A content clause typically contains the main idea of the sentence and can stand on its own grammatically.

Content clauses appear after verbs, adjectives and nouns of saying, feeling and knowing. For example:

- Verbs: האמין *believed*, הניח *assumed*, הֵעיד *testified, indicated*, טען *argued, claimed*, לימד *taught*, סבר *thought, believed, assumed*, צִיֵין *remarked, indicated*, קבע *stated, determined*, תפס *understood, grasped*.
- Nouns: הנחה *assumption, premise*, השערה *hypothesis, assumption*, טענה *argument, claim*, קביעה *statement, assertion, ruling, decision*, תפיסה *understanding*.
- Adjectives: ברור *it is clear*, ידוע *it is known*, כתוב *it is written*.

In the spoken language, -שׁ is more common than כי.

*The content clause is bracketed and the verb, noun or adjective of saying and knowing is
shaded:*

---

(73) מבקש אני **לטעון, כי** [שני הסיפורים קרובים זה לזה מצד נושאם].
I would like to <u>argue</u> that the two stories are very close to each other in their subject.

כי *that* is used after a verb of argument (לטעון) to introduce a content clause. Although
technically subordinate, the clause contains the main idea of the sentence. This is also the
case in the next examples.

(74) בתקופת יַבְנֶה הִתגבשה הַקְּביעה **כי** [במחלוקות בין בית הִלֵּל לבית שמאי הֲלָכה
כבית הִלֵּל.]
In the period of Yavneh, it was decided (literally: the <u>decision</u> was formed) <u>that</u> in the
controversies between the House of Hillel and the House of Shammai, the ruling
would be according to the House of Hillel.

(75) **בָּרוּר כי** [הימים שלאחר החורבָּן היו ימים של מַשְׁבֵּר ומבוכָה.]
It is <u>clear</u> that the days after the destruction were days of crisis and confusion.

(76) **יָדוּע כי** [המלך הורדוֹס שלח גדוד יהודי כדי לסַייע לרוֹמָאים במלחמתם בדרום ערב,
וש]גדוד זה לא שָׁב לארץ ישראל.]
It is <u>known</u> that King Herod sent a Jewish battalion to assist the Romans in their
war in Southern Arabia <u>and that</u> this battalion did not return to the land of Israel.

In this example there are two coordinate content clauses, introduced by different subordinators
(כי and שׁ).

⚠️ Make sure to distinguish between the uses of כי as a subordinator and as the causal
connector *because.*

6.3.2 Dependent clauses without a subordinator
The subordinate clause is not introduced by a subordinator in the following cases:

(a) In a clause beginning with a question word (e.g., מתי, איך, כיצד, איזה/איזו/אילו/אֵילו, הַאִם).

---

(77) בשירתו הוא מסַפר **כיצד** [הֶעניקו לו המוזות את יכולת השירה האלוהית].
In his poetry, he tells <u>how</u> the muses endowed him with the ability of divine
poetry.

(78) במשך מֵאות שנים התווכחו מלומדים על השאלה **האם** [היה אדם בשם הומרוס].
During hundreds of years scholars debated the question of <u>whether</u> there was a
man by the name of Homer.

(b) In a conditional clause beginning with a word of condition (e.g., אִם, אִילוּ, לוּ, אִלְמָלֵא).

---

(79) אֲרוּחה לא הִיתה שְׁלֵמה **אם** [לא נֶאֱכַל בה לחם].
A meal was not complete <u>if</u> bread was not eaten during it.

(c) In a relative clause that begins with an inflected preposition (e.g., בּוֹ, עַלְיו, לוֹ). In this case, the omission of the subordinator – a practice frowned upon by prescriptive grammarians – deprives the reader of a valuable clue to the structure of the sentence. This omission is sometimes offset by a comma placed before the subordinate clause (example 81).

The inflected preposition is bolded:

---

(80) אחד התחומים המִשׁפּטיִים [**בּוֹ** חָלוּ התפתחויות מרובות] הוא משפט המשפחה.
One of the legal areas <u>in which</u> many developments occurred is family law.

(81) בפירושו למקרא מתעמֵת הרמב"ן עם פַּרשׁנים אחרים, [**אותם** הוא מצטט].
In his Bible commentary, Nahmanides confronts other commentators, <u>whom</u> he cites.

(82) הקורא [**אֵלָיו** מכוּוָן הספר] אמוּן על ציות לחוקֵי התורה.
The reader <u>to whom</u> the book is addressed is practiced in obeying the laws of the Torah.

6.4 Strategy for parsing multi-clause sentences

A four-step strategy for parsing multi-clause sentences is suggested below and shown applied to example 63 (reproduced below).

The verbs and the copula are shaded and the subordinating particles are bolded:

---

(63) ראשונֵי הסופרים ההֵלֵניסטיים, **ש**באו בְּמַגע עם היהודים והיהדות, מתארים את היהודים כְּאומה של פילוסופים, **ה**נשלֶטֶת בּידֵי הכוהנים **ו**שׁמֶרכָּזָהּ הוא המִקְדָּשׁ ופוּלְחָנוֹ המיוחד.

Step One: Determine the number of clauses in the sentence
Locate all verbs and copulas – their number is equal to the number of clauses in the sentence.

   In example 63, there are three verbs (באו, מתארים, נשלטת) and a copula (הוא). The sentence comprises, then, four clauses.

Step Two: Locate the verb of the main clause
Locate all subordination and coordination devices, then identify the verb of the main clause – this would be the verb that is <u>not</u> introduced by a subordinator. However, remember that some dependent clauses may not be introduced by a subordinator (6.3.2 above).

In example 63, the subordinators are -שׁ (used twice) and -ה; there is one coordinating conjunction (-ו) joining two subordinate clauses. The verb מתארים is not fronted by a subordinator and is therefore identified as the verb of the main (independent) clause.

<u>Step Three: Match the verb of the main clause with its subject</u>
Match the verb of the main clause with a noun that agrees with it in number and gender and is not preceded by a preposition. Remember that this noun may appear before or after the verb.

In example 63, the plural masculine verb מתארים agrees with ראשוני הסופרים. The noun יהודים, although it is closer to the verb and agrees with it, cannot be designated as the subject because it is preceded by the preposition עם. We determine, then, that the main clause is:

ראשׁוֹנֵי הסופרים הֵלֵנִיסטיים מתארים את היהודים כְּאוּמה שׁל פילוסופים.

<u>Step Four: Match the verbs in the subordinate clauses with their subjects</u>
After the main clause has been identified, the verb in each dependent clause can be matched with its subject. The subject of the verb in the dependent clause may be found within that clause or within the immediately preceding one.

In example 63, the subject of the verb באו (במגע) is ראשׁוֹנֵי הסופרים and the subject of נשׁלטת is אומה; both subjects are found in the main clause. The copula הוא agrees with the subject מרכז.

Once the verbs have been matched with their subjects, the rest of the sentence can be mapped out by identifying the verb complements (objects and adverbs) and various components of the noun phrase (demonstrative pronouns, adjectives, prepositional phrases and quantifiers).

The procedure for parsing multi-clause sentences is further demonstrated in examples 83 and 84 below.

The main clause is shaded, the dependent clauses are bracketed, and the subordinators are bolded:

---

(83) צִיפִּיּוֹת מְשׁיחִיּוֹת שׁ[ליוו את המגורשׁים], לְצַד תְּמוּרוֹת פּוֹליטיוֹת וכלכליוֹת שׁ[יצרו בראשׁית המֵאה השׁשׁ-עשׂרה "מִזרח תיכון חדשׁ"], הפכו את ארץ ישׂראל לְיַעד מֶרכָּזִי ליהודֵי התפוצות.

The Messianic hopes that accompanied the exiles, side by side with political and economic changes that created at the beginning of the 16th century "a new Middle East," turned the Land of Israel into a central destination for the Jews of the Diaspora.

The sentence contains three verbs – הפכו ,יצרו ,ליוו – one in each clause. Since הפכו (in contrast to ליוו and יצרו) is not preceded by a subordinator, it is identified as the verb of the main clause. It agrees with the coordinated subjects ציפיות and תמורות (לצד *side by side with* has the same function as *and*). The main clause is, then:

ציפיות משׁיחיות לצד תמורות פוליטיות וכלכליות הפכו את ארץ ישׂראל ליעד מרכזי ליהודי התפוצות.

Each of the coordinated subjects in the main clause is further expanded via a dependent clause introduced by -שׁ.

(84) ‏ציורי הקיר ש[נמצאו בבית הכנסת בדוּרָא], ש[נֶחֱשָׁבִים כדוגמה בוֹלֶטֶת לשימוש‏
‏נִרְחָב באוֹמָנוּת הדְמוּת], מתארים סְצֵינות מן התנ"ך בלבד.‏

The wall paintings found in the synagogue in Dura, which are considered a promi-
nent example of the widespread use of figurative art, describe only scenes from
the Bible.

As seen in the previous example, the main clause – ‏ציורי הקיר מתארים סצינות מן התנ"ך‏
‏בלבד‏ – is interrupted by two dependent clauses. The three verbs – ‏נמצאו, נחשבים‏ and
‏מתארים‏ have the same subject, ‏ציורי הקיר‏. Note that although the verb ‏נחשבים‏ is in the
present tense, ‏ש-‏ (rather than ‏ה-‏) was used to embed the second clause within the main
clause.

6.4.1 Since very long sentences may prove unwieldy in translation into English, they can be
broken up into shorter units without loss or distortion of meaning. This is the route taken by
the professional translator who rendered the paragraph-long sentence below in four shorter
sentences:

‏מתוך עוֹשר עצום של נושאים שונים שבפרשתנו: הלכות, דינים ומשפטים, המסדירים חיי‏
‏אדם ביחסיו בינו לבין הֶחֶברה, בינו לבין בני עמו, בינו לבין בני עם אחר, בינו לבין חלש‏
‏ממנו או חזק ממנו, בינו לבין שְׁכֵנו, בינו לבין שונאו, בינו לבין הָצֶמַח והחי, המסדירים חיי‏
‏אדם בחוּלוֹ, בעבודתו, בשַׁבָּתוֹ ובמועדיו, והקובעים יחס בינו לבין קוֹנוֹ – נבחר קֶטַע קטן‏
‏לעיון מדויק ומדוקדק בפְרָטָיו.‏

This Sidra is extraordinarily rich in the variety of its themes, the multiplicity of
laws, judgments and statutes governing every facet of human existence. This
comprehensive legislation covers relations between man and society, between
members of the same community and between peoples, between man and man,
man and his enemy, between man and plant and animal. The Torah herein regulates
the life of the Jew at work and at leisure, at Sabbath and festival and relations
between man and his Maker. We shall select just one small sample from this
wealth of material for special study.

From: Nehama Leibowitz, *Studies in Shemot* (translated by Aryeh Newman, Israel, 1976).

✗#6 7. Lexical repetition

Lexical repetition is a sentence expansion device also found in English: a noun in the main
clause is repeated (verbatim or with a slight change). A dash or a comma appears before the
reiterated noun. The repetition allows the writer to append a dependent clause or avoid an
ambiguity of reference.

The reiterated noun is bolded and the dependent clauses are bracketed:

---

(85) חורבן בית שֵני הביא לידי **התערערות** הֶחֶברה היהודית בארץ ישראל – **התערערות,**
ה[מתוארת על ידי התנַאים].

The destruction of the Second Temple caused <u>a weakening</u> of Jewish society in the Land of Israel – <u>a weakening</u> that is described by the Tannaim.

The repetition of התערערות (and not the noun חברה) is the subject of the dependent clause המתוארת על ידי התנאים.

(86) סכְסוך לְאוּמִי עָשׂוּי לְהשׁפּיע על קֶצֶב השינויים בחַיֵי היוֹמיוֹם של תושבֵי העיר, **שינויים**
שֶ[מֵהם יָפִיק תּועֶלֶת אחד מן הצְדָדִים או שְנֵיהם].

A national conflict may influence the pace of <u>changes</u> in the daily life of the people of the city, <u>changes</u> from which one of the sides [in the conflict] or both will benefit.

The reiteration makes it clear that the reference of the pronoun מהם is שינויים (and not חיי היומיום or תושבי העיר).

(87) מוּנָח זה צֵיֵּן **תַהֲלִיך** של אקוּלטוּרציה, שֶ[גוֹרם לאדם או לקבוצה שינוי התנהגות,
עֲרכים מוסָדוֹת וכיו"ב] – **תהליך** שֶ[הִיה תולָדָה מן המַגָע עם היַווֹנוּת].

This term indicated <u>a process</u> of acculturation, which causes in an individual or group a change of behavior, values, institutions etc., <u>a process</u> that was the result of the contact with Hellenism Boston.

The repetition of the noun allows the addition of a second dependent clause.
Note the abbreviation וכיו"ב=וְכַיּוֹצֵא בָּזֶה *etc.*

✗#7   8. Apposition תְּמוּרָה

Apposition is a sentence expansion device that is also found in English. An example is the following sentence "Copley, the painter, was born in Boston," where "Copley" and "the painter" are in apposition.

As this example illustrates, apposition involves the coordination of two consecutive nouns or noun phrases (the appositives) that have the same reference. The second noun (or noun phrase) does not present any new information – it serves to identify, define, particularize or illustrate the first. Therefore, it can be omitted without significant loss of meaning.

The insertion of an appositive may delay the appearance of the verb (examples 92–93) as well as separate the verb from its object (example 31 above).

8.1 Recognizing apposition
Apposition is signaled with punctuation marks (i.e., typographically) or with words (i.e., lexically). Short appositives may not be signaled at all (אהרון הכהן *Aaron the priest* in example 92 below.)

8.1.1 Typographic signals for apposition are commas (example 88 and 93), dashes (examples 89 and 92), colon (example 90) or parenthesis (example 91).

The appositives are bracketed and shaded:

---

(88) [רבי יוסף קארו], [בעל השולחן ערוך], התנגד למנהג.
Rabbi Joseph Caro, the author of the Shulḥan Arukh, objected to the custom.

The appositive identifies Rabbi Joseph Caro as the author of the book; note the use of בעל in the sense of *author*.

(89) לַ[חוֹמֶר] – [בַּיִת, תַּכְשִׁיט, קַנְקַן קָפֶה, אוֹ כְּתַב יָד] – תּוֹחֶלֶת חַיִּים אֲרוּכָה יוֹתֵר מְזוֹ שֶׁל הָאָדָם.
Material – a house, a piece of jewelry, a coffee pot, or a manuscript – has a greater life expectancy than that of a person.

In this example, as also in examples 90 through 92, the appositives proceed from the general to the particular.

(90) הַיִּישׁוּב הַיָּשָׁן הָיָה מְרֻכָּז בְּעִיקָרוֹ בְּ[אַרְבַּע עָרֵי הַקּוֹדֶשׁ]: [יְרוּשָׁלַיִם, צְפַת, טְבֶרְיָה וְחֶבְרוֹן].
The "old Yishuv" was concentrated mostly in the four holy towns: Jerusalem, Safad, Tiberias and Hebron.

(91) בַּגְּנִיזָה טוֹמְנִים [תַּשְׁמִישֵׁי קְדוּשָׁה] ([סִידּוּר, סֵפֶר תַּנַ"ךְ, תְּפִילִּין, מְזוּזוֹת]) פְּגוּמִים שֶׁיָּצְאוּ מִשִּׁימוּשׁ.
In the Geniza are put away defective religious articles (prayer book, Bible, phylacteries, mezuzahs) that are no longer in use.

Note that the second appositive separates the first one (תשמישי קדושה) from its adjective (פגומים).

(92) [שְׁתֵּי מָסוֹרוֹת עַתִּיקוֹת אֵלֶּה] – [הַזֶּבַח הַמְשׁוּתָּף שֶׁל [יִתְרוֹ], [כֹּהֵן מִדְיָן], עִם אַהֲרֹן [הַכֹּהֵן] וְזִקְנֵי יִשְׂרָאֵל וְהַהוֹרָאוֹת בְּעִנְיְנֵי מִשְׁפָּט] – בָּאוֹת לְלַמְּדֵנוּ עַל עִנְיָין זֶה.
These two ancient traditions – the communal sacrifice of Jethro, the Midianite priest, with Aaron the Priest and the elders of Israel, and the instructions in legal matters – come to teach us about this issue.

A short appositive identifying Jethro as the Midianite priest is embedded within a longer appositive whose function is to specify the two ancient traditions: the shared priestly sacrifice and the directives in legal matters. The appositive הכהן *the priest* identifies Aaron.

(93) [הַיִּידִישׁ], [שְׂפַת הַתִּקְשׁוֹרֶת הָעִיקָרִית שֶׁל יְהוּדֵי מִזְרַח אֵירוֹפָּה], הָיְתָה יִיחוּדִית לָהֶם.
Yiddish, the main language of communication of the Jews of Eastern Europe, was unique to them.

⚠ Note that a phrase separated by dashes from the rest of the sentence may be a parenthetical (additional) comment rather than a semantically equivalent appositive.

---

(94) הַדָּתוֹת הַשּׁוֹנוֹת – כָּל אַחַת בְּדַרְכָּהּ – מְתָאֲרוֹת אֶת מַהוּת "יוֹם הַדִּין" וְאֶת סוּגֵי הַשָּׂכָר וְהָעוֹנֶשׁ הַצְּפוּיִים לָאָדָם.

The different religions – each in its own way – describe the nature of the "Day of Judgment" and the kinds of reward and punishment that are expected by man.

The phrase כָּל אַחַת בדרכה is a parenthetical comment. If an appositive were to be used, it might be הַיַּהֲדוּת, הַנַּצְרוּת וְהָאִסְלָאם, to specify what is meant by הַדָּתוֹת הַשּׁוֹנוֹת.

8.1.2 Lexical signals for apposition are the following expressions inserted between the appositives:

- לְמָשָׁל *for example,* כְּמוֹ *like,* כְּגוֹן *such as* offer specific examples after a summative statement.
- קְרֵי, דְּהַיְינוּ, הַיְינוּ, כְּלוֹמַר, זֹאת אוֹמֶרֶת *that is, i.e., namely* explain and elaborate on a general statement.

⚠ Make sure to distinguish in unpointed text between הַיְינוּ *i.e.* (pronounced with the first syllable stressed) and הָיִינוּ *we were* (pronounced with the second syllable stressed).

- בְּעִיקָר, בִּמְיוּחָד, בְּיִיחוּד *particularly* limit the application of a general statement to a special case.

The appositives are bracketed and shaded; words that signal an appositive are bolded:

---

(95) נְוֵה מִדְבָּר הוּא מָקוֹם בַּמִּדְבָּר, שֶׁמָּצוּי בּוֹ [מָקוֹר מַיִם] (**כְּגוֹן** [מַעְיָין]).

An oasis is a place in the desert in which there is <u>a source of water</u> (<u>such as a spring</u>).

(96) שְׁאָר הַמִּתְיַישְּׁבִים הָיוּ [אַשְׁכְּנַזִּים], **כְּלוֹמַר**, [יוֹצְאֵי מִזְרַח אֵירוֹפָּה וּמֶרְכָּזָהּ].

The rest of the settlers were <u>Ashkenazim</u>, <u>that is,</u> <u>natives of Eastern and Central Europe</u>.

(97) לְפִי הַשְׁקָפָתוֹ, [הַלְּאוּמִיּוּת הַיְּהוּדִית], **קְרִי,** [הַצִּיּוֹנוּת], הִיא הַדָּבָר הַיָּחִיד שֶׁיָּעֲנִיק לְחַיֵּינוּ אֶת הַמַּשְׁמָעוּת הַמְּלֵאָה.

According to his view, <u>Jewish nationalism</u>, <u>that is</u>, <u>Zionism</u>, is the only thing that will endow our lives with a full meaning.

(98) בִּתְחִלַּת סֵפֶר בְּרֵאשִׁית מְסוּפָּר עַל הַנָּהָר שֶׁסּוֹבֵב בְּ[עֵדֶן] (**דְּהַיְינוּ בְּ[גַן עֵדֶן]**) וּמַשְׁקָה אֶת הַגַּן.

At the beginning of the Book of Genesis, we are told (literally: it is told) about a river that flows in <u>Eden</u> (<u>i.e.,</u> in <u>the Garden of Eden</u>) and irrigates the garden.

(99) [סִפְרוּת הַחָכְמָה], **בְּעִיקָר** [סֵפֶר מִשְׁלֵי], הִיא סִפְרוּת מְחַנֶּכֶת.
<u>The Wisdom Literature</u>, <u>in particular</u> <u>the Book of Proverbs</u>, is didactic literature.

8.1.2.1 The appositive is sometimes introduced by the pronouns הוּא, הִיא, הֵם, הֵן; the pronoun can be ignored in translation.

(100) הָרַמְבַּ"ן הִכְנִיס בְּפֵירוּשׁוֹ מִ[תּוֹרַת הַנִּסְתָּר], **הִיא** [חָכְמַת הַקַּבָּלָה].
In his commentary, Nahmanides inserted [elements] from <u>mysticism</u>, <u>that is</u>, <u>the Kabbalah</u>.

Note the use of תורה (usually, *Torah*, *Pentateuch*) in the more general sense of *discipline*, *theory*. Similarly, משנה (usually *Mishnah*) is also used in the sense of *doctrine* or *theory*.

(101) בְּפַרְשָׁנוּתוֹ צָעַד בְּעִקְבוֹת ["הַמּוֹרֶה הַגָּדוֹל"] **הֲלוֹא הוּא** [הָרַמְבַּ"ם].
In his commentary, he followed <u>"the great teacher,"</u> <u>namely</u>, <u>Maimonides</u>.

The word הלוא is added for emphasis.

🏋#8 9. Ellipsis השמטה

יָדַע שׁוֹר קֹנֵהוּ, **וַחֲמוֹר אֵבוּס** בְּעָלָיו (ישעיהו א ג)
An ox knows its owner, an ass [knows] its master's crib (Isaiah 1.3)

The term ellipsis refers here to the omission of a noun or a verb in order to avoid repetition. Since the omitted element has already been mentioned, and thanks to the parallelism between the sentence parts, the omitted word can be easily reconstructed by the reader. A dash is sometimes placed where the omitted word would have appeared (example 103).

The shaded brackets indicate the location of the omitted element; the word that is not repeated is bolded:

---

(102) המדינה מחוּלֶּקֶת ל-16 מחוזות, אשר שמונה מהם **נמצאים** מצָפון לנָהָר ושמונה [ ] מדרומו.

The country is divided into 16 regions, eight of which are found north of the river and eight [are found] south of it.

(103) השפה העברית **הייתה נפוצה** בקֶרֶב המַשְכילים ואילו הארמית – [ ] בקֶרֶב פשוּטֵי העָם.

Hebrew was widespread among the educated people, whereas Aramaic [was widespread] among the simple people.

(104) בקהילות קטנות היה על פִּי רוֹב רק בית ספר אחד ואילו בקהילות גדולות היו [ ] רַבים.

In small [Jewish] communities there was usually only one school whereas in large ones there were many.

In this example, the omitted noun has to be reconstructed in the plural:

ואילו בקהילות גדולות היו **בתי ספר** רבים.

Confusables

1. אֲשֶׁר; (בַּ)אֲשֶׁר לְ-; בַּאֲשֶׁר; מֵאֲשֶׁר; לַאֲשֶׁר; כַּאֲשֶׁר

When accompanied by a preposition, the subordinator אשר (a formal alternative for -ש) takes on different meanings.

1.1 -(בַּ)אֲשֶׁר לְ *with regard to*

The preposition -בַּ is optional.

Synonymous expressions are: בְּדָבָר, בְּנוֹגֵעַ לְ, לְגַבֵּי, בְּעִנְיָן.

> (105) קַיֶּימֶת מַחְלוֹקֶת **בָּאשר** למקום הוּלָדְתוֹ.
> There is a controversy <u>with regard to</u> his birthplace.

1.2 בַּאֲשֶׁר *because, since*

> (106) בתחום מדעי החֶברה קשֶׁה להגיע למסְקָנוֹת ברורות **באשר להַשׁעָרַת הַמֶּחְקָר, באשר** הוא איננו מנוהָל בתנאים מבוּקרים הֵיטֵב.
> In the social sciences it is difficult to reach clear conclusions <u>concerning</u> the hypothesis of the study, <u>since</u> it is not conducted under well controlled conditions.
>
> This example illustrates the difference between -באשר ל *with regard to, concerning* and באשר *since, because*.

1.3 מֵאֲשֶׁר *[more] than*

In comparative sentences, מאשר replaces מ/מן before a preposition, an infinitive verb and a clause.

> (107) השימוש בּסְמָלים יהודיים בבית הכנסת היה מרוּבֶּה יותר בארץ ישראל **מֵאֲשֶׁר** בתפוצות.
> The use of Jewish symbols in the synagogue was greater in the Land of Israel <u>than</u> outside it.

1.4 בַּאֲשֶׁר, לַאֲשֶׁר *wherever*

> (108) הגיבור נלחם בָּרֶשַׁע **בַּאשר** הוא.
> The protagonist fights evil <u>wherever</u> it is.

> (109) בַּלָהוֹת הֶעָבָר ממשיכות לרדוֹף את גיבור הסיפור **לַאשר** יֵלֵךְ.
> The horrors of the past continue to pursue the protagonist of the story <u>wherever</u> he goes.

1.5 כַּאֲשֶׁר *when; with, and*

כאשר and its abbreviated (and less formal) form כְּשֶ- introduce adverbial clauses of time (example 110).

כאשר may also be used in the sense of *with*; it is then preceded by a comma (example 111). This use is not considered normative and a careful editor would replace כאשר in this sense with -וְ.

---

(110) הנוצרים היו אלה שיֵסדו את המדינה כאשר בָּנו שם את המִנזָר ואז את העיר.
It was the Christians who founded the state <u>when</u> they built there the monastery and then the city.

(111) העברית היא בדרך כְּלָל שְׂפַת נושׂא-נשׂוּא-מושׂא, כאשר הסֵדֶר גָמיש לְמַדַי וניתָן לשינוי.
Hebrew is generally a subject-verb-object language, <u>with</u> the order being quite flexible and changeable.

(112) יש דרכים מְגוּוָנות להכנסת מֶסֶר סוֹדי לשיר, כאשר הדֶרֶך המפורסֶמֶת ביותר היא הדרך של הֲפיכת השיר. בדרך זו ניתָן לשמוע את המסר הסוֹדי כאשר שומעים את השיר לְאָחור.
There are diverse ways to insert a secret message into a song, <u>and</u> the most famous one is the reversal of the song. In this way, it is possible to hear the secret message <u>when</u> one listens to the song backwards.

In this example we see both uses of כאשר.

#9 2. An initial ה"א (that is not part of the word) has several unrelated functions:

(a) A definite article (*the*) before nouns and adjectives.

(b) A subordinator before a present tense verb (see 6.3.1 (b) above).

(c) A time adverbial (e.g., השנה *this year*).

(d) An interrogative particle (ה"א השאלה) at the beginning of a yes/no question. Common in biblical Hebrew, in modern Hebrew the interrogative ה"א is usually replaced by הַאִם. Neither has a fixed translation equivalent in English (e.g., הידעת? האם ידעת? *did you know?*, היודע אתה? האם אתה יודע? *do you know?*).

הֲלָנֶצַח תֹּאכַל חֶרֶב (שמואל ב ב כו)
Must the sword devour forever? Samuel II, 2.26

הֲרָצַחְתָּ וְגַם יָרָשְׁתָּ (מלכים א כא יט)
Would you murder and take possession? Kings I, 21.19

(113) הֲיֵשׁ תורה באדם פשוט שאינו בן-תורה, שואל המִדְרָשׁ.
The Midrash asks: <u>is there</u> Torah [learning] in a simple man who is not a Torah scholar?

(114) הַאִם ניקוד זה קָבוּעַ או מִשְׁתַּנֶּה?
<u>Is</u> this vocalization fixed or variable?

3. כִּי; כִּי אָז; כִּי אִם; אִם/אַף כִּי; וְכִי #10

3.1 כי has two unrelated functions: a subordinator (*that*) introducing content clauses (see 6.3.1 (c) above), and a causal sentence connector (*because*).
A third function of כי (found in legalistic biblical Hebrew and rare today) is to introduce a condition or time clause (e.g., "וְכִי יְרִיבֻן אֲנָשִׁים" *and if men strive together*, Exodus 21. 18).

3.2 כי אז (colloquially – אז and formally – אֱזַי) introduces the result of a supposition: אם . . . כי; אז *if... then*.

(115) אם תתקבל ההנחה **כי** שַׁמַּאי והלכותיו מְיַיצְגִים את הַהֲלָכָה היותר עתיקה,
בעוד בית הִלֵּל מייצגים את ההלכה היותר "מִתְקַדֶּמֶת," **כי אז** ניתָן להַבְחִין פעם נוֹסֶפֶת
בהתְחַשְּׁבוּת ההלכה התַּלְמוּדִית בילדים בְּשֶׁל הֱיוֹתָם ילדים.
If the assumption <u>that</u> Shammai and his laws represent the more ancient ruling, whereas the school of Hillel represents the more "progressive" law is accepted, <u>then</u> it is possible to notice once more the consideration [given by] Talmudic law to children by virtue of their being children.

Two different meanings of כי are illustrated in this example.

3.3 כי אם *rather* is interchangeable with אֶלָּא (after the negative particles, אַל, לֹא and אֵין; example 116).[9]
When not preceded by a word of negation, כי אם represents two independent components: a subordinator (*that*) followed by a conditional clause beginning with *if* (example 117).

(116) הסיפור מתמקד **לֹא** בפן הטכנולוגי **כי אם** בפן האנושי.
The story focuses <u>not</u> on the technological aspect, <u>but rather</u> on the human aspect.

(117) ההַנָּחָה הרוֹוַחַת היא **כי אם** לא יבוצע החִבְרוּת, תִּפָּגַע הִתְפַּתְחוּתוֹ האישית והחברתית של היָחִיד.
The prevailing assumption is <u>that if</u> socialization does not occur, the individual's personal and social development will be harmed.

---

[9] See Chapter 10, 1.2.

3.4 אַף כִּי, אִם כִּי *though* is an expression of concession (synonymous with אַף עַל פִּי שֶ-).

---

(118) רוב העולים עובדים, **אִם כִּי** רוּבָּם לא במִקְצוֹעוֹתיהם.

Most of the Olim (immigrants to Israel) are employed, <u>though</u> most of them not in their professions.

3.5 וְכִי introduces a rhetorical question or an expression of doubt. Sometimes (in elevated style) the word כְּלוּם is used for this purpose.

---

(119) **וְכִי** זאת התשובה?

And is this the answer?

---

4. Three meanings of אַךְ

(a) אַךְ=אֲבָל *but, however* appears between coordinate clauses (example 120).

(b) אַךְ=רַק *only*. In this sense, אַךְ may be preceded by וְ- (וְאַךְ *and only*). For emphasis, אַךְ וְרַק is used (example 122).

(c) In highly formal use, אַךְ functions as a time expression before a past tense verb, translatable *just as, at the moment that* (e.g., אַךְ זרחה השמש *just as the sun rose*).

---

(120) רוב תושבי מדינת ישראל הם יהודים, **אַךְ** יש בה מיעוט גדול של ערבים מוסלמים, וקבוצות מיעוט אחרות.

Most of the residents of the State of Israel are Jewish, <u>but</u> it has a large minority of Moslem Arabs as well as other minorities.

(121) התלמוד הַבַּבלי הפך לספר הלימוד העיקרי שנלמד בתפוצות ישראל, **וְאַךְ** מעַטים עסקו בתלמוד הירושלמי.

The Babylonian Talmud became the main textbook that was studied in the diaspora, and <u>only </u>few studied the Jerusalem Talmud.

(122) **אַךְ וְרַק** גִּרְסה אחת של שני האֶפּוֹסים הללו נשתמרה.

<u>Only</u> one version of these two epics has been preserved.

References

אורנן, 2000
אלון, 2004
חרל"פ, 2002
עבאדי, 1988
צדקה, 1981
רודריג (שורצולד), 1994

Berman, 1980
Celce-Murcia. & Larsen-Freeman, 1999
Coffin & Bolozky, 2005
Glinert, 1989, 2005
Ornan, 2007
Quirk & Greenbaum, 1975
Richards, Platt, & Platt, 1992
Schwarzwald, 2001.

Chapter 1: Word Order and Sentence Structure – Exercises

Exercise #1: Locating the subject of a simple sentence

The rules to go by (see also section 1):
1. The subject is the noun that (a) agrees with the predicate (verb or verb substitute) in gender and number, and (b) is not preceded by a preposition.
2. When there are several (coordinated) nouns of different genders serving as subjects, the verb agrees with the masculine noun.
3. When the subject is a construct phrase, the verb agrees with the head noun.
4. When the sentence begins with an adverbial or an object complement, the subject usually appears after the verb.
5. The verb and the subject may be far apart.

What to do: select the correct verb form from the alternatives given below the sentence.

Example:

חודשי השנה בלוח העברי **נקבעים** לפי הירח.

נקבע, נקבעת, נקבעים

Explanation: the verb agrees with the plural חודשים, the head noun of the construct phrase.

---

1. המנהג של מִשְׂחֲקֵי פורים (ביידיש, "פורים שְׁפִּיל") _____ בהַשְׁפעת הקַרְנָבָלים באירופה.

   נוצר, נוצרה, נוצרו   was/were created

2. תיאוּר חַיֵּי הָאָבות בספר בְּרֵאשית _____ סיפורים על על מַחסוֹר במים ומְריבות על בְּאֵרות מים.

   כולל, כוללים, כוללות   include(s)

3. שביעות הרצון הכללית מהפרוֹיֶקט של כל המשתתפים _____ על ידי ארבע שאלות סגורות.

   נבדק, נבדקה, נבדקו   was/were examined

Glossary

---

1. מִשׂחקי פורים   Purim games
   הַשפעת הקרנבלים   the influence of the Carnivals
2. תיאור חיי האבות   the description of the life of the Patriarchs
   ספר בראשית   Genesis
   מחסור במים   water shortage
   מריבות על בארות מים   disputes over wells
3. שביעות הרצון הכללית   the general satisfaction
   פרויקט   project
   משתתפים   participants
   שאלות סגורות   closed (multiple choice) questions

4. הֻנַחַת שתי הַחַלוֹת על שולחן השבת החגיגי _____ את כֶּפֶל כמות הַמָן שיָרַד מן השמים לבני ישראל בַּמִדְבָּר כל יום שישי.
מסמל, מסמֶלֶת, מסמלים   symbolize(s)

5. המַצב הַכַּלכָּלי הקשה בפולין והִתגברות כוחות הימין הקיצוני בשנות השלושים _____ את הלַחַץ על היהודים.
הגביר, הגבירה, הגבירו   increased

6. בתקופת התלמוד, בַּמֵאה ה-4 לספירה, _____ בטְבֶּריה החישוב לקְביעת השָנים המעוּבָּרות.
פורסם, פורסמה, פורסמו   was/were publicized

7. בפירושיו של רש"י למקרא ולתלמוד _____ יותר מ-2,000 שמות של כֵּלים, מַכשירים, צמחים ובעלֵי חיים בצרפתית עתיקה.
נזכר, נזכרת, נזכרים   is/are mentioned

8. בסִפרות האֵירופית _____ השפעתו של התנ"ך על השפעת הספרות היְוָונית והרומית.
עולֶה, עולָה, עולות   exceed(s)

Glossary

4.	placement of two challahs הנחת שתי חלות
	the festive Sabbath table שולחן השבת החגיגי
	double the quantity of manna כפל כמות המן
5.	the difficult economic situation in Poland המצב הכלכלי הקשה בפולין
	the strengthening of the extreme right factions התגברות כוחות הימין הקיצוני
	the 1930's שנות השלושים
	pressure לחץ
6.	in the 4th century C.E. במאה ה-4 לספירה
	Tiberias טבריה
	calculation for fixing the leap years חישוב לקביעת השנים המעוברות
7.	Rashi's Bible and Talmud commentaries פירושיו של רש"י למקרא ולתלמוד
	tools, instruments, plants and animals כלים, מכשירים, צמחים ובעלי חיים
	Old French צרפתית עתיקה
8.	European literature ספרות אירופית
	the influence of the Bible השפעתו של התנ"ך
	Greek and Roman literature הספרות היוונית והרומית

9. ‏בְּמָסוֹרֶת הַפַּרְשָׁנִית _____ בְּעִיקָר שָׁלוֹשׁ סִיבּוֹת אֶפְשָׁרִיּוֹת מַדּוּעַ דָּרַשׁ אֱלוֹהִים בִּיצּוּעַ עֲקֵדָה.

הועלה, הועלתה, הועלו   was/were brought up

10. ‏מִפֵּירוּשָׁיו הָרַבִּים שֶׁל רַשְׁבָּ"ם לַמִּקְרָא _____ בְּיָדֵינוּ כַּיּוֹם רַק פֵּירוּשׁוֹ לַתּוֹרָה.

נמצא, נמצאת, נמצאים   is/are found

11. ‏לַטֶּקְסְטִים מְשִׁיחִיִּים רַבִּים _____ הַשִּׁימּוּשׁ בְּמוּשָׂגִים מִן הַשָּׂדֶה הַסֶּמַנְטִי שֶׁל צָבָא וּמִלְחָמָה.

אופייני, אופיינית, אופייניים   is/are characterisic

12. ‏מוֹקֵד נוֹסָף לִפְעִילוּת חֶבְרָתִית לְתִיקּוּן פְּנֵי הַחֶבְרָה _____ הַנּוֹעַר שֶׁל יָמֵינוּ בִּפְעִילוּת לְמַעַן תְּנוּעוֹת שִׁחְרוּר לְמִינֵיהֶן.

מצא, מצאה, מצאו   found

Glossary

9. ‏מסורת פרשנית	exegetical tradition
‏בעיקר	mainly
‏שלוש סיבות אפשריות	three possible reasons
‏מדוע	why
‏דרש ביצוע העקדה	demanded carrying out the binding of Isaac (the Akeda)
10. ‏פירושיו הרבים של רשב"ם	the many commentaries of Rashbam (Rabbi Shmuel ben Meir)
‏מקרא	Bible
11. ‏טקסטים משיחיים	Messianic texts
‏שימוש	use
‏מושגים מן השדה הסמנטי של צבא ומלחמה	concepts from the semantic field of army and war
12. ‏מוקד נוסף	an additional focus
‏פעילות חברתית	social activity
‏תיקון פני החברה	social repair, social reform
‏נוער	youth, young people

Exercise #2: Translating topicalized sentences

> **The rules to go by:** see section 2.
> **What to do:**
> 1. Underline the topicalized element and highlight the pronoun suffix that refers to it.
> 2. Translate the sentences.
> **Example:**
>
> זיקת הגומלין בין ההלכה לאגדה, יסודה במקור וברקע המשותף לשתיהן
>
> The basis for the mutual relationship between the Halakhah and the Aggadah is their common source and background.

1. ישיבה על כיסא האב פירושה לקבל את מקומו במשפחה, את תפקידו ורכושו.

2. הַלֶּקְסִיקוֹלוֹגִיה – עיקר עְנְיָינה הוא תיעוד אוצר המילים במילון.

3. הַמִּסְפָּר "שִׁבְעִים" יְסוֹדוֹ בסיפור אַגָּדָה בְּדְבַר שִׁבְעִים זְקֵנים שהוּזמנוּ על ידי המלך לתַרְגֵם את התורה.

4. לשון זו רֵאשית צְמיחתה נעוּצה כַנראה עוד בימים הראשונים של הבית השני.

5. גַל העלייה הציוני-לאוֹמי הראשוֹן תחילתוֹ בשנת 1882.

6. עֵדים שהִתְקשוּ לענות על השאלות היה נשׂיא בית-הדין בא לעֶזרתָם.

Glossary

1.	ישיבה על כסא האב sitting on the father's chair
	פירוש meaning, significance
	תפקידו ורכושו his role and his property
2.	לקסיקולוגיה lexicology
	עיקר ענייניה its main concern
	תיעוד documentation
	אוצר המילים vocabulary
3.	בדבר שבעים זקנים regarding 70 elders
	הוזמנו על ידי המלך לתרגם את התורה invited by the King to translate the Torah
4.	ראשית צמיחתה נעוצה כנראה ב its inception is apparently traceable to
	הבית השני the Second Temple
5.	גל העלייה הציוני-לאומי הראשון the first Zionist-nationalist immigration wave
	תחילתו its beginning
6.	עדים שהתקשו לענות witnesses who had difficulty answering
	נשיא בית הדין the president of the court
	בא לעזרתם come to their aid

7. הַיֶּלֶד – בִּרְכַּת "שֶׁעָשַׂנִי יהודי" לִיוְּתָה בְּשַׁחַר חַיָּיו אֶת צְעָדָיו הָרִאשׁוֹנִים.

8. לְדַעַת מְחַבֵּר הַסֵּפֶר, דִּימּוּי הָאִשָּׁה כְּנָחוּתָה מְקוֹרוֹ בִּצְרָכִים פְּסִיכוֹלוֹגִיִּים וְכַלְכָּלִיִּים שֶׁל הָאֵלִיטָה הַגַּבְרִית.

9. שִׁימּוּשׁ זֶה שֶׁל "הָרִים" בְּהוֹרָאַת "אֲזוֹרִים," הָאוֹפְיָינִי לִיחֶזְקֵאל, הָאַכָּדִית הִיא בִּרְקָעוֹ.

10. הַיְסוֹדוֹת הַמַּבְדִּילִים בֵּין שְׁנֵי הַדִּיאָלֶקְטִים חוֹתָם הָעַתִּיקוּת טָבוּעַ בָּהֶם.

Glossary

.7	"שעשני יהודי"	"who made me Jewish"
	ליוותה	accompanied
	בשחר חייו	in his early days (the dawn of his days)
	צעדיו הראשונים	his first steps
.8	מחבר הספר	the author
	דימוי האישה כנחותה	the image of the woman as inferior
	צרכים פסיכולוגיים וכלכליים	psychological and economic needs
	האליטה הגברית	the male elite
.9	הלשון האכדית	Akkadian language
	שימוש	use
	בהוראת "אזורים"	in the sense of "regions"
	אופייני ליחזקאל	typical to Ezekiel
	רקע	background
.10	דיאלקטים	dialects
	מבדילים	distinguish
	חותם העתיקות טבוע בהם	they are marked with the stamp of antiquity

Exercise #3: Detecting distant sentence elements

The rules to go by: see section 3.
What to do: underline the separated sentence components and enter the sentence number in the appropriate cell in the chart.
Example:

מאז ומתמיד <u>הייתה</u> החקלאות בארץ ישראל <u>תלויה</u> בגשמים.

Explanation: in this example the components of the verb phrase are separated by the subject; this is due to the fact that the sentence begins with an adverbial.

---

split verb phrase	verb at a distance from its object
example,	

1. בעקבות הנוסע הירושלמי יַעֲקֹב הַלֵוי סָפיר שביקר בגְניזה הקָהירית והוציא ממנה מספר דפים הֵחֵלּוּ אנשים נוספים להוציא חומר מן הגניזה.

2. את רוב החומר אשר מילא את עליית הגג של הגניזה בקהיר הצליח שֶׁכְטֶר להעביר לקיימברידג'.

3. את הקֵץ על קהילות היהודים בספרד הביא הניצָחון של מַלכי ספרד על המוסְלְמים.

Glossary

---

following the Jerusalemite traveler בעקבות הנוסע הירושלמי	.1
Cairo Geniza גניזה קהירית	
took a few pages out of it הוציא ממנה מספר דפים	
began הֵחֵלּוּ	
most of the material רוב החומר	.2
attic עליית הגג	
Schechter שכטר	
transfer to Cambridge להעביר לקיימברידג'	
end קֵץ	.3
the victory of the Kings of Spain over the Moslems הניצָחון של מלכי ספרד על המוסלמים	

4. בְּרְבוֹת הימים הֵחֵל תרגום הַשִּׁבְעִים לשמש בָּסִיס לדְרָשׁוֹת הָאלגוריות של הַיַהֲדות הַהֶלֶניסטית.

5. לעיתים לא הגיעו השליחים בזמן לקהילות המרוחקות שבגולה, ועל־כֵּן נהגו, מתוך סָפֵק, לחוג שְׁנֵי יְמֵי חג.

Glossary

.4	ברבות הימים in the course of time
	תרגום השבעים the Septuagint
	לשמש בסיס serve as a basis
	הדרשות האלגוריות של היהדות ההלניסטית the allegorical interpretations of Hellenistic Jewry
.5	לעיתים sometimes
	שליחים emissaries
	מרוחקות distant
	לחוג שני ימי חג celebrate two festival days

Exercise #4: Identifying impersonal verbs

> **The rules to go by:** see section 4.
> **What to do:** identify the impersonal verb(s) in each paragraph.
> The number of impersonal verbs in each sentence is given in parenthesis.
> The first item is an example (the check mark indicates the correct answer).

1. פירוש רש"י לתורה היה הספר הראשון ש**נדפס** בעברית בשנת 1475 –שלוש מאות ושבעים
שנה לאחר מותו של רש"י. את הספר **הדפיסו** באותיות מיוחדות ש**נקראות** "כתב רש"י", למרות
שרש"י עצמו לא **הכיר** כתב זה. (1)

   __ **נדפס**

   √ **הדפיסו**

   __ **נקראות**

   __ **הכיר**

2. עד גלות בבל **כונו** החודשים במקרא לפי מספרם הסידורי: החודש הראשון, השני וכו'. אולם
לארבעה חודשים **מוצאים** במקרא שמות עבריים. שלושה מהם, **הנזכרים** בקשר לבנין מקדש
שלמה, הם כנראה ממוצא פניקי או כנעני. בכתבי הקודש ש**נכתבו** לאחר גלות בבל **נזכרים** כמה
חודשים בשמותיהם הבבליים. (1)

   __ **כונו**

   __ **מוצאים**

   __ **נזכרים**

   __ **נכתבו**

   __ **נזכרים**

3. בתקופת בית שני וזמן רב לאחריו **היו מקדשים** את החודשים, כלומר **קובעים** את ראשי
החודשים, על-פי עדים ש**ראו** את חרמש הירח **המתחדש** בשמי המערב לפני שקיעת השמש. (2)

   __ **היו מקדשים**

   __ **קובעים**

   __ **ראו**

   __ **מתחדש**

4. **סבורים** שהמנהג להתחפש בפורים **הושפע** גם מן המסורות של העמים הנוצרים. באירופה **נהגו**
לקיים נשפי מסכות באביב, בתקופה שבה **חל** חג הפורים. גם הקרנבל הנוצרי, שראשיתו במאה
ה-12, **נערך** בדרך כלל בתקופה קרובה לחג הפורים ו**נראה** שגם הוא **השפיע** על מנהגי הפורים. (3)

   __ **סבורים**

   __ **הושפע**

   __ **נהגו לקיים**

   __ **חל**

   __ **נערך**

   __ **נראה**

   __ **השפיע**

5. מקדש האלון בחברון, ובמיוחד עץ האלון הענק, **נזכרים** בתרגומים עתיקים ובכתבים נוצריים. בתקופת חז"ל **התקיים** ליד מקדש האלון יריד שנתי שבו **מכרו** בוטנה. (1)

    __ **נזכרים**

    __ **התקיים**

    __ **מכרו**

6. עם תום ארוחה ש**נאכל** בה לחם **אומרים** את ברכת המזון, **הכוללת** שלוש ברכות. במרוצת הדורות **נוספו** לברכת המזון כמה ציטוטים מן המקרא וכמה ברכות חדשות **והותקן** גם נוסח מקוצר של הברכה (בארמית) ש**נועד להיאמר** כאשר לא **יכלו** לומר את הנוסח המלא (למשל, בשעת סכנה). (2)

    __ **נאכל**

    __ **אומרים**

    __ **כוללת**

    __ **נוספו**

    __ **הותקן**

    __ **נועד להיאמר**

    __ **יכלו**

Exercise #5: Locating the subject of the verb in multi-clause sentences

> **The rules to go by:** see section 6.4.
> **What to do:** indicate the subject of each bolded verb.
> **Example:**
> רוח היהדות, ש**גילתה** בכל תמורות הזמנים כוחות התחדשות כמו **הוקפאה** על-ידי היהדות
> החרדית.
> **גילתה** רוח היהדות **הוקפאה** רוח היהדות

1. על ארוחות משותפות של חברי הכת **מעידות** הכַּמויות הגדולות של כְּלֵי אוכל ש**נמצאו**
   מרוכָּזים במקום אחד.
   מעידות _____ **נמצאו** _____

2. בהדלקת נרות חנוכה **השתמר** ככל הנראה אלילי קדום **המשקף** את החשש האנושי
   הטבעי מתהליך התקצרותן של שעות האור בימי החורף.
   השתמר _____ **משקף** _____

3. כש**השתרשה** בישראל האמונה באל אחד **הורגש** הצורך לגשר על המרחק ש**נוצר** בין האל ובין
   העולם הגשמי.
   השתרשה _____ **הורגש** _____ **נוצר** _____

Glossary

> 1. communal meals of the sect members   ארוחות משותפות של חברי הכת
>   testify   מעידות
>   dishes   כלי אוכל
>   found concentrated   נמצאו מרוכזים
> 2. the lighting of the Chanukah candles   הדלקת נרות חנוכה
>   was apparently preserved   השתמר ככל הנראה
>   an ancient pagan custom   מנהג אלילי קדום
>   reflects   משקף
>   natural human fear   החשש האנושי הטבעי
>   the process of the shortening of daylight hours   תהליך התקצרותן של שעות האור
> 3. took root   השתרשה
>   belief in one God   אמונה באל אחד
>   need   צורך
>   bridge the distance   לגשר על המרחק
>   created   נוצר
>   the material world   העולם הגשמי

4. אוסף הגניזה באוניברסיטת קיימברידג' באנגליה **כולל** את שרידי יצירותינו בתחום התרבות וכן
חומר דוקומֶנטָרי רב **המשקף** את התרבות החומרית ואת חיי היום יום והמנהגים של הקהילה
הארץ-ישראלית העתיקה, **שמצאה** מקלט בקהיר לאחר שהחיים במולֶדֶת **לא היו** עוד **אפשריים.**

כולל _____ **משקף** _____ **מצאה** _____ **לא היו אפשריים** _____

5. רשימות ספרים של ספריות פרטיות **שנחשפו** בגניזה **מגלות** את ההיקף הרחב של הַשְׂכָּלה
ותרבות **שאפיינו** את המלומדים היהודים, במיוחד הרופאים שביניהם.

נחשפו _____ **מגלות** _____ **איפיינו** _____

6. כדי לאַפשר את עבודת השחזור של רְבבות הקטעים **שנמצאו** בגניזה **נוסד** בספרייה הלאומית
בירושלים מרכז של תצלומים לכתְבי היד העבריים **המפוזרים** כיום על פני תֵבֵל ומלוֹאה.

נמצאו _____ **נוסד** _____ **מפוזרים** _____

7. הפתיחה של הנוֹבֶלה שבה **מופיעה** הצהרה מפורשת של הגיבור שחייו **מתקרבים** לסופם
מורה על הכיוון שאליו **מובילה** הָעֲלילה.

מופיעה _____ **מתקרבים** _____ **מורה** _____ **מובילה** _____

Glossary

the Geniza collection in Cambridge University	4. אוסף הגניזה באוניברסיטת קיימברידג'
includes	כולל
remnants of our cultural creations	שרידי יצירותינו בתחום התרבות
documentary material	חומר דוקומנטרי
material culture	תרבות חומרית
found refuge in Cairo	מצאה מקלט בקהיר
lists of books in private libraries	5. רשימות ספרים של ספריות פרטיות
were uncovered	נחשפו
reveal	מגלות
a breadth of education and culture	היקף רחב של השכלה ותרבות
characterized	איפיינו
scholars	מלומדים
make possible	6. לאפשר
the work of reconstructing tens of thousands of fragments	עבודת השחזור של רבבות הקטעים
was established	נוסד
manuscripts	כתבי יד
scattered world-wide	מפוזרים על פני תבל ומלואה
long story	7. נובלה
appears	מופיעה
explicit statement	הצהרה מפורשת
are approaching their end	מתקרבים לסופם
indicates the direction	מורה על הכיוון
leads	מובילה
plot	עלילה

8. התביעה לא לאפשר ליהודים להחזיק במשרתים נוצרים **חזרה ועלתה** ואנשים **שפדו** מידי
היהודים עבדים **שהתנצרו, זכו** לתהילה.

חזרה ועלתה _____ **פדו** _____ **התנצרו** _____ **זכו** _____

9. היו עבדים **שזכו** לאמונו המלא של אדונם, ובמקורות **נזכרים** לעתים עבדים **הממלאים**
תפקידים בעלי אחריות רבה.

זכו _____ **נזכרים** _____ **ממלאים** _____

10. הפעילות הספרותית-רוחנית **שנתקיימה** בבית הכנסת הארצישראלי מן המאה השלישית
ועד המאה השביעית לספירה לערך הייתה פעילות דו-לשונית מובהקת, אשר העברית
והארמית **משמשות** בה בערבוביה, **ויעידו** על כך טקסטים רבים **שבאו** לידינו.

נתקיימה _____ **משמשות** _____ **יעידו** _____
באו _____

Glossary

demand	תביעה	.8
make possible	לאפשר
employ Christian servants	להחזיק במשרתים נוצרים
arose repeatedly	חזרה ועלתה
redeemed slaves	פדו עבדים
converted to Christianity	התנצרו
won glory	זכו לתהילה
their master's complete trust	אמונו המלא של אדונם	.9
sources	מקורות
are sometimes mentioned	נזכרים לעתים
fulfill roles of great responsibility	ממלאים תפקידים בעלי אחריות רבה
literary-intellectual activity	פעילות ספרותית-רוחנית	.10
took place	נתקיימה
7th century C.E.	המאה השביעית לספירה
approximately	לערך
distinctive bi-lingual activity	פעילות דו-לשונית מובהקת
are intermixed within it	משמשות בה בערבוביה
will testify, will bear witness	יעידו

11. בפרשנותו למקרא **השתמש** רש"י פעמים רבות במדרשים ש**חיברו** חז"ל בארץ ישראל
מאות שנים לפניו **ושילב** אותם בפירושיו.

השתמש _____ **חיברו** _____ **שילב** _____

12. השינוי מלשון המקרא ללשון חכמים **התחיל** כנראה כבר בלשון הדיבור של תחילת ימי
הבית השני, כאשר גולי בבל, ש**דיברו** בשפה הארמית, **חזרו** לארץ. מאוחר יותר, **נוספו**
לשפות המדוברות בפיהם גם הלשונות היוונית והרומית. כתוצאה מן המזיגה של השפות
הללו ותהליכי שינוי טבעיים ש**קרו** בשפה, **התפתחה** שפה מדוברת ש**היתה שונה** מלשון
המקרא.

התחיל _____ **דיברו** _____ **חזרו** _____ **נוספו** _____

קרו _____ **התפתחה** _____ **היתה שונה** _____

Glossary

11. רש"י   Rashi
פרשנותו למקרא   his exegesis to the Bible
פעמים רבות   many times
חיברו   wrote
חז"ל   Ḥazal (the sages of the Mishnah and Talmud)
שילב   integrated
12. גולי בבל   Babylonian exiles
נוספו   were added
השפות המדוברות בפיהם   the languages spoken by them
כתוצאה מן המזיגה   as a result of the blending
תהליכי שינוי טבעיים   natural processes of change
קרו   occurred
שפה מדוברת   spoken language
לשון המקרא   biblical language

Exercise #6: Identifying lexical repetition

> **The rules to go by:** see section 7.
> **What to do:** select from the bolded words in parenthesis the word that repeats a previously appearing word. Highlight both words.
> **Example:**
> הספר מאיר פרק מרתק בתולדות הפולמוס התיאולוגי על המקומות הקדושים של ארץ הקודש,
> (**פולמוס, פרק, ספר, ארץ**) שנתקיים בין יהודים לנוצרים משחר ימיה של הנצרות.

1. חברה אוטופית זו הקימה ארץ מודרנית המושתתת על כל הטֶכְנוֹלוֹגיה, (**חברה, ארץ, טכנולוגיה**) אשר תושביה נֶהֱנים מחיי חֵירוּת ושִׁוְויוֹן.

2. אחד היסודות החשובים ביותר במַעֲרֶכֶת זו של ארגון קהילָתי יָעיל, (**ארגון, מערכת, יסוד**) האוֹפְיָיני לְמַדי למִבְנֶה כולו, היה – התַקָנָה.

3. הינָוצרוּת הילדוּת והיֵעָלמותה תלויים ביחסם של המבוגָרים אל הילדים, (**ילדות, יחס, מבוגרים, ילדים**) שניתן לגַלותו באמצעות החוק.

4. הָירוֹנימוּס ידע כי היִדָברוּת עם יהודים הֶכְרחית כדי לַחֲלֵץ מפיהם ידיעות על הטקסט הקדוש, (**יהודים, הידברות, ידיעות, טקסט**) שהַכָּרָה טֶכנית בִּלְבָד של השפה איננה יכולה להיות מַפְתח להן.

Glossary

1. חברה אוטופית   utopian society
   מושתתת על   based on
   תושביה נהנים מחיי חירות ושויון   its residents enjoy life of liberty and equality
2. יסודות   elements
   מערכת ארגון קהילתי יעיל   a system of efficient communal organization
   אופייני למדי למבנה כולו   quite typical of the entire structure
   תקנה   ordinance
3. היווצרות הילדות והיעלמותה   the creation and disappearance of childhood
   תלויים ב-   depend on
   ניתן לגלותו באמצעות החוק   can be discovered via the law
4. הירונימוס   Hieronymus
   הידברות   dialogue, discussion
   הכרחית   necessary
   לחלץ מפיהם ידיעות   extract from them information
   הכרה טכנית בלבד של השפה   mere technical knowledge of the language

5. המוּשָׂג "הִתְיַוְּנוּת" מְשַׁמֵּשׁ לִשְׁנֵי עִנְיָנִים הַנִּבְדָּלִים זֶה מִזֶּה: מַשְׁמָעוּת אַחַת הִיא זוֹ הַמְתָאֶרֶת תְּנוּעָה תַרְבּוּתִית, חֶבְרָתִית וּמְדִינִית, מַשְׁמָעוּת אַחֶרֶת מְתָאֶרֶת תוֹפָעָה כְּלָלִית בְּתַרְבּוּיוֹת הָעֵת הָעַתִּיקָה – (**הִתְיַוְּנוּת, מַשְׁמָעוּת, תַרְבּוּת, תּוֹפָעָה**) שֶׁל מִפְגָּשׁ בֵּין-תַּרְבּוּתִי שֶׁהִתְחוֹלְלָה בִּיהוּדָה בַּשְּׁלִישׁ הָרִאשׁוֹן שֶׁל הַמֵּאָה הַשְּׁנִיָּה לִפְסה"נ בְּקֵרוּב.

Glossary

the concept "Hellenism"	המושג "התייונות"
is used for two distinct matters	משמש לשני עניינים הנבדלים זה מזה
movement	תנועה
another meaning describes a general phenomenon	משמעות אחרת מתארת תופעה כללית
Antiquity	העת העתיקה
inter-cultural encounter	מפגש בין-תרבותי
occurred	התחוללה
approximately the first third of the second century B.C.E.	השליש הראשון של המאה השנייה לפסה"נ בקירוב

Exercise #7: Identifying appositives

The rules to go by: see section 8.

What to do: in the blank (appearing in the middle or the end of the sentence) enter the identifying letter of the appositive that matches the framed phrase or word. The answer to the first item is already provided.

the day of the dedication of the Tabernacle	יום חֲנוּכַּת הַמִּשְׁכָּן א.
	שני הנְּמֵלִים הגדולים של ארץ ישראל באותה תקופה ב.
the two large ports of the Land of Israel at that time	
the Enlightenment Movement	תנועת הַהַשְׂכָּלָה ג.
the Yeshiva	הישיבה ד.
the Bible and the Babylonian Talmud	המקרא והתלמוד הבבלי ה.
Babylonian Talmud and Jerusalem Talmud	תלמוד בבלי ותלמוד ירושלמי ו.
the local Arabic and Judeo-Spanish	הערבית המקומית והספרדית-היהודית ז.
Jerusalem, Zefat (Safed), Hebron and Tiberias	ירושלים, צְפַת, חֶברוֹן וּטְבֶריָה ח.
the first of the Bible books	הראשון בספרי המקרא ט.
the Black Death plague	מגפת המוות השחור י.
vegetables, fruit, milk, eggs, cotton, etc.	ירקות, פירות, חלב, ביצים, כותנה, ועוד יא.

.1   שתי לשונות שָׁלְטוּ בדיבור בארץ-ישראל בִּכְלָל ובירושלים בִּפְרַט במאה ה-19: **ז**

.2   הספרדית-היהודית המשיכה להיות בשימוש גם בראשית המאה העשרים בערים הָעַתיקות (או "הקדושות"): __

.3   תיאור חיי האבות בספר בראשית - __ - כולל סיפורים על בצורת ורעב, על מחסור במים ומריבות על בארות מים.

.4   שני מקורותיה החשובים ביותר של תרבות ישראל - __ - הוֹאֲרו באור חדש בזכות מִפעלו הַפָּרשָׁני של רש"י.

Glossary

---

two languages שתי לשונות	.1
reigned שלטו	
in general...in particular בכלל...בפרט	
continued to be in use המשיכה להיות בשימוש	.2
established towns ערים ותיקות	
description of the life of the Patriarchs תיאור חיי האבות	.3
Genesis ספר בראשית	
includes stories about draught and famine כולל סיפורים על בצורת ורעב	
water shortage מחסור במים	
disputes over wells מריבות על בארות מים	
sources מקורות	.4
were illuminated in a new light הוארו באור חדש	
thanks to Rashi's exegetic endeavor בזכות מפעלו הפרשני של רש"י	

‏5. דוגמה ליצירה מרכזית בתרבות ישראל שנכתבה ברובה בארמית היא התלמוד, הכולל
‏   למעשה שני ‏‏תלמודים‏: __ .

‏6. במאה השמונה-עשרה הייתה קהילת ברלין למרכזה של ‏‏תנועה חדשה‏, שנוֹעֲדה לחוֹלֵל
‏   שינויים יְסודיים ביהדות-אֵירוֹפה, היא __ .

‏7. במהלך ימי הביניים באירופה חלה התפתחות אדירה אם כי גם ‏‏אובדן קשה‏ – __ .

‏8. הקיבוצים מייצרים יותר משליש מכל ‏‏המוצרים החקלאיים‏ בארץ (__).

‏9. בקהילות שהיה בהן ‏‏מוסד חינוכי גבוה‏, __ , למדו תלמוד בנים בני 13 ומעלה.

‏10. אוניית מְפָרשים לא הייתה צריכה באותם הימים יותר מעשרה ימים כדי להגיע
‏   מאַלֶכְּסַנְדְרָיָה אל ‏‏עַכּוֹ‏ או אל ‏‏אַשְׁקְלוֹן‏, __ .

‏11. יש איזו דיסְפְּרוֹפּוֹרְצְיָה בין הַחֵטְא לבין העוֹנָשׁ הָאַכְזָר, הבא על שני אחים, ודַוְוקָא במקום
‏   הקדושה ‏‏וביום של חג ושמחה לאומית‏, __ .

Glossary

a central work	יצירה מרכזית	5.
includes in fact	כולל למעשה	
the Berlin Jewish community	קהילת ברלין	6.
movement	תנועה	
was destined to bring about fundamental changes	נועדה לחולל שינויים יסודיים	
in the course of the Middle Ages	במהלך ימי הביניים	7.
an immense development occurred	חלה התפתחות אדירה	
heavy loss	אובדן קשה	
produce more than one third	מייצרים יותר משליש	8.
agricultural products	מוצרים חקלאיים	
an institution of higher learning	מוסד חינוכי גבוה	9.
sailboat	אוניית מפרשים	10.
Alexandria	אלכסנדריה	
Acre	עכו	
Ashkelon	אשקלון	
disproportion	דיספרופורציה	11.
sin	חטא	
cruel punishment	עונש אכזר	
place of holiness	מקום הקדושה	
a day of festival and national celebration	יום של חג ושמחה לאומית	

Exercise #8: Reconstructing elliptical sentences

The rules to go by: see section 9.
What to do: select the missing word from the choices in bold underneath each sentence.
Example:

במסורת היהודית אנו מוצאים גברים המתחפשים לנשים, קבצנים המתחפשים לעשירים,
ופשוטי עם [ ]– למלכים.
(א) מוצאים (ב) המתחפשים (ג) גברים

---

1. לבעייה מדוע "צדיק ורע לו, רָשָׁע וטוב לו" נִיתְנוּ תשובות שונות, אך [ ] העיקרית
   היא – דְחיית נושא הגמול לאַחַר המָוֶות.
   (א) לבעייה (ב) התשובה (ג) המוות

2. העלייה הראשונה זוכה בספר להַעֲרכה מחוּדֶשֶׁת והפעם [ ] חיובית ומַאדירה.
   (א) העלייה (ב) בספר (ג) להעֲרכה

3. בקֵיסָרוּת הרומית היה כל תושב עשׂירי יהודי, ובחֶלְקָה המִזרָחי – כל תושב
   חמישי [ ].
   (א) תושב (ב) היה יהודי (ג) חלק

4. אין סָפֵק שׁ"על הניסים" של חנוכה מַרְשׁימים יותר מ[ ]של פורים.
   (א) ספק (ב) על הניסים (ג) חנוכה

5. ראשי היישוב והמדינה אימצו שם חדש שצליליו דומה לשם המשפחה הקודם. למשל, משה
   שָׁרתוק הפך לשָׁרֶת, גְרין[ ] לבן-גוּריון.
   (א) שם חדש (ב) דומה (ג) הפך

Glossary

1.	righteous man	צדיק
	evil man	רשע
	postponement of the subject of reward till after death	דחיית נושא הגמול לאחר המוות
2.	receives	זוכה
	re-evaluation	הערכה מחודשת
	positive and glorifying	חיובית ומאדירה
3.	The Roman Empire	הקיסרות הרומית
	resident	תושב
4.	without doubt	אין ספק
	[the prayer] "On the Miracles" of Ḥanukkah	"על הניסים" של חנוכה
	impressive	מרשים
	Purim	פורים
5.	the heads of the Yishuv and the State	ראשי היישוב והמדינה
	adopted	אימצו
	its sound is similar to [that of] the previous family name	צלילו דומה לשם המשפחה הקודם

Exercise #9: Differentiating among several functions of an initial ה"א

> **The rules to go by:** see section 2 of the Confusables.
> **What to do:** indicate the function of the initial ה"א by entering the number of the word beginning with -ה in the appropriate cell in the chart. The first sentence is an example.

ה"א השאלה interrogative	part of the word	ה=ש subordinator	definite article before a noun	definite article before an adjective
		3,	1,	2,

1. (1)הלוח (2)הקדום (3)הנזכר בתורה שונה מן הלוח שבימינו.

2. פירושו של (4)הרשב"ם למקרא הוא פירוש פשט, (5)המבוסס על (6)המשמעות (7)הלשונית (8)הפשוטה של (9)הפסוקים.

3. (10)המנהג להתחפש בפורים, (11)המגביר את שמחת החג, מבוסס על מנהגי (12)העמים ועל (13)הסיפור במגילת אסתר.

4. חשובה במיוחד שאלת למדנותם ומידת (14)השכלתם של בני (15)הקהילות. (16)ההיו רבים בני תורה, או שמספרם מועט (17)היה?

Exercise #10: Determining the meaning of כי

> **The rules to go by:** see section 3 of the Confusables.
> **What to do:** indicate the function of כי by entering the number of the sentence in the appropriate cell in the chart. (To make the exercise more challenging, you could cover up the translations.) The first sentence is an example.

that	because	but also	but rather	although
	1,			

1. ‏התפילה מכונה "שמונה עשרה", **כי** במקורה היו בה 18 ברכות.
The prayer is called "Eighteen" _____ originally there were in it 18 blessings.

2. ‏המסקנה העולה מן המחקר היא **כי** לשימוש באינטרנט השפעה ברורה על חיי החברה ופעילות הפנאי.
The conclusion that arises from the study is _____ Internet use has a clear influence on social life and leisure activities.

3. ‏פעילות גופנית מקיפה היום את כל רובדי החברה **כי** רבים רואים בה דרך לשמירה על הבריאות.
Physical activity encompasses today all strata of society _____ many see in it a way to maintain health.

4. ‏מטרתו של לינקולן לא הייתה ביטול העבדות, **כי** אם צמצומה.
Lincoln's goal was not the abolition of slavery _____ its reduction.

5. ‏סיפוריו מיועדים לא רק לילדים כי אם גם למבוגרים.
His stories are meant not only for children _____ for adults.

6. ‏במדינת ישראל המושג "גימנסיה" מקביל לבית ספר תיכון, אם **כי** לא במלואו.
In the State of Israel the term "gymnasia" is equivalent to high school _____ not fully.

2. NOUNS
שמות עצם

This chapter discusses:

- Gender in nouns (section 1)
- Plural suffixes (section 2)
- Definiteness in nouns (section 3)
- Three types of possessive (סמיכות) phrases (section 4)
- Possessive suffixes (section 5)
- Three structural groups: nouns ending with ‑וּת, present tense verb forms functioning as nouns, and action nouns (section 6).

This chapter will help the reader to:

- Uncover the lexical (dictionary) form of nouns with plural and possessive suffixes
- Determine in unpointed text the meaning of an ‑ות ending (‑וֹת or ‑וּת)
- Determine whether an initial ה"א is a definite article (*the*) or part of the noun
- Pronounce correctly ‑יו at the end of a noun
- Identify the referent of possessive suffixes
- Translate ordinary and double construct phrases
- Distinguish between construct and noun+adjective phrases
- Recognize action nouns and relate them to the source verb

Nouns: an overview

Nouns are the largest group among the parts of speech. As is not the case in English, Hebrew nouns have an assigned gender, feminine or masculine. With the exception of animate nouns (people and animals), the assignment to gender is arbitrary; in other words, the gender of the noun is grammatical rather than biological (section 1). Plurality in nouns is indicated by a suffix, ים- /im/ (typically with masculine nouns), ות- (typically with feminine nouns), or – in a few cases – the dual number suffix ־יים/ayim/ (section 2).

A noun can be made definite by appending ה- (the equivalent of *the*) at the beginning of the word (section 3).

When two (or more) nouns are strung together, a construct (סמיכות) phrase is created, usually involving changes in the form and sound of the first (head) noun. Construct phrases are distinguishable from noun+adjective phrases in their formation rules, pluralization and placement of the definite article. Depending on the mechanism of joining the nouns, analytic, synthetic or double construct phrases can be created (section 4).

In formal language, nouns often take possessive suffixes instead of the inflected particle של. There is one set of suffixes for singular nouns and another for plural nouns; these suffixes render the noun definite. The identification of the reference of the suffix is vital for reading comprehension (section 5).

Whereas in the verb system there are seven structural groups (*binyanim*), there are scores of noun groups (called *mishkalim*), created via root and pattern combinations or through suffixation. This chapter discusses three large groups: nouns ending with ות-, nouns based on present tense verb forms, and action nouns (section 6).

1. Gender in nouns: feminine and masculine

While singular masculine nouns have no distinctive marking, singular feminine nouns can be recognized by their ending, ה- or ת-. However, the noun ending is not always a reliable clue to its gender, as there are feminine nouns that do not end with ה- or ת- (e.g., אבן *stone*) and, conversely, nouns that end with ה- or ת- whose gender is, in fact, masculine (e.g., לַיְלָה *night*, בית *house*; in these nouns the stress falls on the penultimate – rather than the final – syllable).

> ⚠ The (usually feminine) ending הָ (/a/) should be distinguished from the ending הֶ (/e/), typically found in masculine nouns (e.g., מוֹרֶה *(male) teacher*, שָׂדֶה *field*, מַעֲשֶׂה *deed; story*). In unpointed text, these endings appear identical.

Similarly in the plural, the typically masculine ים- ending may be found in nouns that are feminine (e.g., נשים *women*, אבנים *stones*), while the usually feminine ות- ending may be found in nouns that are masculine (e.g., אָבוֹת *fathers*, מקורות *sources*).

Note that although the noun ending may be misleading, the ending of the adjective that describes the noun is always in accordance with the gender of the noun, thus serving as a reliable guide to its gender.

For example:

עיר רחוקה *distant city* (f.), לילה טוב *good night* (m.), נשים זקנות *old women* (f.), אבות צעירים *young fathers* (m.).

2. Finding the dictionary form of plural nouns

In most cases, the lexical (dictionary) form of a plural noun is arrived at by removing the plural suffix ים-, or replacing the plural suffix ות- with ה-.
For example: חוקרים → חוקר *researcher(s)*, פעולות → פעולה *action(s)*.
However, as shown in the examples below, the singular form of the noun cannot always be thus derived:

The singular form of מילים *words* is מִילָה (not מיל*)
The singular form of חוזים *contracts* is חוֹזֶה (not חוז*)
The singular form of עיתונאים *journalist* is עִתּוֹנַאי (not עיתונא*)
The singular form of מסורות *traditions* is מסוֹרֶת (not מסורה*)[1]
The singular form of חניתות *spears* is חנית (not חניה*)
The singular form of מקורות *sources* is מקור (not מקורה*)
The singular form of תבניות *patterns* is תבנית (not תבניה*)
The singular form of דמויות *characters, figures* is דמות (not דמויה*).

The various possibilities are summarized in the table below:

7	6	5	4	3	2	1	
-ויות דמויות	-יות תבניות	-ות מקורות	-ות מסורות	-ות פעולות	-ים מילים חוזים	-ים חוקרים	plural
-ות דמות	-ית תבנית		-ת מסורֶת	-ה פעולה	-ה מילָה חוזֶה	חוקר	singular

2.1 "Irregularities" in plural nouns
When looking up in the dictionary a plural noun, be aware of the "irregularities" listed below.

2.1.1 In the transition from singular to plural, there are nouns that change their form. Some examples are:

אִישׁ ← אֲנָשִׁים	*people*
אֱמֶת ← אֲמִיתּוֹת[2]	*truths*
אִשָּׁה ← נָשִׁים	*women*
בַּיִת ← בָּתִּים	*houses*
חֵצִי ← חֲצָאִים	*halves*
עִיר ← עָרִים	*cities*
פְּרִי ← פֵּרוֹת	*fruit*
צַד ← צְדָדִים	*sides*
קָצֶה ← קְצָווֹת	*endpoints, edges*
רַב ← רַבָּנִים	*rabbis*

---

[1] מסורה *Massora* refers to the traditional annotated text of the Bible and has no plural.
[2] אֲמִתָּה means *axiom*.

With the addition of the plural suffix, internal vowel changes may occur as well. However, since these changes do not usually affect the spelling of the word, they do not get in the way of looking it up in the dictionary.

Some examples are:

גְּוָנִים ← גָּוֶן	*colors, hues*
זֵיתִים ← זַיִת	*olives*
מְקוֹרוֹת ← מָקוֹר	*sources*
עִיתִּים ← עֵת	*times*
קְשָׁיִים ← קֹשִׁי	*difficulties, hardships*
תְּכָנִים ← תֹּכֶן	*contents*

2.1.2 Some plural nouns do not have a singular form or have one that is rarely used; others have a singular form whose meaning is different than that of the plural.

Below are some examples from scholarly texts:

(a) Plural nouns without a singular form or with a rarely used one:

אֲשָׁיוֹת	*foundations* (אָשְׁיָה is rare)
יִיסּוּרִים	*torments*
כִּיסּוּפִים	*longings* (כִּיסּוּף is rare)
כְּלוּלוֹת	*betrothal, wedding*
מוֹנִיטִין	*reputation*
נִישּׂוּאִים	*marriage* (also with the Aramaic plural ending: נִישּׂוּאִין)
נְסִיבּוֹת	*circumstances* (נסיבה is rare)
נְעוּרִים	*youth*
נְצוּרוֹת	*hidden things*
נִשְׁכָּחוֹת	*forgotten matters; old memories*
עֲלוּמִים	*youth, youthfulness*
פְּרָעוֹת	*pogrom(s)*
צְפוּנוֹת, צפונים	*secrets*
תַּהְפּוּכוֹת	*vicissitudes* (תהפוכה is rare)
תִּימוּכִין, סִימוּכִין	*source, support, foundation, backing*
תְּפִילִין	*phylacteries*

In this category also fall some nouns with the dual number ending /ayim/. For example, מאזניים *scales*, מַיִם *water*, משקפיים *eye glasses*, צהריים *noon*, שׁוּלַיִים *margins*, שָׁמַיִם *sky* (however, temporal units and body parts have singular forms, e.g., פעמיים-פעם *once-twice*, רגליים-רגל *leg-legs*).

(b) Plural nouns whose singular form has a different meaning from the plural form

plural	meaning of the plural	singular	meaning of the singular
אִישִׁים	*personalities, personages*	אִישׁ	*man*
גֵּירוּשִׁים, גֵּירוּשִׁין	*divorce*	גֵּירוּשׁ	*expulsion*
חַיִּים	*life*	חַי	*lived; alive; living thing*

plural	meaning of the plural	singular	meaning of the singular
כְּתָבִים	writings, written works, oeuvres	כְּתָב	writing system, script; handwriting
כְּתוּבִים	third section of the Bible	כָּתוּב	written; bibilical verse or section
מוֹרָאוֹת	horrors	מוֹרָא	awe, fear
מוֹתָרוֹת	luxuries	מוֹתָר	remainder; superiority, advantage
מְסִיבּוֹת	circumstances[3]	מסיבה	party
מִסְתּוֹרִין	mystery	מסתור	hiding place
מַעְיָינִים	thoughts, attention[4]	מעיין	spring, well
נְקוּדָתַיִם	colon	נקודה	point, period
עֲלִילוֹת	deeds, exploits	עֲלִילָה	plot (of a story); libel[5]
פָּנִים	face	פָּן	aspect
קוֹרוֹת	events, history, chronicles	קוֹרָה	beam, rafter
תּוֹלְדוֹת	history of[6]	תּוֹלָדָה	consequence

2.1.3 A few nouns with distinct meanings share the same plural.
For example:

חובות is the plural of חוב *debt* as well as חובה *obligation*;
מַעֲרָכוֹת is the plural of מַעֲרֶכֶת *set, system, constellation; editorial board* as well as מַעֲרָכָה *war*.

2.1.4 Some nouns have two alternative plural forms, one of which is reserved for use in certain expressions or in construct phrases.
For example:

common form		**special form**	
נָשִׁים → אִישָׁה	women; wives	נשות יעקב	Jacob's wives
יָמִים → יום	days	ימות המשיח	days of the Messiah
שָׁנִים → שָׁנָה	years	שנות השישים	the sixties (NOT: שְׁנֵי הַשִּׁישִׁים*)
מִילִים → מִילָה	words	מילות חיבה	words of affection (NOT: מִילֵי חִיבָּה*)
עִיתִּים → עֵת	times, era	עיתות מצוקה	times of trouble
פִּתְרוֹנוֹת → פתרון	solutions, answers	לאלוהים הפתרונים	God only knows

2.1.5 Nouns whose plural ending is אות- can be found in the dictionary by removing the ות- ending and then replacing the אל"ף with ה"א.
For example:

אַסְמַכְתָּה → אסמכתאות	proofs, support
גִּרְסָה → גרסאות	versions
דּוּגְמָה → דוגמאות	examples
נוסחה → נוסחאות	formulas

---

[3] נְסִיבּוֹת is now more common.
[4] Usually with a pronoun suffix: כל מעייניו *all his thoughts, his entire attention.*
[5] And note: עלילות דם, עלילת דם *blood libel(s).*
[6] This modern use is different from the biblical meaning, *genealogy*; this word appears in construct form only, or with a pronoun suffix (e.g., תולדות העם היהודי *the history of the Jewish people*, תולדותיו *his/its history*).

סְסָמָאוֹת → סִסְמָה   *slogans*
מִקְוָואֹת → מִקְוֶה   *ritual baths*

And note also:

דְּיוֹקָנָאֹת (דיוקנים) → דְּיוֹקָן   *portraits*

Current spelling rules favor the omission of the (Aramaic) אל"ף from the plural (e.g., דוגמות, נוסחות).

2.1.6 The singular form of some plural nouns ending with **אִים-** is arrived at by dropping only the final מ"ם, for example, in nouns indicating professions: עיתונָאִי → עיתונָאִים *journalists*, בַּנָאִי → בַּנָאִים *builders*, and also in תְּנָאִי → תְּנָאִים *conditions* (but the singular form of תַּנָאִים *sages of the Mishnah* is תַּנָּא and of אָמוֹרָאִים *sages of the Talmud* – אָמוֹרָא).
Note also: הֶגֶה → הֲגָאִים *spoken sound(s)* (also הֲגָיִים) and צְבִי → צְבָאִים *deer*.

3. Marking definiteness in nouns

3.1 The definite article -ה *the* is placed before the noun to make it specific (e.g., בַּיִת *a house*, הַבַּיִת *the house*).
When the prepositions ב, כ or ל appear before the noun, the definite article merges with them and they take its vocalization (e.g., בְּבַיִת *in a house* but בַּבַּיִת *in the house*).

3.2 Proper nouns (i.e., names of people or places) are considered definite. The noun is also definite when inflected with a possessive pronoun suffix (e.g., סִפְרוֹ *his book*). Therefore, proper nouns and nouns with a possessive suffix need not (and are not allowed to) take the definite article. In other words, *התל-אביב and *הספרו are not possible.

4. The construct state: x (of) y סמיכות

4.1 The structure of the construct phrase
A construct phrase consists of two (or more) consecutive nouns. Through their proximity, some semantic relationship (e.g., possession, cause, purpose, location, quantity) is established between them.
    There are three types of construct phrases:

(a) Phrases with של (analytic construct – סמיכות פרודה): **noun + של + noun** (4.2 below).

(b) Phrases without של (synthetic construct – סמיכות דבוקה): **noun + noun** (4.3 below).

(c) Phrases with של after a possessive suffix (double construct – סמיכות כפולה): **noun + possessive suffix + של + noun** (4.4 below).

The differences among the three types of construct phrases are a matter of style rather than meaning and cannot be rendered in English:

type	example	structure	translation
analytic construct	הנושאים של הסיפור	noun + שֶׁל + noun	*the subjects of the story*
synthetic construct	נושאי הסיפור	noun + noun	
double construct	נושאיו של הסיפור	noun + possessive suffix + שֶׁל + noun	

4.2 Construct phrases with שֶׁל: הנושא של הסיפור *the subject of the story*

4.2.1 Of the three types of construct phrases, this type – סמיכות with שֶׁל – is the least formal. However, it may be used in the formal written register to avoid a cumbersome phrase made up of several consecutive nouns in the construct form.

4.2.2 The nouns on each side of the particle שֶׁל are usually definite: הנושא של הסיפור *the topic of the story*.
However, the use of a non-specific (indefinite) first noun even when the second noun is specific is possible: נושא של הסיפור *a topic of the story*. This option is not possible in construct phrases without שֶׁל, where the specificity of the second noun unavoidably applies also to the first noun (e.g., נושא הסיפור *the topic of the story*).

4.3 Construct phrases without שֶׁל: נושא הסיפור *the subject of the story*

4.3.1 Noun A (נסמך)

In construct phrases without שֶׁל, the first noun in the sequence is considered the nucleus – the head – of the construct phrase. It is called נסמך (literally: the "supported," or "dependent" noun). Here it will be referred to as Noun A. This noun may undergo some changes in form when within a construct phrase (see 4.3.5 below). In the dictionary, the construct form of the noun is indicated with a hyphen (e.g., דור- *generation [of]*). As shown below, a sequence of several dependent nouns (as many as four in example 3) is possible.

(1) תַּהֲלִיכֵי יְצִירַת תרבות
processes of creation of culture

(2) רֵאשׁית חֵקֶר נוֹהֲגֵי הקבורה
the beginning of the study of burial customs

(3) מִחְשׁוּב תַּהֲלִיך הַנְפָּקַת רישיונות הנהיגה
the computerizing of the process of issuing driving licenses

4.3.2 Noun B (סוֹמֵךְ)

The second (or last) noun in the construct phrase is the סוֹמֵךְ (literally: the "supporting" noun). Here it will be called Noun B. This noun may receive a possessive suffix (e.g., תהליך יצירתו *its creation process*).

Several nouns appearing in a row are separated by commas, and the last one in the sequence will be joined to the rest with וי"ו. These coordinate nouns agree in definiteness, that is, if one has the definite article, so will the other(s) (example 5).

---

(4) הַבְטָחַת שֶׁפַע וּבְרָכָה

[=הבטחה של שפע ושל ברכה]

a promise of plenty and blessing

(5) תחוּמֵי הַהֲלָכָה, הַלָּשׁוֹן, הַפִּיוּט וְהַתִּיאולוֹגיה

[=התחומים של ההלכה, של הלשון, של הפיוט ושל התיאולוגיה]

the fields of law, language, religious liturgy and theology

(6) דַרְכֵי הַסְבָרָה וְהַהִיגָּיוֹן

[=הדרכים של הסברה ושל ההיגיון]

the ways of conjecture and logic

Since the second Noun B – הַהִיגָּיוֹן – is definite, we identify the initial ה"א in the first noun also as a definite article and read it as ה + סְבָרָה *the conjecture*, NOT: הַסְבָּרָה *propaganda, information (in politics)*.

4.3.3 Making construct phrases plural

Ordinarily, construct phrases are made plural by adding the plural suffix to Noun A. However, depending on the desired meaning, Noun B may also take a plural suffix, or both nouns may be pluralized.
For example:

נושאי הסיפור *the **subjects** of the story*
נושא הסיפורים *the subject of the **stories***
נושאי הסיפורים *the **subjects** of the **stories***.

4.3.4 Making construct phrases definite

The definite article appears only once within the construct phrase, before the last noun in the sequence. It renders all the nouns in the construct phrase definite.
For example:

מנהגי חג *holiday customs*
מנהגי החג *the customs of the holiday* (neither *המנהגי החג** nor *המנהגי חג** is allowed).

As illustrated below, this rule can aid the reader in word recognition:

(7) הַמֶּחְקָר עַל יַחֲסֵי הַגּוֹמְלִין שֶׁבֵּין הַדְּמוּת הָרַבָּנִית הַכָּרִיזְמָטִית לְבֵין הַמַּאֲמִינִים הָאוֹרְתוֹדוֹקְסִיִּים בַּמֵּאָה הי"ח עָמַד עַל כָּךְ שֶׁהֵם נָהֲגוּ לְהִישָּׁעֵן עַל הַכְוָונַת רַבָּנֵיהֶם וְעַל הַחְלָטוֹתֵיהֶם בַּתְּקוּפָה זוֹ יוֹתֵר מִבַּעֲבָר.

The study of the reciprocal relationship between <u>the charismatic rabbinical figure</u> and the orthodox believers in the 18th century has found that in this period they were accustomed to rely on the <u>guidance of their rabbis</u> and their decisions more than in the past.

הַדְּמוּת הָרַבָּנִית הַכָּרִיזְמָטִית: By itself, רַבָּנִית could mean *rabbi's wife* (a noun) or *rabbinical* (an adjective). Because the preceding noun – הדמות – is definite, we interpret the sequence הדמות הרבנית as noun + adjective and translate to *the charismatic rabbinical figure*, rather than *the charismatic figure of the rabbi's wife* (possible if the phrase read: דמות הרבנית הכריזמטית).

הכוונת רבניהם: we read *the guidance of their rabbis* (NOT: *the intention of their rabbis*); the initial ה"א in the head noun of the construct phrase must be interpreted as part of the word הַכְוָונָה *guidance*, not as a definite article before the word כַּוָונָה *intention*.

4.3.5 Phonetic changes in construct nouns
Noun A may undergo the following end-of-word changes:

(a) The ending הָ (pronounced /a/) becomes תַ (pronounced /at/). For example,
מְגַמַּת הַמְּחַבֵּר ← הַמְּגַמָּה שֶׁל הַמְּחַבֵּר the *writer's purpose*

⚠️ Note that in nouns ending with הֶ /e/, the ה- does not convert to ת-. For example:
שָׂדֶה פְּעוּלָתוֹ ← שָׂדֶה *his field of action*; מִבְנֵה הַסִּיפּוּר ← הַמִּבְנֶה שֶׁל הַסִּיפּוּר *the structure of the story*.

(b) The plural ending ־ים (pronounced /im/) becomes ־ֵי (pronounced /ei/). For example,
תְּחוּמֵי הַשְׁפָּעָה ← תְּחוּמִים שֶׁל הַשְׁפָּעָה *areas of influence*

The plural ending ־וֹת does not change. For example, הַחְלָטוֹת הַשּׁוֹפֵט *the decisions of the judge*, מְקוֹרוֹת הַמִּנְהָג *the sources of the custom*.

Internal phonetic changes occur in some noun patterns. For example:

דְּבַר- ← דָּבָר	*thing; word*
דִּבְרֵי- ← דְּבָרִים	*things; words*
מִלְחֶמֶת- ← מִלְחָמָה	*war*

בֵּית- → בַּיִת	*house*
בִּרְכַּת- → בְּרָכָה	*blessing*
מוֹת- → מָוֶת	*death*

✦#1   4.3.6 Distinguishing between construct phrases and noun+adjective phrases: סיפורי מלחמה *war stories* versus סיפורים קצרים *short stories*

Two grammatical characteristics distinguish construct phrases from noun+adjective phrases: (1) phonetic changes (occurring only in construct phrases), and (2) gender-number and definiteness agreement (required only in noun+adjective phrases). The table below summarizes the differences.

noun+adjective		construct סמיכות	
example	components	example	components
(ה)חנות (ה)גדולה (the) big shop	**sing. f.** noun + **sing. f.** adjective	חנות (ה)פרחים (the) flower shop	**sing. f.** noun + **pl. m.** noun
(ה)מגדלים (ה)גבוהים (the) tall towers	**pl. m.** noun + **pl. m.** adjective	מגדלי (ה)אבן (the) stone towers	**pl. m.** noun + **sing. f.** noun

4.3.7 Bound construct phrases: בית-ספר *school*

Many construct phrases function as bound expressions (צירופים כבולים), that is, phrases that form a single lexical unit whose meaning is not the sum of the literal meaning of each noun. Such phrases are often marked orthographically, with a hyphen joining the two nouns. They are rendered in English usually by one word. Some examples are:

בן-שיח *farmer*, איש-אדמה *clergymen*, אנשי-דת *ally*, בעל-ברית *animals*, בעלי-חיים *court*, בית-דין *interlocutor*, כתב-יד *manuscript; hand writing*.

⚠ Note that כתב ידו means *his handwriting*; כתב היד שלו may mean either *his handwriting* or *his manuscript*.

4.3.8 Repeated nouns in construct phrases

In a small group of construct phrases, the nouns are repeated to convey the superlative or intensify.
Some examples are:

סודי סודות *uttermost secrets*, שאלת השאלות *the most important question*, תילי תילים *heaps and heaps*, לעולמי עולמים *for ever and ever*, ספר הספרים *the Book of Books (the Bible)*.

4.3.9 Nouns that appear only in the construct state

A few nouns can appear only within a construct phrase, never independently.
For example:

חֵקֶר התנ"ך ,תוֹלְדוֹת המדינה *the history of the State,* רֵאשִׁית הסיפור *the beginning of the story,* *the study of the Bible,* מְלוֹא האפשרויות *the entirety of the possibilities.*

4.3.10 Potential ambiguity in construct phrases
When Noun A is an action noun (see 6.3 below), the construct phrase may be ambiguous; its meaning has to be determined by the context.
For example:

- אהבת אם *mother's love* may mean האם אוהבת *the mother loves* or מישהו אוהב את האם *someone loves the mother, the mother is loved;*
- הערכת המחבר *the evaluation of the author* may mean המחבר העריך *the writer evaluated,* or מישהו העריך את המחבר *someone evaluated the writer, the writer was evaluated;*
- יצירת התרבות *creation of culture* can be construed as התרבות יצרה *the culture created* or משהו/מישהו יצר את התרבות *someone/something created the culture, the culture was created.*

4.3.11 Translating construct phrases into English

4.3.11.1 Construct phrases are translated into English similarly to noun+adjective phrases, with the second noun (Noun B) coming first:
For example:

חומת **אבן** [חומה מאבן] *a stone wall,* רישיון **נהיגה** [רישיון לנהיגה] *a driver's* (literally: *driving*) license, כרטיס **ברכה** [כרטיס עם ברכה] *a greeting card.*

4.3.11.2 If the semantic relationship between the nouns is one of possession (that is, if the nouns can be joined with the particle שׁל), the word *of* can be used in translation and the nouns then appear in the order of their appearance in Hebrew.
For example:

מדיניות השליטים [המדיניות של השליטים] *the policy of the rulers* (OR: *the rulers' policy*).
פקודת המלך [הפקודה של המלך] *the command of the king* (OR: *the king's command*).

4.3.11.3 In some cases, Noun B may (or must) be rendered in translation as an adjective. In other words, the formal distinction between a construct phrase and noun+adjective phrase becomes blurred in translation. This is due to the fact that the function of the second noun of the construct phrase vis-à-vis the first one is essentially adjectival.
Some examples are:

הַשְׁפָּעַת הַסְּבִיבָה	*the influence of the environment* or *the environmental influence*
מִנְהֲגֵי הַדָּת	*the customs of religion* or *the religious customs*
שְׂפַת הַמִּקְרָא	*the language of the Bible* or *biblical language*
עֶרְכֵי יְסוֹד	*basic values*
סִפְרֵי קוֹדֶשׁ	*holy books*
זְכוּיוֹת אֶזְרָח	*civil rights*

4.4 Double construct phrases (סמיכות כפולה): נושאו של הסיפור *the subject of the story*

The double construct, which dates back to Mishnaic Hebrew, is a common stylistic feature of modern formal written and oral language.

As indicated by the name, the dependency relationship between Noun A (נסמך) and Noun B (סומך) is marked <u>twice</u>: once with the possessive suffix attached to Noun A (see discussion of possessive suffixes in section 5 below) and again with the possessive particle של between the two nouns.

4.4.1 Double construct phrases can be formed only when the relationship between the two nouns is that of possession.
For example:

מכתבם של ההורים [המכתב של ההורים] מכתב ההורים *the parents' letter* can be converted into but [מכתב עם ברכה] מכתב ברכה *a letter of greeting* cannot be rendered as a double construct to become מכתבה של הברכה*.

4.4.2 In double construct phrases – as in ordinary ones – the definite article appears only once, before Noun B. For example: מעשיו של הגיבור *the deeds of the protagonist.*

4.4.3 The particle של may be followed by a construct phrase (rather than a single noun).
For example: מעשיו של גיבור הסיפור *the deeds of the protagonist of the story.*

4.4.4 In translation into English, the possessive suffix of the double construct phrase is ignored and the Hebrew word order is retained.
For example: בעיותיה של החברה *the problems of the society* (not: *its problems of the society*).

⚥#2   4.5 Construct phrases with adjectives

4.5.1 Ordinary (synthetic) construct phrases with adjectives
Adjectives come after the construct phrase and may modify either noun A or noun B. Adjective-noun agreement rules help us determine which noun is described by the adjective. However, when both nouns happen to have the same gender and number, an ambiguity may arise. For example:

מנהל המפעל החדש may mean *the manager of the new factory,* OR: *the new manager of the factory.*
The ambiguity can usually be resolved on the basis of the context.

(a) Noun A is described:

---

(8) אֲתָרֵי הַנְצָחָה חדשים

<u>new sites</u> of commemoration (OR: new commemoration sites)
NOT: sites of new commemoration

(9) תפישׂת העָבָר הישׂראלית

<u>the Israeli understanding</u> of the past
NOT: the understanding of the Israeli past

(b) Noun B is described:

---

(10) מוּרְכָּבוּת הַטֶּקְסְט המקראי

the complexity of <u>the biblical text</u>
NOT: the biblical complexity of the text

(11) זְכִירַת מָסוֹרוֹת היסטוריות

remembering of <u>historical traditions</u>
NOT: historical remembering of traditions

(12) תַהֲלִיכֵי גיבוש זֶהוּת חֶבְרָתִית

processes of <u>social identity</u> formation
NOT: social processes of identity formation

The construct phrase is made up of three nouns (תהליכי גיבוש זהות); the feminine singular adjective חברתית agrees with the feminine singular noun זהות.

4.5.2 Double construct phrases with adjectives

In double construct phrases, the adjective can be placed immediately after the noun that is modified; the ambiguity of reference that sometimes occurs in ordinary construct phrases (where the adjective appears at the end of the phrase), is thus avoided.
For example:

תוצאותיה של המלחמה ההרסנית *the outcomes of the destructive war*
תוצאותיה ההרסניות של המלחמה *the destructive outcomes of the war.*

---

(13) עֶמְדָתוֹ הפוליטית של הסוֹפֵר

the author's <u>political stance</u>
NOT: the political author's stance

(14) תושביה של הארץ החדשה

the residents of the <u>new land</u>
NOT: the new residents of the land

(15) חידושו ופריחתו הקצרה של היישוב היהודי

the renewal and <u>brief flourishing</u> of the Jewish settlement
OR: the renewal of the Jewish settlement and its brief flourishing
NOT: the brief renewal and flourishing of the Jewish settlement

---

#3   4.6 Construct phrase as the subject of the sentence

When a construct phrase of any type (analytic, synthetic or double) functions as the subject, the verb (or, in verbless sentences, the verb substitute), agrees with the head (first) noun, the nucleus of the construct phrase.

One exception to this rule is the case in which the head noun is a quantifier: the verb (or verb substitute) then usually agrees with Noun B (examples 23–24).

> Quantifiers indicate quantity or extent. For example: מִסְפָּר *a part,* חֵצִי, מַחֲצִית *a half,* חֵלֶק *a part,* מִסְפָּר *a number (of),* רוֹב, מַרְבִּית *many, most,* מִקְצָת *a little, a portion,* מֵיטַב *the best,* מִבְחַר *a selection,* שׁוּרַת- *a series of.*

The construct phrase is bracketed; the head noun and the verb (or copula) it agrees with are shaded:

(16) [תָּכְנִיּוֹת פעולה] נחשבות כְּכְלי מוּגְדָר של תִכְנוּן מְדִינִיּוּת.
Action <u>plans are considered</u> a specific tool of policy planning.

(17) [מְיַיסֵד התנועה] הציּוֹנית המוֹדֶרְנית היה הֶרְצל.
The <u>founder</u> of the modern Zionist movement <u>was</u> Herzl.

(18) [מוֹעֲדֵי מימוּש התכְנית] לא נקבעו.
The <u>dates</u> for executing the plan <u>were not fixed</u>.

(19) [הכנת תכניות פעולה] היא מְלָאכה מְקצוֹעית.
The <u>preparation</u> of action plans <u>is</u> a professional job.

(20) [מטרות החינוך] בימי הבֵּינַיים היו שונות ממטרות החינוך המַעֲרבי בְּיָמינוּ.
The <u>goals</u> of education in the Middle Ages <u>were different</u> than the goals of Western education in our days.

(21) [קיומן של דֵעות קדוּמות] מֵעִיד על קוֹנְפְליקט בֵּינְעֲדָתי.
The <u>existence</u> of prejudice <u>attests</u> to an inter-ethnic conflict.

(22) במצב זה נִשְׁלֶלֶת [חירוּתוֹ של הַיָּחִיד]
In this situation, the <u>freedom</u> of the individual <u>is taken away</u>.

Note that the verb נשללת comes before the subject חירות.

(23) [רוֹב הנושאים] לא נחקרו.
Most of the <u>topics</u> <u>have not been researched</u>.

The verb agrees with Noun B, not with Noun A, a quantifier.

(24) [שׁוּרַת רעיונות ומוּשׂגים] מְעִידים על הקֶשֶׁר בין קוּמְראן לבין הנַצְרוּת הקַדוּמה.
A series of <u>ideas and concepts</u> <u>attest</u> to the connection between Qumran and early Christianity.

The verb agrees with the רעיונות ומושגים, not with the quantifier -שׁוּרַת.

Examples 25–26 below illustrate the application of the agreement rule (4.6 above) to reading comprehension; the potentially ambiguous word is framed:

---

(25) מודעות עם ישראל לזהותו **היא** גורם קבוע במחשבת המקרא ו**מוצאת** את ביטויה
במאמציהם של סופרי המקרא להסביר את מוצאו של עם ישראל.
The awarenes of the People of Israel of its identity is a fixed element in biblical thought and it finds its expression in the efforts of the biblical writers to explain the origin of the People of Israel.

The feminine singular predicates – the copula היא and the verb מוצאת – require a feminine singular subject; the head noun of the construct phrase מודעות עם ישראל is therefore identified as מודעות *awareness* (rather than the plural מודעות *advertisements, announcements*).

(26) בדתות שאין במרכזן אלוהות אישית הגומלת שָכָר ועונֶש, מצוי לפעמים הרעיון של
מעין סיבתיות קוסמית-מוסרית ה**קובעת** את גורלה ועתידה של הנשמה.
In religions that do not have at their center a personal divinity which rewards and punishes, there is found sometimes the idea of a kind of moral-cosmic causality that determines the fate and future of the soul.

The verb קובעת requires a feminine singular subject.
Therefore, the reading מַעְיָן סיבתיות קוסמית-מוסרית *a spring of moral-cosmic causality*, where the singular masculine noun מעין is the head noun of a construct phrase, must be rejected in favor of the reading מֵעֵין סיבתיות *a kind of causality*.

---

5. Possessive suffixes: סְפְרוֹ = הַסֵפֶר שלו *his book*

5.1 Meaning

While ordinarily possession is indicated with the inflected forms of של (e.g., הספר שלו *his book*), in formal (written and spoken) discourse there is a preference for indicating possession with a possessive suffix attached to the noun (e.g., ספרו instead of הספר שלו).[7]

> When the "possessor" is animate, שלו and שלה are translated *his* and *her*, respectively; with an inanimate "possessor" the translation is *its*.

The (stylistic) difference between הספר שלו and ספרו cannot be rendered in English: in both cases the translation is *his book*.

Foreign (loan) words do not usually take a possessive suffix (example 27).

---

[7] This is somewhat similar to the device of adding -s after a noun in English (e.g., *the boy's book*).

The possessive suffixes and the noun to which they refer are shaded:

> (27) הספר עוסק בחֵקֶר **שְׂפַת הַיִּידִישׁ**, תרבותָהּ, יצירתָהּ הספרותית והפולקלור **שלה**.
> The book deals with the study of Yiddish, <u>its</u> culture, literary creation and folklore.
>
> – פולקלור; **שפת היידיש** and **תרבות** and יצירה receive a suffix (replacing שלה) that refers to שפת היידיש. תרבות and יצירה is not thus inflected. a loan word – is not thus inflected.

#4 5.2 Form

There are two sets of possessive suffixes, one for singular and one for plural nouns. Plural noun suffixes are visually (and phonetically) distinguishable from singular suffixes by the presence of the plural marker י.
For example:

דודו = הדוד שלו *his uncle*, but **דודיו** = הדודים שלו *his uncles*
דודתו = הדודה שלו *his aunt*, but **דודותיו** = הדודות שלו *his aunts*

> Note that for nouns with the plural suffix ות- (as in **דודותיו**) the יו"ד of the possessive suffix is superfluous, since the noun has already been made plural by the suffix.

The two sets of suffixes and the corresponding inflected forms of של are shown in the chart below, followed by information about their pronunciation.

Possessive suffixes for singular nouns

שֶׁלָּהֶן	שֶׁלָּהֶם	שֶׁלָּכֶן	שֶׁלָּכֶם	שֶׁלָּנוּ	שֶׁלָּהּ	שֶׁלּוֹ	שֶׁלָּךְ	שֶׁלְּךָ	שֶׁלִּי
־ן	־ם	־כֶן	־כֶם	־נוּ	־הּ	־וֹ	־ךְ	־ךָ	־י
/an/	/am/	/khen/	/khem/	/enu/	/a(h)/	/o/	/ekh/	/kha/	/i/

Possessive suffixes for plural nouns

שֶׁלָּהֶן	שֶׁלָּהֶם	שֶׁלָּכֶן	שֶׁלָּכֶם	שֶׁלָּנוּ	שֶׁלָּהּ	שֶׁלּוֹ	שֶׁלָּךְ	שֶׁלָּךְ	שֶׁלִּי
־יהֶן	־יהֶם	־יכֶן	־יכֶם	־ינוּ	־יהָ	־יו	־יךְ (־ייך)*	־יךְ	־י (־יי)*
/e(y)hen/	/e(y)hem/	/e(y)khen/	/e(y)khem/	/e(y)nu/	/e(y)ha/	/av/	/a(y)ikh/	/e(y)kha/	/ay/

* full (unpointed) spelling

Pronunciation Notes:

1. <u>Singular nouns</u>: the possessive suffixes in דּוֹדִי, דּוֹדְךָ, דּוֹדוֹ, דּוֹדָהּ are pronounced similarly to the inflected forms of שֶׁל: שֶׁלִּי, שֶׁלְּךָ, שֶׁלּוֹ, שֶׁלָּהּ.
   However, such is not the case in דּוֹדֵךְ, דּוֹדֵנוּ, דּוֹדְכֶם, דּוֹדְכֶן, דּוֹדָם, דּוֹדָן, which do not echo the forms שֶׁלָּךְ, שֶׁלָּנוּ, שֶׁלָּכֶם, שֶׁלָּכֶן, שֶׁלָּהֶם, שֶׁלָּהֶן.
   The inflected forms of the preposition בִּשְׁבִיל serve as a better mnemonic aid than those of שֶׁל, as they are identical in pronunciation to the possessive suffixes. This is illustrated in the table below:

בשבילָם/ן	בשבילכֶם/ן	בשבילֵנוּ	בשבילָהּ	בשבילוֹ	בשבילֵךְ	בשבילְךָ	בשבילי
דוֹדָם/ן	דוֹדכֶם/ן	דוֹדֵנוּ	דוֹדָהּ	דוֹדוֹ	דוֹדֵךְ	דוֹדְךָ	דוֹדִי

2. <u>Plural nouns</u>: the parentheses in the English transcription indicate that in rapid speech the יו"ד /y/ that distinguishes singular from plural nouns is barely, or not at all, pronounced. The pronunciation of the suffixes יַ- and יהָ- is discussed in 5.5 below.

5.2.1 The possessive suffix attaches to the noun in its construct form. This refers, in particular, to end-of-the-word changes (see 4.3.5 (a) and (b) above). Internal vowel changes that occur in the noun in its construct state may or may not be carried over to the pronunciation of the noun when the possessive suffix is attached to it.
For example:

- דְּבָרִים → דִּבְרֵי- → דְּבָרֶיהָ, דִּבְרֵיהֶם: the final מ"ם of the plural suffix does not appear in the construct form דברי- or in the suffixed forms; the internal vowel change evident in the construct form דִּבְרֵיהֶם is not seen in דְּבָרֶיהָ.
- מִלְחָמָה → מִלְחֶמֶת- → מִלְחַמְתָּם: the conversion of the final ה"א in מלחמה to תי"ו in the construct form is seen in the suffixed forms but the internal vowel change (from /a/ to /e/) does not occur.
- בַּיִת → בֵּית- → בֵּיתוֹ, בֵּיתָם: the internal vowel change occurring in the construct form is carried over to the suffixed forms.

5.2.2 As already mentioned in 3.2 above, the definite article ה- cannot be attached to nouns with the possessive suffix, since the suffix already makes the noun specific. In other words, *הספרו is not allowed. As a result, when the prepositions כ, ב and ל introduce a noun with a possessive suffix or a construct phrase whose second noun has a possessive suffix, they are pronounced with a *sheva*. For example: בְּסִיפּוּרוֹ *in his story* (NOT: בַּסִיפּוּרוֹ), בְּסוֹף סִיפּוּרוֹ *at the end of his story* (NOT: בַּסוֹף סיפורו).

5.3 Use
In addition to its role in striking a more formal note, the possessive suffix is often used to avoid repetition when two consecutive construct phrases share the same noun.
For example:

פירוש העבר והבנת העבר can be collapsed with the aid of the possessive suffix into:
פירוש העבר והבנתו. The suffix ו- refers to the shared noun, עבר.

This phrase can be translated in either of two ways: *the interpretation of the past and its understanding,* or *the interpretation and understanding of the past.*
Note that in contrast to English, the sequence – *פירוש והבנת העבר* – is not considered acceptable in Hebrew.

5.4 Potential ambiguities in unpointed text

(a) דודי: *my uncle, my uncles* or *the uncles of?*

In unpointed text, the singular דודי *my uncle* and the plural דודי *my uncles* appear identical, although they are pronounced differently: /i/ with a singular noun (דּוֹדִי) and /ay/ with a plural noun (דּוֹדַי).
To distinguish between the two forms (and meanings), modern plene (full) spelling doubles the יו"ד after a plural noun. Thus:

דודיי ← הדודים שלי
דודי ← הדוד שלי

Even so, a potential ambiguity still remains in unpointed text between the suffixed form דּוֹדִי *my uncle* and the construct form דּוֹדֵי- *the uncles of* (e.g., דודי יעקב could be construed either as *my uncle Jacob* or *Jacob's uncles*).

The doubling of the יו"ד in plene spelling also helps to distinguish between the masculine and feminine second person suffixes (of plural nouns), that is, between דודיך (דּוֹדֶיךָ) *your (m.) uncles* and דודייך (דּוֹדַיִךְ) *your (f.) uncles.*

(b) דודה: *her uncle* or *an aunt?*

Without its special diacritic – the dot inside (called מַפִּיק) – the third person feminine possessive suffix ה- (replacing שלה) could be confused with a final ה"א that is an integral (and non-removable) part of the word.
For example:

מלכה can be read either as מַלְכָּה *a queen* or מַלְכָּהּ = המלך שלה *her/its king*
אישה can be read either as אישה *a woman* or אישהּ = האיש שלה *her man, her husband*
מעמדה is read as מעמדהּ = המעמד שלה *her/its status* (or, possibly, מֵעֶמְדָּה *from a position*), but may be erroneously construed as the non-existent noun מעמדה.

To avoid the ambiguity, the מפיק diacritic is sometimes marked in otherwise unpointed texts.

As illustrated in examples 28–29 below, the ambiguity of the final ה"א can be resolved by attending to grammatical and contextual clues.

(28) סִימָנִים אֵלֶּה מַבְהִירִים אֶת חֶלְקֵי הַבִּנְיָן שֶׁל הַמִּשְׁנָה, וּמְלַמְּדִים עַל **נֻסְחָה**, שֶׁאֵין הוּא מֶחְטִיבָה אַחַת.

These markings clarify the building components of the Mishnah and tell (us) about <u>its textual version</u>, that it is not from one block.

Without vowles נוסחה can be read either as
(a) נוּסְחָה = הַנֻּוסֹח שֶׁלֹה *its textual version*, where נוסח is a masculine noun inflected with the possessive suffix -ה, OR:
(b) נוּסְחָה *a formula*, a feminine noun.
The ambiguity is resolved by the presence of the masculine pronoun הוּא in the subsequent clause.

(29) מַעֲרֶכֶת הָעִצּוּרִים שֶׁל הָעֲרָבִית הַקְלָאסִית קְדוּמָה הִיא; אֲבָל מַעֲרֶכֶת הַפֹּעַל אֵין **מִבְנֶה** קָדוּם.

The consonant system of classical Arabic is ancient, but the structure of the verb system is not ancient (literally: but the verb system, <u>its structure</u> is not ancient)

The correct reading of מבנה is מִבְנָה/מִבְנֶה *its structure*: the topicalized clause[8] מַעֲרֶכֶת הַפֹּעַל אֵין מִבְנֶה קָדוּם requires a pronoun suffix referring back to the head noun of the construct phrase, מערכת הפועל.
The reading מִבְנֶה *structure* would be grammatically possible if the clause were not topicalized:
לְמַעֲרֶכֶת הַפֹּעַל אֵין מבנה קדום.

5.5 Pronouncing ־יו at the end of the noun: /av/, /iv/ or /yo/?

(a) ־יו is pronounced /av/ after a plural noun.
    For example: סְפָרָיו /sefarav/ *his books*, דּוֹדוֹתָיו /dodotav/ *his aunts*.

/av/ is also the pronunciation of the pronoun suffixes in some prepositions (e.g., עָלָיו, לְפָנָיו, תַּחְתָּיו) and in the words עַכְשָׁיו *now*, סְתָיו *autumn*, עָנָיו *humble*, יַחְדָּיו *together*, in which the יו"ד is added in unpointed text.

(b) ־יו is pronounced /iv/ when the יו"ד is integral to the construct form of the noun. The construct form of פֶּה *mouth* is ־פִּי; therefore: פִּיו /piv/ *his mouth*; the construct forms of אָח, אָב and חָם are ־אֲבִי, ־אֲחִי and ־חֲמִי respectively, therefore: אָבִיו /aviv/ *his father* and אָחִיו /ahiv/ *his brother*, חָמִיו /hamiv/ *his father-in-law*.

---

[8] See Chapter 1, 2.

Note that the direct object suffix יו- (replacing אותו) in first person singular past tense verbs is also pronounced /iv/ (e.g., לימדתיו = לימדתי אותו *I taught him.*)

(c) יו- is pronounced /yo/ in words that end with יו"ד (that is, words whose last root letter is י, for example, עינוי *torment*).
For example:

פְּרִי → פִּרְיוֹ /piryo/ *his/its fruit* , עוֹנִי → עוֹנְיוֹ /onyo/ *his/its poverty*, בֶּכִי → בִּכְיוֹ /bikhyo/ *his/its crying*, יוֹפִי → יוֹפִיוֹ /yofyo/ *his/its beauty*, אוֹפִי → אוֹפְיוֹ /ofyo/ *his/its*.
Note that in pointed text a *kamatz katan* diacritic indicates the initial /o/ sound: עָנְיוֹ, יָפְיוֹ, אָפְיוֹ.

5.5.1 The pronunciation of the ending יה- varies along the same lines as that of יו-:

(a) /e(y)ha/ after a plural noun (e.g., סְפָרֶיהָ *her books*, דּוֹדוֹתֶיהָ *her aunts*).

(b) /i-ha/ when the יו"ד belongs to the construct form (e.g., פִּיהָ /piha/ *her mouth*, אָבִיהָ /aviha/ *her father*, אָחִיהָ /aḥiha/ *her brother*);

(c) /ya/ when the יו"ד is part of the word (e.g., פִּרְיָה /pirya/ *her/its fruit*).

🏋#5 **5.6 Locating nouns with a possessive suffix in the dictionary**

To uncover the lexical (dictionary) form of nouns with possessive suffix, the suffix must be removed. For example, after the removal of ו- in מאבקו and יהם- in מאבקיהם, the noun מאבק *struggle* is uncovered.
  Two additional adjustments may be necessary:

(a) When the possessive suffix is attached to a plural noun ending with וֹת-, this ending has to be removed as well and in most – but not all cases – replaced by ה-. (See columns 3–7 in the table in section 2 above).
For example:

פעולותיו → פעולות → פעולה *his/its actions*
מקורותיה → מקורות → מקור *her/its sources*

(b) The תי"ו before the suffix attached to singular nouns has to be converted back into ה"א.
For example:

משפחתם → משפחת→משפחה *their family*
מְכוֹרתו → מכורת → מכורה *his native land*

⚠ However, not every תי"ו remaining after the removal of the possessive suffix is a former ה"א. In some nouns, the final תי"ו is integral to the word, often as part of the וּת- /ut/ and ית- /it/ word endings.

For example:

תּוֹעֶלֶת‎ ‎תוֹעלתם → *their benefit*
בְּדִידוּת‎ ‎בדידותה → *her loneliness*
תַּכְלִית‎ ‎תכליתו → *his/its purpose*

5.7 Possessive suffix rules as an aid in word recognition and dictionary consultation

5.7.1 An initial ה"א: part of the word or a definite article?

Given the rule that nouns with a possessive suffix do not take the definite article (5.2.2 above), an initial ה"א in a noun inflected with a possessive suffix can be automatically interpreted as an integral part of the word (rather than as a removable definite article).

Initial non-removable ה"א commonly occurs in action nouns in the *binyanim* nif'al, hif'il and *hitpa'el.* For example:

non-existent form	in the dictionary (pointed)	in the text (unpointed full spelling)
יעדרות*	הֵעָדְרוּת *absence*	(נפעל) היעדרותה
יווצרות*	הִוָּצְרוּת *formation*	(נפעל) היווצרותם
שפעה*	הַשְׁפָּעָה *influence*	(הפעיל) השפעתו
תנוונות*	הִתְנַוְּנוּת *degeneration*	(התפעל) התנוונותך

Conversely, if a noun is introduced by a definite article, its final ה"א must be identified as part of the word, not as a removable possessive suffix.

---

(30) כַּד חֶרֶס מוּגְדָּל בְּקִדְמַת הַצִּיּוּר וְעָלָיו עִיקָר הַתְּאוּרָה שֶׁל הַתְּמוּנָה.
[There is] an enlarged clay pitcher at the foreground of the painting and on it [falls] the main <u>lighting</u> of the picture.

Reading התאורה של התמונה as *the description of the picture* is incorrect, as it confuses תְּאוּרָה *lighting* with תֵּאוּרָה *its description.*
The spelling provides another clue, since by rule, תֵּאוּר would be written as תיאור.

⚡#5   5.7.2 Is the noun singular or plural?

With the two exceptions noted in 5.5 (b) and (c) above, a יו"ד appearing before the possessive suffix indicates that the noun is plural. It is, therefore, possible to tell at a glance the difference, for example, between דודך *your uncle* and דודיך *your uncles*, or between תפקידם *their role* and תפקידיהם *their roles.*[9]

---

[9] Note, however, that עליו and עליה (when בעל indicates ownership) may refer to a single owner, for example: בעליה של החנות is either *the owner of the store* or *the owners of the store.*

> However, in unpointed text, the decision whether אחיהם means *their brothers* (אֲחֵיהֶם) or *their brother* (אֲחִיהֶם) must be made on the basis of the context. This also applies to the rest of the forms (e.g., אחיו, אחיה).

The presence of the יו"ד in the possessive suffix also tells the reader of unpointed text that **ות-** before the suffix is the plural ending **ות-** /ot/, an inflectional suffix which should be removed for the purposes of dictionary consultation. Conversely, if no יו"ד is present in the possessive suffix, **ות-** is read as **ות-** /ut/, a non-removable derivational suffix in singular feminine (usually abstract) nouns.
For example:

- **קריאותיו** is interpreted as הקריאות שלו – in the dictionary: קריאה *a call, a cry; a reading.*
- **קריאותו** is interpreted as הקריאות שלו – in the dictionary: קריאות *readability.*

Notice that the action nouns in 5.7.1 above – התנוונותן, היווצרותם, היעדרותה – have possessive suffixes without יו"ד, a ready clue that their ות- should be read as ־ות.

> (31) יש במקרא קָרוב לְמֵאָה מִלים, שֶׁ**צורתן** הפונֵטית מרַמֶזֶת על **זרותן**.
> In the Bible there are close to one hundred words <u>whose</u> phonetic <u>form</u> hints at <u>their foreignness</u>.
>
> Since the pronoun suffix in both nouns lacks יו"ד, we determine that both are singular. For the purpose of dictionary look up the תי"ו in צורתן is converted back to the original ה"א – צורה (as explained in 5.6(b) above) but no such change is possible in זרות, since the final תי"ו is an integral part of the word.

#6 & #7   5.8 Strategy for determining the reference of the possessive suffix

5.8.1 The possessive suffix answers the question "whose?," that is, who is the "possessor" of the noun. As is the case with שלו, שלה etc., the identity of the "possessor" is determined on the basis of number (singular-plural) and gender (masculine-feminine) concord between the suffix and some other noun or pronoun in the sentence.
For example:

- the "possessor" in דודו and דודיו is a singular masculine noun (הוא)
- the "possessor" in דודה and דודתה is a singular feminine noun (היא)
- the "possessor" in דודם and דודיהם is a plural masculine noun (הם)
- the "possessor" in דודן and דודיהן is a plural feminine noun (הן)

Usually, the suffix refers <u>backwards</u> (anaphoric reference) to a previously mentioned noun. <u>Forward</u> (cataphoric) reference occurs when the suffixed noun appears (a) within an introductory adverbial phrase (examples 41–43), or (b) in a double construct phrase – the suffix then

refers to the (second) noun within the phrase, that is, the noun that appers after the particle
שֶׁל (examples 36 and 44–46).

5.8.2 A step-by-step procedure for determining the identity of the "possessor" is outlined
below and illustrated in examples 32 through 46.

(a) Determine whether the suffix appears within an adverbial phrase or in a double construct
phrase – the referent will then appear <u>after</u> the suffix.
Otherwise:

(b) Look for a previously-mentioned noun that is nearest to the suffixed noun and agrees with
the suffix in gender and number. Converting the noun into a pronoun – that is, הם ,הוא, היא,
or הן – will be helpful in matching the suffix with its referent.
Bear in mind that:

- A <u>plural</u> possessive suffix may be used to refer to a <u>singular</u> noun representing a collective
entity (e.g., עַם; example 40).
- A possessive suffix that is attached to Noun B of the construct phrase refers to some
noun <u>outside</u> this phrase (in other words, this suffix cannot refer Noun A within the
construct phrase) (example 38).

(c) Determine on the basis of the meaning if the suffix in fact refers to the noun you have
identified.

(d) If the nearest noun is <u>not</u> a plausible referent, look further back in the sentence for a
more likely candidate. It is not unusual for several nouns to be skipped over in the process
(examples 35 and 37) or for the referent to be found in a previous sentence (examples
39–40).

*The possessive suffix is bolded and shaded and the noun to which it refers is shaded; double
construct phrases are bracketed:*

---

(32) הַהֵיעָדְרוּת הממושֶכֶת של **הבעל-הלַמְדָן** מביתו֫ השפיעה על מַעֲמדו֫ בבית ועל יְחָסָיו֫
עם אשתו֫ וילדיו֫.

The lengthy absence of the <u>scholar-husband</u> from <u>his home</u> affected <u>his status</u> at
home and <u>his relationship</u> with <u>his wife and children</u>.

In this example, all suffixes refer backwards to the same noun, הבעל-הלמדן (הוא=).

(33) מַמְלֶכֶת פָּרַס כָּלְלה עמים רבים ושונים זה מזה בדָתָם, בשָׂפתָם ובתַרבוּתָם. מדיניות
השַליטים הפַרסים הייתה סוֹבלָנות דָתית ותַרבותית, ובמִסְגַרתָה הִרְשו לְגולים לשוב
לאַרצם ולבנות את מקדשיהם.

The Persian Empire included many <u>nations</u>, different from each other in <u>their
religion, language and culture</u>. The <u>policy</u> of the Persian rulers was religious and
cultural tolerance and as part of it (literally: within <u>its framework</u>) they allowed the
<u>exiles</u> to return to <u>their land</u> and build <u>their temples</u>.

---

(34) עָלֵינוּ לעסוק בקֶהָל המִתְבּוֹנְנִים בדְיוֹקָנָאוֹת, ביוֹצְרֵיהֶם ובמֵפִיצֵיהֶם.
We should concern ourselves with those who are viewing the <u>portraits</u>, with <u>their creators and distributors</u>.

The possessive suffix in יוצריהם and מפיציהם refers to a plural masculine noun. We identify דיוקנאות (whose feminine ending ות- is misleading) as the referent of the possessive suffix on semantic grounds, since מתבוננים *onlookers* cannot be said to have creators and distributors.

(35) מְסַפְּרִים שפָּעֲלוּ בתקופה מאוחרת הכירו את הסִפְרות שנכתבה בדורות קודמים ויכלו לעשות בה שימוש לצורכֵיהֶם.
<u>Narrators</u> who were active in a later period knew the literature that was written in previous generations and could make use of it for <u>their (own) purposes</u>.

The possessive suffix refers to a plural masculine noun (הם) – in this case – מספרים. Although the nearest masculine plural noun is דורות (like דיוקנאות in the previous example, this is a masculine noun with the plural feminine ending ות-), it must be rejected as a referent on the basis of the meaning.

(36) אין לבחון את [החלטתוֹ של בֵּית המשפט] רק מִזָּוִית מִשפָּטִית צְרוּפָה; משמעוּתָהּ רְחָבָה ונוֹגַעַת לעֶרְכֵי יסוֹד אוניבֶרְסָלִיים ולסוגיוֹת אידאוֹלוֹגיות ופוליטיות.
The court's <u>decision</u> should not be examined only from a purely legalistic viewpoint; <u>its meaning</u> is broad and concerns universal basic values and ideological and political issues.

In this example, one suffix refers forward and another backward. The suffix in החלטתוֹ refers forward, to בית המשפט, the second noun of the double construct phrase. The suffix in משמעותה refers to a feminine singular noun; we determine on the basis of the meaning that the referent is not the immediately preceding noun זווית, but rather החלטה.

(37) כל קֶהִילָּה הייתה מדינה ריבּוֹנית בַּעֲלַת סַמְכות מלאה על חבֵרֶיהָ.
Every <u>congregation</u> was a sovereign state with full authority over <u>its members</u>.

The feminine nouns closest to the feminine suffix in חבריה are סמכות and מדינה but neither is a likely referent: סמכות *authority* cannot be said to have members and similarly מדינה *state* has citizens (אזרחים) or residents (תושבים), but not members (חברים). The referent of suffix must, therefore, be קהילה *congregation*, the first noun in the sentence.

(38) המֶחְקָרים מְתָאֲרים תַּהֲלִיכֵי גיבוּש זֶהות חֶבְרָתית המִתְרַחֲשים בקבוצות מסוימות ומשְתַקְּפים בשימור מוֹרָשְתָּן ובשחזורָהּ.
The studies describe processes of social identity formation which occur in certain <u>groups</u> and are reflected in the preservation of <u>their heritage</u> and <u>its reconstruction</u>.

The suffix in the second noun of the construct phrase שימור מורשתן refers to the preceding plural feminine noun קבוצות; the suffix in שחזורה refers to a singular feminine noun, the immediately preceding noun מורֶשֶת/מוֹרָשָה.

(39) הַמַאֲמָרִים בַּסֵפֶר מַדגִימִים בְּבֵירוּר עַד כַּמָה לֹא רָאוּ כָּל הַזְרָמִים עַיִן בְּעַיִן אֶת **הַזִיקָה לַצִיוֹן**. אֲחָדִים מֵהַזְרָמִים אַף נִיתְקוּ אֶת עַצְמָם בְּמוּדָע מִמֶרכָּזִיוּתָהּ.

The articles in the book clearly illustrate to what extent not all the [ideological] currents were in agreement about <u>the connection to Zion</u>. Some of them even consciously disconnected themselves from <u>its centrality</u>.

The singular feminine possessive suffix in מרכזיותה refers to הזיקה לציון in the previous sentence.

(40) הַצָרוֹת בָּאוּ עַל **עַם יִשְׂרָאֵל** בְּזוֹ אַחַר זוֹ בְּלִי הֶפְסֵק. בְּמַצָבָם הַמוּשפָּל רָאוּ הָאוּמוֹת הוֹכָחָה נִיצַחַת לְצִדְקַת הַנַצְרוּת אוֹ הָאִיסלָאם.

The troubles came upon <u>the people of Israel</u> incessantly, one after another. The nations saw in <u>their degraded situation</u> irrefutable proof of the justness of Christianity or Islam.

The possessive suffix in מצבם refers back to עם ישראל, a collective noun treated as a plural noun (הם rather than הוא), not to the feminine nouns אומות or צרות (if it did, the suffix would be ן-).

(41) לַמרוֹת קְשָׁרָיו הַטוֹבִים עִם מַלכֵי סְפָרַד, לֹא הִצלִיחַ **אַברַבַנאֵל** לְבַטֵל אֶת גְזֵרַת הַגֵירוּש.

Despite <u>his good connections</u> with the Spanish kings, <u>Abrabanel</u> did not succeed in revoking the decree of expulsion.

In this example, as in the next one, the sentence begins with an adverbial of concession and the possessive suffix anticipates the noun that it refers to.

(42) אִם כִּי מוֹצָאָהּ הוּא, כְּכָל הַנִרְאֶה, קֶדֶם-מִקרָאִי, חוֹקְרִים מְנִיחִים כִּי **הָאֱמוּנָה** בַּמַלאָכִים הָיְיתָה מְקוּבֶּלֶת בִּתקוּפַת הַמִקרָא.

Although <u>its origin</u> is, probably, pre-biblical, researchers surmise that the <u>belief</u> in angels was popular in biblical times.

(43) כְּבָר בְּרֵאשִׁית מַסָעָם בַּמִדבָּר מִתלוֹנְנִים **בְּנֵי יִשְׂרָאֵל** וְזוֹכְרִים לְטוֹב אֶת שִׁפעַת הַמָזוֹן בְּאֶרֶץ אוֹיבֵיהֶם.

Already at the beginning of <u>their journey</u> in the desert, <u>the children of Israel</u> complain and remember fondly the plenitude of food in the land of <u>their enemies</u>.

The suffix in מסעם, which is found within an adverbial clause of time, refers forward, to בני ישראל; the suffix in אויביהם refers backward, also to בני ישראל.

(44) הַתַקָנוֹת הָיוּ [פְּרִי תַרבּוּתוֹ, תַלמוּדוֹ וּמָסוֹרוֹתָיו שֶׁל **הָעָם**] כּוּלוֹ.

The *Takkanot* (ordinances) were the fruit of the <u>culture</u>, <u>learning</u> and <u>traditions of the entire people</u>.

The three suffixes in the bracketed double construct phrase refer forward, to עם. As noted in 4.4.4 above, in translation the suffixes are ignored.

(45) [הִתְגַבְּשׁוּתוֹ‎ של הֶסְדֵר‎ זה] ופְעוּלָתוֹ‎ הַמְמוּשֶׁכֶת אינם מתוארים במחקר.
The consolidation of <u>this arrangement</u> and <u>its lengthy operation</u> (OR: the consolidation and lengthy operation of this arrangement) are not described in the study.

The first possessive suffix appears within the double construct phrase and refers forward
while the second suffix refers backwards; both refer to the same noun, הֶסְדֵר.

(46) [בעיותיה‎ של החֶברה] לא באו לידֵי פתרונָן.
The <u>problems of society</u> have not been solved (literally: have not reached <u>their solution</u>)

The first possessive suffix (within the bracketed double construct phrase) refers forward,
to the second noun of the construct phrase, חברה, while the second possessive suffix refers
backwards to בעיות.

🏋#8   6. Three structural groups

Of the many noun groups, three will be discussed here: nouns ending with ‎-וּת, nouns that are
identical in form to present tense verbs, and action nouns.

6.1 Nouns ending with ‎-וּת
Nouns ending with ‎-וּת are singular feminine and usually abstract in meaning (e.g., תרבות
culture, צִיוֹנוּת Zionism, אֱמָנוּת art).

> But note that there are nouns ending with ‎-וּת whose ת is a root letter; these nouns are
> singular masculine. For example: שֵׁירוּת service (שרת), אִיתּוּת spelling (אות), אִיתּוּת signaling
> (אות), חֶבְרוּת socialization (חברת).

Many nouns in this group are created through the addition of the derivational suffix ‎-וּת to
adjectives.
For example:

קיצוניוּת → קיצוני   *extreme – extremism*
מיוּמָנוּת → מיוּמָן   *skilled – skill*
פְּעִילוּת → פָּעִיל   *active – activity*
חֲשִׁיבוּת → חָשׁוּב   *important – importance*
מְתִינוּת → מָתוּן   *moderate – moderation*

> Note that the /u/ vowel in the adjectives חשוב and מתון becomes /i/ in the related, derived,
> noun.

Note also the following derivations:

מַהוּת → מָה   *what – essence*
אֵיכוּת → אֵיך   *how – quality*
כַּמּוּת → כַּמָּה   *how much/many – quantity*
יֵשׁוּת → יֵשׁ   *there is – entity; being*
זֶהוּת → זֶה   *this – identity*

6.2 Nouns modeled upon present tense verb forms: שׁוֹמֵר *he guards; a guard*

Present tense verb forms (participles) may also function as nouns or adjectives.[10] Nouns modeled on present tense forms are often animate (that is, refer to a person).

The reader must decide on the basis of the context whether, in a given sentence, the participle functions as a verb, noun or adjective.

The examples below are culled from scholarly articles; they alternate among singular and plural, feminine and masculine forms in a variety of *binyanim* and verb groups.

participle form	meaning as a noun	meaning as a verb	*binyan*
חוֹקֵר	*researcher*	*studies*	פעל
קוֹרֵאת	*reader* (f.)	*reads*	פעל
שָׁבִים	*returnees*	*return*	פעל
בּוֹנִים	*builders*	*build*	פעל
הוֹגֶה	*thinker*	*thinks*	פעל
אֲהוּבָה	*lover, beloved* (f.)	*loved*	פעול
נִבְחָן	*examinee*	*is examined*	נפעל
מְחַבְּרוֹת	*authors* (f.pl.)	*compose; join*	פיעל
מְחוֹקְקִים	*legislators*	*legislate*	פיעל
מְיַסֵּד	*founder*	*establishes*	פיעל
מְפָרְשִׁים	*commentators, exegetes*	*interpret*	פיעל
מְאַפְיֵן	*characteristic, trait*	*characterizes*	פיעל
מַאֲמִינִים	*believers*	*believe*	הפעיל
מַנְהִיגוֹת	*leaders* (f.pl.)	*lead*	הפעיל
מַרְכִּיב	*component*	*puts together*	הפעיל
מִתְנַדֶּבֶת	*volunteer* (f.)	*volunteers*	התפעל

---

[10] For discussion of the use of present tense verb forms as adjectives see Chapter 4, section 4.1.

Table (*cont.*)

participle form	meaning as a noun	meaning as a verb	*binyan*
מִשְׁתַּנֶּה	*variable*	*changes*	התפעל
מְאוּמָץ	*adoptee*	*is adopted*	פועל
מוּזְמָנִים	*invitees*	*are invited*	הופעל

⚡#9   6.3 Action nouns שמות פעולה

6.3.1 Among the many noun patterns, action nouns, שמות פעולה, comprise a distinct group by virtue of their direct and often predictable relationship to verbs in the *binyanim pa'al, nif'al, pi'el, hitpa'el* and *hif'il*. There are no action nouns related to verbs in the passive *binyanim pu'al* and *huf'al* (as there are also no infinitive forms in these *binyanim*).

Action nouns are created through discontinuous derivation, that is, an alternation of root (consonant) and vowel patterns.
For example:

קְרִיאָה *reading* is derived from לקרוא (*pa'al*) *to read*, דיבּוּר *speaking* is derived from לְדַבֵּר (*pi'el*) *to speak*, הִתְרַגְשׁוּת *excitement* from לְהִתְרַגֵּשׁ (*hitpa'el*) *to be/get excited* and הֲבָנָה *understanding, comprehension* comes from לְהָבִין (*hif'il*) *to understand*.

The usually predictable connection between a source verb and an action noun aids readers in word recognition. In addition, identification of the pattern on which the noun is modeled provides a clue to its phonetic form (pronunciation).

6.3.2 Although by virtue of their close connection to the verb action nouns are similar to English gerunds (-*ing* forms), they cannot always be rendered in English in this way.
For example:

- יְצִירה may be translated as *creating* but also (depending on context) as the product of the act of creating, a *creation* or *work of art*
- סיפּוּר is usually translated as *story*, rather than *story telling*.
- כְּנִיסה may be translated as *entering* or *entrance*
- הַנְהגה is often used in the sense of *leadership*
- רְשִׁימה (from לרשום, *to write down*) means *a list* (rather than *writing down*, which would be רישׁוּם).

6.3.3 Some action nouns are formed in a different *binyan* than the related verb.
For example:

- כניסה *entering, entrance* is in the *pa'al* paradigm, but the related verb, להיכנס, is in *nif'al*.
- תפילה *prayer* is in the *pa'al* paradigm, but the related verb, להתפלל, is in *hitpa'el.*
- The action noun of the *pi'el* verb לְבַקֵּשׁ *to request* is בַּקָשׁה *request*, while the expected form ביקוּשׁ is a term in economics, *demand.*

6.3.4 Like other nouns, action nouns can be used in construct phrases and can take possessive suffixes (e.g., יְצִיאַת מצרים *exodus from Egypt,* הִתְקוֹמְמוּתָם שֶׁל הָעֲבָדִים *the uprising of the slaves*).

6.3.5 With two exceptions (קיטּוּל in פיעל and הֶקְטֵל in הפעיל), action nouns are assigned feminine gender.

6.3.6 The chart below lists the most common action noun patterns by *binyan* and within each *binyan,* by verb group. The chart is followed by explanatory notes.

Action Nouns

pattern	unpointed spelling (bolded if different from pointed spelling)	pointed	*binyan* and root group
(1) קְטִילָה (2) קְטֵלָה (3) קְטָלָה	כתיבה, ירידה, נסיעה, קריאה שאלה שנאה, אהבה **עשייה, עלייה** ריצה	(1) כְּתִיבָה, יְרִידָה, נְסִיעָה, קְרִיאָה (2) שְׁאֵלָה (3) שִׂנְאָה, אַהֲבָה עֲשִׂיָּה, עֲלִיָּה רִיצָה	**פָּעַל** שלמים, פ"י, פ"נ, ל"א ל"ה/ל"י ע"ו
הַקְטָלוֹת	**הִימָּצְאוּת, הֵיעָלְמוּת** **הִיוָּצְרוּת**	הִמָּצְאוּת, הֵעָלְמוּת הִוָּצְרוּת	**נפעל** שלמים, גרוניות פ"י
(1) קִטּוּל (2) קַטָּלָה	**תיקון, ייבוש, ניגון** בקשה, קבלה **שינוי** **וידוא** **ריפוי, מילוי** **תיאור, צירוף** צלצול, שעבוד	(1) תִּקּוּן, יִבּוּשׁ, נִגּוּן (2) בַּקָּשָׁה, קַבָּלָה שִׁנּוּי וִדּוּא רִפּוּי, מִלּוּי תֵּאוּר, צֵרוּף צִלְצוּל, שִׁעְבּוּד	**פיעל** שלמים, פ"י, פ"נ ל"ה/ל"י ל"א ע' גרונית מרובעים

Table (*cont.*)

pattern	unpointed spelling (bolded if different from pointed spelling)	pointed	*binyan* and root group
(1) הַקְטָלָה (2) הֶקְטֵל	התחלה המשך הפניה[11]; **השוואה** המצאה הבנה הוכחה הכרה, **הישג** הכללה	(1) הַתְחָלָה (2) הֶמְשֵׁךְ הַפְנָיָה, הַשְׁוָאָה הַמְצָאָה הֲבָנָה הוֹכָחָה הַכָּרָה, הֶשֵּׂג הַכְלָלָה	**הפעיל** שלמים ל"ה/ל"י ל"א ע"ו/ע"י פ"י פ"נ, פי"צ[12] כפולים
הִתְקַטְּלוּת	התנגדות; התמצאות הסתברות, השתמרות, **הצטיינות**, הזדקנות **התיישבות, התייחסות** התרבות התקוממות התקררות, התמודדות השתחררות, הצטמצמות	הִתְנַגְּדוּת; הִתְמַצְּאוּת הִסְתַּבְּרוּת, הִשְׁתַּמְּרוּת, הִצְטַיְּנוּת, הִזְדַּקְּנוּת הִתְיַשְּׁבוּת, הִתְיַחֲסוּת הִתְרַבּוּת הִתְקוֹמְמוּת הִתְקָרְרוּת, הִתְמוֹדְדוּת הִשְׁתַּחְרְרוּת, הִצְטַמְצְמוּת	**התפעל** שלמים; ל"א שורקות פ"י ל"ה/ל"י ע"ו כפולים מרובעים

6.3.7 Notes on the action noun chart

6.3.7.1 Pronunciation

(a) The ending ‑וּת in *nif'al* and *hitpa'el* is pronounced /ut/.

(b) ה"א at the beginning of the action noun is pronounced הִ /i/ in *hitpa'el* (e.g., הִתְפַּטְּרוּת), הִ /i/ or, before a guttural, /e/, in *nif'al* (e.g., הִימָּצְאוּת, הֵיעָדְרוּת) and הַ /a/ (e.g., הַתְחָלָה) or הֶ /e/ (e.g., הֶמְשֵׁךְ) in *hif'il*.

6.3.7.2 Form

1. *Hif'il*

(a) In *hif'il* there are two patterns, הַקְטָלָה and הֶקְטֵל. In some cases, the co-existence of the two forms allows for a differentiation of meaning.

---

[11] In the construct form, the יו"ד is doubled: ‑הַפְנִיַּת.

[12] The name פי"צ refers to a few roots whose first two letters are יצ: יצב, יצג, יצע, יצת, יצק, יצר. Although their first root letter is יו"ד, these verbs are conjugated (in some *binyamin*) as if they belong to the פ"נ group.

Some examples are:

הַסְכָּמָה	*agreement, consent*; הֶסְכֵּם *agreement* (usually contractual)
הַבְדָּלָה	*Havdalah*;[13] הֶבְדֵּל *difference*
הַפְרָשָׁה	*allocating; secreting*; הֶפְרֵשׁ *difference*
הַסְגָּרָה	*extradition*; הֶסְגֵּר *blockade*
הַסְבָּרָה	*propaganda, publicity*; הֶסְבֵּר *explanation*
הַבָּטָה	*viewing*; היבט (הֶבֵּט) *viewpoint, aspect.*

(b) The הֶקְטֵל pattern is used for the formation of some adverbs (e.g., בְּהֶחְלֵט *absolutely* בְּהֶכְרֵחַ *necessarily*).

(c) Some action nouns in *hif'il* begin with אל"ף, rather than ה"א (e.g., אשלייה *illusion; delusion*), or both forms may exist (e.g., אפלייה, הפלייה *discrimination*, אזהרה, הזהרה *warning*). The אל"ף-ה"א alternation allows, in some cases, for meaning differentiation. For example:

הַבְחָנָה	*differentiation, distinction* and אבחנה *diagnosis*
הַזְעָקָה	*calling urgently, summoning* and אזעקה *(sound of) alarm*
הַבְטָחָה	*promise, assurance* and אבטחה *protection*

2. Action nouns related to weak verbs

The formation rules that apply to the weak (non-*shlemim*) verbs (namely verbs in the groups פ"נ/פי"צ, פ"י, ל"י, ע"ו, ל"א), as well as to מרובעים (four-letter root verbs) and כפולים (roots with identical 2nd and 3rd consonants), apply also to the corresponding action nouns. These rules are detailed below.

(a) Action nouns related to פ"י verbs

- The initial יו"ד becomes a vowel – וֹ /o/ – in *hif'il* and a consonant – וי"ו /v/ – in *nif'al*. For example:
  י.כ.ח. → הוֹכָחָה → להוכיח *proof*
  י.צ.ר. → הַיְווצרות (הִצָּרֵן) → להיוּוצר (הִצָּרֵן) → היווצרות *creation, formation*
- In *pi'el* and *hitpa'el* the initial יו"ד is retained in most cases (e.g., יישוב, התיישבות), but note the following cases where the יו"ד of the root is rendered as וי"ו /v/ in *hitpa'el*: התווספות (הִתְוַסְּפוּת) *addition* (from י.ס.פ.), התווכחות (הִתְוַכְּחוּת) *arguing* (from י.כ.ח.), התוועדות (הִתְוַעֲדוּת) *meeting, conference* (from י.ע.ד.).

(b) Action nouns related to פ"נ verbs

In *hif'il*, the initial נ is usually absorbed into the next consonant. For example:

נ.ב.ט. → היבט (הֶבֵּט) → להביט *aspect*
נ.שׂ.ג. → הישג (הֶשֵּׂג) → להשיג *achievement*

---

[13] Ritual benediction at the conclusion of Sabbaths and festivals.

פי"צ verbs and nouns are formed as if they were פ"נ.
For example:

י.צ.ע → לְהַצִּיעַ → הַצָּעָה *suggestion*

(c) Action nouns related to ע"ו-ע"י verbs

• In *hif'il*, the second root letter (ו or י) is absorbed by the יו"ד of the *binyan*.
For example:

ק.ו.ם → לְהָקִים → הֲקָמָה *founding, establishment*

• In *pi'el* and *hitpa'el*, the יו"ד is often retained (e.g., התקָיְמוּת, קיום). Alternatively, the last letter of the root can be doubled, as if the verb belonged in the כפולים pattern.
For example:

ק.ו.ם → להתקוֹמם → התקוֹמְמות *uprising* is modeled upon:
ב.ל.ל → להתבולל → התבוללות *assimilation*

(d) Action nouns related to ל"ה/ל"י and ל"א verbs

• In *hif'il*, most nouns related to ל"ה/ל"י verbs are formed as if they derived from ל"א verbs.[14] For example, the action noun of להשוות *to compare*, whose root is ש.ו.י, is השואה *comparison, comparing* not *השוויה**.
Additional examples are:

ח.י.י	→	לְהַחֲיוֹת → הַחייאה	*revitalization, reviving; resuscitation*
ע.ל.י	→	להַעֲלוֹת → הַעֲלאה	*lifting; increase, rise*
י.ר.י	→	להוֹרוֹת → הוֹראה	*instruction, teaching; order, command; meaning*
ל.ו.י	→	להלְווֹת → הלוואה	*loan*
ת.ר.י	→	להתרות → התראה	*warning, advance notice*

(But note that הַמצאה *invention* is derived from a ל"א verb, להמציא.)

The root alternation sometimes allows for a differentiation of meaning. An example for this is the verb להודות, each of whose meanings (*to admit* and *to thank*) has its own action noun: הוֹדָאָה *admitting, confession* and הוֹדָיָה *thanking*.

• In *pi'el*, some nouns deriving from ל"א verbs are formed as if they belonged in the ל"ה/ל"י group.
For example:

ר.פ.א → לְרַפֵּא → ריפוּי *healing* (ריפוא is rare)
מ.ל.א → לְמַלֵּא → מילוּי *filling* (NOT: *מילוא**, although מילואים *reserve duty* exists)
ב.ט.א → לבַטֵּא → ביטוּי *expression* (NOT: *ביטוא**)

---

[14] The יו"ד-אל"ף alternation is also found in the verb ה.נ.י in *nif'al*: ה.נ.י → לֵיהָנות → הֲנָאָה *enjoyment*.

A variety of action nouns are seen in the in examples 47–48 below:

The action nouns are shaded:

---

(47) המקוּבָּלִים של צפת היו עורכים סֵדֶר ט"וּ בִּשְׁבָט עם **תפילות**, **שְתיית** יין לבן ואדום **ואכילה** מפירות הָאָרֶץ. בתקופה המודרְנית, ט"וּ בשבט הוא חג **נטיעת** האילָנות ובשנים האחרונות הפך לחג של **התקרבות** לטֶבַע **ושמירה** עליו.

The Cabbalists of Safed used to conduct a Tu Bishvat[15] Seder with <u>prayers, drinking</u> of white and red wine and <u>eating</u> from the fruits of the land. Tu Bishvat is the holiday of tree <u>planting</u> and in recent years has become a holiday of <u>becoming close</u> to nature and <u>preserving</u> it.

Four nouns – שמירה, נטיעה, אכילה, שתייה – are derived from verbs in *pa'al*; תפילה is in the *pa'al* paradigm although the related verb – להתפלל – is in *hitpa'el*. התקרבות is derived from the *hitpa'el* verb להתקרב.

(48) הָעֲרבים דָרשו **הפסקת העֲלייה**, **איסור מכירת** קָרְקעות ליהודים **והקמת** מֶמְשלה ייצוגית לפי הַיַחַס המִסְפָּרי בין הערבים ליהודים.

The Arabs demanded a <u>stop</u> to the <u>immigration</u> [to Israel], a <u>prohibition</u> on the <u>selling</u> of lands to Jews and the <u>establishment</u> of a representative government according to the proportion of Arabs and Jews [in the population].

The nouns הפסקה and הקמה are derived from verbs in *hif'il*, להפסיק and להקים; עלייה and מכירה are from the *pa'al* verbs למכור and לעלות; איסור – an action noun in the *pi'el* paradigm – derives from a *pa'al* verb, לאסור.

In the example below appear (shaded) the three noun types discussed above – nouns ending with -ות, those derived from present tense verbs and action nouns.

---

(49) **מְיַיסֵד** תנועת **הֲחסידות**, ר' ישראל בַּעַל שֵם טוב, הנחיל לבְני דורו את **ההִתְלַהֲבוּת** והדְּבקוּת בעבודת ה'. הוא הנחיל לְמַאֲמיניו את העֶקָרון שֶלְפיו **הריקוד** – המְחַייב את **השתתפות** כל אֵיבְרֵי הגוף – הוא **מרכיב** בלתי-נִפרד מעֲבודת ה'. העֶקָרון המיוחס **למַנהיג** רוחָני זה מוכיח שהריקוד הוא **תפילה** עֲבור הֲחסידות.

The <u>founder</u> of the movement of <u>Hasidism,</u> Rabbi Israel Ba'al Shem Tov, instilled in the people of his generation the <u>enthusiasm</u> and <u>devotion</u> in worship. He bequeathed to his <u>believers</u> the principle according to which <u>dancing</u>, which requires the <u>participation</u> of all body parts, is an inseparable <u>component</u> of worship. The principle that is attributed to this spiritual <u>leader</u> proves that for Hasidism, <u>dancing</u> is <u>praying</u>.

The nouns מנהיג, מרכיב, מאמינים and the noun מייסד are participle verb forms in *hif'il* and *pi'el* respectively. Note that other present tense forms in this text – מוכיח, מיוחס, מחייב – function as verbs.

The two -ות nouns are derived from adjectives, חסידות from חסיד and דבקות from דָּבֵק. The nouns התלהבות and השתתפות are action nouns in *hitpa'el*; ריקוד *dance* or *dancing* is in the *pi'el* paradigm, although the related verb, לרקוד, is in *pa'al*.

References

בליבוים, 1995
שלזינגר, 1994, 2000

Coffin & Bolozky, 2005
Muraoka, 1996
Schwarzwald, 2001

Chapter 2: Nouns – Exercises

exercise #	topic	page
1	Distinguishing between construct phrases and noun+adjective phrases	100
2	Determining which noun of the construct phrase is modified by the adjective	101
3	Identifying the predicate when the subject is a construct phrase	102–103
4	Determining whether nouns with a possessive suffix are singular or plural	104
5	Determining whether an ות- ending is /ut/ or /ot/	105
6	Identifying the reference of the possessive suffix	106–109
7	Selecting the possessive suffix in double construct phrases	110
8	Differentiating among three noun groups	111
9	Translating action nouns and identifying their source verbs	112–113

Exercise #1: Distinguishing between construct phrases and noun+adjective phrases

---

The rules to go by: see section 4.3.6.
What to do:
1. Determine the phrase type and enter its number in the appropriate cell in the chart.
2. Translate the phrases.
Example:

נתונים מהימנים reliable data

Explanation: This is identifiable as noun+adjective sequence because both words agree in number (plural) and gender (masculine) and the ־ים ending of the first word is retained.

---

construct phrases	noun+adjective phrases
	example,

1. אוכלוסיית הכפר

2. תיאורי מלחמה

3. מסורת המקום

4. מסורות מקומיות

5. חֲשִׁיבוּת הִיסְטוֹרִית

6. חשיבות ההיסטוריה

7. דְמוּת הגיבור

8. דמויות ראשיות

9. הוכחות בְּרוּרוֹת

10. מודעות פוליטית

Exercise #2: Determining which noun of the construct phrase is modified by the adjective

---

The rules to go by: see section 4.5.
What to do: highlight the appropriate translation for each construct phrase.
Example:

פריחת היישוב היהודי

(a) the flourishing of the Jewish settlement
(b) the Jewish flourishing of the settlement
Explanation: The correct answer is (a) because the singular masculine adjective יהודי agrees with the singular masculine noun יישוב and not with the feminine singular noun פריחה.

---

1. מַחֲזוֹר הֹחיים הָאֱנוֹשיים

(a) the cycle of human life
(b) the human cycle of life

2. בְּדיקת מָקוֹר עתיק

(a) an examination of an ancient source
(b) an ancient examination of a source

3. גיבוּש זהוּת חֶבְרָתית

(a) formation of a social identity
(b) social formation of an identity

4. צְמיחת התנוּעות הלְאוּמיוֹת

(a) the national growth of movements
(b) the growth of national movements

5. הַשפעות הסָביבה הֶחֶברתית

(a) the social influences of the environment
(b) the influences of the social environment

6. תְחוּשת מָקוֹם ועָבָר מְשוּתָפים

(a) a shared sense of place and past
(b) a sense of a shared place and past

7. בְּנייתה של הבירה החדשה

(a) the new building of the capital
(b) the building of the new capital

8. מְלוּמדי האוניברסיטה העברית

(a) the scholars of the Hebrew university
(b) the Hebrew scholars of the university

9. שינוי המְציאוּת הפוֹליטית

(a) the political change of reality
(b) the change of the political reality

10. סמְלי תרבוּת נוֹסָפים

(a) symbols of an additional culture
(b) additional symbols of culture

11. אוֹפי העילית השׁלְטוֹנית

(a) the nature of the ruling elite
(b) the ruling nature of the elite

Exercise #3: Identifying the predicate when the subject is a construct phrase

---

The rules to go by: see section 4.6.
What to do: highlight the appropriate predicate.
Example:
היעדרותם הממושכת מן הבית של הבעלים הלמדנים (**השפיעה**/השפיע/השפיעו) על מעמדם בבית.
Explanation: The verb השפיעה agrees with the head noun of the double construct phrase, היעדרות, a feminine singular noun. We determine the number and gender of the suffixed head noun on the basis of two clues: the feminine singular adjective ממושכת that follows it, and the absence of a יו"ד from the possessive suffix (as per 5.7.2).

---

1. מְאַפְיֵין אחד של יַהֲדוּת התפוצות (**הוא**/היא/הן) ריבּוּי הגְוְונים שֶבָּהּ.

2. הַשְפָּעַת החֲכָמים על עְנְייני בית הכנסת (היה/**הייתה**/היו) קטנה.

3. כמה ימֵי עיון (הוקדש/**הוקדשו**) לעְנְיינים הקשוּרים במוזאונים.

4. ייחוּס תְכוּנות מַאֲגִיוֹת לחֲפָצים טבעיים (ידוע/**ידועות**/ידועים) בכל תרבות.

5. שְחִיתוּת המְנָהָל הרוֹמי (הסעיר/**הסעירה**/הסעירו) את הרוּחוֹת.

6. מקורותיו הקדומים של המְנָהָג (**אינו ידוע**/אינם ידועים/אינן ידועות)

7. נְוֵוה מִדְבָּר זה (**היה**/הייתה) מֶרְכַּז יְשיבתם של בְּנֵי ישראל במִדְבָּר.

Glossary

---

	characteristic מְאַפְיֵין	1.
	Diaspora Jewry יהדות התפוצות	
	many colors ריבּוּי הגְוְונים	
	the influence of the sages השפעת החכמים	2.
	synagogue matters ענייני בית הכנסת	
	study days ימי עיון	3.
	attribution of magic qualities ייחוס תכונות מאגיות	4.
	natural objects חפצים טבעיים	
	the corruption of the Roman administration שחיתות המנהל הרומי	5.
	its ancient origins מקורותיו הקדומים	6.
	oasis נווה מדבר	7.
the center of the dwelling of the Children of Israel מרכז ישיבתם של בני ישראל במדבר		
in the desert		

8. ‏מַעֲשֵׂהוּ הָרִאשׁוֹן שֶׁל הַמֶּלֶךְ **‏(הָיָה/הָיְתָה/הָיוּ)** בְּנִיָּיתָהּ שֶׁל יְרוּשָׁלַיִם.

9. ‏בְּיִיחוּד **‏(מֶרְכָּזִי/מֶרְכָּזִית/מֶרְכָּזִיִּים)** מַעֲמָדָם שֶׁל יְרוּשָׁלַיִם וְהַמִּקְדָּשׁ בַּהֲלָכָה.

10. ‏הַנְּחִיתוּת הַיַּחֲסִית שֶׁל מַעֲמָדָהּ הָאִישִׁי, הַכַּלְכָּלִי וְהַפּוֹלִיטִי שֶׁל הָאִישָׁה **‏(עוֹמֵד/ עוֹמֶדֶת/ עוֹמְדוֹת)** בְּמוֹקֵד עִיסוּקָן שֶׁל תֵּיאוֹרִיּוֹת וּפְרַקְטִיקוֹת פֵמִינִיסְטִיּוֹת.

Glossary

8.	בנייתה של ירושלים	the building of Jerusalem
9.	בייחוד	particularly
	מעמדם של ירושלים והמקדש בהלכה	the status of Jerusalem and the Temple in Jewish law
10.	נחיתות יחסית	relative inferiority
	מעמדה האישי, הכלכלי והפוליטי	her personal, economic and political status
	במוקד עיסוקן של תיאוריות ופרקטיקות פמיניסטיות	at the center of the occupation of feminist theories and practices

Exercise #4: Determining whether nouns with a possessive suffix are singular or plural

---

The rules to go by: see section 5.2.

What to do:

1. Indicate whether the noun is singular or plural by highlighting the appropriate adjective.
2. Highlight the inflected form of שׁל that the possessive suffix has replaced.
3. Write the dictionary form of the noun.
4. Translate the phrase.

Example:

his sharp criticism ביקורת :במילון   שלו שלה שלהם שלהן   החריפה/החריפות ביקורתו

Explanation: The absence of a יו"ד from the possessive suffix indicates that the noun is singular and therefore it requires a singular adjective; the suffix ו- replaces שׁלו. The final ת —in ביקורת is part of the word (not a converted final ה"א in a construct noun).

---

translation	dictionary entry	whose	singular or plural noun
		שלו שלה שלהם שלהן	1. מנהיגיהם החדש/החדשים
		שלו שלה שלהם שלהן	2. רעיונם החדשני/החדשניים
		שלו שלה שלהם שלהן	3. עמדותיה הנוקשָׁה/הנוקשות
		שלו שלה שלהם שלהן	4. פעולתם האפשרית/האפשריות
		שלו שלה שלהם שלהן	5. שפתו העשירה/העשירות
		שלו שלה שלהם שלהן	6. יצירתם הרוחנית/הרוחניות
		שלו שלה שלהם שלהן	7. מאבקיה הקשה/הקשים
		שלו שלה שלהם שלהן	8. קשריה האישי/האישיים
		שלו שלה שלהם שלהן	9. הגותו המוקדמת/המוקדמות
		שלו שלה שלהם שלהן	10. בדידותן העמוקה/העמוקות

Exercise #5: Determining whether an ‎ות‎- ending is /ut/ or /ot/

> **The rules to go by:** see sections 5.6 and 5.7.2.
> **What to do:**
> 1. Determine whether the noun ending is **/ot/** or **/ut/** and enter the item number in the appropriate cell in the chart.
> 2. In the blank next to each noun, write its dictionary form.
> **Example:**
> הוכחותיו=הוכחות noun /ot/
> במילון: הוכחה
> **Explanation:** the ‎י"ו‎ within the suffix indicates that the noun is plural. To locate the noun in the dictionary both the possessive suffix ‎י-‎ and the plural suffix ‎ות-‎ have to be removed.

‎ות-‎/ut/	‎וֹת-‎/ot/
	example,

‎1. מהימנותו‎ _____

‎2. תעודותיו‎ _____

‎3. עדותם‎ _____

‎4. אישיותה‎ _____

‎5. זהותן‎ _____

‎6. תפוצותיה‎ _____

‎7. נאמנותה‎ _____

‎8. אמונותיהם‎ _____

‎9. מדינותיהם‎ _____

‎10. מדיניותו‎ _____

‎11. מהותו‎ _____

‎12. תקֵפותה‎ _____

Exercise #6: Identifying the reference of the possessive suffix

The rules to go by: see section 5.8.
What to do: select from the list of bolded nouns the one that is referred to by the possessive suffix in the underlined noun(s) in the sentence. The same noun may be selected more than once.
Example:

עֲרָכִים אלה קובעים את הַעֲרָכַת הדמויות ואת <u>הצגתן</u>.

ההצגה של _____

הערכים/ההערכה/הדמויות

Explanation: The suffix ‑ן replaces שלהן, therefore neither הערכה nor ערכים could be the answer as they would require שלה and שלהם, respectively.

1. כל עם יוצר לעצמו היסטוריה ומתאים את מידת <u>נאמנותה</u> למציאות <u>לצרכיו</u>.

הנאמנות של _____

הצרכים של _____

העם/ההיסטוריה/המציאות

2. מֶנְדֶלְסוֹן ראה את <u>ייעודו</u> בחיסול <u>בידודם</u> של היהודים מן התרבות הָאֵירופית ובהַרְחָבַת <u>אופקם</u> הרוּחָני.

הייעוד של _____

הבידוד של _____

האופק של _____

מנדלסון/חיסול/תרבות/היהודים

Glossary

creates	יוצר .1
adjusts	מתאים
the extent of its faithfulness to reality	מידת נאמנותה למציאות
needs	צרכים
mission	ייעוד .2
eradication	חיסול
isolation	בידוד
broadening of their spiritual horizon	הרחבת אופקם הרוחני

3. אַף עַל פִּי שֶׁרָאשֵׁי הַיַּהֲדוּת הַמָּסוֹרְתִית הִתְנַגְּדוּ לְמִפְעָלוֹ שֶׁל מֶנְדֶלְסוֹן, הִתְפַּשֵּׁט עַד מְהֵרָה הַתַּרְגּוּם וְהַבֵּיאוּר וְתָרְמוּ לְעִיצוּבוֹ שֶׁל טִיפּוּס יְהוּדִי חָדָשׁ.

הַמִּפְעָל שֶׁל _____

הָעִיצוּב שֶׁל _____

מֶנְדֶלְסוֹן/רָאשֵׁי הַיַּהֲדוּת הַמָּסוֹרְתִית/ הַתַּרְגּוּם וְהַבֵּיאוּר/טִיפּוּס יְהוּדִי חָדָשׁ

4. מֶרְכַּז הַתּוֹרָה בִּצְפוֹן צָרְפַת עָלָה לִגְדוּלָּה לֹא רַק בִּשֶׁל יְצִירוֹתָיו הָאִישִׁיוֹת שֶׁל רָשִׁ"י, אֶלָּא גַם בְּעִקְבוֹת פְּעוּלָתָם וִיצִירָתָם הַסִּפְרוּתִית שֶׁל תַּלְמִידָיו.

הַיְצִירוֹת שֶׁל _____

הַפְּעוּלָה שֶׁל _____

הַיְצִירָה שֶׁל _____

הַתַּלְמִידִים שֶׁל _____

מֶרְכַּז הַתּוֹרָה/צְפוֹן צָרְפַת/רָשִׁ"י/תַּלְמִידָיו

5. הַמְסַפֵּר הַמִּקְרָאִי מֵנִיחַ לְקוֹרְאָיו לִשְׁפּוֹט אֶת הַדְּמֻיּוֹת הַפּוֹעֲלוֹת בִּיצִירָתוֹ עַל פִּי דִּבְרֵיהֶן וְרַק לְעִתִּים רְחוֹקוֹת יֵאָמֵר דָּבָר מְפוֹרָשׁ עַל תְּכוּנוֹת אוֹפְיָין.

הַקּוֹרְאִים שֶׁל _____

הַיְצִירָה שֶׁל _____

הַדְּבָרִים שֶׁל _____

הָאוֹפִי שֶׁל _____

הַמְסַפֵּר הַמִּקְרָאִי/הַדְּמֻיּוֹת/הַתְּכוּנוֹת

Glossary

.3 רָאשֵׁי הַיַּהֲדוּת הַמָּסוֹרְתִית leaders of traditional Judaism

מִפְעָל undertaking

הַתַּרְגּוּם וְהַבֵּיאוּר the translation and the commentary

הִתְפַּשֵּׁט עַד מְהֵרָה soon spread

תָּרְמוּ contributed

עִיצוּב shaping

טִיפּוּס type

.4 עָלָה לִגְדוּלָּה achieved greatness

בִּשֶׁל because of

בְּעִקְבוֹת following

יְצִירָתָם הַסִּפְרוּתִית their literary creation

.5 הַמְסַפֵּר הַמִּקְרָאִי biblical narrator

מֵנִיחַ lets, allows

לִשְׁפּוֹט judge

הַדְּמֻיּוֹת הַפּוֹעֲלוֹת בִּיצִירָתוֹ the characters acting in his work

לְעִתִּים רְחוֹקוֹת seldom

יֵאָמֵר דָּבָר מְפוֹרָשׁ say something explicit

תְּכוּנוֹת אוֹפִי their character traits

.6 אוּלַי הַשִּׁימוּשׁ הרב בּסַמְלִים יהוּדִים מוּבְהָקִים בּא גם כּתְגוּבָה יהוּדִית לַעֲלִיַּית הַנַּצְרוּת בּסוֹף הָעֵת הָעַתִּיקָה ולהַ<u>שְׁפָּעָתָה</u> על תְּחוּמִים שונים בּחיי העם.

ההשפעה של _____

התגובה/העת העתיקה/הנצרות

.7 זה חָזוֹן קשה של סופר מְזַדְקֵן, שחָזָה מבשרו את <u>עלִיָּיתָה</u> והַ<u>תְמַמְּשׁוּתָה</u> של הציונות, וחוֹשׁשׁ מִפְּנֵי הִתבַּדּוּתוֹ של החזון.

העלייה של _____

ההתממשות של _____

ההתבדות של _____

חזון/סופר מזדקן/ציונות

.8 בין החשובים שבּהיּשֵׂגֵי הַמֶּחְקָר מוֹנִים אנו את הניסיון להגדיר בְּמְדֻיָּק את היחס שׁבֵּין מִמְצָאֵי קוּמְרָאן לַנַּצְרוּת הקְדוּמה. הַצָּעוֹת אחדות ל<u>הַבנתו</u> נִדְחוּ על ידי רוב החוקרים.

ההבנה של _____

המחקר/הניסיון/היחס/הנצרות הקדומה

Glossary

distinctive Jewish symbols	סמלים יהודיים מובהקים .6
Jewish reaction to the rise of Christianity	תגובה יהודית לעליית הנצרות
antiquity	העת העתיקה
various areas	תחומים שונים
harsh vision of an aging author	חזון קשה של סופר מזדקן .7
personally (literally: in the flesh) experienced	חזה מבשרו
realization	התממשות
apprehensive of falsification	חושש מפני התבדות
the achievements of the research	הישגי המחקר .8
we count, we include	מונים אנו
attempt	ניסיון
define exactly	להגדיר במדויק
	היחס שבין ממצאי קומראן לנצרות הקדומה
the relationship between the findings in Qumran and Early Christianity	
several suggestions	הצעות אחדות
were rejected by most researchers	נדחו על ידי רוב החוקרים

9. מַעֲרֶכֶת יְחָסִים זו קשורה גם באֵירוּעים שקָדְמו לְהִשְׁתַּלְטוּת רוֹמָא על הארץ, וגם באֵירוּעים שֶׁנִּתְלַוּוּ לְהִשְׁתַּלְטוּתָה מראשיתה.

ההשתלטות של _____

ראשיתה של _____

מערכת היחסים/האירועים/ההשתלטות/רומא

Glossary

(a system of) relationships מערכת יחסים	9.
אירועים שקדמו להשתלטות רומא על הארץ	
events that preceded Rome's gaining control of the country	
accompanied נתלוו	
from its beginning מראשיתה	

Exercise #7: Selecting the possessive suffix in double construct phrases

---

The rule to go by: see section 5.8.
What to do: select the appropriate form of the suffixed noun.
Example:
נשותיו/נשותיהם/נשותיהן שֶל לַמְדָנִים נֶהֱנוּ מִמִּידָה רבה שֶל סַמְכוּת בניהוּל עִנְייֵנֵי המשפחה.
The scholars' wives enjoyed a great measure of authority in running the affairs of the family.
Explanation:
The possessive suffix in the double construct phrase refers forward, to the masculine plural
noun לַמְדָנים.

---

1. מְתוֹאָר כאן תַהֲלִיך **השתלבותו/השתלבותם/השתלבותה** שֶל היהודים בחֶברה הסוֹבֶבֶת.
The process of the integration of the Jews in the surrounding society is described here.

2. החוקרת מתארת את **התפתחותו/התפתחותם/התפתחותה** שֶל הסיפור האַשְכְּנַזי ביידיש.
The researcher describes the development of the Ashkenazi story in Yiddish.

3. נוֹשֵׂא נוֹסָף במחקר הוא **קיומו/קיומם/קיומן** הקָרוב – אַך הנִבְדָל – שֶל שתי תרבויות.
An additional topic is the close – but separate – existence of two cultures.

4. סיפור זה מבוסס על אגדה ידועה, המתארת את **ייסודם/ייסודו/ייסודה** שֶל מֶרְכז תורה חדש
בְאַשְכְּנַז על רֶקַע **שקיעתו/שקיעתה/שקיעתם** שֶל המרכז בבָבָל.
The story is based on a well-known legend, which describes the founding of a new Torah center
in Ashkenaz against the background of the decline of the Babylonian center.

5. הסיפור חוֹשֵׂף את **התפרצותו/התפרצותה/התפרצותם** שֶל יְצָרים אֲפֵלים.
The story uncovers the breaking out of sinister desires.

6. **גורמיה/גורמיהן/גורמיו** שֶל תמורות אלה בחיי היהודים במאה השמונה עשרה היו הסוֹבְלָנוּת
הדתית, הַהַשְׂכָּלָה והרֶפוֹרְמות בחינוך.
The causes of these changes in the lives of the Jews in the eighteenth century were religious
tolerance, the Enlightenment and the reforms in education.

7. **מניעיה/מניעיו/מניעיהם** שֶל אוכלוסיית העולים אינם מובָנים לַוָתיקים.
The motivations of the immigrant population are not comprehensible to the old-timers.

8. כבר **בשלביה/בשלביו/בשלביהם** הראשונים שֶל החסידות היא לא הונהגה על ידי מנהיג יחיד.
Already in its first stages Ḥasidism was not led by a single leader.

9. בספרו הוא בוחן מחדש את **מקורותיה/מקורותיו/מקורותיהם** שֶל הקיום היהודי.
In his book he re-examines the sources of Jewish existence.

Exercise #8: Differentiating among three noun groups

action nouns	abstract וּת- nouns	nouns modeled on present tense forms
נתינה,		

נתינת שמות מן התנ"ך ליישובים החדשים היה כלי אידֵאולוגי ופוליטי לביסוס הריבּוֹנוּת היהודית בארץ. השמות ביטאו את הדימוי הרוחני של הארץ בתודעת מייסדיה ובוניה, מילאו תפקיד מפתח בהנחלת ערכים ובגיבוש הזהות הלאומית אצל המצטרפים החדשים (העולים החדשים והדור הצעיר) והיוו הכרזה בפני אומות העולם על זכותו של עם ישראל על ארצו. השמות היו על כן אבן פינה בבינוי האומה.

Exercise #9: Translating action nouns and identifying their source verbs

The rules to go by: see section 6.3.
What to do:
1. Underline the action nouns and provide the infinitive form of the corresponding verb. Mark with an asterick nouns whose source verbs are in a different *binyan* than the noun. The number after each paragraph indicates how many action nouns it contains (repeated nouns are counted only once).
2. Translate the noun.
Example:

על סמך <u>מיפוי</u> הכתבים המדעיים של אבן עזרא בחן החוקר את טיבן של התיאוריות המדעיות של אבן עזרא והתחקה אחר <u>הופעתן</u> בכתבים המדעיים ובכתבים הפרשניים-התיאולוגיים. כלומר, הוא ברר לו תכנים מדעיים ובחן את <u>השתקפותם</u> ב<u>דיון</u> המדעי מזה ובדיון הפרשני-התיאולוגי מזה. (4)

מיפוי – למפות *mapping*
הופעה – להופיע *appearance*
השתקפותם – להשתקף *reflection*
דיון* – לדון *discussion*

Explanation: מיפוי is in *pi'el*, הופעה is in *hif'il*, השתקפות is in *hitpa'el*; דיון – modeled on action nouns in *pi'el* – is related to the *pa'al* verb לדון.

1. הַתְחִייה העברית הֵביאה גם לצמיחתה של חוכְמת הלשון העברית; הצְמידוּת בין כתיבת שירה ולימודה הייתה קַיֶּמֶת לאורך כל התקופה. (3)

2. בתקופה הסְפָרַדית היה צוֹרֶך בידיעה טובה של הלשון העברית. עם עלייתה והתפשטותה של שירַת החוֹל נֶעֶשְׂתָה ידיעת העברית הֶכְרֵחית לְשֵם ספיגתם של עֶרכֵי תרבות חילוֹניים לצורך ההשתתפות המְלֵאָה במַעֲמָדים בעֲלֵי אופי חֶבְרָתי. (5)

Glossary

תחייה revival	.1
חוכמת הלשון העברית the science of the Hebrew language	
צמידות closeness, linking	
הייתה קיימת לאורך כל התקופה existed along the entire period	
שירת החול secular poetry	.2
הכרחית essential, necessary	
לשם for the purpose of	
ערכי תרבות חילוניים secular cultural values	
מעמדים בעלי אופי חברתי social occasions	

3. הַחְיָיאת לְשׁוֹן הַמִּקְרָא בִּסְפָרַד הָיְתָה בָּהּ הוֹכָחָה לְכֹשֶׁר הִתְמוֹדְדוּתָהּ שֶׁל הָעִבְרִית עִם הָעֲרָבִית, וְהַחְיָיאת הָעִבְרִית בַּמֵּאָה הי"ט הָיְתָה קְשׁוּרָה לְמִימּוּשׁ הֶחָזוֹן הַצִּיּוֹנִי וְלִשִׁיבָה אֶל הַלָּשׁוֹן כְּאֶמְצָעִי שִׁימּוּשׁ בְּכָל תְּחוּמֵי הַחַיִּים. (6)

4. מִן הַמְּקוֹרוֹת אָנוּ לוֹמְדִים עַל מַצָּבָם הַכַּלְכָּלִי הָאֵיתָן שֶׁל הַיְּהוּדִים, גִּידוּלָן שֶׁל הַקְּהִילּוֹת וּבִיסּוּס שִׁלְטוֹנָן הָעַצְמִי. עוּבְדָּה חֲשׁוּבָה אַחֶרֶת הִיא קִיּוּמוֹ שֶׁל מַגָּע קָרוֹב שֶׁל הַיְּהוּדִים עִם שְׁכֵנֵיהֶם בִּתְחוּמִים שׁוֹנִים: פְּעִילוּת מִסְחָרִית, הַעֲסָקַת מְשָׁרְתִים נָכְרִיִּים בְּבָתֵּיהֶם וְעִסְקֵי יוֹם יוֹם. לַמְרוֹת הַנִּיתּוּק הַדָּתִי וְהָאֵיבָה הַהֲדָדִית לְסֶמְלֵי הַדָּת הָאַחֶרֶת, יֵשׁ אַף מֵידָע עַל הַמָּרוֹת לַנַּצְרוּת. (6)

Glossary

3. כּוֹשֶׁר	ability
הֶחָזוֹן הַצִּיּוֹנִי	the Zionist vision
אֶמְצָעִי	means of
בְּכָל תְּחוּמֵי הַחַיִּים	in all areas of life
4. מְקוֹרוֹת	sources
מַצָּבָם הַכַּלְכָּלִי הָאֵיתָן	their solid economic situation
שִׁלְטוֹנָן הָעַצְמִי	their self rule
עוּבְדָּה	fact
מַגָּע קָרוֹב	close contact
שְׁכֵנֵיהֶם	their neighbors
תְּחוּמִים שׁוֹנִים	different areas
פְּעִילוּת מִסְחָרִית	commercial activity
מְשָׁרְתִים נָכְרִיִּים	non-Jewish servants
לַמְרוֹת	despite
הָאֵיבָה הַהֲדָדִית	mutual hostility
נַצְרוּת	Christianity

3. PRONOUNS
כינויים

This chapter discusses:

- Personal pronouns: אני, אנחנו; אתה; הוא, היא, הם, הן (section 1)
- Demonstrative pronouns: זה, זאת, אלה and their variants (section 2)
- Remote demonstrative pronouns: ההוא; אותו (section 3)
- Indefinite pronouns: אֵיזֶה; אֵיזֶשֶׁהוּ, כָּלְשֶׁהוּ; אִישׁ לֹא, דָּבָר לֹא (section 4)
- Interrogative pronouns: אֵיזֶה, אֵיזוֹ, אֵילוּ (section 5)
- The reflexive pronoun עצמ- (section 6)
- Reciprocity pronouns זה את זה *each other* and their variants (section 7)
- The anticipatory pronoun (section 8)
- זֶה and זֹאת in set expressions (section 9)
- כך in set expressions (section 10)
- Confusables: הֵן; time expressions with זה; expressions with עצם

This chapter will help the reader to:

- Understand the uses of first and second person pronouns in academic writing
- Differentiate among several functions of third person pronouns: for emphasis, as an appositive introducer, and as a remote demonstrative
- Distinguish between similar-looking interrogative and demonstrative pronouns
- Identify the reference of the clausal substitutes זֹאת, הַדָּבָר, הָעוּבְדָה, כָּךְ
- Distinguish between אוֹתוֹ as a direct object and a demonstrative pronoun
- Identify the reference of reflexive and reciprocal pronouns
- Become familiar with various meanings of זה, זאת and כך is set expressions.

1. Personal pronouns

1.1 First person pronouns: אֲנִי; אֲנַחְנוּ, אָנוּ

Writers of scholarly articles often refer to themselves in the first person plural as אָנוּ or אֲנַחְנוּ. This "authorial we" serves to invoke the research community at large and/or include the reader in the scholarly discourse and argumentation, sometimes with an explicit invitation to participate (e.g., הָבָה ננתח *let's analyze*).

Authors often also refer to themselves in the first person when stating their research agenda or conclusions (examples 4 and 14). In these statements of authorial intent the future tense is typically used, and the writer may employ the less formal first person singular אֲנִי rather than אָנוּ/אֲנַחְנוּ (example 4).

---

(1) מְבִינִים אָנוּ אֵפוֹא, שבפסוקים אלה גמר הכותב את רַעְיוֹנוֹ הראשון.
We understand, then, that in these verses the writer has concluded his first idea.

The pronoun, אָנוּ, follows the verb, resulting in a somewhat more elevated tone.

(2) אין בְּיָדֵינוּ נְתוּנִים מַסְפִּיקִים לִקְבִיעַת הַתַּאֲרִיךְ הַמְדוּיָק של יְצִיאַת מִצְרַיִם.
We do not have (literally: there is not in our hands) sufficient data to determine the exact date of the exodus out of Egypt.

The plural first person "we" is expressed through the pronoun suffix. This is also seen in the next example.

(3) בַּשָּׁלָב זה עָלֵינוּ לְהִתְעַכֵּב על פְּרָט חָשׁוּב.
At this stage, we must spend some time on an important detail.

(4) בְּמַאֲמָר זה אֶתְבַּסֵּס על הַמִּמְצָא הָאַרְכֵאוֹלוֹגִי וְכֵן אֶעֱשֶׂה שימוש בִּידִיעוֹת הִיסטוריות.
In this article I will base [my investigation] on archeological findings and I will also make use of historical information.

1.1.1 The pronoun אֲנִי is represented by the ‎נִי- suffix in the following present tense verb forms that express an opinion or belief: סְבוּרַנִי *I think*, חוֹשְׁבַנִי, כִּמְדוּמַנִי, דּוֹמַנִי, *it seems to me, in my opinion* (when the speaker is a woman the suffix is ‎תְנִי-: סְבוּרַתְנִי).

---

(5) דּוֹמַנִי שאפשר לְהַצִּיע הֶסְבֵּר אחֵר, מְשַׁכְנֵעַ יותר מִבְּחִינָה סִפְרוּתִית.
It seems to me that it is possible to suggest another explanation, more convincing from a literary viewpoint.

1.2 Second person singular pronoun: אתה

Similarly to English, in scholarly writing the pronoun אתה *you* is indefinite, referring to *one* (rather than to the present reader).

---

(6) בְּמָקוֹם מְקוּדָּש צָרִיך אתה לצַפּוֹת לנִסִים.
In a sacred place <u>one</u> (OR: <u>you</u>) should expect miracles.

⚡#1   **1.3 Third person singular and plural pronouns: הוא, היא, הם, הן**

The third person singular pronouns **הוא** and **היא** are translated, respectively, as *he* and *she* or, when referring to inanimate nouns, as *it*. The plural pronouns **הם, הן** are translated as *they*.

In the past and future, the mention of the third person pronoun is obligatory. For example, whereas קראתי את הספר *[I] read the book* does not require the pronoun אני, omitting the pronoun הוא in *קרא את הספר* *[he] read the book* and in *יקרא את הספר* *[he]will read the book* is not possible. (It would be possible, however, in literary style when the identity of the "doer" is known from a previous sentence.)

Note, however, that sentences with a plural masculine verb (in any tense) but without the pronoun הם are legitimate; they are considered impersonal sentences[1]

The third person pronouns also function as copulas, that is, a substitute for the "missing" verb "to be" in nominal (verbless) present tense sentences. In this role, הוא and היא are translated as *is*, הם and הן are translated as *are*.[2]

For example:

עברית היא שפה שמית *Hebrew is a Semitic language*
עברית וערבית הן שפות שמיות *Hebrew and Arabic are Semitic languages.*

1.3.1. Emphatic uses of the third person pronouns

The third person pronouns may be used to express contrastive emphasis: an implied alternative is rejected in favor of an explicitly stated one. Three instances of this use are illustrated below.

1.3.1.1   הוא/היא/הם/הן -ש

it is he/she/they [and not another] who/that… (a cleft sentence)

In this construction, the subject (a noun) is "echoed" by a pronoun, which in turn is followed by a subordinate clause. The subordinate clause is introduced with -שֶׁ or אֲשֶׁר (examples 7–8) or, before a present tense verb, with -ה (example 9).

If the pronoun and the subordinator are omitted, the sentence remains grammatical and conveys the same information (albeit without the emphasis).

---

[1] See Chapter 1, 5.
[2] See full discussion of the use of the third person pronouns as copulas in Chapter 7, 1.

---

(7) אֵירוּעִים חִיצוֹנִיִּים **הֵם שֶׁקָּבְעוּ** אֶת גּוֹרָלָם שֶׁל הַיְּהוּדִים.
<u>It was external events that</u> determined the fate of the Jews.

The pronoun הם echoes אירועים. Without emphasis the sentence would read:
אירועים חיצוניים קבעו את גורלם של היהודים

(8) אֱלוֹהִים **הוּא אֲשֶׁר** נֶחֱלָץ לְסַיֵּיעַ לָעָם.
<u>It is God who</u> comes to the aid of (literally: to assist) the people.
Without emphasis: אלוהים נחלץ לסייע לעם

(9) דְּבוֹרָה **הִיא הַמְעוֹרֶרֶת** אֶת הָעָם לְמִלְחֶמֶת חֵירוּת, **הִיא הַמַּפְעִילָה** אֶת בָּרָק.
<u>It is Deborah who</u> arouses the people to a war of liberation, <u>it is she who</u> arouses Barak to action.

Without emphasis: דבורה מעוררת את העם למלחמת חירות ומפעילה את ברק

1.3.1.2 -הוא הוא/היא היא/הם הם/הן הן ש
it is/was the... who/that...

The repetition of the pronoun creates an emphatic statement implying a rejection of some unstated (contradictory) proposition.

---

(10) מְצִיאוּת קָשָׁה זוֹ **הִיא הִיא** הַמְשַׁמֶּשֶׁת רֶקַע לַהֲבָנַת פְּעוּלָתוֹ שֶׁל הַנָּבִיא.
<u>It is this</u> difficult reality <u>that</u> serves as a background for understanding the action of the prophet.

(11) יַלְדֵי הַפְּרָחִים **הֵם הֵם אֲשֶׁר** חוֹלְלוּ אֶת תְּנוּעַת הַשְּׂמֹאל הָעוֹלָמִית.
<u>It was the</u> flower children <u>who</u> brought about the international Left movement.

(12) הַהֲגִיָּיה שֶׁל הַבֵּית הָרָפָה כְּדֹגוּשָׁה נָבְעָה כַּמּוּבָן מִן הַהַשְׁקָפָה שֶׁדֶּגֶם הַהֲגִיָּיה הָעַרְבִית **הוּא הָרָאוּי** לְאִימּוּץ, מִשּׁוּם **שֶׁהוּא הוּא** הַקָּרוֹב לַהֲגִיָּיתָה הַקְּדוּמָה שֶׁל הָעִבְרִית.
The pronunciation of the "v" consonant as "b" stemmed, of course, from the view that <u>it is the pattern</u> of Arab pronunciation <u>that</u> is worth adopting, since <u>it is the [one] that</u> is closest to the original pronunciation of Hebrew.

In this example we find both emphatic devices: the cleft sentence (הוא הראוי לאימוץ) and the repeated pronoun (הוא הוא הקרוב).

1.3.1.3 [Noun +Possessive suffix]+personal pronoun: *his own, their own...*
לשונם הם *their own language*

In this construction, the possessive suffix that is attached to the noun (לשונם) is echoed by the following personal pronoun (הם).The suffixed noun and the personal pronoun may be joined with a hyphen (example 14). The pronoun and the possessive suffix have the same reference, creating, from an informational point of view, a redundancy.

This rhetorical device has the effect of underscoring the possessive force of the suffix. Alternatively, to achieve this effect, the inflected form of שֶׁל may be used instead of a pronoun (e.g., יצירותיו הוא=יצירותיו שלו *his own works*).

---

(13) כַּמָּה הוֹגִים יְהוּדִים מוֹדֶרְנִיִּים נָטוּ לְהַגְדִּיר אֶת הַמָּסוֹרֶת הַיְּהוּדִית עַל פִּי **רְאִיָּיתָם הֵם**.
Several modern Jewish thinkers have tended to define Jewish tradition according to <u>their own view</u>.

(14) נָדוּן בכל אֱמָן בִּפְנֵי עַצְמוֹ, עַל רֶקַע **יצירותיו-הוא**.
We will discuss each artist separately, on the basis of (literally: on the background of) <u>his own works</u>.

(15) מַבָּט מִנְּקוּדַת הַתַּצְפִּית שֶׁל **יָמֵינוּ-אָנוּ** מְאַפְשֵׁר בִּיקּוֹרֶת לְלֹא מַשּׂוֹא פָנִים שֶׁל הֶעָבָר.
A view from the vantage point of <u>our own days</u> makes an unbiased criticism of the past possible.

1.3.2 Third person pronoun before an appositive

Third person personal pronouns are sometimes used to introduce an appositive. The pronoun agrees with the following noun in gender and number. In translation, it can be ignored.

Appositives are units (usually noun or noun phrases) that have the same reference and one of them can be omitted without loss of meaning (see Chapter 1, section 8).

---

(16) הַפִּיּוּט כָּתוּב בלשון הָאֲרָמִית, **הִיא לְשׁוֹן** הַדִּיבּוּר בְּאוֹתָהּ תְקוּפָה.
The liturgical hymn is written in the Aramaic language, the spoken language at that period.

(17) מַכִּירִים אָנוּ יָפֶה רק אֶת קָדֵשׁ בַּרְנֵעַ, **הוּא הָאֵזוֹר** הֶעָשִׁיר בַּמַּעְיָינוֹת בדרום אֶרֶץ כְּנַעַן.
We know well only Kadesh Barne'a, the area rich in springs in the south of Canaan.

1.4 Idiomatic expressions with הוא and היא

וְלֹא הִיא, וְהִיא הַנּוֹתֶנֶת *this is not so*

נַהֲפוֹךְ הוּא *quite the opposite*

הוּא הַדִּין בְּ- *the same applies to*

The pronouns היא and הוא in the above expressions are gender neutral, that is, they do not refer to any particular previous noun, but rather to a whole idea unit.

(18) בסֵפֶר שְׁנֵי חֲלָקִים שׁוֹנִים בְּאוֹפְיָים וּלְפִיכָך הָיוּ חוֹקְרִים שֶׁסָּבְרוּ כִּי הֵם מֵשֶּׁל מְחַבְּרִים שׁוֹנִים; **וְלֹא הִיא**: אוֹפְיָים הַשּׁוֹנֶה נוֹבֵעַ מִמַּהוּתָם.

The book has two distinct parts (literally: two parts of different character) and therefore there were scholars who believed that they were by different authors. <u>This is not so:</u> Their different character derives from their nature.

(19) טָעוּת הִיא לַחְשׁוֹב שֶׁהָעֲגָה נְמוּכַת דֶּרֶג הִיא, נְחוּתָה. **נַהֲפוֹך הוּא.**

It is a mistake to think that slang is of low status, inferior. <u>The opposite is the case.</u>

✗#2   2. Demonstrative pronouns: זֶה, זֹאת, אֵלֶּה and their variants

	Masculine	Feminine
Singular: *this*	זֶה	זֹאת, זוֹ
Plural: *these*	אֵלֶּה, אֵלּוּ הַלָּלוּ	

Demonstrative pronouns follow the noun and refer to it, or replace it altogether. These reference and substitution functions are discussed below.

2.1 Demonstrative pronouns used for reference
Similarly to adjectives, referential demonstrative pronouns follow the noun directly (unless an adjective intervenes, as in האיש הטוב הזה *this good man*) and agree with it in number and definiteness.

> However, lending the style a Mishnaic flavor, an indefinite demonstrative pronoun is sometimes found <u>before</u> a <u>definite</u> noun.
> For example:
> כל אחד מאלה הספרים (rather than כל אחד מן הספרים האלה) *each of these books*;
> בזו הפעם מרחם הנביא על העם (rather than בפעם הזו) *this time the prophet takes pity on the people.*

Gender distinction occurs in the singular (e.g., האיש הזה, האישה הזאת) but not in the plural (e.g., האנשים האלה, הנשים האלה).

2.1.1 זֹאת, זוֹ; אֵלֶּה, אֵלּוּ
The difference between **זֹאת** and **זוֹ** and between **אֵלֶּה** and **אֵלּוּ** is historical: זֹאת and אֵלֶּה are biblical, whereas זוֹ and אֵלּוּ belong to Mishnaic Hebrew. In modern Hebrew the two sets of pronouns are used interchangeably (example 40).

Grammarians prescribe adherence to historical usage in the following way: הָאֲנָשִׁים הָאֵלֶּה (biblical) or אֲנָשִׁים אֵלּוּ (Mishnaic), and frown on the historical hybrids הָאֲנָשִׁים הָאֵלּוּ and אֲנָשִׁים אֵלֶּה.

2.1.2 הַלָּלוּ is the plural form of the Mishnaic הַלָּה *that person*. The definite article -ה is integral to the pronoun (that is, *לָלוּ does not exist), and the following plural noun, therefore, is always definite (e.g., הָאֲנָשִׁים הַלָּלוּ). הַלָּלוּ is considered more formal or literary than אֵלֶּה and אֵלּוּ. It can be translated as either *these* or *those* (examples 23 and 46).

2.1.3 Demonstrative pronouns and the definite article -ה
Although the demonstrative pronoun already makes the noun definite (specific) in meaning, both the noun and the pronoun may (redundantly) take the definite article -ה (e.g., רעיון זה can be rendered as הָרַעְיוֹן הַזֶּה).

In formal style, there seems to be a preference for <u>not</u> using the definite article. In any case, the difference between the definite and indefinite options cannot be reflected in translation.

The rule that the noun and the demonstrative pronoun must <u>both</u> take – or not take – the definite article can help in word recognition. In other words, if the demonstrative pronoun appears without the definite article, the ה"א before the noun is construed as part of the word.

For example:

הסדר **הסדר זה** in הַסֵּדֶר **הסדר** means *this arrangement* (הַסֵּדֶר), NOT: *the order* (הַ+סֵדֶר)

העמדה **העמדה זאת** in העמדה means *placing* (הַעֲמָדָה), NOT: *the position* (הַ+עֶמְדָּה).

This rule also guides the pronunciation of the prepositions בכ"ל before the noun: they are pronounced with a *sheva* when the demonstrative pronoun lacks the definite article (examples 21–22).

---

(20) כבר התנ"ך הִדְגִּישׁ אֶת <u>הָרַעְיוֹן הַזֶּה</u>.
The Bible has already emphasized <u>this idea</u>.

(21) <u>תְּכוּנוֹת אֵלֶּה</u> שֶׁל הָעִבְרִית אֵינָן מְצוּיוֹת <u>בְּצֵרוּפָן זֶה</u> בִּלְשׁוֹן שֵׁמִית אַחֶרֶת.
<u>These</u> characteristics of Hebrew are not found in <u>this</u> combination in any other Semitic language.

Note that although the noun צירופן is definite (due to the presence of the possessive suffix), the definite article -ה need not appear before the demonstrative pronoun; in other words, *בצירופן הזה is not possible.

---

(22) סָבִיר שהַשֵׁם הַמִּקְרָאִי "לֵאָה" מִתְיַיחֵס **לְשׁוֹרֶשׁ זה בְּמַשְׁמָעוּת זוֹ.**

It is plausible that the biblical name "Leah" is related to <u>this</u> root with <u>this</u> meaning.

Since זה and זו are indefinite, the prepositions are pronounced בְּ and לְ, rather than בַּ and לַ, as would be the case if the demonstrative pronouns were definite (i.e., לַשׁוֹרֶשׁ הזה, בַּמשמעות הזאת).

(23) **הַנְּתוּנִים הַלָּלוּ** לא הוּסְבְּרוּ בצוּרה מַסְפֶּקֶת.

<u>These</u> data were not sufficiently explained.

With הללו the plural noun is always definite.

2.1.4 כָּזֶה, כָּזֹאת, כָּאֵלֶּה/כָּאֵלּוּ
like this/these, such as this/these

כְּ- (the short form of כְּמוֹ like) merges with the demonstrative pronouns to produce the forms **כָּזֶה, כָּזֹאת** in the singular, and **כָּאֵלֶּה** or **כָּאֵלּוּ** in the plural. These pronouns follow the noun and agree with it.[3] Although the form incorporates a definite article (כְּ+הַ+זֶה←כָּזֶה), the noun does not take the article (הַמחקר כזה* is not possible). Sometimes, -שֶׁ is added (i.e., שֶׁכָּזֶה); it is ignored in translation (example 25).

The pronoun and the noun with which it agrees are bolded:

(24) דוגמה **לְמִדְבָּר כָּזֶה** הוא מִדְבַּר יהודה.

An example for <u>such</u> a desert (OR: a desert such as this) is the Judea Dessert.

(25) מופיעים במקורות גם **הַסְבֵרים שֶׁכָּאֵלֶה.**

<u>Such</u> explanations (OR: explanations as these) also appear in the sources.

2.2 Demonstrative pronouns used for substitution

Demonstrative pronouns are often used to avoid a verbatim repetition of a previously mentioned noun. The pronoun agrees with this noun in number and gender. If the noun would have been introduced by a preposition, this preposition appears before the demonstrative pronoun (examples 26–28).

In their role as noun substitutes, the demonstrative pronouns are usually translated as *that*, (for זה and זו/זאת), *those* (for אלה/אלו) or, in some cases, *the latter* (example 29).

---

[3] Colloquially the pronouns may come before the noun.

The pronoun and the noun it substitutes for are shaded:

---

(26) הָאֵזוֹר הָפַךְ לִשְׂדֵה קְרָב בֵּין **הָאִימְפֶּרְיָה** הַפַּרְסִית **לְזוֹ** הָרוֹמִית.
[זוֹ=הָאִימְפֶּרְיָה]
The region became a battlefield between the Persian Empire and the Roman [Empire].

(27) לְמַרְבִּית הַחַיּוֹת, גַּם הַגְּדוֹלוֹת שֶׁבָּהֶן, **תּוֹחֶלֶת חַיִּים** נְמוּכָה **מִזֹּאת** שֶׁל בְּנֵי אָדָם.
[זֹאת=תּוֹחֶלֶת חַיִּים]
Most animals, even the largest among them, have a lower life expectancy than that of humans.

(28) דְּמוּתוֹ שֶׁל הַמְסַפֵּר הִיא בַּעֲלַת **מְאַפְיֵנִים** מִשֶּׁל עַצְמָהּ, וְ**אֵלֶּה** אֵינָם זֵהִים בְּהֶכְרֵחַ **לְאֵלֶּה** שֶׁל הַמְחַבֵּר.
[אֵלֶּה=מְאַפְיֵנִים]
The figure of the narrator has its own characteristics, and these are not necessarily identical with those of the author.

(29) הַשָּׂטָן מַצִּיב אֶתְגָּר לִפְנֵי **יֵשׁוּעַ**, לְאַחַר שֶׁ**זֶּה** צָם אַרְבָּעִים יוֹם וְאַרְבָּעִים לַיְלָה.
[זֶה=יֵשׁוּעַ]
Satan places a challenge before Jesus, after the latter has fasted forty days and forty nights.

2.2.1 Before שֶׁל, the demonstrative pronoun may be omitted, but the preposition is retained.

---

(30) הַנָּשִׁים דָּרְשׁוּ **זְכֻיּוֹת** פּוֹלִיטִיּוֹת וּמִשְׁפָּטִיּוֹת שָׁווֹת **לְשֶׁל** הַגְּבָרִים.
[זְכֻיּוֹת שָׁווֹת לִזְכֻיּוֹת **שֶׁל הַגְּבָרִים** = זְכֻיּוֹת שָׁווֹת **לְאֵלֶּה שֶׁל הַגְּבָרִים** = זְכֻיּוֹת שָׁווֹת לְשֶׁל הַגְּבָרִים]
Women demanded political and legal rights equal to those of men.

(31) **צוּרָתוֹ** שֶׁל הַסֵּמֶל **כְּשֶׁל** מְשֻׁלָּשׁ.
[צוּרָתוֹ שֶׁל הַסֵּמֶל **כְּשֶׁל צוּרָה** שֶׁל מְשֻׁלָּשׁ = צוּרָתוֹ שֶׁל הַסֵּמֶל **כְּשֶׁל זֹאת** שֶׁל מְשֻׁלָּשׁ = צוּרָתוֹ **כְּשֶׁל** מְשֻׁלָּשׁ]
The shape of the symbol is like that of a triangle.

2.3 זֹאת used as pro-clause (and other clausal substitutes)

זֹאת can be used to refer to a previous statement, that is, to an entire clause rather than a single noun or noun phrase. (In colloquial language, זֶה (אֶת) is more common.) Although זֹאת is feminine in form, in its function as a clause substitute it is gender-neutral. In translation, *so, thus, that* or *this* may be used.

The reference of זאת is shaded:

---

(32) **את הַשְׁקָפָתוֹ עַל הַגָּלוּת הִבִּיעַ** ר' יהודה הלוי בשירים רבים, אבל בְּיֶתֶר פֵּירוּט עשה
זאת בחיבורו הַהֲגוּתִי הַגדוֹל, ספר הכּוּזָרִי.
Rabbi Yehuda Halevi expressed his opinion of the exile in many poems, but he did
<u>so</u> with greater detail in his great philosophical work, the Kuzari.

(33) בהַכְרָזַת הָעַצמָאוּת **נקבע שֶׁשֵׁם המדינה הַחדשה יהיה "ישראל" וּבְזאת** בּוּטַל השם
"פַּלֶשתִינה".
In the Declaration of Independence it was determined that the name of the new
state would be "Israel" and <u>thus</u> the name "Palestine" was annulled.

✗#3   **2.3.1** Other words that function as clausal
substitutes are כֵּן, כָּך *this, thus,* הַדָּבָר *this thing* (example 37)
and הָעוּבְדָה *the fact* (example 38).
These words may either follow or anticipate the statement that
they replace (as seen in examples 34 and 35, כָּך refers backward, while שֶׁ- כָּך anticipates).

> כֵּן (rather than כָּך) is often
> preferred after the verb
> לַעשׂוֹת (example 36).

---

(34) אַבְּרַבַּנְאֵל ניסה **לבטֵל את גזירת הגֵּירוּש**, אך לא הצליח **בְּכָך**.
Abrabanel tried to rescind the decree of expulsion, but did not succeed (<u>in this</u>).

(35) מְסוּפָּר בספר שְׁמוֹת על **כָּך שֶׁמֶלֶך מצרַים היה נוהֵג להגיע לנילוס**, כַּנראֶה כְּדֵי להתרחֵץ.
It is recounted in the Book of Exodus <u>that</u> the king of Egypt used to arrive to the
Nile, apparently to bathe.

The reference of כָּך שֶׁ- is always forward. In translation, כָּך is ignored.

(36) היו תקופות שבָּהֶן **צוּיְרוּ אוֹ נֻרקְמוּ דְמוּיוֹת וּבעלֵי חיים על פָּרוֹכוֹת** והיו תקופות שבהן
נמְנְעוּ מלעשוֹת **כֵּן**.
There were periods in which figures and animals were drawn or embroidered on
curtains of the Ark and there were periods in which they [people] refrained from
doing <u>so</u>.

(37) בִּשְׁנַת 1871 **נשרפה העיר כְּמעט לַחֲלוּטִין בדְלֵקה עֲנָקית**. **הַדָּבָר** אפשר את בנְיָיתה
של העיר מֵחָדָשׁ.
In 1871 the city was almost completely destroyed in a huge blaze. <u>This</u> made its
rebuilding possible.

---

(38) כִּינּוּיוֹ שֶׁל כְּתַב רַשִׁ"י נוֹבֵעַ מִן **הָעוּבְדָה** שֶׁהַסֵּפֶר הָרִאשׁוֹן שֶׁהוּדְפַּס בִּכְתָב זֶה הָיָה פֵּירוּשׁוֹ **שֶׁל רַשִׁ"י.**

The Rashi script is called by this name due to <u>the fact that</u> the first book printed in this script was Rashi's commentary.

(39) כְּתוֹצָאָה מִן הַגִּידוּל הַמָּהִיר בָּאוּכְלוּסִיַּית הַשְּׁכוּנָה **הִיא הָפְכָה לִמְקוֹם מְגוּרִים צָפוּף וּמוּזְנָח. לְכָךְ** גַּם תָּרְמָה הָעוּבְדָה שֶׁלְּאַחַר מִלְחֶמֶת הָעַצְמָאוּת וַחֲלוּקַת יְרוּשָׁלַיִם **הָיְתָה "מֵאָה שְׁעָרִים"** סְמוּכָה מְאֹד לִגְבוּל **הַיַּרְדֵּן, דָּבָר** שֶׁפָּגַע בַּחֲזוּתָהּ וּבְמַעֲמָדָהּ.

As a result of the fast growth in the population of the neighborhood, it became a crowded and neglected residential area. <u>To this</u> also contributed the fact that after the War of Independence and the partition of Jerusalem Meah Shearim was very close to the Jordanian border, <u>[something] which</u> harmed its appearance and status.

לכך refers backwards to הפכה למקום מגורים צפוף ומוזנח; the preposition -ל is required by the verb תרמה. דבר also refers backwards – to the fact that the neighborhood was close to the border.

2.4 Plural demonstrative pronoun before a subordinate clause
אלו/אלה ש-/אשר/ה- ... *those who*

Before a clause introduced by -ש or אשר, the plural demonstrative pronouns אלה and אלו are translated as *people, those,* or *anyone*. Alternatively, -ש מי *anyone, whoever* may be used; it is treated as singular (example 41) or plural (example 42).

(40) הַמֵּידָע הַמָּצוּי בְּיָדֵינוּ לְגַבֵּי תְּקוּפָה מְסוּיֶּמֶת לָקוּחַ בְּעִיקָרוֹ שֶׁל דָּבָר מִדִּבְרֵיהֶם שֶׁל **אֵלּוּ אֲשֶׁר** נָטְלוּ חֵלֶק בְּאוֹתָם אֵירוּעִים, אוֹ **אֵלֶּה אֲשֶׁר** כָּתְבוּ עֲלֵיהֶם לְאַחַר זְמַן.

The information that we have with regard to a certain period is taken mostly from the words of <u>those who</u> took part in those events, or <u>those who</u> wrote about them later.

This example illustrates the interchangeability of אלו and אלה, and the use of אותם as a remote demonstrative (see 3.2 below). Note also the two different meanings of דבר: עיקרו של דבר=*mostly, in the main,* and דבריהם=*their words.*

(41) כּוֹרֶשׁ הִנְהִיג אֶת הָאֲרָמִית כִּלְשׁוֹן הַמִּנְהָל וְכָל **מִי שֶׁנָּשָׂא** וְנָתַן עִם הַשִּׁלְטוֹן הָיָה חַיָּיב בִּידִיעָתָהּ.

(King) Cyrus introduced Aramaic as the language of administration and <u>anyone who</u> had dealings with the authorities was obligated to know it.

(42) יֵשׁ כַּמּוּבָן הֶבְדֵּל נִיכָּר בֵּין **מִי שֶׁהֵם** דּוֹר שֵׁנִי וּשְׁלִישִׁי לְנִיצוֹלֵי שׁוֹאָה, לְבֵין **מִי שֶׁאֵינֶנּוּ** כָּזֶה.

There is of course a considerable difference between <u>those who</u> are a second and third generation of Holocaust survivors, and <u>someone who</u> is not.

In this example, מי refers, first, to a plural entity (מי שהם) and then to a single entity (מי שאיננו כזה, rather than מי שאינם כאלה).

3. Remote demonstrative pronouns: *that, those*

3.1 ההוא, ההיא, ההם, ההן

With the addition of a definite article, the third person personal pronouns הוא, היא, and הם, הן become the remote demonstratives *that* and *those*, respectively. The pronouns follow a definite noun and agree with it in number and gender (e.g., השאלה ההיא *that question*, בַּיָּמִים ההם *in those days*).

3.1.1 In elevated style, הַלָּה (and rarely, הַלָּז or הַלָּזֶה) may be used instead of ההוא when referring to a person; it is translated as *that one* or *the latter* (example 44).

---

(43) התַּקָּנוֹת אִפְשְׁרוּ לִיהוּדֵי **הַתְּקוּפָה הַהִיא** לְחֵיוֹת חַיֵּי קְהִילָה תְּקִינִים וּמְאוּרְגָנִים.
The Takkanot (ordinances) made it possible for the Jews of <u>that period</u> to conduct regulated and organized community life.

(44) בָּלָק פָּחַד מֵהִתְקָרְבוּתוֹ שֶׁל עַם יִשְׂרָאֵל לִגְבוּלוֹ וּבִיקֵּשׁ מִבִּלְעָם בֶּן בְּעוֹר שֶׁיְּקַלֵּל אֶת עַם יִשְׂרָאֵל. **הַלָּה** סֵירֵב בַּתְּחִילָה לָבוֹא אֵלָיו.
Balak feared the approach of the Israelites to his border and asked Balaam son of Beor to curse them. <u>The latter</u> refused at the beginning to come to him.

✗#4 3.2 אותו, אותה, אותם, אותן
that, those; the same, similar

In their role as demonstrative pronouns, the inflected third person forms of אֶת – namely, אותו, אותה, אותם, אותן – have two, context-determined functions:

(a) As remote demonstratives (*that* and *those*), equivalent to ההוא, ההיא, ההם, ההן (example 45), or

(b) To indicate sameness or similarity (examples 46–47).

In other words, אותו מקום could be understood either as *that place* or as *the same/a similar place*.

These pronouns precede the noun they refer to, and agree with it in number and gender. A definite article before the noun is optional (e.g., אותו המקום or אותו מקום).

(45) מִמְצָאִים אַרְכֵאוֹלוֹגְיִים מְעִידִים עַל הִתְפַּתְחוּתָם שֶׁל שְׁנֵי טִיפּוּסִים עִיקָרִיִּים שֶׁל **אוֹתוֹ מָקוֹם** קָדוֹשׁ שֶׁבּוֹ אוּחְסְנוּ סִפְרֵי תּוֹרָה.

Archeological findings testify to the development of two main types of <u>that</u> holy place in which Torahs were stored.

(46) שְׁנֵי הַסְּפָרִים הַלָּלוּ חוּבְּרוּ **בְּאוֹתָה תְּקוּפָה וּבְאוֹתָה סְבִיבָה**.

These two books were composed at <u>the same</u> period and in <u>the same</u> environment.

(47) הַמַּדְרִיכִים הַמְּקוֹמִיִּים הוֹבִילוּ אֶת הַנּוֹסְעִים הָאֵירוֹפִים **לְאוֹתָם הָאֲתָרִים**, הֶרְאוּ לָהֶם **אוֹתָם הַדְּבָרִים** וְסִיפְּרוּ לָהֶם **אוֹתָם הַסִּיפּוּרִים**.

The local guides lead the European travelers to <u>the same</u> sites, showed them <u>the same</u> things and told them <u>the same</u> stories.

⚠️ **3.2.1** The demonstrative pronouns אוֹתוֹ, אוֹתָה, אוֹתָם, אוֹתָן are distinguishable from the inflected forms of the preposition אֶת in that they can be preceded by a preposition (even by אֶת) and are followed by a noun.
For example:

הוּא הִסְבִּיר אֶת הַמִּילָה→ הוּא הִסְבִּיר <u>אוֹתָהּ</u> *he explained the word* (direct object pronoun)
הוּא הִסְבִּיר (אֶת) <u>אוֹתָהּ (הַ)מִּילָה</u> *he explained the same* (OR: *that*) *word* (demonstrative pronoun).

(48) קְשָׁרָיו הַמִּשְׁפַּחְתִּיִּים קֵרְבוּ **אוֹתוֹ** אֶל **אוֹתָם אֲנָשִׁים** שֶׁעִיצְבוּ אֶת הַהִיסְטוֹרְיָה שֶׁעָלֶיהָ כָּתַב.

His family connections brought <u>him</u> close to <u>those</u> people who shaped the history about which he wrote.

אוֹתוֹ is a direct object pronoun; אוֹתָם is a demonstrative pronoun.

🏋 #5   4. Indefinite pronouns

4.1   אֵיזֶה, אֵיזוֹ, אֵילוּ *some*

	Masculine	Feminine
Singular	אֵיזֶה	אֵיזוֹ
Plural	אֵילוּ אֵי-אֵלֶּה, אֵי-אֵלּוּ	

4.1.1 Indefinite pronouns come before the noun and are translated as *some*. Gender distinctions can be made only in the singular: אֵיזֶה for masculine nouns, אֵיזוֹ for feminine nouns. For example: אֵיזֶה הֶסְבֵּר *some explanation,* אֵיזוֹ תְּשׁוּבָה *some answer,* אֵילוּ הֶסְבֵּרִים, אֵילוּ תְּשׁוּבוֹת *some explanations, some answers.*

The hyphenated pronouns אֵי-אֵלּוּ and אֵי-אֵלֶּה *some, a few, a number of* are infrequent alternatives to אֵילוּ (example 51).

> The biblical question word אֵי (a short form of אַיֵּה *where*) is a component also in אֵימָתַי *when*, אֵי־שָׁם *somewhere*, and אֵי־פַּעַם *some time*.
>
> ⚠ In unpointed text, אֵי should be distinguished from the negation prefix אִי (e.g., אי אפשר *impossible*).

---

(49) הָיָה בָּאֲוִירַת הַבַּיִת **אֵיזֶה** כּוֹבֶד.
There was <u>some</u> heaviness in the atmosphere of the home.

(50) הָעִבְרִית מֵעוֹלָם לֹא מֵתָה מִיתָה גְּמוּרָה, וּבְ**אֵילוּ** זְמַנִּים וּבְ**אֵילוּ** אֲרָצוֹת שִׁמְּשָׁה לְשׁוֹן דִּיבּוּר בִּשְׁעַת לִימּוּד אוֹ בְּהִזְדַּמְנוּיּוֹת אֲחֵרוֹת.
Hebrew never completely died, and in <u>some</u> periods and <u>some</u> countries served as a spoken language during study or on other occasions.

(51) רַעְיוֹן הַלְּאוּמִיּוּת מְבוּסָּס עַל זְכוּתָם שֶׁל אֲנָשִׁים הַחוֹלְקִים **אֵי אֵלּוּ** מֵהַמְּאַפְיֵינִים הַבָּאִים: תַּרְבּוּת, שָׂפָה, טֶרִיטוֹרְיָה וְהִיסְטוֹרְיָה.
The idea of nationalism is based on the right of people who share <u>some</u> of the following characteristics: culture, language, territory and history.

4.1.2 Instead of אֵילוּ, the quantifiers אֲחָדִים and אֲחָדוֹת *several, some* or, less formally כַּמָּה, may be used. For example: אֵילוּ אֲרָצוֹת, אֲרָצוֹת אֲחָדוֹת, כַּמָּה אֲרָצוֹת *several countries*.

A small quantity may also be indicated with (a) מְעַטִּים, מְעַטּוֹת *few* (e.g., אֲנָשִׁים מְעַטִּים *few people*, אֲרָצוֹת מְעַטּוֹת *few countries*), (b) מְעַט *few, little* (e.g., מְעַט אֲנָשִׁים *few people*, מְעַט מַיִם *little water*), or (c) מִסְפַּר *a [small] number of*, appearing before or (more formally) after a plural noun (e.g., אֲרָצוֹת מִסְפָּר, מִסְפַּר אֲרָצוֹת *few people*, אֲנָשִׁים מִסְפָּר, מִסְפַּר אֲנָשִׁים *few countries*).

4.2
אֵיזֶשֶׁהוּ *some*
כָּלְשֶׁהוּ *some, any*

> The pronunciation of כלשהו follows that of the word כֹּל, i.e., with /o/.

	Masculine	**Feminine**
Singular	אֵיזֶה שֶׁהוּא, אֵיזֶשֶׁהוּ כָּלְשֶׁהוּ, כָּל...שֶׁהוּא	אֵיזוֹ שֶׁהִיא, אֵיזוֹשֶׁהִי כָּלְשֶׁהִי, כָּל...שֶׁהִיא
Plural	אֵיזֶה שֶׁהֵם כָּלְשֶׁהֶם, כָּל... שֶׁהֵם	אֵיזֶה שֶׁהֵן כָּלְשֶׁהֶן, כָּל... שֶׁהֵן

4.2.1 Form

- The indefinite pronouns in this group are made up of three elements:
  כל/איזה + שׁ + 3rd person pronoun (הוא, היא, הם, הן).
  This set of pronouns allows for gender distinction both in the singular and plural.
  In the blended forms איזשהו, איזושהי, כלשהו, כלשהי, the final אל"ף of הוא and היא is omitted.
- The components of כלשהו and איזשהו may be separated to straddle the noun (example 56). The final אל"ף then returns (e.g., שהוא).

4.2.2 Meaning

- **איזשהו** and **איזושהי** are equivalent to איזה and איזו, respectively; **איזה שהם, איזה שהן** are equivalent to אילו. They are rendered in English as *some, some kind of.*
- **כלשהו, כלשהי, כלשהם, כלשהן** can be used in the sense of *somewhat, a small measure of* to diminish the scope of the noun (example 53) – this is despite the fact that כל is typically used for inclusion (as in כל אחד *everyone*, הכל *everything*).
- When כל and שהוא are separated (example 55), and when they appear (separated) in negative and interrogative sentences, the translation is *any* (example 56).

---

(52) בְּמֶרְכָּזָהּ שֶׁל הָאֱמָנוּת הַקוֹנְסֶפְּטוּאָלִית יֵשׁ אֵיזוֹ שֶׁהִיא "אֲמִירה".
At the center of conceptual art there is <u>some kind of</u> "statement".

(53) יֵשׁ דְּמְיוֹן כָּלְשֶׁהוּ בֵּין הסיפורים.
There is <u>some</u> (OR: small measure of) resemblance between the stories.

(54) יֵשְׁנוֹ רק יום מוֹעֵד אחד במסוֹרֶת העברית הנקרא על שמה של אישיות היסטורית כָּלְשֶׁהִי.
There is only one calendar day in Jewish tradition that is called after <u>some</u> historical personality.

(55) מִכֵּיוָן שהמשפחה הִיא המִסְגֶרֶת הַחֶבְרָתִית הַבְּסִיסִית ביותר, הֲבָנָתָהּ הִיא חֵלֶק חשוב בניתוח של כל חֶברה שהיא.
Since the family is the most basic social unit (literally: frame), its understanding is an important part of the analysis of <u>any</u> society.

(56) בימים הראשונים לגלות בָּבֶל עדיין לֹא קיבלו היהודים אוטונומיה שיפוטית או דָתית כלשהי.
In the first days of the Babylonian exile, the Jews had not yet received <u>any</u> judicial or religious autonomy.

4.3

מִישֶׁהוּ, מִישֶׁהִי *someone*
מַשֶׁהוּ *something*
אִיש לֹא, אָדָם לֹא, אַף אֶחָד לֹא *no one*
דָבָר לֹא, מְאוּמָה לֹא, כְּלוּם לֹא *nothing*

4.3.1 **מישהו, מישהי** *someone* and **משהו** *something* are indefinite pronouns that refer to animate and inanimate nouns, respectively.

A formal alternative to משהו is דְּבַר-מָה (example 58).

מה after a noun indicates a vague or small quantity (e.g., דמיון-מה *some similarity*, זמן-מה *(for) some time*, במידת-מה *to some extent*).

4.3.2 *No one* is expressed as איש לא (example 59), אדם לא or, less formally, as אף אחד לא.

4.3.3 *Nothing* and *anything* are rendered with כלום (שום), דבר and more formally with מאומה (or its less common variant, מאום, example 61) accompanied by a word of negation, לא or אין, placed before the verb.

For example:

הוא איננו יודע דבר/כלום/מאומה; דבר/כלום/מאומה הוא איננו יודע *he does not know anything*
לא קרה (שום) דבר; (שום) דבר לא קרה, מאומה לא קרה *nothing happened*

---

(57) לְפִי אֱמוּנָה טְפֵלָה אַחַת, אָסוּר לִדְרוֹךְ עַל צֵל שֶׁל **מִישֶׁהוּ**.
According to one superstition, it is forbidden to step on <u>someone's</u> shadow.

(58) סָטִירָה הִיא יְצִירָה אָמָנוּתִית שמַטְּרָתָהּ לָשִׂים **דְּבַר-מָה** (אֱמוּנָה, הִתְנַהֲגוּת, מִפְלָגָה פוֹלִיטִית וכו') לְלַעַג.
A satire is an artistic work whose purpose is to mock <u>something</u> (a belief, a behavior, a political party, etc.).

(59) וַעֲדַת הַשֵּׁמוֹת קָבְעָה לַמָּקוֹם שֵׁם עברי, "רָמִים," אַך **אִיש לֹא** קָרָא כך לקיבּוּץ.
The naming committee set a Hebrew name, "Ramim," for the place, but <u>no one</u> called the kibbutz by that name (literally: called the kibbutz thus).

(60) הַחוֹלוֹת הללוּ כּוּנּוּ "דְיוּנוֹת הַמָּוֶת," דְיוּנוֹת שֶׁלֹּא צָמַח בָּהֶן **מְאוּמָה**.
These sands were called "the death dunes," dunes in which <u>nothing</u> grew.

(61) בשׁוֹאָה חָרְבָה הַקְּהִילָה בָּעֲיָירָה **וְלֹא** נוֹתַר מִמֶּנָּה **מְאוּם**.
In the Holocaust, the Jewish community in the town was destroyed and <u>nothing</u> was left of it.

(62) במקרא **לֹא** נֶאֱמַר **דָּבָר** עַל תּוֹכְנוֹ שֶׁל הַגֵּט וְעַל צוּרָתוֹ.
<u>Nothing</u> was said in the Bible about the content of the Get (divorce certificate) or its form.

⚡#5   5. Interrogative pronouns: אֵילוּ ,אֵיזוֹ ,אֵיזֶה *which one(s)?*

In addition to their use as indefinite pronouns in the sense of *some,* אֵילוּ ,אֵיזוֹ ,אֵיזֶה are used as interrogative pronouns asking *which (one)?* or *what kind of?*

Similarly, the meaning of the word כמה varies with the sentence type: in interrogative sentences it means *how many?* while in declarative sentences it means *some, several* (compare כמה אנשים היו שם? *how many people were there?* with כמה אנשים היו שם *several people were there.*)

אֵיזֶה and אֵיזוֹ come before singular masculine and feminine nouns, respectively; אֵילוּ is used with plural nouns, both masculine and feminine. However, colloquially (and, in formal written discourse, carelessly) אֵיזֶה is used also with feminine singular nouns and plural nouns (example 67).

> ⚠ Note that in unpointed text אֵילוּ *which* and אִילוּ *if* (hypothetical) appear identical.

Like other question words, אֵיזֶה, אֵיזוֹ and אֵילוּ can be introduced by a preposition (examples 64 and 66).

---

(63) לא הוחלט **אֵיזֶה** מהדְגָלים יהיה דֶגֶל לְאוּמי.
It was not decided <u>which</u> of the flags would be the national flag.

(64) עַל הָאָדָם לְהַכְריע בְּעַצמו **בְּאֵיזוֹ** משתי הדְרָכים הוא חָפֵץ ללכת.
Man has to determine for himself in <u>which</u> of the two roads he wishes to walk.

The interrogative pronoun אֵיזוֹ agrees with the feminine noun דרך.

(65) לא ידוע **אֵילו** מן החיבורים מקוּמְרָאן נתחַבְּרו בקֶרֶב הכַּת מַמָּש.
It is not known <u>which</u> of the works from Qumran were actually written within the sect.

(66) המשנה קובעת **בְּאֵילו** חומָרים אפשר להשתמש לעֲשיית נֵרות שבת וּבְאֵילו חומרים אי אפשר להשתמש.
The Mishnah determines <u>which</u> materials can be used to make Sabbath candles and <u>which</u> ones cannot be used.

(67) הפְּרָט בוחר **אֵיזה** מצוות לקבל כְּמְחַיְּיבות.
The individual decides <u>which</u> [religious] commands to accept as binding.

אֵיזה instead of the normative אֵילו (before a plural noun) was used here.

The chart below summarizes the pronouns discussed in sections 2 through 5 above:

singular masculine & feminine	plural masculine & feminine	translation	type of pronoun
זֶה, זֹאת זֶה, זוֹ	אֵלֶּה אֵלוּ	*this, these*	demonstrative
כזה, כזאת	כאלה, כאלו	*like this, like these*	
ההוא, ההיא	ההם, ההן	*that, those*	remote demonstrative
אותו, אותה	אותם, אותן	*that, those; the same*	
אֵיזֶה? אֵיזוֹ?	אֵילוּ?	*which?*	interrogative
אֵיזֶה, אֵיזוֹ איזה שהוא, איזו שהיא; כלשהו, כלשהי	אֵילוּ, אֵי-אֵלֶּה, אֵי-אֵלוּ איזה שהם, איזה שהן כלשהם, כלשהן	*some* *some, some kind of* *some, any*	indefinite
מישהו, מישהי		*someone*	
איש לא, אדם לא, אף אחד לא		*no one*	negative
דבר לא, מאומה לא, כלום לא		*nothing, anything*	

6. Reflexive pronouns -עצמ: *himself, herself, itself...*

אדם קרוב אצל **עצמו** (סנהדרין ט)
A man is close to (thinks first of) ***himself*** (Tractate Sanhedrin 9)

6.1 Reflexive pronouns appear after a verb (or an adjective acting as a verb) and its preposition and refer back to the subject through a personal pronoun suffix.

The preposition before the reflexive pronoun is the one required by the verb. However, as a stylistic option, the preposition את is often omitted (example 70).

Reflexive action may also be expressed in *binyan hitpa'el*: התרחץ=רחץ את עצמו.
Note the reflexive meaning of the idiomatic expression -חזר בו מ *went back on, changed one's mind* (e.g., הם חזרו בהם מהחלטתם *they went back on their decision*), where the meaning is reflexive but -עצם is not used.

The reference of the pronoun suffix (the subject) is shaded:

---

(68) הַמֶּמְשָׁלָה נָטְלָה עַל עצמה לפתור את הבעיות הכַּלְכָּלִיות של המדינה.
The government took upon <u>itself</u> to solve the economic problems of the state.

(69) הַגִּיבּוֹר מְתָאֵר אֶת עצמו כְּטיפוס בּוֹדֵד וְאינְטְרוֹסְפֶּקְטיבי.
The protagonist describes <u>himself</u> as a lonely and introspective type.

(70) הוא הִקְדיש עצמו לפילוֹסוֹפיה מִנְעוּרָיו.
He devoted <u>himself</u> to philosophy from his youth.

6.2 When appearing directly after a noun or a pronoun (rather than after a verb), the suffixed forms of עצמ- have an emphatic function; the suffix refers to the noun.

If עצמ- is omitted, the emphasis would be lost, but the sentence would remain grammatical. Alternatively, inflected forms of the noun גוף *body* – גופו, גופם and so on – may be used (example 73).

---

(71) בעבודת הגמר התלמיד מְסַפֵּר עַל עצמו, על תַהֲלִיך הכְּתיבה, ועל העבודה עצמה.
In the final thesis, the student tells <u>about himself</u>, about the process of writing, and about <u>the thesis itself</u>.

This example illustrates the two uses of עצמ-+pronoun suffix: as a reflexive pronoun after a verb (התלמיד מספר על עצמו), and as an optional emphatic device after a noun (העבודה עצמה). These two uses are seen side by side also in the next example.

(72) כְּיום דוֹבְרֵי האמְהָרית כְּשְׂפַת אֵם מְכוּנים על ידי זָרים בשם אמהרים אך הם עצמם מתייחסים לעצמם בשם אֶתיוֹפים.
Today the speakers of Amharic as a native language are called by outsiders Amharas but <u>they themselves</u> refer <u>to themselves</u> by the name Ethiopians.

Two uses of עצמ- are seen here.

(73) בשעה שֶׁבָּאים לחקור תשובות אלה יש לחזור אל כְּתָב-היד גופו.
When one investigates these responses, it is necessary to return to the manuscript <u>itself</u>.

---

7. Reciprocity pronouns: זה + preposition + זה
each other, one another

Reciprocity is commonly expressed in Hebrew by repeating the pronoun זה (other options are shown in the table below), and linking the repeated words with a preposition.

The preposition is the one required (grammatically) by the verb or adjective, or is determined by the meaning (example 78).

In reciprocal phrases, זה is often gender and number neutral, that is, it refers to masculine or feminine, singular or plural nouns. However, as shown below, gender and number distinctions can be made.

masculine (singular and plural) nouns	זֶה . . . זֶה
	(a) שֵׁנִי(ה) . . . אֶחָד(ה)
	(b) אֶחָד . . . חֲבֵרוֹ/רֵעֵהוּ/אָחִיו
	איש . . . חברו/רעהו/אחיו
	אֶחָד . . . מִשְׁנֵהוּ
	(c) אדם . . . זוּלָתוֹ
feminine (singular and plural) nouns	זוֹ . . . זוֹ
	(ה)אחת . . . (ה)שנייה
	אחת . . . חֲבֶרְתָּהּ/רְעוּתָהּ/
	אֲחוֹתָהּ
	אישה . . . חֲבֶרְתָּהּ/רְעוּתָהּ/
	אֲחוֹתָהּ
	אַחַת . . . מִשְׁנָהּ
masculine and feminine plural nouns	אֵלּוּ . . . אֵלּוּ
	אֵלֶּה.. אֵלֶּה

Note that:

(a) אֶחָד . . . שֵׁנִי is considered colloquial.

(b) חבר and רֵעַ *friend* as well as אח *brother*, and their feminine equivalents, do not denote friendship or family relationship (example 77) and may be used with animate as well as inanimate nouns (examples 78–80).

(c) On its own, הַזּוּלָת means *one's fellowman, another person*. (The adverb זוּלַת – synonymous with מִלְּבַד[4] – means *other than, beside*.)

The reciprocal pronouns are shaded and the prepositions are bolded; the verb and its required preposition are given in brackets below the sentence:

> (74) החינוך והתרבות יוצרים **זה את זה**.
> [יוצר את]
> Education and culture create <u>each other</u>.
>
> (75) פשוטו של מקרא ומדרשו שונים **זה מזה** אך אין הם שוללים **זה את זה**.
> [שונה מן, שולל את]
> The simple meaning of the Bible and its exegetic meaning are different from <u>each other</u> but they do not negate <u>each other</u>.

---

[4] See Chapter 10, Confusables 6.2 (b).

(76) כָּךְ הוֹלְכִים שני נְבִיאִים כֹּה שונים **זֶה מִזֶה** – אֵלִיָּהוּ וֶאֱלִישָׁע – וּמִתְדַמִּים **אִישׁ לְרֵעֵהוּ**.
[שׁוֹנֶה מִן, מִתְדַּמֶּה ל]
In this way two prophets so different <u>from each other</u> – Elijah and Elisha – gradually become similar <u>to each other</u>.

For stylistic variety, both זה...זה and איש ...רעהו are used in the same sentence.

(77) הוֹיְכּוּחִים הַפּוּמְבִּיִּים בֵּין אַנְשֵׁי הַכְּמוּרָה וּבֵין חֲכָמִים יְהוּדִים הֵבִיאוּ אֵת שני הַצְּדָדִים לְהַכִּיר **אִישׁ אֵת** תּוֹרַת **רֵעֵהוּ**.
[מַכִּיר אֵת]
The public debates between the churchmen and the Jewish sages brought them to know <u>each other's</u> doctrines.

The singular pronouns איש and רע refer to plural nouns – אנשי כמורה and חכמים יהודים.

(78) בְּמֶשֶׁךְ הַזְּמַן הִתְחִילוּ לְהַגִּיהַּ נוּסְחָה אַחַת **עַל פִּי** חֲבֶרְתָּהּ, לְהַכְנִיס תּוֹסָפוֹת מִן **הָאַחַת לְתוֹךְ הַשְּׁנִיָּה**.
In the course of time, they began to correct <u>one</u> version <u>according to another</u>, to introduce additions <u>from one into the other</u>.

(79) הַדּוֹבֵר עוֹבֵר **מֵרָמַת** לשון **אַחַת לַחֲבֶרְתָּהּ** וּמִמִּשְׁלָב **אֶחָד לְרֵעֵהוּ**.
[עוֹבֵר מ...ל]
The speaker switches <u>from one</u> language level <u>to another</u> and <u>from one</u> register <u>to another</u>.

(80) לְשׁוֹנוֹת בְּמַגָּע מַשְׁפִּיעוֹת **זוֹ עַל זוֹ** וּמוּשְׁפָּעוֹת **זוֹ מִזּוֹ**. הַהַשְׁפָּעָה הַנִּכֶּרֶת בְּיוֹתֵר הִיא בַּתְּחוּם הַמִּילוֹן, שֶׁבּוֹ מִילִים נוֹדְדוֹת **מִלָּשׁוֹן אַחַת לִרְעוּתָהּ**.
[מַשְׁפִּיעַ עַל, מוּשְׁפָּע מִן, נוֹדֵד מ... ל]
Languages in contact influence <u>each other</u> and are influenced <u>by each other</u>. The most visible influence is in the area of the lexicon, in which words wander <u>from one</u> language <u>to another</u>.

This example demonstrates the rule that the preposition between the reciprocal pronouns is determined by the verb: לְהַשְׁפִּיעַ **עַל**, מוּשְׁפָּע **מ**.

(81) הוּא הֶאֱמִין כִּי כּוֹחוֹת שָׁמֵימִיִּים וְכוֹחוֹת טֶבַע אֵינָם סוֹתְרִים **אֵלֶּה אֶת אֵלֶּה**, כִּי אִם פּוֹעֲלִים בְּצוּרָה הַרְמוֹנִית **זֶה לְצַד** זֶה.
[סוֹתֵר אֵת]
He believed that celestial powers and the powers of nature do not contradict <u>each other</u> but rather work harmoniously side by side (literally: <u>next to each other</u>).

In this example, the plural nouns כוחות are referred to first with אלה and then with זה.

> (82) חֵלֶק גדול מִסְפְּרֵי הַמַּסָעות אֵינו אלא פְּלגיאַט של אנשים אשר לא ביקרו בארץ ישראל
> או בַאֲתָרים שתֵיארו וכל שעָשו היה לְהַעתיק **אִיש מִמִּשְׁנֵהו.**
> [מעתיק מ . . .]
> A large portion of the voyage literature (literally: books) is nothing but plagiarism by
> people who did not visit the Land of Israel or the sites they described and all they
> did was to copy from <u>each other</u>.

7.1 זה או זה

When the repeated pronouns are linked by או, choice (rather than reciprocity) is expressed.
A synonymous expression for זה או זה is זה או אחר (feminine: זו או אחרת; זו או זו; plural:
אלה או אלה, אלה או אחרים).

> (83) לפי נְטִיָּיתו האישית של החוקר הוּדְגַש צַד **זה או זה.**
> According to the researcher's personal preference, <u>this or that</u> aspect was given
> emphasis.

8. Anticipatory (proleptic) pronoun

A preposition inflected with a pronoun suffix sometimes anticipates the noun that the suffix
refers to. This stylistic device results in a redundancy, since the preposition appears twice, once
with the suffix and once with the noun. In translation, the anticipatory pronoun is ignored.

> (84) הַמֶּסֶר בסיפור בָּרוּר: אין **לו ליהודי** לִבְטוֹח בְּאיש שאֵינו מבְּנֵי בְּריתו.
> The message of the story is clear: the Jew should not trust anyone who is not a
> Jew.
>
> See also example 5 in Chapter 8.

8.1 The phenomenon of an anticipatory pronoun is also seen in double construct phrases,[5]
where the pronominal suffix that is attached to the first noun refers to the next noun (e.g.,
in שאלתו של החוקר *the researcher's question* the pronoun suffix ו- anticipates the noun
חוקר).

9. זה and זאת in set expressions

The original meaning of זאת and זה is often altered or lost when they function as components
within sentence connectors and set expressions. Below are some examples.

---

[5] See Chapter 2, 4.4.

זֹאת אוֹמֶרֶת	*that is to say*
אֵי לָזֹאת	*accordingly, consequently*
יְתֵרָה מזאת, זֹאת וְעוֹד	*moreover*
לְבַד מזאת	*apart from this, in addition to*
בְּכָל זֹאת	*nonetheless*
(יחד) עִם זֹאת/זֶה, למרות זֹאת	*however*
אין זֹאת כי	*this could only mean that…*
כַּיּוֹצֵא בָּזֶה/בָּזֹאת/בָּאֵלֶּה	*and such, etc.*
בִּכְלָל זֶה/זֹאת	*including*
זֶה אוֹ אַחֵר (זוֹ אוֹ אחרת)	*this or that*
אַף זוֹ/גַם זֹאת	*this also*
בָּזֹאת, בָּזֶה	*in this respect, at this opportunity*
בָּזֶה אחר זה	*one after another*
לֹא . . . כְּהוּא זֶה	*not one iota*
לֹא זוֹ אַף זוֹ	*in addition, also*
במקום/תחת זֹאת	*instead of this*
בְּעִקְבוֹת זֹאת	*following/as a result of this*
אַךְ זֶה	*just now, not too long ago*[6]
מזה וּ . . . מזה	*on one hand…and on the other*

10. כך in set expressions

בְּשֶׁל כך	*therefore*
אֵי לְכך	*hence, therefore*
אִם כך	*consequently*
אִם כך ואם כך	*either way*
אַחַר כך	*later*
בֵּין כך וּבֵין כך	*in any case; in the meantime*
בְּתוֹך כך	*in the meantime; whilst doing so*
מתוֹך כך	*through this*
כל כך	*so, so much*
כך וכך	*such and such*
כך אוֹ כך	*one way or another*
כְּכל שֶׁ . . . כך	*the more…the more*
כְּשֵׁם שֶׁ . . . כך	*as…so also*
נוֹסף לכך	*in addition to this*
דָּבָר שֶׁל מה בְּכך	*a thing of little importance*

---

[6] See example 13 in Chapter 7.

Confusables

1. הֵן

In addition to *they* (a pronoun) and *are* (a copula), הן has the following meanings:

- *indeed, truly*, a rhetorical confirmation synonymous with הֲרֵי (example 85);
- הֵן (וְ) . . . הֵן *both, as well as* (example 86);
- כֵּן *yes* (in Mishnaic Hebrew).

---

(85) **הֵן** כָּךְ הַמַּצָּב בתרגום השומרוני.
<u>Indeed</u> this is the case in the Samaritan translation.

(86) בְּאֶמְצָעוּת הַדְּרָשָׁה הִצְלִיחוּ הַחֲכָמִים לְעוֹרֵר אֶת עְנְיָנָם שֶׁל היהודים **הֵן** בתורה **וְהֵן** בְּעִנְיָנֵי דְיוֹמָא.
Through the sermon the sages succeeded in arousing the interest of the Jews <u>both</u> in the Torah and in everyday affairs.

---

2. זה (usually *this*) appears as a non-translatable component in the following time expressions:

- (מִ)זֶה שָׁנִים, (מִ)זֶה זְמַן *for years, for a long time* (where זה followed by a time unit indicates duration)
- זֶה (מִ)כְּבָר *long ago.* זה לא מִכְּבָר, זה מִקָּרוֹב, זה עַתָּה, אַךְ זה *recently, not long ago;*

---

(87) **מִזֶה שָׁנִים** עֵרִים הַחוֹקְרִים לָעוּבְדָה, שֶׁהָאָמָּנוּת יְכוֹלָה לְשַׁמֵּשׁ מָקוֹר לִידִיעוֹת הִיסְטוֹרִיּוֹת חֲדָשׁוֹת וּלְהַצִּיעַ הֶסְבֵּרִים לָעוּבְדוֹת הַיְדוּעוֹת לָנוּ **מִזֶה זְמַן**.
Researchers have been aware <u>for many years</u> that art can serve as a source of new historical information and offer explanations for facts that we have known <u>for a long time</u>.

(88) חֲלוּקָה זֹאת לְשָׁלוֹשׁ קְבוּצוֹת עוֹמֶדֶת וְקַיֶּמֶת **זה כמה וכמה דורות**.
This division into three groups has existed <u>already for several generations</u>.

Note the repetition – כמה וכמה – as an intensifying device.

(89) לַמַּאֲמָר שֶׁנִּכְתַּב לִפְנֵי שְׁלוֹשִׁים שָׁנָה נוֹסְפוּ **זה לא מכבר** עִדְכּוּנִים.
Updates have been <u>recently</u> added to the article that was written thirty years ago.

---

3. עֶצֶם (ה-); כְּשֶׁלְּעַצְמוֹ, בִּפְנֵי עַצְמוֹ, בְּעַצְמוֹ; מֵעַצְמוֹ; בְּעֶצֶם; עַצְמִי

3.1 עצם (ה-) *(the) very*

When the noun **עצם** *thing, object* appears as the first noun in a construct phrase, its function is to intensify the second noun of the phrase. In this role, עצם is translated as *the/this very* (e.g., עד עצם היום הזה *to this very day*).

(90) רֶצַח של ראש מדינה הוא אִיּוּם על עצם מַהוּתָהּ של הַדֶּמוֹקְרַטְיָה.
The murder of a head of state is a threat to <u>the very</u> essence of democracy.

3.2 כְּשֶׁלְּעַצְמוֹ *in and of itself, per se*
בִּפְנֵי עצמו *in itself*

The components -כש and לעצמו may be separated by a personal pronoun referring to the subject (example 93).

(91) הַשֵּׁירוּת בַּצָּבָא הפך להיות עֵרֶךְ **בפני עצמו.**
Army service became a value <u>in itself</u>.

(92) לַיָּחִיד אין עֵרֶךְ מוּחלט **כְּשֶׁלְעַצְמוֹ.**
The individual does not have an absolute value <u>in and of himself.</u>

(93) הַדֶּרֶךְ המתודית, שֶׁבָּה בָּחַר, מוֹשֶׁכֶת **כְּשֶׁהִיא לְעַצְמָהּ.**
The methodological route that he chose is attractive <u>in and of itself</u>.

היא refers to דרך.

3.3 בעצמו *by itself/himself/oneself, on its/his own*

(94) פִּינְסְקֶר טָעַן שֶׁהיהודים חַיָּיבִים לפעול **בעצמם** למען עַצְמָאוּת לאומית.
Pinsker argued that the Jews must act <u>by themselves</u> for national independence.

3.4 מֵעַצְמוֹ *of one's own accord, by itself*

(95) אפשר היה לַצָּפוֹת שֶׁהכל יסתדר **מעצמו.**
It could be expected that everything would be settled <u>by itself</u>.

3.5 בעצם *in fact*

בעצם is an adverbial that is used to comment on the statement made in the sentence. When appearing at the beginning of the sentence, it is separated from it with a comma.

(96) כאן **בְּעֶצֶם** מתחיל הַפֶּרֶק האחרון בחייו.
Here <u>in fact</u> begins the last chapter of his life.

3.6 עַצְמִי, עצמית, עצמיים, עצמיות

The adjective עצמי is translated as *self-*. For example:

בְּטָחוֹן עצמי	*self-confidence*
דְּיוֹקָן עצמי	*self-portrait*
הֲגָנָה עצמית	*self-defence*
שִׁלְטוֹן עצמי	*self-rule*

⚠ Make sure to distinguish the adjective from the reflexive pronoun עצמי *myself*.

⚠ **3.6.1** Distinguish also עַצְמִי from the differently spelled and pronounced adjective עַצְמָאִי *independent*.

References

דורון, 1991
שורצולד (רודריג), 1994

Coffin & Bolozky, 2005
Glinert, 1989
Muraoka, 1998

Chapter 3: Pronouns – Exercises

exercise #	topic	page
1	Determining the function of third person pronouns	143–144
2	Determining the reference of the demonstrative pronoun	145–146
3	Determining the reference of כך	147–148
4	Distinguishing between אותו as pronoun and as preposition	149
5	Distinguishing among אלה/אלו, אֵילו, אֵילו	150–151

Exercise #1: Determining the function of third person pronouns

---

The rules to go by: see section 1.3 and Confusables, section 1.
What to do:
1. Indicate the function of the bolded pronoun(s) in each sentence by entering the sentence number in the appropriate cell in the chart.
2. Translate the sentences.

Example:

העברית והערבית ועוד לשונות יוצרות משפחה אחת של לשונות, <u>היא</u> משפחת הלשונות השמיות.

Hebrew, Arabic and other languages create one family of languages, the family of Semitic languages. (היא introduces an appositive and can be ignored in translation).

---

personal pronoun (he, she, it, they)	copula (is, are)	emphatic copulas	appositive introducer	its/his/her/their own	both
			example,		

1. ההיסטוריון סוקר את המקבילות בין חורבן הבית הראשון ובין תקופתו **הוא**.

2. הר סיני, **הוא** הר חוֹרֵב, כּוּנָה "הר האלוהים".

3. אַהֲבַת חַיִּים, שִׂמְחַת חיים, צימאון לחיים – **הן-הן** התכונות שאִפְיְינו את ציוריו וגם את אישיותו.

4. אין מסוֹרֶת מקוּבֶּלֶת אחת שקוֹבַעַת איזה הר **הוא** הר סיני הָאֲמִיתי.

Glossary

---

the historian reviews	ההיסטוריון סוקר .1
parallels	מקבילות
the destruction of the First Temple	חורבן הבית הראשון
was called	כּוּנה .2
thirst for life	צימָאון לחיים .3
qualities, characteristics	תכונות
characterized	אִפְיְינו
his drawings	ציוריו
his personality	אישיותו
accepted tradition	מסורת מקובלת .4
states, determines	קובעת
the real Mount Sinai	הר סיני האמיתי

5. הַגַּרְזֶן היה **הן** כְּלִי עבודה שימושי **והן** כלי נֶשֶׁק.

6. המאורע של נפילת בָּבֶל בידֵי כּוֹרֶשׁ (א)**הוא** שנתפס על-ידי הנָביא כְּבַעַל מַשְׁמָעוּת היסטוֹרית-תֵּאולוֹגית ובו (ב)**הוא** רואה התְגַשְׁמוּת של הנבואה.

7. גם דִבְרֵי נבואה ושירה וגם תעודות וחיבורים היסטוריים שהוּעֲלוּ על הכְּתָב לאַחַר זמן, (א)**הם** בבְחִינַת "מְקוֹרוֹת," (ב)**הן** בְּיַחַס לעוּבְדוֹת ההיסטוֹריוֹת (ג)**והן** בַּיַחַס לפֵירוּשָׁן.

Glossary

.5	גַּרְזֶן axe
	כְּלִי עבודה שימושי useful work tool
	נֶשֶׁק weapon
.6	מאורע event
	נפילת בָּבֶל בידֵי כּוֹרֶשׁ the fall of Babylon in the hands of Cyrus
	נתפס על ידי הנביא understood by the prophet
	התגשמות של הנבואה fulfillment of the prophecy
.7	דברי נבואה ושירה words of prophecy and poetry
	תעודות וחיבורים היסטוריים historical documents and writings
	הועלו על הכתב were put in writing
	לאַחַר זמן at a later date (time)
	בבחינַת מקורות have the status of sources
	בְּיַחַס לעוּבְדוֹת היסטוריוֹת with regard to historical facts
	פירושן their interpretation

Exercise #2: Determining the reference of the demonstrative pronoun

---

The rules to go by: see section 2.
What to do:
1. In each sentence, highlight the reference of the bolded pronoun.
2. Translate the sentence.
Example:

זהותם הָאֶתְנִית של יהודים בבוֹסטוֹן ובפילַדֶלפיה חזקה יותר מזו של יהודים בלוֹס אַנְגֶ'לֶס.

The ethnic identity of Jews in Boston and Philadelphia is stronger than that of Jews in Los Angeles.

---

1. ב-1950 הושווּ זכויותיהן (וחוֹבוֹתיהן) של הנשים לאלו של הגברים.

2. הוא אָמְנָם לְפְעָמים גֵּירֵש דיבוקים, אך פעל זאת בקדושת ספר תורה ובתפילות, ולא בדרכים אחרות.

3. מוטיב זה מופיע בכל הנוסחים המוכָּרים, והללו אינם מועָטים.

4. יהודים נָשְׂאו שֵמות זרים, וכאלה נשְׁתַמרו אף במקרא.

5. חֲשיבותו של המְשוֹרֵר עולה על זו של הכְּרוֹניקוֹן.

6. רש"י מפרֵש את הפסוק בדֶרך שונה לַחֲלוּטין מזו המקובלת כּיום.

Glossary

---

were made equal הושווּ	.1
rights זכויות	
duties, obligations חובות	
exorcised Dibbuks (demons) גירש דיבוקים	.2
did, acted פעל	
holiness of a Torah book and prayers קדושת ספר תורה ותפילות	
known versions נוסחים מוכרים	.3
few מועטים	
had (carried) נשאו	.4
were preserved נשתמרו	
the importance of a poet חשיבותו של משורר	.5
surpasses עולה על	
chronicler כרוניקון	
Rashi interprets the verse רש"י מפרש את הפסוק	.6
completely different way דרך שונה לחלוטין	
customary מקובלת	

7. דַּרְכָּהּ שֶׁל הַתְּנוּעָה סָטְתָה מִדַּרְכָּם שֶׁל רִאשׁוֹנֵי הַתְּנוּעָה וַאֲפִילוּ **מִזֹּאת** שֶׁל מְאוּחָרִים יוֹתֵר.

8. קָשֶׁה לִמְצוֹא הַקְבָּלָה שֶׁל מַמָּשׁ בֵּין הַפְּעִילוּת הַסִּפְרוּתִית שֶׁנַּעֲשְׂתָה בַּקְּהִילּוֹת אַשְׁכְּנַז בַּמֵּאוֹת הָעֲשִׂירִית וְהָאַחַת-עֶשְׂרֵה וּבֵין **זוֹ** שֶׁנַּעֲשְׂתָה בְּאוֹתָם יָמִים בִּסְבִיבָתָן.

9. הַסְּטָטִיסְטִיקָה מְעִידָה כִּי חֶלְקָהּ שֶׁל הָאִשָּׁה בַּסִּיפּוּר רַב **מִזֶּה** שֶׁל הַגֶּבֶר.

10. בָּבֶל וְרוֹמָא הִשְׁתַּמְּשׁוּ בַּהַגְלָיָה הַמוֹנִית שֶׁל עַמִּים שְׁלֵמִים כָּעוֹנֶשׁ עַל מְרִידוֹת בָּהֶן **וְזֹאת** מִתּוֹךְ הֲנָחָה כִּי עַם הַמְנֻתָּק מֵאַרְצוֹ יִתְפּוֹרֵר וְיֵיעָלֵם.

11. כְּשֶׁהַמַּצָּב הַכַּלְכָּלִי הָיָה טוֹב לֹא דָּרְשׁוּ הַסְּפָרַדִּים מִן הָאַשְׁכְּנַזִּים לְהִשְׁתַּתֵּף בַּתַּשְׁלוּמֵי הַמַּס לַשִּׁלְטוֹנוֹת, אַךְ מִשֶּׁהוּרַע הַמַּצָּב נֶאֶלְצוּ לִתְבּוֹעַ מֵהֶם הִשְׁתַּתְּפוּת מְלֵאָה בַּנֵּטֶל, לְמוֹרַת רוּחָם שֶׁל **הַלָּלוּ**.

Glossary

.7	תנועה	movement
	סטתה	diverged, strayed
	ראשוני התנועה	the first (founders) of the movement
.8	הקבלה של ממש	real parallels
	פעילות ספרותית	literary activity
	קהילות אשכנז	the communities in Germany
	בסביבתן	around them
.9	סטטיסטיקה	statistics
	מעידה	tells, indicates
	חלקה של האישה	the woman's role
.10	בבל ורומא	Babylon and Rome
	הגלייה המונית	mass exiling
	עונש על מרידות	punishment for rebellions
	מתוך הנחה	out of the assumption
	מנותק	disconnected, uprooted
	יתפורר וייעלם	will disintegrate and disappear
.11	המצב הכלכלי	the economic condition
	דרשו	demanded
	להשתתף בתשלומי המס לשלטונות	participate in the tax payments to the authorities
	משהורע המצב	when the situation worsened
	נאלצו לתבוע	were obliged to require
	השתתפות מלאה בנטל	full participation in the burden
	מורת רוח	displeasure

Exercise #3: Determining the reference of כך

The rules to go by: see section 2.3.
What to do: highlight the reference of כך in each sentence.
Example:

שמו של היישוב ניתן לו על כך שבאזור בו ממוקם היישוב ישב פעם שבט אפרים

---

1. השפה מיוחדת ב**כך** שהיא לא השתנתה במידה רבה מאז המאה ה-13.

2. עם התפתחות האינטרנט החלו בפרסום מודעות "דרושים" באינטרנט באתרים המיוחדים ל**כך**.

3. כלכלנים רבים הציעו בעבר תֵיאוֹריות שונות כיצד המַשבֵּרים הפינַנסיים מתפתחים וכיצד ניתן למנוע מ**כך** לקרות.

4. לאזרחי המדינה יש זכות לעזוב את המדינה ואף לחזור אליה בכל עֵת שירצו ב**כך**.

5. במשך השנים הבא פרוֹיֶקט "שוֹרָשים" ל**כך** שכל בני המשפחה עזרו באיסוּף יֶדַע על המש־פחה.

6. הסיפוֹרֶת נבדלת מהשירה בעיקר ב**כך** שחוקֵי הכתיבה שלה דומים יותר לדיבור יומיומי ותוֹכנה הוא לָרוב סיפורי.

Glossary

.1	במידה רבה to a great extent, greatly
	השתנתה changed
	מאז המאה ה- 13 since the 13th century
.2	התפתחות האינטרנט development of the Internet
	החלו began
	פרסום מודעות "דרושים" publishing "help wanted" ads
	אתרים sites
.3	כלכלנים economists
	משברים פיננסיים financial crises
	כיצד ניתן למנוע how it is possible to prevent
.4	אזרחי המדינה citizens of the state
	זכות right
	בכל עת שירצו whenever they wish
.5	פרויקט "שורשים" "Roots" project
	איסוף ידע collection of information
.6	סיפורת prose
	נבדלת is different from
	תוכנה its content
	לרוב סיפורי usually narrative

.7 אִרְגּוּנִים פִילַנְתָרוֹפְּיִים יהודיים בארצות הברית הבדילו את עצמם ממוֹדלים מוּקְדָּמִים יותר של צְדָקָה
יהודית, **בכך** שפעלו מחוץ למסגרות של בית הכנסת.

.8 הפִילַנְתָרוֹפִיה נעשתה למעין תַחֲלִיף של השוּתָּפוּת הדתית של היהודים וגם הֶחֵלָה לשקף את
ההבדלים המעמדיים והאִידֵאוֹלוֹגִיים הקיימים בתוכם, וּ**בכך** אפשר לראות בה חלק מתהליכי
המוֹדֶרְנִיזָצְיָה והחילוּן של יְהוּדֵי אמריקה.

Glossary

philanthropic organizations אִרְגּוּנִים פִילַנְתָרוֹפְּיִים	.7
distinguished themselves הבדילו את עצמם	
earlier models מוֹדלים מוּקְדָּמִים יותר	
Jewish philanthropy צְדָקָה יהודית	
frameworks מסגרות	
a kind of substitute מעין תַחֲלִיף	.8
religious fellowship שוּתָּפוּת דתית	
to reflect לשקף	
class and ideological differences הבדלים מעמדיים ואִידֵאוֹלוֹגִיים	
exist קיימים	
processes of modernization and secularization תהליכי המודרניזציה והחילוּן	

Exercise #4: Distinguishing between אותו as pronoun and as preposition

---

The rules to go by: see section 3.2.
What to do: determine the meaning of אותו, אותה, אותם, אותן and enter the number in the appropriate cell in the chart.

---

the preposition את	*that, those*	*the same*

1. במובן המצומצם יותר מתייחס המושג "שארית הפליטה" (1)**לאותם** 250 אלף יהודים אשר
יצאו ממחנות הכפייה, הריכוז וההשמדה, והפגינו רצון עז במיוחד להגר מאירופה לארץ
ישראל. (2)**אותו** רצון עז לעלות לארץ ישראל ייחד (3)**אותם** מיתר שרידי יהדות אירופה.

2. הרעיון הציוני מצא ביטוי ביצירותיהם של אמנים מן התקופה של ראשית הציונות. ביצירו־
תיהם ביטאו (4)**אותם** אמנים את הרעיון כי יהודה זוכה לשְׁחְרוּר על (5)**אותה** אֲדָמָה שבה
נִשְׁבְּתָה: אדמת ארץ ישראל.

3. שני החיבורים והציבורים שׁ(6)**אותם** הם מייצגים משתמשים (7)**באותן** מפות מוּשָׂגים.

4. הצורך בתבלינים היה מֵנִיעַ מֶרְכָּזִי במסעות למִזְרח בימי הבֵּינַיים על ידי סוחרים אירופאיים.
(8)**אותם** מסעות הם שהובילו בהֶמְשֵׁךְ אף לגילוי אמריקה.

Glossary

---

1. מחנות הכפייה, הריכוז וההשמדה   the forced labor and concentration camps
הפגינו רצון עז במיוחד להגר   demonstrated a particularly strong desire to immigrate
ייחד   set apart
יתר שרידי יהדות אירופה   the rest of the remnants of European Jewry
2. מצא ביטוי ביצירותיהם של אמנים   found expression in the works of artists
יהודה זוכה לשחרור   Judea wins liberation
נשבתה   was taken into captivity
3. חיבורים   compositions
ציבורים   publics
מייצגים   represent
מפות מושגים   conceptual maps
4. הצורך בתבלינים   the need for spices
מניע מרכזי   a central motive
מסעות למזרח   voyages to the East
ימי הביניים   the Middle Ages
סוחרים אירופאיים   European merchants
הובילו בהמשך אף לגילוי אמריקה   later on lead even to the discovery of America

---

Exercise #5: Distinguishing among אלה/אלו, אֵילוּ, אִילוּ

> **The rules to go by:** see section 4.1 and 5.
> **What to do:**
> 1. Determine the meaning of the bolded word(s) in each sentence and enter the sentence number in the appropriate cell in the chart.
> 2. Translate the sentence.

these	*which*	*if* (hypothetical)	*each other*

1. מִמְצָאִים **אלה** בהחלט מעודדים.

2. **אילו** אירועים השפיעו על הדמוּת?

3. החוק קובע **אילו** חובות וזכויות חלות על האזרחים.

4. **אילו** הופעלה התוכנית, ייתכן שמצבו של החינוך היה היום טוב יותר.

5. היו **אלו** ימים של שַׁלְווה והיטָהרות.

6. החכמים החליטו (א)**אֵילוּ** ספרים ייכָּללוּ בתנ"ך (ב)**ואילו** לֹא ייכָּללוּ בו.

7. המשׁטָר הסוֹבייֵטי והיָמין הלאוּמי בפולין האשימו **אלה** את **אלה** בפוגרוֹם.

Glossary

> 1. ממצאים   findings
> מעודדים בהחלט   certainly encouraging
> 2. אירועים   events
> השפיעו על הדמות   influenced the character
> 3. קובע   determines
> חובות וזכויות   obligations and rights
> חלות על האזרחים   apply to the citizens
> 4. הופעלה   was activated, was executed
> מצבו של החינוך   the state of education
> 5. שלווה והיטהרות   tranquility and purification
> 6. ייכללו   will be included
> חכמים   sages
> 7. משטר סובייטי   Soviet regime
> הימין הלאומי בפולין   the nationalist Right in Poland
> האשימו   blamed

8. ‏(א)**אילו** אירועים היסטוריים חשובים התְרחשו בתַאֲריכים (ב)**אלו**?

9. לְהַחְלטות **אלו** אין הַשפעה רבה בקְביעת אופְייה של המדינה לקְראת המאה הבאה.

10. ייצור הַמצות במכונה עוֹרֵר ברֵאשיתו מַחלוֹקֶת קשה בין הרַבָּנים בַּאֲשר לשְאֵלה אם **אלו** מצות כְּשֵרות.

Glossary

.8	התרחשו took place
	תאריכים dates
.9	השפעה influence
	קביעת אופייה של המדינה determining the character of the state
	לקראת המאה הבאה toward the next century
.10	ייצור מצות במכונה machine production of Matzahs
	עורר מחלוקת aroused controversy
	בראשיתו at its beginning
	באשר לשאלה with regard to the question
	כשרות kosher

4. ADJECTIVES
תוארי שם

This chapter discusses:

- Attributive and predicative functions of the adjective (overview and 1.2.1)
- Noun-adjective agreement (section 1)
- "Stand-alone" adjectives (section 2)
- Adjective strings (section 3)
- Adjective structural groups (section 4)
- Adjectives with a semantic prefix (section 5)
- Confusables: רב; words ending with ־י and ־ית.

This chapter will help the reader to:

- Apply adjective-noun agreement rules to resolve problems in word recognition and translation
- Recognize superlative phrases
- Recognize adjectives by their structural characteristics
- Translate adjective strings, hyphenated adjectives and prefixed adjectives
- Distinguish among various meanings of רב
- Determine the meaning of words ending with ־י and ־ית

Adjectives: an overview

Adjectives describe the noun that precedes them and are part of the noun phrase. In this role, they are called "attributive". Adjectives can also function as the predicate in verbless sentences, and in this role they are called "predicative." This dual role is seen in the following saying (based on Ecclesiastes 7, 1): טוֹב שֵׁם מִשֶּׁמֶן טוֹב *a reputation* (literally: name) *is better than riches* (literally: good oil), where טוֹב first functions predicatively (before the subject) and then attributively.

Adjectives agree with the noun in gender (masculine-feminine) and number (singular-plural); each adjective has, therefore, four forms. Attributive adjectives must also agree with the noun in definiteness.

The relevance of noun-adjective agreement rules to word recognition and reading comprehension is discussed in section 1 below. In section 2 are noted the exceptions to the rule that the (attributive) adjective directly follows the noun it describes. Section 3 distinguishes among three types of adjective strings (coordinated, stacked and hyphenated). Section 4 presents four major morphological (structural) adjective groups: adjectives deriving from present tense verb forms (participles), adjectives ending with -י, adjectives in the פָּעִיל pattern, and construct (סמיכות) adjectives. Section 5 discusses adjectives that have semantic (meaning-bearing) prefixes.

1. Noun-adjective agreement

1.1 Gender and number agreement

In contrast to so-called "irregular" gender markings in nouns, where a masculine noun may have a feminine ending and vice versa, adjective gender suffixes always match the gender of the noun. The gender suffix of the adjective is, therefore, a reliable indicator of the gender of the noun.

For example:

אבן גדולה	אבנים גדולות	*large stone(s)*	אבן is feminine
עיר רועשת	ערים רועשות	*noisy town(s)*	עיר is feminine
לילה טוב	לילות טובים	*good night(s)*	לילה is masculine
מקור חדש	מקורות חדשים	*new source(s)*	מקור is masculine

1.1.1 If two (or more) nouns of different genders are described by the same adjective, it takes the plural <u>masculine</u> suffix. For example: הגדרות והסברים חלקיים *partial definitions and explanations* (הסבר is masculine), מוסדות וקהילות יהודיים *Jewish institutions and communities* (מוסד is masculine).

1.1.2 When following a construct phrase (a phrase consisting of two or more nouns), the adjective may describe and agree in gender and number with either noun, depending on the desired meaning.

For example, in the phrase שינויי המפה הפוליטית, the adjective פוליטית agrees with the feminine singular noun מפה. The correct reading is, therefore, *changes in the political map*, NOT: *political changes in the map*.

When the nouns of the construct phrase have the same gender and number, the reader must determine on the basis of the context which one is described by the adjective. For example: מנהיגת המפלגה החדשה may mean *the new leader of the party* or *the leader of the new party.*

1.2 Noun-adjective definiteness agreement

1.2.1 The noun and the modifying (attributive) adjective also agree in definiteness. In contrast, when the adjective functions as a predicate, that is, in lieu of a verb, it does not take a definite article even when the noun (the subject) is definite (examples 1–2). This rule allows us to distinguish between sentences and non-sentences (phrases).
For example:

- Sentence: the noun is definite, but the adjective is not – the adjective is predicative
  הספר מעניין *The book is interesting*
- Phrase: the noun and the adjective agree in definiteness – the adjective is attributive
  ספר מעניין   *an interesting book*
  הספר המעניין   *the interesting book*

The position of the adjective vis-à-vis the noun is another indicator of its syntactic role: when the adjective comes <u>before</u> the noun, it has a predicative function.
For example:

מעניין במיוחד הסיפור הבא *The following story is particularly interesting*

1.2.2 An attributive adjective is required to take the definite article -ה even when the definiteness of the noun is expressed by means other than the definite article. In other words, an adjective modifying a proper noun (e.g., name of a person or place) or a noun with a possessive suffix must take the definite article even though the noun does not.
For example: in the phrase העיר העתיקה *the old city* both noun and adjective take the definite article -ה, but in יפו העתיקה *Old Jaffa* and עירם העתיקה *their old city* only the adjective does (example 3).

The adjective and the noun are shaded:

---

(1) יַצִיבָה יותר מחוזקה של הַחֶרֶב הייתה הַהֶגְמוֹנְיָה התרבותית של מסופוטומְיָה על האֵזור כּוּלוֹ.
The cultural <u>hegemony</u> of Mesopotamia over the entire region <u>was</u> more <u>stable</u> than the power of the sword.

The predicative adjective יַציבה is not definite and appears before the definite subject ההגמוניה. The second adjective, תרבותית, is attributive: it follows the noun it modifies and agrees with it in definiteness.
Note that when the predicate is an adjective, the past tense is expressed with the verb "to be" (here – הייתה); as seen here, this verb may appear after the adjective and at a distance from it.[1]

---

[1] See discussion of split verb phrases in Chapter 1, 3.3.

---

(2) הַיְסוֹד הַלִּירִי מְשֻׁתָּף לִשְׁלוֹשֶׁת הַסּוֹפְרִים.
The lyrical element is shared by the three authors.

In this example, לירי *lyrical* is an attributive adjective describing the noun יסוד *element*; both are definite. The adjective מְשׁוּתָף *common* functions as the predicate in the sentence and is, therefore, indefinite.

(3) בַּסֵּפֶר מְתוֹאָרִים טִיבָה וּקְדוּשָׁתָה הַמְיוּחָדִים שֶׁל הָעִיר.
In the book are described the special nature and holiness of the city.

The (attributive) adjective מיוחדים has a definite article, while the definiteness of the nouns טיב and קדושה is expressed via the possessive suffix (the final ה in each).
This example also illustrates the rule in 1.1.1 above that an adjective describing nouns of different genders (here, the masculine טיב and the feminine קדושה) takes the masculine form. Notice that the verb מתוארים, too, takes the masculine form.

1.3 The contribution of noun-adjective agreement rules to word recognition in unpointed text

1.3.1 The obligatory agreement in number between the adjective and the noun helps readers of unpointed text determine whether ות- at the end of the word should be read as וֹת- /ot/, an inflectional plural suffix, or וּת- /ut/, a derivational suffix which is part of the word and therefore – unlike וֹת- – is not removed when the word is looked up in the dictionary.
For example:

By itself, מעורבות can be read either as מְעוֹרָבוּת *involvement*, a singular feminine noun, or מְעוֹרָבוֹת *involved*, the plural feminine form of the adjective מְעוֹרָב *involved*. However, within the phrase מעורבות חזקה, the singular feminine form of the adjective indicates that the correct reading is מעורבות.

1.3.2 The obligatory agreement in definiteness between the noun and the attributive adjective helps the reader determine the lexical (dictionary) form of nouns and adjectives that begin with ה"א: if the adjective does not have a definite article, an initial ה"א in the noun must be identified as an intrinsic part of the word.
For example:

In the phrase השאלה תרבותית the adjective is indefinite; we therefore read השאלה as *borrowing* (הַשְׁאָלָה), not as *question* (הַ+שְׁאֵלָה). (See also example 32 below.)

Conversely, if the adjective begins with ה"א but the noun is indefinite, we interpret the initial ה"א as part of the adjective.
For example:

The adjective הגותיות in the phrase יצירות הגותיות cannot be interpreted as ה+גותיות *the gothic* because the noun יצירות is indefinite; the correct reading is, then, יצירות הֲגוּתִיּוֹת *philosophical writings*.

1.4 Adjective-noun agreement is an aid in distinguishing between noun+adjective phrases and noun+noun construct (סמיכות) phrases. In construct phrases, in contrast to noun+adjective phrases, no number, gender or definiteness agreement between the components of the noun phrase is required.[2]

2. "Stand-alone" adjectives

There are two circumstances in which the (attributive) adjective does not directly follow the noun it describes: when the adjective takes on the role of the noun, and when the adjective appears in a superlative phrase.

2.1 Adjectives used as nouns
Some adjectives may stand on their own, replacing the modified noun; they agree with that noun in gender and number. Such stand-alone adjectives are often definite.

The adjective replaces the noun in the following circumstances:

(a) The noun is inferable from the immediate context and has been omitted to avoid repetition (examples 4–5).

(b) The implied noun is אנשים *people* (example 6). Some adjectives that belong in this group are: רבים *many*, מעטים, אחדים *few*, חשובים *important*, אחרים *others*.

(c) The implied noun is non-specific, *something, that which*. For example: הָאָמוּר לְעֵיל *the above said [thing], that which is said above* (example 7).

The adjective is shaded:

---

(4) לבעיה זאת ניתנו תשובות שונות, אך **העיקרית** היא זאת:
[=לבעיה זאת ניתנו תשובות שונות, אך התשובה העיקרית היא זאת:]
Different answers were given to this problem, but the <u>main</u> answer (OR: <u>the main one</u>) is this:

The adjective agrees with the implied noun, תשובה.

(5) הם התגיירו אף על פי שידעו כי מעשה זה איננו מן **הקלים**.
[=הם התגיירו אף על פי שידעו כי מעשה זה איננו מן המעשים הקלים]
They converted to Judaism even though they knew that this deed was not among <u>the easy ones</u>.

The adjective קלים *easy* agrees with the implied noun מעשים.
איננו *is not* is translated here as *was not* to abide by English tense consistency rules.

---

(6) **רבים** עזבו משפחות וחברים, **אחרים** עברו תְּלָאוֹת קשות בדרך ואיבדו את **היקרים** להם.
<u>Many</u> left families and friends; <u>others</u> underwent severe hardships en route and lost their <u>dear ones</u>.

(7) **הסָּתוּם** מרוּבֶּה מן **המפוֹרָשׁ** בנוֹשֵׂא הנידוֹן.
The <u>unknown</u> is greater than the <u>known</u> (literally: the explicit) in the topic under discussion.

⚠**2.1.1** A shift in meaning sometimes occurs when the adjective becomes "stand-alone". For example:

- The adjectives הראשון *the first* and האחרון *the last* mean *the former* and *the latter*, respectively (examples 8–10).
- In the plural, הראשונים and האחרונים may refer, respectively, to early and later Jewish legal authorities.
- In the context of the Mishnah and Talmud, החכמים are *the sages* or *the rabbis*, not just any *wise men*. (Note also: תלמיד חכם *a Talmudic scholar*, NOT: *a clever student*.)
- הזקנים *the old* (men) may mean *the elders*.
- האדם הקדמון means *early man*, but הקדמונים are *the ancients*.

(8) נַקְדִּים כמה דברי מָבוֹא לְהַבְהָרַת המוּשָׂגִים "סִפְרוּת האַגָּדָה" ו"חז"ל," ונפתח **בָּאַחֲרוֹן**.
We shall start with introductory words to clarify the concepts "the literature of the Aggadah" and "Ḥazal," and open with the <u>latter</u>.

(9) כְּתוֹבוֹת באַרָמית התגַלוּ בכל רַחֲבֵי המזרח התיכון ואַסיה המֶרְכָּזית, כּוֹלל מצְרַים. **לאחרונה** יש מַשְׁמָעוּת חשוּבָה משׁוּם שתוֹדוֹת לאַקְלִימָהּ החַם והיָבֵשׁ שָׂרְדוּ שָׁם כְּתוֹבוֹת רַבּוֹת.
Inscriptions in Aramaic were found all over the Middle East and Central Asia, including Egypt. <u>The latter</u> has important significance since thanks to its hot and dry climate, many inscriptions survived there.

Note that the initial ד in למ"ד in **לאחרונה** goes with **יש**; in other words, לאחרונה here is not read as the adverb *recently*.

(10) אפשר לְהַשְׁווֹת את מַעֲשֵׂה ההַחְיָיאָה של לשוֹן המִקְרָא בסְפָרַד למעשה ההחייאה של העברית בסוף המאה הי"ט, אלא שבָּרַאשׁוֹן היתה שיבָה סִפרוּתית אל לשׁוֹן המקרא ואילוּ **האחרון**, כַּיָדוּע, הֲרֵיהוּ שיבָה אל הלשון כאֶמְצָעִי שימוּש בכל תְּחוּמֵי החיים.
It is possible to compare the revival of biblical language in Spain to the revival of Hebrew at the end of the nineteenth century, but in the <u>former</u> there was a literary return to the language of the Bible, whereas the <u>latter</u>, as is well known, was a return to the language as an instrument of use in all areas of life.

בראשון *in the former* refers to the revival of biblical Hebrew in Medieval Spain, while האחרון *the latter* refers to its revival at the end of the 19th century.

2.2 Adjective before noun in superlative phrases

In superlative phrases with ביותר *the most*, rather than follow the noun directly, the adjective may anticipate it as well as be separated from it.

---

(11) הַקָּשָׁה ביותר היא שאלת מוֹצָאָהּ של המילה.
The most difficult question is (that of) the origin of the word.

2.2.1 When the scope of the superlative is stated explicitly, the word ביותר may be omitted. The superlative meaning is then conveyed solely by the definite article before the adjective. The noun that delimits the scope of the superlative is introduced by the preposition -בְּ (sometimes preceded by -שֶׁ, examples 14 and 15).
For example:

In **בישראל** תל אביב היא העיר **העשירה בישראל** *Tel Aviv is the most affluent city in Israel*, provides the scope of the superlative, allowing for the dropping of ביותר.

To express *one of the most*, a plural noun and the preposition מִן/-מִ are used.
For example:

ההר הוא **מן הגבוהים בעולם** *the mountain is one of the highest in the world.* Alternatively, if אחת or אחד are added, מן can be dropped: ההר הוא **אחד הגבוהים בעולם**.

In comparative sentences too, יותר *more* may be omitted. The comparison is then signaled by the preposition (מ(ן). This is seen in טוב שם משמן טוב (above, in the chapter overview) as well as in the following:

טוֹבִים הַשְׁנַיִם מִן הָאֶחָד (קהלת ד ט)
The two are better than the one (Ecclesiastes 9.4)

The adjective is shaded and the noun that provides the frame of reference for the superlative is bolded:

---

(12) הוא היה הפּוֹרֶה בסופרי דורו.
He was the most prolific among the writers of his generation.

The phrase בסופרי דורו indicates the scope of the superlative.

(13) הַמַּעֲרֶכֶת האוּניבֶרסיטָאית החשובה והמשפיעה בעולם מְצויה באַרצות הברית.
The most important and influential university system in the world is found in the United States.

(14) החשובים שבכל קהילה הוזמנו לבוא לכֶנֶס.
The most important people in each congregation were invited to attend the convention.

---

(15) הַסֵפֶר עוֹסֵק בְּאַחַת הַבְּעָיוֹת הַקָּשׁוֹת וְהַמּוּרְכָּבוֹת בְּיוֹתֵר בַּהִיסְטוֹרְיָה הָאִינְטֶלֶקְטוּאָלִית,
אִם לֹא **הַקָּשָׁה שֶׁבָּהֶן.**

The book deals with one of <u>the most difficult and complex</u> problems in intellectual
history, if not <u>the most difficult (problem)</u> among them.

Here both the noun בעיות and the superlative word ביותר are omitted on second mention.

2.2.2 The superlative can also be expressed with an evaluative adjective (e.g., גדול, חשוב, טוב, יפה)
followed by a definite plural noun; the adjective then takes the construct (סמיכות) form.
For example:

גְּדוֹל הַמְלַחִינִים → הַמַּלְחִין הַגָּדוֹל בְּיוֹתֵר	*the greatest composer*
טוֹבֵי הָרוֹפְאִים → הָרוֹפְאִים הַטּוֹבִים בְּיוֹתֵר	*the best doctors*
חֲשׁוּבַת הַסּוֹפְרוֹת → הַסּוֹפֶרֶת הַחֲשׁוּבָה בְּיוֹתֵר	*the most important female author*

Another possibility is to repeat the noun; on its first occurrence the noun is in the construct
form (e.g., שאלת השאלות *the most important question*).

⚠ **2.2.3** Note that when ביותר appears with a <u>non</u>-definite adjective, it means *very* or *most*
(NOT: <u>*the most*</u>).
For example:

שאלה קשה ביותר *a very (most) difficult question*, but: **השאלה הקשה ביותר** *the most difficult
question.*

---

(16) קִיּוּם הַנֵּדֶר נֶחֱשַׁב לְחוֹבָה **קְדוֹשָׁה בְּיוֹתֵר,** שֶׁשּׁוּם דָּבָר שֶׁבָּעוֹלָם אֵינוֹ יָכוֹל לְשַׁחְרֵר מִמֶּנָּה.
The fulfillment of the vow was considered <u>a most sacred</u> duty from which nothing
in the world could release.

🏋#1   **3. Adjective strings**

When two or more adjectives describe the same noun, they may be either coordinated or
stacked. The implications of this distinction for comprehension and translation are discussed
below.

3.1 Coordinated adjectives
Coordinated adjectives are coequal in describing the noun. They are separated from each other
by commas and the last one in the sequence is joined to the previous one with ו- *and*. Coordinated adjectives are translated into English in the order of their appearance in Hebrew.

---

(17) סיבות אישיות **ו**כלליות

personal and general reasons

(18) דִּיּוּן מְחוּדָּשׁ**,** גָּלוּי וּבִלְתִּי-שִׁגְרָתִי

a renewed, open and unconventional discussion

3.2 Stacked adjectives

Stacked adjectives are hierarchical: in a sequence of two, the second adjective describes the preceding noun+adjective phrase. Stacked adjectives follow each other seamlessly, without commas or "and".

Unlike coordinated adjective strings, which are translated in the order of their appearance in Hebrew, stacked adjectives are translated backwards, beginning with the last one in the sequence.

The noun+adjective phrase that is modified by the stacked adjective is bracketed and shaded:

(19) חדשה [חֲשִׁיבָה צִיּוֹנִית]

new Zionist thinking
(NOT: Zionist new thinking)

(20) אוּטוֹפִּית [תּוֹכְנִית חִינּוּכִית]

a utopian educational plan
(NOT: an educational utopian plan)

(21) הַיָּחִיד [הַמִּפְגָּשׁ הַפּוֹלִיטִי הַרִשְׁמִי]

the sole official political encounter

3.2.1 Coordinated and stacked adjectives may occur in different configurations within one noun phrase.

The noun+adjective phrase that is modified by the stacked adjective(s) is shaded:

(22) פְּעִילִים וְדִינָמִיִּים [חַיִּים סִפְרוּתִיִּים]

active and dynamic literary life

(23) מְפוֹרָטִים וּמְדוּיָּיקִים [פְּרָטִים מֶרְחָבִיִּים]

particularized and accurate spatial details

(24) גְּדוֹלָה וַחֲזָקָה [מַמְלָכָה יְהוּדִית עַצְמָאִית]

a large and strong independent Jewish kingdom

(25) מְהֵימָנִים [יְסוֹדוֹת הֲלָכָתִיִּים, אַגָּדִיִּים וְהִיסְטוֹרִיִּים]

reliable halakhaic, aggadic, and historical elements

(26) עֲשִׁירָה, מַעֲמִיקָה וּרְחָבָה [הַשְׁוָואָה טֶקְסְטוּאָלִית וּלְשׁוֹנִית]

a rich, profound, and broad textual and linguistic comparison

(27) עֲמוּקָה [מַשְׁמָעוּת הִיסְטוֹרִית, תַּרְבּוּתִית וְרִגְשִׁית]

a deep historical, cultural and emotional significance

3.2.2 Although two (or more) coordinated adjectives that describe the same noun as a rule follow each other sequentially, on occasion they may be interrupted by parenthetical material.

> (28) חז"ל הוא כינוי כְּלָלִי – ראשֵׁי תֵּיבוֹת שמַּשְׁמָעם: חֲכָמֵינוּ זִכְרָם לברכה – וּמְאוּחָר יַחֲסִית.
> Ḥazal is a <u>general</u> and relatively <u>late</u> name – an acronym whose meaning is "our sages of blessed memory".

3.3 Hyphenated adjectives

Hyphenated adjective pairs (sometimes triplets, as in example 30) are conceptually related. The definite article – if required – usually appears only once, before the first adjective (example 31), but may also be added to the second adjective (example 33). All the adjectives in the string agree with the preceding noun in gender and number.

The ordering of the hyphenated adjectives in translation is often a matter of choice (what sounds best in English).

The hyphenated adjectives are shaded:

---

(29) חֶבְרָה פְּלוּרָלִיסְטִית-לִיבְּרָלִית
a <u>liberal-pluralistic</u> (OR: pluralistic-liberal) society

(30) כְּתָבִים פַּרְשָׁנִיִּים-תֵּיאוֹלוֹגִיִּים-פִילוֹסוֹפִיִּים
<u>exegetic-theological-philosophical</u> writings

(31) השיטה הַבִּיקּוֹרְתִּית-הַשְׁוָואָתִית
the <u>critical-comparative</u> method

The initial ה in הַשְׁוָואָתִית is part of the word, not a definite article.

(32) הֶקְשֵׁרִים סוֹצְיוֹ-תרבותיים
<u>socio-cultural</u> contexts

Since the phrase סוֹציו-תרבותיים is not definite, we read הֶקְשֵׁרִים as *contexts*, not as ה+קשרים *the connections*.
Note that -סוֹציו, the first component of the adjective string, is directly borrowed from English and (exceptionally) does not conform to Hebrew adjective formation rules.

(33) המודֶרְניזַצְיה הַכַּלְכָּלִית-הַחֶברתית
the <u>socio-economic</u> modernization

Both adjectives have a definite article.

(34) חוק בַּלְשָׁנִי-חֶבְרָתִי בְּסִיסִי
a basic <u>sociolinguistic</u> law

(35) דיאלוֹג תרבותי יהודי-ערבי
<u>Jewish-Arab</u> cultural dialogue

The hyphenated adjective is stacked.

(36) פעילות היסטורית חֶברתית-דתית מקיפה
a comprehensive <u>socio-religious</u> historical activity

𝞡#2 & #4   4. Adjective structural groups

Adjectives fall into a number of structural (morphological) groups. Four major groups are discussed below: adjectives identical with present tense verb forms (participles), adjectives ending with ‎י- (pronounced /i/), adjectives in the פָּעִיל pattern, and construct (סמיכות) adjectives.

4.1. Adjectives identical with present tense verb forms (participles)

4.1.1 Below are examples of adjectives identical with present tense forms in each of the seven *binyanim*, as well as in *pa'ul* (the passive participle form of *pa'al*):

רוֹוֵחַ, רוֹוַחַת, רוֹוְחִים, רוֹוְחוֹת	פָּעַל	*common, widespread*
יָדוּעַ, יְדוּעָה, יְדוּעִים, יְדוּעוֹת	פָּעוּל	*known, famous*
נָפוֹץ, נְפוֹצָה, נְפוֹצִים, נְפוֹצוֹת	נִפְעַל	*widespread*
מְבַטֵּל, מְבַטֶּלֶת, מְבַטְּלִים, מְבַטְּלוֹת	פִּיעֵל	*dismissive*
מְגוּוָן, מְגוּוֶנֶת, מְגוּוָנִים, מְגוּוָנוֹת	פּוּעַל	*varied*
מִתְקַדֵּם, מִתְקַדֶּמֶת, מִתְקַדְּמִים, מִתְקַדְּמוֹת	הִתְפַּעֵל	*advanced*
מַרְשִׁים, מַרְשִׁימָה, מַרְשִׁימִים, מַרְשִׁימוֹת	הִפְעִיל	*impressive*
מוּבְהָק, מוּבְהֶקֶת, מוּבְהָקִים, מוּבְהָקוֹת	הוּפְעַל	*distinctive*

4.1.2 The adjectives in this group are inflected for gender and number like the matching verbs. However, a few feminine singular forms are an exception:

- In *nif'al*, נֶהֱדֶרֶת *wonderful* is patterned on נִכְנֶסֶת (the נִקְטֶלֶת paradigm) while נִפְלָאָה (also *wonderful*) is modeled on the alternative נִקְטָלָה pattern.
- In *hif'il*, a few feminine singular adjective forms are modeled on the מַקְטֶלֶת paradigm, rather than the more common מַקְטִילָה.
  For example: סִיבָּה מַסְפֶּקֶת *sufficient reason*, סְקִירָה מַקֶּפֶת *comprehensive survey*, חֲשִׁיבוּת מַכְרַעַת *critical importance*, הַלָּשׁוֹן הַמַּשְׁפַּעַת *the influential language*.

The מַקְטֶלֶת form is typically used when the adjective has an attributive (rather than predicative) function.

> Since the third root letter of מכרעת and משפעת is the guttural ע, the second and third root consonants are sounded /a/ (rather than /e/). (This phenomenon is also seen in יוֹדַעַת versus כּוֹתֶבֶת.)
> Note also the verb form מַגַּעַת (rather than מגיעה) in the expression עד כמה שהיד מַגַּעַת *to the extent possible* (literally: *to the extent that the hand reaches*).

4.1.3 Not all adjectives in this group have corresponding past or future verb forms. For example:

מוּבהק *distinctive* does not have a corresponding past tense form, *הוּבהק,
מקוּבל *accepted, customary, popular* does not have the corresponding past tense form קוּבל*,
מְמוּשך *lengthy* does not have the corresponding past tense form מוּשך*.

⚠ In addition, although verb-derived adjectives are usually related in meaning to the verb, there are some whose meaning differs from that of the verb of origin.
For example: יש דמיון **ניכר** בין השניים *there is considerable similarity between the two* versus **ניכר** דמיון בין השניים *a similarity between the two is apparent.*

---

(37) "המְגילות הגְנוזות" של מְדבָּר יהודה גרמו להְתרגשות נִיכֶּרֶת בקהל הרחב ולפעילוּת קַדַחְתָּנית של חוקרים רבים.
The Dead Sea Scrolls caused <u>considerable</u> excitement in the general public and feverish activity among many scholars.

In this example, ניכרת – an attributive adjective – means *considerable*.

(38) רש"י היה דמות מרכָּזית בתרבות יהודֵי אַשכְּנז והשפעתו נִיכֶּרֶת מֵעֵבֶר לזמנו ולמקומו.
Rashi was a central figure in the culture of the Jews of Ashkenaz and his influence <u>is seen</u> beyond his time and place.

In this example, ניכרת is used as a verb, in the sense of *is seen, is apparent.*

Below are listed additional examples of participle forms whose meaning varies (to a lesser or greater extent) depending on whether they function in the sentence as an adjective or present tense verb.

participle	*binyan*	meaning as a verb	meaning as an adjective
שולט	פעל	*rules*	*dominant*
נֶעְלָם	נפעל	*disappears*	*hidden, secret*
מְאַלֵף	פיעל	*trains (animals)*	*instructive*
מְבַטֵל	פיעל	*cancels; dismisses*	*dismissive*
מְבוּסָס	פועל	*is based on*	*well-founded, proven, established*
מְצוּיָן	פועל	*is noted, pointed out*	*excellent*
מְסוּיָם	פועל	*is finished, completed[3]*	*certain*
מיוּחָס	פועל	*is attributed to*	*of distinguished lineage*
מַקִיף	הפעיל	*encompasses, surrounds*	*comprehensive, extensive*
מַכְרִיעַ	הפעיל	*determines, decides*	*decisive*
מוּרְכָּב	הופעל	*is made up of, consisting of*	*complex*
מוּשְׁלָם	הופעל	*is finished, completed*	*perfect; complete*
מוּחְלָט	הופעל	*is decided*	*absolute, total, complete*

---

[3] This meaning is rare.

4.2 Adjectives ending with ‎יִ-‎[4]

4.2.1 The adjectives in this group often derive from nouns.[5]
For example:

דָּתִי ← דָּת *religion* → *religious*, מְקוֹמִי ← מָקוֹם *place* → *local*.

Identifying the source noun is helpful in understanding the adjective. For example, סִיפּוּרִי (derived from סִיפּוּר *story*) means *narrative*, while סִפְרוּתִי (derived from ספרות *literature*) means *literary*.

4.2.1.1 Many adjectives in this group are foreign (loan) words.
For example:

פּוֹלִיטִי	*political*
מִיתִי	*mythical*
הֶטֶרוֹגֶּנִי	*heterogeneous*
אֶסְתֵטִי	*esthetic*
תֵּאוֹרֶטִי	*theoretical*

> Notice the omission of final "c" and "cal" in the borrowed adjectives (e.g., "political" does not become פּוֹלִיטִיקִי*).

4.2.2 When the source word ends with ‎הָ-‎, it may be converted into ‎ת-‎ to create the adjective.
For example:

בְּעָיָיתִי ← בְּעָיָה *problem* → *problematic*, חֶבְרָתִי ← חֶבְרָה *society* → *social*,
but: כַּלְכָּלִי ← כַּלְכָּלָה *economy* → *economic*.

4.2.3 Some adjectives in this group end with ‎נִי-‎.
For example:

רוּחָנִי ← רוּחַ *spirit* → *spiritual*, אוֹפְיָינִי ← אוֹפִי *character, personality* → *typical*,
עִירוֹנִי ← עִיר *city* → *urban*, תּוֹרָנִי ← תורה Torah → *religious* (e.g., סופר תורני *religious writer*).

The ‎נִי-‎ ending sometimes denotes an ideology (in some cases with pejorative overtones, for example, לוחמני, *combative, belligerent*). Note, therefore, the distinction between לְאוּמִי *national* and לְאוּמָנִי *nationalist*, or between שְׂמָאלִי *left-handed* and שְׂמָאלָנִי *leftist*. Note also the difference between פָּשׁוּט *simple* and פַּשְׁטָנִי *simplistic* and between חדש *new* and חדשני *innovative*.

4.2.4 Care should be taken to distinguish between an ‎יִ-‎ ending that is part of the adjective (e.g., מְקוֹמִי *local*) and the first person singular pronoun suffix (e.g., מְקוֹמִי *my place*).

4.2.5 The singular feminine form of adjectives in the ‎יִ-‎ group is invariably ‎ית-‎.
For example: פּוֹלִיטִית, דָּתִית, בְּעָיָיתִית, אוֹפְיָינִית, רוּחָנִית, כַּלְכָּלִית.

---

[4] The grammatical term for this adjective formation is *nisbeh*.
[5] Exceptionally, the adjectives נשי *feminine* and אימהי *mother-like, motherly* are derived from <u>plural</u> nouns: נשים and אימהות, respectively.

In the feminine plural, the ending is יות-, pronounced /iyot/.

For example: פוליטיות, דתיות, בעייתיות, אופייניות, רוחניות, כלכליות.

⚠ **4.2.6** Note the difference between דתית *religious*, an adjective (e.g., אידֵאולוֹגיה דתית *religious ideology*), and דתִיָה *a religious woman*, a noun, and similarly between יהודית (e.g., ספרות יהודית *Jewish literature*) and יהודיה *a Jewish woman*.

4.2.7 In the masculine plural form, the letter יו"ד appears twice: the first יו"ד is part of the adjective, the second is part of the plural suffix ים-. Thus: בעייתיים *problematic*, הטרוגניים *heterogeneous*, פוליטיים *political*.

The doubled יו"ד enables us to distinguish between certain adjectives and nouns.

For example:

- יהודיים *Jewish*, but יהודים *Jews* (e.g., כתבי יד יהודיים *Jewish manuscripts*, ההיסטוריה של היהודים *the history of the Jews*)
- נָשִׁיים *feminine* but נָשִׁים *women*
- זמניים *temporary*, but זמנים *times*.

4.3 Adjectives in the פָּעִיל pattern

The פָּעִיל pattern is frequently used nowadays to mint Hebrew equivalents for English adjectives with the "-able" suffix. The adjectives in this group are related to verbs in a variety of *binyanim*.

For example:

אָכִיל	*edible*	(אכל *eat*)
אָמִין	*credible, reliable*	(האמין *believe*)
הָפִיך	*reversible*	(הפך *turn over*)
זָנִיחַ	*negligible*	(הזניח *neglect*)
יָצִיג	*representative*	(ייצג *represent*)
יָשִׂים[6]	*applicable*	(יישׂם *apply*)
נָגִישׁ	*accessible*	(ניגש *approach*)
סָבִיר	*plausible*	(סבר *think, hypothesize*)
עָדִיף	*preferable*	(העדיף *prefer*)
קָבִיל	*acceptable*	(קיבל *accept*)

To create an antonym, the semantic prefix בִּלְתִי is typically used (e.g., בלתי הפיך *irreversible*).

---

(39) משפט זה איננו קָבִיל בעברית בת-זמננו.
This sentence is not <u>acceptable</u> in contemporary Hebrew.

Unlike the related verb form, קיבל, the adjective has no *dagesh* in the second root letter.
Note also the difference in meaning between קָבִיל – *acceptable* and מְקוּבָּל – *accepted, customary, prevalent, popular*.

---

6   ⚠Make sure to distinguish the adjective from the future verb tense form יָשִׂים *he will put*.

> **(40)** ההבדל בין שני הנוסחים אינו <u>זָנִיחַ</u>.
> The difference between the two versions is not <u>negligible</u>.
>
> **(41)** רואים אנו כי גבולותיה של ארץ ישראל הם עניין <u>גמיש</u> ואף <u>"נָזִיל"</u>.
> We see that the borders of the Land of Israel are a <u>flexible</u> and even <u>"fluid"</u> matter.

4.3.1. The פָּעִיל adjective pattern should be distinguished from two other similar sounding adjective groups:

(a) Adjectives ostensibly in the פָּעִיל pattern that do not have the "-able" meaning and are not related to verbs.
For example: בָּרִיא *healthy*, וָתִיק *veteran*, חָדִישׁ *modern*, מָהִיר *swift*.

(b) Adjectives whose initial /a/ sound is represented by a short rather than a long vowel (that is, by פַּתַח rather than קָמָץ), and is followed by a consonant with a *dagesh*.
For example: עַתִּיק *ancient*, יַצִּיב *stable*.

4.4 Two-word construct (סמיכות) adjectives

> יְפֵה עֵינַיִם וְטוֹב רֹאִי (שמואל א טז יב)
> *bright-eyed and good-looking* (Samuel I,16.12)

Two-word construct adjectives, formed by joining an adjective and a noun, date back to biblical Hebrew. They are somewhat similar to English "adjective + of + noun" phrases (e.g., *large of build*).

These construct adjectives have the following characteristics:

- The first word – though an adjective – follows noun construct formation rules whereby final הָ- (/a/) becomes תַ- (/at/) and final ים- (/im/) becomes יֵ- (/ei/).[7]
  For example:
  אישה **טובת** לב ← אישה טובָה *good-hearted woman*
  אנשים **טובֵי** לב ← אנשים טובים *good-hearted men*
- Certain internal vowel changes may also occur, just as they would if the adjective were a noun (e.g., -יְפַת ← יָפֶה, -יְפֵה ← יָפֶה).
- The adjective describes the quality of the next adjacent noun (לב in איש טוב לב), but it agrees in gender and number with the preceding noun, the one that is ultimately modified by this two-word construct adjective. Therefore:
  נשים טובות לב – אנשים טובֵי לב – אישה טובת לב – איש טוב לב *good-hearted man/woman/ men/women*.
- Construct adjectives are made definite by attaching the definite article -ה to the second element, namely, to the noun.

---

[7] See Chapter 2, 4.3.5.

For example:

האנשים טובי הלב ← אנשים טובי לב *(the) good-hearted people* (examples 45 and 48).

- A hyphen is sometimes inserted between the components of the construct adjective to signal that they constitute one lexical unit (e.g., איש טוב-לב).

4.4.1 The adjectives that are typically used to create construct adjectives are so-called "primary" adjectives such as קל *light; easy*, רב *great, much*, גדול *big*, כָּבֵד *heavy*, עָבֶה *thick*, רָחָב *wide* (examples 42–46), as well as verb-derived (present participle) adjectives (see 4.1 above) and adjectives in the פָּעוּל group (examples 47–49).

4.4.2 Some construct adjectives are metaphorical, that is, a literal translation of their individual components does not yield their meaning. For example, רְחַב ידיים cannot be translated as *wide handed*; it means *spacious*.

Other examples are: רְחַב אוֹפָקִים *broad-minded*, רְחַב יָד *generous*, חַד עין *perceptive*, קְצַר רוח *impatient*, קַר רוח *not excitable, composed*, צַר עַיִן *miserly; envious*.

The four forms of the adjective are shown in parentheses:

(42) שינוי **קל עֵרֶךְ**
(קַל-, קַלַּת-, קַלֵּי-, קַלּוֹת-)
<u>slight</u> change
(43) מַמְלָכָה **רַבַּת-עוֹצְמָה**
(רַב-, רַבַּת-, רַבֵּי-, רַבּוֹת-)
<u>powerful</u> kingdom
(44) כַּדֵּי קְבוּרָה **גְדוֹלֵי מְמַדִּים**
(גְדוֹל-, גְדוֹלַת-, גְדוֹלֵי-, גְדוֹלוֹת-)
<u>sizable</u> (literally: of large dimensions) burial urns
גדולי agrees with כדים, the first noun of the construct phrase כדי קבורה.
(45) השאלה **כְּבָדַת-הַמִּשְׁקָל**
(כָּבֵד-, כִּבְדַת-, כִּבְדֵי-, כִּבְדוֹת-)
the <u>weighty</u> question
(46) סְפָרִים **עָבֵי כָּרֵס**
(עַב-, עֲבַת-, עֲבֵי-, עֲבוֹת-)
<u>thick</u> books (literally: paunchy)
(47) פְּעוּלָה **טְעוּנַת מַשְׁמָעוּת**
(טָעוּן-, טְעוּנַת-, טְעוּנֵי-, טְעוּנוֹת-)
<u>significant</u> (literally: loaded) action
(48) הַנָּבִיא **עֲלוּם הַשֵּׁם**
(עֲלוּם-, עֲלוּמַת-, עֲלוּמֵי-, עֲלוּמוֹת-)
the <u>anonymous</u> prophet

(49) תְּסִיסָה חֶבְרָתִית **רְוִוּיַת מְתָחִים**
(רְווּי-, רְווּיַת-, רְווּיֵי-, רְווּיוֹת-)
tension-filled (literally: tension-saturated) social fermentation

(50) דֶּגֶם **יוֹצֵא דוֹפֶן**
(יוֹצֵא-, יוֹצֵאת, יוֹצְאֵי-, יוֹצְאוֹת-)
unusual (OR: out of the ordinary) model

4.5 Construct adjectives with -בַּעַל/-בַּעֲלַת/-בַּעֲלֵי/-בַּעֲלוֹת and
-חֲסַר/-חֲסָרַת/-חַסְרֵי/-חַסְרוֹת

Before a concrete (tangible) noun, the words בַּעַל and חֲסַר (both in the construct form) indicate, "having" and "not having," respectively. For example: דְּמוּת בעלת כְּנָפַיִם *a figure with wings, a winged figure*, חֲסַר בַּיִת *homeless*.

Before abstract nouns, -בעל and -חֲסַר create adjectives expressing, respectively, the existence or lack of a certain quality. For example: בעל סַבְלָנוּת *patient*, חַסְרֵי פְּנִיּוֹת *unbiased*.
In translation, the word -בעל is either ignored or rendered as *with*; -חסר is usually represented by a negative prefix (in-, ir-, un-) or suffix (-less).

(51) בְּמָרוּצַת הַמֵּאָה הָעֶשְׂרִים "גִּילְתָה" תַּרְבּוּת הַמַּעֲרָב אֶת הָאִינְדִּיָאנִים כְּקְבוּצָה אֶתְנִית **בַּעֲלַת חוֹכְמָה וְיָדַע**.
In the course of the twentieth century, western culture "discovered" the Indians as a wise and knowledgeable ethnic group (OR: as an ethnic group with wisdom and knowledge).

(52) אל"ף אִילֶמֶת הִיא **חֲסַרַת נִיקּוּד**.
A silent aleph is unpointed (OR: does not have vowels).

4.5.1 Note that not every adjective formed with -בעל has an opposite with -חסר, and vice-versa (e.g., חסר פניות *unbiased* does not have as an opposite בעל פניות*).

4.5.2 Adjectives with בעל can be intensified with the addition of the adjectives רב, מרובה or גדול. After חסר, the word כל (translated *any*) is used to intensify.
For example:

בַּעַל/בַּעֲלַת/ בַּעֲלֵי/בַּעֲלוֹת משמעות רבה/מרובָה   *very significant*
בַּעַל/בַּעֲלַת/ בַּעֲלֵי/בַּעֲלוֹת השפעה גדולה/מרובָה   *very influential*
חֲסַר/חֲסָרַת/חַסְרֵי/חַסְרוֹת כל כוח   *completely powerless, without any power*
חֲסַר/חֲסָרַת/חַסְרֵי/חַסְרוֹת כל משמעות   *completely insignificant, without any significance*

4.5.3 When a construct adjective with -בעל and -חסר is followed by another adjective, the words -בעל and -חסר are usually translated according to their literal sense of "having" and "not having". In other words, -בעל is rendered as *with* or *of*, and -חסר is translated as *lacking* or *without*.

For example:

בעל מְמַדִּים *large, sizable*, but: בעל ממדים מיתיים *with/of mythical dimensions*;
חֲסַר מַצְפּוּן *conscienceless, unscrupulous*, but: חֲסַר מַצְפּוּן חֶבְרָתִי *lacking/without social conscience*
or *socially unscrupulous*.

---

(53) אֲמִירָה בַּעֲלַת מַשְׁמָעוּת חֶבְרָתִית-דָּתִית נוֹעֶזֶת
a statement <u>with</u> a daring social-religious meaning

Compare with אמירה בעלת משמעות *a meaningful statement*.

(54) אוֹסֶף מִסְמָכִים חֲסַר עֵרֶךְ הִיסְטוֹרִי
a document collection <u>without </u>(OR: lacking) historical value

Compare with אוסף מסמכים חסר ערך *a worthless document collection*.

(55) פְּצָצַת הָאָטוֹם הִיא נֶשֶׁק בַּעַל עוֹצְמַת הֶרֶס וְהֶרֶג חֲסַרַת תַּקְדִים.
The atomic bomb is a weapon <u>with </u>(OR:<u> of</u>) unprecedented power of destruction
and killing.

4.6 Alternative expressions to -בעל and -חסר

(a) The verb נושא (literally: *bears, carries*) may sometimes be used instead of בעל.
(e.g., האגדה נושאת אופי ביוגרפי → האגדה בעלת אופי ביוגרפי *the legend has a biographical
nature*).

(b) A variant of חסר is מְחוּסָר (e.g., מחוסר יסוד *without basis, baseless, unfounded*).

(c) In certain set expressions, adjectives other than חֲסַר may indicate lack; they include:
נְטוּל-, חֲשׂוּךְ-, מְשׁוּלָל-, נֶעֱדָר-.
For example: נְטוּל פָּנִיּוֹת *unbiased*, נְטוּלַת אידֵאוֹלוֹגְיָה *non-ideological*, נְטוּלֵי חָזוֹן
lacking in vision, חֲשׂוּכֵי מַרְפֵּא *incurable*, מְשׁוּלָל תּוֹקֶף *invalid, unfounded*,
נֶעֱדָר עִנְיָין *uninteresting*.

4.6.1 The adjectives דַּל and מְעוּט are used with certain nouns to indicate paucity
(e.g., דַּל תּוֹכֶן *content-poor*, מְעוּט אֶמְצָעִים *poor*). In contrast, the adjectives עָשִׁיר, רַב and עָתִיר
indicate abundance (e.g., רַב אֶמְצָעִים *[a person] of means, wealthy*, עָתִיר מֶתַח *suspenseful*).

⚠ **4.6.2** חָסֵר/חֲסֵרָה/ חֲסֵרִים/חֲסֵרוֹת **as a verb and an adjective**
Care should be taken to distinguish (in unpointed text) between the adjective constituent
-חֲסַר, on one hand, and חָסֵר, on the other. חָסֵר functions as a verb (example 56) or an adjective (example 57) and is translated as *missing, lacking* or *absent*. A similar distinction should
be made (in unpointed text) between -חַסְרוֹת and חֲסֵרוֹת.

---

(56) לא **חֲסֵרוֹת** לכך דוגמאות.
There is no paucity of examples for this (OR: examples for this <u>are not lacking</u>).

(57) תַּפְקִיד אחד של הסְלֶנג הוא השלָמת מילים **חֲסֵרוֹת** בשָׂפָה.
One role of the slang is filling-in for words that are <u>absent</u> in the language.

4.7 Set expressions with בעל

בעל is also used in certain set expressions to indicate the following: ownership (e.g., בעל חנות *store owner*), a role or an activity (e.g., בעל תפילה *prayer leader*, בעל משפחה *a family man*, בעל דין *litigant*), authorship (e.g., בעלי המילון *the authors of the dictionary*), and an opinion, belief or trait (e.g., בעל אמונה *a believer*, בעל דמיון *imaginative*, בעל חלומות *dreamer*).

4.8 -בן and -בר

The nouns בֵּן and בַּר (from Aramaic) are used (sometimes interchangeably) to create two-word adjectives of the "-able" type (e.g., בן-ביצוע, בר-ביצוע *feasible, attainable*; בר השוואה *comparable*). And note also: בן חֲלוֹף *ephemeral*, בר סָמְכָא *expert, an authority*, בן חוֹרִין *free*, בן שׂיח *interlocutor*, בנות בְּרית *allies*, בני עֲרוּבה *hostages*.

The feminine singular form is בַּת; the plural forms are בְּנֵי (masculine) and בְּנות (feminine).

---

	(58) יַעַד **בַּר-הֲשָׂגָה**
	(יעדים בני-השגה)
an <u>attainable</u> goal	
	(59) הֶסְכֵּם **בַּר-קַיָּימָא**
	(הסכמים בני-קיימא)
a <u>durable</u> agreement	

4.8.1 With numbers, בן indicates age (בן מאה *a hundred years old*) or a time span (e.g., חודש בן שלושים יום *thirty-day month*, שנה בת שלושה עשר חודשים *a thirteen-month year*).

4.8.2 בן is also used to express the notion of belonging to a place, period or group. For example:

בני זמננו *our contemporaries*, בן הדור *member of the generation*, המציאות בת הזמן *contemporary reality*, בני משפחה *family members*, בנות העיר *the woman residents of the town*.

4.9 In a small sub-group of two-word adjectives, a preposition (-ל or -ב) intervenes between the adjective and the noun. The adjective then does not take the construct form. The definite article, if used, is appended only to the adjective (example 61).

---

(60) חֲשִׁיבוּת **גְּלוּיָה לָעַיִן**

<u>obvious</u> importance (literally: obvious to the eye)

(61) הדבר **הָרָאוּי לְצִיּוּן**

the <u>noteworthy</u> thing

(62) דַּקְדְּקָנוּת **רְאוּיָה לְשֶׁבַח**

<u>praiseworthy</u> meticulousness

(63) מוֹנִיטִין **שְׁנוּיִים בְּמַחְלוֹקֶת**

<u>controversial</u> reputation

(64) הֶבְדֵּל **נִיתָּן לְתֵיאוּר**

<u>describable</u> difference

(65) תַּהֲלִיךְ **יָחִיד בְּמִינוֹ**

<u>unique</u> process

In the example below appear adjectives of several patterns:

---

(66) עליית תרמ"ב הייתה תוצאתן של יוזמות **אישיות** וקבוצתיות שהיו **חַסְרוֹת דְּפוּס אִרְגּוּנִי** **מְלֻכָּד**.

The *Aliya* of 1882[8] was the result of <u>personal</u> and <u>collective</u> initiatives that were <u>lacking in</u> a <u>cohesive organizational</u> pattern.

Adjectives in the ־י group: אישיות, קבוצתיות, ארגוני
A present participle adjective: מלכד
A two-word adjective: חסרות דפוס

✗#4 & #2   5. Adjectives with a semantic prefix

Adjectives in this group have semantic (meaning-bearing) prefixes indicating spatial, temporal, quantity, attitude and other attributes. For example: ־בֵּין inter, ־רַב *multi*, ־עַל *super,* ־קְדָם *pre,* אַנְטִי־ *anti,* ־פְּנִים *intra-,* חוּץ־ *extra-*. These prefixes, whose prevalence is ascribed to the influence of English, are typically appended to adjectives in the ־י group.

5.1 As always, the adjective takes gender and number inflections to agree with the modified noun; however, the prefix remains unchanged.
For example: תשובות **חַד-מַשְׁמָעִיּוֹת**, תשובה **חַד-מַשְׁמָעִית** *unambiguous answer(s).*

---

[8] For the conversion of Hebrew dates (in letters) into Gregorian calendar dates see Appendix I.

5.2 The definite article (when used) appears only at the beginning of the adjective, appended to the prefix. This is an indication that the two elements, the adjective and its prefix, constitute one lexical unit.
For example:

*הרוֹמָן הפוֹסט-מוֹדרני *the post-modern novel* NOT: הרומן הפוסט-המודרני
הקֶשֶר הרב-דורי *the multigenerational connection* NOT: *multigenerational context.*

(This rule also applies to *הבעיה *the more important problem* NOT: הבעיה הַיוֹתֵר חשובה :יותר
היוֹתֵר החשובה.)

5.3 The writing conventions for prefixed adjectives vary:
A hyphen between the prefix and the adjective is optional. For example: בין תחומי or בֵּין-תְּחוּמִי *interdisciplinary.*
    In some cases, the prefix and the adjective blend into one word. For example:

בֵּינְלְאוּמִי, בין-לאומי	*international*
רַבְגוֹנִי	*variegated* (literally: *multi-colored*)
אַנְטִישֵׁמִי	*anti-Semitic*

5.4 Many semantic prefixes are foreign borrowings. For example:

פְּרוֹטוֹ-שֵׁמִי	*proto-Semitic*
פּוֹסְט-מוֹדֶרְנִי	*post modern*
אַ-פּוֹלִיטִי	*apolitical*
פְּרֶהִיסְטוֹרִי	*prehistoric*
פַּן-ערבי	*pan-Arab*

5.5 Some prefixes are Aramaic in origin. For example:

תַּת-הַכָּרָתִי	*subconscious*
בָּתַר-מִקְרָאִי	*post-biblical*
תְּלָת-מְמַדִּי	*three-dimensional*
חַד-מַשְׁמָעִי	*unambiguous*
דּוּ-לְשׁוֹנִי	*bilingual*

5.6 Negation is often expressed with the prefix בִּלְתִּי (e.g., בלתי ידוע *unknown*).

5.7 The words סָפֵק, כמעט, כְּאִילוּ, כמו may be used as prefixes for hedging a statement or expressing doubt and uncertainty; they are equivalent to *quasi-, pseudo-* or *semi-* in English (e.g., רעיון ספק מקורי *quasi-original idea*).

5.8 Below are listed examples of prefixed adjectives culled from scholarly articles:

אֵין-סוֹפִי	*infinite*
בּוֹ זְמַנִּית	*simultaneous*
בֵּין-אִישִׁיִּים	*interpersonal*

בִּלְתִּי אֶפְשָׁרִיוּת	*impossible*
דּוּ-מַשְׁמָעִי	*ambiguous*
חַד כִּיווּנִית	*unidirectional*
כְּלַל-אַרְצִיִּים	*countrywide*
לֹא רֶלֶוַוונְטִיוּת	*irrelevant*
עַל-אֱנוֹשִׁי[9]	*superhuman*
פְּנִים-קְהִילָתִית	*intra-congregational*
רַב-לְשׁוֹנִיִּים	*multilingual*
תַּת-אֱנוֹשִׁיוּת	*subhuman*

5.9 Note that some semantic prefixes occur also with nouns (e.g., קְדַם-דְּרִישָׁה *prerequisite*, אִי-סוֹבְלָנוּת *intolerance*, רב-לשוניוּת *multilingualism*, עַל-זמניוּת *timelessness*, דּוּ-קִיּוּם *co-existence*).

---

[9] עַל may also be used as a semantic suffix (e.g., מַעֲצֶמֶת-עַל *super-power*, מטרות-על *overall goals*).

Confusables

1. רב

Several uses and meanings of רב have to be distinguished from each other:

(a) An attributive adjective after a noun: **רב, רבָּה, רבִּים, רבּוֹת** *great, many* or *much*.
For example: עניין רב *great interest,* מספר רב *large number,* דורות רבים *many generations,* שאלות רבות *many questions.*

(b) A predicative adjective (e.g., בתקופה זו הייתה השפעת הארמית על העברית רבה *in this period, the influence of Aramaic on Hebrew was great*).

(c) The first word in a construct adjective: **רב-, רבַּת-, רבֵּי-, רבּוֹת-**.
For example: דיון רב-עניין *very interesting discussion,* מדינה רבת אוכלוסין *densely populated state,* שאלות רבות-בְּרֵרָה *multiple-choice questions,* ספרים רבֵּי מֶכֶר *bestsellers,* בתים רבי קומות *high-rise buildings*).

(d) A non-changing semantic prefix before an adjective, translated as *multi*.

For example: חברה רב עדָתית ורב תרְבּוּתית *multi-ethnic and multi-cultural society.* רב לאומי *multinational,* רב לְשוני *multilingual,*

(e) A semantic prefix before a noun indicating a military or police rank (e.g., רב אַלּוּף *lieutenant general,* רב חוֹבֵל *captain*) or a high professional standing (e.g., רב אוּמָן *master craftsman*).

(f) רַב *rabbi* (plural – רבנים).

(g) רָב *quarrel* – present and past tense singular masculine forms of the verb לריב.

(h) רַב *increase* (e.g., הרעש רב *the noise increased*; in formal use).

(i) רֹב (רוב) a *majority*.

(j) רבות functions also as an adverb, synonymous with הרבה *much*;[10] רבים has the meaning of *public* in the expressions ברבים *in public, publicly* and רשות הרבים *public domain.*

⚠ Make sure to distinguish רבות from the לְרַבּוֹת *including, inclusive of* and note the opposite, לְמַעֵט *excluding.*

---

2. י- and ית- endings

2.1 In unpointed text, <u>masculine singular adjectives</u> ending with י- (pronounced /i/) appear identical to <u>plural nouns</u> with the construct ending י- (pronounced /ei/). For example: זמְנִי *temporary* and זמְנֵי *the times of.*

---
[10] See Chapter 5, 2.3.2.

These endings can be differentiated by the position of the word in relation to the adjacent noun:

(a) If the word appears <u>after</u> a singular masculine noun, it is an adjective.

(b) If the word comes <u>before</u> another noun, it is a plural noun in the construct form.

Thus:

(a) מצב זמני *a temporary situation* – זְמַנִּי is an adjective after a singular noun.

(b) זמני קריאת התורה *the times of reading the Torah* – זְמַנֵּי is a plural noun in the construct form before another noun.

2.2 Adjectives belonging to the ־ִי structural group should also not be confused with the following:

(a) nouns that end with ־ִי or ־ִית. For example: אוֹפִי *character*, קוֹשִׁי *difficulty*; תַכְלִית *purpose*, תַמְצִית *extract*; *summary*, עִילִית *elite* (also *upper*, an adjective).

(b) names of languages (e.g., ארמית *Aramaic*).

(c) adverbs that are fashioned after the feminine form of adjectives.[11] For example: מַעֲשִׂית *practically*, כְּלָלִית *generally*.

References

ברי, תשמ"ח, 1988
הלוי, 7.1.03
שלזינגר, 1994, 2000
רודריג (שורצולד), 1994

Glinert, 1989
Quirk. & Greenbaum, 1975.

Chapter 4: Adjectives – Exercises

exercise #	topic	page
1	Translating adjective strings	179–180
2	Identifying adjectives	181–182
3	Matching adjectives derived from foreign words with their English equivalent	183
4	Changing the gender or number in adjectives of different patterns	184–185

Exercise #1: Translating adjective strings

The rules to go by: see section 3.
What to do: translate the phrases into English.
Example:

תמורה תרבותית דרמטית

dramatic cultural change

---

1. הֶיבֵּט בַּלְשָׁנִי מְקוֹרִי

2. התגובה הספונטנית הראשונה

3. רעיונות לאומיים מְשִׁיחִיים

4. תיעוד אַרְכִיוֹני וסִפְרוּתי עשיר

5. תעודה פוליטית מובהקת

6. עולם פנימי עשיר ומעניין

7. אֲווירָה עירונית חַיָה ונוֹשֶׁמֶת

8. פעילוּת חֶברתית וכלכלית מְגוּוֶנֶת

9. ניצָחון מְדיני, כלכלי וצְבָאי גדול

10. מִתְקָנים חקלָאיים ותעשייתיים יְשָנים

11. כּוֹחַ פוליטי וצְבָאי ניכָּר

12. מפגש רב-תרבותי טעון

Glossary

aspect	הֵיבֵט	1.
reaction	תגובה	2.
ideas	רעיונות	3.
documentation	תיעוד	4.
document	תעודה	5.
atmosphere	אווירה	7.
activity	פעילות	8.
victory	ניצחון	9.
installations	מתקנים	10.
power	כוח	11.
encounter, meeting	מפגש	12.

13. יצירה ספרותית ואינטלקטואלית לא-יהודית

14. סביבה חֶברתית פתוּחה, סוֹבְלָנית ורב-תרבותית

Glossary

13. יצירה	work
14. סביבה	environment

Exercise #2: Identifying adjectives

> **The rules to go by:** see sections 4 and 5.
> **What to do:**
> 1. Identify the adjectives in each sentence. The number of adjectives in the sentence is indicated in parentheses (hyphenated adjectives are counted as one adjective).
> 2. Underline the adjectives borrowed from English.
> 3. Translate the sentences.
> **Example:**
>
> הַסֵפֶר כּוֹלֵל סְקִירָה מַקִּיפָה וּמְעַנְיֶינֶת שֶׁל הָעִיתוֹנוּת הַיְּהוּדִית בָּאֲרָצוֹת הַקֵּיסָרוּת הָאוֹסְטְרִית עַל כָּל גְּוָונֶיהָ הַלְּשׁוֹנִיִּים, הַדָּתִיִּים וְהַפּוֹלִיטִיִּים. (7)
>
> The book includes a comprehensive and interesting survey of Jewish journalism in the countries of the Austrian Empire with all of its linguistic, religious and political varieties.

1. עוֹלָה הַשְׁאֵלָה בְּדָבָר הַיַחַס בֵּין כּוֹחוֹ הַמָאגִי וְכוֹחוֹ הַסְפִּירִיטוּאָלִי שֶׁל הַבַּעַל-שֵׁם-טוֹב, וְחֶלְקָם הַפְּרוֹפוֹרְצְיוֹנָלִי בִּפְעוּלוֹת הָרִיפּוּי. (3)

2. בְּפִילוֹסוֹפְיָה שֶׁלוֹ הָיָה שִׁילוּב שֶׁל שַׁמְרָנוּת תַּרְבּוּתִית וְאֶסְתֶטִית וְרָדִיקָלִיוּת חֶבְרָתִית וּפוֹלִיטִית. (4)

3. סָפֵק אִם יֶשְׁנוֹ בְּתַרְבּוּת הַמַּעֲרָב הוֹגֶה דֵעוֹת שָׁנוּי בְּמַחְלוֹקֶת, אַמְבִּיוַוֹלֶנְטִי וּבַעַל פָּנִים רַבּוֹת יוֹתֵר מִפְרִידְרִיך נִיטְשֶׁה. (3)

4. אָז גַם נוֹדְעוּ פְּרָטִים נוֹסָפִים עַל הַתַּגְלִית, אוּלָם מֵידָע זֶה הָיָה כּוֹלְלָנִי וּבִלְתִי מְדוּיָיק. (3)

Glossary

1. יחס   relationship
   הבעל-שם-טוב   the Ba'al Shem Tov (the founder of the Chassidic movement)
   פעולת הריפוי   the act of healing
2. שילוב   combination, integration
   שמרנות   conservatism
3. ספק אם   it is doubtful whether
   הוגה דעות   philosopher
   פרידריך ניטשה   Friedrich Nietzsche
4. נודעו   became known
   פרטים   details
   תגלית   discovery
   מידע   information

5. צָרִיךְ לִזְכּוֹר כִּי הַכְּנַעֲנִיּוּת – מְקוֹרִית, מְרַתֶּקֶת, אוֹ מַרְגִּיזָה כְּכָל שֶׁתִּהְיֶה – הִיא רַק רְכִיב אֶחָד בְּתוֹךְ מַעֲרֶכֶת שֶׁל מְתָחִים חֶבְרָתִיִּים וְתַרְבּוּתִיִּים שֶׁאָנוּ נְתוּנִים בָּהּ. (5)

6. טֶקְסְטִים רַבִּים – הֵן הַסִּפְרוּתִיִּים וְהֵן הָאוֹתֶנְטִיִּים (יוֹמָנִים, מִכְתָּבִים וְכַדּוֹמֶה) – אֵינָם מְבַטְּאִים חֲוָיָה אִישִׁית, אֶלָּא נִכְתָּבִים כְּדֵי לְהִתְאִים לְמוֹדֶל הַדּוֹמִינַנְטִי. (5)

7. חוֹפֶשׁ הָרָצוֹן נִבְחָן בַּסֵּפֶר הֵן מִנְּקוּדַת רְאוּת מַדָּעִית, פִילוֹסוֹפִית וְתֵאוֹרֶטִית, וְהֵן מִנְּקוּדַת רְאוּת מָסוֹרְתִית וּמוּסָרִית-אִישִׁית. (5)

8. זֶהוּ סֵפֶר קָרִיא, בָּהִיר וְנָגִישׁ, מְעַנְיֵן וְשָׁקוּל, אַף שֶׁלֹּא נֶעֱדֶרֶת מִמֶּנּוּ נִימָה אֲפוֹלוֹגֶטִית. (6)

9. הַסִּפּוּר מִתְרַחֵק מִפָּתוֹס גַּס וּמוּגְזָם מֵאַחַר שֶׁהוּא מְאֻפָּק, מָמוּתָן וּמְפוֹרָט וְנָע תָּמִיד בֵּין הַמִּשְׁלָבִים – הַפָּתֶטִי, הַקּוֹמִי, הַטְרִיוִויָאלִי וְהַנִּשְׂגָּב. (9)

10. בָּעֲלִיָּיה הָרִאשׁוֹנָה נִקְבְּעוּ רִאשׁוֹנֵי הַדְּפוּסִים הַתַּרְבּוּתִיִּים שֶׁל הַחֶבְרָה הַיִּשְׂרְאֵלִית בֶּעָתִיד. כְּבָר אָז עֻצְּבָה דְּמוּת הָאָדָם הָעִבְרִי הֶחָדָשׁ, כְּבָר אָז הִתְקַיֵּים מִפְגָּשׁ בֵּין-עֲדָתִי, כְּבָר אָז נִרְאוּ מְגַמּוֹת כְּנַעֲנִיּוֹת, שֵׁמִיוֹת וּמִזְרָחִיּוֹת בַּלְּאוּמִיּוּת הָעִבְרִית. (10)

Glossary

.5	כנעניות	Cannanism (an Israeli political-ideological movement)
	רכיב	component
	מתחים	tensions
.6	חוויה	experience
.7	חופש הרצון	free will
	נבחן	is examined
	נקודת ראות	viewpoint
.8	נעדרת ממנו	absent from it
	נימה	overtone
.9	משלבים	registers
.10	דפוסים	patterns
	עוצבה	was formed
	התקיים מפגש	an encounter took place
	לאומיות	nationality

Exercise #3: Matching adjectives derived from foreign words with their English equivalent

> **The rule to go by:** see section 4.2.1.1.
> **What to do:** match the English adjective with the number of its Hebrew equivalent. The first one is an example.

6	aesthetic	אוניברסלי	.1
	allegorical	אותנטי	.2
	ambivalent	אינטלקטואליים	.3
	apologetic	אלגורית	.4
	authentic	אמביוולנטי	.5
	comic	אסתטית	.6
	dominant	אפולוגטית	.7
	ethical	אתי	.8
	intellectual	דומיננטי	.9
	mystical	טכנולוגיים	.10
	physical	מיסטיות	.11
	pathetic	פיזיים	.12
	proportional	פרופורציונלי	.13
	romantic	פתטי	.14
	technological	קומיות	.15
	theological	רומנטית	.16
	theoretical	תאולוגי	.17
	universal	תאורטיות	.18

Exercise #4: Changing the gender or number in adjectives of different patterns

> **Summary of the rules to go by** (see sections 4 and section 5):
> • Adjectives derived from present tense verb forms are inflected for gender and number like the matching verbs.
> • Adjectives of the -י group are inflected with -ת in the feminine singular, -ים in the masculine plural, and -ות in the feminine plural.
> • In two-word construct adjectives, the second word (the noun) remains unchanged; the first word (the adjective) agrees with the noun that is described.
> • Hyphenated adjectives agree with the noun (and with each other) in gender and number.
> • Semantic prefixes do not inflect for number and gender, but can take a definite article.
> **What to do:** change the adjective to agree with the given noun; retain the definite article (if used).
> **Example**:
>
> מצב רווי מתחים — אווירה רוויַת מתחים
> *tension-saturated (very tense) situation/atmosphere*

_____	שינוי	שינויים פְּעוּטֵי-עֵרֶךְ *insignificant changes*	1.
_____	תופעות	תוֹפָעָה רַבַּת חֲשִׁיבוּת *important phenomenon*	2.
_____	מקרים	מִקְרֶה מְעוֹרֵר גיחוּך *funny* (literally: *laughter-arousing*) *event*	3.
_____	נשים	אנשים מַשְׂכִּילים ויוֹדְעֵי סֵפֶר *well-educated and literate people*	4.
_____	יַהֲדוּת פולין	יהודֵי פולין לְמוּדֵי הַסֵּבֶל *Polish Jews versed in suffering*	5.
_____	שינויים	שינוי מַרְחיק לֶכֶת *far-reaching change*	6.
_____	התפתחות	הִתְפַּתְחוּיוֹת חַסְרוֹת תַקְדים *unprecedented developments*	7.
_____	עיתונאים	עיתונַאי קל הִתְרַשְׁמוּת *impressionable journalist*	8.
_____	הקוראת	הקוראות בנות הזמן *the contemporary readers*	9.
_____	תכניות	תכנית נְטוּלַת אידאולוגיה *non-ideological program*	10.
_____	היישוב	היי-שובים הלא-קוֹלֶקְטיביים הראשונים *the first non-collective settlements*	11.

_____	בעיות	12. בעייה חברתית-תרבותית *socio-cultural problem*
_____	כוח	13. כוחות פוליטיים-דמוגרפיים *political-demographic powers*
_____	מסרים	14. מֶסָר בלתי רֶלֶוַונְטִי *irrelevant message*
_____	מקור	15. מקורות חוּץ-לְשׁוֹניים *extra-linguistic sources*
_____	משוררות	16. מְשׁוֹרֵר בָּרוּךְ-כִּישָׁרוֹן *talented poet*
_____	מעשים	17. מעשה הָרֵה-אסון *disastrous deed*

5. ADVERBS
תוארי פועל

This chapter discusses:

- The meanings, forms and uses of adverbs (section 1)
- Various structural types of adverbs of manner (section 2)
- Adverbial verbs and internal objects used as adverbial expressions (section 3)
- Adverbs of time (Appendix)

This chapter will help the reader to:

- Recognize adverbs of manner by their structural characteristics
- Distinguish between adjectives and adverbs
- Recognize and translate verb phrases with adverbial functions

1. Adverbs: use, meaning and form

1.1 An adverb is a word, phrase or clause that describes a verb (example 1), an adjective (example 2) or another adverb (example 3).

Adverbs that are more than one word long are referred to as adverbials. Clauses with adverbial function indicate cause, condition, result, purpose, contrast and the like.

The adverb is shaded:

---

(1) הָעִנְיָין נִזְכָּר **בְּקִצְרָה** בְּפֶרֶק הראשׁון.
The matter is mentioned <u>briefly</u> in the first chapter.

(2) עוּבְדָה זאת מְעַנְיֶינֶת **בְּאוֹפֶן מְיוּחָד** וּמוּבְלֶטֶת **בְּצֶדֶק** על ידי המְחַבֵּר.
This fact is <u>particularly</u> interesting and is <u>rightly</u> emphasized by the author.

The first adverb describes the adjective מעניינת, the second adverb describes the verb מובלטת.

(3) הרוֹב הָאֶתְנִי מחזיק לְמַעֲשֶׂה **בִּלְעָדִית** בכּוֹח הפוליטי.
The ethnic majority holds political power, <u>in effect, exclusively</u>.

The adverb למעשה modifies the adverb בלעדית.

1.2 Adverbs typically answer the questions "when?" (adverbs of time), "where?" (adverbs of place), "how?" (adverbs of manner) and "to what extent?" (adverbs of degree). Some examples are:

Adverbs of time: תמיד *always,* מִזְמַן *long ago;*[1]
Adverbs of place: שָׁם *there,* פנימה *inside;*
Adverbs of manner: בקצרה *briefly,* באופן מיוחד *especially;*
Adverbs of degree: (עד) מאוד כֹּה, כָּל כָּךְ *so,* *very* (much), יותר *more,* בְּיוֹתֵר *most,* דַי, לְמַדַי *quite, sufficiently,* מִדַּיי *too (much),* בְּהַרְבֵּה *by much.*

> The final ה"א in פנימה, known as the directional ה"א, replaces the directional prepositions -לְ or אֶל. Other examples are: צפונה *to the north,* אַרְצָה *to the Land (of Israel).*

1.3 Some adverbs, called sentential or comment adverbs (also: disjuncts), evaluate or comment on the entire sentence (examples 4–6). When they appear at the beginning of the sentence, they are followed by a comma.
Some examples for comment adverbs are:

כָּאָמוּר[2]	*as has been said/mentioned*
כַּיָּדוּעַ	*as is (well) known*
כַּנִּרְאֶה	*apparently*

---

[1] See appendix at the end of the chapter for a comprehensive list by category of adverbs of time.
[2] See discussion of כזכור, כאמור and כידוע in Chapter 11, 2.3.1.

כַּזָּכוּר	as you may remember (literally: as is remembered)
כַּמּוּבָן	of course
כִּכְלָל	in general, as a rule
לִכְאוֹרָה	supposedly
לְלֹא סָפֵק	undoubtedly
לְמַעֲשֶׂה	in fact
לְסִיכּוּם	in summary
לָרוֹב	usually, generally, in most cases

> ⚠️ Another meaning of **לָרוֹב** (when appearing at the end of the clause) is: *in abundance, in great numbers, many* (e.g., הוא כתב ספרים לָרוב *he wrote many books*).
> Make sure to distinguish the adverb from the noun רוב *majority* when it appears with an incidental preposition (e.g., הוא שייך לָרוב הדומם *he belongs to the silent majority*; לְרוב הקוראים הוא ידוע בשם העט שלו *to most readers he is known by his pen name*).

---

(4) **לְמַרְבֵּה הַצַּעַר**, נשתמרו רק דפים אחדים מכְּתַב היד.
Unufortunately, only a few pages of the manuscript were preserved

The adverb expresses the writer's attitude to the information that is conveyed in the sentence. This is also seen in the next two examples.

(5) **מִבְּחִינָתֵנו**, המִמְצָא הזה הוא רַב מַשְׁמָעוּת.
From our point of view, this finding is very significant.

(6) חידושם של המְחַברים הוא **קוֹדֶם כל** חידוש שבגישה.
The innovation of the authors is, first of all, in the approach.

1.4 Unlike adjectives, which agree in gender (masculine or feminine) and number (singular or plural) with the noun they modify, adverbs have a fixed form. This rule helps the reader determine the part of speech – adjective or adverb – of some words that can function as both (see 2.3.2–2.3.4 below).

1.4.1 However, a few adverbs (e.g., לְבַד *alone*, לְאַט *slowly*, עוֹד *still*, דַי *enough*, בְּעִיקָר *mainly*), may receive, in formal style, pronominal suffixes; these refer to the subject.

(7) הַחֶבְרָה הַיִּשְׂרְאֵלִית חֲזָקָה דַּיָּהּ לְנַהֵל בְּתוֹכָהּ אֶת הַמַּחֲלוֹקוֹת הַחֲרִיפוֹת עַל זֶהוּתָהּ.
Israeli society is <u>sufficiently</u> strong to conduct within itself the intense controversies about its identity.

The suffix refers to חברה.
An alternative wording would be: הַחֶבְרָה הַיִּשְׂרְאֵלִית דִּי חֲזָקָה
The pointed and unpointed full spelling of the third person inflected forms of דַּי are:
דַּיּוֹ (דיו), דַּיָּהּ (דייה), דַּיָּם (דיים), דַּיָּן (דיין)
(In the Passover Haggadah: דַּי דַּיֵּינוּ *sufficient for us*.)

(8) כְּלָלִים אֵלֶּה עוֹדָם תְּקֵפִים.
These rules are <u>still</u> valid.

The suffix refers to כללים.
The third person inflected forms of עוֹד are: עוֹדָן, עוֹדָם, עוֹדָהּ/עוֹדֶנָּה, עוֹדוֹ/עוֹדֶנּוּ.
An alternative wording (where the adverb – עֲדַיִן – is not inflected) would be: כְּלָלִים אֵלֶּה
עֲדַיִן תְּקֵפִים

(9) הָעֲגָה שֶׁל דּוֹר תָּש"ח דָּעֲכָה לְאִיטָּהּ.
The slang of the 1948 generation <u>slowly</u> died out.

The suffix refers to עגה. Alternatively: דעכה לְאָט.

(10) פָּרָשַׁת כִּיבּוּשׁ הָאָרֶץ כְּפִי שֶׁהִיא מוּצֶגֶת בְּסֵפֶר יְהוֹשֻׁעַ הִיא בְּעִיקָרָהּ קוֹנְסְטְרוּקְצִיָּה סִפְרוּתִית-תֵּאוֹלוֹגִית.
The story of the conquest of the Land of Israel as it is presented in the Book of Joshua is <u>mainly</u> a literary-theological construction.

The suffix refers to פרשה; בעיקר could be used here instead.

(11) צַוֵּוי הַגֵּרוּשׁ לֹא קוּיְּמוּ בִּמְלוֹאָם.
The orders of expulsion were not carried out <u>in full</u>.

The suffix refers to צווים.

(12) פְּרוֹזָה הִיא סִגְנוֹן כְּתִיבָה וְדִיבּוּר הַדּוֹמֶה בִּיסוֹדוֹ לְדִיבּוּר הַיּוֹמְיוֹמִי.
Prose is writing and speaking style that <u>essentially</u> is similar to every day speech.

The suffix refers to סגנון.

2. Adverbs of manner: structural types

Adverbs of manner merit special discussion since they appear frequently in scholarly writing and are structurally very heterogeneous.

These adverbs answer the question: "how (does the action take place)?" and usually appear directly after the verb.

Alongside a small and closed group of primary adverbs of manner such as שׁוּב *well,* הֵיטֵב
again, לְאַט *slowly,* מַהֵר *fast,* there exist many derived (created) adverbs which fall into a number of structural groups. These are presented in the next section.

2.1 Many adverbs are created by **prefixing a preposition to a noun or an adjective.**
This is a derivational mechanism somewhat akin to the addition in English of the -ly suffix to
an adjective in order to create an adverb.

> Some adverbs – not all of them adverbs of manner – are formed with more than one
> preposition (e.g., לַבַּסוֹף *finally,* מִלְכַתְּחִילה *from the start,* מִלְמַעְלה *from the top*).

2.1.1 מִ-, לְ-, כְּ-, בְּ- + adjective or noun
The four prepositions referred to mnemonically as בַּכְלָ"ם create adverbs of manner when
prefixed to adjectives or nouns. In this role, the prepositions lose their original grammatical
and semantic meaning.

Some noun-derived adverbs are:

בְּהַדְרָגָה	*gradually*
בְּוַודָּאוּת	*with certainty*
בְּנֶאֱמָנוּת	*faithfully*
לְעֵרֶךְ, בְּעֵרֶךְ; בְּקֵירוּב	*approximately*
לַהֲלָכָה	*theoretically*

Some adjective-derived adverbs are:

בְּמוּדע	*consciously*
בְּגָלוּי	*openly*
בְּמַפְתִּיעַ	*surprisingly*
כַּנִּרְאֶה	*apparently*
מֵחָדָשׁ	*anew*

Note that in some cases a different preposition changes the meaning of the adverb:

- בְּרָצוֹן *gladly, willingly;* מֵרָצוֹן *voluntarily*
- כַּהֲלכה *properly;* לַהֲלכה *theoretically*

> ⚠ Be aware that neither לַהֲלכה nor כַּהֲלכה mean *according to the Ḥalakhah* (Jewish law);
> this meaning would be expressed by לפי ההלכה.

2.1.2 As illustrated in examples 13–17, an initial ambiguity could arise due to the dual role of the preposition, whether it is a component of the adverb, or an independent part of speech linking a verb, an adjective or a noun to an object complement.

The ambiguous word is shaded:

---

(13) לְעִתִּים יוֹדְעִים אָנוּ בְּפֵירוּשׁ שֶׁהָאָמָן הַמְצַיֵּיר לֹא הָיָה מִבְּנֵי-בְּרִית.
Sometimes we know <u>explicitly</u> that the artist was a non-Jew.

We read בפירוש as an adverb, not a noun preceded by a preposition, since the reading *we know in the explication* does not make sense. (The reading *according to the explication* would require the phrase לפי הפירוש.)

(14) הַמִּמְצָא הָאַרְכֵאוֹלוֹגִי שֶׁל סַמָּנֵי תַרְבּוּת נוֹסָפִים כְּגוֹן צְמָחִים אוֹ בַּעֲלֵי חַיִּים יַעֲזוֹר בְּפֵירוּשׁ הֶעָבָר וּבַהֲבָנָתוֹ.
The archeological discovery of additional cultural markers, such as plants or animals, will help <u>in explicating</u> and understanding of the past.

In this example, פירוש is the first noun in the construct phrase פירוש העבר. The preposition בְּ- links the verb יעזור to the nouns פירוש and הבנה.

(15) הוּא הִטִּיף לִדְבֵקוּת נֶחֱרֶצֶת בְּעִיקָר קִיּוּמָן שֶׁל מִצְווֹת הַתּוֹרָה.
He preached resolute adherence to <u>the principle</u> of observing the commandments of the Torah.

Similarly to the previous example, בְּ- is a linking preposition (required by דבקות) to the word עיקר *principle*, <u>not</u> an integral part of the adverb בעיקר *mainly* (which does not appear in this example).

(16) הַשֵּׁם "מָקוֹר" מְכֻוָּון לִשְׁתֵּי קְבוּצוֹת שֶׁל צוּרוֹת שֶׁהֵן בְּפוֹעַל שָׁלוֹשׁ.
The term "infinitive" refers to two groups of forms which are, <u>in effect</u>, three.

The word בְּפוֹעַל is an adverb. The reading בַּ+פוֹעַל *in the verb* (or בְּ+פוֹעַל *in a verb*) would be here contrary to fact (the Hebrew verb system does not have three groups of infinitive forms).

(17) הָיָה אֶפְשָׁר לְהִשְׁתַּמֵּשׁ בְּסִפּוּרוֹ כְּדֵי לָדוּן בַּלַּהַט, וְאוּלַי בְּטֵירוּף, שְׁמוּנָחִים בַּבָּסִיס הַצִּיּוֹנוּת.
It may have been possible to use his story in order to discuss <u>the fervor,</u> and perhaps <u>the madness,</u> that lie at the base of Zionism.

Since the text is unpointed, בלהט and בטירוף may be initially read as adverbs – בְּלַהַט *fervently* and בְּטֵירוּף *madly* – both describing the verb לדון. However, as we continue to read the sentence, we re-interpret these words as nouns – להט *fervor* and טירוף *madness* – that function as the subject of the verb מונחים *lie* in the subordinate clause. The preposition בְּ- is required by the verb לדון and is pronounced with an /a/ (בַּלַּהַט, בַּטֵּירוּף) rather than a *sheva* (בְּלַהַט, בְּטֵירוּף), as it would be if it were part of the adverb.

(18) במוֹקְדָה שֶׁל הַמְּשִׁיחִיּוּת נִיצֶבֶת דְּמוּת שֶׁל מַנְהִיג דָּתִי, הַמֵּבִיא בְּכוֹחַ פְּעִילוּתוֹ לְשִׁינוּי עֲרָכִים בְּתוֹךְ הַמְּצִיאוּת הַהִיסְטוֹרִית.
At the center of Messianism stands the figure of a religious leader, who brings about <u>through the force</u> of his activity a change of values in the historical reality.

In this example, בכוח cannot be interpreted as the adverb *forcibly* (as seen in the next example), since כוח *force, power* functions as the first noun in the construct phrase כוח פעילותו.

(19) הַכּוֹבְשִׁים הֵמִירוּ בְּכוֹחַ אֶת תּוֹשְׁבֵי הַמָּקוֹם לְנַצְרוּת.
The conquerors <u>forcibly</u> converted the local inhabitants to Christianity.

⚠️ Note also the use of בכוח in the sense of *potential* (after a noun), the opposite of בפועל *in actual fact, in effect*.
For example: מספר המשמעויות של הטקסט כמספר הקוראים בכוח *the number of the meanings of the text is the same as the number of the potential readers*.

2.1.3 When an adverb of manner of the +ב pattern is followed by an adjective, it is usually translated verbatim, that is, "with+noun".

(20) הַמִּדְרָשִׁים הָרַבִּים מְתוֹאָרִים בְּדַקְדְּקָנוּת רבה.
The many Midrashim are described <u>with great meticulousness</u>.

If the adjective רבה were not used, the translation would be: described meticulously.

2.1.4 A number of adverbial expressions are created with prepositions other than בכל"ם. Some examples are:

(ב)עַל כּוֹרְחוֹ	*unwillingly*
מִתּוֹךְ בִּיקוֹרֶת	*critically*
עַל הָרוֹב, עַל פִּי רוֹב	*in most cases, generally*
עַל נְקַלָּה	*easily*
אֶל נָכוֹן	*certainly, without doubt*
מִן בָּרוּר (rare)	*clearly*

2.1.5 To express the *lack* of a certain quality, the following negating words are used before a noun or an adjective: בְּחוֹסֶר, (מְ)בְּלִי, בְּאִי, (שֶׁ)לֹא ב, לְלֹא.

For example:

בְּחוֹסֶר רָצוֹן	*unwillingly*
(מ)בְּלִי כַּוָּונָה	*unintentionally*
בְּאִי הֲבָנָה	*uncomprehendingly*
לֹא בְּמַפְתִּיעַ	*not surprisingly*
לְלֹא סָפֵק	*undoubtedly*

2.1.5.1 Note, however, that לְאֵין has a positive meaning. Examples are:

לְאֵין עֲרוֹךְ	*to a great extent*
לְאֵין שִׁיעוּר	*immeasurably*

> לֹא אַחַת and לֹא פעם similarly have a positive meaning: *more than once, often* (rather than *never*), as does the expression בלי די *much, a great deal* (rather then *insufficiently*). This is also the case with אֵין סְפוֹר *innumerable, countless, numerous* (e.g., המחזה זכה לאין ספור פרסים *the play won numerous prizes*).

2.1.5.2 The word בְּיֶתֶר is used before an abstract noun for intensification:

בְּיֶתֶר שְׂאֵת	*more strongly, with greater vigor*
בְּיֶתֶר דִיוּק, לְיֶתֶר דיוק	*more accurately, with greater accuracy*

> Note the expression בֵּין הַיֶּתֶר *among other things* (synonymous with בין השאר).

2.2 בְּדֶרֶךְ/בְּצוּרָה + adjective (f.sing.), בְּאוֹפֶן/בְּאוֹרַח + adjective (m.sing.)

Many adverbs are created by adding an adjective to an expression that means *in a manner, in a way*.

There are four such expressions: באופן, באורח, בדרך, בצורה.

באופן and באורח require a masculine (singular) adjective; בדרך and בצורה require a feminine (singular) adjective.

באופן מַשְׁמָעוּתִי	*significantly*
באורח הֲדָדִי	*mutually*
בצורה זְהִירה	*cautiously*
בדרך עֲקִיפה	*indirectly*

> דרך can be followed by a noun (rather than an adjective) to form an adverb; the preposition בְ- is optional then.
> For example: (ב)דרך כלל *usually*, (ב)דרך קֶבַע *regularly*, (ב)דרך אקראי *accidentally, by chance*. Note also דרך משל *for example*.

2.2.1 Preceded by a preposition, the nouns בְּחִינה[3] *aspect* and נוסַח *style* likewise may be used with an adjective to form an adverb of manner.

מִבְּחִינה מוּסָרית   *morally, from an ethical point of view*
בנוסח שירי   *poetically*

2.2.2 Two (or more) adverbs of this type can be created through coordination of adjectives without repeating the introducing expression:

בְּאופֶן מִקְרִי וְחֶלְקִי   *accidentally and partially*

2.3 Adverbs in the form of adjectives

Some adverbs of manner are identical in form to adjectives, but no gender-number agreement is entailed (e.g., הם עובדים קשה *they work hard*, not: *הם עובדים קשים*).

Note, then, the difference in meaning between היא עובדת מצוין *she works very well (excellently)* and היא עובדת מצוינת *she is an excellent worker.*

Three groups of adverbs that have the same form as adjectives are listed below.

2.3.1 Adverbs identical in form to **singular masculine adjectives**:

as adjective		as adverb
בָּרוּר	clear	clearly
טוב	good	well (in formal style, הֵיטֵב is preferred to טוב)
רע	bad	badly
יפה	nice	nicely
מצוין	excellent	very well, with excellence
קשה	hard, difficult	with difficulty; strongly; harshly; hard
קָרוֹב	close	near, nearby
רָחוֹק	distant, remote	far
מאוחר	late	late
נָכוֹן	correct	correctly

⚠️ As an adjective, מאוחר does not refer to people, that is, *הוא מאוחר* is incorrect (it should be: הוא בא/הגיע מאוחר *he arrived late*), while שעה מאוחרת *late hour* is possible. Similarly, *הוא נכון* is not possible (הוא צודק *he is right* should be used), while פתרון נכון *a correct solution* and לפתור נכון *solve correctly* are right.

⚠️ **2.3.1.1** Note also the difference between the adverb כָּלִיל *completely, entirely* (e.g., העיר נהרסה כליל *the city was completely destroyed*), and the adjective כליל *complete, total* (appearing only in construct adjective phrases):[4] ספר כְּלִיל שְׁלֵמוּת *a perfect book.*

---

[3] See further discussion of בחינה in Chapter 11, 10.2.
[4] See Chapter 4, 4.4.

2.3.2 Adverbs modeled on **plural feminine adjectives**:

תְּכוּפוֹת	*often* (adjective: *frequent*)
גְּלוּיוֹת	*openly* (adjective: *open*)
חֲלִיפוֹת	*by turns, alternately* (no adjective)
יְשִׁירוֹת	*directly* (adjective: *direct*)
קְצָרוֹת	*briefly* (adjective: *short*)
רַבּוֹת	*much, greatly* (adjective: *many*)
מְמוּשָּׁכוֹת	*for a long time, at length* (adjective: *lengthy*)

2.3.3 Adverbs that look like **singular feminine adjectives, usually in the -ית** pattern:

כְּלָלִית	*generally* (adjective: *general*)
יַחֲסִית	*relatively* (adjective: *relative*)
עֶקְרוֹנִית	*in principle* (adjective: *fundamental, basic*)
זְמַנִית	*temporarily* (adjective: *temporary*)
אִינְטוּאִיטִיבִית	*intuitively* (adjective: *intuitive*)
בִּלְעָדִית	*exclusively* (adjective: *exclusive*)

And also:

אַחֶרֶת	*differently; otherwise* (adjective: *different*) הם חשבו אחרת *they thought differently*
רִאשׁוֹנָה	*firstly, before others; in the first place* (adjective: *first*) הוא יצא ראשונה *he came out first*
אַחֲרוֹנָה	*lastly* (adjective: *last*) הוא דיבר אחרונה *he spoke last*

⚠ Note that when ראשונה and אחרונה appear with the prepositions -בּ or -ל they become adverbs of time.
For example: לָרִאשׁוֹנָה *for the first time,* בָּרִאשׁוֹנָה *at first, in the beginning,* לָאַחֲרוֹנָה, בָּאַחֲרוֹנָה *recently, lately.*

נֶאֱמָנָה	*faithfully* (adjective: *faithful*) הוא עשה את מלאכתו נאמנה *he did his work faithfully*
נְכוֹנָה	*correctly* (adjective: *correct*) הוא ענה נכונה על השאלות *he answered the questions correctly*
נְכוֹחָה	*properly, correctly* (No adjective; the form נכוח* does not exist.) הוא ראה את הדברים נכוחה *he saw things properly* (typically used with verbs of cognition or saying, such as לדבר, להבין, לראות.

🏋 #2   **2.3.4 Distinguishing adverbs from adjectives**

The adverb can be distinguished from the identically looking adjective on the basis of grammatical clues: its lack of agreement with a preceding noun, and its location in the sentence,
specifically, its proximity to the verb.
For example:

- הוא חשב אחרת *he thought differently* (אחרת is an adverb) versus הם ניסו שיטה אחרת *they
  tried a different method* (אחרת is an adjective).
- הקהל הנלהב הריע ממושכות *the enthusiastic audience cheered at length* (ממושכות is an adverb)
  versus המנצח זכה לתשואות ממושכות *the conductor received lengthy applause* (ממושכות is an
  adjective).

Below are some examples in which the grammatical status of the word appears initially ambiguous because the adjective and the adverb share the same form.

---

(21)   לַתמונה זאת יש להוסיף עוד תְמוּרה דֶמוֹגְרָפִית, זו המתחוֹלֶלֶת בַּיַהֲדוּת העולם בִּכְלָלָה.
גם אם יַתְמִידוּ המְגַמוֹת הנוֹכְחִיוֹת וישראל תהיה בְּהַדְרָגָה פחות יְהוּדית בְּהֶרְכֵּב אוֹכְלוּסִיָּיתָה,
היא תהיה דֶמוֹגרפית לְמֶרְכָּז הַיַהֲדוּת העוֹלָמית.

To this picture should be added another demographic change that is taking place in
world Jewry in general. Even if the current tendencies persist and Israel will gradually become less Jewish in the composition of its population, demographically it will
become the center of world Judaism.

In the first sentence, דמוגרפית is an adjective, modifying the noun תמורה. In the second sentence, דמוגרפית functions as an adverb after the verb תהיה, answering the question "how/
in what respect (will Israel become the center of world Judaism)?"

(22)   בְּהֵיעָדֵר הַבָּסיס של זֶהוּת ישראלית עקבית בִּיסוֹדָה, כְּתיבת ההיסטוריה של ישראל
כְּחֶברה מְאוּחֶדֶת, אֶתנית ותרבותית, תהיה בְּעָיָיתית עוד יותר.

Absent (OR: in the absence of) the basis of a fundamentally consistent Israeli
identity, the writing of Israeli history as an ethnically and culturally unified society,
will be even more problematic.

אתנית ותרבותית function here as adverbs describing the adjective מאוחדת. The reading חברה
מאוחדת, אתנית ותרבותית as a sequence of three coordinated adjectives – *a unified, ethnic
and cultural society* – though grammatically possible, must be rejected for incoherence.
A less ambiguous phrasing would have been: חברה מאוחדת מבחינה אתנית ותרבותית.

(23)   ניסָיון לַעֲקוב אַחַר מְקורותיו של הַסְטָטוּס קְווֹ מְתַסְכֵּל אֱמְפּירית אך מְרַתֵּק תֵאוֹרֶטית.
An attempt to trace the origins of the status quo is empirically frustrating but theoretically fascinating.

אמפירית and תאורטית cannot be read as adjectives since they do not follow (or agree with)
a noun. The adverbs מבחינה תאורטית and מבחינה אמפירית could be substituted here.

2.4 Adverbs with the (Aramaic) suffix ין-

Some examples are:

בַּעֲקִיפִין	*indirectly*
בְּמֵישָׁרִין	*directly*
לַחֲלוּטִין	*absolutely*
לַחֲלוּפִין	*alternatively*
בְּיוֹדְעִין	*knowingly*
לִמְקוּטָעִין	*in fits and starts, brokenly*
לְסֵרוּגִין	*alternately*
לַחֲצָאִין	*by halves*

Some of these adverbs may also appear with the ים- ending:
במישרים, ביודעים, למקוטעים, לסרוגים, לחצאים.

2.5 Aramaic expressions used as adverbs

Some examples are:

כִּדְבָעֵי	*properly, fittingly*
לָאו דַּוְקָא	*not necessarily*
בְּדִיעֲבַד	*after the event, a posteriori*
בְּעָלְמָא	*merely*
בְּלָאו הֲכֵי	*in any case*
גְּרֵידָא	*merely, only*
בְּאַקְרַאי, באופן אַקְרָאִי	*by chance*

⚠ Note the use of אַקְרַאי (without a preposition) in construct phrases (e.g., הערת אקראי *a chance comment*), and the adjective אַקְרָאִי *random, coincidental* (e.g., תהליך אקראי *random process*).

2.6 Adverbs created through repetition (exact, approximate or synonymous).

Some examples are:

אֶחָד אֶחָד	*one by one*
בָּרֹאשׁ וּבָרִאשׁוֹנָה	*first and foremost*
טִיפִּין טִיפִּין	*little by little*
יוֹתֵר וְיוֹתֵר	*more and more*
לֹא...כְּלָל וּכְלָל, לֹא...כְּלָל וְעִיקָר[5]	*not at all*
לְפֶתַע פִּתְאוֹם	*suddenly*
מִכֹּל וָכֹל	*entirely*
שׁוּב וָשׁוּב	*repeatedly*
בַּד בְּבַד	*at the same time, along with*

---

[5] See Chapter 10, Confusables section 3 for other expressions with כלל.

| אַךְ וְרַק | *only* |
| שְׁלַבִּים שְׁלַבִּים | *gradually, in stages* |

2.7 Some adverbs are **fixed idiomatic expressions**, for example:

פֶּה אֶחָד	*unanimously*
(בְּ)דֶרֶךְ אַגַּב	*by the way, incidentally*
מִן הַקָּצֶה אֶל הַקָּצֶה	*extremely, entirely*
פִּי כַּמָּה (וְכַמה)	*many times over*

> When appearing with a (masculine) number פִי indicates multiplication, for example: פי שניים *twice as much, twice as many.*

2.8 Different forms for the same adverb

The same adverb can be formed in several ways without a change in meaning:

יְשִׁירוּת, בְּאוֹפֶן יָשִׁיר, בְּצוּרָה יְשִׁירָה	*directly*
גְּלוּיוֹת, בְּאוֹפֶן גָּלוּי, בָּאוֹרַח גָּלוּי, בְּגָלוּי	*openly, candidly*
רִשְׁמִית, בְּאוֹפֶן רִשְׁמִי, בָּאוֹרַח רִשְׁמִי, בְּצוּרָה רִשְׁמִית	*formally*
לְאַט, בְּאִטִּיּוּת	*slowly*
בַּעֲקִיפִין, בדרך עקיפה	*indirectly*
בצורה זְהִירָה, בִּזְהִירוּת	*cautiously*
(בְּ)דֶרֶךְ קֶבַע, באוֹפֶן קָבוּעַ, בִּקְבִיעוּת	*regularly*

2.8.1 However, on occasion a change of form entails a change in meaning. For example:

בְּקוֹשִׁי *with difficulty,*[6] but קָשׁוֹת *severely*;
בָּאוֹרַח קַל, קַלּוֹת *easily,* but קַלּוֹת, בְּנָקֵל *lightly.*

> (24) רק בְּקוֹשִׁי אפשר להבחין בַּהֶבְדֵּלִים.
> Only <u>with difficulty</u> is it possible to notice the differences.
>
> (25) באותה תקופה סָבְלוּ יהוּדֵי פּוֹלִין קָשׁוֹת מֵרְדִיפוֹת.
> At that period, the Jews of Poland suffered <u>greatly</u> from persecutions.

---

[6] Also – colloquially – *hardly, barely.*

2.9 Coordinated adverbs

Adverbs belonging to different structural types may appear side by side:

---

(26) קשה להצביע בְּבִטְחה ובאופן חַד-מַשְמָעִי על מָקור אחד לכל היסודות.

It is difficult to point <u>with confidence</u> and <u>unambiguously</u> at a single source for all the elements.

בבטחה is formed by prefixing a preposition to a noun; באופן חד-משמעי is created by appending an adjective to באופן.

---

3. Alternative ways of expressing manner: adverbial verbs and internal objects

3.1 Adverbial verbs: finite verb+infinitive

Certain (finite) verbs have a built-in adverbial meaning and their function is to describe the manner of execution of another, adjacent (infinitive) verb. These adverbial verbs are often lexically related to primary adverbs.

For example: לְהַרְבות is related to הַרְבֵה *much*, לְהֵיטיב is related to הֵיטֵב *well*, לְמַעֵט/לְהַמְעיט are related to מְעט *little*, לְהִתקַשות is related to קשה *difficult*.

3.1.1 Adverbial verbs may appear in any tense (as well as in the infinitive form), but the following verb – the main verb – is always in the infinitive (alternatively, an action noun may be used, for example: להרבות בדיבור or לְהַרְבות לְדַבֵּר *to speak much*).

3.1.2 In translation to English, the inflected (adverbial) verb is often rendered by means of the related adverb.

---

(27) הוא הֵיטיב לתָאֵר את רגשותיה.
[=הוא תיאר היטב את רגשותיה]
He <u>described</u> her feelings <u>well</u>.

(28) על מותָן של נשים אין המִקרָא מַרְבֶּה לסַפֵר.
[=המקרא אינו מספר הרבה על מותן של נשים]
The Bible does not <u>tell much</u> about the death of women.

(29) המְסַפֵר מְמַעט לתָאֵר את רגשותיו של הגיבור.
[=המספר מתאר מעט את רגשותיו של הגיבור]
The narrator <u>little describes</u> the feelings of the protagonist.

(30) קהילות אשכנז הגדילו לעשות והוסיפו את התקנָה לנוסח הכְּתובה.
The German congregations <u>did even more</u> (OR: <u>surpassed themselves</u>) and added the ordinance to the wording of the marriage contract.

The expression הגדיל לעשות or, more formally, הגדיל עֲשות is used to qualify the next (coordinate) verb (here – הוסיפו); both verbs (הגדילו והוסיפו) are in the same tense (here: in the past) and have the same subject (here: קהילות אשכנז).

---

(31) המְשׁוֹרֵר **הִפְלִיא עֲשׂוֹת** בשינויים, הָעֲשָׁרָה וּמְצִיאַת מַקְבִּילוֹת מִלְּשׁוֹן הַמִּקְרָא.
The poet <u>did wonders</u> in changing (literally: changes), enriching and finding parallels from the language of the Bible. (OR: the poet <u>wonderfully</u> changed, enriched and found parallels from the language of the Bible.)

In this example, the adverbial verb הפליא is related to the noun פלא *wonder* (rather than to an adverb as in the previous examples); it is followed by the infinitive construct form[7] עשות.

(32) הממשלה **הִשְׂכִּילה לִפְתֹחַ** בעיר מקורות תעסוקה.
The government <u>succeeded</u> in developing (OR: <u>successfully</u> developed) in the town sources of employment.

Before another (infinitive) verb, the finite (conjugated) form of להשכיל (usually in the sense of *become wise, acquire knowledge; instruct*) indicates that the action of the infinitive verb was successful.

3.2 Adjective+infinitive verb as an adverbial
Certain adjectives (e.g., חכם *wise*, מצליח *successful*, תמים *naïve*) pair with the verb **להפליא** to create an adverbial expression wherein להפליא is translated as *amazingly, wonderfully, incredibly*.
For example:

הוא היה מלחין פורה להפליא *he was an incredibly productive composer.*

Other infinitive verbs that function in the same way are להחריד *frighteningly, horribly* (e.g., תנאים קשים להחריד *horribly difficult conditions*) and להקסים *enchantingly* (e.g., שִׁיר שָׁנוּן להקסים *enchantingly witty poem*).

✗#3   3.3 Internal object phrases (cognate accusative)
Three-word adverbials of manner consist of a verb "echoed" by a direct object from the same root and followed, in turn, by an adjective. For example: הפתיע הפתעה רבה. Since English stylistics does not allow for the appearance of same-root words in close proximity, verbatim translation of internal object phrases violates English language norms. In other words, the translation *surprised a great surprise* for הפתיע הפתעה רבה would be unacceptable. The reader is therefore advised to ignore the noun (the internal object) and translate the adjective as an adverb: *greatly surprised.*

---

[7] See Chapter 6, 1.1.

(33) הַהֶכֵּרוּת עם תרבות המזרח הִשְׁפִּיעָה הַשְׁפָּעָה חיובית על יְצִירָתוֹ.
The acquaintance with the culture of the Orient <u>affected</u> his work <u>positively.</u>

(34) תְּחִיַּית העברית וּתְקוּמַת עם ישראל בארצו שימשו לא אַחַת את החוקרים כְּדֵי **לְהָבִין** את ההיסטוריה היהודית ואת סִפְרוּתה הֲבָנָה חדשה.
The revival of Hebrew and the revival of the people of Israel in its land were often used by researchers to <u>understand anew</u> Jewish history and its literature.

As seen in this example, the verb and the object of the same root may be separated.

(35) ביטול הבְּחִינה הפְּסִיכוֹמֶטְרִית צָפוּי **לִפְגּוֹעַ פגיעה מהותית** בְּמידת הַהַתְאָמָה של המתְקַבְּלים ללימודים לְמַסְלוּלֵי הלימוד השונים.
The abolition of the psychometric exam is expected to <u>harm substantially</u> the degree of suitability of those admitted to [university] studies in the various tracks.

Appendix of time expressions by category[8]

in the beginning	בִּפְרוֹס (הַשָּׁנָה, הַמֵּאָה), בָּרִאשׁוֹנָה, בְּרֵאשִׁית, בַּשַּׁחַר[9] (הַהִיסְטוֹרְיָה), בַּתְּחִלָּה, בִּתְחִלַּת ה-, הֵחֵל בְּ[10]
in the end	בְּסוֹף, לְבַסּוֹף, בְּסִיּוּם, בַּעֲרוֹב (יָמָיו)[11]; בְּשִׁלְהֵי (הַמֵּאָה), בְּתוֹם (ה-), (וְ)כַלֵּה בְּ[12]
before, beforehand	(בְּ)טֶרֶם, לִפְנֵי,[13] לִפְנֵי כֵן, קוֹדֶם ל, קוֹדֶם לָכֵן, קוֹדֶם שֶׁ-
after, afterwards	אַחַר, אַחַר כָּךְ, אַחֲרֵי (שֶׁ), אַחֲרֵי כֵן, לְאַחַר (זֹאת, זְמָן, מִכֵּן), לְיָמִים;[14] מְאוּחָר יוֹתֵר,[15] בְּעוֹד,[16] כַּעֲבוֹר
often, frequently	לֹא פַעַם,[17] לֹא אַחַת,[18] לְעִתִּים מְזוּמָּנוֹת, לְעִתִּים קְרוֹבוֹת, לְעִתִּים תְּדִירוֹת, תָּדִיר,[19] (לְעִתִּים) תְּכוּפוֹת
infrequently, rarely, seldom	לְעִתִּים נְדִירוֹת, לְעִתִּים רְחוֹקוֹת
sometimes	יֵשׁ אֲשֶׁר, יֵשׁ וְ,[20] יֵשׁ שֶׁ; כָּל (פַּעַם, שָׁנָה), (לְ)עִתִּים, לִפְעָמִים, לִפְרָקִים, מִזְּמָן לִזְמָן, מֵעֵת לְעֵת, מִפַּעַם לְפַעַם, (מִדֵּי) פַּעַם כְּפַעַם, פְּעָמִים
every	כָּל (פַּעַם, שָׁנָה), מִדֵּי (פַּעַם, שָׁנָה)[21]
when, while, during, within, at the time that	(בְּ)עֵת (שֶׁ-), (בְּ)שָׁעָה שֶׁ-, בִּזְמַן (שֶׁ-), בָּרֶגַע (שֶׁ-), בִּשְׁעַת; תּוֹךְ (יוֹם, שָׁנָה),[22] תּוֹךְ (שֶׁ-), בְּתוֹךְ (כָּךְ); כַּאֲשֶׁר, כְּשֶׁ..., לִכְשֶׁ..(+עָתִיד); מִשֶּׁ..(+עָבַר); בְּ+infinitive construct (בְּבוֹא הַיּוֹם=כַּאֲשֶׁר הַיּוֹם בָּא/יָבוֹא, בְּדַבְּרוֹ=כַּאֲשֶׁר הוּא דִּיבֵּר/מְדַבֵּר/יְדַבֵּר), עִם+infinitive construct (עִם רֶדֶת הַלַּיְלָה=כַּאֲשֶׁר הַלַּיְלָה יָרַד/יוֹרֵד/יֵירֵד);[23] עִם+noun (עִם הַמַּהְפֵּכָה=בִּזְמַן הַמַּהְפֵּכָה, עִם הַכְּתִיבָה=בִּזְמַן הַכְּתִיבָה)

---

[8] For the reader's convenience, partial pointing was added to the full spelling.

[9] בשחר *at the beginning*; literally: *at (the) dawn*.

[10] החל ב *beginning with*.

[11] בערוב *toward the end of*; literally: *at the draw (evening) of*.

[12] וכלה ב *and ending with*.

[13] לפני followed by a time unit is variably translated as *ago* (when the unit of time is indefinite, e.g., לפני מאה שנה *one hundred years ago*) or *before* (e.g., לפני המאה העשרים *before the twentieth century*).

[14] לימים *after a long time, eventually*.

[15] מאוחר יותר *later*.

[16] בעוד followed by a time unit is used with a time unit (e.g., שנה, יום) to refer to the future; otherwise it serves as a contrastive sentence connector, *while*. Note the expression מבעוד יום *before dark*.

[17] This expression has a positive meaning – *more than once, often*, distinct from אף פעם לא *never*.

[18] לא אחת *more than once, every now and then, not infrequently*.

[19] Also used as an adjective: נושא תדיר *a frequent topic*.

[20] יש ו is considered incorrect, יש ש and יש אשר are preferred.

[21] מדי פעם – *each time, every so often*; מדי שנה – *each year*.

[22] תוך (שנה) *within a year*.

[23] See discussion of the infinitive construct in adverbial expressions in Chapter 6, 1.2.

in the course of (time)	בְּמַהֲלַךְ (הזמן, השנים, הדורות),²⁴ בִּמְרוּצַת (הזמן, השנים, הדורות), בְּמֶשֶׁךְ, בְּרְבוֹת (הימים, השנים)²⁵
at the same (time) as	אַגַּב; בְּאוֹתוֹ (ה)יום, בְּאוֹתָן (ה)שנים; עִם שֶׁ-, תוֹךְ כְּדֵי
simultaneously	בָּה בָּעֵת, בְּעֵת וּבְעוֹנָה אַחַת, בּוֹ בַּזְּמַן, בּוֹ זְמַנִית, בַּד בְּבַד, בה בשעה ש-
whenever, anytime	(ב)כל פעם שֶׁ-, כל אֵימַת שֶׁ-
never, ever	אַף פַּעַם לא, מֵעוֹלָם לא,²⁶ לְעוֹלָם לא;²⁷ מִיָּמָיו/מִיָּמֶיהָ/מִימֵיהֶם/מימיהן לא, מֵעוֹדוֹ/מֵעוֹדָה/מֵעוֹדָם/מֵעוֹדָן לא
always	בכל (עת, שעה, דור), מֵעוֹלָם, לְעוֹלָם, תָּמִיד, תְּמִידִית²⁸
then	אָז, דְּאָז, בְּאוֹתוֹ (ה)יום, בזמן ההוא, בימים ההם, בִּשְׁעָתוֹ/בִּשְׁעָתָה/בשעתם/בשעתן
since	מֵאָז, מֵרֶגַע שֶׁ-, מִזְּמַן שֶׁ-, משעה ש-
already	(מ)זֶה²⁹ (שנה, דורות, עִידָן וְעִידָנִים),³⁰ כְּבָר
long ago, in the past	מֵאָז וּמֵעוֹלָם, מִדּוֹרֵי דורות, מִזְּמַן, מִימֵי קֶדֶם, מִיָּמִים יְמִימָה, מִיָּמִים מִשֶּׁכְּבַר, מִקַּדְמַת דְּנָא, תְּמוֹל שִׁלְשׁוֹם
at some time (in the past or future)	באחד הימים, בִּזְמַן מִן הַזְּמַנִּים, לְיָמִים, פעם
as long as	כל זמן שֶׁ-, כל עוד, עד שֶׁ-/אשר
lately, recently	אַךְ זֶה, בָּאַחֲרוֹנָה, לָאַחֲרוֹנָה, זֶה לא מִכְּבָר, זֶה עַתָּה, עתה זה
now	כַּיּוֹם, כָּעֵת, עַכְשָׁיו, עתה
until now	עד כֹּה, עד עכשיו, עד עתה
in the meantime	בֵּינְתַיִם, לְפִי שָׁעָה;³¹ לְעֵת עתה
just, as soon as	אַךְ; רַק
soon	בִּמְהֵרָה, בְּקָרוֹב, עַד מְהֵרָה
(not) yet, still	עוֹד/עֲדַיִן (לא)³²

---

²⁴ במהלך ה-, במרוצת ה- in the course of.
²⁵ ברבות הימים, ברבות השנים over the years, with the passage of time.
²⁶ מעולם לא with past tense verbs.
²⁷ לעולם לא with present and future tense verbs.
²⁸ The adverb תמידית always, constantly, looks like the feminine adjective meaning constant.
²⁹ מזה is considered non-standard.
³⁰ מזה עידן ועידנים for ages.
³¹ לפי שעה for the time being.
³² עדיין still; עדיין לא not yet.

Historical dates	בִּשְׁנַת in the year
	עַד שְׁנַת until the year
	בֵּין הַשָּׁנִים between the years
	בִּשְׁנוֹת הַ-[33] in the (specified decade)
	בַּמֵּאָה הַ- in the (specified) century
	B.C.E. (לִפְנֵי סְפִירַת הַנּוֹצְרִים) לפסה"נ ,(לִפְנֵי הַסְּפִירָה) לפנה"ס
	C.E. לַסְּפִירָה

---

[33] Followed by multiples of ten, e.g., בשנות השלושים *in the 1930's.*

References

אבינרי, תשכ"ב
אילני, 2001
בליבוים, 1995
בן-אשר, תשל"ג
צדקה, 1997
קדרי, 1985
(רודריג) שורצולד, תשמ"ט
שלזינגר, 2000

Glinert, 1989
Richards, Platt, & Platt, 1992
Schwarzwald, 2001

Chapter 5: Adverbs – Exercises

exercise #	topic	page
1	Identifying and translating adverbs	208–209
2	Distinguishing between adjectives and adverbs	210–211
3	Translating internal object phrases	212

Exercise #1: Identifying and translating adverbs

> **The rules to go by:** see sections 2 and 3.2.
> **What to do:** identify and translate the adverb(s) in each sentence (the number in parenthesis indicates how many there are).
> **Example:**
>
> המחברת סוקרת **בשיטתיות** מִגְוָון רחב של נושאים. בשיטתיות – systematically

1. בַּכַּלְכָּלָה מוּצָר ציבּוּרי הוא מוצר שניתן לשימוש על יְדֵי כולם באוֹפן חוֹפשי. (1)

2. אפילו המתיישבים שומרי המָסוֹרֶת לא נֶאֶמְנוּ דיים על אֲדוּקי ירושלים. (1)

3. הוא חזר שוב ושוב על גְרְסָתו, כשסיפורו מושפע ללא ספק מן הדיאַלוֹג המוּסָרי-פוליטי שֶׁבְּרֶקַע. (2)

4. בעיקר ניסתה הציונות להגדיר מחדש את היהדות במושגים של לְאוֹם, ארץ ותרבּוּת. (2)

5. העָמָל הרב והיצירָתיות שהוּשׁקעוּ ביצירת חֶברת מוֹפֵת הוֹלידוּ באורח פרדוקסלי חברה "נורמלית" שהקימה ביעילוּת ובמהירוּת ארץ מודרנית. (3)

Glossary

economics	כלכלה 1.
public good	מוצר ציבורי
can be used	ניתן לשימוש
the (religiously) observant settlers	המתיישבים שומרי המסורת 2.
were trusted	נאמנו
the Orthodox of Jerusalem	אדוקי ירושלים
repeated	חזר על 3.
his version	גרסתו
influenced from	מושפע
background	רקע
tried	ניסתה 4.
to define	להגדיר
religious terms	מושגים דתיים
nationality	לאום
labor	עמל 5.
creativity	יצירתיות
invested	הושקעו
creation of a model society	יצירת חברת מופת
gave birth to	הולידו

6. עַל פִּי גִישַׁת כּוּר הַהִיתּוּךְ, צִיפּוּ מִן הַיֶּלֶד לְהִיטָּמַע לְשׁוֹנִית, חֶבְרָתִית וְתַרְבּוּתִית בַּהֲוָיָיה הַיִּשְׂרְאֵלִית. (3)

7. עִם הִתְעוֹרְרוּת הַקַּנָּאוּת הַדָּתִית, קְהִילּוֹת יְהוּדִיוֹת רַבּוֹת נִפְגְּעוּ קָשׁוֹת וּלְעִתִּים אַף הוּשְׁמְדוּ כָּלִיל. (3)

8. הוּא מְתָאֵר קִיּוּם יְהוּדִי קְהִילָתִי בָּעִיר אִיטַלְקִית פּוֹרַחַת מִבְּחִינָה כַּלְכָּלִית וְסוֹבְלָנִית מִבְּחִינָה דָּתִית. (2)

9. מַרְבִּית שִׁבְטֵי הָאִנְדִיאָנִים בַּחֶבֶל אֶרֶץ נִרְחָב זֶה עוֹדָם פְּרָאִים לְהַפְלִיא. (2)

10. שְׁלוֹשָׁה גוֹרְמִים חָבְרוּ בַּהַדְרָגָה לְהַשְׁפִּיעַ לְרָעָה עַל מַעֲמָדָם הַמְּדִינִי וְהַחֶבְרָתִי שֶׁל הַיְּהוּדִים וּבְעִקִּיפִין גַּם עַל יְצִירָתָם שֶׁל חֲכָמִים, כָּל זֹאת לַמְרוֹת שֶׁלֹּא חָל בַּפּוֹעַל שִׁינּוּי בְּמַעֲמָדָם הַמִּשְׁפָּטִי. (4)

Glossary

6.	גִישַׁת כּוּר הַהִיתּוּךְ	the melting pot approach
	צִיפּוּ מִן הַיֶּלֶד	it was expected from the child, the child was expected
	לְהִיטָּמַע	to be assimilated
	הֲוָיָיה	existence
7.	הִתְעוֹרְרוּת הַקַּנָּאוּת הַדָּתִית	the rise of religious fanaticism
	נִפְגְּעוּ	were hurt
	הוּשְׁמְדוּ	were destroyed
8.	קִיּוּם קְהִילָתִי יְהוּדִי	communal Jewish existence
	עִיר אִיטַלְקִית פּוֹרַחַת	flourishing Italian city
	סוֹבְלָנִית	tolerant
9.	שִׁבְטֵי הָאִנְדִיאָנִים	the Indian tribes
	חֶבֶל אֶרֶץ	region
	פְּרָאִים	uncivilized
10.	גוֹרְמִים	factors
	חָבְרוּ	joined
	מַעֲמָדָם הַמְּדִינִי וְהַחֶבְרָתִי	their social and political status
	יְצִירָתָם	their work
	חֲכָמִים	sages
	חָל	occurred
	מַעֲמָדָם הַמִּשְׁפָּטִי	their legal status

Exercise #2: Distinguishing between adjectives and adverbs

The rules to go by: see section 2.3.4.
What to do:
1. Indicate whether the bolded word is an adjective or an adverb (enter the sentence number in the appropriate cell in the chart).
2. Translate the bolded word.
The first two sentences are an example.

---

adverb	adjective
2 – at length,	1 – long,

1. הַחֲסִידִים נֶעֶדְרוּ מִבֵּיתָם לִתְקוּפוֹת **אֲרוּכּוֹת.**

2. הֵם דיברו **אֲרוּכּוֹת.**

3. לְכָל יֶלֶד נקבעה תכנית לימודים **אִישִׁית.**

4. מִלְּבַד הַפְּרָטִים הַהִיסְטוֹרִיִּים הוֹסִיף הַסּוֹפֵר לָעֲלִילָה יְרִיבוּת **אִישִׁית** בֵּין הָאַחִים.

5. עֲלִיַּית הַסִּגְנוֹן הַקְּלָאסִי הוּא חֵלֶק מִתְּמוּרָה **כְּלָלִית** בְּתַרְבּוּת הָאֵירוֹפָאִית בְּאֶמְצַע הַמֵּאָה הַ-18.

6. **כְּלָלִית,** אֵין שִׁנּוּיִים מַהוּתִיִּים בֵּין הַמַּהֲדוּרָה הָרִאשׁוֹנָה וְהַשְּׁנִיָּיה שֶׁל הַסֵּפֶר.

7. אַלְפְרֶד דְּרַייפוּס זוֹכֶה **סוֹפִית** עַל יְדֵי בֵּית הַמִּשְׁפָּט לַעֲרְעוּרִים בְּצָרְפַת.

8. שֵׁם הַשִּׁיר שׁוּנָה בְּגִרְסָתוֹ **הַסּוֹפִית.**

Glossary

1.	were absent	נעדרו
3.	a program of study was fixed	נקבעה תוכנית לימודים
4.	details	פרטים
	plot	עלילה
	rivalry	יריבות
5.	the rise of classical style	עליית הסגנון הקלאסי
	change	תמורה
6.	fundamental changes	שינויים מהותיים
	edition	מהדורה
7.	Alfred Dreyfus	אלפרד דרייפוס
	was acquitted	זוכה
	court of appeals	בית המשפט לערעורים
8.	its version	גרסתו
	was changed	שונה

9. ‏עיר הבירה וושינגטון כְּפוּפה **ישירות** לְמִמְשַׁל הַפֶדֶרָלי.

10. ‏ראש העיר נבחר בבְחירות **ישירות.**

11. ‏התחריטים עזרו **רבות** בפְענוּח אופְייה של תרְבות המאיה וההיסטוריה שלה.

12. ‏העיר ניטְשה שנים **רבות** לפני הַגָעַת הכובשים הסְפרדים אל חופֵי אמריקה.

Glossary

	subordinate to	‏כפופה	.9
	the federal government	‏הממשל הפדרלי	
	mayor	‏ראש עיר	.10
	elections	‏בחירות	
	engravings	‏תחריטים	.11
	decoding	‏פענוח	
	its character	‏אופיה	
	Mayan culture	‏תרבות המאיה	
	was abandoned	‏ניטשה	.12
	before the arrival of the Spanish conquerors	‏לפני הגעת הכובשים הספרדיים	
	the shores of America	‏חופי אמריקה	

Exercise #3: Translating internal object phrases

> **The rules to go by:** see section 3.3.
> **What to do:** identify the internal object phrase and translate the sentence.

1. הֲקָמָתָם שֶׁל מוּזֵיאוֹנִים מְקוֹמִיִּים קְשׁוּרָה קֶשֶׁר יָשִׁיר לַחֲשִׁיבוּתוֹ הַגּוֹבֶרֶת שֶׁל עֲנַף הַתַּיָּירוּת.

2. הוּא הִתְנַגֵּד לַרַעְיוֹנוֹת אֵלֹּה הִתְנַגְּדוּת נִמְרֶצֶת.

3. אֵין לְהַפְרִיד בֵּין הַמּוּשָׂגִים הַפְרָדָה בְּרוּרָה.

4. מִמְצָאֵי הַגְּנִיזָה תָּרְמוּ תְרוּמָה עֲצוּמָה לְחֵקֶר הַיַּהֲדוּת.

5. הַמִּתְקָפָה הַיָּמִית נִכְשְׁלָה כִּשָּׁלוֹן מוּחְלָט.

6. עַל חֵטְא זֶה נֶעֶנְשׁוּ הָאַחִים עוֹנֶשׁ כָּבֵד.

6. VERBS
פעלים

This chapter discusses:

- Infinitive verb forms used as nouns and as time adverbials (section 1)
- Direct object suffixes (section 2)
- Verb phrases with modal, aspectual and conditional meanings (section 3)
- Idiomatic verb phrases (section 4)
- Present tense verb forms (participles) (section 5)
- Some non-modern verb forms found in modern scholarly writing (section 6)
- The functions of the letter נו"ן at the beginning of a verb (section 7)
- Confusables: וְלוּ; לוּ; אִילוּ; כְּאִילוּ; וְאִילוּ; אֵילוּ; אִם, בְּאִם; הַאִם

This chapter will help the reader to:

- Translate verbal nouns and adverbial time clauses
- Distinguish between direct object suffixes and conjugational (tense) suffixes
- Determine the reference of pronoun suffixes in verbs
- Recognize and translate expanded verb phrases
- Differentiate among different uses of "to be" in the past tense
- Translate "unreal" (hypothetical) condition sentences
- Recognize and translate idiomatic verb phrases
- Determine the grammatical role of the present participle in the sentence
- Distinguish among various verb forms beginning with נו"ן

Verbs: an overview

Sections 1 and 2 discuss two grammatical phenomena that are found nowadays primarily in formal, scholarly and literary discourse: infinitive verb forms used as verbal nouns and time adverbials (section 1) and direct object suffixes (section 2). Section 3 discusses verb phrases with various meanings, including conditional, repeated, continued, gradual, habitual and intended action. Section 4 contains an inventory of idiomatic verb phrases gleaned from scholarly articles. Section 5 deals with the different syntactic functions of present tense verb forms (participles). The next section lists some verb forms that are found in academic writing, but are rare in everyday use, and the last section of the chapter differentiates among several verb forms that begin with the letter נו"ן.

Matters relating to the "nuts and bolts" of the verb system, namely, root groups (strong and weak verbs) and pattern groups (*binyanim*), are not discussed here as they are dealt with extensively in other grammar books.[1]

In any case, for the purposes of reading comprehension, the identification of the person is far more instructive than that of the root, the *binyan* and the tense, since knowing the gender and number of the verb allows the reader to match it with the subject, a necessary initial step in the syntactic parsing of the sentence.

1. An infinitive verb without -ל (infinitive construct) as a verbal noun and an adverbial of time

1.1 The infinitive without -ל as a verbal noun

> הִנֵּה מַה טּוֹב וּמַה נָּעִים **שֶׁבֶת** אַחִים גַּם יַחַד (תהלים קלג א)
> *How good and how pleasant it is, the dwelling of brothers together* (Psalms 133.1).

An infinitive verb form without its initial -ל is a verbal noun similar to the English gerund (-ing) form. In the example above, the verbal noun is שֶׁבֶת *sitting, dwelling* (directly related to לָשֶׁבֶת *to sit*).

1.1.1 Verbs in the passive *binyanim pu'al* (פּוּעַל) and *huf'al* (הוּפְעַל) do not have verbal noun forms as they do not have infinitive verb forms.

1.1.2 Like all nouns, verbal nouns can participate in construct phrases (hence the name "infinitive construct," מְקוֹר נָטוּי) (examples 1–3). They can also take pronoun suffixes (examples 4–6). The suffixes are identical in form to those used to indicate possession in <u>singular</u> nouns.[2]

---

[1] For information about the verb system, the reader is referred to Glinert, "Modern Hebrew: An Essential Grammar" (Routledge, 2004), and Coffin & Bolozky, "A Reference Grammar of Modern Hebrew" (Cambridge University Press, 2005).

[2] See Chapter 2, 5.2.

The verbal nouns are bolded; the possessive suffix (where it appears) and its reference are shaded:

‫(1) בַּהֲלָכָה הַיְהוּדִית **צֵאת** הַכּוֹכָבִים מְצַיֵּין אֶת תְּחִילַת הַלַּיְלָה.‬
In Jewish law, the <u>appearance</u> of the stars indicates the beginning of the night.

The infinitive form is ‫לָצֵאת‬ *to come out.*

‫(2) הַבְּעָיָה הָעִיקָרִית הִיא **הֵיעָדֵר** מְקוֹרוֹת הִיסְטוֹרִיִּים.‬
The main problem is the <u>absence</u> of historical sources.

The infinitive form is ‫לְהֵיעָדֵר‬ *to be absent.*

‫(3) מָה גָּרַם **לְהֵיעָדֵר** בָּתֵּי כְנֶסֶת בַּתְּקוּפָה הָעַתִּיקָה?‬
What was the cause of (OR: what caused) the <u>absence</u> of synagogues in the ancient period?

Note that the ‫-ל‬ before ‫היעדר‬ is the preposition required by the verb ‫לגרום‬, NOT part of the infinitive form ‫להיעדר‬ *to be absent.*

‫(4) כֵּיוָון שֶׁהַמִּילָה אֲרָמִית הִיא, מוּבָן **הִימָצְאָה** בִּשְׁטָרוֹת אֲרָמִיִּים.‬
Since the word is Aramaic, <u>its presence</u> on Aramaic legal documents is understandable.

The noun ‫הימצא‬ is related to the *nif'al* infinitive ‫להימצא‬ *to be found*; the possessive suffix pronoun ‫-ה‬ refers backwards to ‫מילה‬ *word.*
Alternatively, the action noun ‫הימצאות‬ could be used here (it would entail a change in the verb form from the masculine ‫מובן‬ to the feminine ‫מובנת:‬
‫כיוון שהמילה ארמית היא, מובנת הימצאותה בשטרות ארמיים.‬

‫(5) הַסֵּפֶר מְתָאֵר אֶת **הֵיעָלְמָן** שֶׁל **הַדָּתוֹת** הָאֵלִילִיּוֹת וְאֶת הוֹפָעַת הַמּוֹנוֹתֵיאִיזְם.‬
The book describes the <u>disappearance of</u> the pagan religions and the appearance of Monotheism.

‫היעלם‬ is related to the *nif'al* infinitive ‫להיעלם‬ *to disappear*; the possessive suffix pronoun ‫-ן‬ refers forward to ‫דתות‬ *religions.* Alternatively, the action noun ‫היעלמות‬ could be used:
‫הספר מתאר את היעלמותן של הדתות האליליות ואת הופעת המונותיאיזם.‬

‫(6) רַבִּים מֵהַחֲכָמִים הִתְפַּרְנְסוּ מֵעֲבוֹדַת כַּפַּיִים בְּנוֹסָף **לִהְיוֹתָם** מוֹרִים וּפוֹסְקֵי הֲלָכָה.‬
Many of the sages made a living from manual labor in addition to <u>their being</u> teachers and legal authorities.

‫היותם‬ is related to the infinitive form ‫להיות‬ *to be*; the suffix refers to ‫חכמים‬ *sages.*
Note that similarly to example 3 above, the preposition ‫-ל‬ is required by the previous word (‫בנוסף ל-‬ *in addition to*) and is not part of the infinitive form ‫להיות‬.

1.2 The infinitive without -לְ as an adverbial of time

בִּנְפֹל אוֹיִבְךָ, אַל תִּשְׂמָח (משלי כד יז)
When your enemy falls, do not rejoice (Proverbs 24.17)

When the preposition -בְּ (sometimes -כְּ) introduces an infinitive construct form, an adverbial time clause (that is, a clause that answers the question "when?") is created. In paraphrase, the preposition -בְּ can be replaced with כַּאֲשֶׁר, and the verb is then assigned a tense.
For example:

בְּצֵאת יִשְׂרָאֵל מִמִּצְרַיִם *upon the departure of Israel from Egypt* could be reworded as: כאשר יִשְׂרָאֵל יצא(ו) ממצרים. Similarly, כְּבוֹא הָאָבִיב *at the arrival of spring* can be rephrased as כאשר האביב בא/יבוא.

1.2.1 Other prepositions or adverbs of time may be used (instead of -בְּ or -כְּ).
For example:

לִפְנֵי, (בְּ)טֶרֶם, קֹדֶם לְ- *since,* מֵאָז *till,* עַד *from the moment of,* מֵרֶגַע *with,* עִם *at the time of,* בְּעֵת *before,* לְאַחַר/אַחַר/אַחֲרֵי *after* (examples 9–12, 14).

1.2.2 In translation, the infinitive construct can be converted into a noun or a gerund (-ing). Alternatively, a finite verb may be used; its tense would be the same as that of the verb in the main clause.

The adverbial time clauses are shaded; an alternative wording with כאשר is shown in brackets:

---
(7) בְּבוֹא הַמַּלְאָכִים לִסְדוֹם, מַפְצִיר בָּהֶם לוֹט לְהִתְאָרֵחַ אֶצְלוֹ.
[=כאשר המלאכים באים]
Upon the arrival of the angels [OR: when the angels arrive] in Sodom, Lot entreats them to be his guests.

בבוא is related to לבוא; it can be translated with a noun (*arrival*) or a verb (*arrive*) in the present tense, the same tense as the verb מפציר in the main clause.

(8) כְּבָר בִּתְקוּפַת הַתַּנָּאִים, בִּהְיוֹת לְשׁוֹן חֲכָמִים לָשׁוֹן חַיָּה, הִיא לֹא הָיְתָה לָשׁוֹן אֲחִידָה.
[=כאשר לשון חכמים הייתה לשון חיה]
Already in the period of the *Tannaim*, when Mishnaic language was a living language, it was not a homogenous language.

היות is related to להיות. In translation, the past tense in used, in concord with the tense of the main clause: היא לא הייתה לשון אחידה.
---

(9) **עִם גָּדוֹל אוכלוסיית השכונה**, נבנו בתים נוֹסָפים.
[=כאשר אוכלוסיית השכונה גדלה]
With the growth of the population of the neighborhood [OR: as the population of the neighborhood grew], additional houses were built.

גָּדוֹל is related to לִגְדּוֹל; it can be translated with a noun (*growth*) or a verb in the past tense (*grew*), the same tense as that of the verb נבנו in the main clause.

(10) את השערים נהגו לסגור **עִם רֶדֶת הלילה** ולפתוח שוב בבוקר.
[=כאשר הלילה ירד]
They used to close the gates at night fall and reopen in the morning.

רדת is related to לָרֶדֶת.

(11) מְדוּבָּר כאן באירוע שאירַע **בְּטֶרֶם עֲלוֹת בן-יהודה אַרְצָה.**
[=בטרם בן יהודה עלה]
The event discussed here took place before Ben-Yehuda's immigration [OR: before Ben-Yehuda immigrated] to the Land of Israel.

עֲלוֹת is related to לַעֲלוֹת; it can be translated as a noun (*immigration*) or a verb (*immigrated*). Alternatively, the action noun עלייה could be used:
... בטרם עלייתו של בן-יהודה ארצה.

𝌆#1 & #2   1.3 -בְּ + verbal noun + pronoun suffix

ודברת בם **בְּשִׁבְתְּךָ** בביתך **וּבְלֶכְתְּךָ** בדרך **וּבְשָׁכְבְּךָ וּבְקוּמֶךָ** (דברים ו ז)
Recite them when you are sitting at home, walking in the road, going to bed and waking up
(Deuteronomy 6.7).

The forms שׁבֶת, לָלֶכֶת, לִשְׁכַּב and קוּם are related to the forms שבתך, לכתך, שכבך and לקום. The pronoun suffix -ךָ refers to the second person masculine singular, אתה *you*.

עַל נַהֲרוֹת בָּבֶל שָׁם יָשַׁבְנוּ גַּם-בָּכִינוּ **בְּזָכְרֵנוּ** אֶת צִיּוֹן (תהלים קלז א)
By the rivers of Babylon, there we sat down and wept, when we remembered Zion
(Psalms 137.1)
The form זכרנו is related to לִזְכּוֹר. The suffix -נו refers to the first person plural speakers, אנחנו *we*.

As seen in the biblical examples above, a pronoun suffix can be added to the infinitive construct appearing within a temporal clause. The reference of the suffix is to the subject of the sentence (found in the main clause).

The pronoun suffix and its reference (the subject of the sentence) are shaded:

---

(12) **הוּא וּבָנָיו** הוֹסִיפוּ לָשֵׂאת שֵׁמוֹת עִבְרִיִּים גַּם **לְאַחַר רִדְתָּם** מִצְרָיְמָה.
[=אחרי שירדו]

He and his sons continued to bear Hebrew names even after their <u>descent</u> [OR: after they went down] to Egypt.

רִדְתָּם is related to the infinitive form לָרֶדֶת. The pronoun suffix ם- refers to the subject of the sentence, הוא ובניו [הם].

(13) כָּךְ נָדַר **יַעֲקֹב בְּעָזְבוֹ** אֶת בֵּית אָבִיו.
[=כַּאֲשֶׁר עָזַב אֶת בֵּית אָבִיו]

So vowed Jacob <u>upon leaving</u> [OR: when he left] his father's house.

עזבו is related to the infinitive לעזוב. The pronoun suffix refers to יעקב [הוא], the subject of the sentence. Note that בְּעָזְבוֹ is pointed with a קָמָץ קָטָן /o/ (see 1.2.4(b) below).

(14) **הַמִּילָה** הָאֲרַמִּית הָלְכָה וְנָפוֹצָה בַּשָּׂפָה הָעִבְרִית **עַד הַגִּיעָהּ** לִלְשׁוֹן יָמֵינוּ.

The Aramaic word gradually became current in the Hebrew language <u>until its arrival</u> (OR: <u>until it arrived</u>) in contemporary Hebrew.

The pronoun suffix ה- refers to the subject מילה.
Note that the unpointed הגיעה is read as הַגִּיעָהּ *its arrival* (as in לְהַגִּיע), not הִגִּיעָה *[it] arrived*. This second reading would have been possible if עד ש- had been used:
המילה הארמית הלכה ונפוצה בשפה העברית **עד שֶׁהִגִּיעָה** ללשון ימינו.

(15) **בִּהְיוֹתָהּ** לְשׁוֹן דִּיבּוּר יוֹמְיוֹמִית שֶׁל יְהוּדִים, הָיְתָה **הַסְּפָרַדִּית-הַיְּהוּדִית** מוּכֶּרֶת לְתוֹשְׁבֵי הָאָרֶץ אַף יוֹתֵר מִן הָעִבְרִית הַמִּתְחַדֶּשֶׁת.

<u>Being</u> a daily language of speaking among Jews, Judeo-Spanish was familiar to the residents of the Land [of Israel] even more than the revitalized Hebrew.

בהיותה is related to the infinitive להיות; the pronoun suffix ה- refers to the language, ספרדית-יהודית.
Note that in this sentence the adverbial clause indicates cause, rather than time.

1.4 The pronunciation of verbal nouns with suffixes

When a pronoun suffix is attached to the verbal noun, the following phonetic (pronunciation) changes occur in the verb stem.

(a) The stress moves forward, from the second to the third root letter. Thus: בהיוול**דה** ← **ל**היוולד, בְּעָזְ**בו** ← **ל**עזוב (the bolding indicates where the stress falls).

(b) In verbs in *binyan pa'al*, the /o/ vowel, which in the infinitive form appears between the second and third root letters, moves backwards, appearing now between the first and second root letters. Thus:
לשמור: בְּשָׁמְרִי, בְּשָׁמְרְךָ, בְּשָׁמְרֵךְ, בְּשָׁמְרוֹ, בְּשָׁמְרָהּ, בְּשָׁמְרֵנוּ, בשמרכם/ם, בשמרם/ן

Note, however, that there is no such shift in verbs belonging to the ל"ה/ל"י group (e.g., (להיות – בהיותו, לרצות – ברצותה).

The /o/ vowel sound is often indicated in unpointed text with a וי"ו (e.g., בשומרו), although this spelling is not approved by the Academy of the Hebrew Language.[3]

(c) If the first letter of the verb root is יו"ד (in verbs belonging to the חסרי פ"י group), there are two alternative forms, one without יו"ד (similarly to the infinitive verb form, where the יו"ד is not retained) and one with יו"ד (retaining the first root letter).
For example:

בְּיוֹשְׁבוֹ, בשִׁבְתוֹ *sit* לָשֶׁבֶת
בְּיוֹדְעָם, בדַעְתָּם *know* לָדַעַת
בִּיוֹצְאָהּ, בצֵאתָהּ *go out* לָצֵאת
בְּיוֹרְדָן, בְּרִדְתָּן *go* down לָרֶדֶת

Some פ"נ verbs (as well as the verb לקח) also have two alternative forms:

בנוֹתְנוֹ, בְּתִיתוֹ *give*[4] לָתֵת
בנוֹשְׂאוֹ, בְּשֵׂאתוֹ *carry* לָשֵׂאת
בְּלוֹקְחָם, בְּקַחְתָּם *take* לָקַחַת

(d) In the *binyanim nif'al, pi'el* and *hitpa'el*, the long vowel /e/ in the second root letter shortens (is reduced), becoming a (mobile) *sheva*. (This is caused by the shift of the word stress to the last syllable after the addition of the suffix.)

נפעל: להיכָּנֵס – בהיכָּנְסָהּ
פיעל: לדַבֵּר – בדַבְּרוֹ
התפעל: להתפַּלֵּל – בהתפַּלְּלָם

Binyan hif'il remains unchanged: להַסְכִּים – בהַסְכִּימְךָ.

2. The direct object suffix (accusative pronoun suffix) כינוי המושא

2.1 Meaning and use
The inflected forms of את (e.g., אותו, אותם) may be replaced by a pronoun suffix attached to the verb. The suffix is known as the direct object suffix.
For example:

הוא קרא את הסיפור הוא קרא **אותו** → הוא קְרָאוֹ → **הוא קְרָאוֹ**: the inflected preposition אותו is replaced by the pronoun suffix -וֹ; both refer to the direct object סיפור.

The difference between הוא קרא אותו and הוא קְרָאוֹ cannot be rendered in English: they are both translated as *he read it*.

---

[3] See chapter 11, 3.3 for an example of the impact of this spelling rule on word recognition.
[4] This form is quite rare now.

The direct object suffix can be attached to the verb in any tense, as well as to the infinitive and imperative forms. Very common in biblical Hebrew, the suffix is found in modern Hebrew primarily in formal and literary registers, and then most likely only with the infinitive and third person past tense verb forms.[5]

זָכָר וּנְקֵבָה **בְּרָאָם** וַיְבָרֶךְ אֹתָם (בראשית ה ב)

[בראם=ברא אותם]

Male and female he created them, and He blessed them (Genesis 5.2)

The suffix is attached to the past tense verb בְּרָא.

זָכוֹר אֶת יוֹם הַשַּׁבָּת **לְקַדְּשׁוֹ** (שמות כ ז)

[לקדשו=לקדש אותו]

Remember the Sabbath day to sanctify it (Exodus 20.7)

The suffix is attached to the infinitive verb form לקדש.

2.1.1 The verbs that can take the object suffix are typically those that require את before a definite object (that is, transitive verbs in the *binyanim pa'al, pi'el* and *hif'il*).

Occasionally (and due to historical variations in preposition usage), the suffix at the end of the verb may replace the preposition -ל, rather than the preposition את.
For example:

הֶרְאָנוּ=הֶרְאָה לָנוּ *[it/he] showed us*
מְסַיַּעְתּוֹ=מְסַיַּעַת לוֹ *[it/she] assists him*
קָרָהוּ=קרה לוֹ *[it] happened to him*

2.1.2 The direct object suffixes are similar to the possessive suffixes of singular nouns (with one exception, the first person singular). Their meaning, however, is different.
For example:

The נו- suffix is translated as שלנו *our* when it appears with a noun, but as אותנו *us* when it is attached to a verb. Therefore, compare הוא מורנו=הוא המורה שלנו *he is our teacher*, with הפסוק מורנו=הפסוק מורה אותנו *the verse teaches us*.

The table below (read from left to right) shows the suffixes and the inflected forms of את that they replace.

me	you (m.)	you (f.)	him	her	us	you (m.)	you (f.)	them (m.)	them (f.)
נִי-	ךָ-	ךְ-	וֹ-/הוּ-/נּוּ-*	הָ-/הָ-/נָּה-*	נוּ-	כֶם-	כֶן-	ם-	ן-
אותי	אותךָ	אותךְ	אותו	אותה	אותנו	אתכם	אתכן	אותם	אותן

* The נה- and נו- suffixes can be used only in the future.

---

5 This is the conclusion arrived at by מוצ'ניק (1992) on the basis of an analysis of newspaper writing. She believes that the limited use of the direct object suffix today is due to the complexity of the phonetic changes in the verb brought about by the addition of the suffix.

2.2 Pronunciation

(a) If the last letter of the root does not already have a vowel, the vowel sound before the suffixes ־ם and ־ן is /e/ in the future and imperative, and /a/ in the inifiitive, present and past.
For example:

יוֹצִיאֵם/ן, **יְלַמְּדֵם/ן**, **יִשְׁמְעֵם/ן** (future) and **שָׁמְעֵם/ן**, **לַמְּדֵם/ן**, **הוֹצִיאֵם/ן** (imperative), but **מוֹצִיאָם/ן**, **מְלַמְּדָם/ן**, **שׁוֹמְעָם/ן** (present), **לְהוֹצִיאָם/ן**, **לְלַמְּדָם/ן**, **לְשׁוֹמְעָם/ן** (infinitive), **הוֹצִיאָם/ן**, **לִימְּדָם/ן**, **שְׁמָעָם/ן** (past).

(b) The suffix ־ו has several pronunciations, depending on the preceding:
/o/ (לִימְּדוֹ *he taught him*), /iv/ (לִימַּדְתִּיו *I taught him*) or /u/ (לִימְּדַתְהוּ, לִימְּדָתּוּ *she taught him*).

The addition of the direct object suffix entails a number of phonetic changes affecting vowel pronunciation and word stress in the verb. These changes are described in grammars of classical Hebrew and will not be dealt with here.

➤#3 & #4   **2.3 Identifying the reference of the direct object suffix**
The identification of the reference of the direct object suffix is important for reading comprehension. The suffix refers to a previously mentioned noun (the direct object) that agrees with it in number and gender.

A quick identification of the reference of the suffix is often facilitated by the fact that the direct object has already been introduced elsewhere in the sentence with the preposition את.

This is seen in the biblical verse cited above, "זָכוֹר אֶת יוֹם הַשַּׁבָּת לְקַדְּשׁוֹ", where the reference of the direct object suffix in לקדשו is יום השבת, already introduced with את (see also examples 17, 19, 22, 25 and 28 below).

In the second verse, "זָכָר וּנְקֵבָה בְּרָאָם וַיְבָרֶךְ אֹתָם", the inflected preposition אותם appears <u>after</u> the direct object suffix in בראם.

The suffix and its reference are shaded; the verb is shown "unpacked" in brackets:

---

(16) חז"ל הִדְגִּישׁו את עֶקרוֹן "מִידָה כְּנֶגֶד מִידה" – **מַטְבֵּעַ לָשׁוֹן** שֶׁהם יְצָרוּהוּ.
[יצרו אותו]
Ḥazal stressed the principle of "measure for measure" – an expression that they created.

(17) בִּימֵי הכּוֹהן עוּזִי, תפס עֵלִי את **הַמִּשְׁכָּן** וְהֶעֱבִירוֹ לשילה.
[העביר אותו]
In the days of the priest Uzi, Eli seized the tabernacle and moved <u>it</u> to Shiloh.

(18) חז"ל הִנְהִיגו **ברכה** מיוחדת שׁיש לְאָמְרָהּ לפני אכילת לֶחֶם.
[לאמור אותה]
Ḥazal instituted a special blessing that should be said before the eating of bread.

2.4 Distinguishing between direct object suffixes and conjugational (tense) suffixes

In unpointed text, the direct object suffixes that replace אותו, אותה and אותנו appear identical to the following conjugational endings:

(a) ו- (3rd person plural masculine, הם)
(b) ה- (3rd person singular feminine, היא)
(c) נו- (1st person plural, אנחנו)

Examples for each of these potential ambiguities are the following:

(a) פירשו could be read as:
    (1) פֵּירְשׁוֹ *he interpreted it*, OR:
    (2) פֵּירְשׁוּ *they interpreted*

(b) הסבירה could be read as:
    (1) הִסְבִּירָהּ *he explained it*, OR:
    (2) הִסְבִּירָה *she explained*
To help readers determine the function of the final ה-, the מַפִּיק diacritic (a dot within the ה) is sometimes added even in otherwise unpointed text.
(Note the different pronunciation of הִסְבִּירָהּ and הִסְבִּירָה: in הסבירה, the stress falls on the last syllable, in הסבירה it falls on the next to the last syllable).

(c) שלחנו could be read as:
    (1) שְׁלָחָנוּ *he sent us*, OR:
    (2) שָׁלַחְנוּ *we sent*

2.4.1 The table below shows potentially ambiguous verbs forms side by side in the past, future and present. (Some imperative forms also lend themselves to misinterpretation, but since they are not likely to occur in scholarly writing they are not listed here.)

conjugational suffix	direct object suffix	verb forms in unpointed text	*binyan*
(הם) שָׁלְחוּ (היא) שָׁלְחָה (אנחנו) שָׁלַחְנוּ	שְׁלָחוֹ (הוא שלח אותו) שְׁלָחָהּ (הוא שלח אותה) שְׁלָחָנוּ (הוא שלח אותנו)	שלחו שלחה שלחנו	פעל עבר
(הם) יִשְׁלְחוּ	יִשְׁלָחוֹ (הוא ישלח אותו)	ישלחו	פעל עתיד
(הם) בִּקְּרוּ (היא) בִּקְּרָה (אנחנו) בִּקְּרְנוּ	בִּקְּרוֹ (הוא ביקר אותו) בִּקְּרָהּ (הוא ביקר אותה) בִּקְּרָנוּ (הוא ביקר אותנו)	בקרו/ביקרו* בקרה/ביקרה* בקרנו/ביקרנו*	פיעל עבר
(הם) יְבַקְּרוּ	יְבַקְּרוֹ (הוא יבקר אותו)	יבקרו	פיעל עתיד
(הם) הִסְבִּירוּ (היא) הִסְבִּירָה	הִסְבִּירוֹ (הוא הסביר אותו) הִסְבִּירָהּ (הוא הסבירה אותה)	הסבירו הסבירה	הפעיל עבר
(היא) מַסְבִּירָה	מַסְבִּירָהּ (הוא מסביר אותה)	מסבירה	הפעיל הווה
(הם) יַסְבִּירוּ	יַסְבִּירוֹ (הוא יסביר אותו)	יסבירו	הפעיל עתיד

* Plene (full) spelling requires an additional יו"ד to indicate the /i/ sound in פיעל.

2.4.2 To determine the function of the suffix, first identify the subject of the verb with the suffix. This procedure is shown in examples 19–22 below.

The direct object suffix and its reference are shaded; the verb is shown "unpacked" in brackets below the sentence:

---

(19) הַקָּהָל קיבל את **החידוש** וְאַף **עודדו**.
[עודד אותו]

The public accepted the innovation and even <u>encouraged it</u>.

The reading עודדוּ *they encouraged* is not possible because the subject is the singular noun קהל (which would require the form עודד). Therefore, we read עודדוֹ=עודד אותו *he encouraged it*.

(20) בְּמִקְרֶה זה אין לְפָנֵינוּ **הוֹסָפָה**, שהמשורר נִזְכַּר בה בְּאיחור וְהוֹסִיפָהּ.
[הוסיף אותה]

In this case we do not have before us an addition that the poet remembered belatedly and <u>appended [it]</u>.

The reading הוסיפה *she added* is not possible because the subject of the clause, מְשׁוֹרֵר, is masculine. We, therefore, read הוסיפה *he appended it*.

(21) לביטוי **"הן...הן"** נִיתְּנוּ כמה הֶסְבָּרים. בֶּן-יְהוּדָה במילונו **כְּלָלוֹ** בְּעֵרֶךְ השלישי של "הן".
[כלל אותו]

Several explanations were given to the expression הן...הן. Ben Yehuda <u>included it</u> in his dictionary in the third entry for "הן".

The verb כללו cannot be read as כָּלְלוּ *[they] included* since the subject of the sentence is Ben Yehuda (singular masculine).

(22) את **היהודי** חֲסַר השורשים לא רִיתֵּק שום דָבָר לִכְפָרוֹ או לַעֲיָירָתוֹ, והכול משכו לַכְּרַךְ הגדול.
[משך אותו]

Nothing bound the rootless Jew to his village or town, and everything <u>pulled him</u> to the big metropolis.

We read משכו as מָשְׁכוֹ=מָשַׁךְ אותו *[it] attracted him* rather than מָשְׁכוּ *[they] attracted* because the subject of the clause, הכול *everything*, requires a singular verb form.
The interpretation of הכול as *everything* rather than *everyone* (a formal variant of כולם requiring a plural verb form) is based on the its contrast with שום דבר *nothing* in the first clause. In addition, the reading הכל מָשְׁכוּ *everyone attracted* would require a direct object – משכו אותו.

#5 & #6   **2.5 Distinguishing among three types of pronoun suffixes**

2.5.1 Direct object suffixes versus subject suffixes

With the exception of the first person singular, the direct object suffixes are identical in form to the suffixes that attach to verbal noun forms and refer to the subject. The distinction between these suffixes is, therefore, vital for reading comprehension. The differences are summarized below:

(a) Direct object suffixes can attach to a transitive verb (that is, a verb that can take an object complement) in any of its forms, that is, past, present, future, infinitive and imperative. The suffix answers the questions את מי? את מה?.

(b) Subject suffixes can attach only to an infinitive construct form (that is, infinitive verb minus the initial -ל), which is typically preceded by the prepsotion -ב (or by other prepositions or adverbs that indicate time, for example, כ-, עם, עד, לפני, אחרי, בטרם). The suffix answers the question מי?.

2.5.2 Verb suffixes versus noun suffixes

The distinction between the two types of verb suffixes, on one hand, and the similar looking noun (possessive) suffixes, on the other hand, is made on the basis of the grammatical identity of the word that takes the suffix, that is, whether it is a verb or a noun. Noun suffixes answer the questions של מי? or של מה?.

The flow chart below provides further help in determining the function of the suffix. It can be used to determine the meaning of the suffixes in examples 23–28 below.

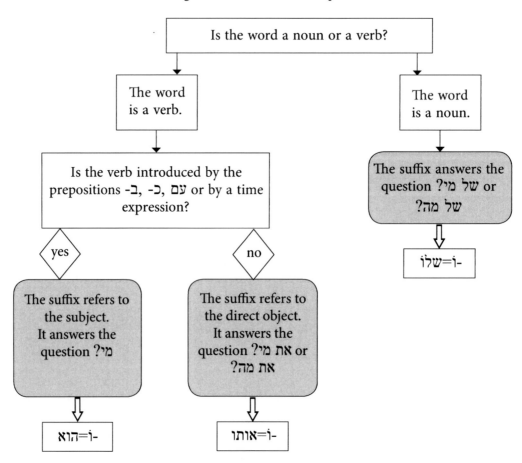

The suffixed words are shaded and the suffixes are bolded; the suffixed forms are shown "unpacked" in brackets below the sentence:

---

(23) **בְּצֵאתָם** מֵהַר ה' מֹשֶׁה נוֹשֵׂא וְנוֹתֵן עִם חוֹבָב חוֹתְנוֹ הַמִּדְיָינִי, כְּדֵי **לְצָרְפוֹ** לְמַסַּע ישראל אל הארץ החדשה.

[בצאתם=כאשר הם (משה וחובב) יצאו, לצרפו=לצרף אותו (את חובב)]

When <u>they</u> leave [OR: upon leaving] God's Mountain, Moses negotiates with Hovav, his Midianite father-in-law, in order to include <u>him</u> as a participant in the voyage of the Israelites to the new land.

(24) הַמְחַבֵּר **מַעֲמִידֵנוּ** על הקשיים העומדים בפנינו **בְּנַסּוֹתֵנוּ** ללמוד על העולם הרוּחָני של גְּאוֹנֵי בָּבֶל מן השאלות והתשובות כְּפִי שֶׁהִגִּיעוּ **לְיָדֵינוּ**.

[מעמידנו=מעמיד אותנו, בנסותנו=כאשר אנחנו מנסים, ידינו=הידיים שלנו]

The author presents <u>us</u> with the difficulties (that stand) before us when <u>we</u> try [OR: when trying] to learn about the spiritual universe of the Babylon Geonim from the responsa as they came into <u>our hands</u>.

(25) לוּ רצה אָדָם להתעלם **מִיָּלְדָיו** (**לְנוֹטְשָׁם אוֹ לְמוֹכְרָם**) ולא לָזון את ילדיו, היה בית הדין כּוֹפֶה על האָב **לְזוּנָם** עד **הַגִּיעָם** לגיל שְׁתֵּים-עֶשְׂרֵה.

[ילדיו=הילדים שלו; לנוטשם, למוכרם, לזונם=לנטוש, למכור, לזון אותם, עד הגיעם=עד שהם יגיעו]

If a person wanted to ignore <u>his children</u> (to abandon <u>them</u> or sell <u>them</u>) and not feed <u>his children</u>, the court would compel the father to feed <u>them</u> until <u>they</u> reached the age of twelve.

(26) **תְּחוּשָׁתָם** של היהודים הייתה שהקדוש-ברוך-הוא עצמו שָׁלַח אֵשׁ **בְּמִקְדָּשׁוֹ וְהֶחֱרִיבוֹ**.

[תחושתם=התחושה שלהם, מקדשו=המקדש שלו, החריבו=החריב אותו]

The feeling of the Jews (<u>their</u> feeling) was that God himself had sent fire to <u>His temple</u> and destroyed <u>it.</u>

(27) השורה "הֱיֵה אדם **בְּצֵאתְךָ** ויהודי **בְּאֹהֳלְךָ**" מתוך **שִׁירוֹ** של יל"ג משנת 1863 הפכה **לְסִיסְמָתָהּ** של תנועת הַשְׂכָּלה.

[בצאתך=כאשר אתה יוצא, באהלך=באהל שלך, שירו=השיר שלו, סיסמתה=הסיסמה שלה]

The line "be a human being in public (literally: when <u>you</u> go out) and a Jew at home (literally: within <u>your</u> tent) from Yehuda Leib Gordon's 1863 poem became the slogan of the [Jewish] Enlightenment movement (<u>its</u> slogan).

(28) **בְּסַיְּימוֹ** את **סִפְרוֹ** "תולדות יצחק" **נְתָנוֹ** יצחק קארו בידי סופר שֶׁ**יַּעְתִּיקוֹ וִיבִיאוֹ** לדפוס.

[בסיימו=כאשר הוא סיים, ספרו=הספר שלו, נתנו=נתן אותו, יעתיקו=יעתיק אותו, יביאו=יביא אותו]

When <u>he finished</u> (OR: upon finishing) <u>his book</u> "Toledot Yitzhaq", Isaac Caro <u>put it</u> in the hands of a scribe who would <u>copy it</u> and <u>publish it</u>.

In this example, the pronoun suffix -וֹ has 3 different functions: (a) in בסיימו it refers to the subject, יצחק קארו, and translated as *he*, (b) in ספרו it is a possessive suffix translated as *his*, (c) in נתנו, יעתיקו and יביאו it is a direct object suffix, translated as *it*. Note that without points there is a risk of misreading נתנו, יעתיקו, יביאו as נָתְנוּ *they gave*, יעתיקו *they will copy*, יביאו *they will bring* (see 2.6 above); this can be averted by identifying יצחק קארו as the subject of the verb נתנו, and סופר *scribe* as the subject of the verbs יעתיקו and יביאו.

3. Expanded predicates נשוא מורחב

This section discusses three types of two-word verb phrases:

(a) Finite verb + infinitive verb (3.1)

(b) Finite verb *and* finite verb (3.2)

(c) Past tense of "to be" + a main verb in the present tense (3.3 and 3.4)

> A finite verb is a verb that has a tense – past, present or future.

3.1 Finite verb + infinitive verb
In verb phrases that are made up of a finite verb and an infinitive verb, the first (finite) verb has an aspectual function: it describes the action of the main (infinitive) verb in terms of its beginning, continuation or end.

The aspectual verbs in this group include:

(a) הֵחֵל, התחיל *began* (alternatively, this verb may be followed by a present tense verb, example 30).

(b) הוסיף, הִמְשִׁיךְ *continued* (note that before an infinitive verb, להוסיף no longer means *to add*).

(c) חָדַל, סִיֵּם, הפסיק, פָּסַק, גָּמַר, כִּילָה *stopped, ceased*.

3.1.1 When the sentence begins with an adverbial, the finite and infinitive verbs may be separated by the subject (examples 30, 32–33).

The verb phrase is shaded:

---

(29) באמצע שְנות העשרים הֵחֵלוּ להתגבש אַרבַּע התנועות הקיבוציות.
In the middle of the 1920's, the four Kibbutz movements <u>began to consolidate.</u>

(30) בשְנת 1882 הֵחֵלוּ עולֵי גל העלייה הראשון מגיעים לארץ ישראל.
In the year 1882, the immigrants of the first immigration wave <u>began arriving</u> to the Land of Israel.

Both החלו להגיע and החלו מגיעים are possible.

(31) שַעֲרֵי העיר הוסיפו להיות סגורים בלֵילות.
The city gates <u>continued to be</u> closed at night.

(32) לְאַחַר קום המדינה הִמְשִיכָה התנועה הקיבוצית להתרחב.
After the establishment of the State [of Israel], the Kibbutz movement <u>continued to expand.</u>

---

(33) בְּסוֹף שְׁנוֹת הַתִּשְׁעִים חדל הַיִּישׁוּב לתפקד כְּקִיבּוּץ.
At the end of the 1990's, the settlement <u>ceased functioning</u> as a kibbutz.

3.1.2 Expanded verb phrases referring to the future: עָמַד, הִתְעַתֵּד, אָמַר, עָתִיד + infinitive

To indicate an intended action in the near future or future within the past, the verb עמד is utilized before a main verb in the infinitive. In this use, עמד is translated as *was about to* rather than *stood* (example 34).

3.1.2.1 The verb התעתד indicates an intention with regard to the future action expressed in the main verb (example 35). Another way of indicating intention or future plan is to use the verb אמר before the main verb (e.g., אמר לחזור *intended to return*, NOT: *said*).

3.1.2.2 To indicate a remote future action, עתיד before main verb in the infinitive is used (example 36).

(34) כָּל אֵימַת שֶׁעָמְדוּ להתקין תַּקָּנָה דְּרוּשָׁה הָיְתָה הַסְכָּמַת כָּל חָבֵר וְחָבֵר שֶׁל כָּל קְהִילָה וּקְהִילָה.
Whenever <u>they were about to</u> institute a new ordinance, the consent of each and every member of each congregation was required.

(35) חֶבֶר הַלְּאוּמִים התעתד להקיף אֶת כָּל אֻמּוֹת הָעוֹלָם.
The League of Nations <u>intended to</u> encompass all of the world's nations.

(36) הַמִּדְרָשׁ עתיד להופיע בְּמַהֲדוּרָה בִּיקּוֹרְתִית.
The Midrash <u>will appear</u> in a critical edition.

3.1.3 In another group of verb phrases of the "finite verb + infinitive verb" type, the first verb is semantically related to an adverb and therefore has an adverbial role, namely, to describe <u>how</u> the action of the second (infinitive) verb takes place.
For example, in הֵיטִיב לְתָאֵר *described well* the verb היטיב is related to היטב *well*.[6]

#7   3.2 Finite verb *and* finite verb
הלך ו-
חזר ו-, שב ו-
המשיך ו-, הוסיף ו-

The verbs הלך, חזר (or שב), and המשיך (or הוסיף) indicate, respectively, gradual, repeated and continued aspects of the action expressed by the adjacent (main) verb.

> An alternative way of signaling repeated (or strong) action is by repeating the verb (e.g., דיבר ודיבר *spoke for a long time*, OR: *spoke a great deal*).

---

[6] See further discussion in Chapter 5, 3.1.

The two coordinated verbs in this phrase "mirror" each other in form: they share the same tense, person and number, or are both infinitives.

With the exception of הלך, the aspectual verb always comes first. When הלך is positioned <u>after</u> the main verb, the tone is elevated (example 39).

Note that the coordination of two <u>synonymous</u> verbs is a separate phenomenon from the one described here, as those comprise a single lexical concept (e.g., צף ועלה *emerged*).[7]

3.2.1 When the sentence begins with an adverbial, the two verbs in the sequence are likely be separated, straddling the subject (examples 38 and 41).

3.2.2 The use of המשיך and הוסיף *continued* with a coordinated finite verb is perceived as more formal than with an infinitive verb form, as seen in 3.1 above. In other words, הוסיף ודיבר is more formal than הוסיף לדבר, but the meaning is the same: *continued to speak*.

3.2.3 In translation, the aspectual verb is not rendered verbatim (e.g., הלך is not translated as *went*; שב is not translated as *returned*). Instead, the verb may be replaced by an adverb (e.g., *gradually* for הלך, *again* for הוסיף), or a prefix (*re-* for שב and חזר).

---

(37) יְדִיעַת הָעִבְרִית <mark>הָלְכָה וּפָחֲתָה</mark>.
Knowledge of Hebrew <u>gradually decreased</u>.

(38) בְּאוֹתָה תְקוּפָה <mark>הָלְכוּ הָאֵירוּעִים הָאַנְטִישֵׁמִיִּים וְתָכְפוּ</mark>.
Anti-Semitic events <u>grew more frequent</u> during that period.

After an adverbial (בְּאוֹתָה תְקוּפָה) the verb phrase is split, and the verbs straddle the subject. This is also seen in example 41.

(39) הַשְׁפָּעָתָם שֶׁל אַנְשֵׁי הַהָגוּת וְהַמַּדָּע, הַמְשׁוֹרְרִים וְהַסּוֹפְרִים בַּחֶבְרָה <mark>נִתְרַחֲבָה וְהָלְכָה</mark> מֵאָז הַמְצָאַת הַדְּפוּס וְהִתְפַּשְּׁטוּתוֹ.
The influence on society of thinkers and scientists, poets and writers, <u>gradually expanded</u> since the invention and spread of print.

(40) בִּשְׁנוֹת הַ-40 שֶׁל הַמֵּאָה הַ-19 <mark>מַמְשִׁיכָה</mark> הָאוּכְלוּסִיָּה הַיְּהוּדִית בָּאָרֶץ לִגְדֹּל בְּקֶצֶב <mark>הוֹלֵךְ וְגוֹבֵר</mark>.
During the forties of the 19th century, the Jewish population in the Land (of Israel) <u>continues to grow</u> at an accelerating <u>(gradually increasing)</u> pace.

This sentence contains two types of aspectual verb phrases: הולך וגובר and ממשיכה לגדול.

(41) אֵלִיָּהוּ <mark>שָׁב וּמִתְגַּלֶּה</mark> בָּאֵירוּעִים שׁוֹנִים כְּדֵי לְלַמֵּד חָכְמָה וּמוּסָר.
Elijah <u>reappears</u> at different events in order to teach wisdom and moral behavior.

---

[7] See discussion of binomials in Chapter 11, Part C.

> (42) בְּזוֹהַר **חוֹזֶרֶת וְנִשְׁנֵית** הַהֲנָחָה שֶׁבְּנֵי הָעוֹלָם מְצוּיִים עַל פִּי רוֹב בְּמַצָּב שֶׁל שֵׁינָה.
> The notion that mortals are usually found in a state of slumber <u>recurs</u> in the Zohar.

3.2.4 The idiomatic expression **מְמַשְׁמֵשׁ וּבָא**, also in this pattern, indicates the imminent beginning of an event.
For example:

קִיצָהּ שֶׁל הַדְּמוֹקְרַטְיָה מְשַׁמֵּשׁ וּבָא *the end of democracy was (fast) approaching.*

3.2.5 A rather formal and literary variation of the "verb *and* verb" phrase is a three-verb sequence, where the first verb – a finite (conjugated) verb (example 43) or an infinitive verb (example 44) – is followed by two coordinated verbs in the infinitive absolute form.
The second of the two coordinated verbs has the same root and *binyan* as the first verb in the sequence.
The first of the two coordinated verbs – usually the verb חָזוֹר – is aspectual: it describes the repetitive nature of the action expressed by the verbs with the shared root and *binyan* (in the examples below, the verb pairs הֵפֵרוּ-הָפֵר, נֶעֶנְשׁוּ-הֵיעָנֵשׁ and לְהַזְהִיר-הַזְהֵר).
In translation, the three-verb sequence can be converted to a single verb followed by an adverb that conveys the repetitiveness of the action.

> Like the regular infinitive, the infinitive absolute (מָקוֹר מוּחְלָט) has a fixed form in each *binyan*, not dependent on tense or person. The regular infinitive and infinitive absolute differ from each other in that (a) the infinitive absolute is not introduced by a למ"ד and (b) in two *binyanim* (*pa'al* and *hif'il*) their forms are not identical.
> The infinitive absolute occurs mostly in biblical Hebrew, where one of its functions is to emphasize the action.

> (43) בְּנֵי יִשְׂרָאֵל נָטוּ אַחַר הָאֱלִים הַזָּרִים וּבְכָךְ **הֵפֵרוּ חָזוֹר וְהָפֵר** אֶת בְּרִיתָם עִם אֱלוֹהֵי יִשְׂרָאֵל וְלָכֵן **נֶעֶנְשׁוּ חָזוֹר וְהֵיעָנֵשׁ** עַל חֲטָאֵיהֶם.
> The Children of Israel followed the foreign gods, and in doing so <u>repeatedly violated</u> their covenant with the God of Israel, and therefore were <u>repeatedly punished</u> for their sins.

The aspectual verb חזור (in the infinitive absolute form of *binyan pa'al*) indicates the repeated nature of the action expressed by main verbs, נענשו, היענש and הפרו, הפר. The first and third verbs in each sequence share the same root and *binyan* but vary in form: הפרו and נענשו are in the past tense (in the *binyanim hif'il* and *nif'al*, respectively), while the echoing verbs הָפֵר and הֵיעָנֵשׁ are in the infinitive absolute.

> (44) מַה מֵּנִיעַ אֶת הָאֵם לְהַזְהִיר אֶת בְּנָהּ **חָזוֹר וְהַזְהֵר**?
> What impels the mother to <u>warn</u> her son <u>again and again</u>?

✗#8   3.3   היה + **present tense verb**

Verb phrases made up of the verb "to be" in the past tense and a present tense verb have two (unrelated) uses: they express (a) habitual action in the past, and (b) hypothetical and non-factual statements.

These two functions of the past tense of the verb "to be" (discussed in 3.3.1 and 3.3.3 below) should be distinguished from its use to indicate ordinary past time in nominal (verbless) sentences and יש/אין sentences, as well as with certain verbs whose present tense is phonetically identical to the past tense (e.g., היה נחשב *was considered* instead of just נחשב).

3.3.1 Habitual action in the past – *used to, would*

Habitual or typical action in the past can be expressed by means of time adverbials such as תמיד *always,* בדרך כלל *usually,* and לעתים קרובות *often.* Alternatively, the verb "to be" in the past tense followed by another (main) verb in the present tense may be employed. Often, a specific past time frame or setting for the actions or events is mentioned, with the implication that they no longer take place.

3.3.1.1 The auxiliary verb "to be" may be separated from the main verb by one or more words (example 46). An inversion of the order (whereby the auxiliary "to be" appears <u>after</u> the main verb) is a stylistic variation that tends to elevate the tone (example 47).

---

(45) על פי התיאור במשנה, בחג הסוכות **היו מדליקים** במקדש את מנורות הזהב.

According to the description in the Mishnah, in the holiday of Succoth, they <u>would light</u> the gold candelabras in the Temple.

Note that היו מדליקים is impersonal (i.e., subjectless). An alternative translation – in the passive[8] – is: *The gold candelabras would be lighted in the temple.*

(46) עם שַׁחַר **הָיְתָה** תהלוכה גדולה של אנשי ירושלים ועולֵי רֶגֶל, בראשה כוהנים ובתוכה מְנַגְּנִים בחֲצוֹצְרוֹת ותוקעים בשופר, **צוֹעֶדֶת** למַעְיָין השילוֹחַ שֶׁלְמַרְגְלוֹת הַר הזֵיתים.

At dawn, a large procession of Jerusalemites and pilgrims, with priests at its head and trumpet players and shofar (horn) blowers within it, <u>would march</u> to the Shiloah Spring at the foot of Mount Olive.

(47) שַׁבָּת הַמַּלְכָּה **הָיְתָה** מתקבלת בִּשְׁקִיעַת הַחַמָּה בזְמִירוֹת והַקָּפוֹת על-יְדֵי המְקוּבָּלים, וגם בצֵאתָה **מְלֻוָּה הָיְתָה** בשירָה ובריקוד.

Sabbath the Queen <u>would be received</u> at sundown with singing and rounds of dancing by the Cabbalists, and also upon its departure it <u>would be accompanied</u> by singing and dancing.

3.3.1.2 Following its use in Mishnaic Hebrew, היה + present tense verb is occasionally employed to indicate a continuous (rather than habitual) past.

---

[8] See Chapter 1, 5(a).

> (48) מֹשֶׁה הִתְיַישֵׁב בְּמִדְיָן, וּבְיוֹם מִן הַיָּמִים **הָיָה יוֹשֵׁב** עַל יַד אַחַת הַבְּאֵרוֹת אֲשֶׁר בְּאוֹתָהּ הָאָרֶץ.
>
> Moses settled in Midian, and one day he <u>was sitting</u> by one of the wells in this country.

3.3.2 Habitual or customary action with נהג + infinitive

Where an established past custom is referred to, the verb נהג in the past tense paired with a main verb in the infinitive may be used (example 49). Another (somewhat redundant) option is a three-verb sequence: "to be" in the past tense followed by נהג in the present tense, and a main verb in the infinitive (examples 50–51).

When נהג is in the present tense, it refers to a current custom or practice (example 52).

3.3.2.1 When נהג is <u>not</u> followed by a verb in the infinitive, it is translated as *(to be) customary, it is the custom to* (example 53).

> (49) בְּנֵי יִשְׂרָאֵל, כַּשֵּׁמִיִּים בִּכְלָלָם, **נָהֲגוּ לְהַבְטִיחַ** לָאֵל הַבְטָחָה-עַל-תְּנַאי – הַבְטָחָה זוֹ נִקְרֵאת בְּשֵׁם נֵדֶר.
>
> The Israelites, like the Semites in general, <u>used to</u> make God a conditional promise – this promise is called *"neder"* (a vow).
> OR: <u>it was the custom</u> among the Israelites, as also the Semites in general, to make God a conditional promise.
>
> (50) בִּתְקוּפַת הַמִּשְׁנָה וְהַתַּלְמוּד **הָיוּ נוֹהֲגִים לְתַרְגֵּם** אֶת הַתּוֹרָה בְּשָׁעָה שֶׁקָּרְאוּ בָּהּ.
>
> In the period of the Mishnah and the Talmud they <u>used to</u> (OR: the custom was to) translate the Torah when reading it.
>
> (51) כֶּנֶס כָּזֶה **הָיָה נוֹהֵג לַחֲזוֹר וּלְהַתְקִין** כָּל הַתַּקָנוֹת הַקּוֹדְמוֹת **וְהָיָה מוֹסִיף** עֲלֵיהֶן תַּקָנוֹת חֲדָשׁוֹת.
>
> Such an assembly <u>used to</u> reinstate all the previous ordinances and <u>would add</u> to them new ones.
>
> Note the use of the coordinated verbs לחזור ולהתקין to indicate repeated action, as discussed in 3.2 above.
>
> (52) מִבְנִים רַבִּים **נוֹהֲגִים** לְהַבְלִיט אֶת אֶבֶן הָרֹאשָׁה אוֹ לְקַשְּׁטָהּ.
>
> In many structures <u>it is the custom to</u> make the keystone protrude or to adorn it.
>
> (53) מָסֹרֶת זוֹ **נָהֲגָה** בַּקְּהִילּוֹת שׁוֹנוֹת.
>
> This tradition <u>was customary</u> (OR: was the custom) in various congregations.
>
> An alternate wording would be: מסורת זו הייתה נהוגה בקהילות שונות.

⚠️ **3.3.2.2** Be sure to distinguish between the uses of נהג to express custom and its other meanings:

(a) *To behave* (synonymous with להתנהג) or *treat someone in a certain way* (also expressed by להתייחס אל), when followed by the prepositions -ב or עם (e.g., השליט נהג עימם/בהם ביד רכה *the ruler treated them leniently*).

(b) *To drive a vehicle.*

3.3.3 Past tense of "to be" in "unreal" conditional sentences

Conditional sentences are made up of two clauses: a condition clause introduced by "if" and a result clause.

In "real" conditional sentences, the fulfillment of the condition may or may not occur. In "unreal" (or "hypothetical") conditional sentences, it is expected that the condition will <u>not</u> be fulfilled.

The two types of condition sentences differ in Hebrew in their use of tense and the introductory particle "if".

3.3.3.1 Tense in conditional sentences

"Real" condition sentences usually require in Hebrew the future tense in <u>both</u> clauses (example 54). The present tense may be used when a general circumstance is referred to. In contrast, "unreal" conditions employ the past tense of the verb "to be" and a present tense verb. There are two possibilities:

(a) Non-symmetrical configuration:
  [if + past tense verb] + [past "to be" + present tense verb]
  אילו למדת, היית מצליח בבחינה
  The verb "to be" appears only in the result clause

(b) Symmetrical configuration:
  [if + past "to be" + present tense verb] + [if + past "to be" + present tense verb]
  אילו היית לומד, היית מצליח בבחינה
  The verb "to be" appears twice, in the conditional and the result clauses

---

Both configurations are translated in the same way: *if you had studied for the exam, you would have succeeded*. The difference between the two options is stylistic, the non-symmetrical configuration perceived as being more formal.

3.3.3.2 Varieties of the particle "if"

(a) "Unreal" condition sentences are introduced (in formal or careful style) by the particles **אילו** or **לו**.

(b) **אם** is reserved for "real" condition clauses (example 54); however, in informal style it may be used instead of אילו and לו.
When this happens, a symmetrical clause configuration (that is, "to be" in the past tense used twice) is <u>obligatory</u> (example 57).

> לו is biblical, **אילו** is post-biblical. Note that לו, when followed by a future tense verb, expresses a wish: לו יְהִי (poetic) *if only it were so.*

Other expressions that introduce a "real" condition are: בְּמִידָה שֶׁ-/ו- *to the extent that,* בְּמִקְרֶה שֶׁ- *in case that,* בִּתְנַאי שֶׁ- *on condition that,* וּבִלְבַד שֶׁ- *provided that,* אֶלָּא אִם *unless,* כָּל עוֹד *as long as,* וְהָיָה כִּי *should this be the case* and בְּאִם *if* (considered non-normative).

(c) To express negative hypothetical condition – אִילוּ לֹא *if not* – the particles לוּלֵא, אִלְמָלֵא or אִילוּלֵא may be used (an alternative spelling is with יו"ד rather than אל"ף at the end: אִלְמָלֵי, אִילוּלֵי, לוּלֵי). Occasionally, the word לֹא is (redundantly) added (e.g., אלמלא לא, example 59).

Negative hypothetical condition sentences usually adhere to the non-symmetrical pattern, where היה is used only once, in the result clause.

The condition part of the sentence may be a noun phrase, rather than a clause (example 61).

A well known biblical example is Samson's words:
לוּלֵא חֲרַשְׁתֶּם בְּעֶגְלָתִי, לֹא מְצָאתֶם חִידָתִי (שופטים יד יח)
If you had not plowed with my heifer, you would not have found out my riddle
(Judges 14.18)
In the biblical example, there is no auxiliary verb and both main verbs are in the past tense.

In translation into English it is not possible to distinguish among the different conditional particles – they are all translated as *if*.

3.3.3.3 Translating "unreal" conditional sentences into English
Hebrew conditional sentences in the past tense are ordinarily interpreted – and translated – as referring to events that can no longer take place (examples 55–56).

On occasion, if the probability of the event is perceived within a given context as low, but not zero, the translator may use the English conditional structure of improbability (see example 25 above).

Negative hypothetical sentences (*if not*) with לולא, אלולא and אלמלא are always understood (and translated) as truly "unreal" (impossible) conditions (examples 58–61).

Note also that following אילו and its varieties, the verb tends to appear before the subject (examples 59–60), requiring – in translation – a word order reversal.

(54) אם נצליח להתחקות אחר דרכי הקבורה של אנשי ירושלים, נוכל להכיר טוב יותר את החברה הירושלמית.
<u>If we succeed</u> to trace the burial methods of the residents of Jerusalem, <u>we will be able to</u> know better the society in Jerusalem.

(55) לְפִי אַגָּדָה אַחַת, **לוּ הָיוּ** שְׁלוֹשׁ מֵאוֹת כּוֹהֲנִים **עוֹמְדִים** בהר הַזֵּיתִים **וְאוֹמְרִים** בִּרְכַּת כּוֹהֲנִים, **הָיָה הַמָּשִׁיחַ** בָּא.
According to one legend, <u>if</u> three hundred priests <u>had stood</u> on the Mount of Olives and <u>said</u> the priestly benediction, the Messiah <u>would have come</u>.

The two elements of the verb phrase – the auxiliary "to be" and the main verb – straddle the subject in both clauses. Note also that the auxiliary "to be" is not repeated with each main verb (הָיוּ עוֹמְדִים וְאוֹמְרִים); this economy is also seen in example 57.

(56) נְתָאֵר לְעַצְמֵנוּ מה **הָיָה** גוֹרלה של העברית הקדומה **אילו הָיְיתָה מוֹסִיפָה לְהִתְקַיֵּים** בְּפִי הָעָם בְּאַרְצוֹת פְּזוּרָיו הַמְרוּבּוֹת, מִן הַסְּתָם לא לָשׁוֹן עברית אחת **הָיְיתָה** לָנוּ אֶלָּא לְשׁוֹנוֹת לְשׁוֹנוֹת.
Let's imagine what <u>would have been</u> the fate of ancient Hebrew if it <u>had continued</u> to exist as a spoken language (literally: in the mouth of the people) in the many diasporas. Probably we <u>would have had</u> not one Hebrew language, but many.

Given the hypothetical conditional clause אילו הָיְיתָה מוֹסִיפָה לְהִתְקַיֵּים, we understand מה הָיָה גוֹרלה and לא לָשׁוֹן אחת הָיְיתָה לָנוּ as hypothetical result clauses and translate *what would have been its fate* and *we would have had not one language but many*, rather than: *what was its fate* and *we did not have one language but many*.

Note the doubling of the noun לְשׁוֹנוֹת to indicate *many*.

(57) **אם הָיָה מַצְלִיחַ** – **הָיָה מַמְשִׁיךְ** לארץ ישראל **וכוֹתב** שָׁם הֲלָכָה בְּרוּרָה לִקְרַאת שְׁנַת תקמ"א.
<u>Had he succeeded</u>, he <u>would have continued</u> to the Land of Israel <u>and written</u> there a clear ruling for the year 1781.[9]

In this example, the less formal אם is used instead of אילו or לוּ; the symmetrical configuration (הָיָה מַצְלִיחַ – הָיָה מַמְשִׁיךְ וכוֹתב) is, therefore, obligatory.

(58) **אילו לא הִתְנַצֵּר לא הָיָה יָכוֹל** בנימין דיזראלי **לְהִיכָּנֵס** לחיים הפוליטיים.
If he <u>had not converted</u> to Christianity, Benjamin Disraeli <u>would not have been able</u> to enter the political life.

(59) **אלמלא לא פָּגַע** הַסְּכְסוּךְ אָבוֹת-בָּנִים בְּעֶצֶם לִיבָּהּ של החסידות, אֶפְשָׁר שֶׁכָּל דַּרְכָּהּ של הַתְּנוּעָה **הָיְיתָה שׁוֹנָה** מאוד.
If the fathers-sons conflict <u>had not struck</u> at the very heart of the Ḥasidic movement, it is possible that its entire course <u>would have been</u> very different.

Note the redundant use of לא after אלמלא (3.3.3.2 (c) above).

---

⁹ For the conversion of Hebrew dates in letters into Gregorian calendar dates see Appendix I.

---

(60) הַיִּשׁוּב **לֹא הָיָה שׂוֹרֵד אלמלא הַצְּלִיחָה** הַמִּלְחָמָה בְּמָלַרְיָה.
The settlement <u>would not have survived</u> if the war on the malaria <u>had not succeeded.</u>

(61) הַיְּצִירָה מְתָאֶרֶת אֶת הָעוֹלָם **שֶׁיָּכוֹל הָיָה לְהִתְקַיֵּים לוּלֵא** הַחֵטְא הַקַּדְמוֹן.
The work describes the world that <u>could have existed</u> if not for original sin.

3.3.3.4 Past tense of "to be" + present tense verb in counter-factual statements

The past tense of "to be" and a main verb in the present tense are also used to indicate that a statement is contrary to fact. In a factual statement, the main verb would be in regular past tense.

---

(62) הַקֶּשֶׁר רָחָב יוֹתֵר **הָיָה מְסַיֵּיעַ** בְּזִיהוּי מָהִיר יוֹתֵר שֶׁל הַשִּׁיר.
A wider context <u>would have aided</u> in a quicker identification of the poem.

With the verb לְסַיֵּיעַ in the past tense and without the auxiliary הָיָה the sentence would have the opposite meaning:
הקשר רחב יותר <u>סייע</u> בזיהוי מהיר יותר של השיר *A wider context aided in a quicker identification of the poem.*

3.4 הָיָה in modal expressions

The use of הָיָה in conjunction with a modal expression (e.g., מוּכְרָח, חַיָּב *obligated,* צָרִיךְ *must,* יָכוֹל *can,* מְסוּגָל *capable,* עָשׂוּי *may,* אָמוּר *supposed to*) may create an ambiguity, as it may signal either the past tense of the modal or a counter-factual statement.
For example:

הוּא יָכוֹל לְהָבִין (now) *he can understand*
הוּא הָיָה יָכוֹל לְהָבִין *he was able to understand* (factual statement in the past), or: *he could have understood* (but did not) (non-factual statement).

Since both meanings are served by the same form, the writer's intention must be inferred from the context beyond the sentence level. For instance, when the phrases הָיָה כְּדַאי and הָיָה רָאוּי appear in a book review, they refer to what the author failed (in the critic's opinion) to do, and are translated as *it would have been worthwhile/ appropriate* rather than *it was worthwhile/ appropriate* (examples 64–65).

---

(63) תַּרְגּוּם יְצִירוֹת מוֹפֵת מִגֶּרְמָנִית אוֹ מִצָּרְפָתִית לְעִבְרִית **עָשׂוּי הָיָה** לִבְנוֹת גֶּשֶׁר תַּרְבּוּתִי לְאַקוּלְטוּרַצְיָה שֶׁאִפְיְּינָה אֶת הַשְׂכָּלַת בֶּרְלִין בַּמֵּאָה הי"ט.
The translation of classical literary works from German or French into Hebrew <u>could build (OR: could have built)</u> a cultural bridge for the acculturation that characterized the Berlin Enlightenment movement in the 19th century.

In this example, the translation of עָשׂוּי הָיָה as *could,* to indicate past possibility, or as *could have,* to indicate unrealized past possibility, depends on the historical facts presented in the article: whether the translation of German and French literary works into Hebrew in fact contributed to Jewish acculturation, or only had the potential to do so.

> (64) כָּאן נִרְאֶה לִי רָאוּי הָיָה לְהַרְחִיב בְּדִיּוּן בִּמְקוֹרוֹת חוּץ-יְהוּדִיִּים.
> Here, it seems to me, <u>it would have been appropriate</u> to extend the discussion of non-Jewish sources.

> (65) פֶּרֶק זֶה שֶׁל הַסֵּפֶר הָיָה יָכוֹל לְהִיקָּרֵא בְּשֵׁם אַחֵר.
> This chapter of the book <u>could have been called</u> by another name.

3.4.1 Paired with the verb "to be" in the past tense, the verb רצה, announces the speaker's wish or intention more modestly: הייתי רוצה *I would like* contrasts with the more direct אני רוצה *I want*. Writers often use this phrase when they discuss their scholarly agenda.

> (66) לְסִיכּוּם, הָיִיתִי רוֹצֶה לְמַקֵּם אֶת הַנּוֹשֵׂא בְּהֶקְשֵׁר רָחָב יוֹתֵר.
> In summarizing, <u>I would like</u> to place the topic in a wider context.

4. Idiomatic verb phrases

Idiomatic verb phrases are fixed verb + noun sequences; some can be translated word-for-word into English (e.g., הגיע למסקנה *came to a conclusion*), while others cannot (e.g., זרה אור על *spread light on* is translated as *threw light on* or *illuminated*).

The participating verb may be a rarely encountered verb that co-occurs only with certain nouns (e.g., זרה אור, מתח ביקורת, שטח טענה), or, conversely, a very common verb, such as בא, יצא, עשה, עמד, נתן, whose original meaning is modified or lost when it becomes part of the idiomatic verb phrase (e.g., עמד על טעותו *realized his mistake*).

Often, the phrase has a parallel one-verb equivalent that is lexically related to the noun (e.g., הִשְׁוָוה ← עָרַךְ הַשְׁוָואָה *compared*).

Below is an (unexhaustive) list of idiomatic verb phrases gleaned from scholarly articles.[10] Where possible, synonymous one-word alternatives are given in brackets.

בָּא לְ-/לִידֵי גִיבּוּשׁ	[הִתְגַּבֵּשׁ] *consolidated*
בָּא עַל תִּיקּוּנוֹ	[תּוּקַּן] *was remedied*
גָּמַר אֶת הַהַלֵּל עַל	[הִילֵּל] *praised*
הִגִּיעַ/בָּא לְ-/לִידֵי בִּיטּוּי	[הִתְבַּטֵּא] *was expressed*
הִגִּיעַ לְמַסְקָנָה	[הִסִּיק] *concluded, came to a conclusion*
הִגִּיעַ לְקִיצּוֹ	[הִסְתַּיֵּים] *ended, came to its end*
הִטִּיל סָפֵק בְּ-	*doubted*
הִילֵּךְ קֶסֶם עַל	[הִקְסִים] *fascinated, charmed*
הָלַךְ שׁוֹלָל אַחֲרֵי	*was misled by*
הֶעֱלָה עַל הַכְּתָב	[כתב] *wrote, put down in writing*
הֶעֱלָה עַל נֵס	*praised, extolled*
הֶעֱמִיד בְּסִימָן שְׁאֵלָה	*questioned, doubted*
הֵקֵל רֹאשׁ בְּ-	*treated lightly, slighted*

---

[10] For a comprehensive treatment of multi word lexical units consult עברית בדגש לקסיקלי by רבקה הלוי, הוצאת אקדמון, ירושלים, 1994

יָצָא לָאוֹר	[התפרסם, פורסם]	was published; was revealed
יצא בביקורת על, מָתַח ביקורת על	[ביקר]	criticized, leveled criticism at
לבש ופשט צורה		changed form, was transformed
ניטש מַאֲבָק		a struggle took place
נקט עֶמְדָה/גִישָׁה/הַשְׁקָפָה/מדיניות		took, adopted (position, approach, view, policy)
נָשָׂא אוֹפִי		was characterized
נתן את הדַעַת על	[חשב על]	thought about, considered
נתן את אוֹתוֹתָיו ב-		left its mark on
סתם את הגוֹלל על		put the lid on, i.e., put an end to
עבר תַהֲלִיך		underwent a process
עלה בְּיָדָיו	[הצליח]	he succeeded
עמד בְּסְתִירָה ל-	[סָתַר]	contradicted
עמד על טָעוּתוֹ		realized his mistake
עָרַך הַשְׁוָואָה	[הִשְׁוָוה]	compared
עשה שימוש ב-	[השתמש]	used
עשה שַׁמּוֹת ב-		destroyed, ruined
קנה מוֹנִיטִין	[התפרסם]	earned a reputation, became famous
קרא תִיגָר על		challenged, criticized
רָקַם תָּכְנית	[תכנן]	made (devised) a plan
שטח טענה	[טען]	argued
שיוָוה אוֹפִי ל-	[אפְיֵין]	lent a character, characterized
שָׂם דָגֵשׁ על	[הִדְגִישׁ]	emphasized

♣#9 5. Present participles used as verbs

Present tense verb forms have multiple word class (=part of speech) membership: they can function as verbs, adjectives or nouns. (Hence the alternative term בינוני *present participle* for הווה *present tense*.)
For example:

The present tense form **מחנכת** could function in the sentence as

- a verb: האם מחנכת את בניה *the mother educates her sons*,
- a noun: המחנכת נכנסה לכיתה *the homeroom teacher entered the class*, or
- an adjective: ספרות דידקטית היא ספרות מחנכת *didactic literature is an educational/instructive literature*.

Similarly, the present tense form **מדוברת** could be used as

- a verb: עברית מדוברת היום על ידי כשמונה מיליון אנשים בעולם *Hebrew is spoken today by about eight million people worldwide*, or
- an adjective: אליעזר בן יהודה לחם למען הפיכת העברית לשפה מדוברת *Eliezer Ben Yehuda fought for turning Hebrew into a spoken language*.

One (or several) of the following grammatical conditions obtain when the present participle form functions in the sentence as a verb (rather than an adjective):

1. There is no other verb in the clause/sentence;
2. The sentence remains grammatical when put in the past tense;
3. The present tense form has a comma immediately before it (an adjective cannot be thus separated from the noun it describes);
4. The present tense form is introduced by -ה while the immediately preceding noun is indefinite (this -ה is a subordinator, replacing -ש or אשר before a present tense verb, NOT a definite article before an adjective);[11]
5. The present tense form is followed by a preposition: by את after verbs in the active *binyanim pa'al, pi'el* and *hif'il* and by על ידי, בידי or -מ after verbs in the passive *binyanim nif'al, pu'al* and *huf'al* (these prepositions link the present tense verb with its object complement).

Examples 67–71 demonstrate the application of the above criteria in order to determine the grammatical status of the present tense form.

The present participle form is shaded:

---

(67) מַטְרָתֵנוּ הָעִיקָרִית הִיא לִסְקוֹר אֶת הָעוֹלָם הַסִּפְרוּתִי וְהַתַרְבוּתִי הַמַקִיף אֶת סִפְרוּת הָאַגָדָה שֶׁל חז"ל.

Our main goal is to survey the literary and cultural world <u>that surrounds</u> the aggadic literature of Ḥazal.

NOT:... *to survey the comprehensive literary and cultural world.*

מקיף is a verb linked by את to the object complement ספרות האגדה של חז"ל (condition 5). Its identification as a verb can be further confirmed by putting the sentence in the past tense (condition 2): ... הָעוֹלָם הסִפרוּתי והתרבוּתי שהקיף את ספרוּת האגדה של חז"ל.

(68) הדיון בספר שלפָנינו הוא מְאַלֵף וּמַדְגִיש אֶת שְׁאִיפַת הַמְחַבֵּר לתרוֹם להיסטוריה הַחֶברָתית והתרבוּתית שֶׁל התקוּפה.

The discussion in the book before us <u>is instructive</u> and <u>emphasizes</u> the author's wish to contribute to the social and cultural history of the period.

NOT: *The discussion in the book before us trains and emphasizes...*

Put in the past tense (condition 2), the sentence would read

*הדיון בספר שלפנינו אילף והדגיש את שאיפת המחבר לתרום להיסטוריה החברתית והתרבותית של התקופה

**the discussion in the book before us trained and emphasized the author's wish to....*מאלף is, therefore, translated as an adjective (*instructive*), and מדגיש as a verb (*emphasizes*).

---

[11] See Chapter 1, 6.3.1(b).

(69) הֲקָמַת הָאִימְפֶּרְיָה הָאַשּׁוּרִית **מְזַעֲזַעַת** אֶת תְמוּנַת הָעוֹלָם **הַמְּיוּשָׁב**, **הַמְּתוֹאֶרֶת** בְּשִׁירַת "הַאֲזִינוּ" בִּדְבָרִים ל"ב.

The establishment of the Assyrian Empire <u>unsettles</u> the picture of the <u>inhabited</u> world that <u>is described</u> in the song of "Ha'azinu" in Deuteronomy 32.

מזעזעת is followed by את and is, therefore, read as a verb (condition 5);
מתוארת is also read as a verb since a present tense verb form preceded by a comma cannot be an adjective (condition 3);
המיושב is an adjective modifying the noun העולם; both agree in definiteness (condition 4).

(70) הַצַּד הַשָּׁוֶה שֶׁל רֹב מְגִילוֹת הַתַּנָ"ךְ, הוּא שֶׁהֵן **מוּרְכָּבוֹת** מִסִּפּוּרִים בּוֹדְדִים הַקַּיָּימִים בִּפְנֵי עַצְמָם.

The common denominator (literally: side) of most of the biblical Scrolls is that they <u>are made up of</u> single stories that stand on their own.

We translate מורכבות as a verb (*made up of, consisting of*), NOT as an adjective (*complex*) on the basis of condition 5: a passive verb form followed by the preposition -מ. In addition, the sentence remains grammatical when put in the past tense (condition 2):
הצד השוה של רוב מגילות התנ"ך, הוא שהן הורכבו מסיפורים בודדים שהיו קיימים בפני עצמם.

(71) לְדַעֲתוֹ זָכוּ יִשְׂרָאֵל לְמַעֲמָדָם בִּגְלַל מוֹצָאָם **הַמְאוּשָּׁשׁ** בְּוַודָאוּת עַל יְדֵי מָסוֹרוֹת מְהֵימָנוֹת.

In his opinion, the people of Israel won their [privileged] status because of their origin, which <u>is supported</u> with certainty by trustworthy traditions.

מאושש is followed by על ידי and, therefore, must be read as a verb (condition 5); the reading *Israel won their status because of their strengthened origin* is therefore erroneous.
The appropriate reading can be further confirmed by re-phrasing the sentence in the past:
לדעתו זכו ישראל למעמדם בגלל מוצאם, שאושש בוודאות על ידי מסורות מהימנות.
If a comma were employed by the writer, the reader would have been immediatelty alerted to the function of the participle:
לדעתו זכו ישראל למעמדם בגלל מוצאם, המאושש בוודאות על ידי מסורות מהימנות.

6. Some non-modern verb forms

Writers who favor Mishnaic style sometimes adopt its verb forms. Some examples are:

- יְהֵא, תְהֵא instead of יהיה, תהיה *will be* (example 72)
- מָצִינוּ instead of מצאנו *we find, we infer that*
- לִיכָּנֵס instead of להיכנס *enter*
- לִיתֵן instead of לתת *give*
- Plural ending ין- instead of the ים- (e.g., יש מקדימין את התאריך *there are those who set the date earlier*)
- ה- ending (instead of ת-) in feminine present tense verbs (example 73).

---

(72) דַעְתֵּנוּ **תְּהֵא** נְתוּנָה לַנּוֹשְׂאִים הבאים.

We will discuss (literally: our mind will be given to) the following topics.

The modern form would be תהיה.

(73) שירה זו **מְבַטְאָה** את עולמו של הפְּרָט.

This poetry expresses the world of the individual.

The more common form is מבטאת.

6.1 The נתפעל *nitpa'el* form – a past tense version of *hitpa'el* originating in Mishnaic Hebrew – is common in academic writing. It tends to occur in verbs that would be translated into English in the passive mode.

---

(74) חוֹמֶר רב מן היצירה המִדְרָשית של יְמֵי הַבֵּינַיִם **נתגלה** בגְנִיזת קָהיר.

A large amount of material from the homiletic creation of the Middle Ages <u>was discovered</u> in the Cairo Geniza.

(75) צורה זו **נשְׁתַּמְרָה** לא רק בכְתבי-יד עתיקים אלא גם במסורות שֶׁבְּעַל-פֶּה.

This [word] form <u>was preserved</u> not only in old manuscripts, but also in oral traditions.

✗#10   7. The letter נו"ן at the beginning of the verb

Care should be taken to distinguish between the different functions of the letter נו"ן in initial position (when it is not the first root letter):

(a) The נו"ן belongs to נתפעל, as discussed above (examples 74–75).

(b) The נו"ן indicates first person plural (we) in the future tense of all *binyanim* (examples 76–78).

(c) The נו"ן belongs to *binyan nif'al* in the past or present (examples 79–80).

---

(76) אנו **נתמַקֵד** בעֵדויות הארְכֵאולוֹגִיות.

<u>We will focus</u> on the archeological evidence.

נתמקד cannot be read as נתפעל since its subject is אנו *we* not the third person singular masculine הוא.

(77) אם **נִתְבּוֹנֵן** בִּמְשִׂימַת הַהִיסְטוֹרְיוֹן הֶעָתִידִי שֶׁל הַהִיסְטוֹרְיָה הַיְּהוּדִית בַּת זְמַנֵּנוּ, **נִמְצָא** שֶׁהַפַּעַר בֵּין הַהִיסְטוֹרְיָה הַיְּהוּדִית לְזוֹ הַיִּשְׂרְאֵלִית יָכוֹל רַק לְהִתְרַחֵב.

If <u>we contemplate</u> the task of the future historian of contemporary Jewish history, <u>we will find</u> that the gap between Jewish and Israeli history can only widen.

Since the sentence begins with אם, we know to read both nouns as future tense forms (see 3.3.3.1 above).

(78) כְּפִי שֶׁנִּרְאֶה לְקַמָּן הִשְׁפִּיעָה אַגָּדָה זוֹ עַל הַמָּסוֹרֶת הַמּוּסְלְמִית הַשְׁפָּעָה רַבָּה.

As <u>we shall see</u> below, this legend greatly influenced the Moslem tradition.

(79) אַחֲרֵי סִילוּק הַצַּד הָאַגָּדָתִי שֶׁבַּסִּיפּוּר **נִרְאֶה** שֶׁבֶּאֱמֶת **נִתַּרְגְּמָה** הַתּוֹרָה בִּידֵי חֶבֶר מְתַרְגְּמִים.

After removing the legendary element from the story, <u>it appears that</u> the Torah <u>was</u> indeed <u>translated</u> by a team of translators.

The reading of נראה as *it appears* rather than *we will see* (as in 78) is based on the fact that the sentence is taken from a lexicon entry, where the use of the first person is generally avoided.
ניתרגמה is in נתפעל.

(80) בְּמֶרְכַּז הַדֶּגֶל **נִמְצָא** נֶשֶׁר.

In the middle of the flag <u>is found</u> (there is) an eagle.

Confusables

1. ‏לוּ; וְלוּ‏

‏לוּ‏ *if* (interchangeable with ‏אִילוּ‏) should be distinguished from ‏וְלוּ‏ *even, even if it be*, an expression that tends to appear in parenthetical comments. Its less formal equivalent is ‏אֲפִילוּ‏.

> ‏(81) הַנָּבִיא אֵינוֹ מְהַסֵּס, וְלוּ לְרֶגַע.‏
> The prophet does not hesitate, <u>even</u> for a minute

2. ‏אִילוּ; וְאִילוּ; כְּאִילוּ; אֵילוּ‏

2.1 ‏וְאִילוּ‏ *whereas* is distinct from the hypothetical conditional ‏אִילוּ‏ in both form and meaning: its initial ‏וי"ו‏ is an integral part of the word, and its function is to indicate contrast between two sets of opposites (as such it is distinct from ‏אבל‏ *but*, for which one set of opposites is sufficient).

> ‏(82) הַשָּׂפָה הַמְּדוּבֶּרֶת הִתְפַּתְּחָה, וְאִילוּ הַשָּׂפָה הַכְּתוּבָה לֹא הִשְׁתַּנְּתָה כִּמְעַט בִּכְלָל.‏
> The spoken language has evolved, <u>whereas</u> the written language has hardly changed at all.
>
> ‏וֹאילו‏ indicates two contrasts: between the spoken and written language, and between evolution and lack of change.

2.2 ‏כְּאִילוּ‏ *as if, seem to be*
Alternative expressions are ‏כְּמוֹ‏ and ‏מָשָׁל‏.

> ‏(83) יֵשׁ הַמְּנַסִּים לִקְרוֹא אֲחָדִים מִסִּיפּוּרָיו שֶׁל עַגְנוֹן כְּאִילוּ הֵם רוֹמָן מַפְתֵחַ.‏
> There are those who try to read several of Agnon's stories <u>as if</u> there were a roman à clef.
>
> ‏(84) חֵקֶר הַשָּׂפוֹת הַשְּׁמִיּוֹת וְחֵקֶר הַמִּקְרָא כְּאִילוּ כְּרוּכִים יַחְדָּיו.‏
> The study of Semitic languages and Bible research <u>seem</u> to be bound together.

2.2.1 When ‏כאילו‏ appears directly before a noun or an adjective, it corresponds to the English semantic prefix "pseudo" (e.g., ‏כְּאִילוּ-מַשְׂכִּיל‏ *pseudo-educated*).

⚠️**2.3** In unpointed text, ‏אֵילוּ‏ *which* appears identical to ‏אִילוּ‏ *if.* The reader must rely on the context to select the appropriate meaning.

(85) אִילוּ אֶפְשָׁר הָיָה לְהַצִּיג תֵּאוּר מַשְׁוֶוה בֵּין הַצַּבָּר הַמּוּבְהָק וּבֵין כְּלַל צִיבּוּר בְּנֵי הָאָרֶץ, הָיָה בְּכָךְ כְּדֵי לְהָאִיר אֶת עֵינֵינוּ אֵילוּ עֲרָכִים הוּפְנְמוּ וְאֵילוּ כְּלָלֵי הִתְנַהֲגוּת לֹא הוּפְנְמוּ בִּכְלַל הַצִּיבּוּר שֶׁל בְּנֵי הָאָרֶץ.

If it were possible to present a comparative description of the prototypical Sabra and the general community of Israelis, it would enlighten us as to which values were internalized and which rules of behavior were not internalized by the general community of Israelis.

3. אִם, בְּאִם; הַאִם

בְּאִם is viewed by some as a more formal variant of אִם *if* (though this form is considered non-normative by prescriptive grammarians); both forms are distinguishable from הַאִם, a question word that introduces a yes/no question. Unlike question words that elicit answers other than "yes" or "no" (e.g., אֵיךְ *how*, אֵיפֹה *where*), הַאִם does not have a fixed English translation, but varies with the sentence.

(86) הַאִם לֹא נוּכַל לְגַלּוֹת קְשָׁרִים סְמוּיִים בֵּין הַמְּסוֹרוֹת?
Will we not be able to discover hidden connections between the traditions?

(87) הַאִם הוּא יָדַע אֶת הַתְּשׁוּבָה לְכָךְ?
Did he know the answer for this?

When a negative answer is expected, the question may be introduced by כְּלוּם.

(88) הַהִתְרַכְּזוּת בְּמִפְעַל אֶרֶץ יִשְׂרָאֵל כְּלוּם הִיא כְּרוּכָה בְּהִינָתְקוּת מִן הַמְּצוּקָה הַיְּהוּדִית הַמְּיָידִית בְּאֵירוֹפָּה?
Does the focus on the enterprise in the Land of Israel entail disengagement from the immediate distress of the Jewish masses in Europe?

References

בן-אשר, תשל"ג
גלינרט, 1981
הלוי, 1994
מוצ׳ניק, 1992
צדקה, 1981
רודריג, תשמ"ט
שלזינגר, 1994

Celce-Murcia and Larsen-Freeman, 1999
Coffin & Bolozky, 2005
Glinert, 1989
Quirk and Greenbaum, 1975
Rosen, 1966
Schwarzwald 2001
Weingreen, 1959

Chapter 6: Verbs – Exercises

exercise #	topic	page
1	"Unpacking" infinitive forms with pronoun suffixes	246
2	Determining the reference of the pronoun suffix in adverbial time clauses	247–248
3	Determining the reference of the direct object suffix	249–250
4	Selecting the direct object suffix	251
5	Determining the reference of the pronoun suffix: subject or direct object	252
6	Distinguishing among possessive, direct object and subject suffixes	253–254
7	Adding an aspectual verb in expanded verb phrases	255–256
8	Distinguishing among different uses of היה	257–258
9	Identifying the function of the present participle: verb or adjective	259–261
10	Identifying the function of an initial נו"ן	262–263

Exercise #1: "Unpacking" infinitive forms with pronoun suffixes

> **The rules to go by:** see section 1.2.3.
> **What to do:** rewrite the infinitive as a past tense verb and indicate the "doer".
> **Example:**
>
> בכתבם=הם כתבו
>
> **Note:** to indicate the /o/ vowel after the first letter of the root, some writers add (in defiance of the prescribed rule) the letter וי"ו: בכותבם. This spelling is adopted in item 7 below.

1. בראותו _____

2. בהוסיפם _____

3. בסָפרה _____

4. בהתקבלם _____

5. בהגיעה _____

6. בנסותו _____

7. ביודען _____

8. בהיעדרם _____

Exercise #2: Determining the reference of the pronoun suffix in adverbial time clauses

---

The rules to go by: see section 1.2.3.

What to do:

1. Rewrite the bolded verb form as a phrase made up of a subject and a finite verb (verb with a tense).
2. Translate the sentence.

Example:

לְפִי דַעַת הרמב"ן חָטְאָה רָחֵל **בִּרְצוֹתָהּ** שיתפלל בעלה עליה.

רחל רצתה שיתפלל בעלה עליה.

In the opinion of the Ramban, Rachel sinned when she wanted (OR: by wanting) her husband to pray for her.

‎1. הַחוֹקְרִים הִצִּיעוּ לקבוע את תקופת הָאָבוֹת בַּמֵּאָה הארבע-עשרה, **בְּהַסְתַּמְכָם** עַל מִנְיַן הדורות במקרא.

‎2. הרצל בנה את מוֹסְדוֹת התנועה מתוך הַכָּרָה שֶׁיֵּשׁ לדאוג לקיומה גם **לְאַחַר לֶכְתּוֹ.**

‎3. הַמֶּלֶךְ שׁוֹאֵל שאלות על מַהוּת הַיַּהֲדוּת, הֶחָכָם מֵשִׁיב, וְיֵשׁ שֶׁשְּׁנֵיהֶם מִתְוַוכְּחִים **בְּחַפְּשָׂם** את הָאֱמֶת.

‎4. **בְּצַפּוֹתָם** בכּוֹכָבִים הִבְחִינוּ בני האדם בשינוי מקומם וּמַצָּבָם וַיְיַחֲסוּ לְכָךְ הַשְׁפָּעוֹת שׁוֹנוֹת עַל הארץ ועל החיים בה.

Glossary

‎1. לקבוע את תקופת האבות	to date the period of the Patriarchs
מניין	counting
‎2. מוסדות התנועה	the institutions of the (Zionist) movement
הכרה	awareness
לדאוג לקיומה	take care of (ensure) its existence
‎3. מהות היהדות	the nature of Judaism
ויש ש	sometimes
מתווכחים	argue
אמת	truth
‎4. הבחינו	noticed
שינוי מקומם ומצבם	change in their place and situation
ייחסו לכך	attributed to this
השפעות שונות	various influences

5. הַיהודים תלויים היו בִּרצוֹנם הטוב של בִּישוֹפים שונים **בְּבַקָשָׁם** להתיישב בְּעָריהם וּבִרְצוֹתָם לקבל זְכוּיוֹת שונות.

6. **בְּעֵת דוּנָה** בלשונות כתובות וּמֵתוֹת מִשְׁתדלת הבלשנות החדישה לחְדוֹר – מְבַּעַד לסְמָלֵי הכְּתב – אל הדיבור.

7. בסוף המאה ה-18 ובראשית המאה ה-19 התרחשו מאורעות שונים בארץ ישראל, אשר **בהצטרפם** יחד מסמלים ראשיתה של העת החדשה בארץ ישראל.

Glossary

5. תלויים היו	were dependent on
רצונם הטוב	the good will of
בישופים	Bishops
להתיישב	to settle
זכויות	privileges
6. לשונות כתובות ומתות	written and dead languages
הבלשנות החדישה	modern linguistics
משתדלת לחדור	attempts to penetrate
בעד לסמלי הכתב	through the written symbols
דיבור	speech, spoken language
7. התרחשו	took place
מאורעות	events
מסמלים	symbolize
ראשיתה של העת החדשה	the beginning of modernity

Exercise #3: Determining the reference of the direct object suffix

> **The rules to go by:** see section 2.5.
> **What to do:**
> 1. "Unpack" the suffixed verb and indicate the noun that the suffix refers to.
> 2. Translate the sentence.
> **Example:**
>
> חריגותו של המן מתבטאת בנסיונות **להשוותו** אל המוּכָּר.
> להשוותו=להשוות אותו; את המן
> The exceptionality of the manna is expressed by the attempts to compare it to the familiar.

1. בכל הדורות הצליחו מְשׁוֹרְרִים וסופרים לחדור לעולמן הפְּנימי של נשים **וּלְתָאֲרוֹ.**

2. הוא מְקַבֵּל את מִצְווֹת הדָת **וּמְקַיְּימָן.**

3. מֶחְקָר מַשְׁוֶוה כָּזֶה עָשׂוּי **לְקָרְבֵנוּ** למוֹצָא הצוּרוֹת הלשוֹניוּת.

4. על פי המסורת הרווחת ניתנה התורה לישראל בהר סיני, לאחר **שֶׁהוֹשִׁיעָם** ה' משעבוד מצרים.

5. למסורת העתיקה נמצא הד בנוסח המקורי של הספר, כפי **שֶׁשִׁחֲזַרְנוּהוּ** לעיל.

6. התַקָּנוֹת שהיו נוֹהֲגוֹת או **שֶׁהִתְקִינוּן** בְּפְרוֹס המֵאה הי"א הן מְשׁלוֹשה סוּגים.

Glossary

.1	poets and writers	מְשׁוֹרְרים וסופרים
	to penetrate	לחדור
	their inner world	עולמן הפנימי
.2	the commandments of religion	מצווֹת הדת
.3	comparative research	מחקר משווה
	may	עשוי
	the origin of the language forms	מוֹצא הצוּרות הלשוֹניות
.4	the common tradition	המסורת הרווחת
	enslavement	שעבוד
.5	echo	הד
	original version	נוסח מקורי
	above	לעיל
.6	ordinances	תקנות
	were in place	היו נוהגות
	at the beginning of	בפרוֹס
	kinds	סוגים

7. ‏המן לא היה חריג משאר הניסים, **ועושהו**, האלוהים, לא ברא יש מֵאַיִן.

8. ‏כשהאם רוצה לקחת את הָאתרוג לידה אין מַרְשים לה לָגַעת בו אלא רק **להָריחו**.

Glossary

7. ‏המן	the manna
‏חריג	exceptional
‏ניסים	miracles
‏ברא יש מאין	created something out of nothing
8. ‏לקחת את האתרוג לידה	take the *ethrog* (citron) into her hand
‏אין מרשים לה לגעת בו	she is not permitted to touch it

Exercise #4: Selecting the direct object suffix

> **The rules to go by:** see section 2.5.
> **What to do:** select the appropriate direct object suffix.
> **Example:**
>
> הוא מקבל את מצוות הדת ומקיימ‑ו, ‑ה, ‑ם, **‑ן**
>
> **Explanation:** The direct object is מצוות (feminine plural); therefore, the suffix is ‑ן.

1. בַּעַל כְּתָב‑יָד זֶה לֹא הִשְׁמִיט בדרך כְּלָל אֶת הַשְּׁאֵלוֹת ולֹא **קִיצֵּר**‑ו, ‑ה, ‑ם, ‑ן, אלָא **הֵבִיא**‑ו, ‑ה, ‑ם, ‑ן בִּשְׁלֵמוּתָן.

2. אֵין זֶה מֵחוֹבָתוֹ שֶׁל הַהִיסְטוֹרְיוֹן לְהַעֲרִיך אֶת נוֹשְׂאֵי עֲבוֹדָתוֹ מִבְּחִינוֹת מוּסָרִיוֹת, דָתִיוֹת אוֹ לְאוּמִיוֹת, אלָא **לְהָבִין**‑ו, ‑ה, ‑ם, ‑ן **וּלְהַסְבִּיר**‑ו, ‑ה, ‑ם, ‑ן.

3. בני ישראל פונים אל אהרון בבקשה כי יעשה להם אלוהים אשר **יוביל**‑ו, ‑ה, ‑ם, ‑ן במדבר.

4. מֶנְדֶּלְסוֹן תרגם את התנ"ך לְגֶרְמַנִית וְהִדְפִּיס את התרגום באותיות עבריות, כדי שכל יהודי יוכַל **לִקְרֹא**‑ו, ‑ה, ‑ם, ‑ן וללמוד מִמֶּנּוּ גרמנית.

5. ההנהגה המסורתית נאלצת להיכנע לתכתיבו של יפתח **וְלָמַנּות**‑ו, ‑ה, ‑ם, ‑ן למנהיג בימי מלחמה ולשליט עליון אף בימי שלום.

6. כל אחד מן השניים פגש באישה ונתפתה. זה **פגש**‑ו, ‑ה, ‑ם, ‑ן על אם הדרך וזה בשוק.

Glossary

1.	manuscript כתב יד
	omitted השמיט
	in their entirety בשלמותן
2.	the historian's duty מחובתו של ההיסטוריון
	to evaluate the subjects of his research להעריך את נושאי עבודתו
	from moral, religious or national viewpoints מבחינות מוסריות, דתיות או לאומיות
3.	turn to פונים
	will lead יוביל
4.	translated תרגם
	printed הדפיס
	Hebrew letters אותיות עבריות
5.	the traditional leadership ההנהגה המסורתית
	was compelled to give in to נאלצה להיכנע
	Jephthah's dictate תכתיבו של יפתח
	appoint למנות
	leader מנהיג
	supreme ruler שליט עליון
6.	was seduced נתפתה
	crossroads אם הדרך

Exercise #5:   Determining the reference of the pronoun suffix: subject or direct object

---

The rules to go by: see section 2.7.1.
What to do: determine whether the pronoun suffix in the shaded verb refers to the subject or direct object.
Example:

הוא הציל את חיי המלך בְּגַלוֹתוֹ את הקשר שנתרקם נגדו. **הוא/אותו** (הוא גילה)
He saved the king's life by uncovering the conspiracy that was hatched against him.

---

1. אברהם **בְּשַלְחוֹ** את הָגָר לְמִדְבָּר נתן לה לחם ומים. **הוא/אותו**

2. אביו **שוֹלְחוֹ** לשאול בְּשָלוֹם אֶחָיו שיצאו לקרב. **הוא/אותו**

3. הפסוק **מְלַמְדֵנוּ** כי הלֶחֶם היה מזון בְּסִיסִי בתקופת המקרא. **אנחנו/אותנו**

4. חז"ל הִנְהִיגו ברכה מיוחֶדֶת שיֵשׁ **לְאָמְרָהּ** לפני אכילת לחם. **היא/אותה**

5. הם הפְרִישׁוּ קומֶץ מן העיסָה **וְהֵנִיחוּהוּ** על המִזבח. **הוא/אותו**

6. מְקוּבָּל שלא להשליך את פירורי הלחם אלא **לְאָסְפָּם** בקְפִידה. **הם/אותם**

7. **בְּהִיכָּנְסם** לארץ ישראל הפסיקו בני ישראל לאכול את הָמָן. **הם/אותם**

8. לא ה' מְנַסֶּה את ישראל כי אם הם מְנַסִים אותו **בְּבַקְשָם** ממנו לחם ובשר. **הם/אותם**

9. **בְּהַגִיעוֹ** לעיר, מבקש הנָביא אליָהו מן האישָה **לְכַלְכְּלוֹ**. **הוא/אותו, הוא/אותו**

Glossary

1. הָגָר   Hagar
   מדבר   desert
2. לשאול בשלום אחיו   to ask after his brothers
   יצאו לקרב   went into battle
3. פסוק   verse
   מזון   food
4. הנהיגו   instituted
5. הפרישו קומץ מן העיסה   set aside a handful from the dough
   הניחו   placed
   מזבח   altar
6. להשליך   to discard
   פרורי הלחם   bread crumbs
   לאסוף בקפידה   gather carefully
7. מן   manna
8. מנסה, מנסים   try
9. הנביא אליהו   the prophet Elijah
   לכלכל   to feed

Exercise #6: Distinguishing among possessive, direct object and subject suffixes

---

The rules to go by: see section 2.7.
What to do: identify the reference of the suffix in the bolded words (select the correct option from the words in parenthesis) and highlight it.
Example:

הוא לא התעכב לראות מה יהיו תוצאות הספר **והדפסתו** (<mark>שלו</mark>, אותו, הוא) אלא **מסרו** (שלו, <mark>אותו</mark>, הוא) בידי איש נאמן ויצא לדרך.

---

1. בעבר הרחוק נתקיימה מסורת שנימקה את אכילת המצות בפסח ברצון לזכור את **עינויים** (שלהם, אותם, הם) של ישראל במצרים ואת המזון **שהאכילום** (שלהם, אותם, הם) **שוביהם** (שלהם, אותם, הם) **בעבודתם** (שלהם, אותם, הם).

2. רבות עסקו חז"ל בלחם ו**באכילתו** (שלו, אותו, הוא) וזאת בשל **היותו** (שלו, אותו, הוא) המזון המרכזי שבחיי האדם.

3. לפי סיפור התורה ירד אברהם עם כל **משפחתו** (שלו, אותו, הוא) למצרים בשל הָרָעָב הכָּבֵד בארץ כנען **ביודעו** (שלו, אותו, הוא) כי אשתו היא "יפת תואר", וּמֵחֲשָׁשׁ פֶּן **יהרגוהו** (שלו, אותו, הוא) המצרים **ויקחוה** (שלה, אותה, היא) ממנו, הוא מבקש ממנה לומר שהיא **אחותו** (שלו, אותו, הוא).

4. בָּרֶדֶת משה מן ההר **ובראותו** (שלו, אותו, הוא) את העם החוגג לפני העגל הוא משבר את לוחות הברית, שורף את העגל, **טוחנו** (שלו, אותו, הוא) וזורה את **אפרו** (שלו, אותו, הוא) על פני המים.

Glossary

---

1. נתקיימה מסורת שנימקה	a tradition existed that gave the reasons for
עינוי	torture
שובים	captors
2. רבות עסקו חז"ל	Ḥazal dealt much with
3. בשל הרעב הכבד	because of the great famine
יפת תואר	good looking
מחשש פן	for fear lest
4. חוגג לפני העגל	celebrating before the (golden) calf
משבר את הלוחות	smashes the tablets
שורף	burns
טוחן	grinds
זורה	scatters
אפר	ashes

‫5. הצירוף "לחם עוני" הולם את מאכלם של אסירים, שהרי את אלה מרעיבים כדי להרבות את‬
‫**סבלם** (שלהם, אותם, הם) אך **לשמרם** (שלהם, אותם, הם) בחיים.‬

Glossary

the expression "bread of affliction"	‫5. הצירוף "לחם עוני"‬
fits	‫הולם‬
the food of prosinoers	‫מאכלם של אסירים‬
starve (someone)	‫מרעיבים‬
increase	‫להרבות‬

Exercise #7: Adding an aspectual verb in expanded verb phrases

---

The rules to go by: see section 3.2.
What to do:
1. Provide the missing aspectual verb (the aspect is indicated after each sentence).
2. Translate the sentence.
Example:

repeated action הריקוד _____ והוחזר, בִּפְרָט לחג שמחת תורה

הריקוד שב (אוֹ: חזר) והוחזר, בפרט לחג שמחת תורה

Dancing was re-introduced, in particular to the festival of Simchat Torah.

Explanation: the aspectual verb לשוב (OR: לחזור) agrees in tense with the main verb הוחזר; both agree in gender and number with the subject ריקוד.

---

1. לאט לאט _____ השכונה וגדלה   gradual action

2. עם פילוג הממלכה _____ שבט אפרים ותופס מקום חשוב ביותר   repeated action

3. בשנות השלושים_____ המשבר הכלכלי והחריף.   gradual action

4. גן האמנות _____ וצומח וקולט דרך קבע פסלים חדשים   continued action

5. הטְקָסים השְׁנָתִיים הקבועים בבתי-הספר ש _____ ונשנו מִדֵּי שנה נַעֲשׂו בעלֵי אופִי אָחִיד.   repeated action

6. מאמצע החודש ועד סופו הירח _____ ופוחת.   gradual action

7. ליקוי ירח אורך מספר שעות ובסופו הירח _____ ומתגלה.   repeated action

Glossary

---

1. שכונה   neighborhood

2. פילוג הממלכה   the splitting of the kingdom
   שבט אפרים   the tribe of Ephraim
   תופס מקום חשוב ביותר   occupies a very important place

3. שנות השלושים   the 1930's
   המשבר הכלכלי החריף   the economic crisis worsened

4. גן האמנות   the art garden
   צומח וקולט פסלים חדשים   grows and absorbs new sculptures

5. הטקסים השנתיים הקבועים   the regular annual ceremonies
   נעשו בעלי אופי אחיד   became uniform

6. ירח   moon
   פוחת   lessens

7. ליקוי ירח אורך מספר שעות   a lunar eclipse lasts several hours
   מתגלה   appears

256   6. VERBS

8. כך _____ שני נביאים כה שונים זה מזה – אליהו ואלישע – ומתדמים איש
   לרעהו.   gradual action

9. בסיפור זה _____ ומגולֶמֶת הָרְגִישׁוּת הַחֶבְרָתִית והמוּסָרִית הַמְאַפְיֶינֶת את הסְפְרוּת
   העברית והישראלית.   repeated action

Glossary

שני נביאים כה שונים זה מזה	two prophets so different from each other .8
מתדמים איש לרעהו	resemble each other
מגולמת הרגישות החברתית והמוסרית	the social and moral sensitivity is embodied .9
מאפיינת	characterizes

Exercise #8: Distinguishing among different uses of היה

The rules to go by: see section 3.3.
What to do:
1. Determine the meaning of היה in each sentence and enter the sentence number in the appropriate cell in the chart.
2. Translate the sentence.
Example:

מנהג זה לא **היה** יכול להתקיים אלמלא זכה בתמיכת הקהל וראשיו.

This custom could not have existed if it had not received the support of the community and its leaders (unreal condition).

---

habitual (*used to*)	unreal condition	past tense (*was, were*)
	example,	

1. כבר בעת העתיקה **היה** בַּעַל חיים זה סֵמֶל יהודי מובהָק.

2. בִּפְרוֹס הַמֵּאָה הי"א רַבֵּנוּ גֵרשׁוֹם חבר חשוב מאוד בכְּנָסים הָאַרְצִיים של הקהילות.

3. תַכְלִיתָן הכְּלָלִית של התַקָנוֹת **הָיְיתָה** לתַקֵן פְּגָם חָמוּר בחייהם המאוּרְגָנים של היהודים באותה תקופה.

4. את הַהֲלָכוֹת **היו** מסדרים למיניהן ולסוגיהן, כל אחד על פי דַרְכוֹ ושיטָתוֹ.

5. הם **היו** חולצים את נַעֲליהם בחָצֵר בטֶרֶם ייכנסו לאוּלָם התפילה.

Glossary

---

1. בעת העתיקה in antiquity
   בעל חיים animal
   סמל יהודי מובהק distinctive Jewish symbol
2. בפרוס at the beginning
   רבנו גרשום Rabenu Gershom
   כנסים ארציים national conventions
3. תכליתן הכללית their general purpose
   לתקן פגם חמור fix a serious flaw
   חייהם המאורגנים their institutional life
4. הלכות (Jewish) laws
   מסדרים למיניהן ולסוגיהן classify
   דרכו ושיטתו his way and method
5. חולצים את נעליהם remove their shoes
   בטרם before
   אולם התפילה prayer hall

---

6.   קשה להַניח שהמִשׁנָה **היתה** שומרת את זֵכֶר שְׁמו היָוָוני, אילו היה לו גם שֵׁם עברי.

7.   בנוּסָחים השונים של תפילת "על הניסים" **היו** מְסַיְימים בדְבְרֵי בַּקָשָׁה.

8.   אין זה בָּרוּר אם הפעוּלה **היתה** זוֹכָה לאישוּר הַמֶמשָׁלָה.

9.   לולֵא **היו** מְחַיֵי העברית רוּבּם דוברֵי יידיש, **היתה** העברית שלנו היום נשמעת ונראית שפה שונָה   מאוד.

10.   קשה להניח שבלֹא עידוּדו המפוֹרש של רש"י **היתה** זוכה היצירה הַפַּרשנית לפריחה כה גדולה עוד במֵאה ה-11.

Glossary

it is difficult to assume קשה להניח	.6
memory of his Greek name זכר שמו היווני	
versions נוסחים	.7
the prayer of "On the Miracles" תפילת "על הניסים"	
words of supplication דברי בקשה	
act פעולה	.8
received זוכה	
government approval אישור הממשלה	
those who revived Hebrew מְחיי העברית	.9
Yiddish speakers דוברי יידיש	
it is difficult to assume קשה להניח	.10
without Rashi's explicit encouragement בלֹא עידודו המפורש של רש"י	
exegetic creation יצירה פרשנית	
attain such great flourishing זוכה לפריחה כה גדולה	

Exercise #9: Identifying the function of the present participle: verb or adjective

---

The rules to go by: see section 5.
What to do:
1. Determine whether the bolded present participle functions in the sentence as a verb or an adjective (enter the sentence number in the appropriate cell in the chart).
2. Translate the sentence.

Example:

גם בקְטָעִים מלשון המִשְׁנה (א) **הַמְחַקִּים** בניסוּחָם את השירה המקראית (ב) **נִכֶּרֶת** זיקָה ללשון המקרא.

Even in Mishnaic texts <u>that imitate</u> biblical poetry in their style <u>is seen</u> an affinity to the language of the Bible.

---

verb	adjective
example א and ב,	

1. מַצָּבים מְדיניים-לְאומיים **מוּגְדָרים** במוּנָחים דָתיים בסְפרי הנְביאים.

2. הסֵפר סוֹקֵר מְסַפֵּר תֵיאוֹריוֹת, **המוּגְדָרות** על ידי החוקרים כְּחַדְשָׁניוֹת.

3. בדיוּנים שוֹנים על תְחִיַּת הלְשון העברית **מוּדְגָּשים** חֶלְקָה של היידיש והַשְׁפעתה.

4. ההתוועדות החסידית (א)**כּוללת** לעיתים קרובות ביקורת אישית (ב)**מוּדגשת.**

Glossary

.1	מצבים מדיניים-לאומיים political-national situations
	מונחים דתיים religious terms
.2	סוקר reviews
	תיאוריות theories
	חדשניות innovative
.3	דיונים שונים various discussions
	תחיית הלשון העברית the revival of the Hebrew language
	חלקה של היידיש והשפעתה the role of Yiddish and its influence
.4	התוועדות חסידית Ḥasidic gathering (*farbrengen*)
	לעיתים קרובות often
	ביקורת אישית personal criticism

5. מַדָע כַּדוּר הָאָרֶץ משתמש בפיזיקה, מתמטיקה, ביולוגיה וכימיה כדי לאפשר הבנה **כוללת** של כדור הארץ.

6. מָסוֹרוֹת אַגָדִיוֹת שונות **מַקְדִימוֹת** את רֵאשִית הַיִישוּב היהודי בגֶרמַניה עוד לתְקופת הבית הראשון.

7. מבצעים צבאיים (א)**כוללים** לרוב תכנון (ב)**מקדים**.

8. הָעִברית הִשפיעה על הסְפָרדית-הַיהודית הַשפעה **ניכֶּרֶת** בתְחומים שונים.

9. השפעות הַסַנְסְקריט **ניכרות** בכל השפות שהתפתחו ממנה.

10. תשובה **מְבוּסָסֶת** על שאלות מסוג זה נוכל לקבל רק כאשר יהיה בידינו מַאֲגָר אֶלֶקְטְרוֹני גדול וְיָצִיג של העברית המְדוּבֶּרֶת.

11. הַהֶסבֵּר המקובּל למִנהָג לטבול את הלחם במלח **מבוסס** על פסוק בספר ויקרא.

12. בסֶקֶר משנות ה-70 של המאה ה-19 **מצוין** שבתקופה זו מגיעים ארצה מְדֵי שנה בשנה בין 1000 ל-1500 יהודים.

Glossary

.5	מדע כדור הארץ	earth science
	לאפשר	make possible
	הבנה	understanding
.6	מסורות אגדיות	legendary traditions
	ראשית היישוב	the beginning of the Jewish settlement
	תקופת הבית הראשון	the period of the First Temple
.7	מבצעים צבאיים	military operations
	לרוב	usually
	תכנון	planning
.8	השפעה	influence
	תחומים	areas
.9	סנסקריט	Sanskrit
	התפתחו ממנה	developed from it
.10	שאלות מסוג זה	questions of this kind
	מאגר אלקטרוני	electronic corpus
	יציג	representative
	עברית מדוברת	spoken Hebrew
.11	לטבול את הלחם במלח	dip the bread in salt
	פסוק בספר ויקרא	a verse in Leviticus
.12	סקר	survey
	תקופה	period
	מגיעים ארצה	arrive in Israel
	מדי שנה בשנה	every year

‫13.‬ ‫שמואל בן יהודה אבן תיבון נודע כמתרגם **מצויין** של יְצירות חכְמי ישראל בימי הביניים.‬

‫14.‬ ‫בסֵפר תמונה **מקיפה** של פיגורה לשונית מרכזית – הדימוי.‬

‫15.‬ ‫החיבור **מקיף** את הֲגות היהודית בימי הביניים.‬

Glossary

‫שמואל בן יהודה אבן תיבון‬ Shmuel Ben Yehuda Ibn Tibon	‫13.‬
‫נודע‬ was known	
‫מתרגם‬ translator	
‫יצירות חכמי ישראל‬ the works of Jewish sages	
‫ימי הביניים‬ Middle Ages	
‫פיגורה לשונית מרכזית‬ a central (linguistic) figure of speech	‫14.‬
‫דימוי‬ simile	
‫חיבור‬ (written) work	‫15.‬
‫הגות יהודית‬ Jewish thinking/philosophy	

Exercise #10: Identifying the function of an initial נו"ן

> **The rules to go by**: see sections 6.1 and 7; for item 5 see Chapter 7, 5.2.1.
> **What to do**: identify the origin the initial נו"ן and translate the verb.
> **Example:**
>
> כבן 25 **נתעשר** ועמד בראש הקהילה היהודית.
> נתעשר – נתפעל; became rich

"אנחנו" בעתיד	נפעל	נתפעל
		example,

1. בעשור הראשון בתולדות מדינת ישראל **נתעצבה** דמותה של המדינה בכל התחומים.

2. כֵּיוָן (א)**שֶׁנִּתְקַבֵּל** התַּלמוּד וּפָשַט בישראל, (ב)**נעשׂתה** אף לשון חֲכָמים לְמְיוּחֶדֶת.

3. להבהרת העניין **נסתייע** בהַשְׁוָוָאָה.

4. ארוחה לא הייתה שְׁלֵמָה אם לא **נאכל** בה לֶחֶם.

5. בסְפרוּת ילדים **נעשׂה** שימוש נרחב בהַאֲנָשת בעלֵי חיים.

6. (א)**נַקדים** כמה דברֵי מָבוא להַבהרת המוּשָׂגים "אגדה" ו"חז"ל" ו(ב)**נפתח** באחרון.

7. סיום הסיפור מַדגיש כי הנֵס **נתקיים**.

Glossary

1. העשור הראשון   the first decade
   דמותה של המדינה   the character of the State
2. פשט   spread
   לשון חכמים   the language of the sages (Mishnaic Hebrew)
3. להבהרת העניין   to clarify the matter
   השוואה   comparison
4. שלמה   complete
5. ספרות ילדים   children's literature
   שימוש נרחב   extensive use
   האנשת בעלי חיים   personification of animals
6. דברי מבוא   introductory words
   הבהרת המושגים   clarification of the terms
7. סיום הסיפור   the end of the story
   מדגיש   emphasizes
   נס   miracle

פְּרָטִים שׁוֹנִים מִטְקְסֵי בֵּית הַמִּקְדָשׁ **נִשְׁתַּמְּרוּ** בְּתוֹכֵנוּ בְּחַיֵּי הַיּוֹמִיוֹם. .8

בַּמִּקְרָא **נִמְצָא** עֵדֻיּוֹת נוֹסָפוֹת לִתְפִיסָה זֹאת. .9

בַּפּוּלְחָן שֶׁ**נִּצְטַוּוּ** בְּנֵי יִשְׂרָאֵל לְקַיֵּים בְּמִשְׁכָּן בְּמִדְבָּר מְמַלֵּא הַלֶּחֶם כַּמָּה תַּפְקִידִים מֶרְכָּזִיִּים. .10

הַמְּגִילוֹת **נִמְצְאוּ** בִּמְעָרָה בַּמִּדְבָּר. .11

שִׂיאוֹ שֶׁל הַמּוֹדֶל הַפִילוֹסוֹפִי הַזֶּה **נִמְצָא** בְּמִשְׁנַת הָרַמְבַּ"ם. .12

בְּחֶלְקוֹ הַשֵּׁנִי שֶׁל הַמַּאֲמָר **נִתְמָקֵד** בְּטַעֲנָה הָרוֹוַחַת בַּמֶּחְקָר. .13

נִתְבּוֹנֵן הֵיכָן מוֹפִיעָה מִילָה זוֹ בַּסִּפְרוּת הַמִּקְרָאִית. .14

בֶּעָבָר **נִטְעַן** כִּי נָשִׁים חֲלָשׁוֹת מִכְּדֵי לַעֲסוֹק בַּפּוֹלִיטִיקָה. .15

אִם (א)**נְנַסֶּה** לְהַגְדִּיר זַ׳אנֶר מְסֻיָּם לַשִּׁירָה, (ב)**נִתְקַשֶּׁה** לַעֲשׂוֹת כֵּן. .16

Glossary

	various details	פְּרָטִים שׁוֹנִים	.8
	rituals of the Temple	טְקְסֵי בֵּית הַמִּקְדָשׁ
	among us	בְּתוֹכֵנוּ
	Bible	מִקְרָא	.9
	additional testimonies	עֵדֻיּוֹת נוֹסָפוֹת
	notion, idea	תְּפִיסָה
	ritual	פּוּלְחָן	.10
	to observe	לְקַיֵּים
	Tabernacle	מִשְׁכָּן
	fulfills central roles	מְמַלֵּא תַּפְקִידִים מֶרְכָּזִיִּים
	scrolls	מְגִילוֹת	.11
	cave in the desert	מְעָרָה בַּמִּדְבָּר
	the apex of this philosophical model	שִׂיאוֹ שֶׁל הַמּוֹדֶל הַפִילוֹסוֹפִי הַזֶּה	.12
	the work of Maimonides	מִשְׁנַת הָרַמְבַּ"ם
	the second part of the article	חֶלְקוֹ הַשֵּׁנִי שֶׁל הַמַּאֲמָר	.13
	an argument that is widespread in the research	טַעֲנָה הָרוֹוַחַת בַּמֶּחְקָר
	where	הֵיכָן	.14
	appears	מוֹפִיעָה
	in biblical literature	בַּסִּפְרוּת הַמִּקְרָאִית
	in the past	בֶּעָבָר	.15
	women are too weak to engage in politics	נָשִׁים חֲלָשׁוֹת מִכְּדֵי לַעֲסוֹק בַּפּוֹלִיטִיקָה
	define a specific genre	לְהַגְדִּיר זַ׳אנֶר מְסֻיָּם	.16

7. COPULAS
אוגדים

This chapter discusses:

- The use of third person pronouns as copulas in verbless sentences (section 1)
- The use of אֵין as a negative copula (section 2)
- Emphatic copulas (section 3)
- Verbal copulas (section 4)
- Verbs of becoming (section 5)
- Confusables: הֲרֵי; הֲרֵי שֶׁ-; שֶׁהֲרֵי; לֹא הֲרֵי . . . כַּהֲרֵי

This chapter will help the reader to:

- Distinguish between the use of הוּא, הִיא, הֵם, הֵן as pronouns and as copulas
- Comprehend and translate sentences with a negative copula, emphatic copulas and verbal copulas
- Recognize and translate verbs of becoming

The copula: an overview

In Hebrew, the verb להיות *to be* does not have present tense forms. Therefore, English sentences that employ the verbs *is* and *are* would be verbless in Hebrew. Verbless sentences are called משפטים שֵׁמָניים *nominal sentences*.[1]
For example:

חַיִּים וּמָוֶת בְּיַד הַלָּשׁוֹן (משלי יח כא)
Life and death [are] in the hand of (powered by) the tongue (Proverbs 18.21)

To compensate for the "missing" verb, a substitute – called copula (אוֹגֵד) – is often used. As the name indicates, the function of the copula is to link the subject to the rest of the sentence (the predicate).

The copula is found in biblical and Mishnaic Hebrew; however, its greater incidence in modern Hebrew is thought to be English-influenced.

Words that function as copulas are:

(1) The third person pronouns הוא, היא, הם, הן (section 1);
(2) The negative word אין, often inflected with personal pronoun suffixes (section 2);
(3) The emphatics הֵינוֹ and הֲרֵיהוּ (section 3);
(4) The verbs להַווֹת and לִשַׁמֵשׁ(כ-) (section 4).

Verbs of becoming – להיות ל-, להֵיעָשׂות (ל-), לַהֲפוֹך (ל-) – are also included here (section 5).

1. הוא, היא as *is* and הם, הן as *are*

The pronouns הוא, היא, הן, הם have two different functions:

(a) As personal pronouns (*he, she, it, they*) they replace animate and inanimate nouns.

(b) As copulas they stand in for *is* and *are* in present tense sentences.
     This second function is discussed below.

1.1 The need for the copula
In the absence of a verb, it is sometimes difficult – particularly in longer sentences – to determine where the subject ends and the predicate begins. This is demonstrated in examples 1–4 below.

---

[1] See also Chapter 1, section 4.

The predicate is shaded:

(1) יְסוֹדָהּ שֶׁל הַמַּחְלוֹקֶת סְבִיב מִנְהָג זֶה בַּמָּסוֹרוֹת שׁוֹנוֹת מִימֵי הַמִּשְׁנָה וְהַתַּלְמוּד.
The basis for the controversy around this custom [is] <u>in different traditions from the days of the Mishnah and Talmud.</u>

(2) יָמֶיהָ שֶׁל הַפַּרְשָׁנוּת לַמִּקְרָא כִּמְעַט כִּימֵיהֶם שֶׁל סִפְרֵי הַמִּקְרָא עַצְמָם.
Biblical exegesis [is] almost as old as the Bible itself (literally: The days of biblical exegesis [are] almost as (many as) the days of the books of the Bible themselves).

(3) כְּכָל הַיָּדוּעַ לָנוּ רֵאשִׁית בִּיּוּתוֹ שֶׁל הַחֲזִיר בִּירִיחוֹ בִּשְׁנַת 6000 לפנה"ס.
As far as we know, the first domestication of the pig [is] <u>in Jericho in 6000 B.C.E.</u>

(4) מִלִּים זָרוֹת אֶמְצָעִי בָּדוּק לְשַׁחְזוּר פְּרָטִים בַּהִיסְטוֹרְיָה הַתַּרְבּוּתִית וְהַחוֹמְרִית שֶׁל עַם.
Foreign words [are] <u>a proven means for reconstructing details in the cultural and material history of a people.</u>

#1 1.2 The use of third person pronouns as copulas

To assist in sentence segmentation and link the subject to the predicate, modern Hebrew often uses the third person pronouns as copulas. In this role, the pronouns הוּא, הִיא are translated as *is*, and הֵם, הֵן as *are*.

Sometimes, instead of a pronoun, a dash is used to mark the end of the subject and the beginning of the predicate (e.g., [2] הַשָּׁלוֹם – צַוָּואָתוֹ *Peace [is] his legacy* and example 11).

Like any verb, the copula must agree with the subject in gender (feminine or masculine) and number (singular or plural). When the subject is a construct phrase, the agreement is, in most cases, with the head noun (examples 10–11). When two (or more) coordinated nouns of different genders are the subject, the copula agrees with the masculine noun.

1.2.1 In equation sentences, namely, sentences indicating equivalence between the subject (a noun) and the predicate (also a noun), the copula is usually obligatory (examples 5–6). It is also required before a clausal predicate (examples 7–8).

Although the copula is not obligatory when the predicate is an adjective (e.g., הַבַּיִת גָּדוֹל *the house [is] large*), an adverb (e.g., הַבַּיִת שָׁם *the house [is] there*) or a prepositional phrase (e.g., הַבַּיִת בַּפִּנָּה *the house [is] on the corner*), there is a preference for using it even in these cases after a long subject phrase (examples 9–10).

---

[2] This sentence appears on the memorial at the site of Premier Rabin's assassination.

The subject and the predicate are shaded and the copula is bolded:

---

(5) הַדְּמוּיוֹת הַמֶּרְכָּזִיּוֹת בָּרוֹמָן זֶה **הֵן** נְכָדִים שֶׁל מְיַיסְדִים.
The central characters in this novel <u>are</u> grandchildren of founding fathers.

The copula הֵן agrees with the subject, the feminine plural noun דמויות, not with the adjacent predicate, the masculine plural noun נכדים.

(6) דְּקְדּוּקָהּ הָרִשְׁמִי שֶׁל הָעִבְרִית הַחֲדָשָׁה **הוּא** דִּקְדּוּק הַבָּנוּי בְּעִיקָרוֹ עַל לְשׁוֹן הַמִּקְרָא.
The official grammar of modern Hebrew <u>is</u> (a grammar) built principally on biblical Hebrew.

The copula agrees with the masculine singular noun דקדוק. Note that the final ה"א in דקדוקה is the possessive suffix (הדקדוק שלה=דקדוקה), not a gender marker for a feminine noun.

(7) הַקּוֹשִׁי **הוּא** לִמְצוֹא לְכָךְ הוֹכָחָה.
The difficulty <u>is</u> to find a proof for this.

The copula introduces an infinitive clause.

(8) הַדֵּעָה **הִיא**, שֶׁלֹּא הָיָה לַתּוֹכְנִית סִיכּוּי.
The opinion <u>is</u> that the plan did not have a chance.

A comma separates the copula from the predicate, a finite clause.

(9) הַנִּיתוּחַ שֶׁל תּוֹכֶן הָעִיתוֹנִים וְכִתְבֵי הָעֵת הַשּׁוֹנִים **הוּא** מְקוּצָּר מְאוֹד.
The analysis of the contents of the various newspapers and periodicals <u>is</u> much abbreviated.

The predicate is an adjective.

(10) בְּעָיַית הַיַּחַס שֶׁבֵּין הַדִּקְדּוּק הָרִשְׁמִי לָעִבְרִית הַיְלִידִית **הִיא** סְבוּכָה וְרַבַּת-אַנְפִּין.
The issue of the relationship between the official grammar and the native [spoken] Hebrew <u>is</u> complex and multi-faceted.

The copula agrees with בעייה, the head noun of the construct phrase.

(11) מְקוֹם הַהִתְרַחֲשׁוּת הַמֶּרְכָּזִי שֶׁל הָעֲלִילָה, תל אביב או ירושלים – **מַשְׁמָעוּתִי לְגַבָּיו**.
The main site where the plot takes place, Tel Aviv or Jerusalem, <u>is</u> significant for him.

The dash could be replaced by the copula הוא.

1.3 Using the demonstrative pronoun as a copula

The demonstrative pronoun **זה** as well as the blended forms זוֹהִי (זו+היא) זֶהוּ (זה+הוא) and זֹהִי (זו+היא) may replace the copulas הוא and היא. In the blended forms, the final אל"ף of הוא and היא is dropped. This option is more colloquial.

(12) ‎כָּל מַה שֶׁהוּא מְבַקֵּשׁ זֶה לְהַעֲמִיד דְּבָרִים עַל תִּיקוּנָם.
All that he wants <u>is</u> to redress the situation.

It is likely that ‎זה is utilized here as a copula (instead of ‎הוא) because of the neutrality of ‎מה, or so as not to use ‎הוא twice in the same sentence in two different senses, *he* and *is*.

(13) ‎הַפְּגִישָׁה שֶׁל בֶּן הָאָרֶץ עִם פְּלִיטֵי הַשּׁוֹאָה שֶׁאַךְ זֶה הִגִּיעוּ לָאָרֶץ – זֶהוּ הָרֶקַע לַסִּיפּוּר.
The meeting of the native Israeli with the survivors of the Holocaust who have just arrived to Israel – <u>this is</u> the background for the story.

The demonstrative pronoun ‎זהו agrees in this example with the predicate ‎רקע, not with the distant subject ‎פגישה. An alternative wording would be:

‎הפגישה של בן הארץ עם פליטי השואה שאך זה הגיעו לארץ <u>היא</u> הרקע לסיפור.

⚡#2 1.4 Distinguishing between a copula and a pronoun
The copula is easily differentiated from the pronoun: when the clause already has a verb, the words ‎הוא, היא, הם, הן function as pronouns, not as copulas.
Alternatively, the sentence may be re-worded in the past (or future) tense: if the pronoun can be replaced by past (or future) forms of "to be" (e.g., ‎היה, יהיה), it is a copula.

(14) ‎הָאַגָּדָה הִיא סוּגָה רְחָבָה הַרְבֵּה יוֹתֵר מִן הַהֲלָכָה וְהִיא מַקִּיפָה נוֹשְׂאִים רְחָבִים עַד מְאוֹד.
The Aggadah <u>is</u> a much broader genre than the Halakhah, and <u>it</u> encompasses extensive subject matter.

‎היא functions as a copula in the first (verbless) clause, and as a pronoun – the subject of the verb ‎מקיפה – in the second clause.

1.5 Word order in sentences with a copula
The typical word order in verbless sentences is "subject-copula-predicate". However, the subject and the copula may appear at a considerable distance from each other (example 15).

1.5.1 For reasons of emphasis (on the predicate), cohesion or sentence length, the subject and the predicate may exchange places, resulting in "predicate-copula-subject" word order (example 16).

1.5.2 Another word order option, which lends the sentence an emphatic tone, is to place the copula last, at the very end of the clause, so that the order is "subject-predicate-copula" (example 17).

The subject and the predicate are shaded and the copula is bolded:

---

(15) הָאֱמוּנָה בִּגְמוּל, זאת אומרת, האמונה שהאֵל מְשַׁלֵּם שָׂכָר טוב בְּעַד מַעֲשִׂים טובים
ומַעֲנִישׁ בעד מעשים רעים, **היא אַחַת** מֵעִיקָרֵי הָאֱמוּנָה של היהודים.
The belief in reward, that is, the belief that God rewards (for) good deeds and punishes (for) bad ones, is one of the basic tenets of Jewish faith.

The copula is at a considerable distance from the subject due to the introduction of an appositive phrase[3] that elaborates on the meaning of אמונה בגמול.

(16) מעטים **הם הָאֲתָרִים** שבָּהֶם נמצאו כְּתוֹבוֹת עם שם האיש הַמְּקְרָאִי.
Few are the sites where inscriptions with the name of the biblical figure were found.

If the subject were to come first, many words would separate it from the predicate:
הָאתרים שבהם נמצאו כתובות עם שם האיש המקראי הם **מעטים**.

(17) **מוּשָׂג זה בִּינְלְאֻמִי הוא**.
This concept is international.

The placement of the copula at the very end of the sentence lends the predicate emphasis. This nuance cannot be rendered in translation.

1.5.3 Due to the flexibility of word order in Hebrew, it cannot be assumed that in equation sentences (that is, in noun-coupla-noun sequences), the first noun is the subject. The identity of the subject in these sentences is determined on the basis of two grammatical properties: definiteness and agreement. In other words, the subject is the noun that is definite and that agrees with the copula.

---

(18) **גוֹרֵם** ראש וראשון במַעֲשׂה השיבה אל העברית **היא הַבְּחִינָה** הרַעְיוֹנִית.
The ideological aspect is the first and foremost reason for the return to Hebrew.

In this example, the definiteness of the noun הבחינה and its agreement with the copula היא identify it as the subject.

1.6 מַהוּ, מִיהוּ

The copulas הוא/היא/הם/הן may blend with the question words מה and מי, producing the forms מַהוּ/מַהִי/מַהֶם/מָהֶן *what is, what are,* and מיהוּ/מיהי/מיהֶם/מיהֶן *who is, who are,* respectively. Note the spelling without the final אל"ף of הוא and היא. The copula component agrees with the following noun.

---

[3] See Chapter 1, 8.1.2.

(19) לֹא יָדוּעַ **מַהִי** סִיבָּתוֹ שֶׁל הַסִּכְסוּךְ.
It is not known <u>what</u> the reason for the conflict <u>is</u>.

מהי agrees with the adjacent סיבתו (סיבה).

(20) **מָהֵן** הַתְּכוּנוֹת הַמְאַפְיִּינוֹת אֶת גִּיבּוֹר הַסִּיפּוּר?
<u>What are</u> the traits that characterize the protagonist?

מהן agrees with תכונות.

⚠ **1.6.1** In unpointed text, make sure to distinguish the question words מֶהֶם and מֶהֶן (a blend of מה+הם/הן) from the identical looking מֵהֶם and מֵהֶן (a blend of מן+הם/הן).

(21) גַּם בְּדוֹרוֹת הַבָּאִים אָנוּ שׁוֹמְעִים בִּיטּוּיִים שׁוֹנִים, **מֵהֶם** בְּשִׁבְחָהּ שֶׁל הָאַגָּדָה **וּמֵהֶם** בְּהִסְתָּיְיגוּת מִמֶּנָּה.
In the following generations too we hear different expressions, <u>some of them</u> in praise of the Aggadah, <u>and some of them</u> with reservations.

Note in this example the use of the preposition מ- in the sense of *part of, some of*.[4]

2. Negative copula אוגד שלילי - אין

2.1 The negation of the predicate is accomplished in verbless sentences colloquially with לֹא, and in written and formal style with אֵין, translated as *is not* or *are not*. The personal pronouns that refer to the subject merge with אֵין to produce the following inflected forms:

אֲנִי לֹא = **אֵינִי/אֵינֶנִּי**
אַתָּה לֹא = **אֵינְךָ**
אַתְּ לֹא = **אֵינֵךְ**
הוּא לֹא = **הוּא אֵינוֹ/אֵינֶנּוּ**
הִיא לֹא = **הִיא אֵינָהּ/אֵינֶנָּה**
אֲנַחְנוּ לֹא = **אֵינֶנּוּ**
אַתֶּם לֹא = **אֵינְכֶם**
אַתֶּן לֹא = **אֵינְכֶן**
הֵם לֹא = **הֵם אֵינָם**
הֵן לֹא = **הֵן אֵינָן**

The reason for the existence of two alternative forms is historical: איני, אינו, אינה are biblical, אינני, איננו, איננה are Mishnaic.

⚠ Note that (a) אין+הוא and אין+אנחנו are identical in form (איננו) and (b) in the third person, the pronouns הוא, היא, הם, הן are retained before the inflected form of אין.

---

4 See also Chapter 8, 2.3.4.(b), examples 33-34.

The negative copula is bolded and the predicate is shaded:

---

(22) מַעֲמָדָם הֻחֻקִּי בְּיִשְׂרָאֵל **אֵינוֹ** מַעֲמַד שֶׁל עֵדָה דָּתִית עַצְמָאִית.
Their legal status in Israel <u>is not</u> the status of an independent religious community.

(23) סֵדֶר יְמֵי הַשִּׁלְטוֹן שֶׁל הַמְּלָכִים **אֵינֶנּוּ** מְדֻיָּק.
The chronology of days of the Kings' rule <u>is not</u> accurate.

2.1.1 When placed <u>before</u> the subject, אין is not inflected. This option is more formal (examples 24 and 26).

---

(24) **אין** פירוש מילה זו יָדוּעַ.
(או: פירוש מילה זו אינו/איננו ידוע)
This meaning of this word <u>is not</u> known.

#3   **2.2** אין also replaces the more colloquial לא before present tense verbs. Except when the verb is passive (example 28), the translation is *do not* or *does not* (examples 25–26) rather than *is not* or *are not*, the translation of אין in verbless sentences.

---

(25) תפילה זו **איננה** מופיעה בתלמוד.
This prayer <u>does not</u> appear in the Talmud.

(26) **אין** המקרא מדגיש במיוחד את חשיבותם של המלאכים.
(או: המקרא איננו מדגיש במיוחד את חשיבותם של המלאכים)
The Bible <u>does not</u> particularly emphasize the importance of angels.

(27) על פי ביקורת המקרא, המקרא **איננו** חיבור אחיד והוא חובר על ידי כותבים שונים. **איננו** יודעים את שמות הכותבים ו**איננו** יודעים בדיוק את זמנם.
According to Bible [textual] criticism, the Bible <u>is not</u> a uniform composition and was composed by various writers. <u>We do not</u> know their names and <u>we do not</u> know exactly their time.

(28) בֵּיתָר **איננה** נזכרת בתנ"ך אבל נזכרת בתרגום השבעים ליוונית.
[The fortress of] Betar <u>is not</u> mentioned in the Bible but is mentioned in the Septuagint translation into Greek.

人#4 3. Emphatic copulas

3.1 הַבּוֹ/הַנָּה/הַנָּם/הַנָּן[5]

The copulas הַבּוֹ/הַנָּה/הַנָּם/הַנָּן are created by blending the word הִנֵּה *here* with the third person pronoun suffixes. In full (plene) spelling, the letter יו"ד is usually added: הינו/הינה/הינם/הינן. The use of these copulas as alternatives to הוא/היא/הם/הן is often a matter of stylistic choice or additional emphasis.

The copula is bolded and the subject is shaded:

(29) התחבורה העירונית **הינה**, ללא ספק, אחת הבעיות המורכבות ביותר של החברה המודרנית.
Urban transportation <u>is</u>, undoubtedly, one of the most complex problems of modern society.

In this example, היא could have been used instead of הינה.

(30) ההֶסבֵּר למְנָהג להשאיר לֶחֶם על השולחן **הוא** שה**ינו** ביטוי של הכָנָסת אורחים כְּלַפֵּי עוברי דרכים ושל צְדָקה לעניים.
The explanation for the custom to leave bread on the table <u>is</u> that it <u>is</u> an expression of hospitality toward travelers and charity for the poor.

By using הינו the writer avoids employing הוא twice in succession:
ההסבר למנהג להשאיר לחם על השולחן הוא שהוא ביטוי של הכנסת אורחים

(31) המֶתָח הזה שבין שתֵי המְגַמות הללו היה **וה**ינו גורֵם חָשוב לעיצוב המִבְנֶה האינטֶלֶקטוּאַלי של עַמֵנו.
This tension between these two tendencies <u>was and [still] is</u> an important factor in shaping the intellectual makeup of our people.

הינו serves as the present tense counterpart of היה.

3.2 הֲרֵיהוּ/הֲרֵיהִי/הֲרֵיהֶם/הֲרֵיהֶן

These copulas are the result of the blending of הֲרֵי *here is; indeed* with the pronouns הוא/היא/הם/הן. In the blended forms, the final אל"ף of הוא and היא is omitted.
This copulas has a confirmatory tone, and can be rendered in translation as *indeed* or *in fact*.

The copula is bolded and the subject is shaded:

(32) מגילת רות לפי אוֹפְיָה הסִפרותי **הֲרֵיהי** סיפור קָצָר.
By its literary character, the Book of Ruth is (<u>in fact</u>) a short story.

---
[5] Also הַנֵּהוּ (m.) and הַנֵּה or הַנֵּהִי (f.). Note the use of וְהַנֵּה *lo and behold* to introduce an unexpected event or idea, and the adverb הֵנָּה *to here, hither*.

3.2.1 The inflected forms of הרי may also be used for emphasis with a present tense verb. In translation they may be ignored or rendered as *truly, indeed, in fact, then*.[6]

---

(33) מִכֵּיווָן שֶׁאֵלִיָּהוּ, הַמְבַקֵּשׁ לְהַעֲנִישׁ אֶת עַם יִשְׂרָאֵל, אֵינֶנּוּ יָכוֹל לְהוֹצִיא אֶת הָעָם אֶל הַמִדְבָּר, **הֲרֵיהוּ** מֵבִיא אֶת הַמִדְבָּר אֶל הָאָרֶץ וְקוֹרֵא לַבַּצּוֹרֶת.

Since Elijah, who seeks to punish the people of Israel, cannot take the people out into the desert, <u>he (then) brings</u> the desert to the land, calling for a drought.

(34) בְּסוֹפוֹ שֶׁל דָּבָר הַתַּרְגוּם הוּא חֵלֶק מִסִּפְרוּת חז"ל, אַךְ הוּא נִיצָּב בְּשׁוּלֶיהָ, **וַהֲרֵיהוּ** מְגַלֶּה אֶת הַפָּן שֶׁהִיא מַפְנָה לְכִיווּן הַמּוֹנֵי הָעָם. וּכְשֵׁם שֶׁהַמְתֻרְגְּמָן הוּא הַמְתַוֵּוךְ בֵּין הָאֵלִיטָה הָרוּחָנִית לְבֵין הֶהָמוֹן, כָּךְ הַתַּרְגוּם **הֲרֵיהוּ** צִינּוֹר חָשׁוּב וּמֶרְכָּזִי בְּהַעֲבָרַת תּוֹרָתָם שֶׁל חֲכָמִים אֶל הַשְּׁכָבוֹת הָרְחָבוֹת שֶׁל הַמַּאֲמִינִים.

In the final analysis, the Targum is part of the literature of Ḥazal but it stands in its margins, and <u>(in fact)</u> reveals its popular aspect (literally: reveals the face that it turns toward the masses). And just as the translator is the mediator between the intellectual elite and the masses, so also the translation <u>is</u> an important and central channel for transmitting the learning of the sages to the broader strata of believers.

In this example, הֲרֵיהוּ is used in the first sentence emphatically before the verb מגלה and can be ignored in translation or rendered as *in fact*.
In the second sentence, הֲרֵיהוּ is used as a copula, *is*.
Note also in this example the uses of הוא and היא as copula and pronoun:
(a) copula – *is* – in: הַמְתֻרְגְּמָן <u>הוּא</u> הַמְתַוֵּוךְ, הַתַּרְגוּם <u>הוּא</u> חֵלֶק מִסִּפְרוּת חז"ל
(b) pronoun – *it* – in: הַפָּן <u>שֶׁהִיא</u> מַפְנָה לַהֲמוֹנֵי הָעָם, <u>הוּא</u> נִיצָּב בְּשׁוּלֶיהָ

火#4 4. Verbal copulas

4.1 לִהֱווֹת *to constitute*

When the item is a member of a group of similar items, the verb לִהֱווֹת *to constitute* can be used. Its present tense forms, מְהַוֶּוה/מְהַוֵּוֶה/מְהַוּוים/מְהַווֹת, may come in lieu of the pronoun copulas הוא/היא/הם/הן.

The past and future forms (e.g., יֶהֱווֹה, תֶּהֱווֶה, יֶהֱווּ and הָיָוֶוה, הַיְּווֹתָה הָיוּ) correspond to past and future forms of "to be".

The subject is shaded and the copula is bolded:

---

(35) הַיְּהוּדִים מְהַוּוים כַּיּוֹם 0.2 אֲחוּזִים מֵאוֹכְלוּסִיַּית הָעוֹלָם.
The Jews <u>constitute</u> (OR: are) today 0.2 percent of the world population.

(36) בְּיָמֶיהָ הָרִאשׁוֹנִים שֶׁל אַרְצוֹת הַבְּרִית הִיא לֹא הָיְווֹתָה יַעַד הֲגִירָה מוּעֲדָף.
In its first days, the United States <u>did not constitute</u> (OR: was not) a preferred immigration destination.

<hr>

[6] For additional uses of הרי, see the Confusables section below.

4.1.1 Note that when the root הוה is conjugated in *hitpa'el*, the resulting verb is לְהִתְהַוּוֹת, whose meaning is *to be formed, to come about, to transpire*.

For example: בספרד הִתְהַוָּה מרכז חדש *in Spain a new center was formed.*

4.2 (-כ) לשמש *serve as, be used as*

The verb לשמש *serve as, be used as* can be employed instead of past, present and future forms of the verb "to be". In other words, מְשַׁמֵּשׁ can be replaced by הוא (example 37), שימש can be replaced by היה and יְשַׁמֵּשׁ can be substituted by יהיה. The preposition -כ after the verb is optional (examples 37 and 39).

The copula is bolded and the subject is shaded:

---

(37) התנ"ך **משמש** מקור הַשְׁרָאָה לתַרבויות שונות.
(או: התנ"ך הוא מקור השראה לתרבויות שונות)
The Bible <u>serves as</u> (OR: is) a source of inspiration for various cultures.

(38) הארמית אף **שימשה** כשְׂפַת הדיפְּלוֹמַטְיָה.
(או: הארמית אף הייתה שפת הדיפלומטיה)
Aramaic also <u>served as</u> (OR: was) the language of diplomacy.

(39) בְּשנות העשרים **שימשו** השמות ההיסְטוֹריים יְסוֹד לשמות היישובים החדשים בארץ.
(או: בשנות העשרים היו השמות ההיסטוריים יסוד לשמות היישובים החדשים)
In the 1920's, the historical names <u>were used as</u> (OR: were) a basis for the names of new settlements in the country.

Note that after the time adverbial, the verb precedes the subject.

(40) בית הכנסת פָּסַק **לשמש** מקום מֶרכָּזי לתפילה.
(או: בית הכנסת פסק להיות מקום מרכזי לתפילה)
The synagogue ceased to <u>serve as</u> (OR: to be) a central place for prayer.

⚠️ **4.2.1** Note, however, that when לשמש is followed by prepositions other than -כ, specifically, לשמש ל-, לשמש ב-, לשמש **את**, it does not substitute for a copula: its translation then is *serve* or *be used, be employed*.

To express this meaning, the phrase להיות בשימוש is often used, for example: מילה זו **הייתה בשימוש** בתקופת המקרא, מילה זו **שימשה** בתקופת המקרא *this word was in use/ was used in the biblical period.*

---

(41) צורה זו **משמשת** בעיקר בעברית של יום יום.
This form <u>is used </u>mainly in everyday Hebrew.

Note also the expression לשַׁמֵּשׁ בְּעִרְבּוּבְיָה *be intermixed.*

4.2.2 The meaning of לשמש may not be immediately apparent when neither -כ (which is optional) nor את (which does not appear with an indefinite direct object) are present.

To test whether לְשַׁמֵּשׁ functions as a copula in a given sentence, the reader is advised to insert the preposition -כְ after the verb, or replace the verb with a copula – the sentence then should remain grammatical. This procedure is illustrated in example 42.

---

(42) "הַר הָאֱלוֹהִים" היה **מָקוֹם מְקוּדָּשׁ שֶׁשִׁימֵּשׁ** שְׁבָטִים וּקְבוּצוֹת אֶתְנִיּוֹת שׁוֹנוֹת בָּאֵזוֹר.
"God's Mountain" was a sacred place that <u>served</u> (OR: was used by) tribes and ethnic groups in the area.

Since both the insertion of the preposition -כְ and the substitution of שִׁימֵּשׁ by היה would result in a nonsensical sentence, we determine that the שִׁימֵּשׁ does <u>not</u> function here as a copula:

* "הר האלוהים" היה מקום מקודש שֶׁשִׁימֵּשׁ <u>כְּ</u>שבטים וקבוצות אתניות שונות באזור.
* "הר האלוהים" היה מקום מקודש שֶׁ<u>הָיָה</u> שבטים וקבוצות אתניות שונות באזור.

✗#4　5. Verbs of becoming: -לִהְיוֹת ל,(-ל) לְהֵיעָשׂוֹת ל-/לְהֵיהָפֵךְ ל-/לַהֲפוֹךְ (ל-) *to become, to turn into*

These verbs indicate becoming; except in the case of נהפך ל- and היה ל-, the preposition may be omitted. When the previous state is specified – for example, הפך מ-... ל-... – the translation is *turned from...into* (example 54).

5.1　-נֶהֱפַךְ ל[7] /(-הָפַךְ (ל

When followed by the preposition -ל, the verb לַהֲפוֹךְ *to turn* means *to become, to turn into*. The preposition is optional (example 44); when used, it may appear at a distance from the verb (example 45). To express the notion of becoming, the verb הפך may also appear in *nif'al:* -נֶהֱפַךְ ל (example 46).

The subject is shaded and the copula is bolded:

---

(43) צֶמַח הַצַּבָּר **הָפַךְ** לְדִימוּי שֶׁל יְלִידֵי הָאָרֶץ.
The cactus plant <u>became</u> the metaphor for native-born Israelis.

(44) הַפְּרִיפֶרְיוֹת בָּאֵזוֹר **הָפְכוּ** מֶרְכָּזִים.
The peripheries in the region <u>became</u> centers.

(45) בְּתוֹךְ עֲשׂוֹרִים סְפוּרִים **הָפְכָה** הָעִבְרִית – שָׂפָה שֶׁלֹּא הָיוּ לָהּ דּוֹבְרִים יְלִידִים וְשֶׁנֶּחְשְׁבָה לְ"שָׂפָה מֵתָה," הַמִּתְקַיֶּימֶת בְּעִיקָר בְּטֶקְסְטִים כְּתוּבִים – **לְשׂפה** לְאוּמִית, דּוֹמִינַנְטִית וְהֶגְמוֹנִית.
Within few decades, Hebrew – a language that did not have native speakers and that was considered a "dead language" existing mainly in written texts – <u>became</u> a national, dominant and hegemonic language.

(46) יש בין הדיבוקים גם רוּחוֹת שֶׁל מֵתִים שלא באו למנוחה וְנֶהֶפְכוּ למזיקים.
Among the Dibbukim there are also spirits of dead people who did not find a resting place and <u>became</u> evil spirits.

---

[7] נֶהֱפַךְ is also possible.

5.1.1 If a direct object complement is added – הפך (את) . . . לְ- – the translation is *turned (someone/something) into*. This meaning can also be expressed by עשה (את) . . . לְ-.

---

(47) **מְאַפְיינים** אלה הם שהפכו **את** העיר **לְאַתר** תיירות פופולרי.
It is these characteristics that turned the city into a popular tourism site.

✗#5   5.2 (-לְ) נעשה

Becoming can also be expressed with the *nif'al* form of the root עשה: לְהֵיעָשׂוֹת. The preposition לְ- is optional, usually omitted before an adjective (example 49).

---

(48) מְקוֹמוֹת אלה **נַעשׂוּ** באוֹפֶן טבעי **לִיַעֲדֵי** עֲלִיָּיה לָרֶגֶל נוֹצריים.
These places naturally <u>became</u> Christian pilgrimage destinations.

(49) מצב היהודים בעיר **נעשָׂה** קשה יותר ויותר.
The situation of the Jews in the city <u>became</u> more and more difficult.

⚠ **5.2.1** The verb לְהיעָשׂוֹת also functions as the passive counterpart of לעשׂות, in the sense of *to be made, to be done* (rather than *to become*).

This meaning can be discerned when בידי, על ידי *by* or בְּעֶזְרַת *with the aid of* are present, introducing the "doer," or when the verb is followed by the preposition מ/מן (נעשׂה מן *made from*). Otherwise, the reader must rely on the context to determine the intended meaning of the verb.

---

(50) **חידושים** מַדְעיים **נַעשׂים** בדֶרֶך שיטָתית.
Scientific innovations <u>are made</u> systematically.

The reading *scientific innovations <u>become</u> systematically* is not possible.

(51) **תרגומים** עתירי אַגָדות **נַעשׂוּ** לא רק לתורה אלא גם לנביאים ולסְפרֵי המגילות.
Legend-rich translations <u>were made</u> not only for the Torah but also for the Prophets and (the books of) the Scrolls.

The reading *legend-rich translations <u>became</u> not only the Torah but also the Prophets and the books of the Scrolls*, while grammatically possible, must be rejected as contrary to fact.

In unpointed text, there are four alternatives for interpreting the form נעשה:
(a) נַעֲשָׂה (*nif'al* past tense, 3rd person masculine singular: *he/it became/was made*).
(b) נַעֲשֶׂה (*nif'al* present tense, masculine singular: *I/you/he/it is becoming/is made*).
(c) נַעֲשֶׂה (*pa'al* future tense, 1st person plural: *we will make/do*).
(d) נֵעָשֶׂה (*nif'al* future tense, 1st person plural: *we will become/be made*; however, in full spelling this form appears with a יו"ד: ניעשה.

5.2.2 Note the expression ‫שימוש‬ ‫נעשה‬ ‫ב-‬ (literally: *use was made of*), where the noun ‫שימוש‬ functions as the subject of the verb.

---

(52) ‫לראשונה‬ **‫נעשה‬ ‫שימוש‬** ‫בזכוכית‬ ‫לייצור‬ ‫תכשיטים‬ ‫באזור‬ ‫מסופוטמיה.‬
Glass <u>was used</u> (literally: <u>use was made</u> of glass) for the first time to manufacture jewelry in the region of Mesopotamia.

⚡L#6   5.3   ‫היה‬ ‫ל-‬

```
‫אֶבֶן‬ ‫מָאֲסוּ‬ ‫הַבּוֹנִים‬ ‫הָיְתָה‬ ‫לְרֹאשׁ‬ ‫פִּנָּה‬ (‫תהילים‬ ‫קיח‬ ‫כב‬)
A Stone which the builders rejected has become the chief corner-stone (Psalms 118.22)
```

The preposition ‫ל-‬ is essential for converting ‫היה‬ from a verb of being – *was* – to a verb of becoming. The verb ‫היה‬ and the preposition ‫ל-‬ may be separated by the subject.

---

(53) ‫במאה‬ ‫השמונה-עשרה‬ **‫הייתה‬ ‫קהילת‬ ‫בֶּרְלִין‬ ‫למֶרְכָּזָה‬** ‫של‬ ‫תְנוּעת‬ ‫ההַשְׂכָּלָה.‬
In the 18th century, the Jewish community of Berlin <u>became</u> the center of the Enlightenment Movement.

(54) **‫מעיר‬ ‫קטנה‬ ‫בלבו‬ ‫של‬ ‫מָחוֹז‬ ‫כַּפְרִי‬ ‫ואוכלוסיה‬ ‫של‬ 8,000–10,000 ‫נֶפֶשׁ‬ ‫בראשית‬ ‫המאה,‬ ‫הייתה‬ ‫ירושלים‬** ‫לעיר‬ ‫הראשית‬ ‫של‬ ‫ישראל.‬
<u>From</u> a small town at the heart of a rural region and a population of 8,000–10,000 people, Jerusalem <u>became</u> the main city of Israel.

⚠️ **5.3.1** Make sure to distinguish between the two meanings of ‫היה‬ ‫ל-‬: *had* and *became*: in "have" sentences, the preposition ‫ל-‬ tends to come <u>before</u> the verb (example 55), whereas in "becoming" sentences the preposition always comes <u>after</u> the verb (example 56).

---

(55) **‫לחוקר‬ ‫לא‬ ‫היה‬** ‫הסבֵּר‬ ‫לכך.‬
The researcher <u>did not have</u> an explanation for this.

(56) ‫זה‬ **‫היה‬** ‫להסבר‬ ‫המקוּבָּל.‬
This <u>became</u> the accepted explanation.

5.4 ‫נהיה‬ (‫ל-‬)

Binyan nif'al provides the present tense forms ‫נִהְיֶה/נִהְיֵית/נִהְיִים/נִהְיוֹת.‬ The preposition ‫ל-‬ is optional (example 58).
This verb also has past tense forms – ‫נִהְיָה/נִהְיֵיתָ/נִהְיוּ‬ (equivalent to ‫ל-‬ ‫(היה/הייתה/היו‬ – but there are no future tense forms.

⚠️ As with נעשה, there are several alternatives for interpreting the form נהיה in unpointed text:

(a) נִהְיָה (*nif'al* past tense, 3rd person singular masculine, *he/it became*; examples 57-58).
(b) נִהְיֶה (*nif'al* present tense, singular masculine, *I/you/he/it become(s)*; example 59).
(c) נִהְיֶה (*pa'al* future tense, 1st person plural, *we will be*; example 60).

---

(57) החור בשכְבַת האוזון נהיה לנושא מֶרְכָּזִי בּאֵיכות הסְביבה העולָמית.
The hole in the ozone layer <u>became</u> a central topic in world environmentalism.

The choice between past (*became*) and present (*becomes*) is made on the basis of extra-linguistic (world) knowledge, while in examples 58-59 it is based on grammatical clues (the tense of other verbs in the sentence).

(58) אדם נהיה מנהיג אם היה בראש משפחה גדולה ועשירה.
A man <u>became</u> a leader if he was at the head of a large and rich family.

(59) החוקר מנתֵח את הדינָמיקה ההופֶכֶת אָדָם אחד לקָדוש בעֵיני הקהילָה בְּעוד שְׁאַחֵר אֵינו נהיֶה כָּזֶה.
The researcher analyzes the dynamic that turns one person into a holy man in the eyes of the community while another does not <u>become</u> such.

(60) תרגום המשפט בהגָדָה של פֶּסַח "הַשַׁתָּא עַבְדֵי לשנה הבאה בּנֵי חורין" הוא: "עכשיו אנחנו עבָדים, בשנה הבָּאה נהיֶה בּנֵי חורין".
The translation of the phrase from the Passover Haggadah is: "now we are slaves, next year <u>we will be</u> free."

5.5 The verbs נִשְׁאַר and נוֹתַר *remained* are also considered verbal copulas, but with the built-in meaning of stasis, in contrast to the dynamism implied by copulas of becoming.

---

(61) הם נשארו מְבודָדים.
They <u>remained</u> isolated.

(62) שְׁאלה זו נותרה ללא מַעֲנֶה.
This question <u>remained</u> unanswered.

Confusables

הֲרֵי; הֲרֵי (שֶׁ-); שֶׁהֲרֵי; לֹא הֲרֵי . . . כַּהֲרֵי

1. הרי *here it is* emphasizes a subsequent statement and can be translated as *indeed* or *in fact*. This purpose is also served by the words הֲלוֹא, הִנֵּה and הֵן.

---

(63) הרי לְפָנֵינוּ סֵמֶל נוֹצְרִי מוּבְהָק.
We, <u>in fact</u>, have before us a distinctive Christian symbol.

---

2. הֲרֵי (-שֶׁ) links a dependent adverbial clause of supposition, contrast, cause or concession to the main clause. This function is also be served by אָז, כִּי אָז, אֲזַי as well as הִנֵּה (example 68) or הֵן.

For example:

אִם . . . הרי (-שֶׁ) *if this is the case . . . then* (examples 64–65)
בְּנִיגוּד לְ-. . . הרי (-שֶׁ) *in contrast to,* הרי . . . בְּעוֹד *while* (examples 66–67), כְּ- שֶׁלֹּא *unlike*
מִכֵּיוָן שֶׁ-/מֵאַחַר שֶׁ-/הֱיוֹת וּ-[8] . . . הרי (-שֶׁ) *since*
עַל אַף/לַמְרוֹת/אַף עַל פִּי שֶׁ-/אַף שֶׁ- . . . הרי (-שֶׁ) *despite, even though*

Except when paired with אִם, הרי (שֶׁ-) is usually ignored in translation (examples 66–67).

---

(64) הַהַשְׁקָפָה הַמִתְפַּתַחַת בְּאוֹתָה תְקוּפָה הִיא שֶׁאִם אַתָּה בָּא לִירוּשָׁלַיִם, וְאַתָּה חַי בָּהּ וְלוֹמֵד בָּהּ, הרי שֶׁהַגּוֹלָה צְרִיכָה לְסַפֵּק לְךָ אֶת מְקוֹרוֹת פַּרְנָסָתְךָ.
The evolving view at that period is that <u>if</u> you come to Jerusalem and you live and study in it, <u>then</u> the Diaspora should provide you with your sources of livelihood.

(65) אִם הַמַסְקָנוֹת הָאֵלֶּה נְכוֹנוֹת, הֲרֵי הֵן מְחַיְּבוֹת בְּדִיקָה מְחוּדֶּשֶׁת שֶׁל הֲנָחוֹת הַיְסוֹד שֶׁהוּצְבוּ עַד כֹּה בַּמֶּחְקָר.
<u>If</u> these conclusions are correct, <u>then</u> they require a re-examination of the basic assumptions that have until now been posited in the research.

(66) בְּנִיגוּד לַהֶסְבֵּר פְּסִיכוֹלוֹגִי-סוֹצִיוֹלוֹגִי זֶה, הֲרֵי הַהֶסְבֵּר הַשֵּׁנִי שֶׁנָּבִיא גֵּיאוֹגְרָפִי הוּא בִּיסוֹדוֹ.
<u>In contrast to</u> this psycho-social explanation, the second explanation that we will give is, fundamentally, geographical.

(67) בְּעוֹד שֶׁבַּתַרְגּוּם הָרִאשׁוֹן עוּבְרְתוּ שְׁמוֹת הַגִּיבּוֹרִים, הרי בַּתַרְגּוּם הַשֵּׁנִי הֵם נוֹתְרוּ בַּמָקוֹר הַגֶּרְמָנִי.
<u>Whereas</u> in the first translation the names of the protagonists were hebraized, in the second one they remained in their original German.

---

[8] הֱיוֹת וּ- is considered non-normative by prescriptive grammarians.

> **(68)** אַף כִּי ביסוד המצוות ניצֶבֶת הָאֱמוּנה הדתית המחייבֶת את הָאָדָם לקיום המצוות, הִנֵּה הביטוי העיקרי לאמונה הדתית היא התפילה.
> <u>Even though</u> at the basis of the [religious)] commands stands the religious faith that requires man to observe them, prayer is the main expression of religious faith.

3. שֶׁהֲרֵי is synonymous with שֶׁכֵּן *since, because*; it introduces the reason for a previous statement.

> **(69)** הוא נמנע משימוש במונָחים טֶכְניים, שהרי אלה אינם מוּבנים לקוראים רבים.
> He avoids using technical terms, <u>since</u> those are not understood by many readers.

4. לֹא הֲרֵי ... כַּהֲרֵי is an expression that stresses the contrast between two items: *this is not the same as that; this case is different from the other.*

> **(70)** לֹא הרי מִקְדָּשׁ שני כהרי מִקְדָּשׁ ראשון.
> The Second Temple <u>is different from</u> the First Temple.

References

בליבוים, 1995
טרומר, תשנ"ט

Coffin & Bolozky, 2005
Glinert, 1989

■

Chapter 7: The Copula – Exercises

exercise #	topic	page
1	Selecting the copula that is in agreement with the subject	284–286
2	Distinguishing between pronouns and copulas	287–288
3	Translating אין	289–290
4	Recognizing and translating copulas other than הוא, היא, הם, הן	291–292
5	Distinguishing among different meanings of נעשה	293–294
6	Distinguishing between *had* and *became*	295–296

Exercise #1: Selecting the copula that is in agreement with the subject

The rules to go by: see section 1.2 and remember also:
(a) When the subject is a construct phrase, the copula agrees with the first (head) noun.
(b) Names of countries and cities are considered feminine.
(c) ה at the end of the noun may be a possessive suffix (equivalent to שלה) attached to a masculine noun (rather than a feminine ending).
(d) Nouns ending with ות- are feminine singular.
What to do: select the appropriate copula.
Example:

המורכבות של היחסים בין היהודים, הנוצרים והמוסלמים בימי הביניים הוא/<u>היא</u>/הם/הן אחד הפרקים המעניינים ביותר בהיסטוריה של ספרד.

Explanation: The copula היא is selected, in agreement with מורכבות, as per (d) above.

1. הקיבוץ הוא/היא/הם/הן צורת חיים מקיפה.

2. הדרשה בציבור הוא/היא/הם/הן מנהג קדום.

3. היהדות הוא/היא/הם/הן צירוף ייחודי של דת ואומה.

4. לפי הַמָּסוֹרֶת הַבַּבְלִית בָּבֶל הוא/היא/הם/הן מקום החיבור בין שָׁמַיִם לארץ.

5. הַתַּעֲמוּלָה והַתִּקְשׁוֹרֶת הוא/היא/הם/הן האמצעי ולא המטרה.

6. כל הַדְּמֻיּוֹת שברוֹמָן הוא/היא/הם/הן קורבנותיו של סדר חברתי המוּשָׁתַת על הַיַּרַרְכְיָה.

Glossary

1.	comprehensive way of life צורת חיים מקיפה
2.	public sermon דרשה בציבור
	an ancient custom מנהג קדום
3.	unique blend צירוף ייחודי
	religion and nationality דת ואומה
4.	Babylonian tradition מסורת בבלית
	Babylonia בבל
	the place of connection מקום החיבור
5.	propaganda תעמולה
	communications תקשורת
	means אמצעי
	goal מטרה
6.	characters דמויות
	novel רומן
	the victims of a social order קורבנותיו של סדר חברתי
	based on hierarchy מושתת על היררכיה

7. הַמוֹטִיבַציה של העלייה היהודית לארץ ישראל הוא/היא/הם/הן בְּעִיקַר דתית.

8. גידול האוכְלוסיה היהודית הוא/היא/הם/הן הגורם הבולט והחשוב ביותר בהתְפַתחותה של ירושלים בעֵת החדשה.

9. נושְׂאו של ספר זה הוא/היא/הם/הן סִפְרות הַהַשְׂכָּלָה.

10. יְמות המִדְבר הוא/היא/הם/הן ימים של כְּפיות טוֹבה בִּלְתי-פוֹסקת.

11. שני המְאוֹרעות הגדולים בשַׁחַר ההיסטוריה של עַם ישראל הוא/היא/הם/הן יציאַת מצרים ומעמד הר סיני.

12. השילוב שבין דת ופוֹליטיקה הוא/היא/הם/הן קַרְקַע פוֹרייה לצְמיחתה של קַנָאות דתית אלימה בעולם כולו.

13. דְמות אחרת במִקְרא שהִתְאַפְיינה בקַנָאות דתית הוא/היא/הם/הן אֵלִיָהו הנביא.

Glossary

.7	מוֹטיבַציה motivation
	בעיקר דתית mainly religious
.8	גידול האוכלוסיה the population growth
	גורם cause
	בולט outstanding, prominent
.9	נושׂא topic
	ספרות ההשׂכלה the Enlightenment literature
.10	ימות המדבר the desert days
	כפיות טובה בלתי פוסקת incessant ingratitude
.11	מאורעות events
	שחר ההיסטוריה dawn of history
	יציאת מצרים Exodus (out) of Egypt
	מעמד הר סיני the giving of the Torah at Mount Sinai
.12	שילוב integration
	קרקע פורייה fertile ground
	צמיחה growth
	קנאות דתית אלימה violent religious zealotry
.13	דמות figure, character
	התאפיינה was characterized by
	קנאות דתית religious zealotry

14. ההתעַנְיְינוּת בתולדות הרפואה בארץ וּמְאפְיֵינְיה ‏הוא/היא/הם/הן‎ התפתחות של העת האחרונה.

15. שְׁמָהּ של שָׂפָה ‏הוא/היא/הם/הן‎ מוּסְכָּמָה המְעוּגֶנֶת במסורת היסטורית ובזהוּת תרבותית.

16. פריחתם של מוזאונים ואתרים המוקדשים להצגת תולדות החלוציוּת בארץ ‏הוא/היא/הם/הן‎ חלק מנַחְשוֹל נוֹסְטַלְגִיָה השוטף את העולם.

Glossary

14. התעניינות בתולדות הרפואה	interest in the history of medicine
מאפייניה	its characteristics
התפתחות של העת האחרונה	a recent development
15. מוסכמה	convention
מעוגנת	anchored in
זהות תרבותית	cultural identity
16. פריחתם (פריחה)	flourish, boom
אתרים	sites
מוקדשים להצגת תולדות החלוציות	dedicated to presenting the history of pioneering
נחשול נוסטלגיה השוטף את העולם	a wave of nostalgia washing over the world

Exercise #2: Distinguishing between pronouns and copulas

> **The rules to go by:** see section 1.4.
> **What to do:**
> 1. Determine the appropriate translation for the bolded pronoun (enter the sentence number in the appropriate cell in the chart).
> 2. Translate the sentence.
> **Example:**
>
> הניגוד בין האבות והבנים **הוא** הניגוד שבין ארץ ישראל הישנה ובין ארץ ישראל החדשה
>
> The contrast between fathers and sons <u>is</u> the contrast between the old and the new Land of Israel.

it	*they*	*is*	*are*
		example,	

1. .הרבה לפני שהמשפחות המסורתיות במזרח אירופה הושפעו ממגמות המודרניזַציה, **הן** הושפעו מפעולתם של גורמים פְּנימיים בחברה היהודית.

2. .המקור החשוב ביותר לידיעת העברית המקראית **הוא** ההשוואה ללשונות השֵׁמיות האחרות.

3. .מאפיין אחד של יהדות התפוצות **הוא** ריבוי הגְוונים שָׁבה.

4. .מִסְפר בתי הכנסת והמֵידע שהם מְסַפקים לְגבי אוֹפי היהדות של קְהילה כָּלְשֶׁהי מוּגבָּלים **הם**.

Glossary

traditional families	משפחות מסורתיות	.1
modernization trends	מגמות המודרניזציה
were influenced	הושפעו
internal elements	גורמים פנימיים
source	מקור	.2
biblical Hebrew	עברית מקראית
comparison	השוואה
Semitic languages	לשונות שמיות
characteristic	מאפיין	.3
Diaspora Jewry	יהדות התפוצות
its many varieties (colors)	ריבוי הגוונים שבה
information	מידע	.4
provide	מספקים
character	אופי
limited	מוגבלים

5. אַף עַל פִּי שֶׁהָעִבְרִית הוּשְׁפְּעָה מִלְּשׁוֹנוֹת שֶׁאֵינָן שֵׁמִיּוֹת, (א)**וְהִיא** עֲדַיִן מוּשְׁפַּעַת מֵהֶן, (ב)**הִיא** לֹא אִיבְּדָה אֶת אוֹפְיֵיהּ הַשֵּׁמִי.

6. הַסִּפּוּר "הִסְתַּלְּקוּת" (א)**הוּא** פְּנִינָה; (ב)**הוּא** מְתָאֵר אֶת הִסְתַּלְּקוּתָהּ הָאִיטִית שֶׁל הַסַּבְתָּא.

7. אֶפְשָׁרֻיּוֹת אֲחֵרוֹת לְמִיּוּן הַסִּיפּוּרִים (א)**הֵן** מִצַּד הַתֵּימָטִיקָה שֶׁלָּהֶם וְכֵן מִצַּד הַדְּמֻיּוֹת (ב)**שֶׁהֵם** מְתָאֲרִים.

8. עִיקַּר מוֹצָאָהּ שֶׁל הָאֱמוּנָה בַּמַּלְאָכִים (א)**הוּא** כְּכָל הַנִּרְאֶה, קְדַם-מִקְרָאִי, (ב)**וְהִיא** מוֹפִיעָה בּוֹרִיאַצְיוֹת שׁוֹנוֹת בְּדָתוֹת מֶסוֹפּוֹטָמִיּוֹת.

Glossary

even though	אַף עַל פִּי שֶׁ 5.
was influenced by non-Semitic languages	הוּשְׁפְּעָה מִלְּשׁוֹנוֹת שֶׁאֵינָן שֵׁמִיּוֹת
still	עֲדַיִן
lost its Semitic character	אִיבְּדָה אֶת אוֹפְיֵיהּ הַשֵּׁמִי
demise	הִסְתַּלְּקוּת 6.
here: a gem	פְּנִינָה
describes	מְתָאֵר
slow	אִיטִית
grandmother	סַבְתָּא
other possibilities	אֶפְשָׁרֻיּוֹת אֲחֵרוֹת 7.
from the thematic point of view	מִצַּד הַתֵּימָטִיקָה
from the point of view of characters	מִצַּד הַדְּמֻיּוֹת
describe	מְתָאֲרִים
its main origin	עִיקַּר מוֹצָאָהּ 8.
the belief in angles	הָאֱמוּנָה בַּמַּלְאָכִים
pre-biblical	קְדַם-מִקְרָאִי
appears	מוֹפִיעָה
different variations	וָרִיאַצְיוֹת שׁוֹנוֹת
Mesopotamian religions	דָתוֹת מֶסוֹפּוֹטָמִיּוֹת

Exercise #3: Translating אין

> **The rules to go by:** see section 2.2.
> **What to do:** determine the correct translation for each form of אין (enter the sentence number in the appropriate cell in the chart).
> **Example:**
>
> הנשמה (א)**אינה** רעבה, צמאה ועייפה ו(ב)**אינה** סובלת מכאב.
> The soul <u>is not</u> hungry, thirsty and tired and <u>does not</u> suffer from pain.

is not	are not	does not	do not
example א,		example ב,	

1. ההיסטוריונים **אינם** בטוחים באֲמִיתוּת הטַעֲנָה.

2. לא ניתן להבין את הנבואה בשֵׂכֶל והיא **אינה** מלמדת אמיתות פילוסופיות.

3. באֲזורים הצְפוניים השֶׁמֶשׁ **אינה** זורחת כְּלָל.

4. רוב המדינות המוּסלמיות בעולם **אינן** ערביות.

5. מקור המילה "אַרְמוֹן" בשפה העברית (א)**אינו** ברור, והיא (ב)**אינה** מבוססת על שורש ידוע בשפה העברית.

6. השתייכותו של אדם לקבוצה (א)**אינה** סוּבְּיֶיקְטִיבית – האדם (ב)**איננו** מחליט בעצמו אם הוא שייך לקבוצה או לא.

Glossary

1.	veracity of the claim אמיתות הטענה
2.	it is not possible to understand prophecy by logic לא ניתן להבין את הנבואה בשכל
	philosophical truths אמיתות פילוסופיות
3.	northern regions אזורים צפוניים
	shines זורחת
4.	most Muslim countries רוב המדינות המוסלמיות
5.	origin מקור
	clear ברור
	based on מבוססת על
	a known root שורש ידוע
6.	belonging (השתייכות) השתייכותו
	subjective סוביייקטיבית

7. הָעוֹלִים מִבְּרִית הַמוֹעֵצוֹת לְשֶׁעָבַר **אֵינָם** מִשְׁתַּלְבִים בַּחֶבְרָה הַיִשְׂרְאֵלִית וכך נוֹצְרָה בה קהילה חדשה.

Glossary

former USSR	ברית המועצות לשעבר	7.
integrate	משתלבים	
was created	נוצרה	
community	קהילה	

Exercise #4: Recognizing and translating copulas other than הוא, היא, הם, הן

> **The rules to go by:** see sections 3, 4 and 5.
> **What to do:** identify the copula in each sentence and determine its type (enter the number of the sentence in the appropriate cell in the chart).
> **Example:**
>
> אשת הגיבור <u>משמשת</u>, במידה רבה, תחליף אם.
>
> The protagonist's wife <u>serves</u>, to a great extent, as a substitute mother.

verbal copula *constitute*	verbal copula *serve as*	"becoming" copulas	emphatic copulas
	example,		

1. בלי סָפֵק מהווה הספר ציון דֶרֶךְ בידיעתנו את העיתונות העברית באוֹסְטְריה.

2. מיזוג זה של יַהֲדות ונַצרות נעשה שַליט ביצירתו של שאגאל.

3. רוֹמָן זה הינו הראשון בסִדְרַת הרומנים ההיסטוריים שפרסם.

4. הוא היה לא רק לגָדוֹל סוֹפְריה של סְפרד אלא גם לאבי הרומן המודרני, האֵירוֹפִי.

5. בחַייו ובמותו הפך דוגמה וסֵמֶל לנוֹער הצִיוֹני.

Glossary

without a doubt	בלי ספק .1
landmark	ציון דרך
our knowledge	ידיעתנו
Jewish journalism in Austria	העיתונות העברית באוסטריה
fusion, blend	מיזוג .2
Christianity	נצרות
here: dominant	שליט
the work of Chagall	יצירתו של שאגאל
the series of novels	סידרת הרומנים .3
published	פרסם
the greatest Spanish author	גדול סופריה של ספרד .4
father of the modern novel	אבי הרומן המודרני
in his life and death	בחייו ובמותו .5
example and symbol	דוגמה וסמל
youth	נוער

6. הָאֲרָמִית שימשה בִּימֵי קֶדֶם כלשון הַמַשָׂא-וּמַתָן בין עַמֵי הַמִזְרָח.

7. בַּהַשְׁפָּעַת גולֵי בָּבֶל נהיה הלוּח הירחי ללוח הדתי המקוּבל במסורת היהודית.

8. סְפָרוּת המסעות הריהי מקור מֵידע על אֶרץ ישראל בַּמֵאה ה-19.

9. זִכְרונותיו של בֶּנְיָמין מהווים צוֹהַר חשוב להַכָּרת חיי הקהילות היהודיות בזְמנו.

10. הפְּתיחה הינה אֶקְסְפּוֹזיצְיָה הַמַצִיגָה את הָרֶקַע לבְעָיָה ואת הנְפָשוּת הפוֹעלות.

Glossary

6.	ארמית	Aramaic
	בימי קדם	in antiquity
	לשון המשא ומתן	language of negotiation
	עמי המזרח	the peoples of the East
7.	בהשפעת גולי בבל	through the influence of the Babylonian exiles
	הלוח הירחי	the lunar calendar
	מקובל	customary, accepted
8.	ספרות המסעות	voyage literature
	מקור מידע	source of information
9.	זכרונותיו של בנימין	Benjamin's memoirs
	צוהר חשוב	important window
	הכרת חיי הקהילות	learning about the life of the communities
10.	פתיחה	opening
	אקספוזיציה	exposition
	מציגה את הרקע	presents the background
	נפשות פועלות	characters (in a story)

Exercise #5: Distinguishing among different meanings of נעשה

> **The rules to go by:** see section 5.2.
> **What to do:**
> 1. Determine the meaning of נעשה in each sentence (enter the number of the sentence in the appropriate cell in the chart).
> 2. Translate the sentences.

become(s)/became	made

1. הַפִילַנְתְרוֹפִיה **נעשתה** לְמֵעֵין תַּחֲלִיף שֶׁל הַשׁוּתָפוּת הַדָתִית שֶׁל הַיְהוּדִים.

2. "אֵין עֵד **נעשה** דַיָן" הוּא כְּלָל בְּמִשְׁפָּט הָעִבְרי.

3. רַבִּים מִסַּרְטָיו **נעשו** בְּמָסוֹרֶת הַקוֹמֶדְיָה הָאִיטַלְקִית.

4. הַנִּיסָיוֹן הָרִאשׁוֹן לְהַגִּיעַ לְפִסְגַת הָהָר **נעשה** עַל יְדֵי מִשְׁלַחַת אֲמֵרִיקָנִית.

5. בְּאַרְצוֹת הַבְּרִית **נעשה** שִׁימוּשׁ פּוֹלִיטִי בְּמִפְקָדִים הָחֵל מֵרֵאשִׁית יְמֵי הרפּוּבְּלִיקָה בַּמֵּאָה ה-17.

6. עִיבּוּד נְתוּנִים **נעשה** בְּיָמֵינוּ בְּאֶמְצָעוּת מַחְשֵׁב.

7. כְּלִי זֶה **נעשה** פּוֹפּוּלָרִי בַּשָׁנִים הָאַחֲרוֹנוֹת.

Glossary

.1	מעין תחליף של השותפות הדתית a kind of substitute for the religious fellowship
.2	עד witness
	דיין judge
	כלל במשפט העברי rule in Jewish law
.3	סרטיו his movies
	מסורת הקומדיה האיטלקית the tradition of Italian comedy
.4	ניסיון ראשון first attempt
	להגיע לפסגת ההר to reach to mountain top
	משלחת אמריקנית American mission
.5	מפקדים censuses
	החל מראשית ימי הרפובליקה במאה ה-17 since the first days of the Republic in the 17th century
.6	עיבוד נתונים data processing
	באמצעות מחשב via computer
.7	כלי instrument
	בשנים האחרונות in recent years, lately

8.   השימוש הראשון בנֶשֶק כִימי **נעשה** במלחמת העולם הראשונה על ידי הגרמנים.

9.   בסִפְרוּת יְלָדים **נעשה** שימוש רב בהַאֲנָשת בַּעֲלֵי חיים.

10. העבודה **נעשתה** בידי צֶוֶת בונים מְיוּמָן.

Glossary

.8	נשק כימי chemical weapon
.9	ספרות ילדים children's literature
	האנשת בעלי חיים personification of animals
.10	צוות בונים מיומן a skilled team of builders

Exercise #6: Distinguishing between *had* and *became*

The rules to go by: see section 5.3.1.
What to do: identify the meaning of the bolded sequence **היה/הייתה/היו** + **ל** and enter the sentence number in the appropriate cell in the chart.

---

became	*had*

1. אדם **היה** למַנְהיג אם עמד בראש משפחה גדולה ועשירה.

2. לטָעוּת זו **היו** הַשלָכות אֶסְטְרָטֶגיות מַרְחיקות לֶכֶת.

3. עם סוף מלחֶמֶת העולם השנייה **היו** ל"קוֹל אמֶריקה" 39 משדרים ברַחֲבֵי העולם.

4. מְחוזות אלו **היו** לקוֹנְפֶדֶרַצִיה של שמונה מדינות.

5. בקֶטע זה מְסופר גם כי לְיֵשׁוּ **היו** חמישה תלמידים.

6. לארמון **היו** שני מִפְלָסים.

7. העיר **הייתה** לבירת המדינה.

Glossary

---

1. מנהיג   leader
2. טעות   error
   השלכות אסטרטגיות מרחיקות לכת   far-reaching strategic implications
3. "קול אמריקה"   Voice of America
   משדרים   transmitters
   ברחבי העולם   world-wide
4. מחוזות   districts
   קונפדרציה   confederation
5. קטע   section
   מסופר   it is told
   ישו   Jesus
6. ארמון   palace
   מפלסים   levels
7. בירת המדינה   the capital

8. בִּמְקוֹמוֹת רַבִּים **הָיָה** לִימוּד הַפָּרָשָׁה עִם פֵּירוּשׁ רַשִׁ"י **לִדְרִישָׁה** מְקוּבֶּלֶת מִכָּל יֶלֶד יְהוּדִי הַלּוֹמֵד בַּחֶדֶר.

9. לִקְרַאת סוֹף הַמֵּאָה הַ-18 מִסְפַּר יְהוּדֵי הָעִיר הוּכְפָּל וְעַד מַחֲצִית הַמֵּאָה הַ-19 **הָיָה** לְ-1,000.

Glossary

8. לימוד הפרשה	the study of the Torah portion of the week
פירוש רש"י	Rashi commentary
דרישה מקובלת	a customary requirement
חדר	Heder (religious elementary school)
9. לקראת	toward
הוכפל	was doubled
מחצית המאה ה-19	the middle of the 19th century

8. PREPOSITIONS
מילות יחס

This chapter discusses:

- The formal characteristics of the prepositions (section 1)
- The meanings of the prepositions (section 2)
- The use of prepositions within the sentence (section 3)
- Confusables: ליד; לפי; לפני; של; תוך; בלעדי; אל
- Less commonly used prepositions (Appendix)

This chapter will help the reader to:

- Distinguish between translatable and non-translatable prepositions
- Choose the correct translation for prepositions with multiple meanings
- Determine whether nouns preceded by the prepositions ב,כ,ל are definite or indefinite
- Identify the reference of inflected prepositions in relative clauses
- Use prepositions as an aid in reading comprehension

Prepositions: an overview

Prepositions link verbs, nouns and adjectives to nouns. Unlike Hebrew nouns, verbs and adjectives, prepositions have no number or gender markings. The preposition may be attached to the noun or stand on its own as an independent word. The prepositions -בְּ, -כְּ and -לְ merge with the definite article -הַ.

In Hebrew, a preposition cannot be followed by a pronoun – instead, it is inflected with the appropriate pronoun suffix.

Some prepositions have a fixed meaning and are, therefore, translatable into English. Others – usually those that are required by the verb and as such are considered part of it (in fact, the preposition may change the meaning of the verb) – may be ignored in translation, or may have different translation options in different linguistic environments.

1. The forms of the prepositions

The prepositions fall into three structural groups:

(a) One-letter prepositions that are affixed to the noun (these are referred to nemonically as בַּכְּלָ"ם).

(b) One-syllable prepositions that are written as a separate word (e.g., עִם, עַל, אֶל, מִן, מוּל, כְּמוֹ, בֵּין, אֶת).

(c) Multi-syllable prepositions, some of them created through compounding of several prepositions (e.g., (לְ)אַחַר after, (כְּ)נֶגֶד against, (מִ)לִפְנֵי before, לְעוּמַת against, in contrast to, (מִ)סָבִיב around, בִּשְׁבִיל for, (עַל) אוֹדוֹת about, לְקְרַאת toward, אֵצֶל at, מִמּוּל vis-à-vis).

1.1 Merging of prepositions and pronouns
A preposition cannot be followed by a personal pronoun. Instead, it is inflected by a personal pronoun suffix. For example, בְּ+הוּא becomes בּוֹ (בהוא* is not possible).

The reference of the suffix can be determined on the basis of its gender and number agreement with a previously mentioned noun (on occasion, however, the inflected pronoun may anticipate the noun, as seen in example 5).

The inflected preposition and the noun it refers to are shaded:

(1) בשבעת יְמֵי הָאֵבֶל אין הָאֲבֵלים מכינים לְעצמם את מְזוֹנָם, וקרוֹבֵיהם והקהילה דואגים לָהֶם.
During the seven days of mourning <u>the mourners</u> do not prepare for themselves their food, and their relatives and the community take care <u>of them</u>.

(2) מוֹטיבַציָה אינְטֶגרטיבית היא המְניעה מְהַגרים הבאים לְאֶרֶץ חדשה להשְׁתלב בָּהּ בְּאוֹפֶן מלֵא.
It is integrative motivation that impels immigrants arriving in a <u>new country</u> to integrate <u>in it</u> fully.

‎(3) שֶׁגְּשׁוּגָה הַכַּלְכָּלִי שֶׁל <u>אַרצות הברית</u> משך <u>אֵלֶיהָ</u> מְהַגְרִים רבים.

The economic prosperity of <u>the United States</u> attracted <u>to it</u> many immigrants.

‎(4) באימוץ השֵׁם היְוָוני היה מֶסֶר בָּרוּר <u>לַחֶברָה הַהֶלֶניסטית</u>, מֶסֶר של פְּתיחוּת <u>כְּלַפֶּיהָ</u>, וּנְכוֹנוּת להִזְדָהוֹת <u>עִמָּה</u> ולהידָמוֹת <u>אֵלֶיהָ</u>.

In the adoption of the Greek name there was a clear message to <u>the Hellenistic society,</u> a message of openness <u>toward it</u>, and a willingness to identify <u>with it</u> and be similar <u>to it</u>.

‎(5) אין <u>בָּהּ</u> <u>בַּהַצהָרָה</u> זו שום כַּוָונָה של כינון אוטונומְיָה ליהודים ביהודה.

<u>In this declaration</u>, there is no intention of establishing autonomy for the Jews in Judea.

The word בה anticipates בהצהרה; in translation, it is ignored (for another instance of the anticipatory pronoun, see example 20 below and Chapter 3, example 84).

#1 1.1.1 The pronoun suffixes that inflect the prepositions are similar in form to those used to indicate possession in nouns.[1]

Most prepositions take the suffixes that mark possession in singular nouns: compare, for example, סביבָם *around them* with דוֹדָם *their uncle,* or עֲבוּרָהּ *for her* with דוֹדָהּ *her uncle.*

Prepositions that end with יו"ד (e.g., לפני, אחרי, לגבי, כלפי, על ידי) and those that end with וֹת- (e.g., בעקבות, אודות), as well as the prepositions אֶל *to* and עַל *on/about* are inflected like plural nouns. Thus: עליה *about her/it,* בעקבותיה *after her/it,* לפניה *before her/it* are inflected like דודיה *her uncles;* עליהם *about them,* בעקבותיהם *after them,* לפניהם *before them* are inflected like דודיהם *their uncles.*

#2 1.1.2 Some irregular inflected forms are listed alphabetically below (only the third person singular and plural forms – those most likely to appear in academic writing – are shown). Note that:

(a) בֵּין, כְּמוֹ and מִן have unique inflectional sets.

(b) אֶת and (מ)בְּלִי change their base form when inflected.

(c) עִם has a second set of inflected prepositions, based on the biblical אֵת *with.*

אֶת – אותו, אותָהּ, אותָם, אותָן
בֵּין – בֵּינוּ, בֵּינָהּ, בֵּיניהֶם/בֵּינָם, בֵּיניהֶן/בֵּינָן
(מ)בְּלִי – (מ)בִּלעָדָיו, (מ)בִּלעָדֶיהָ, (מ)בִּלעָדֵיהֶם, (מ)בִּלעָדֵיהֶן
כְּמוֹ – כָּמוֹהוּ/כְּמוֹתוֹ, כָּמוֹהָ/כְּמוֹתָהּ, כְּמוֹהֶם/כְּמוֹתָם, כְּמוֹהֶן/כְּמוֹתָן

---

[1] See Chapter 2, 5.2.

> The uninflected form כְּמוֹת is found before personal pronouns introduced by -שֶׁ. For example: הציורים מתארים את נושאיהם כמות-שהם *the paintings describe their subjects as they are*.

מִן — מִמֶּנּוּ, מִמֶּנָּה, מֵהֶם, מֵהֶן

> Note that מִמֶּנּוּ refers to both הוא and אנחנו; therefore, מֵאִתָּנוּ is commonly used for מִן+אנחנו (based on the older form מִן=מֵאֵת).
> Writers with an affinity for Mishnaic style sometimes use the forms הֵימֶנּוּ, הֵימֶנָּה instead of ממנו, ממנה.

עִם — אִתּוֹ, אִתָּהּ, אִתָּם, אִתָּן

or, more formally

עִמּוֹ, עִמָּהּ, עִמָּם/עִמָּהֶם, עִמָּן/עִמָּהֶן

By rule, the unpointed forms of the inflected preposition are spelled in the same way as the pointed ones, but the spelling איתו, איתה, איתם, איתן and עימו, עימה, עימם, עימן (with a יו"ד to indicate the initial /i/ sound) is also found.

1.1.3 Due to shift in word stress, some prepositions undergo internal vowel changes when inflected (e.g., דֶּרֶךְ[2] → דַּרְכּוּ *through*, נֶגֶד → נֶגְדָּם *against*, בְּקִרְבָּה → בְּקֶרֶב *among, within*).

#3   1.2 Merging of the prepositions בכ"ל with the definite article

The prepositions -ב, -כ and -ל (בכ"ל) merge with the definite article -ה and assume its **pronunciation** (e.g., בְּ+הַ → בַּ).

   The lexical (word meaning) and phonetic (pronunciation) implications of this rule are discussed below.

> בכ"ל are **typically pronounced** with a *sheva* (בְּ, לְ, כְּ) or, when the word already begins with a *sheva*, with the /i/ vowel (בִּ, לִ, כִּ). (This is because two consecutive initial *shevas* are not permissible.)

1.2.1 Lexical implications

Any ה"א following -ב, -כ, -ל can be automatically interpreted as an intrinsic part of the word.

---

[2] דרך is also a noun, *road*.

---

(6) בְּהֶקְשֵׁר‎ של הסבל הכללי

in the <u>context</u> of the general suffering...

The correct reading is הקשר *context*, NOT: קֶשֶׁר *connection*.

(7) החלטה בנוגֵעַ לַהֲגירה‎

a decision with regard to <u>immigration</u>

(8) השלבים בְּהִתְהַוּוּתוֹ‎ של עם ישראל

the stages in the <u>formation</u> of the people of Israel

(9) בְּהַקְדָּמתה‎ לשירה

in her <u>introduction</u> to her poem

In this example and the preceding one, the ה"א can be ruled out as a definite article also on the grounds that nouns with a possessive pronoun suffix cannot take a definite article.[3]

1.2.2 Phonetic implications

In unpointed text, it is not immediately evident whether a noun fronted by בכ"ל is definite or indefinite. The issue is not only one of accurate meaning (the difference between *in a place* and *in the place*, both written במקום), but also of accurate pronunciation (בְּמקום or בַּמקום).

⚠️ Make sure to distinguish בְּמקום and בַּמקום from בִּמְקוֹם *instead of* (followed by a noun or pronoun suffix).

A reliable clue that the noun is definite (and the preposition should then take the pronunciation of the definite article) is the presence of a definite article before the modifying adjective or the demonstrative pronoun that follow the noun (example 10).
For example:

בַּמָקוֹם החדש *in <u>the</u> new place* NOT: בְּמָקוֹם החדש* (בְּמָקוֹם חדש *in <u>a</u> new place* is correct);
בַּתחום הזה *in <u>this</u> area* NOT: בְּתחום הזה* (בְּתחום זה *in this new area* is correct).

Note, however, that before proper nouns (names) and nouns inflected with the possessive suffix – both considered definite – בכ"ל do not take a definite pronunciation.[4]
For example:

לְתֵל אביב *to Tel Aviv* NOT: לַתֵל אביב*;
בְּספרו *in his book,* NOT: בַּספרו*;
בְּתחומם *in their area,* NOT: בַּתחומם*.

---

[3] See Chapter 2, 3.2.
[4] Certain place names, namely these to which -ה is always pre-posed, are an exception: for example, בַּנגב ב+הנגב → *in the Negev*.

Similarly, בכ"ל take the indefinite pronunciation before definite construct phrases (e.g., בְּעִיר הבירה *in the capital city*, NOT: בָּעִיר הבירה*). This is because in construct phrases the preposition and the definite article are not contiguous: the preposition is affixed to the first noun, while the definite article appears before the second (or last) one.

---

(10) **לְ**ביזור רחב זה של הסְפרות העברית היו מִסְפָּר סיבות.
This wide decentralization of Hebrew literature had several reasons.

In this example, since neither the adjective nor the demonstrative pronoun have a definite article, we determine that the preposition should take the indefinite pronunciation.

(11) **בַּ**סֵפֶר מתוארים שלושה שלבים **בְּ**תולדותיו של עם ישראל.
In the book are described three stages in the history of the people of Israel.

בַּסֵפֶר is a product of the merging of the ב+הסֵפר (a book referred to earlier in the text). The preposition in בְּתולדותיו takes the indefinite pronunciation because the noun is inflected with the possessive suffix (בַּתולדותיו* would be wrong).

(12) המלְחָמָה והמַהְפֵּכָה הֵביאו **לַ**הֶרֶס הפיסי של המֶרכָּז ולְ**ש**יתוק כִּתְבֵי העֵת ובָתֵי ההוצָאָה.
The war and the revolution caused the physical destruction of the center and the paralysis of the periodicals and publishing houses.

The prepositions before the nouns הרס and שיתוק are pronounced differently: /la/ before הרס as per the rule that the preposition merges with the definite article and assumes its pronunciation (ל+הַהרס הפיסי=לַהרס הפיזי), /le/ before שיתוק, as per the rule that such merging is not possible in a construct phrase.

#4 2. The meanings of the prepositions

2.1 Translating prepositions
Depending on its role in the sentence, any given preposition may be ignored, changed, or translated verbatim.

2.1.1 Non-translatable prepositions
Prepositions whose sole function is grammatical, namely, to link a verb to an object complement, are considered an intrinsic part of the verb. They are called "governed" prepositions. As such, they do not have an independent (semantic) meaning of their own and can be ignored in translation. (Their translatability – or lack thereof – relates to the language of translation rather than any inherent Hebrew-specific trait.)

Chief among the non-translatable prepositions is את, obligatory before a definite direct object, and without any meaning other than its grammatical function to mark the definite direct object. As such, it has no English equivalent.

Some examples of verb-governed, untranslatable prepositions are:

להתחקות אחר *trace,* לעזור ל- *help,* להשתמש ב- *use,* להמליץ על *recommend,*
לשמור על *guard, keep,* לגרום ל- *cause,* ליהנות מן *enjoy,* להתעלם מן *ignore,*
לוותר על *renounce, give up,* להיתקל ב- *encounter,* להתנגד ל- *oppose,*
לזכות ב-/ל- *win, earn, merit, receive.*

Note that the prepositions ב-, כ-, ל-, מ- do not have an independent, translatable meaning when affixed to a noun or adjective for the purpose of creating an adverb. For example: בִּמְיוּחָד *especially,* כַּהֲלָכָה *properly,* לְעִיתִים *sometimes,* מִזְמַן *a long time ago* (see Chapter 5, 2.1).

2.1.1.1 The preposition required by the verb is often the same one required by a related noun or adjective.
For example:

להשפיע על *to influence,* השפעה על *influence on* (but מושפע מן *influenced by*)
להתגאות ב- *be proud of,* גאה ב- *proud of,* גאווה ב- *pride in*
להתייחס ל-/אל *treat; refer to* התייחסות ל-/אל *treatment of, reference to*
להתנגד ל- *oppose,* התנגדות ל- *opposition to.*

2.1.2 Translatable prepositions

Translatable prepositions have an intrinsic, semantic, meaning. They express relations of time, place, cause, etc., between a verb and a noun or between two nouns. In this group belong prepositions with one fixed meaning such as בְּלִי *without,* מְסָבִיב *around,* בְּתוֹך *inside,* מֵאֲחוֹרֵי *behind,* מ(ו)ל *across from,* לְקְרָאת *toward.*

2.1.3 If the English verb too requires a preposition, whether a different one from Hebrew or (by happenstance) an equivalent one, this would be the preposition used in translation.
Some examples for different prepositions used in Hebrew and English are:

להגיב על *react to,* NOT: *react on,* למרוד ב- *rebel against,* NOT: *rebel in.*

Examples for prepositions that happen to be parallel in Hebrew and English and therefore translatable verbatim into English are the following:

להאמין ב-	*believe in*
להזדהות עם	*identify with*
להישען על	*lean on*
לסבול מן	*suffer from*
להשתייך ל-	*belong to*
להשתתף ב-	*participate in*
להקדיש ל-	*devote to*
לבסס על	*base on*

2.2 Prepositions and verb meaning

The addition or change of a preposition may alter the meaning of the verb (sometimes also the adjective). This is akin to the role of the preposition in some English phrasal verbs, e.g., *put off, put away, put out, put on, put up with.*
For example:

- With the addition of various prepositions, the verb לעמוד *to stand* acquires the following meanings: לעמוד **על** *discuss; comprehend; insist on,* לעמוד **מאחורי** *stand behind, support,* לעמוד **ב**- *withstand, endure.*
- The addition of -ל to the adjective יפה *beautiful* changes its meaning to *beneficial.*
- In the example below, the addition of the preposition -ל after the verb לעשות *do, make* changes its meaning to *work for, strive for.*

---

(13) הַמַשְׂכִּילִים עשו לשימורה של המוֹרֶשֶׁת הקבוּצָתית בכֵלים חַדְשָׁניים.
The Maskilim <u>worked for</u> the preservation of the collective heritage with innovative tools.

Other verb pairs whose meanings vary with the preposition are listed below:

דן (את)	*judged*	דן ב-	*discussed*
האמין ל-	*believed (someone)*	האמין ב-	*believed in; trusted*
הביא (את)	*brought*	הביא ל-	*brought about, caused*
הבחין ב-	*noticed*	הבחין בין . . . ו(בין)/לבין	*distinguished between . . . and*
הודה ל-	*thanked*	הודה ב-	*admitted*
היה	*was*	היה ל-	*became*
הכיר (את)	*knew, recognized*	הכיר ב-	*acknowledged*
הניח	*assumed, supposed; placed*	הניח ל-	*allowed; left alone*
הפך (את)	*turned*	הפך ל-	*became*
הצביע ל-/בעד	*voted for*	הצביע על	*pointed out/at*
השיג (את)	*overtook; obtained; achieved*	השיג על	*disagreed, argued with*
השלים (את)	*completed*	השלים עם	*reconciled with, made one's peace with*
התיישב ב-	*settled in*	התיישב עם	*was congruent with*
חתר ל-	*strove for*	חתר תחת	*undermined, subverted*
פתח (את)	*opened*	פתח ב-	*began*
ראה (את)	*saw*	ראה ב-	*considered, regarded*
רדף (את)	*persecuted*	רדף אחרי	*chased*
שאל (את)	*asked (a question)*	שאל מן	*borrowed*

2.2.1 Alternative prepositions

In a few cases, alternative prepositions exist, but there is no change of verb meaning.
For example:

בחר ב-/את   *chose; voted for*
הֶחֱזִיק ב-/את   *held*
הסתכל ב-/על   *watched*
הִשְׁווה (את) ל-/עם   *compared with*
חשש מ-/מן/מפני   *was apprehensive of*
נזהר מ-/מן/מפני   *was wary of*
נֶחְשַׁב ל-/כ-   *considered as*
נלחם ב-/נגד   *fought*
שלט ב-/על   *ruled*

2.3 Prepositions with multiple meanings

Some of the most common prepositions, notably בכל"ם and על, have multiple meanings and,
therefore, different translation options.

2.3.1 Different meanings of ב-

(a) *in* or *at* – to indicate time and place before nouns (e.g., בימי הביניים *in the Middle Ages*,
    באתר *at the site*) and also before infinitive construct verbs[5] (e.g., בְּשׁוּבוֹ *when he returned*,
    בְּהתקרב הזמן *when the time approaches*).

(b) *through, by, by means of* – before an action noun (example 15).

(c) *with* – to indicate means (e.g., כָּתוּב בְּעִפָּרוֹן *written with a pencil*; example 14). Alternative
    prepositions for expressing means are: בְּאֶמְצָעוּת *by means of*, על ידי *by* and בְּעֶזְרַת *with*
    the help of.

(d) *among* – before a plural noun or pronoun (e.g., הוא הגדול בסופרי דורו/בהם *he is the*
    greatest among writers of his generation; example 16). Alternatively, בֵּין(מ) may be used
    (e.g., הוא הגדול (מ)בֵּין סופרי דורו).

(e) *by* – to indicate change in price, quantity or measure (example 17).

---

(14) בְּאחד משיריו הוא מַבִּיע את עִנְיַן נִצְחִיוּת עַמּוֹ בדימוי נָאֶה.
<u>In</u> one of his poems he expresses the idea of the immortality of his people <u>with</u> a
nice metaphor.

(15) בַּהֲפִיכַת המיתוֹס למציאות נֶחשָׂפוֹת כל סַכָּנוֹתיו.
<u>By</u> turning the myth into reality all of its dangers are exposed.

---

[5] See Chapter 6, 1.2.

(16) הַסֵּפֶר עוֹסֵק בְּאַחַת הַבְּעָיוֹת הַקָּשׁוֹת וְהַמּוּרְכָּבוֹת בְּיוֹתֵר בַּהִיסְטוֹרְיָה הָאִינְטֶלֶקְטוּאָלִית, אִם לֹא הַקָּשָׁה שֶׁבָּהֶן: אֵיךְ הוֹפְכִים רַעְיוֹנוֹת לְכוֹחַ מַשְׁפִּיעַ בַּהִיסְטוֹרְיָה.

The book deals <u>with</u> one of the most complex and difficult problems <u>in</u> intellectual history, if not the most difficult <u>among them</u>: how ideas become an influencing force <u>in</u> history.

We see here three different uses of ‎ב:

(a) ‎עוסק ב- – the preposition is required by the verb
(b) ‎בהיסטוריה – *in* (time adverbial)
(c) ‎בהן – *among one of (them)*. Alternatively, ‎ביניהן could be used.

(17) מִפְלָס הַכִּינֶּרֶת עָלָה בְּמֶטֶר לְאַחַר הַגְּשָׁמִים.

The water level of the Sea of Galilee went up <u>by</u> one meter after the rains.

#5   2.3.2 **Different meanings of ‎-כ**

(a) *like, in the same way as, similarly, alike* – in this sense ‎-כ is a short form of ‎כמו (examples 18–20). Dissimilarity is expressed with ‎שלֹא כ- *unlike* (example 21).

(b) *as, in the role of, in the status of* – in this sense ‎-כ is synonymous with ‎בְּתוֹר *in the capacity of, qua* (example 22). It appears with certain verbs and adjectives that indicate status (e.g., ‎נוֹדַע/מוּכָּר כ- *be known as,* ‎לְשַׁמֵּשׁ כ- *serve as,* ‎לְהֵיחָשֵׁב כ- *be considered as,* ‎לְהֵירָאוֹת כ- *be seen as,* ‎-be).

(c) *approximately*, before a number (example 23).

(18) לִדְבָרָיו, אֶרֶץ יִשְׂרָאֵל אֵינֶנָּה כִּשְׁאָר הָאֲרָצוֹת.

According to him, the Land of Israel is not <u>like</u> other lands.

(19) הַדְּרָקוֹן הִילֵּךְ קֶסֶם עַל כָּל אַנְשֵׁי יְמֵי הַבֵּינַיִים, יְהוּדִים כְּנוֹצְרִים.

The dragon fascinated all people of the Middle Ages, Jews and Christians <u>alike.</u>

(20) גִּיבּוֹר הָרוֹמָן, כָּמוֹהוּ כַּמְחַבֵּר, הוּא צָעִיר שֶׁנּוֹלַד לְאָב מִמִּשְׁפָּחָה יְרוּשַׁלְמִית דָּתִית.

The protagonist of the novel, <u>just like </u>the author, is a young man who was born to a father from a religious Jerusalemite family.

The preposition appears twice – once before a pronoun suffix and once before a noun – for emphasis.

(21) שֶׁלֹּא כְּרַבִּים מִן הַתַּנָּאִים, הוּא אֵינוֹ מְזוֹהֶה בְּשֵׁם אָבִיו.

<u>Unlike</u> many of the Tannaim he is not identified by his father's name.

(22) הַדָּת הַמּוֹנוֹתֵיאִיסְטִית מַנִּיחָה אֶת שִׁלְטוֹן הָאֵל כְּשִׁלְטוֹן עֶלְיוֹן.

Monotheistic religion posits God's rule <u>as</u> a supreme rule.

In this function, ‎-כ could be replaced by the word ‎בְּתוֹר: בתור שלטון עליון.

(23) בְּמַהֲלָךְ הַמֶּחְקָר ביקרתי בְּכְשִׁשִׁים מוּזֵיאוֹנִים.

In the course of the research, I visited <u>about</u> sixty museums.

As seen here, -כְ in the sense of *approximately* may appear after another preposition.

2.3.2.1 Note that -כְ is ignored in translation when affixed to -שֶׁ in -כְּשֶׁ *when, at the time when* (a short form of כַּאֲשֶׁר) and in -לִכְשֶׁ *when* (for future events).

2.3.3 Different meanings of -ל

(a) *to* – a directional preposition (example 24).

With certain verbs (and the related nouns) **אֶל** is optionally interchangeable with -ל. For example:
פנה לאיש, פנה **אל** האיש *turned to the man*; however, אל is obligatory with the personal pronoun: פנה אליו *turned to him*, NOT: פנה לו*.

(b) *for* – after certain nouns (e.g., סיבה *reason*, תנאי *condition*, דוגמה *example*, הסבר *explanation*, רקע *background*) (example 25).

(c) *of* – to indicate belonging (example 26).

(d) *for the purpose of, in order to* – instead of כדי before an action noun (example 27).

(e) *in* – in the idiomatic expression -לְדַעַת *in the opinion of*.

(f) *by* – to indicate authorship (e.g., מִשְׁנֶה תורה לרמב"ם *Mishneh Torah by Maimonides*).

(24) דֵעוֹתָיו של הַמְחַבֵּר מוּצָגוֹת **לַ**קּוֹרֵא.
The opinions of the author are presented <u>to</u> the reader.

(25) הסיבות **לְ**בִיזוּר רחב זה של הסְפרות העברית היו אֲחָדוֹת.
There were several reasons <u>for</u> this wide decentralization of Hebrew literature.

(26) הוא היה בֶּן **לְ**משפחת כוהנים חשובה.
He was the son <u>of</u> an important family of priests.

(27) **לְ**הַדְגָּמַת הַטַעֲנָה, בָּחַרנו בְּכַמָּה דוּגְמָאוֹת.
<u>In order to</u> (OR: <u>to</u>) illustrate our argument, we chose several examples.

Alternatively:...כדי להדגים את הטענה

⚠️ **2.3.3.1** Note that -ל is not translatable as a preposition when it is part of a "have" sentence (e.g., -היה ל, נעשה ל- יש/אין ל-, examples 28–30), or a verb of becoming (e.g., הפך ל- *became*).

---

(28) לְמַעֲמָדוֹ הַנִשְׂגָב כַּיוֹם **אֵין** כל קֶשֶׁר לְמַעֲשֶׂה הַבְּרִיאָה.
His lofty status today <u>has</u> no relation to the act of creation.

The preposition -ל first occurs as part of a "have" phrase (-ל . . . אֵין), then as an obligatory preposition after קֶשֶׁר, where it is translated as *to*.

(29) **לַ**צוֹרֶךְ בִּידִיעָה טוֹבָה שֶׁל עברית בתקופה הסְפָרַדִית **הָיְתָה** גם בְּחִינָה חֶבְרָתִית.
During the Spanish period, the need for a good knowledge of Hebrew also <u>had</u> a social aspect.

The preposition and the verb are far apart.

(30) **לִ**קבוּצַת סוֹפרים זו שֵׁמוֹת מְזַהִים אֲחָדים.
This group of authors <u>has</u> several identifying names.

"Having" is indicated by the preposition alone.[6]

The following example illustrates a variety of functions (and translations) of -ל within one sentence.

---

(31) **לְ**דעת יְהוּדָה הַלֵוי, בכל השאלות הנוגעות **לָ**אֱלוֹהוּת או **לַ**יַחַס שבין הָאֱלוֹהוּת והבריאה יש **לְ**תורת ישראל עֲדִיפוּת מוּחְלֶטֶת ואין היא זְקוּקָה **לְ**סִיוּעָם שֶׁל כִּתְבֵי אריסטוֹ.
<u>In</u> the opinion of Judah Halevi, in all questions regarding the deity or the relationship between the deity and creation, the Torah <u>has</u> absolute advantage and it does not need the assistance of the writings of Aristotle.

The various functions of -ל in this sentence are the following:

(a) לְדַעַת *in the opinion of* (idiomatic usage; -ל is translated as *in*)
(b) לָאֱלוֹהוּת, לַיחס and לסיוּעם: non-translatable preposition required by the verb נוֹגֵעַ and the adjective זְקוּקָה, respectively
(c) לתורת ישראל – part of -יש ל *has*

2.3.4 Different meanings of מ-/מִן

-מִ (pronounced -מֵ before א, ה, ח, ע, ר) is a short form of מִן; the forms are identical in meaning and are usually interchangeable, although מִן tends to appear before a definite article

---

[6] See Chapter 9, 2.2.

(example 52) and is obligatory (though not translatable) in certain idiomatic expressions (e.g., מִן הָרָאוּי *it is appropriate,* מִן הַסְתָם *probably*).

(a) *from* – in time and space adverbials, and complemented by -לְ *to* (example 32) or עד(לְ) *to, till,* when an end point is specified. לְמִן (instead of מִן) is sometimes used with time expressions (e.g., לְמן המאה הי"ז וָאֵילָךְ *from the seventeenth century on*).

(b) *one of, some of* – part of a whole, before a plural (or collective) noun or pronoun. For example: אחד מהקבוצה *one of the group,* אחד מהם *one of them* (examples 33–34).

(c) *than* – in comparative sentences, after יותר *more* and פחות *less* (example 35); when יותר is (optionally) omitted, the meaning of the comparison rests entirely on the preposition (example 36). Before a preposition or an infinitive verb form, מֵאֲשֶׁר is often preferred to מ/מן (example 37).

(d) *on* – in מימין *on the right,* משמאל *on the left,* BUT: מִדרום *south of.*

(e) *when, at the time that* – when affixed to -שׁ (-מִשֶׁ) (example 39); this is a formal alternative to -כְּשֶׁ.

---

(32) מֵחורבן לְחורבן לא פָסקו מִלהַעֲלות את הַהַתחָלָה הַבלתי נשכַּחַת.
From destruction to destruction they did not cease to bring up the unforgettable beginning.

Note that the sequence -מל (מִלהעלות) is created by the placement of the preposition -מ (optionally accompanying the verb פסקו and not tranlsatable) before the infinitive form of the verb.

(33) תֵיאורה של הסבתא הוא מֵהתֵיאורים המופלאים שבנמצא.
The description of the grandmother is (one) of the (most) wonderful descriptions in existence.

(34) בכל מחוזותיה של ארץ-ישראל נוצְרו גם לשונות-כלאיים. לשונות כלאיים אלה, מֵהֶן היו עשויות רכיבי עברית ויידיש, מהן היו בנויות אֲריחֵי יידיש וערבית, מהן היו שְלובות יְסודות של עברית, עֲרבית, יידיש וסְפרדית-יהודית.
In all regions of the Land of Israel, hybrid languages were also created. Some of them were made up of Hebrew and Yiddish components, some of them had Yiddish and Arabic as their building blocks, (and) some of them were interlaced (with) elements of Hebrew, Arabic, Yiddish and Judeo-Spanish.

(35) סיפור זה מענְיין יותר מקודמו.
This story is more interesting than the previous one.

(36) רָמַת ההשכָּלָה של כָּלל היהודים באָרצות המזרח בתקוּפת הגאונים הייתה גבוהה מִשֶׁל שכניהם המוסלמים, אבל נְמוכָה משל אָחֵיהם בסְפרד.
The educational level of most Jews in the Orient during the time of the Geonim was higher than that of their Moslem neighbors but lower than that of their brethren in Spain.

The comparative יותר was omitted.

(37) השימוש בסָמָלים יהודיים בבית הכנסת היה מרובה **יותר** בארץ ישראל **מֵאֲשֶר** בתפוצות.

The use of Jewish symbols in the synagogue was <u>greater</u> in the Land of Israel <u>than</u> in the diasoporas.

Before a preposition (**בתפוצות**), מאשר is used.

(38) מונָח זה, "השיבָה המלֵאָה אל העברית," נראֶה לי הולֵם **יותר**, **מן** הבחינה הבַּלשנית הצרופָה, **מן** המונח "תחְיַית העברית," ובְוודאי **מן** המונָח "החיָאַת העברית".

This term, "the full return to Hebrew," appears to me <u>more</u> appropriate, <u>from</u> the pure linguistic aspect, <u>than</u> the term "the revival of Hebrew," and certainly (<u>more</u>) <u>than</u> the term "the resuscitation of Hebrew".

In this example, מן has two different functions. On its first occurrence, it is part of the adverbial expression מן הבחינה *from the point of view*.[7] On its second and third occurrences, מן is part of a comparative phrase, and is translated as *than*. Note that while the preposition is repeated, the comparison word יותר appears only once.

(39) תחילָה התגוררו התֵימָנים בסוכות בחורשַת האֵקליפטוסים שליד הוַואדי. **מֶשהגיע** החורף עברו לגור ברפתות ובאורוות של איכָּרי המושבָה.

At the beginning, the Yemenites lived in huts in the eucalyptus grove near the wadi. <u>When</u> the winter arrived, they moved to the cowsheds and stables of the farmers in the settlement.

2.3.4.1 When affixed to other prepositions, -מ does not alter their meanings and is ignored in translation. Some examples are: מבלי, בלי *without,* מסביב, סביב *around,* מעל, על *above,* מלְפני, לפני *before,* מתחת, תחת *below.*

⚖#6   2.3.5 Different meanings of על

(a) **on, upon** – with adverbials of place (e.g., על בָּמת ההיסטוריה *on the stage of history*); sometimes: על גבֵּי (see example 5 in the Appendix below).

(b) **about, regarding.** For example: לדבר על *talk about.*

(c) **must, have to, it is incumbent upon** – followed by a noun or pronoun and then by an infinitive verb, על indicates an obligation (examples 40–41 and 53). In ornate style, the expression שׂוּמָה על may be found (example 42).

(d) **(together) with, including** – synonymous with עִם (example 43).

(e) **because of, for** in the sense of *on the basis of* (example 44).

(f) **after** – with the word שם (e.g., הוא נקרא על שם אביו *he is called after his father*).

---

[7] See Chapter 11, 10.2.

> (40) בסיפור הקצר **עַל** כל מילה, **עַל** כל פיסקה, להיות חיונית.
> In the short story every word, every paragraph, <u>must</u> be essential.
>
> (41) כדי שהסיפור ימשוך את לִבָּם של הקוראים, **עָלָיו** לדבר בִּלשוֹנָם.
> In order for the story to attract the readers, it <u>has to</u> speak their language.
>
> (42) רְחֲבַת העיר מילאה את כל התפקידים שֶשׂוּמה היה **עַל** בניין מֶרכזי למלא.
> The city square fulfilled all the roles that a central building <u>had to</u> fulfill.
>
> (43) יש לָתֵת את הדעת לרַב-מֵימַדיוּתוֹ של הפַשיזם עצמו, **עַל** תכָנָיו האינטלקטואליים, **עַל** גְוָוניו ורבָדיו וְ**עַל** שלַבֵי התפתחותו.
> Attention should be given to the multi-dimensionality of fascism itself, <u>including</u> its intellectual content, its varieties and layers, and its stages of development.
>
> (44) **עַל** חֵטא זה נֶעֶנשו האחים עוֹנש כָּבֵד.
> <u>Because of</u> (OR: <u>for</u>) this sin, the brothers were heavily punished.

2.3.5.1 עַל is also used as a semantic prefix or suffix, meaning *super* (e.g., עַל-אֱנוֹשי *superhuman*, עַל-קוֹלי *supersonic*; מַעֲצֶמֶת-עַל *super-power*).

2.3.5.2 Note that עַל is a non-translatable component in several compound prepositions, (e.g., עַל אוֹדוֹת *about*, עַל פִּי *according to*, עַל יד *next to*, עַל יָדֵי *by*) as well as in adverbial expressions (e.g., עַל אַף *despite*, אַף עַל פִּי כֵן *despite this*, -ש עַל פִּי אַף *even though*, עַל כי, עַל שוּם, עַל כֵּן *therefore*, עַל מְנָת *in order to*, עַל אחת כַּמָּה וכמה *moreover*, עַל הרוב *mostly, generally*). Note also (ב)עַל פה *orally*; *by heart, from memory* and עַל סָמך *based on, on the basis of*.

3. Syntactic aspects of preposition use

3.1 Verbs followed by two (or more) prepositions
Many verbs accommodate (or require) two object complements, usually one direct and the other indirect (not necessarily in this order). The direct object (if definite) is linked to the verb with את, the indirect object is linked to it by other prepositions.
Some examples are:

ביקר (את) . . . עַל . . .	*criticized (something/someone) for*
האשים (את) . . . בְּ- . . .	*accused (someone) of*
הודה (ל-) . . . עַל . . .	*thanked (someone) for*
הוסיף (את) . . . לְ- . . .	*added (someone/something) to*
העדיף (את) . . . עַל (פְּני) . . .	*preferred (something/someone) over* (example 46)
הפך (את) . . . מִ- . . . לְ-. . .	*turned (someone/something) from . . . into* (example 47)
השווה (את) . . . עם/לְ- . . .	*compared (something/someone) to*
התייחס לְ-\אֶל . . . כְּ- (אֶל)	*treated (someone) as* (example 45)
ייחס לְ- . . . (את) . . .	*attributed (something) to*

כפה (את) ... על ...ֹ   *imposed (something) on*
מינה (את) .... ל-...   *appointed (someone) to*
מנע (את) ... מ-...   *withheld (something) from*
נתן ל-... (את) ...   *gave (something) to*

---

(45) יְהוּדֵי רוּסְיָה שֶׁהִגְּרוּ בְּסוֹף הָעִידָן הַסּוֹבְיֵיטִי הִתְיַיחֲסוּ לְיִשְׂרָאֵל כְּמִפְלָט זְמַנִּי.
The Russian Jews who immigrated at the end of the Soviet era <u>treated</u> Israel <u>as</u> a temporary asylum.

In this example there are two indirect object complements; their order of appearance is fixed: **כ...ל\אל** להתייחס *treat [someone] as*

(46) סִפְרוּת זוֹ הֶעֱדִיפָה אֶת הָאִידֵיאָלִיזַצְיָה עַל פְּנֵי תֵּיאוּר הַהֲוָיָה הַמַּמָּשִׁית.
This literature <u>preferred</u> idealization <u>over</u> the description of actual reality.

(47) הַיְּהוּדִים הָפְכוּ אֶת מַשְׁמָעוּת הַסֵּמֶל מִשְׁלִילִית לְחִיּוּבִית.
The Jews <u>turned</u> the meaning of the symbol <u>from</u> negative <u>to</u> positive.

3.2 The placement of the preposition

The preposition may either precede or follow the verb, whether directly or at a distance. Naturally, it appears at the beginning of the sentence when the object is pre-posed (examples 48–50). In interrogative sentences, the preposition directly precedes the question word (example 51).

The preposition and the verb that requires it are shaded:

---

(48) בְּדֵעָה זוֹ מַחֲזִיקִים חֲכָמִים רַבִּים.
Many sages hold this opinion.

(49) לְנוֹשֵׂא זֶה לֹא הִקְדִּישׁ הַמֶּחְקָר תְּשׂוּמֶת לֵב מַסְפֶּקֶת.
The research has not devoted enough attention <u>to</u> this topic.

(50) בְּמַעֲמָדָם הַמְיוּחָד שֶׁל יְרוּשָׁלַיִם וְהַמִּקְדָּשׁ הִכִּירוּ אַף הַמְּלָכִים הַהֶלֶנִיסְטִיִּים, כְּשֵׁם שֶׁהִכִּירוּ בּוֹ לִפְנֵי כֵן מַלְכֵי פָּרָס.
Even the Hellenistic kings acknowledged the special status of Jerusalem and the Temple, as did the Persian kings before them.

(51) עַל מָה מְבַסֵּס הַסּוֹפֵר אֶת כְּתִיבָתוֹ עַל הַיְחָסִים שֶׁבֵּין יְהוּדִים וּפוֹלָנִים?
<u>On</u> what does the author base his writing about relationships between Jews and Poles?

3.3 Repetition of identical prepositions

בְּרֵאשִׁית בָּרָא אֱלֹהִים אֵת הַשָּׁמַיִם וְאֵת הָאָרֶץ (בראשית א א)
In the beginning God created the heaven and the earth (Genesis 1.1)

אִישׁ תַּחַת גַּפְנוֹ וְתַחַת תְּאֵנָתוֹ (מלכים א, ה ה)
Everyone under his own vine and his own fig tree (Kings I 5.5)

As the above citations illustrate, in Hebrew there is a preference for repeating identical prepositions. This practice facilitates the identification of multiple object complements emanating from the same verb.

The verb and the preposition(s) it requires are shaded:

---

(52) התרגום שואב הרבה מלשון המקרא, מן השירה המקראית העתיקה ומן הנבואה.
The translation draws much <u>from</u> biblical language, (<u>from</u>) ancient biblical poetry and (<u>from</u>) prophecy

Before the definite article ה-, מן is preferred to the shorter -מ.

(53) על המתיישבים היה להתמודד עם המהפך באורחות חייהם, עם עבודות שדה, ועם אקלים נוקשה וזר.
The settlers had to grapple <u>with</u> the dramatic change in their way of life, (<u>with</u>) the agricultural work, and (<u>with</u>) a harsh and foreign climate.

🏋#7   3.4 Inflected prepositions in relative clauses

When the verb in a relative clause requires a preposition, this preposition can neither be omitted nor left to "dangle" (as it might in English). Instead, it is inflected with a pronoun suffix. The suffix refers back to the antecedent noun in the main clause, and agrees with it in gender and number.

For example:

The sentence זאת בעיה שרבים התמודדו עמה *this is a problem with which many have grappled* is the result of two simple sentences: זאת בעיה and רבים התמודדו עם הבעיה. In the combined sentence, the word בעיה is not repeated, but is referred back to by means of a pronoun suffix attached to the (required) preposition עם.

Neither the sentence *זאת בעיה שרבים התמודדו עם (the equivalent of *this is a problem many have grappled with*) nor *זאת בעיה שרבים התמודדו (which ignores the preposition altogether) is acceptable in Hebrew.

3.4.1 The placement of the preposition and clause word order

The word order in relative clauses with an inflected preposition is quite flexible. The preposition may appear before or after the verb.

When the inflected preposition is placed <u>before</u> the verb, it appears at the beginning of the clause, immediately following the subordinating particle -שׁ (or its more formal variant אֲשֶׁר, example 57). In this arrangement, the verb is likely (and expected by rule) to precede the subject (e.g., זאת בעיה **שעמה התמודדו רבים**, and examples 54 and 57).

When the preposition appears <u>after</u> the verb, the verb may follow the subject and the preposition is then the last word of the clause (e.g., זאת בעיה **שרבים התמודדו עמה**, and example 56). Alternatively, the verb may precede the subject and the preposition is then the penultimate word in the clause, positioned between the verb and the subject (e.g., זאת בעיה **שהתמודדו עמה רבים**).

In many cases, when the inflected preposition is in initial position in the relative clause, the subordinating particle -שׁ (or its more formal variant אֲשֶׁר) is omitted (example 55). The omission of the subordinator is frowned upon by prescriptive grammarians as non-normative. It also has the disadvantage of depriving the reader of a valuable clue to the structure of the sentence, although the absence of a subordinating particle can be offset by placing a comma before the preposition to mark the beginning of the subordinate clause (example 58).

---

(54) הָאֲדָמָה **שֶׁעָלֶיהָ** יושב הַמִּקְדָּשׁ הָיְתָה בעבר יער.
The land <u>on which</u> the temple stands (literally: sits) was in the past a forest.

The third person feminine suffix in עליה refers to אדמה; the verb יושב in the relative clause comes before the subject מקדש.

(55) שְׁאִיפַת הַמַּשְׂכִּילִים הַיְּהוּדִים הָיְתָה לְהִשְׁתַּלֵּב בָּעַמִּים **בְּקִרְבָּם** הִתְגּוֹרְרוּ.
The aspiration of the Jewish Maskilim was to integrate into the nations <u>among whom</u> they dwelled.

(56) נֻסַּח סְפָרַד מְקֻבָּל בְּאַרְצוֹת **שֶׁיְּהוּדֵי** סְפָרַד הִשְׁתַּקְּעוּ **בָּהֶן** לְאַחַר גֵּירוּשׁ סְפָרַד.
The Sephardic version [of the prayer book] is customary in the countries <u>where (OR: in which)</u> Sephardic Jews settled after the expulsion from Spain.

Since the inflected preposition appears at the end of the relative clause there is no inversion of the subject-verb word order.

(57) הַנּוֹשֵׂא הָעִיקָּרִי בַּסֵּפֶר הוא דִּיּוּן בִּצְדָדִים שׁוֹנִים של ניגוד בין **רַעְיוֹן הָאֵל, אֲשֶׁר עָלָיו** מֻשְׁתֶּתֶת הַיַּהֲדוּת, לבין הַהַשְׁקָפָה הַפִילוֹסוֹפִית.
The main theme in the book is a discussion of the different facets of the conflict between the idea of God, <u>on which</u> Judaism is founded, and the philosophical perspective.

אֲשֶׁר is used in stead of -שׁ; the verb in the relative clause (מושתתת) precedes the subject (היהדות).

⚠ 3.4.2 שֶׁ+-לוֹ versus שֶׁלּוֹ

A distinction should be made between שֶׁ+-לוֹ (where לוֹ refers back to one of the nouns in the main clause and -שֶׁ is the subordinating particle) and שֶׁלּוֹ *his* (the result of merging שֶׁל with הוּא). To avoid the ambiguity, a comma may be added to separate the subordinate clause from the main clause (example 58), or -שֶׁ could be replaced by אֲשֶׁר.

---

(58) כּוֹחָהּ שֶׁל הַיְצִירָה הַסִּפְרוּתִית הוּא בָּאֶמְצָעֶיהָ הָאֲמָנוּתִיִּים, שֶׁלָּהֶם נִיתֶּנֶת הַבְּכוֹרָה.
The power of the literary work is its artistic means, <u>to which</u> the priority is given.

שֶׁלָּהֶם is segmented as שֶׁ+-לָהֶם *to which* (the comma before שֶׁלָּהֶם alerts the reader to such a reading), NOT: שֶׁל+הֶם *their*; the preposition -לְ is required by the verb לָתֵת, its pronoun suffix refers to אמצעים אמנותיים

(59) הַסִּיפּוּרִים שֶׁלָּהֶם מוּקְדַּשׁ מַאֲמָר זֶה הִתְפַּרְסְמוּ לְאַחַר מוֹת מְחַבְּרָם.
The stories <u>to which</u> this article is devoted were published after the death of their author (posthumously).

NOT: *their stories*; -לְ is required by the verb מוּקְדָּשׁ.
If a comma or אֲשֶׁר – instead of -שֶׁ – were used, the (potential) ambiguity of the form שלהם could be avoided.

3.5 Using prepositions as an aid in reading comprehension

Although often ignored in translation, prepositions provide valuable grammatical information, helping readers differentiate between subject and object, detect the presence of object complements, and recognize adverbials. Prepositions can also aid in lexical decoding of homographs (unrelated words that appear identical in unpointed text), and in choosing the context-appropriate meaning of polysemous (multi-meaning) words.

Readers, therefore, should attempt to account for the presence of each preposition encountered in the text and determine its function and provenance. This strategy is demonstrated in examples 60–66 below.

The ambiguous word is framed and the clue to its meaning is shaded:

---

(60) לֹא בְּפַרְשָׁנוּת בִּלְבַד עוֹסֶקֶת הָאַגָּדָה הַמִּקְרָאִית, אֶלָּא אַף בַּתֵּיאוּר הַמַּשְׁלִים אֶת הַמְסוּפָּר בַּמִּקְרָא.
The biblical legend is occupied not only with exegesis, but also with description <u>that complements</u> what is told in the Bible.

The preposition אֶת provides the necessary clue for reading משלים as a verb – מַשְׁלִים *complements* (rather than הַמְּשָׁלִים *the fables*).

(61) בבתי-כנסת בָּאָרֶץ מתגלָה נְטִייָה גדולה יותר מֵאֵלוּ שבתפוצות לאומנות דְמוּת בַּעֲלת אוֹפִי פַּגאני מוּבהָק.

In synagogues in the Land of Israel, more than in those in the diaspora, a greater propensity is evident for figurative <u>art</u> of a distinctly pagan nature.

We read לאומנות as ל-+אומנות, (rather than לאומנות *nationalism*); the initial -ל is the preposition required by the noun נטייה. Note that the preferred (normative) spelling of word is אמנות, to distinguish it from אומנות *craft, craftsmanship*.

(62) שְׁאלה זו קְשׁורה לְטיב זיקָתָה של התורה שבְּעל פֶּה לתורה שבּכְתָב וּלמידת תְּלוּתה של זו בזו.

This question is related to the nature of the connection between oral and written Torah and the <u>extent</u> of their interdependency.

We read למידת as ל-+מידת, where the initial -ל is the preposition required by the adjective קשורה and מידת is the construct form of מידה *extent*, NOT: -למידת *the learning/study of* (where the initial למ"ד is an integral part of the word למידה).
We are alerted to the prepositional function of the initial למ"ד by the fact that previously in the sentence it connects the adjective קשורה to the noun טיב, with which מידה is coordinated by means of -ו *and*; recall (3.3 above) that the preposition is required to repeat before each complement, thus: קשורה לטיב . . . ו(קשורה) למידת.

(63) פְּעולָה זו, כמו גם עֶצֶם השבתה של אֶרֶץ ישראל לשִׁלטון יהודי, נַעֲשׂית תוך מַאֲבָק קָשֶׁה.

This act, as well as the very <u>restoration</u> of Jewish rule to the land of Israel, is carried out through a difficult struggle.

Without the points, השבתה could be read either as (a) הַשְׁבָּתָה, the action noun of להשבית *lock out [in a strike]*, or (b) הֲשָׁבָתָה, the action noun הֲשָׁבָה (from להשיב *bring back, restore*) inflected with a feminine singular possessive suffix referring to ארץ ישראל.
The first reading will leave the preposition -ל before שלטון יהודי unaccounted for; the second (correct) reading is based on the fact that the preposition -ל is required by the noun השבה (as is it by the related verb -להשיב ל *bring back to*; see 2.1.1.1 above).

(64) בּמַאֲמרנו נבחַן מסְפר הֶיגֵדים, המוּצגים כּפַרשָׁנוּת לכָּתוב המִקראָי. לכל ההיגדים הללוּ מְכַנֶה מְשׁוּתָף – הם נראים בעיון רִאשׁוֹני כחיבור מְלאכוּתי וּמאוּלָץ בֵּין הטֶקסְט המקראָי למסוֹרֶת קַיֶּימֶת.

In our article we will examine a number of statements which are presented as interpretation for the biblical writing. All these statements have a common denominator – at first glance they seem as an artificial and forced <u>joining</u> of the biblical text to an existing tradition.

The presence of the prepositions -ל . . . בֵּין indicates that חיבור should be read as *joining, connecting* rather than *composition, essay*.

(65) כָּךְ נוֹצָר מוֹדֶל שָׁגוּר שֶׁל בִּיקוּר בָּאֶרֶץ יִשְׂרָאֵל, וּמִכָּאן גַּם הַ‏דמיון בֵּין סִפְרֵי הַמַּסַּע הַשׁוֹנִים שֶׁל הַנוֹסְעִים הַמַּעֲרָבִיִּים.

So was created a common model of a visit in the Land of Israel, and hence also the <u>similarity</u> among the different voyage books [written] by the Western travelers.

We understand דמיון as *similarity* (rather than *imagination*) due to presence of the preposition בֵּין.

(66) בַּתְּפוּצוֹת אָנוּ עֵדִים לִצְמִיחָתָם שֶׁל מֶרְכָּזִים קְהִילָתִיִּים גְּדוֹלִים, שֶׁנּוֹסָף לְתַפְקִידָם כִּמְקוֹם לִתְפִילָה הֵם מרכזים גַּם אֶת כָּל הַתַּפְקִידִים הָאֲחֵרִים שֶׁהָיוּ פַּעַם תַּפְקִידֵיהֶן שֶׁל הַקְּהִילוֹת.

In the diasporas, we witness the rise of large community centers, which in addition to their role as a place of prayer, they <u>concentrate</u> all the other functions that once belonged to the congregations.

The preposition אֶת guides the reading מרכזים as a verb (מְרַכְּזִים) rather than a noun (מֶרְכָּזִים *centers*).

Confusables

The prepositions and conjunctions listed in sections 1–3 below are created through the pre-fixation of a preposition to the construct form of a noun whose literal meaning – יד *hand*, פה *mouth*, and פנים *face* – was by and large lost when it became a component of the preposition or conjunction.

✗L#8   1. לְיַד-, עַל יַד-; עַל יְדֵי, בִּידֵי; לִידֵי

(a) לְיָד, עַל יָד *next to, near, by* indicate proximity (example 67).

(b) עַל יְדֵי (literally *on the hands of*) is translated as ***by, by means of, through*** after a passive verb (examples 68 and 71) or an action noun (examples 69–70) when the "doer" is identified. The abbreviated form is ע"י.

Note that with some passive verbs utilize other prepositions to introduce the "doer," for example: נעזר ב- *helped by,* הושפע מ- *influenced by* (example 74), מכובד על *respected by.*

> To indicate authorship, מֵאֵת (rather than עַל ידי) is used.
> For example: ספר חדש מאת עמוס עוז *a new book by Amos Oz.*

With a pronoun suffix, עַל ידי may or may not retain the final יו"ד. In other words, both עַל ידיו and עַל ידו *by him* are possible.

⚠ However, עַל ידו is potentially ambiguous, as it may also means *next to him* (עַל יד+ pronoun suffix). The presence of a passive verb would then serve as a clue that עַל ידו has the same meaning as עַל ידיו *by him.*

(c) Literally, בִּידֵי means ***in the hands of*** (example 71). Otherwise, it is used in the same way as עַל ידי to specify the "doer" of the action, typically with verbs of physical action (e.g., נכתב בידי *written by,* נכבש בידי *conquered by*; example 72).

(d) לִידֵי *to, to a state of, to a point of* usually collocates (regularly appears) with the verbs להביא *bring, bring about,* לבוא *come,* and להגיע *arrive* (example 73).

---

(67) עַד לְהֲקָמַת הַגֵּטָאוֹת בְּאֵירוֹפָה בְּמֵאָה הט"ז לִסְפִירָה, הָיוּ כל הַמוֹסָדוֹת מְרוּכָּזִים עַל-יַד בֵּית הכנסת.
Until the establishment of the ghettos in Europe in the 16ᵗʰ century, all the [Jewish] institutions were concentrated <u>next to</u> the synagogue.

(68) הָאַגָדָה מְסַפֶּרֶת על שִבְעִים זְקֵנִים שֶהוּזְמְנוּ עַל ידי הַמֶלֶך לתרגם את התורה ליוָונית.
The legend tells about seventy elders who were invited <u>by</u> the king to translate the Torah into Greek.

(69) סִיפּוּר מִצְרִי עַתִיק מְתָאֵר את כיבוש יָפוֹ עַל ידי צָחוּתי.
An ancient Egyptian story describes the conquest of Jaffa <u>by</u> Djehuti.

(70) ביקוֹרֶת הַמִּקְרָא שׁוֹאֶפֶת לְשַׁחְזֵר אֶת הַטֶּקְסְט וּלְקָרְבוֹ לְצוּרָתוֹ הָרִאשׁוֹנִית **עַל יְדֵי הֲסָרַת** שִׁנּוּיִּים וְ"תִיקּוּנִים".
Biblical [textual] criticism aspires to reconstruct the text and bring it closer to its original form <u>through</u> the removal of (OR: <u>by</u> removing) changes and "corrections".

(71) הַשִּׁלְטוֹן הַמֶּרְכָּזִי שֶׁל הַמְּדִינָה מָצוּי **בִּידֵי** הַמֶּלֶךְ, וְהַשִּׁלְטוֹן הַמְּקוֹמִי נִמְצָא **בִּידֵי** מוֹשְׁלִים אֲשֶׁר מְמוּנִּים **עַל יָדוֹ**.
The central rule of the state is <u>in the hands</u> of the king, and local rule is <u>in the hands</u> of governors who are appointed <u>by</u> him.

(72) מִכְתְּבֵי תֵּל-עַמַרְנָה נִכְתְּבוּ בְּאַכָּדִית **בִּידֵי** אֲנָשִׁים שֶׁדִּיבְּרוּ וְחָשְׁבוּ כְּנַעֲנִית.
The Tel-Amarna Letters were written in Accadian <u>by</u> people who spoke and thought in Canaanite.

(73) זִכְרוֹנוֹתָיו הֵבִיאוּ **לִידֵי** צִיּוּרָן שֶׁל תְּמוּנוֹת הֲוַי יְהוּדִיּוֹת רַבּוֹת.
His memories lead <u>to</u> the painting of many pictures of Jewish life.

2. לְפִי, עַל פִּי; כְּפִי; מִכְּפִי; לְפִי שֶׁ-, לְפִיכָךְ; פִּי; עַל פִּי רוֹב; אַף עַל פִּי שֶׁ-, אַף עַל פִּי כֵן; כְּלַפֵּי

(a) **לְפִי, עַל פִּי** *according to* (examples 74–75).

⚠ Note the different meaning of לפי in expression לְפִי שָׁעָה *for the time being*.

(b) **כְּפִי** *as*, is synonymous with כְּמוֹ (example 75).

(c) **מִכְּפִי** appears as a component in a comparative phrase instead of שֶׁ- מִ(מַה) and is ignored in tranlsation: קָשֶׁה יוֹתֵר **מִ(מַה) שֶׁחָשַׁבְנוּ**=קָשֶׁה יוֹתֵר **מִכְּפִי שֶׁחָשַׁבְנוּ** *harder than we thought*.

(d) **לְפִי שֶׁ-** *because*, is synonymous with מִפְּנֵי שֶׁ- (but less frequent and more literary in flavor); **לְפִיכָךְ** *therefore* is synonymous with לָכֵן.

(e) **פִּי** + numeral *multiplied by*, (a number of) times more; **פִּי כַּמָּה (וְכַמָּה)** means *much more, many times over*.

(f) **עַל פִּי רוֹב** *usually, most of the time* (synonymous with לָרוֹב and עַל הָרוֹב).

(g) **אַף עַל פִּי שֶׁ-** *even though*; in abbreviated form: אעפ"י. **אַף עַל פִּי כֵן** *despite this, nevertheless* refers to the content of the previous clause.

(h) **כְּלַפֵּי** *toward* (similar to אֶל), or *vis-à-vis* (similar to בְּיַחַס לְ- and לְגַבֵּי) usually appears after nouns indicating attitude or feeling (e.g., יַחַס *attitude*, מְדִינִיּוּת *policy*, גִּישָׁה *approach*, בִּיקּוֹרֶת *criticism*, חוֹבָה *obligation*, מְחָאָה *protest*, עוֹיְנוּת *hostility*, רֶגֶשׁ *feeling*, שִׂנְאָה *hate*, אֲדִישׁוּת *indifference*).

---

(74) עַיִן הָרַע הִיא מוּשָׂג מִיסְטִי, **לְפִיו** גּוֹרָלוֹ שֶׁל אָדָם מוּשְׁפָּע מֵרִגְשֵׁי הַזּוּלַת **כְּלַפָּיו**, וּבִפְרָט מֵרִגְשֵׁי קִנְאָה.

The evil eye is a mystical concept <u>according to which</u> one's fate is influenced by the feelings of another person <u>towards him</u>, and particularly feelings of envy.

(75) הִלֵּל הֶעֱבִיר אֶת הַלּוּחַ הָעִבְרִי לִקְבִיעוּת **עַל פִּי** חֶשְׁבּוֹן, בִּמְקוֹם **עַל פִּי** רְאִיַּית הַלְּבָנָה, **כְּפִי** שֶׁהָיָה מְקוּבָּל עַד אָז.

Hillel moved the Hebrew calendar to permanence <u>according to</u> mathematical calculation, instead of <u>according to</u> the sighting of the moon, <u>as</u> was customary till then.

---

3. (מ)לִפְנֵי; בִּפְנֵי; מִפְּנֵי; מִפְּנֵי שֶׁ-; עַל פְּנֵי (מ)

(a) **לִפְנֵי** *before* is used for both time and place; before a time unit without a definite article it is translated as *ago* (e.g., לִפְנֵי עָשׂוֹר *a decade ago,* לִפְנֵי הַמֵּאָה הָעֶשְׂרִים *before the 20ᵗʰ century,* לִפְנֵי הַמְּאוֹרָע *before the event*). **מִלִּפְנֵי** is *from…ago* (example 76).

(b) **בִּפְנֵי** *in front of, before, facing* (example 77). Note that לַעֲמוֹד בִּפְנֵי has two meanings: *to face* and *to resist.*

(c) **מִפְּנֵי** *from, of, against* is an alternative for מִן/מ with verbs and (the related nouns) indicating caution (e.g., לְהִיזָּהֵר), defense (e.g., לְהָגֵן, לְהִתְגּוֹנֵן) and fear (e.g., לַחֲשׁוֹשׁ, לִפְחֹד) (examples 78–79). Another translation is *in favor of* (example 80).

(d) **מִפְּנֵי שֶׁ-** *because* introduces a clause of cause or reason. Before a noun, the particle -שֶׁ is omitted and מִפְּנֵי is then interchangeable with the more colloquial בִּגְלַל (example 81).

(e) **עַל פְּנֵי** *over, on the surface of* (עַל alone may be used) (examples 82–83). The literal sense, *on the face of,* is preserved in the English-influenced expression עַל פָּנָיו *on its face.*

---

(76) יֵשׁ עֵדוּיּוֹת **מִלִּפְנֵי** אַלְפֵי שָׁנִים לְהִתְיַישְּׁבוּת בַּמָּקוֹם.
There is evidence <u>from</u> thousands of years <u>ago</u> for settlement in this place.

(77) רֹאשׁ הַמֶּמְשָׁלָה מַצִּיג אֶת הַמֶּמְשָׁלָה **בִּפְנֵי** הַכְּנֶסֶת.
The prime minister presents the government <u>to</u> (literally: <u>before</u>) the parliament.

(78) הַתְּנוּעָה בַּשַּׁיָּירוֹת אִפְשְׁרָה לְסוֹחֲרִים לְהִתְגּוֹנֵן **מִפְּנֵי** שׁוֹדְדִים.
Travelling in caravans allowed merchants to defend themselves <u>against</u> highwaymen.

(79) יֵשׁ לְהִיזָּהֵר **מִפְּנֵי** הַכְּלָלוֹת.
One should beware <u>of</u> generalizations.

(80) הַנּוּסְחָה הַקּוֹדֶמֶת נִדְחֲתָה **מִפְּנֵי** הַנּוּסְחָה הַחֲדָשָׁה.
The previous version was rejected <u>in favor of</u> the new one.

(81) מִפְּנֵי מִשְׁנִיּוּתָהּ שֶׁל הָאִישָׁה בַּמִּקְרָא, אֲפִילוּ סְפָרִים שֶׁנִּקְרְאוּ עַל שֵׁם גִּבּוֹרוֹתֵיהֶם,
רֵאשִׁיתָם בְּאִישׁ וְסוֹפָם בְּאִישׁ.
<u>Because of</u> the secondary status of women in the bible, even books that were
named after their heroines begin and end with a man.

(82) הָעֵדֻיּוֹת נִפְרָסוֹת עַל פְּנֵי תְּקוּפָה שֶׁל קָרוֹב לְאֶלֶף שָׁנִים.
The evidence extends <u>over</u> a period of close to a thousand years.

(83) הוּא אֵינוֹ מַעֲדִיף פֵּירוּשׁ זֶה עַל פְּנֵי קוֹדְמוֹ.
He does not prefer this interpretation <u>to</u> (OR: <u>over</u>) the previous one.

4. שֶׁל, מִשֶּׁל; בִּשֶׁל

(a) **מִשֶּׁל** *of one's own*: when מ- is added to **שֶׁל** *his,* the meaning is altered. Thus: מִשֶּׁלּוֹ *of his*
own (rather than *his*), מִשֶּׁלָּהּ *of her own* (rather than *her(s)*) (example 84).

(b) **בִּשֶׁל** *because, on account of* is a causal word; it can be inflected with personal pronouns
(example 86).

The reference of the suffix is shaded:

(84) סוֹפְרִים רַבִּים קִיבְּלוּ אֶת הַשְׁרָאָתָם מִן הַתַּנַ"ךְ וְהוֹסִיפוּ פַּרְשָׁנוּת מִשֶּׁלָּהֶם לְמוֹטִיבִים אוֹ
גִּיבּוֹרִים תַּנַכְּיִּים.
Many authors received their inspiration from the Bible and added <u>their own</u> inter-
pretations to biblical motifs or protagonists.

(85) הַבְּרִיטִים כָּבְשׁוּ אֶת אֶרֶץ יִשְׂרָאֵל בַּשָּׁנִים 1917–1918 בִּשֶׁל חֲשִׁיבוּתָהּ הָאֶסְטְרָטֶגִית.
The British occupied the Land of Israel in the years 1917–1918 <u>because</u> of its
strategic importance.

(86) לַמֶּרֶד הָיוּ סִיבּוֹת שֶׁלֹּא נִיתַּן הָיָה לְסַלְּקָן בִּדְרָכִים מְדִינִיּוֹת רְגִילוֹת, וּבִשְׁלָהֶן הָפַךְ הַמֶּרֶד
לְבִלְתִּי-נִמְנָע.
The rebellion had causes that could not be removed by ordinary political means,
and <u>because of them</u> it became unavoidable.

5. (ב)תוֹךְ, תוֹךְ כְּדֵי, בְּתוֹךְ כָּךְ; מִתּוֹךְ; תּוֹךְ-

(a) **בְּתוֹךְ** indicates location in place – *inside, within* (example 87), or in time – *within, during*
(example 88).
When duration is indicated, the preposition ב- may be omitted (example 89).
Before a noun (usually, an action noun), תוֹךְ is translated as *while, at the same time as*
(example 90). Parallel action is indicated with **בְּתוֹךְ (כְּדִי) כָּךְ** and **תוֹךְ כְּדֵי** (examples
91–92).

(b) **מִתּוֹךְ** *of, from, out of* (examples 93–94).

(c) **תוֹךְ-** *intra-* is a semantic prefix before an adjective (e.g., הַבְדֵּלִים תּוֹךְ-מְדִינָתִיִּים *intra-state*
differences).

(87) בֶּעָבָר בּוּשַׁל הַמַאֲכָל **בְּתוֹך** סִיר שֶׁהֻטְמַן **בְּתוֹך** בּוֹר.
In the past, the dish was cooked <u>in</u> a pot that was buried <u>inside</u> a pit.

(88) **בְּתוֹך** זְמַן קָצָר רָכַשׁ לוֹ רַשִׁ״י פִּרְסוּם רַב וְעֶמְדָּה חֲשׁוּבָה בַּקְּהִילּוֹת צָרְפַת הַצְּפוֹנִית.
<u>Within</u> a short time Rashi acquired great reputation and important status in the communities of Northern France.

(89) **תוֹך** מֵאוֹת סְפוּרוֹת אָבְדוּ הַשָּׂפָה הָאַכָּדִית וְשִׁיטַת הַכְּתִיבָה שֶׁלָּהּ.
Accadian and its writing system were lost <u>within</u> a few centuries.

(90) הַמִּיתוֹלוֹגְיָה הָרוֹמִית הִיא הַמִּיתוֹלוֹגְיָה שֶׁנּוֹצְרָה בְּרוֹמָא הָעַתִּיקָה **תוֹך** עִרְבּוּב שֶׁל מִיתוֹסִים, אַגָּדוֹת עַם, אֵלִים שֶׁל עַמִּים כְּבוּשִׁים, וְהַעְתָּקָה שֶׁל הָאֵלִים בַּמִּיתוֹלוֹגְיָה הַיְּוָנִית **תוֹך** שִׁינּוּי שְׁמוֹתֵיהֶם.
Roman mythology is the mythology that was created in ancient Rome <u>through</u> fusing myths, legends and gods of vanquished nations, and the copying of the gods of Greek mythology <u>while</u> changing their names.

(91) מַטְרָתָהּ שֶׁל הַמִּפְלָגָה הִיא לְהַמְשִׁיך בָּרֶפוֹרְמוֹת הַדֶּמוֹקְרָטִיּוֹת בַּמְּדִינָה, **תוֹך כְּדֵי** שְׁמִירָה עַל מְדִינִיּוּת רְוָוחָה.
The objective of the party is to continue the democratic reforms in the state <u>while</u> preserving the welfare policy.

(92) קְבוּצוֹת אֵלֶּה הִסְתַּיְּיגוּ מִמּוֹסַד הַמִּשְׁפָּחָה **וּבְתוֹך כָּך** מִן הַקְּבוּרָה הַמִּשְׁפַּחְתִּית.
These groups had reservations about the institution of the family and <u>at the same time</u>, about family burial.

(93) הַמִּפְלָגָה זָכְתָה בַּעֲשָׂרָה מוֹשָׁבִים **מִתּוֹך** 120 הַמּוֹשָׁבִים שֶׁל בֵּית הַנִּבְחָרִים.
The party received ten <u>out of</u> the 120 seats in the parliament.

(94) הָעֲמוּתָה נוֹלְדָה **מִתּוֹך** צוֹרֶך בְּמַתַּן תְּמִיכָה לַמִּשְׁפָּחוֹת.
The charity fund was born <u>out of</u> the need to give support to the families.

6. (מִ)בַּלְעֲדֵי; בִּלְעָדִי

(a) **(מִ)בַּלְעֲדֵי** *without* is a biblical (and now) formal variant of בְּלִי(מִ). It employed as the base for all inflected forms of בְּלִי (e.g., (מִ)בַּלְעֲדֵיהָ ,(מִ)בַּלְעָדָיו *without him, without her*) regardless of register.

(b) In unpointed text, בַּלְעֲדֵי appears identical to the adjective **בִּלְעָדִי** *exclusive, only* (example 96); note also the derived adverb בְּאוֹפֶן בִּלְעָדִי *exclusively*.

(95) לַמְּקוֹמוֹת הַקְּדוֹשִׁים וְלַחֲפָצִים הַקְּדוֹשִׁים אֵין תּוֹקֶף **מִבַּלְעֲדֵי** הַיְּהוּדִי.
The holy places and holy objects have no validity <u>without</u> the Jew.

(96) הַמִּקְרָא הוּא כִּמְעַט הַמָּקוֹר **הַבִּלְעָדִי** לְתוֹלְדוֹת יִשְׂרָאֵל בִּתְקוּפַת הַמִּקְרָא.
The Bible is almost the <u>only</u> source for the history of Israel in the biblical period.

7. אֶל; אַל; אֵל; מֵאֵלָיו; יש/אין לְאֵל יָדוֹ

(a) In unpointed text, the following appear identical:

- אֶל *to, toward* (a variant of a directional -לְ)
- אַל *(do) not* is used instead of לֹא in negative imperative phrases, before a verb in the future form (e.g., אַל תירא *do not fear*); note also the expression לשים לְאַל *nullify, render worthless*
- -אַל – *a-, no, not, in-* a semantic prefix (e.g., אַל-אֱנוֹשִׁי *inhuman*, נקודת אַל-חֲזוֹר *a point of no return*)
- אֵל *god* or *God* (plural: אֵלִים *gods*).

(b) When the preposition -מ is added to the inflected forms of the preposition אל (e.g., מֵאֵלָיו, מֵאֵלֶיהָ, מֵאֵלֵיהֶם, מֵאֵלֵיהֶן) the meaning is *of/by itself, automatically, naturally,* (e.g., מוּבָן מאליו *self-understood*; example 97).

(c) The expression יש לְאֵל יָדוֹ followed by an infinitive verb indicates ability: *he can do something; it is within his means*; the "doer" is expressed via the pronoun (e.g., אֵין לְאֵל יָדָהּ לעזור *she cannot help*).

---

(97) רק לְאַחַר שבעה ימים מַכַּת הַדָּם הִפְסִיקָה מֵאֵלֶיהָ.
The plague of blood stopped <u>of itself</u> only after seven days.

Appendix of less common prepositions

Below are listed in alphabetical order some less common prepositions and their English translations; where possible, the more commonly occurring equivalent is indicated.
With the exception of three prepositions – באמצעות, בקרב, לקראת – which take singular suffixes, all the prepositions listed below take plural suffixes.

1. על אודות, על=אודות *about, regarding*

---

(1) לְפִי שָׁעָה יְדִיעוֹתֵינוּ **אוֹדוֹת** דְּמוּתוֹ, **אוֹדוֹת** פְּעִילוּיוֹתָיו וְ**אוֹדוֹת** הַשְׁקָפוֹתָיו הֵן כְּלָלִיּוֹת בְּיוֹתֵר.
At present, our knowledge <u>about</u> his character, (about) his activities and (about) his views is very general.

Note the repetition of the identical prepositions.

---

2. עַל יְדֵי=בְּאֶמְצָעוּת *through, by means of, via*

---

(2) הַמֶּסֶר שֶׁל הַשְׁמִירָה עַל הַסְּבִיבָה מוּעֲבַר **בְּאֶמְצָעוּת** סִיּוּרִים וְהַרְצָאוֹת.
The message of preserving the environment is transmitted <u>through</u> trips and lectures.

(3) סוֹלְלוֹת עָפָר שִׁמְּשׁוּ בְּמִצְרַיִם הָעַתִּיקָה עַל מְנָת לְהָרִים **בְּאֶמְצָעוּתָן** אֶת הָאֲבָנִים הַכְּבֵדוֹת שֶׁשִּׁמְּשׁוּ לִבְנִיַּית הַפִּירָמִידוֹת.
Dirt dikes were used in ancient Egypt to lift up <u>by their means</u> the heavy stones used to build the pyramids.

---

3. בְּשֶׁל, בִּגְלָל=בְּגִין *because of*

בגין has a legalistic flavor.

---

(4) הַסִּיבּוֹת שֶׁ**בְּגִין** תִּיקְנוּ אֶת הַתַּקָנוֹת הָיוּ שׁוֹנוֹת וּמְגוּוָנוֹת.
The reasons <u>for which</u> the ordinances were legislated were varied.

(5) בִּתְקוּפַת הָרוֹמָאִים הָיָה נָהוּג לִכְתּוֹב אֶת פִּשְׁעוֹ שֶׁל הַנִּצְלָב, **בְּגִינוֹ** הוּצָא לַהוֹרֵג, עַל גַּבֵּי הַצְּלָב, לְמַעַן יִרְאוּ וְיִירָאוּ.
In the period of the Romans it was customary to write the crime <u>because of which</u> the crucified person was executed on the crucifix, so that [people] would see and be forewarned (literally: be afraid).

---

4. כְּתוֹצָאָה מִ(ן); אַחֲרֵי=בְּעִקְבוֹת *following, in the footsteps of; as a consequence of*

> (6) העלייה השלישית באה בעקבותיה של השנייה.
> The Third Aliya came <u>in footsteps</u> of the Second.

Note that the related עֵקֶב *as a result of, due to* cannot be inflected with pronoun suffixes.

> (7) שְׁחיקה לעיתים מוּאֶצֶת עקב פעילוּתו של האדם.
> Erosion is sometimes accelerated <u>due to</u> human activity.

5. בְּתוֹךְ=בְּקֶרֶב *among, in the midst of*

> (8) היהודים דיברו בשׂפות העמים שבקרבָּם ישבו.
> The Jews spoke the languages of the people in the midst of whom they lived.

6. לְגַבֵּי *concerning, regarding*

Synonymous with . . . בְּיַחַס ל, בנוגע ל

> (9) הדֵעות חלוּקות לגבי שימוּשׁו המְקורי של המבנֶה.
> Opinions are divided <u>regarding</u> the original use of the structure.

⚠Note the difference between לגבי and עַל גַּבֵּי *upon, on* (example 5 above).

7. אֶל=לִקְרַאת *toward(s)*

> (10) כאשר מתברר ליעקב שעֵשָׂו בא לקראתו בראש קבוצה של ארבַּע מֵאות איש איש הוא חוֹשׁשׁ מאוד.
> When Jacob finds out that Esau is coming <u>toward him</u> at the head of a group of four hundred men he is very fearful.
>
> Note that beginning with number 11, a singular (rather than plural) noun is allowed with units of measurement (e.g., עשׂרים שקל *twenty shekel*) and time (e.g., שׁלושׁים יום *thirty days*, מאה שׁנה *one hundred years*), and also with the words נפשׁ *person* and (as seen in this example) אישׁ *man*.

8.   בִּשְׁבִיל, לְמַעַן=(בַּ)עֲבוּר *for*

> (11) הַמַּעֲבָר מִמִּסְחָר לעבודת אֲדָמָה היה קֶשֶׁה עֲבוּר העולים.
> The transition from commerce to agriculture was difficult <u>for</u> the immigrants.
>
> (12) "נְזִיד עֲדָשִׁים" היה המַאֲכָל שבַּעֲבוּרוֹ מָכר עֵשָׂו ליעקב את הבְּכוֹרָה.
> Lentil stew was the dish <u>for which</u> Esau sold his birthright to Jacob.

⚠ Make sure to differentiate – in unpointed text – the preposition עבור from the time adverbial עבור *passing*, for example: אחרי עֲבוֹר שנה, כַּעֲבוֹר שנה *after (the passing of) a year*.

9.   תַּחַת, מִתַחת (ל-) *below, beneath, under; instead of*

In the sense of *below* or *under*, תחת and מתחת (ל-) are interchangeable (examples 13–14). In the sense of בִּמְקוֹם *instead of*, only תחת can be used (example 15).
This preposition may take singular or plural pronoun suffixes (e.g., תחתיו or תחתו).

> (13) הַמִּשְׁנָה מַרְשָׁה להַציל בשבת שֶׁקָּבוּר אָדָם מתחת לעֲרִימָה של אֲבָנִים וייתָכֵן שהוא חי.
> The Mishnah permits to save on the Sabbath a man who is buried <u>under</u> a pile of stones and may still be alive.
>
> (14) תחת הכיבוש הנאצי, נוסדו בעֲיָירה מחנה שבויים ומַחנֶה ריכוז לעבודת כְּפייה.
> <u>Under</u> the Nazi occupation, a prison camp and a concentration camp for forced labor were established in the town.
>
> (15) העורכים נמְנְעו מלהַעֲמִיס על הטֶקְסְט הֶעָרות והֶאָרות. תחת זאת הם הִסְתפְּקו במִסְפָּר מְצוּמְצָם של הַבְהָרות.
> The editors refrained from overloading the text with footnotes and comments. <u>Instead</u>, they limited themselves to a small number of clarifications.

10.   בִּמְקוֹם=תְּמוּרַת *in exchange for*

> (16) "סְחורה תמורת דם" היא עִסְקה להַצָּלת יַהֲדות הונגריה במַהֲלך השואה.
> "Goods <u>in exchange for</u> blood" is a transaction for saving Hungarian Jewry during the Holocaust.

Alternatively, בתמורה ל- can be used (*e.g.*, בתמורה לעמלו מקבל הסופר שכר סופרים *in exchange for his labor the author receives royalties*).

⚠ Note that the noun תמורה means (a) *return, compensation* (e.g., הַלְאָמָה נעשתה ללא הַלְאָמָה תמורה הולֶמֶת *the nationalization was done without appropriate compensation*) or (b) *change, transformation* (often in the plural), for example, עידן של תמורות *an era of change(s)*.

References

בליבוים, 1995
צדקה, 1993
שלזינגר, 1994

Coffin & Bolozky, 2005
Glinert, 1989
Quirk & Greenbaum, 1975
Schwarzwald, 2001

Chapter 8: Prepositions – Exercises

exercise #	topic	page
1	Identifying the referent of preposition suffix	329
2	Choosing the correct form of the inflected preposition	330–331
3	Determining the pronunciation of the prepositions בכ"ל	332
4	Choosing the correct translation of the preposition	333–334
5	Choosing the correct translation of the preposition כ-	335–336
6	Choosing the correct translation of the preposition על	337–338
7	Choosing the correct form of the inflected preposition in relative clauses	339–340
8	Translating על ידי and על יד	341–342

Exercise #1: Identifying the referent of preposition suffix

> **The rules to go by:** see section 1.1.
> **What to do:**
> 1. Give the uninflected form of the bolded preposition.
> 2. Select the reference of the pronoun suffix.
> **Example:**
>
> 1. היהודים עשו כל מאמץ להתקרב לחברה הגרמנית ולהוכיח את נאמנותם **לה**.
>   **ל- מאמץ, חברה, נאמנות**

1. גם מי שלא יקבל את כל טענותיו של המְחַבר יוכל להסכים **עימו**.
   _____ הטענות, המחבר

2. המחבר מַצביע על אוֹפְיָין המיוחד של הַהַבְטָחות האלוהיות ליַעֲקֹב בסיפור המקורי **אודותיו**.
   _____ המחבר, יעקב, הסיפור

3. קיים מְתאָם מְסוּיָם בין הֲבָנת יידיש והשימוּש בה לבין העֶמְדה **כלפיה**.
   _____ ההבנה, היידיש, העמדה

4. עַמֵי אֵירופה ראו ביהודים מיעוּט זָר ושונה המְאַיים **עליהם**.
   _____ עמי אירופה, היהודים, מיעוט

5. תופָעת הלאומיות היא חלק בלתי נְפְרד מצמיחתה של אירופה המודֶרנית. **בלעדיה** לא ניתן להסביר את השינויים שהִתְחוללו במַפַּת אירופה מִתְחילת המֵאה ה-18 ועד יְמֵינו.
   _____ תופעת הלאומיות, צמיחתה של אירופה

Glossary

the author's arguments	טענות המחבר	.1
points at	מצביע על	.2
the special character of the divine promises	אופיין המיוחד של ההבטחות האלוהיות	
certain correlation	מתאם מסוים	.3
position, attitude	עמדה	
a foreign and different minority	מיעוט זר ושונה	.4
threatening	מאיים	
the phenomenon of nationalism	תופעת הלאומיות	.5
inseparable part	חלק בלתי נפרד	
the growth of modern Europe	צמיחתה של אירופה המודרנית	
it is not possible	לא ניתן	
the changes that occurred	השינויים שהתחוללו	
the map of Europe	מפת אירופה	

Exercise #2: Choosing the correct form of the inflected preposition

> **The rule to go by:** see section 1.1.2.
> **What to do:** select the appropriate form of the inflected preposition.
> **Example:**
> הרצל ביסס את התנועה הציונית והפך **אותו, אותה, אותם** מתנועת יחידים לתנועה הזוכה בהכרה בינלאומית.

1. עד כֹּה טֶרֶם נמצאה מילה חֲלוּפִית למילה "חילוֹני" וסופרים והעיתונאים משתמשים **בו, בה, בהם** בצוּרה שִׁגרָתית.

2. הלְאוּמִיוּת היהוּדית הוּשְׁפְּעה ממְאפְייני היְסוֹד של הלְאוּמיוּת הכְּללית ואימְצה לעצְמה חֵלֶק גדול **ממְנה, מהן, מהם.**

3. הנוֹעַר ראה בבוּרגנוּת חֶבְרה מתחַסֶדֶת וצְבוּעה וביקש למְרוֹד **בו, בה, בהם** ולהָקים חברה צוֹדקת ומוּסרית יותר.

4. היֵידיש, שְׂפת התְּקֶשׁוֹרֶת העִיקרית של יהוּדֵי מזרח אירופה, הייתה יְחוּדית **לו, לה, להם.**

5. היהוּדי עקר את עצמו מן המסורת היהודית, אך לחברה הגדולה לא הצליח להתקבל, ושעָרים רבים נשארו נעוּלים **בפָניו, בפניה, בפניהם.**

Glossary

so far	עד כה	1.
an alternative word has not yet been found	טרם נמצאה מילה חלופית	
secular	חילוני	
routinely	בצורה שגרתית	
Jewish nationalism	הלאומיות היהודית	2.
was influenced	הושפעה	
fundamental characteristics	מאפייני היסוד	
general (non-Jewish) nationalism	הלאומיות הכללית	
adopted	אימצה	
young people	הנוער	3.
bourgeoisie	בורגנות	
a sanctimonious and hypocritical society	חברה מתחסדת וצבועה	
wished to rebel	ביקש למרוד	
establish a just and moral society	להקים חברה צודקת ומוסרית	
the main language of communication	שפת התקשורת העיקרית	4.
Jews of Eastern Europe	יהודי מזרח אירופה	
unique	יחודית	
uprooted himself	עקר את עצמו	5.
be accepted by	להתקבל	
gates	שערים	
remained locked	נשארו נעולים	

6. תִּקְשׁוֹרֶת הַהֲמוֹנִים פתחה בפני הציבור הרחב ערוצֵי מֵידע וביטוי שהיו חסומים **בפניו, בפניה, בפניהם** בעבר, ואיפשרה **לו, לה, להם** לקחת חלק במַעֲשֶׂה הפוליטי.

7. יותר מִמַּחֲצִית מכ-6000 השפות שבעולם נמצאות בסַכָּנַת הַכְחָדָה, וְעמו, **עמה, עמן** תֵיעָלם גם המוֹרֶשֶׁת התַרבותית המִתְלַווה **אליו, אליה, אליהן**.

8. בין שניצחו הנוצרים או המוסלמים, הַיישׁוּב היהודי היה הסוֹבֵל. שני המחנות היריבים סחטו **ממנו, מהם, מהן** כסף, שהיה דרוש **לו, להם, להן** למלחמותיהם, ושניהם חשדו **בו, בהם, בהן.**

9. אצל עמים אחרים, גם אם לא כל העם נמצא במולדתו ההיסטורית, הֲרֵי שחלק גדול **ממנו, ממנה, מהם** יושב **בו, בה, בהם** ומחובר אליו, **אליה, אליהם** פיזית.

Glossary

mass communications	תקשורת ההמונים	6.
the wider public	הציבור הרחב	
channels of information and expression	ערוצי מידע וביטוי	
blocked	חסומים	
made possible	איפשרה	
take part in the political action	לקחת חלק במעשה הפוליטי	
danger of extinction	סכנת הכחדה	7.
will disappear	תיעלם	
the cultural heritage	המורשת התרבותית	
accompanies	מתלווה	
won	ניצחו	8.
the Jewish community was the sufferer	היישוב היהודי היה הסובל	
the two rival camps	שני המחנות היריבים	
extorted	סחטו	
required	דרוש	
suspected	חשדו	
historical homeland	מולדתו ההיסטורית	9.
attached	מחובר	
physically	פיזית	

Exercise #3: Determining the pronunciation of the prepositions בכ"ל

> **The rules to go by:** see section 1.2.
> **What to do:** choose the correct pronunciation of the bolded preposition.

1. לאחרונה נדפסו מִסְפָּר ספרים המְתָיַיחסים לַתּוֹפעה/לְתוֹפעה זו.

2. תגליות אלה יוכלו להתברר רק הודות לַתֵיאוֹרְיָה/לְתֵיאוֹרְיָה המקיפה שהעמיד המחבר.

3. משְׁנוֹת העשרים ואילך נעשתה השירה הלירית לַמִבְצָרָן/לְמִבְצָרָן של נשים יוצְרות בעברית.

4. עם כְּניסתה של השירה העברית לַעידן/לְעידן היצירה המודרנית לא נמצאה אף מְשׁוֹרֶרֶת עברית אחת.

5. **בַּהֶמשכו/בְּהֶמשכו** של הדיון נִסָּה להשיב תשובה מלאה על שאלות אלו.

6. כאן ימצא הקורא התייחסות לָעוֹלם/לְעוֹלם האינטֶלֶקְטוֹאלי של הגְּאוֹנים, לַמְגוון/לְמְגוון השפות שעשו בהן שימוש ולִתְחוּמֵי/לַתְּחוּמֵי הִתעַנְיְינוּתם.

7. הַהַשְׂכָּלָה גרמה לְמוֹדֶרְניזַצְיָה/לַמודרניזציה יהודית.

8. **בְּכל/בַּכל** מדינה על כל האֶזרחים לקחת חלק פעיל **בְּחיים/בַּחיים** הפוֹליטיים.

9. הצִיּוֹנים המְדיניים האמינו **בִּפְעילוּת/בַּפְעילות** דיפּלוֹמטית **כִּתְנאי/כַּתְנאי** בְּסיסי **לְהתיישבות/לַהתיישבות** היהודית בארץ ישראל.

Exercise #4: Choosing the correct translation of the preposition

> **The rules to go by:** see section 2, the Confusable section and the Appendix.
> **What to do:** write next to each preposition the number of the sentence in which its Hebrew equivalent (shown bolded) appears. The first one is an example.

preposition	sentence number	preposition	sentence number
0 (no translation)	2	out of	
according to		from among	
among		of itself	
before		of their own	
by		toward	
by means of, through		under	
for		within	

1. לְאַרְצוֹת הַבְּרִית הוּבָא זֶרֶם הָרֵפוֹרְמָה **עַל יְדֵי** הַמְּהַגְּרִים הַיְּהוּדִים שֶׁהִגִּיעוּ מִגֶּרְמַנְיָה בְּאֶמְצַע הַמֵּאָה הַ-19.

Reform Judaism was brought to the United States _____ the Jewish immigrants that arrived from Germany in the middle of the 19th century.

2. אֶזְרָחֵי הַמְּדִינָה לוֹקְחִים חֵלֶק פָּעִיל בַּחַיִּים הַפּוֹלִיטִיִּים וְנֶהֱנִים **מִן** הַזְּכֻיּוֹת הַנִּיתָנוֹת לָהֶם.

The citizens of the state take an active part in the political life and enjoy _____ the rights that are given to them.

3. הַקְּהִילָה הִתְנַהֲלָה **עַל פִּי** חֻקֵּי הַהֲלָכָה.

The community behaved _____ the rules of Jewish law.

4. הַמִּפְלָגוֹת הָאַנְטִישֵׁמִיּוֹת הֶעֱמִיקוּ אֶת שִׂנְאַת הַיְּהוּדִים **בְּקֶרֶב** הַהֲמוֹנִים.

The anti-Semitic parties deepened the anti-Semitism _____ the masses.

5. הַסּוֹצְיָאלִיסְטִים הַיְּהוּדִים הֶאֱמִינוּ **מִתּוֹךְ** לַהַט מַהְפְּכָנִי כִּי נִצָּחוֹן הַסּוֹצְיָאלִיזְם יָבִיא לְעוֹלָם צוֹדֵק יוֹתֵר.

The Jewish socialists believed _____ revolutionary fervor that the victory of socialism will bring about a more just world.

6. עַמֵּי אֵירוֹפָּה נָטְשׁוּ אֶת הַשָּׂפָה הַלָטִינִית וְהֵחֵלּוּ לְפַתֵּחַ שָׂפוֹת **מִשֶּׁלָּהֶם.**

The peoples of Europe abandoned Latin and began to develop languages _____.

7. **בִּפְנֵי** מַנְהִיגֵי הַתְּנוּעָה עָמְדָה דִּילֶמָה מוּסָרִית וּפוֹלִיטִית.

_____the leaders of the movement stood an ethical and political dilemma.

8. הַשְּׁאֵלָה הָיְיתָה אם לְהֵיאָבֵק לְהֲשָׂגַת זְכֻיּוֹת כְּמִיעוּט לְאוּמִי **עֲבוּר** יהודי אירופה.

The question was whether to struggle to achieve rights as a national minority_____
the Jews of Europe.

9. חַבְרֵי התנועה השתתפו בוויכוח על דרכה של התנועה הציונית, וביקשו לְהַשְׁפִּיעַ על הדור הצעיר
בְּאֶמְצָעוּת חינוך לְאוּמִי.

The members of the movement participated in the debate about the path of the Zionist movement and wished to influence the young generation _____ national education.

10. רוב יהודי צרפת גילו אדישות **כְּלַפֵּי** דרייפוס בזמן "הפרשה" מתוך חשש לעורר יְצָרִים אנטיש־
מִיים.

Most French Jews displayed indifference _____ Dreyfus during the "[Dreyfus] affair"
out of fear of arousing anti-Semitic sentiments.

11. הָאִיכָּרִים עבדו **תַּחַת** פיקוח מְקצוֹעִי של מְנַהֵל הַחַוָּוה.

The farmers worked _____ the professional supervision of the farm manager.

12. עם קַבָּלַת הַשִּׁוְויוֹן שוּלְבוּ היהודים **בְּתוֹךְ** הַמַּעֲרָךְ הפוליטי-פַּרְלָמֶנְטָרי של אוסטריה.

Upon receiving equal rights, the Jews were integrated _____ the political-
parliamentarian system of Austria.

13. תוך שנה עלו לארץ ישראל כאלף וחמש מאות עולים **מִקֶּרֶב** יהדות תֵּימָן.

Within a year about 1,500 immigrants came to Israel _____ the Jewry of Yemen.

14. בָּאנטישמיות ראו יהודי צרפת מוּצָר מיוּבא מגֶּרמניה, חוּלְשָׁה חֶבְרָתית שֶׁתחלוֹף **מֵאֵלֶיהָ**.

French Jews regarded anti-Semitism as an imported product from Germany, a social weakness
that would depart_____.

Exercise #5: Choosing the correct translation of the preposition כ-

---

The rules to go by: see section 2.3.2.
What to do: select the correct translation for the bolded preposition. (Enter the sentence number in the appropriate cell in the chart.) The first one is an example.

---

like	*as*	*approximately*
	1,	

1. הציונים המדיניים האמינו בפעילות דיפלומטית **כ**תנאי בסיסי להתיישבות בארץ ישראל.

2. בכל התנועות הלאומיות הושם דגש על השפה הלאומית **כ**מרכיב מרכזי בזהותו הלאומית של העם.

3. התנועה היהודית ביקשה, **כ**כל התנועות הלאומיות האחרות, לטפח מסורות מן העבר.

4. **כ**-70 שנה לְאחר הופעתן של התנועות הלאומיות הראשונות באירופה הקים העם היהודי תנועה לאומית משלו.

5. התנועה הלְאומית היהודית שאפה לקבל הכרה **כ**"לְאום"(א) ולהיות עם **כ**כל(ב) העמים.

Glossary

1. פעילות דיפלומטית diplomatic activity
   תנאי בסיסי basic condition
   התיישבות settlement
2. תנועות לְאומיות national movements
   הושם דגש על emphasis was put on
   מרכיב מרכזי central component
   זהותו הלאומית של העם the national identity of the people
3. לטפח מסורות מן העבר cultivate traditions from the past
4. לאחר הופעתן after their appearance
   הקים established
5. שאפה לקבל הכרה aspired to receive recognition
   לְאום nation

6. **כ**קהילה נהנו היהודים מסובלנות דתית ומאוטונומיה קהילתית.

7. לְאַחַר הַמַּפָּלָה שֶׁל מֶרֶד בַּר כוכבא, **כ**שליש מן האוכלוסיה היהודית נהרגו או הוגלו.

Glossary

enjoyed	6. נהנו
religious tolerance	סובלנות דתית
communal autonomy	אוטונומיה קהילתית
the defeat of the Bar Kochba revolt	7. המפלה של מרד בר כוכבא
one-third of the Jewish population	שליש מן האוכלוסיה היהודית
were killed or exiled	נהרגו או הוגלו

Exercise #6: Choosing the correct translation of the preposition על

> **The rules to go by:** see section 2.3.5.
> **What to do:** select the appropriate translation for the bolded preposition. (Enter the sentence number in the appropriate cell in the chart.) The first one is an example.

about	for	with	must	on	no translation
			1,		

1. בן יהודה האמין כי **על** העם היהודי ללמוד לדבר בשפתו.

2. בכל מדינה **על** כל האזרחים לקחת חלק פעיל בחיים הפוליטיים.

3. משוררים לאומיים כתבו **על** נושאים לאומיים שונים ומגוונים.

4. הגולה נתפסה כעונש מידי שמיים **על** חטאי העם.

5. מטרת החוק הייתה להגן **על** יהודים מפגיעה חמורה במקור פרנסתם.

6. אי אפשר להתעלם מההשפעה הרבה שהיתה לחיים בשכנות לתרבות המארחת **על** אורח חייהם של היהודים.

Glossary

1. בן יהודה   Ben Yehuda
ללמוד לדבר בשפתו   learn to speak its language
2. אזרחים   citizens
לקחת חלק פעיל   take an active part
3. משוררים לאומיים   national poets
נושאים לאומיים שונים ומגוונים   different and varied national topics
4. גולה   exile
נתפסה כעונש מידי שמים   was perceived as punishment from heaven
חטאי העם   the sins of the people
5. מטרת החוק   the purpose of the law
להגן   protect
פגיעה חמורה במקורות פרנסתם   severe harm to their sources of income
6. להתעלם   ignore
חיים בשכנות לתרבות המארחת   life in proximity to the hosting culture
אורח חיים   way of life

.7 עַל פִּי חז"ל, מרים דאגה לא רק לשלום אחיה משה אלא לְהַמְשָׁכְיוּת הָעָם בְּכלל **וְעַל** מעשיה אלה זכתה שדוד המלך יהיה אחד מִצֶּאֱצָאֶיהָ.

.8 בימים הראשונים לְגָלוּת בבל לא הקימו היהודים עָרים ויישובים משלהם; לכן לא עמדה עוד לרשוּתָם רחבת העיר, שנתקיימה בעריהם במולדתם, **עַל** התפקידים הציבוריים החשובים שמילאה.

Glossary

דאגה לשלום אחיה משה	.7 was concerned about the welfare of her brother Moses
הַמְשָׁכיות העם בכלל	the continuity of the people in general
זכתה	merited
צאצאיה	her descendents
עמדה לרשותם	.8 was at their disposal
רחבת העיר	town square
נתקיימה בעריהם במולדתם	existed in their towns in their homeland
התפקידים הציבוריים החשובים שמילאה	the important public roles that it fulfilled

Exercise #7: Choosing the correct form of the inflected preposition in relative clauses

> **The rules to go by:** see 3.4.
> **What to do:** select the appropriate form of the preposition. The first one is an example.

1. נוכל אולי לזהות את הנמל הארץ-ישראלי ש(**אליו, אליה, אליהם**) היו פניו של יהודה הלוי מועדות.

2. ההיסטוריון אינו רשאי לראות את מקורותיו כספרות קודש שאין לערער (**עליו, עליה, עליהן**).

3. כל מושבה כתבה ספר תקנות ש(**ממנו, ממנה, מהן**) אפשר היה לעמוד על אופייה.

4. היהודים נהנו מאוטונומיה יהודית שהיו (**בו, בה, בהן**) כל הסממנים של שלטון פנימי יהודי.

5. החסידים שעלו לארץ ביקשו לקרב את בוא המשיח על ידי תפילות הצדיקים ש(**לו, להם, להן**) יֵדַע הכַּוונות הנכונות.

6. ההפרדה בין דת ומדינה בארצות הברית איפשרה ליהודים לקיים את אמונתם מתוך חופש מלא, שלא היה דומה (**לו, לה, להן**) באף מדינה אחרת.

Glossary

.1	לזהות identify
	נמל port
	פניו היו מועדות he was heading to
.2	אינו רשאי is not allowed
	מקורותיו his sources
	ספרות קודש divine literature
	לערער refute, doubt
.3	מושבה settlement
	ספר תקנות a book of ordinances
	לעמוד על אופייה understand its character
.4	נהנו מאוטונומיה enjoyed autonomy
	סממנים characteristics, traits
	שלטון פנימי internal (self) rule
.5	ביקשו לקרב את בוא המשיח sought to hasten the arrival of the Messiah
	ידע הכוונות הנכונות knowledge of the proper devotions
.6	הפרדה בין דת ומדינה separation of religion and state
	לקיים את אמונתם מתוך חופש מלא observe their faith with full freedom
	דומה similar

7. הוא התיישב בירושלים וביטא את אהבתו לעיר בשיריו המקוריים ובמחקריו על המשלים שנכתבו **(אודותיו, אודותיה, אודותיהם).**

Glossary

settled	7. התיישב
expressed his love	ביטא את אהבתו
his original poems and his research	שיריו המקוריים ומחקריו
fables	משלים

Exercise #8: Translating על יד and על ידי

The rules to go by: see Confusable, section 1.
What to do: select the appropriate translation for the prepositions. (Enter the sentence number in the appropriate cell in the chart.) The first one is an example.

---

by	*next to*	*on the hand(s)*
	1,	

1. תפקידו של בית הדין היה לפקח על צורכי רבים, **ועל-ידו** התרכזו כל המוסדות המיועדים לשרת את הרבים.

2. כתב העת נערך **על ידו** עד לפטירתו.

3. מריחת החינה **על ידיה** של הכלה מסמלת פוריות.

4. הנהר מפורסם בעקבות הקרב שהתרחש **על ידו.**

5. בתי השכונה נבנו על ידי משפחות ערביות נוצריות ואוכלסו **על ידן.**

Glossary

1. תפקידו של בית הדין   the role of the court
לפקח על צורכי הרבים   supervise the needs of the public
התרכזו   were concentrated
מוסדות   institutions
מיועדים לשרת   designed to serve
2. כתב העת   periodical
נערך   was edited
פטירתו   his death
3. מריחת החינה   daubing of henna
כלה   bride
מסמלת פוריות   symbolizes fertility
4. הנהר מפורסם   the river is famous
בעקבות   following
קרב   battle
התרחש   took place
5. בתי השכונה   the houses of the neighborhood
נבנו   were built
משפחות ערביות נוצריות   Christian Arab families
אוכלסו   populated, inhabited

6. כל צעדיו של הנביא מוכתבים **על ידי** האל.

7. בהרבה תרבויות אירופאיות מקובל להפגין כבוד **על ידי** לחיצת יד.

8. רחבת העיר ש**על יד** שער העיר הייתה מוסד ציבורי.

9. לארצות הברית הובא זֶרֶם הָרֶפוֹרמה **על ידי** המהגרים היהודים שהִגיעו מגֶּרמניה באֶמצע המאה ה-19.

Glossary

6. צעדיו של הנביא	the prophet's steps
מוכתבים	are dictated
7. תרבויות אירופאיות	European cultures
מקובל	it is customary
להפגין כבוד	demonstrate respect
לחיצת יד	handshake
8. רחבת העיר	town square
שער	gate
מוסד ציבורי	public institution
9. הובא	was brought
זרם הרפורמה	The Reform movement
מהגרים	immigrants

9. "BEING" AND "HAVING" SENTENCES
משפטי יש/אין

This chapter discusses:

- "Being" sentences with יש and אין (sections 1.1–1.6)
- Alternative ways of expressing "being" (section 1.7)
- "Having" sentences with יש ל- and אין ל- (section 2.1–2.3)
- Alternative ways of expressing "having" (section 2.4)
- Additional uses of יש and אין: ability, possibility, and prohibition (sections 3.1–3.2)
- יש ש-/יש ו- *sometimes* (section 3.3)
- אין instead of לא (section 4)
- Confusables: מצוי; נמצא; קיים; אין

This chapter will help the reader to:

- Differentiate between "be" and "have" sentences and translate them
- Identify "be" and "have" sentences without יש
- Recognize "being" and "having" notions in sentences with expressions other than יש and אין
- Distinguish among various uses of יש and אין and translate the phrases in which they appear

Sentences with יש and אין: an overview

In the present tense only, the words יש and אין are used to create existential ("being") and possession ("having") sentences. Although יש and אין are not strictly verbs (some call them "verboids"), they fulfill the function of the predicate in the sentence. Unlike verbs, יש and אין do not conjugate for tense and person, although they may be inflected with personal pronoun suffixes (1.5 and 4.1).

In "being" sentences, יש expresses the notions of presence (in a particular place) or existence, and אין expresses absence or non-existence (section 1).

In possession sentences, namely, sentences expressing the notions of "having" and "not having," the preposition -ל accompanies יש and אין (section 2). The preposition may precede or follow these words. When -ל comes first, it is separated from יש and אין by a noun or a pronoun suffix. The noun (or pronoun suffix) that comes immediately after the preposition refers to the "possessor" (or the "non-possessor," in the case of אין).

In the past and future tense, יש and אין are replaced by the third person forms of the verb "to be" and, in addition, אין becomes לא. In contrast to יש and אין, whose form is invariable, the past and future forms of the verb "to be" must agree in gender and number with other sentence elements – with the subject in "being" sentences, and with the "possessed" in possession sentences.

In formal style, יש may be omitted and the meaning of the sentence – whether "being" or "having" – rests on the preposition alone: on -ב in "being" sentences and on -ל in "having" sentences (1.1.1, and 2.2).

When incorporated in certain set expressions, יש and אין assume meanings other than "being" and "having;" these are discussed in section 3. Section 4 discusses the use of אין for negation instead of לא.

1. "Being" sentences

"Being" sentences are of two types:

- Presence (-יש ב) and absence (-אין ב)
- Existence (יש) and non-existence (אין)

#1 & #2   **1.1 Presence and absence sentences:** *there is/are (not)*

אין ... ב-	יש ב ... -
ב- ... אין	ב- ... יש
אין בּוֹ/בָּהּ/בָּהֶם/בָּהֶן[1]	יש בּוֹ/בָּהּ/בָּהֶם/בָּהֶן

-יש ב indicates presence in a place, and -אין ב indicates absence from a place. The preposition -ב is followed by a noun or a pronoun suffix (בּו, בה בהם, בהן).

---

[1] In the first person: יש/אין בִּי, יש/אין בָּנו; in the second person: יש/אין בְּךָ, יש/אין בָּך, יש/אין בָּכֶם, יש/אין בָּכֶן. יש/אין בְּךָ, יש/אין בָּך

For example:

בָּעִיר **יֵשׁ** גנים גדולים, אבל **אֵין בָּהּ** מוּזֵאוֹן *there are large parks in the city, but there is no museum (in it).*

The word order is flexible: יֵשׁ and אֵין may appear before or after the preposition (example 3), adjacent to it or at a distance (example 4).
In translation, יֵשׁ and אֵין are rendered as *there is/are (not)*, or – usually when the subject is inanimate – as *has/have (not)*.

---

(1) **יֵשׁ** בַּמִּקְרָא לָשׁוֹן מוּקְדֶּמֶת **וְיֵשׁ בּוֹ** לָשׁוֹן מְאוּחֶרֶת.
<u>There is</u> in the Bible early language and there is in it late language.
OR: The Bible <u>has</u> both early and late language.

(2) בְּנִיגוּד לְשָׂפוֹת אֲחֵרוֹת, **יֵשׁ בָּעֲרָבִית** כְּבָעִבְרִית מַעֲרֶכֶת בִּנְיָינִים.
In contrast to other languages, <u>there is</u> in Arabic, as (there is) in Hebrew, a system of *binyanim*.
OR: In contrast to other languages, Arabic, like Hebrew, <u>has</u> a system of *binyanim*.

(3) **יֵשׁ בְּיָדֵינוּ** דוּגְמָאוֹת נוֹסָפוֹת, שֶׁאַף **בָּהֶן יֵשׁ** מַשְׁמָעוּת.
<u>We have</u> (literally: there is in our hands) additional examples, which also <u>have</u> signi☐cance (literally: in which also there is significance).

(4) בַּגַּן הָעֵדֶן **אֵין** בּוּשָׁה **וְאֵין** אִיסוּר **וְאֵין** אַשְׁמָה.
In the Garden of Eden <u>there is no</u> shame and <u>no</u> prohibition and <u>no</u> guilt.

🏋 #3   **1.1.1** In formal style, the word יֵשׁ can be omitted (and must be reconstructed in translation); the notion of presence is then conveyed solely through the preposition בְּ- (sometimes through בֵּין *among*, example 7).

---

(5) **בַּ**סֵּפֶר חֲמִישָׁה פְּרָקִים.
(=**יֵשׁ** בַּסֵּפֶר חֲמִישָׁה פרקים)
<u>There are</u> five chapters in the book (OR: the book <u>has</u> five chapters).

(6) דוּגְמָאוֹת הַרְבֵּה לַגִּישָׁה זֹאת **בְּ**חֵקֶר לְשׁוֹן הַמִּקְרָא.
(=**יֵשׁ** בחקר המקרא דוּגמאות הרבה לגישה זאת)
<u>There are</u> many examples for this approach in biblical language research.

Note the use of הרבה *many* after the noun; in a more colloquial style הרבה would appear before the noun (e.g., הרבה דוגמות).

(7) **בֵּין** הַמִּמְצָאִים הָאַרְכֵאוֹלוֹגִיִּים הַמּוּצָגִים בַּמּוּזֵאוֹן מֹאזְנַיִם וּמִשְׁקָלוֹת.
(=**בֵּין** הממצאים הארכאולוגיים המוצגים במוזאון **יֵשׁ** מאזניים ומשקלות)
Among the archeological findings exhibited in the museum <u>[there] are</u> scales and weights.

🏋 #1 & #2   **1.2 Existence and non-existence sentences:** ‏יש/אין‏ *there is/are (not)*

When ‏יש‏ expresses absolute existence, rather than presence in a place, the preposition ‏-ב‏ need not appear (since no specific place is indicated). This applies also to ‏אין‏ (example 10). Existence (and non-existence) sentences are translated as *there is/there are (not)*. Another option is to use the verb ‏קיים‏ *exists* (examples 25–26).

---

(8) ‏יש‏ סוגים שונים של סמלים.
There are different kinds of symbols.
OR: Different kinds of symbols exist.

(9) ‏יש‏ תפוצות שלא הצליחו להקים מדינות משל עצמן.
There are diasporas that did not succeed in establishing states of their own.
OR: There exist diasporas that did not succeed in establishing states of their own.

1.3 "Being" sentences in the past and future

In the past and future, ‏יש‏ and ‏אין‏ are replaced by third person forms of the verb "to be": ‏(לא) היה/היתה/היו‏ and [2] ‏(לא) יהיה/תהיה/יהיו/תהיינה‏, respectively. The choice of verb form is according to the gender and number of the subject of the clause.

For example

Past: בעיר **היו גנים** גדולים אבל **לא היה** בה **מוזאון**
Future: בעיר **יהיו** גנים גדולים אבל **לא יהיה** בה מוזאון

‏היו‏ and ‏יהיו‏ agree with the plural ‏גנים‏; ‏היה‏ and ‏יהיה‏ agree with the singular masculine ‏מוזאון‏. For a feminine singular subject ‏היתה‏ and ‏תהיה‏ in the past and future, respectively, would be used.

---

(10) **לא היתה** אֶפְשָרוּת, וְעַדַיִין **אין** אֶפְשָרוּת, לבלום את הַהֲגִירה.
There was no possibility – and there still is no possibility – to curb the immigration.

(11) באותה תקופה **לא היו** בעיר יהודים רבים.
At that period, there were not many Jews in the city (OR: at that period, the city did not have many Jews).

---

[2] ‏תהיינה‏ (f.pl.) is not often used in modern Hebrew.

1.4 *There are those who...*

⚡#1 1.4.1 (רבים) פועל + -ה/אֲשֶׁר-/שֶׁ + יש

In this construction, the plural masculine verb is subjectless; the subject, a non-specified group of people, is understood from the context. -שֶׁ (or אֲשֶׁר) are used before the verb in any tense; -ה can be used only before a verb in the present tense.

In the past and future, היו and יהיו, respectively, replace יש (example 13).

‏(12) בראש השָׁנָה **יש שאוכלים** פְּרי חָדָש שעֲדַיין לא נֶאֱכַל בעונה הזו, **ויש המברכים** בְּרָכָה מְיוחֶדֶת על לבישת בֶּגֶד חָדָש.

On Rosh Ha-Shanah (the Jewish New Year) <u>there are those who</u> eat a new fruit that has not yet been eaten in this season, and <u>there are those who</u> say a special blessing for wearing a new garment.

‏(13) **היו שתָמְכו** ביצירת חֶבְרָה סוֹציאָליסטית, **והיו שהתנגדו** לְכָך.

There were <u>those who</u> supported the creation of a socialist society, and <u>those who</u> objected to it.

1.4.2 (פועל (יחיד או רבים + -שֶׁ + מי + יש

When מי is inserted after יש, the verb is introduced by -שֶׁ (אֲשֶׁר and -ה cannot be used). Whether the verb is in the singular or plural form, the translation is the same:

יש מי שחושבים, יש מי שחושב *there are those who think (that)....*

‏(14) **יש מי שחושב** שדוברֵי לשון חז"ל היו דו-לְשוֹניים ודיברו ארמית ועברית.

<u>There are those who</u> think that the speakers of Mishnaic Hebrew (literally: the language of Ḥazal) were bilingual and spoke both Aramaic and Hebrew.

⚡#1 1.5 Inflected יש: יֶשְׁנוֹ/יֶשְׁנָהּ/יֶשְׁנָם/יֶשְׁנָן *there is/are*

אומרים יֶשְׁנָהּ ארץ (טשרניחובסקי)
They say, there is a land... (Tchernichowsky)

יֶשְׁנוֹ עַם אחד מְפוּזָר ומְפוֹרָד בין העמים (אסתר ג ח)
There is a certain people, scattered and dispersed among the other people
(Book of Esther 3.8)

יש may be inflected with the third person pronouns; the pronoun anticipates the subject and agrees with it in number and gender. This form allows the use of a definite noun (e.g., הספרים ישנם על השולחן, but הספרים יש על השולחן* is not possible).

From an informational point of view, the pronoun is redundant, since the subject is immediately specified. This variant of יש (found in both "existence" and "presence" sentences) is, therefore, a stylistic option and, as such, cannot be rendered in translation.

The subject is shaded:

> (15) יֶשְׁנָם **ספרים** שונים העוסקים ב"שְׁאֵלה היהודית".
> There **are** different books that deal with the "Jewish question".
>
> (16) יֶשְׁנָה במגילה **שורת** רַעְיוֹנוֹת ומושָׂגים הַמְּעִידים על הַקֶשֶׁר בין קומראן לבין הַנַּצְרוּת הַקְּדוּמה.
> There **is** in the scroll a series of ideas and concepts that testify to the connection between Qumran and early Christianity.
> OR: The scroll has a series of ideas and concepts....

1.6 יש/אין ב- ...מִשׁוּם

have something of..., have a certain amount of.../ not have any of...

The word מִשׁוּם is added to יש ב-/אין ב- to qualify the statement and make it more tentative. A similar rhetorical function may be fulfilled by the expressions (כְּ)מִין, כְּעֵין, מֵעֵין, בְּגֶדֶר and בִּבְחִינַת.

> (17) יש בדברים אלה **משום** פישוט.
> There **is** in these words <u>some</u> simplification.
>
> (18) בפְּסִיקה היה **משום** עִידוד ליהודים לעסוק בעֲנף פַּרְנָסָה זה.
> In the ruling <u>there was</u> <u>some</u> encouragement for the Jews to work in this occupation.
>
> (19) אין בכך **משום** סְתירה.
> There is <u>no real</u> contradiction in this.

1.7 Alternative ways of expressing presence and existence

1.7.1 נִמְצָא/נִמְצֵאת/נִמְצָאִים/נִמְצָאוֹת ב-
מָצוּי/מְצוּיָה/מְצוּיִים/מְצוּיוֹת ב-
יש/אין בַּנִּמְצָא

Presence in a place may be indicated with the verb להִימָצֵא ב- *be found in* or with the related adjective מָצוּי ב-.[3]

The notion of existence is expressed with יש/אין בנמצא (examples 23–24).

> *The expected participle form מָצוֹא does not exist. מָצוּי reflects the root alternation between ל"ה-ל"י and ל"א carried over from Mishnaic to modern Hebrew.

---

[3] For another meaning of מָצוּי see below, Confusables section 1.

(20) מילה זאת **נמצאת** כבר בתנ"ך.
This word is already <u>found in</u> the Bible.

(21) **מצויה בידינו** גִּרְסָה מַקְבִּילָה.
<u>We have</u> (literally: [there is] found in our hands) a parallel version.

This expression is synonymous with יֵשׁ בידינו (example 3 above).

(22) יש מלים **המצויות** רק במקרא ואינן **מצויות בלשון** חז"ל.
There are words that <u>are found</u> only in the Bible and <u>are not found</u> in the language of Ḥazal.

(23) בראשית שנת תרס"ט (1908) **היו בנמצא** רק ארבע המַחברות הראשונות של המילון.
At the beginning of 1908 only the first four notebooks of the dictionary <u>were in existence.</u>

(24) מִכֵּיוָן שלא **היו** אז סְפְרֵי לימוד בעברית **בנמצא**, כתבו מורֵי בית הספר את סְפְרֵי הלימוד.
Since Hebrew language textbooks <u>did not exist</u> then, the teachers wrote the books.

1.7.2 קַיָּם, קַיֶּמֶת, קַיָּמִים, קַיָּמוֹת (ב-) *exist(s) (in)*

This adjective is an alternative to יֵשׁ and indicates both presence (example 25) and existence (example 26). In the latter case, the preposition -בְּ is not used.

(25) בכל דת **קיימת** ספרות עֲנֵפָה בנושא זה.
In every religion <u>there exists</u> (OR: <u>there is</u>) a rich literature on this subject.

(26) יש תְּפוּצוֹת שלא הצליחו להָקים מְדִינות מִשֶּׁל עַצְמָן, וּמִצַּד שֵׁנִי **קַיָּמוֹת** תפוצות הקשורות למדינת-לְאוֹם.
<u>There are</u> diasporas that did not succeed in establishing states of their own, and on the other hand <u>there exist</u> (OR: <u>there are</u>) diasporas that are connected to a national state.

יֵשׁ and קיים are used here side by side for stylistic variation.

2. "Having" (possession) sentences

יש ל-... /ל-...יש   אין ל-... /ל-...אין
יש לו/לה/להם/להן   אין לו/לה/להם/לנו/להם

Possession sentences are created by using the preposition -לְ in conjunction with יֵשׁ (for having) and אֵין (for not having). The preposition is either attached to a noun (the "possessor"), or is inflected with a pronoun suffix that refers to this noun. In normative Hebrew, the noun without the preposition is considered the subject, but in colloquial use it is treated as the object (hence יֵשׁ לי את הספר).

2.1 Word order

The word order in possession sentences is flexible:

(a) When -ל is attached to a noun, יֵשׁ and אֵין may appear <u>before</u> the preposition (e.g., **יש/אין** לסיפור מקורות עתיקים *the story has/does not have ancient sources*, or – and this option is the more likely in written style – <u>after</u> it (e.g., לסיפור **יש/אין** מקורות עתיקים). In the latter case, the preposition may appear at a distance from יֵשׁ and אֵין, requiring the reader to scan the sentence ahead to uncover the function of the preposition (example 28).

(b) When the preposition is inflected with a pronoun suffix, יֵשׁ and אֵין appear first, just before the preposition (e.g., **יש לו** מקורות עתיקים/אֵין **לו** מקורות עתיקים).
By putting the preposition first (e.g., **לו אין** מקורות עתיקים/**לו יש** מקורות עתיקים), an emphasis is achieved.

---

(27) יצירות פוליטיות מוגְדָּרות כיצירות שיש **להן** מֶסֶר פוֹליטי יָשיר.
Political works are defined as works that <u>have</u> a direct political message.

(28) **למקומות** הקְדושים ולחֲפָצים הקדושים **אֵין** בָּסיס במָסורֶת.
The holy places and the holy objects <u>do not have</u> basis in the tradition.

The preposition is repeated.

(29) **לצָרותיו שאֵין להן** קֵץ **יכולה להיות** רק מַשְמָעות אחת.
His troubles, that <u>have no</u> end, <u>can have</u> only one meaning.

The subordinate clause אֵין להן קץ *they have no end*, is embedded within another "have" clause – לצרותיו **יכולה להיות** רק משמעות אחת *his troubles can have only one meaning* – where, after the modal יכולה *can*, יֵשׁ converts into להיות *to be*.

🏋#3 2.2 Omission of יֵשׁ

As already noted in 1.1.1, the word יֵשׁ may be omitted altogether. "Having" is then signaled by the preposition -ל alone. The reader must identify the function of the preposition (namely, to indicate possession) and determine where in the sentence the omitted יֵשׁ would have appeared.

A reconstructed sentence with יֵשׁ is given in parentheses:

---

(30) **לסיפור** שני חלָקים בְּרורים.
(=לסיפור יש שני חלקים ברורים)
The story <u>has</u> two distinct parts.

(31) סיפורים אלו לובשים צורות שונות ולהם נושאים, מְגמות ותפקידים מְגוּונים.
(=סיפורים אלה לובשים צורות שונות ויש להם נושאים, מגמות ותפקידים מגוונים)
These stories take various forms and <u>have</u> diverse subjects, purposes and functions.

---

(32) סְגְנוֹנוֹ הַנְּבוּאִי שֶׁל יְחֶזְקֵאל זִיקָה **לוֹ** לַסִּגְנוֹן שֶׁל הַבָּבְלִית הַסִּפְרוּתִית.

(=לְסִגְנוֹנוֹ הַנְּבוּאִי שֶׁל יְחֶזְקֵאל יֵשׁ זִיקָה לַסִּגְנוֹן שֶׁל הַבָּבְלִית הַסִּפְרוּתִית)

Ezekiel's prophetic style <u>has</u> affinity to the style of literary Babylonian.

The inflected preposition לוֹ conveys the notion of "having"; it refers back to the topicalized noun[4] סגנון.

(33) **לַבַּצוֹרֶת, לַלֶּחֶם, לַמַּאֲכָל וְלַנִּסִּים** הַכְּרוּכִים בָּהֶם תַּפְקִיד מֶרְכָּזִי בַּסִּיפּוּר.

(=לַבצורת, ללחם, למאכל ולנסים הכרוכים בהם **יֵשׁ** תפקיד מרכזי בסיפור)

The drought, the bread, the food and the miracles that they entail <u>have</u> a central role in this story.

2.3 Possession sentences in the past and future

In the past and future, third person forms of the verb "to be" (היה, הייתה, היו) replace יֵשׁ and אֵין, and אֵין becomes לֹא; the verb agrees with the "possessed," rather than (as it is in English) with the "possessor".

After the modal יָכוֹל *can*, the infinitive לִהְיוֹת replaces יֵשׁ and אֵין (example 29 above).

As is the case in the present tense (see 2.1 above), the word order is flexible: the verb may be placed <u>before</u> the preposition -ל (e.g., **הָיוּ** לַסִּיפּוּר מְקוֹרוֹת עַתִּיקִים) or <u>after</u> it (e.g., לַסִּיפּוּר עַתִּיקִים מְקוֹרוֹת **הָיוּ** *the story had ancient sources*). In addition, the verb and the preposition may be separated (e.g., **הָיוּ** מְקוֹרוֹת עַתִּיקִים לַסִּיפּוּר), sometimes appearing at a considerable distance from each other (example 35). This feature of written style necessitates reading ahead far into the sentence to determine the function of the preposition -ל.

The "possessed" is shaded:

---

(34) לַתְּחוּמִים אֵלֶּה **הָיְתָה** חֲשִׁיבוּת מַדָּעִית וּתֵאוֹלוֹגִית כְּאַחַת.

These areas <u>had</u> both scientific and theological importance.

(35) לְגִיּוּס הָאוֹרְיֵנוּת לְטוֹבַת הַהַבְנָיָה הַלְּאֻמִּית הַמּוֹדֶרְנִית – עֵקֶב הַהֲגִירָה הַנִּמְשֶׁכֶת לְיִשְׂרָאֵל – **הָיוּ** הַשְׁפָּעוֹת עַל שִׁיטוֹת הַהוֹרָאָה וְעַל תּוֹכְנִית הַלִּמּוּדִים.

The mobilization of literacy for the sake of the modern national building – due to the continuing immigration to Israel – influenced (literally: <u>had</u> influences on) the methods of teaching and the curriculum.

2.4 Alternative ways of expressing "having" and "not having"

2.4.1 בַּעַל/בַּעֲלַת/בַּעֲלֵי/בַּעֲלוֹת = יֵשׁ לוֹ/לָהּ/לָהֶם/לָהֶן

חֲסַר/חֲסָרַת/חַסְרֵי/חַסְרוֹת = אֵין לוֹ/לָהּ/לָהֶם/לָהֶן

---

[4] See discussion of topicalization in Chapter 1, section 2.

> אֵין חָכָם כְּבַעַל הַנִּיסָּיוֹן (מִלֵּי דְּאָבוֹת י)
> *There is no one as wise as the experienced person* (Mile de-Avot)

When the words בַּעַל and חֶסַר (in the construct form) are followed by a noun or a noun+adjective phrase, "having" or "possessing" and "lacking" or "being deficient in," respectively, are indicated.[5]

---

(36) כּוֹתְבֵי הָאוּטוֹפִּיוֹת צִיְּירוּ חֶבְרָה **בַּעֲלַת תַּרְבּוּת מוֹדֶרְנִית**.
(=חברה שיש לה תרבות מודרנית)
The writers of the utopias drew a society <u>with</u> (OR: <u>that has</u>) a modern culture.

(37) הָאוּטוֹפִּיָה מְתָאֶרֶת עוֹלָם לְלֹא מִלְחָמוֹת, עוֹלָם **בַּעַל אֵיכוּת חֲדָשָׁה**.
(=עולם שיש לו איכות חדשה)
The utopia describes a world without wars, a world <u>with</u> (OR: <u>that has</u>) a new quality.

(38) רוֹפְאִים קוֹנְוֶונְצְיוֹנַלְיִּים רַבִּים טוֹעֲנִים כִּי הָרְפוּאָה הַהוֹלִיסְטִית **חֲסֵרַת כָּל בָּסִיס מֶחְקָרִי** וְעַל כֵּן **חֲסֵרַת יְכוֹלֶת** לְסַיֵּיע לִבְנֵי אָדָם.
Many conventional doctors argue that holistic medicine <u>has no</u> empirical basis and therefore is <u>unable</u> (literally: <u>lacks the ability</u>) to help people.

2.4.1.1 Where a quantity (and an inanimate noun) is involved, the notion of "having" is conveyed by בן rather than בעל.
For example:

בַּיִת בֶּן שָׁלוֹשׁ קוֹמוֹת *a house with three stories* (*a three-story house*)
מַחְבָּרוֹת בְּנוֹת מֵאוֹת דַּפִּים *notebooks with hundreds of pages.*

2.4.2 נודע ל- + Noun
The use of נודע ל- in the sense of "have" is restricted to certain nouns (e.g., חשיבות *importance*, משקל *weight*, משמעות *significance*, תוצאות *consequences*); these nouns are often accompanied by the adjective רב/רבה/רבים/רבות *great, many/much.*

---

(39) לַמָּקוֹם **נוֹדַעַת** חֲשִׁיבוּת רַבָּה בָּעוֹלָם הַיְּהוּדִי מִפְּנֵי שֶׁהוּא בֵּיתָהּ שֶׁל קְהִילָה יְהוּדִית גְּדוֹלָה.
The place <u>has great importance</u> in the Jewish world because it is the home of a large Jewish community.

(40) תַּקָּנוֹת אֵלּוּ **נוֹדְעָה לָהֶן** מַשְׁמָעוּת רַבָּה.
[=לתקנות אלו נודעה משמעות רבה]
These ordinances <u>had great significance</u>.

The sentence is topicalized.

---

5 See also discussion in Chapter 4, section 4.5.

⚠️This meaning of נודע should be distinguished from its use as an adjective (e.g., סופרים נודעים *famous authors*) or impersonal verb (whose form does not change) in the sense of *it became known* (e.g., נודע להם על הגירוש *they learned about the expulsion*).

2.4.3 With an inanimate subject, the verb **להחזיק** *to hold, to contain* also expresses "having" (e.g., הספר מחזיק שמונה פרקים *the book contains (has) eight chapters*).

2.4.4 The verb לָשֵׂאת *to carry* indicates "having" when it co-occurs with certain nouns (e.g., אוֹפִי *character*, מַשְׁמָעוּת, מוּבָן *meaning*, כותרת *headline*, תואר *title*, שם *name*, כינוי).

---

(41) המילה "עָרִיץ" **נוֹשֵׂאת** עִמָּהּ קוֹנוֹטַצְיָה שְׁלִילִית.
The word "tyrant" <u>has</u> (literally: carries with it) a negative connotation.

(42) דְּמוּיוֹתָיו **נוֹשְׂאוֹת** אֶלֶמֶנְטִים רֵיאָלִיסְטִיִּים.
His characters <u>have</u> realistic elements.

2.4.5 -להיות שַׁיָּךְ לְ/לְהִשְׁתַּיֵּךְ לְ *belong to*
Ownership or belonging (as distinct from possession) is indicated with the adjective -שייך ל or the verb -להשתייך ל.

---

(43) המקום **היה שייך** לאָדָם (אוֹ למשפחה) בשֵׁם זה.
The place <u>belonged to</u> a person (or family) by this name.

(44) העברית **מִשְׁתַּיֶּכֶת** לעָנָף הַכְּנַעֲנִי של הַשָׂפוֹת הַשֵׁמִיוֹת.
Hebrew <u>belongs to</u> the Canaanite branch of the Semitic languages.

2.4.5.1 The notion of belonging, "being a member of," can also be expressed with בֶּן. For example:

בן משפחה *family member*, בני העיר *the people of the town*, בת המזרח *woman of the orient*.

3. Additional uses of יש and אין

3.1 Expressions of ability with -יש/אין ב

🏋️#1 & #2   **3.1.1** יש/אין ביכולתו, יש/אין בכוחו, יש/אין באפשרותו, יש/אין בידיו/בידו
(לעשות) *can/cannot (do)*
When these expressions are followed by an infinitive verb they indicate ability (or inability) to perform the action.

On occasion, יש may be omitted (e.g., בכוחו/בידיו/ביכולתו/באפשרותו לעשות זאת *[he] can do it*); rarely, לְאֵל is added:[6] יש לְאֵל ידו לעשות זאת *he can do it, it is within his power to do it.*

Note that when a verb is not present, יש בידינו and אין בידינו indicate, respectively, "having" and "not having" (e.g., אין בידינו הוכחה ברורה לכך *we do not have clear proof for this* and example 3 above).

---

(45) פעולה מַעֲשית ביישוב הארץ **יש בכוחה לקרֵב** את הגאולה.
Practical action in the settlement of the land <u>can</u> hasten the redemption.

(46) ללא סימנֵי פיסוק, **אין בידי** הקורא **להַכריע** איך לקרוא את המשפטים.
Without punctuation marks, the reader <u>cannot</u> determine how to read the sentences.

(47) **אין ביכולתו** של רוב בקהילה **לבַטֵל** את מנהָגָיו של המיעוט.
The majority in the community <u>cannot</u> invalidate the customs of the minority.

🏋 #1 & #2   3.1.2   כדי ...-ב אין/יש *can/cannot*

After יש ב- and אין ב-, the word כדי loses its customary meaning of *in order to* and the entire phrase now indicates ability (or inability).

When כדי is omitted, the infinitive form of the verb – required after כדי – provides the clue to the meaning of the phrase (example 49).

Sentences with this expression are often topicalized[7] – the inflected forms בו/בה/בהם/בהן refer back to the noun at the head of the sentence (example 50).

---

(48) **יש בסיפור כדי להָעֵיד** על אֵירועים שקדמו לו בכמאתיים שנה.
The story <u>can</u> attest to events that preceded it by about two hundred years.

(49) הקורא נקלע לתוך עולָמה של הפַנטזָיה שאין בה להָאיר את חייו שלו.
The reader falls in a world of fantasy which <u>cannot</u> illuminate his own life.

(50) המבנֶה של החֶברה והאידֵאָלים שלה **יש בהם כדי** הֶסבֵּר לעֵרֶך הרב שתָפסו הקהיּלה ומוסדותיה בתודעתָם של בנֵי אַשכּנַז באותם ימים.
The structure of the society and its ideals <u>can</u> explain the great value that the community and its institutions occupied in the consciousness of the Jews of Germany in those days.

In this example, an action noun הסבר – rather than an infinitive verb (להסביר) – follows כדי. בהם refers back to the topicalized nouns מבנה and אידיאלים.

---

[6] אֵל – in this expression in the sense of *power* – should be differentiated from אַל, see Chapter 8 Confusables 7(a).
[7] See Chapter 1, 2.

3.2. Modal meanings of יש/אין + infinitive: obligation, possibility, impossibility, prohibition

𝍄#1   3.2.1 יש + infinitive

When followed by an infinitive verb, יש expresses impersonal obligation: *one must, one should*; it is a more formal alternative to צריך.

By adding the preposition -ל inflected with a personal pronoun, the obligation can be personalized (example 52).

---

(51) יש **לאַתֵּר** את ים סוף בְּאֵזור זה.

The Red Sea <u>should be located</u> in this area.

(52) יש לנו **לבדוק** את הָעִנְיָן מִקָרוֹב.

<u>We should examine</u> the matter closely.

3.2.1.1 When followed by verbs of cognition or belief (e.g., להאמין *assume*, להניח, לשער *believe*), יש expresses possibility, rather than obligation.

---

(53) יש **להניח** שהמְנהָג הוּבָא על יְדֵי שליחים מארץ ישראל.

<u>It can be assumed</u> that the custom was brought by emissaries from the Land of Israel.

𝍄#2   3.2.2 אין + infinitive

Followed by an infinitive verb, אין is understood – depending on the context – as *should not* (examples 54–44) or *cannot* (example 56).

Note that when אלא is inserted after אין, the meaning changes from prohibition (*should not*) to obligation (*should, must*; example 57).

By adding an inflected form of -ל the prohibition is personalized (example 58); with this addition, אין may be replaced by אַל (example 59).

---

(54) אין **לחפש** אֶצלו חידושים לעומת קודמָיו.

One <u>should not</u> look in his work for innovations vis-à-vis his predecessors.

(55) ההיסטוריון אינ‌נו יכול להתְיַיחס למְקורותיו כסְפרות קודש שאין **לערער** עליה.

The historian cannot treat his sources as sacred literature that <u>should not</u> be doubted.

(56) הַאִם אין **לקרוא** את הרוֹמָן על הַמֵאָה העשירית כמבַשֵּׂר מְאורָעות של המֵאָה העשֹרים?

<u>Cannot</u> the novel about the tenth century be read as heralding events of the twentieth century?

> (57) **אֵין אֶלָּא לִבְחֹן** בִּקְפִידָה אֶת הַמְמֻצָּאִים הַכְּתוּבִים.
> One <u>must</u> examine carefully the written findings.
>
> (58) **אֵין לָנוּ** עוֹד **לָשִׂים לֵב** לְכָךְ.
> We <u>need not</u> pay attention to this anymore.
>
> (59) **אַל לָנוּ** לְהִתְעַלֵּם מֵחֶסְרוֹנוֹתֶיהָ שֶׁל מְדִינַת הַסַּעַד.
> We <u>should not</u> ignore the shortcomings of the welfare state.

🏋#1   3.3 **יֵשׁ ש-/יֵשׁ ו-** [8] *sometimes, at times*

Before -שׁ or -ו, יֵשׁ takes on an adverbial meaning, equivalent to לִפְעָמִים *sometimes*.

> (60) **יֵשׁ שֶׁ**הַגְּמוּל הוּא קוֹלֶקְטִיווִי **וְיֵשׁ שֶׁ**הוּא אִישִׁי.
> <u>Sometimes</u> the reward is collective, and sometimes it is personal.
>
> (61) **יֵשׁ ו**הַמְסַפֵּר הַמִּקְרָאִי מְעַצֵּב אֶת הַדְּמוּת כְּאַנְטִיתֵזָה לִדְמוּת אַחֶרֶת.
> The biblical narrator <u>sometimes</u> forms the character as the antithesis of another character.

4. אֵין instead of לֹא

🏋#2   אֵין replaces the more colloquial לֹא in the following cases:

- In nominal (verbless) sentences (where it is translated as *is/are not*)[9]
- Before present tense verbs (where it is translated as *does/do not* or *is/are not* when the verb has a passive meaning).

Unless it appears at the beginning of the clause, אֵין is inflected with a personal pronoun suffix that refers to the subject.
For example:

אֵין הַחוֹקְרִים מְקַבְּלִים דֵּעָה זוֹ or הַחוֹקְרִים אֵינָם מְקַבְּלִים דֵּעָה זוֹ *the researchers do not accept this opinion.*

4.1 When אֵין appears in conjunction with אֶלָּא, an emphatic positive statement is made.
For example:

אֵין זוֹ אֶלָּא הַשְׁעָרָה, זוֹ אֵינָהּ אֶלָּא הַשְׁעָרָה *this is only/none other than a conjecture.*[10]

---

[8] יֵשׁ ו- is considered non-normative by prescriptive grammarians.

[9] See discussion of negative copula in Chapter 7, 2.

[10] See also Chapter 10, section 1.1.

Confusables

1. ‏מָצוּי ב-/אצל‎; מצוי

1.1 With a human subject, ‏מצוי אצל‎ and ‏מצוי ב-‎ mean *familiar with* (rather than the locative sense, *found in*, as seen in examples 21–22 above).

> ‏(62) הוא היה חָכָם **הַמָצוּי אצל** המקורות.‎
> He was a Talmudic scholar <u>familiar with</u> the sources.
>
> ‏(63) חֵלֶק מן הכותבים החילוניים **אינם מצויים** במקורות היהודיים הבָּתַר-מִקרָאיִים.‎
> Some of the non-religious writers <u>are not familiar with</u> the post-biblical Jewish sources.

1.2 ‏מָצוּי/מְצוּיָה/מְצוּיים/מְצוּיוֹת‎
Used as an adjective, ‏מצוי‎ means *common*.

> ‏(64) ירידָתָם של שבטֵי נודדים בִשנת בַצוֹרֶת למצוא מִרעֶה לעֶדרֵיהם היא תופָעָה **מצוייה**.‎
> The migration of nomadic tribes during a drought year in order to find pasture for their flocks is a <u>common</u> phenomenon.

2. ‏נמצא ל-‎; נמצא ש-

Followed by ‏ל-‎ or ‏ש-‎, the verb ‏נמצא‎ does not mean *found, located*

2.1 ‏נמצא ל-‎ *available to*

> ‏(65) הָאֶפשָרות להַפריד בין המושָא לפֹועַל **נמצאת לעברית** מן המקורות.‎
> The possibility to separate the object from the verb <u>is available to</u> Hebrew from the sources.

2.2 ‏נמצא ש-‎
This impersonal expression, which literally means *it is/was found that*, is used in academic writing to sum up a point: *it can be inferred, we may conclude that*. Alternatively, the first person plural may be used: ‏נמצאנו לְמֵדים‎ or [11]‏מָצינו‎ *we (may) learn (from this)*.

Another possible reading of ‏נמצא‎ – depending on the context – is *we will find* (the verb is interpreted as first person plural future in *pa'al*).

---

[11] This form is due to ‏ל"א-ל"ה/ל"י‎ root alternation.

3. קַיָּם; לְקַיֵּם; לְהָקִים; לְהִתְקַיֵּם

The adjective קַיָּם (*exists*; without vowel points – קיים) should not be confused with other words from the same root in the *binyanim pi'el, hif'il and hitpa'el*:

(a) קִיֵּם, קַיָּם (לְקַיֵּם (לקיים)) *to fulfill* (a promise, a duty); *to observe* (a law, a commandment); *to maintain, preserve* (ties, connection). The related noun קִיּוּם may mean – depending on the context – *fulfillment; observance, maintenance* or *existence*.

(b) הֵקִים (לְהָקִים) *to establish, to found*. The action noun is הֲקָמָה *establishment, founding*.

---

(66) **קִיּוּם** הַנֶּדֶר נֶחֱשָׁב לְחוֹבָה קְדוֹשָׁה בְּיוֹתֵר.
The <u>fulfillment</u> of the vow is considered a most holy obligation.

(67) הִתְפַּתְּחָה אָז אֱמוּנָה בְּהֶמְשֵׁךְ **קִיּוּמָהּ** שֶׁל הַנֶּפֶשׁ.
A belief in the continued <u>existence</u> of the soul developed then.

(c) Note also the various meanings of לְהִתְקַיֵּם: *to take place; to be carried out; to exist; to live, to survive; to subsist*.

4. -מֵאַיִן, בְּאֵין; מֵאַיִן; לְאַיִן; אֵין

4.1 מֵאֵין and בְּאֵין mean *in the absence of, for lack of, without*. Synonymous expressions are: מֵהֶעְדֵּר, בְּחוֹסֶר.

---

(68) **מֵאֵין** יְכוֹלֶת לָדוּן כָּאן בְּכָל הַתּוֹרוֹת הַשּׁוֹנוֹת, נָדוּן רַק בְּאַחַת.
<u>For lack of</u> ability to discuss here all the various doctrines, we will discuss only one [of them].

(69) הַפְּגִישָׁה בֵּין הָאִישָׁה לַמַּלְאָךְ מִתְרַחֶשֶׁת **בְּאֵין** רוֹאֶה.
The meeting between the woman and the angel takes place <u>in the absence of</u> witnesses (literally: without anyone seeing).

4.2 מֵאַיִן (מאין) *where from?*

⚠️ In unpointed text without full (plene) spelling, מֵאַיִן (otherwise: מאין) and מֵאֵין appear identical.

4.3 לְאַיִן is a component in the adverbs לאין עֲרוֹךְ and לאין שִׁיעוּר *immeasurably*.[12]

4.4 -אֵין is used as a negative semantic prefix before certain adjectives (e.g., אֵין-סוֹפִי or אֵינסוֹפִי *infinite*).

---

[12] See Chapter 5, 2.1.5.1.

References

בן אשר, תשל"ג
בן-חיים, תשנ"ב
צדקה, 1981, 1997
שוורצולד (רודריג), 1988

Adler, 2006
Glinert, 1989

Chapter 9: "Being" and "Having" Sentences – Exercises

exercise #	topic	page
1	Identifying different meanings of יֵשׁ	361–362
2	Identifying different meanings of אֵין	363–364
3	Reconstructing sentences with an omitted יֵשׁ	365–366

Exercise #1: Identifying different meanings of יש

> **The rules to go by:** see sections 1, 3.1, 3.2.1, 3.3.
> **What to do:**
> 1. Determine the meaning of יש and enter the sentence number in the appropriate cell in the chart.
> 2. Translate the sentence.
> **Example:**
>
> יש לשים לב לעובדה כי רבות מן המסורות מופיעות בתקופות מעבר.
>
> It **should** be noted (literally: the fact should be noted) that many of the traditions appear in periods of transition.

there is/ there are	have/ has	there are those who...	can	sometimes	should/ must
					example,

1. כדי להבין סֵמֶל **יש** להכיר את העולם התרבותי אשר בו נכתבה היצירה.

2. **יֶשְׁנָם** סְמָלים מקוּבָּלים וידוּעים לכל.

3. לא לכל הסמלים **יש** פֵּירושים אחידים וחַד-מַשְׁמָעיים.

4. **יש** לבחון את ההשפעה היְשירה של רַעיונות אוטופיסטיים מסוּיָמים על בניָין מדינת ישראל.

5. **יש** שֶׁשְׁתֵי לשונות קרובות מְכוּנות בשְׁנֵי שֵׁמות.

6. שְׁתֵי הלשונות כה קרובות, עד שֶׁ**יש** הרואים בהן לָשׁון אחת.

7. **יש** בסיפורים אלו כדי ללמדֵנו על זמן סיפורם.

Glossary

1. סֵמֶל	symbol
	עולם תרבותי cultural world
	יצירה work (of art)
2. מקובלים וידועים לכל	accepted and known to all
3. פירושים	interpretations, meanings
	אחידים וחד משמעיים uniform and unambiguous
4. השפעה ישירה	direct influence
	רעיונות אוטופיים מסויימים certain utopian ideas
	בניין מדינת ישראל the building of the State of Israel
5. לשונות	languages
	מכונות called
6. כה קרובות	so close
7. זמן סיפורם	the time of their telling

8. בכל פְּעִילוּת פַּרְשָׁנִית **יש** אֶלֶמֶנְטִים יְצִירָתִיִּים.

9. לִקְשָׁרִים בֵּין הַקְּהִילּוֹת **יש** מַשְׁמָעוּת פּוֹלִיטִית רבה.

10. **יש** הַמַּפְרִיזִים בְּהַשְׁפַּעת הַאֲרָמִית עַל לשון חז"ל, וְיֵשׁ הַמְצַמְצְמִים אוֹתָהּ.

11. לִשְׁנֵי הַמְאַפְיְינִים **יש** לְהוֹסִיף מְאַפְיֵין שְׁלִישִׁי.

12. **יש** בִּידֵינוּ דּוּגְמָאוֹת הֵן מִן הַמִּקְרָא וְהֵן מִמְּקוֹרוֹת אֲחֵרִים.

13. סִיפּוּרִים אֵלֶה מַדְגִּישִׁים אֶת תְּחוּשַׁת הָרִיחוּק בֵּין מַה **שֶׁיֵּשְׁנוֹ** לְבֵין מַה שֶׁהָיָה.

14. לַתַּחְפּוֹשׂוֹת וְלַמָּסוֹרוֹת **יש** כַּנִרְאֶה גַם מָקוֹר לֹא יְהוּדִי.

Glossary

8. פעילות פרשנית	exegetic activity
אלמנטים יצירתיים	creative elements
9. קשרים בין קהילות	connections among communities
משמעות פוליטית	political significance
10. מפריזים	exaggerate
השפעת הארמית על לשון חז"ל	the influence of Aramaic on the language of Ḥazal
מצמצמים	minimize
11. מאפיינים	characteristics
להוסיף	add
12. מקרא	Bible
מקורות אחרים	other sources
13. תחושת הריחוק	sense of distance
14. תחפושות	costumes
מסורות	traditions
כנראה	apparently

Exercise #2: Identifying different meanings of אֵין

The rules to go by: see sections 1, 3.1, 3.2.2, 4.1.
What to do:
1. Determine the meaning of אֵין and enter the sentence number in the appropriate cell in the chart.
2. Translate the sentence.
Example:

אֵין לדעת אם יש יסוד להאשמות אלה.

It is **not possible** to know whether there is a basis for these accusations.

there is no(t)	do not have/ does not have	cannot/ not possible	are not	does not
		example,		

1. לתיאור זה **אֵין** כל קֶשֶׁר לרעיון העיקרי.

2. שלוש הדוגמאות שהבאתי **אֵין** בהן כדי לְמַצות את הנִמְצא במִקְרָא.

3. עֵל פי רוב **אֵין** להכיר מתוך צורתן החיצונית של המילים, אם חדשות הן או עתיקות.

4. למסורת זו **אֵין** ביטוי גלוי בספר התורה משום שיש בָּה יותר מֵאָבָק של מיתוס.

5. **אֵין** בידינו די נתונים לקבוע את מקום חיבור המִדְרש.

6. טֶקְסְט שֶ**אֵין**(א) לו תפקיד ליטורגי מוגְדר, **אֵין**(ב) לומַר עליו כי מקורו בסידור.

7. רוב הׂשָׂפות שבבסַכָּנת הַכְחָדָה **אֵינָן**(א) מְלֻווׂת בכתָב וְ**אֵין**(ב) תַעְתיק כָּתוב של הֲגָית מִלוׂתיהן.

Glossary

1.	תיאור	description
	רעיון עיקרי	main idea
2.	למצות	to exhaust
3.	על פי רוב	usually
	צורתן החיצונית של המילים	the external form of the words
4.	מסורת	tradition
	ביטוי גלוי	open expression
	אבק של מיתוס	trace (literally: dusting) of myth
5.	נתונים	data
	לקבוע את מקום חיבור המדרש	determine the place of composition of the Midrash
6.	תפקיד ליטורגי מוגדר	a defined liturgical role
	מקורו בסידור	its origin is in the Siddur (prayer book)
7.	סכנת הכחדה	in danger of extinction
	מלווות בכתב	accompanied by a writing [system]
	תעתיק כתוב של הגיית מילותיהן	written transcription of the pronunciation of their words

8. **אין**(א) לנו סֵפֶר אחד במִקְרא שׁ**אינו**(ב) מֵכיל מֵטָפוֹרוֹת.

9. **אין**(א) דרך לכַמֵּת תופָעות לְשׁוניוֹת אלה כל עוד **אין**(ב) בידינו מַאֲגָר מדוּבָּר של העברית.

Glossary

contains metaphors מכיל מטפורות	8.
to quantify linguistic phenomena לכמת תופעות לשוניות	9.
as long as כל עוד	
spoken corpus מאגר מדובר	

Exercise #3: Reconstructing sentences with an omitted יֵשׁ

> **The rules to go by:** see sections 1.1.1 and 2.2.
> **What to do:** insert יֵשׁ within each sentence.

1. לַלָּשׁוֹן הַמְשַׁמֶּשֶׁת בְּהִתְכַּתְּבוּת אֶלֶקְטְרוֹנִית אִפְיוֹנִים אֲחָדִים מִשֶּׁלָּהּ.

2. שְׁתֵּי פָּנִים לִתְפִילָתָם שֶׁל הַיְּהוּדִים.

3. פָּנִים רַבּוֹת לִדְמוּתוֹ שֶׁל שְׁלֹמֹה הַמֶּלֶךְ בַּמִּקְרָא.

4. לְכָל הַהֶיגֵּדִים הָאֵלֶּה מְכַנֶּה מְשׁוּתָּף.

5. שְׁתֵּי סִבּוֹת עִיקָרִיּוֹת לְהַשְׁפָּעָה הַזָּרָה.

6. בַּתְּקוּפָה זוֹ לַיְּהוּדִים בִּסְפָרַד הַמּוּסְלְמִית מְקוֹרוֹת פַּרְנָסָה מְגֻוָּונִים.

7. לַמָּסוֹרֶת הַמְשׁוּחְזֶרֶת בַּדָּבָר הֱיוֹתוֹ שֶׁל שִׁמְשׁוֹן עֲנָק בֶּן אֱלֹהִים וּבַת אֱנוֹשׁ מַקְבִּילוֹת בָּעוֹלָם הַתַּרְבּוּתִי הַסּוֹבֵב אֶת יִשְׂרָאֵל.

8. לַמְּסַפֵּר אֶת סִיפּוּרֵנוּ דְּרָכִים מְגֻוָּונוֹת לְשַׁכְנֵעַ אֶת הַקּוֹרֵא כִּי הַנִּיצָּחוֹן אָכֵן מוּשָׂג בְּסִיּוּעַ שָׁמַיִם.

Glossary

.1	מששמש בהתכתבות אלקטרונית	used in electronic correspondence
	איפיונים	characteristics
.2	שתי פנים	two aspects
.3	דמות	character
	מקרא	Bible
.4	היגדים	statements
	מכנה משותף	common denominator
.5	סיבות עיקריות	main reasons
	השפעה זרה	foreign influence
.6	ספרד המוסלמית	Moslem Spain
	מקורות פרנסה מגוונים	diverse sources of livelihood
.7	מסורת משוחזרת	reconstructed tradition
	בדבר	regarding
	היותו של שמשון	Samson's being
	ענק בן אלוהים ובת אנוש	a giant son of God and a mortal woman
	מקבילות	parallels
	העולם התרבותי הסובב את ישראל	the cultural world surrounding Israel
.8	מספר	narrator
	דרכים מגוונות	varied ways
	לשכנע את הקורא	convince the reader
	הניצחון אכן מושג בסיוע שמים	victory is indeed attained through divine help

9. בְּפֵירוּשָׁיו שֶׁל רַשִׁ"י לתלמוד נדונים עִנְיָינִים שֶׁלָּהֶם זיקה לְיַחְסֵי הַכְּפִיפוּת בֵּין רַב לתלמיד.

Glossary

פירושיו של רש"י לתלמוד	Rashi's commentaries to the Talmud
נדונים	discussed
עניינים	matters
זיקה	association, connection
יחסי הכפיפות בין רב לתלמיד	the relationship of subordination between student and teacher

10. DISCONTINUOUS SENTENCE CONNECTORS
קישורים מסורגים

Discontinuous sentence connectors come in two complementary parts that may be separated by any amount of text, ranging from a single word to an entire clause. Some connectors are made up of identical (repeated) elements. Others have more than one complementation option.

These connectors fulfill various semantic functions: emphasis, addition, contrast and comparison.

Although in some instances (noted in sections 2, 3, 5, 8, 10, 11, 13 and 14) complementation is optional, as a rule, when readers encounter the first component of these sentence connectors, they should scan the text forward to locate its mate.

This chapter presents the following fourteen discontinuous sentence connectors and their variants.

Discontinuous sentence connectors

1. לֹא/אֵין . . . אֶלָּא   *not . . . but rather; none other than; only; not only . . . but also*
2. לַהֲלָכָה. . . .לְמַעֲשֶׂה   *in theory . . . in fact, actually*
3. אָמְנָם . . . אַךְ   *although, even though, yet; but*
4. כְּשֵׁם שׁ- . . . כָּךְ (גַם)   *in the same way as, just as*
5. כְּכָל שׁ- . . . כֵּן/כָּךְ   *the more . . . (the more)*
6. הֵן . . . (וְ)הֵן   *as well as, both*
7. מֵחַד (גִּיסָא) וְ . . . מֵאִידָךְ (גִּיסָא) . . .   *on one hand . . . on the other*
8. בִּכְלָל . . . בִּפְרָט   *in general . . . in particular*
9. בֵּין (אִם) . . . (וּ)בֵין (אִם)   *whether . . . or*
10. הַאִם . . . אוֹ (שֶׁמָּא?)   *whether . . . or (perhaps?)*
11. בֵּין . . . לבין/וּבין/וְ-/לְ-   *between, among*
12. לֹא . . . וְלֹא   *neither . . . nor*
13. הָחֵל בְּ-/מֵ-. . . . וְכַלֵּה בְּ-   *beginning with . . . and ending with*
14. רֵאשִׁית, . . . , שֵׁנִית, . . .   *first(ly), . . . second(ly)*

Confusables

1. אֶלָּא שֶׁ-; אֶלָּא אִם (כֵּן); אֵלֶּה
2. רֵאשִׁית
3. כְּלָל, כְּכְלָל, בִּכְלָל; בְּדֶרֶךְ כְּלָל; לִכְלָל; כְּלָל-; כְּלָלִי, כּוֹלֵל, כּוֹלְלָנִי; לִכְלוֹל, לְהִכָּלֵל, לְהַכְלִיל
4. בִּפְרָט; פְּרָט לְ-; פְּרָט, פְּרִיט; פְּרָטִי
5. אָמְנָם; הַאָמְנָם
6. בִּלְבַד; לְבַד; לְבַד מִן, מִלְּבַד; וּבִלְבַד שׁ-

⚡#1   1. לא/אין ... אלא

There are three types of sentence connectors made up of a word of negation – אֵל or אֵין, לֹא –
followed by אֶלָא. Their different functions are discussed below.

1.1 לא/אין – אלא *only, none other than*

> אין כוחו **אלא** בפיו (במדבר רבה כ)
> *His might is only in his mouth* (Be-Midbar Rabbah 20)
>
> אין זקן **אלא** חכם (קידושין לב)
> *[The meaning of] old is none other than a sage* (Kiddushin 32)

This emphatic structure implicitly rejects one alternative, to explicitly accept and affirm another.
The sum of לֹא/אֵין and אֶלָא is, then, positive.

Both לֹא (or אֵין) and אֶלָא may be omitted without altering the meaning of the sentence. For
example: כוחו (הוא) בפיו=אין כוחו אלא בפיו.

If אֶלָא alone is omitted, the sentence remains grammatical, but with an opposite intent (e.g.,
אין כוחו בפיו *his might is not in his mouth*).

1.1.1 The two components, the negating particle לֹא/אֵין and אֶלָא, may be adjacent (examples
1–2), or separated (examples 3–4).

1.1.2 In translation, the negating particle is ignored. Whether the translation should be *only*
(to diminish) or *none other than* (to emphasize) depends on the context.

---

(1) אִיתוּר דֶּרֶךְ הַנְּדוּדִים שֶׁל בְּנֵי יִשְׂרָאֵל בַּמִּדְבָּר **אֵינוֹ אֶלָא** מְשׁוֹעָר.
Locating the route of the wanderings of the Israelites in the desert <u>is only</u>
conjectural.

The possibility that the route of the Israelites in the desert is known – rather than conjectural –
is implicitly rejected.
With the removal of אֵינוֹ אֶלָא the sentence retains its meaning:
איתור דרך הנדודים של בני ישראל במדבר [הוא] משוער
If אֶלָא is omitted, an opposite meaning is conveyed:
איתור דרך הנדודים של בני ישראל במדבר אינו משוער *locating the route of the wanderings
of the Israelites in the desert is not conjectural.*

(2) הַחְלָטָתוֹ שֶׁל "הֶחָבֵר," לַעֲלוֹת לְאֶרֶץ-יִשְׂרָאֵל וּפְרֵידָתוֹ מִמֶּלֶךְ הַכּוּזָרִים **אֵינָן אֶלָא** הַחְלָטָתוֹ
שֶׁל הַמְּשׁוֹרֵר עַצְמוֹ וּפְרֵידָתוֹ מִמּוֹלַדְתּוֹ.
The decision of the "friend" to go to the Land of Israel and his leave-taking from
the King of Kuzar <u>are none other than</u> the decision of the poet himself and his own
leave-taking from his homeland.

(3) **אֵין** בֵּית הכנסת בָּאָרֶץ **אֶלָא** מקום תפילה בלבד.
In Israel, the synagogue is a place <u>only</u> for prayer.

The sentence implicitly rejects the possibility that the synagogue in Israel has uses other than prayer. The word בלבד is added for emphasis. If both אֵין and אֶלָא are omitted, the meaning remains the same:
בית הכנסת בארץ (הוא) מקום תפילה בלבד
If אֶלָא alone is omitted, the opposite meaning is expressed:
the synagogue is not only a place of prayer. אין בית הכנסת בארץ מקום תפילה בלבד

(4) הַתְקָפוֹת הטילים **לֹא** נִסְתַּיְּמוּ **אֶלָא** לְאַחַר כִּיבּוּשׁ הָאֵזוֹר בִּידֵי הַצָּבָא.
The missile attacks ended <u>only</u> after the occupation of the area by the army.

לֹא (rather than אֵין) is used when the predicate is a verb in the past or the future (see also example 6).

1.2 לֹא/אֵין/אַל (א) אֶלָא/כִּי אִם (ב) *not (a) but rather (b)*

לֹא יִקָּרֵא שִׁמְךָ עוֹד יַעֲקֹב **כִּי אִם** יִשְׂרָאֵל יִהְיֶה שְׁמֶךָ, וַיִּקְרָא אֶת שְׁמוֹ יִשְׂרָאֵל. (בראשית לה י)
Thy name shall not be called any more Jacob, but Israel shall be thy name; and he called his name Israel (Genesis 35.10)

אַל תסתכל בַּקַּנְקַן **אֶלָא** בְּמַה שֶׁיֵּשׁ בּוֹ (משנה אבות ד כז)
Do not look at the pitcher, but at what is in it (Mishnah Aboth 4, 27)

With the words לֹא, אֵין or אַל one alternative is explicitly rejected in order to accept a second one, introduced by אֶלָא or כִּי אִם, both translated as *but (rather)*.

כִּי אִם is biblical, אֶלָא is Mishnaic. In modern Hebrew they are used interchangeably.

In contrast to 1.1 above, the two components of the connector link two parallel phrases (e.g., יִקָּרֵא שִׁמְךָ יעקב – ישראל יִהְיֶה שְׁמֶךָ).
   Another difference is that the omission of אֶלָא (or כִּי אִם) will render the sentence ungrammatical (e.g., אל תסתכל בקנקן במה שיש בו*).

The parallel phrases are shaded:

(5) רבים באו לִידֵי הָרַעְיוֹן, שהַגְמוּל העִיקָרִי **אֵינוֹ** בעולם הזה, **אֶלָא** בעולם הבָּא.
Many came to the belief (literally: notion) that the main reward is <u>not</u> in this world, <u>but rather</u> in the next world.

(6) בִּימֵי הַלֵּוִי **לֹא** שָׁלְטוּ **מוסלמים** בירושלים כי אם **נוצרים**.
In the days of Halevi, <u>not</u> Moslems, <u>but rather</u> Christians, ruled Jerusalem.

(7) רוּבָּהּ הגדול של האגָדָה התלמודית **אינו** עומד ברשות עַצמו **אלא** מְשָׁרֵת את המקרא.
The bulk of the Talmudic Aggadah does <u>not</u> stand on its own, <u>but rather</u> serves the Bible.

1.3 (ב) **לֹא רק** (א) **אלא גם/אלא אַף/כי אם גם**
(ב) **אלא גם/אלא אַף/כי אם גם** (א) **לֹא זֹאת/זוֹ בִּלְבַד שֶׁ-**
not only (a) but also (b)

This connector is additive and emphatic: both alternatives are explicitly stated and accepted. The words גם and אַף may not appear (אלא . . . לֹא רק; example 11).

(8) היא הייתה מְשׁוֹרֶרֶת שהושפְּעָה **לֹא רק** מֵהַיַהֲדוּת **כי אם גם** מֵהַנַצְרוּת.
She was a poet who was influenced <u>not only</u> by Judaism, <u>but also</u> by Christianity.

(9) בְּמֶשֶׁךְ רוב התקופה מאז חוּרבן בית שֵׁנִי ועד תְחִיָּיתָהּ בסוף המאה ה-19, השתמשו בעברית **לֹא רק** כלשון קריאה **אלא גם** כלשון לכְתיבה.
During most of the period since the destruction of the Second Temple and its revival at the end of the 19th century, Hebrew was used <u>not only</u> as the language of reading, <u>but also</u> of writing.

(10) **לא זו בלבד** שֶׁמוּתָר, לפי דַעַת חז"ל, לשַׁנוֹת ולְהוֹסִיף בְּ"נוּסַח הקָבוּעַ" של התפילה, **אלא אַף** רָצוּי לַעֲשׂוֹת כֵּן.
<u>Not only</u> is it permissible, according to Ḥazal, to change and add to the fixed version of the prayer, <u>but it is also</u> desirable to do so.

(11) בְּעָיית הַהֲגירה הַהֲמוֹנית היתה **לֹא רק** של יהוּדֵי גֶרמניה, שנרְדְפוּ על ידי המִשְׁטָר הנאצי, **אלא** של מיליוֹני יהוּדֵי פולין וגם יהוּדֵי הוּנגריה.
The problem of mass immigration was <u>not only</u> that of German Jews, who were persecuted by the Nazi regime, <u>but [also]</u> of millions of Polish Jews and also the Jews of Hungary.

2. לַהֲלָכָה . . . לְמַעֲשֶׂה *in theory…in fact, actually*

2.1 This two-part adverbial expression presents, side by side, two propositions: the first one is rejected in favor of the second, which states the true state of affairs as the speaker sees it.
The rejected proposition may be introduced by any of the following synonymous expressions:

⚠️Note that the expression הלכה למעשה *in practice*, serves to reinforce, rather than contradict. In this expression the two words must follow each other without interruption.

לַהֲלָכָה	*in theory*
לִכְאוֹרָה	*apparently, supposedly*
כִּבְיָכוֹל	*so to speak, as it were, supposedly*
לְמַרְאִית עַיִן	*apparently, on the surface*
בְּמַבָּט רִאשׁוֹן	*at first glance*
עַל פָּנָיו	*on its face*

The speaker's view can be (optionally) affirmed with the expressions listed below:

לְמַעֲשֶׂה	*in fact, actually*
בְּפוֹעַל	*in practice, really*
לַאֲמִיתּוֹ שֶׁל דָּבָר	*in truth*
בְּעֶצֶם	*in fact.*

2.2 אוּלָם/אַךְ/אֲבָל (and the more formal בְּרַם) – all meaning *but* – may be used in the second clause instead of, or in addition to, the confirmatory expressions listed above.

---

(12) הַסֵּפֶר בָּנוּי מִשְּׁלוֹשָׁה חֲלָקִים, שֶׁכָּל אֶחָד מֵהֶם הוּא **לִכְאוֹרָה** סִיפּוּר עַצְמָאִי, **אַךְ לְמַעֲשֶׂה** שְׁלוֹשְׁתָּם קְשׁוּרִים זֶה בָּזֶה.
The book is constructed of three parts, each of which is <u>seemingly</u> an independent story, <u>but in fact</u> the three of them are interconnected.

(13) **לַהֲלָכָה** אֵין הֶבְדֵּל בֵּין הַשְּׁנַיִים **אוּלָם** אֵין הַדָּבָר כָּךְ.
<u>In theory</u>, there is no difference between the two, <u>but</u> this is not so.

2.3 The words לִכְאוֹרה and כביכול may be used to qualify a single noun or adjective (rather than an entire idea unit) in the sense of *supposed, so called, as it were*. In this role, they usually appear directly after the qualified word.
For example:

הַצְלָחָה כביכול *supposed success,* בלתי-מְשׁוּחָד כביכול *supposedly unbiased,*
בחירה חופשית-לכאורה *supposedly free will.*

This meaning may also be conveyed (less formally) with כמו or כְּאִילוּ, appearing <u>before</u> the noun or adjective (e.g., כמו-סתירה *supposed/so called contradiction*).

---

(14) הַפְּעוּלָה הַפְּשׁוּטָה **לכאורה**, שֶׁל יְצִיאַת אדם מבֵּיתו לְתקוּפת-מָה מְכִילָה בתוֹכָה פְּרידות רבות-עוֹצְמָה.
The <u>supposedly</u> simple act of leaving one's home for a short period of time contains powerful partings.

(15) בסְפרו הוא מְיישֵׁב את הסְתירות **לכאורה** הקַיָּימות בֵּין הדָּת והפילוֹסוֹפיה.
In his book he resolves the <u>supposed</u> contradictions that exist between religion and philosophy.

3. אֲמְנָם . . . אַךְ/אֲבָל/אוּלָם/אֶלָּא שֶׁ- *although, even though, yet; but*

3.1 This expression is used to privilege the second opinion over the first one.
In translation into English, the expressions *though, although,* or *yet* render אמנם; alternatively, אמנם can be ignored and *but* would be used to connect the clauses (example 17).

> Note that אֲמְנָם is pronounced /omnam/ and therefore sometimes spelled with וי"ו: אומנם.

---

(16) הַיְּהוּדִים הָיוּ אמנם בַּעֲלֵי זְכוּיוֹת אֶזְרָח, אַךְ לֹא זָכוּ לְשִׁוְיוֹן פּוֹלִיטִי מָלֵא.
Although the Jews did have citizenship rights, they did not gain full political equality.
OR: The Jews had citizenship rights, <u>yet</u> did not gain full political equality.

(17) הַמְּשׁוֹרֵר אמנם מִשְׁתַּמֵּשׁ בְּבִדְיָה, אבל לְמַעֲשֶׂה הוּא מַעֲבִיר אֶת הָאֱמֶת בְּאֹפֶן מְדֻיָּק, בְּשָׁעָה שֶׁהַכְּרוֹנִיקוֹן אמנם נִרְאֶה כְּדוֹבֵר אֱמֶת אבל לְמַעֲשֶׂה דְּבָרָיו אֵינָם מְדֻיָּקִים.
Even though the poet makes use of fiction, he in fact communicates the truth accurately, while the chronicler of events appears to be telling the truth, <u>but</u> in fact his words are not accurate.

#2 **3.2** Note that when אמנם appears on its own, not complemented by a word of negation, it has a confirmatory meaning: *truly, indeed, in fact.* It may appear at the beginning of the clause or in the middle. The word אָכֵן is a close synonym (example 19).

---

(18) הֶעְדֵּרָן שֶׁל דֻּגְמָאוֹת אמנם מַחֲלִישׁ אֶת טִעוּנָיו.
The absence of examples <u>indeed</u> weakens his arguments.

(19) בֵּית הַמִּשְׁפָּט קָבַע כִּי הַסֵּפֶר הוּא אכן זִיּוּף.
The court determined that the book was <u>indeed</u> a forgery.

---

4. כְּשֵׁם שֶׁ-...כֵּן/כָּךְ (גַּם), כְּ-...כֵּן/כָּךְ (גַּם), כְּדֶרֶךְ שֶׁ-...כֵּן (גַּם), מָה...אַף/גַּם
in the same way as, just as...so (also)

These sentence connectors have a comparative function.

---

(20) כְּשֵׁם שֶׁקָּשֶׁה לַעֲמוֹד בְּדִיּוּק עַל טִיבוֹ שֶׁל הַשֵּׁם "אגדה," כָּךְ קָשֶׁה לְהַגְדִּיר גַּם אֶת מַהוּתָה.
<u>Just as</u> it is difficult to determine exactly the nature of the name "Aggadah" <u>so also</u> it is difficult to define its character.

> (21) **כשם שאין** בסיפור דיוק בזמנים, **כן** אין דיוק במֶמַד המֶרחָב.
> <u>Just as</u> there is in the story no chronological accuracy, <u>so also</u> there is no accuracy in the spatial dimension.
>
> (22) **כתנ״ך**, **כן גם** "מורֶה נבוכים" מופיע לפנינו בצורה מסורתית עם פירושים המכַתרים אותו.
> <u>Like</u> the Bible, <u>so also</u> "Guide for the Perplexed" appears in a traditional form with commentaries framing it.
>
> (23) **מה** שָם מְשַמשים המכונית ובַעל-המוסָך כסמָלים של אֶנֶרגיה, **כך** כאן מופיעה אותה מַעֲרֶכֶת סמָלים במשמעות דומָה.
> <u>Just as</u> there the car and the garage owner serve as symbols of energy, <u>so also</u> here, the same set of symbols appears with similar meaning.
>
> (24) **מה** האָדָם אתה מוצא באופְיו קַוֵוי-יְסוד וקַוֵוי-מִשנֶה, שלא תמיד הם מתיַישבים עם קַוֵוי היסוד, **אף** הלָשון כך.
> <u>Just as</u> you find in man's character primary traits and secondary traits that are not always congruent with the primary ones, <u>so also</u> in a language.

5. כְּכָל שֶ- ... (כֵּן/כָּךְ) *the more... (the more)*

This is an expression of extent; complementation with כן or כך is optional.

> (25) **כְּכָל שֶ**גּוֹבֶרֶת ההִתעַנינות של הדור הצעיר בשוֹאָה, **כך** מֵעִזים יותר ויותר אנשים צעירים "לָגַעַת" בה.
> <u>The more</u> the interest of the young generation in the Holocaust grows, <u>so</u> more and more young people dare "touch" it.
>
> (26) **ככל ש**גדֵלות הדרישות מֵהלומֵד, גָדֵל הלַחַץ החֶברָתי וגובֶרֶת החֲרָדָה.
> <u>The more</u> the demands on the learner increase, [the more] the social pressure and the anxiety increase.

6. הֵן ... (ו)הֵן *as well as, both*

6.1 Like לֹא רק ... אלָא גם (1.3 above), this is an additive connector, synonymous with the more colloquial גם ... וגם. The וי"ו between the two (sometimes three) parts of the expression may be omitted.

⚠️ Note that הֵן in this structure is unrelated to the feminine pronoun הֵן.

(27) ‫הן אֵירופה והן אַסיה קיבלו את שמן מאישה.‬

<u>Both</u> Europe and Asia were named after a woman (literally: received their name from a woman).

(28) ‫הָהָר מְהַוֶּה מוֹקד תַּיָּירוּתי הן בקיץ, הן בחורף, והן בעונות האָביב והסְתָיו.‬

The mountain is a tourist attraction in the summer <u>and</u> the winter, <u>as well as</u> in the spring and fall seasons.

6.2 The words כְּאֶחָד (masculine) and כְּאַחַת (feminine) also mean *both*. They are usually used when the joined entities are in contrast. Another synonym is גַּם יַחַד; it may or may not indicate contrast.

(29) ‫חוקרים רבים, יהודים ולא יהודים כאחד, נוטים עֲדַיין לְהַבחין בין היסטוריה "כְּלָלית" להיסטוריה "יהודית".‬

Many researchers, Jewish and non-Jewish <u>alike</u>, still tend to distinguish between "general" history and "Jewish" history.

כאחד agrees in gender with חוקרים.

(30) ‫לְיצירות אלה הָייתה חשיבות מדעית ותֵיאוֹלוֹגית כאחת.‬

These works had scientific <u>as well as</u> theological importance.

כאחת agrees in gender with the feminine חשיבות.

(31) ‫לשליט הָייתה סַמכות בנושאים דָּתיים וחילוניים גם יחד.‬

The ruler had authority in <u>both</u> religious and secular matters.

7. מֵחַד (גִּיסָא) וּ . . . מֵאִידָךְ (גִּיסָא), מִצַּד אֶחָד וּ . . . מִצַּד שֵׁנִי/אַחֵר, מִכָּאן וּ . . . מִכָּאן, מִזֶּה וּ . . . מִזֶּה
on the one hand . . . on the other (hand)

With these expressions, two points of view or alternatives are presented.
מִנֶּגֶד *in contrast* is an alternative for מצד שני/אחר *on the other hand* (example 38).

(32) ‫במהלך חייו הוא מָשַׁךְ קולות רבים של מַעריצים, מצד אחד, וֹשל מְבַקרים חריפים, מצד שני.‬

In the course of his life, he attracted the voices of many admirers, <u>on one hand</u>, and sharp critics, <u>on the other</u>.

---

(33) **מחד גיסא** הִגְבִּירוּ עוֹלֵי גֶּרְמַנְיָה מְאוֹד אֶת כּוֹחוֹ שֶׁל הַיִּשּׁוּב; **מֵאִידָךְ גִּיסָא**, הֵם הִתְבַּדְּלוּ מִמֶּנּוּ וְשִׁמְרוּ אֶת תַּרְבּוּתָם.

On one hand, the immigrants from Germany strengthened greatly the Yishuv, <u>on the other hand</u>, they kept themselves apart from it and preserved their culture.

(34) אוֹפְּטִימִיּוּת **מֵחַד גִּיסָא** וְאֱמוּנָה כִּי הַחִינּוּךְ מְעַצֵּב אֶת הָאָדָם **מֵאִידָךְ גִּיסָא** הֵן תְּכוּנוֹת יְסוֹד שֶׁל כּוֹתְבֵי הָאוּטוֹפִיּוֹת הַחִינּוּכִיּוֹת.

Optimism, <u>on the one hand</u>, and a belief that education shapes man, <u>on the other</u>, are basic characteristics of the writers of educational utopias.

(35) הַמִּשְׁפָּחָה הַמָּסוֹרְתִּית הוּשְׁפְּעָה מִפְּעוּלָּתָם שֶׁל גּוֹרְמִים פְּנִימִיִּים: הַחֲסִידוּת **מִכָּאן** וְהַלַּמְדָנוּת **מִכָּאן.**

The traditional family was influenced by the actions of internal factors: Ḥasidism <u>on the one hand</u> and Torah study <u>on the other</u>.

(36) לְאוֹר הַכָּתוּב לְעֵיל נָקֵל לְהָבִין אֶת תַּהֲלִיךְ הִתְפַּתְחוּתוֹ שֶׁל בֵּית הַכְּנֶסֶת בָּעֵת הַחֲדָשָׁה בָּאָרֶץ **מִזֶּה**, וּבַתְּפוּצוֹת – וּבְעִיקָר בְּאַרְצוֹת הַבְּרִית – **מִזֶּה.**

In light of the above, it is easy to understand the process of development of the synagogue in the modern era in Israel <u>on one hand</u> and in the Diaspora – and particularly in the United States – <u>on the other</u>.

(37) כַּלְכָּלַת הַמְּדִינָה מְשַׂגְשֶׂגֶת בְּיַחַס לִמְדִינוֹת אַפְרִיקָה הָאֲחֵרוֹת. **מִנֶּגֶד**, הַמִּשְׁטָר נוֹטֶה לְרוֹדָנוּת וְהוּאַשַּׁם בְּשַׁחִיתוּת.

The economy of the country is flourishing in relation to other African countries. <u>On the other hand</u>, the regime leans toward tyranny and has been accused of corruption.

---

8. בִּכְלָל ... בִּפְרַט *in general... in particular*

The order of the components is not fixed: בפרט ... בכלל or בכלל ... בפרט.
בפרט *in particular, particularly* may also appear on its own, unaccompanied by בכלל (example 39). Synonymous words are בעיקר and במיוחד, בייחוד *specially, mainly*.
Note also the expression מן הפרט אל הכלל *from the particular to the general.*

---

(38) הַמּוּזֵאוֹן מַצִּיג אֶת הַהִיסְטוֹרְיָה שֶׁל הַיְּהוּדִים בְּהוֹלַנְד **בִּפְרַט** וּבְרַחֲבֵי הָעוֹלָם **בִּכְלָל.**

The museum presents the history of Jews in Holland <u>in particular</u> and throughout the world more generally.

(39) הַמִּיתוֹסִים הַכְּתוּבִים בְּאַכָּדִית מוּשְׁוִוים לְעִתִּים קְרוֹבוֹת לְסִיפּוּרֵי הַתַּנַ"ךְ (**בִּפְרָט** לְסִיפּוּרֵי סֵפֶר בְּרֵאשִׁית).

The myths written in Accadian are often compared to the stories of the Bible (in <u>particular</u> to the stories of Genesis).

9. בֵּין (אָם)...(וּ)בֵין (אָם), בֵּין שֶׁ-...(וּ)בֵין שֶׁ-...., בֵּין שֶׁ-...אוֹ, אָם...(וּ)אָם #3
whether...or

These expressions serve to introduce two alternatives that are considered equally valid.

---

(40) נְשִׂיאַת שֵׁמוֹת זָרִים הִיא בִּיטוּי לְמַגָּע בֵּין-תַּרְבּוּתִי, **בֵּין** שִׁטְחִי **בֵין** עָמוֹק.
Bearing foreign names is an expression of an inter-cultural contact, <u>whether</u> superficial <u>or</u> profound.

(41) תלמיד הוא אדם שלומד, **בֵּין אם** זה נַעֲשֶׂה בְּעֶזְרַת מורים **ובֵין אם** זה נעשה באופן עַצְמָאי.
A student is someone who learns, <u>whether</u> it is done with the help of teachers <u>or</u> independently.

(42) הַמֶּמְשָׁלָה הִמשיכה לראות ביהודים אֶלֶמֶנְט מסוכָּן – **בֵּין שהם** קָפִּיטָלִיסטים **ובֵין שהם** קוֹמוניסטים.
The government continued to view the Jews as a dangerous element – <u>whether</u> they were capitalists <u>or</u> communists.

(43) **בֵּין שׁ**ניצחו הנוצרים **אוֹ** המוסְלְמים, היישוב היהודי היה הסוֹבל.
<u>Whether</u> the Christians <u>or</u> the Moslems won, it was the Jewish community that was the sufferer.

(44) בדתוֹת שונות קַיֶּימֶת הָאֱמוּנָה שמַּעֲשָׂיו של אדם, **אם** טובים **אם** רעים, קובעים את גוֹרָלו.
In various religions there exists the belief that man's deeds, <u>whether</u> good <u>or</u> bad, determine his fate.

---

10. הַאָם....אוֹ (שֶׁמָּא?) *whether...or (perhaps?)*

Two equally valid alternatives are presented, phrased as a (rhetorical) question.
The addition of שמא *could it be that, perhaps* before the second alternative implies doubt or lesser desirability.

> By itself, שמא can be rendered as *lest, for fear that*; it often appears after words that express worry or concern.

---

(45) אחת משאלות היְסוֹד של התֵיאוֹלוֹגְיה היא **הַאָם** האדם רַשַׁאי לבְחור בין טוב לְרע **אוֹ שמא** נגזר עליו הכל משָׁמַיִם.
One of the basic questions of theology is <u>whether</u> man is permitted to choose between good and evil, <u>or perhaps</u> everything is predetermined from heaven.

---

(46) פַּרְשְׁנֵי הַמִּקְרָא נֶחְלְקוּ בִּשְׁאֵלָה **אִם** הַבָּנִים רַק הוּעֲבְרוּ בָּאֵשׁ **אוֹ שֶׁמָּא** הֵם נִשְׂרְפוּ חַיִּים בְּמְדוּרוֹת הַפּוּלְחָן.

The commentators on the Bible disagreed on <u>whether</u> the sons were just passed through fire <u>or perhaps</u> were burnt alive in the ritual bonfires.

✗#3   11. -‏בֵּין . . . לְבֵין/וּבֵין/ו-/ל‏ *between; among*

11.1 Several complements for בֵּין *between* are possible: -‏לְבֵין, וּבֵין, ו-, ל‏. All are translated as *and*.

By itself (that is, without complementation), בֵּין is translated as *among* (examples 51–53). The inflected forms בֵּינָם/בֵּינָן (example 51) and בֵּינֵיהֶם/בֵּינֵיהֶן (example 53) are interchangeable.

(47) סֵפֶר בְּרֵאשִׁית מְסַפֵּר לָנוּ עַל מַעַרְכוֹת הַיְחָסִים **בֵּין** קַיִן **וְהֶבֶל**, יַעֲקֹב **וְעֵשָׂו**, וְיוֹסֵף **וְאֶחָיו**.

The Book of Genesis tells us about the relationships <u>between</u> Cain <u>and</u> Abel, Jacob <u>and</u> Esau, and Joseph <u>and</u> his brothers.

(48) לַמְרוֹת הַדִּמְיוֹן **בֵּין** הָאֳמָנוּת הַיְהוּדִית **לְאֳמָנוּת** הַכְּלָלִית, קַיָּמִים הֶבְדֵּלִים קַלִּים **בֵּינֵיהֶן**.

Despite the similarity <u>between</u> Jewish <u>and</u> non-Jewish art, there exist slight differences <u>between them</u>.

(49) הַדִּמְיוֹן **שֶׁבֵּין** הַסִּיפּוּר הֶחָדָשׁ **לְבֵין** מְקוֹרוֹ הוּא כַּדִּמְיוֹן **שֶׁבֵּין** דְּמוּת וּבְבוֹאָתָהּ בַּמַּרְאָה.

The similarity <u>between</u> the new story <u>and</u> its source is akin to the similarity <u>between</u> a figure <u>and</u> its reflection in a mirror.

In the same sentence, the writer used two complementation options: ‏בֵּין . . . לְבֵין‏ and ‏בֵּין . . . ו‏.

(50) יֵשׁ לְהַבְחִין **בֵּין** אַגָּדָה הַנִּזְקֶקֶת לְתַנַ"ךְ, **לְבֵין** אַגָּדָה הִיסְטוֹרִית הַמְסַפֶּרֶת עַל אִישִׁים וְעַל מְאוֹרָעוֹת מִן הַתְּקוּפָה הַבָּתַר-מִקְרָאִית, **לְבֵין** הָאַגָּדָה הַמּוּסָרִית-דִּידַקְטִית.

A distinction should be made <u>between </u>an Aggadah that is based on the bible, a historical Aggdah that tells about people and events from the post-biblical period, <u>and</u> the moral-didactic Aggadah.

This sentence contains a three-way comparison.

(51) לַקְּשָׁרִים **בֵּין** הַקְּהִילוֹת הַשּׁוֹנוֹת וּבֵין לְבֵין הַחֵלֶק שֶׁל הָעָם שֶׁנּוֹתַר בַּמּוֹלֶדֶת יֵשׁ מַשְׁמָעוּת פּוֹלִיטִית רַבָּה.

The ties <u>among</u> the various communities, and <u>between them and</u> the portion of the people that remained in the homeland, have great political significance.

(52) **בֵּין** מְיַיסְדֵי הַקְּבוּצָה הָיוּ אָב וּבְנוֹ.
Among the founders of the group were a father and his son.

(53) בְּסוֹף יְמֵי בַּיִת שֵׁנִי דָּחֲקָה הָאֲרָמִית אֶת רַגְלֵיהֶן שֶׁל הַשָּׂפוֹת הַלְּאוּמִיּוֹת **וּבֵינֵיהֶן** גַם הָעִבְרִית.
At the end of the Second Temple period, Aramaic encroached upon the national languages, among them also Hebrew.

11.2 The questions ?...לְבֵין ... בֵּין מַה and ? מַה בֵּינֵיהֶם/ן, ask: *what is the relationship, what is the connection, between...?*

11.3 בֵּין- also functions as the semantic prefix *inter-.*[1]
For example: בֵּין-תַּרְבּוּתִי *intercultural* (example 40 above), בֵּין-תְּחוּמִי *inter-disciplinary.*

(54) הֶיעָדֵר קֶשֶׁר **בֵּין-אִישִׁי** אוֹהֵב **בֵּין** הַתִּינוֹק **לַמְטַפֵּל** בּוֹ גּוֹרֵם לְנָכוּת רִגְשִׁית קָשָׁה.
The absence of a loving inter-personal connection between the baby and its caretaker causes severe emotional disability.

In this example, בֵּין appears twice: as a semantic prefix, *inter-* and adjective, *between.*

11.4 Note the following expressions with בֵּין: בֵּין הַשְּׁאָר, בֵּין הַיֶּתֶר *among other things,* כָּךְ וּבֵין כָּךְ *in any case.*

12. לֹא...וְלֹא *neither...nor*

With this expression, both alternatives are rejected.

(55) לְלֹא הִתְבּוֹנְנוּת קְבוּעָה וּשִׁיטָתִית הַנַּעֲשֶׂה בַּלָּשׁוֹן, אֵין **לֹא** הַתִּכְנוּן **וְלֹא** הַתִּקְנוּן אֶפְשָׁרִיִּים.

Without a regular and systematic scrutiny of what is happening in the language, neither planning nor standardization is possible.

The word אֵין negates the predicate אֶפְשָׁרִיִּים while לֹא...וְלֹא negate the subjects of the clause, תִקְנוּן and תכנון.

---

[1] See also Chapter 4, 5.

13. הֵחֵל בְּ-/מִ- . . . וְכַלֵּה בְּ-/וּגְמוֹר בְּ-/וְעַד
beginning in/with . . . and ending in/with; from . . . to/and up to
לְמִן . . . וְעַד *from . . . and till*
הַמְשֵׁךְ בְּ- . . . / עֲבוֹר לְ- . . . /דֶּרֶךְ *continuing with*

The adverbial expressions הֵחֵל מִ-/בְּ- and לְמִן *beginning with* mark the beginning of a series of events; וְעַד, וּגְמוֹר בְּ-, וְכַלֵּה בְּ- *and until, and ending with* mark the last in the series. To indicate an intermediate point, דֶּרֶךְ *through*, הַמְשֵׁךְ בְּ-, עֲבוֹר לְ- *continue with* are used.

---

(56) תֵּיאוּרֵי הַשָּׂכָר בָּעוֹלָם הַבָּא מְגֻוָּנִים מְאוֹד – **הָחֵל בַּתֵּיאוּר** מְגֻשָׁם וְקוֹנְקְרֶטִי **וְעַד לַתֵּיאוּר** הָרוּחָנִי.
The descriptions of the rewards in the afterlife are very varied – <u>from</u> the physical and concrete <u>to</u> the spiritual.

(57) לְהַלָּן יֵיעָשֶׂה נִסָּיוֹן לִסְקֹר אֶת מוּשַׂג הַ"יַּלְדוּת" בָּעַם הַיְּהוּדִי בְּעֵת הָעַתִּיקָה **הָחֵל מִן** הַמְּקוֹרוֹת הַמִּקְרָאִיִּים **וְכַלֵּה** בַּמְּקוֹרוֹת הָרַבָּנִיִּים מִסִּפְרוּת הַמִּשְׁנָה וְהַתַּלְמוּד.
What follows is an attempt to survey the Jewish concept of "childhood" in antiquity, <u>beginning with</u> the biblical sources and <u>ending with</u> the Rabbinical sources from the Mishnah and Talmud.

(58) הַיַּחַס לְעוֹרְכוֹת דִּין הָיָה מִקְצוֹעִי פָּחוֹת, **הָחֵל בָּעֵדִים** הַמּוֹפִיעִים בַּמִּשְׁפָּט, **עֲבוֹר לְעוֹרְכֵי** הַדִּין הַיְּרִיבִים **וְכַלֵּה בְּבֵית** הַמִּשְׁפָּט עַצְמוֹ.
The attitude to women lawyers was less professional, <u>beginning with</u> the witnesses who appeared at the trial, <u>continuing with</u> the opposing lawyers and <u>ending with</u> the court itself.

(59) מְאַפְיֵין מֶרְכָּזִי שֶׁל הַפּוֹלִיטִיקָה **הָחֵל מֵאֶמְצַע** הַמֵּאָה הַ-19 וּבְיֶתֶר שְׂאֵת בַּמַּחֲצִית הַמֵּאָה הָאַחֲרוֹנָה הוּא הִשְׁתַּתְּפוּת הַצִּבּוּר הָרְחָב בַּחַיִּים הַפּוֹלִיטִיִּים.
A central characteristic of politics <u>beginning with</u> the middle of the 19th century and increasingly in the second half of the last century is the participation of the public in the political life.

הֵחֵל מִ- has no end-point complementation because the process is ongoing.

---

14. רֵאשִׁית, . . . שֵׁנִית, . . . *first(ly), . . . second(ly), . . .*

To introduce the first point in a series, רֵאשִׁית *first(ly)* (sometimes רִאשׁוֹנָה, but never רִאשׁוֹן) is used. The second point is introduced by שֵׁנִית *second(ly)* (rather than שֵׁנִי or שְׁנִיָּה *second*), and thereafter, the feminine ordinal numbers are employed (e.g., שְׁלִישִׁית *third(ly)*, רְבִיעִית *fourth(ly)*).

---

(60) **רֵאשִׁית**, נַגְדִּיר אֶת הַמּוּשָׂג, **שֵׁנִית**, נַצִּיג דֻּגְמָאוֹת אֲחָדוֹת.
<u>First</u>, we will define the concept, <u>secondly</u>, present several examples.

⚠️ Note that on its own, the adverb שֵׁנִית (or בַּשֵׁנִית) means *the second time, again* (e.g., שנית מסדה לא תיפול *Masada shall not fall again*).

Confusables

1. אֶלָּה ;(כֵּן) אֶלָּא אִם ;-אֶלָּא שֶׁ

1.1 -אֶלָּא שֶׁ
-אֶלָּא שֶׁ is the equivalent of *but*; in contrast to אֶלָּא *but rather*, it is not accompanied by a word of negation.

> (61) בְּמָקוֹר הָיוּ בְּסֵדֶר שֶׁבַע מַסֶּכְתּוֹת, **אֶלָּא שֶׁמַּסֶּכֶת נְזִיקִין** שֶׁפְּתָחָה אֶת הַסֵּדֶר פּוּצְלָה לִשְׁלוֹשׁ בִּשֶׁל גוֹדְלָה הָרַב.
> Originally there were in the order (of the Mishnah) seven tractates, <u>but</u> the Tractate Nezikin was split in three because of its large size.

1.2 אֶלָּא אִם (כֵּן) *unless*

> (62) הַמּוֹנַרְךְ שׁוֹלֵט עַד מוֹתוֹ, **אֶלָּא אִם** הוּא מוּפָּל וְתַפְקִידוֹ נִלְקָח מִמֶּנּוּ.
> The monarch rules till his death <u>unless</u> he is toppled and his role is taken away from him.
>
> (63) אֲמָנַת זְכוּיוֹת הַיֶּלֶד מַגְדִּירָה יֶלֶד כְּכָל יְצוּר אֱנוֹשִׁי מִתַּחַת לְגִיל 18, **אֶלָּא אִם כֵּן** חוֹק הַמְּדִינָה קוֹבֵעַ גִּיל צָעִיר יוֹתֵר.
> The Convention on the Rights of the Child defines a child as any human being below the age of 18, <u>unless</u> the law of the state sets a younger age.

1.3 אֵלֶּה
Make sure to distinguish אֶלָּא (pronounced: /ela/) from the demonstrative pronoun אֵלֶּה *these* (pronounced: /ele/).

𐀪#4   2. רֵאשִׁית

The adverb רֵאשִׁית *first(ly)* should be distinguished from:

(a) The feminine adjective רָאשִׁית (pronounced: /rashit/) *primary, main, principal* (e.g., הַסִּבָּה הָרָאשִׁית *the main reason*).

(b) The noun רֵאשִׁית *beginning* (e.g., רֵאשִׁית הַמֵּאָה הָעֶשְׂרִים *the beginning of the twentieth century,* רֵאשִׁית חַיָּיו *the beginning of his life, his early life*). Hence בְּרֵאשִׁית *at the beginning.*

✗#5 **3.** כְּלָל, בִּכְלָל; לֹא...כְּלָל ;בִּכְלָל; בְּדֶרֶךְ כְּלָל; לִכְלָל, כְּלָל-; כְּלָלִי, כּוֹלֵל, כּוֹלְלָנִי; לִכְלוֹל, לְהִכָּלֵל, לְהַכְלִיל

3.1 As a noun, כְּלָל means *rule*: hence יוצא מן הכלל *exception to the rule; exceptional*, and בִּכְלָל *as a rule*.

⚠ In unpointed text, make sure to distinguish between כְּלָל *rule* and the verb כָּלַל *[he] included*.

3.2 כְּלָל is also a quantifier, *all, the entire*, before a definite noun (e.g., כלל אוכלוסיית התלמידים *the entire student population*, כלל המידע ההיסטורי *all of the historical information*, כלל ישראל *the [whole of] Jewish people*).

3.3 לֹא . . . כְּלָל, לֹא . . . בִּכְלָל, לֹא . . .כְּלָל וּכְלָל, לֹא . . . כְּלָל וְעיקר *not at all*
When לֹא is accompanied by כלל, the negative statement is emphatic: *(not) at all*. The word of negation (i.e., לֹא, אין) may appear before or after (ב)כלל (e.g., (ב)כלל לֹא or (ב)כלל לֹא...(ב). Repetition (לֹא . . . כלל וכלל) and the expression לֹא . . . כלל ועיקר convey additional emphasis (examples 66–67).
בכלל *at all* tends to appear in questions and indicates doubt or incredulity (example 68).

---

(64) מַשְׁמָעוּת הַסֶּמֶל לֹא הָיְתָה בְּרוּרָה כְּלָל.
The meaning of the symbol was <u>not at all</u> obvious.

(65) במדינה יש אוֹצְרוֹת טבע רַבִּים שֶׁחֶלְקָם אֵינָם מנוּצָל בכלל.
In the country there are many natural resources, some of which are <u>not</u> exploited <u>at all</u>.

(66) הַשֵּׁם אֵינוֹ קשוּר כלל וכלל לְתוֹכְנוֹ של הסיפור.
The title is <u>not at all</u> connected to the content of the story.

(67) תֵּיאוּר זה אֵינוֹ מדוּיָק כְּלָל וְעיקָר.
This description is <u>not at all</u> accurate.

(68) נשאלת השְׁאֵלָה:הָאִם בְּכְלָל צריך חינוך מיוחָד?
The question is asked: is special education <u>at all</u> needed?

3.4 In declarative sentences, when a word of negation is not present, בכלל means *in general* (example 69). As seen in section 8 above, it is often paired with בפרט *in particular*. Another meaning – before a pronoun – is *among, including* (examples 71–72). Note the expression ועד בכלל *including* (example 73).

(69) אֱלֶגְיָה הִיא שִׁיר עַל אָדָם שֶׁמֵּת אוֹ עַל עֶצֶב בִּכְלָל.
An elegy is a poem about a man who died, or about sorrow <u>in general</u>.

(70) הַמִּקְרָא מְמַעֵט לְהַזְכִּיר אֶת קִיּוּמָן שֶׁל יְשֻׁיּוֹת עַל-טִבְעִיּוֹת בִּכְלָל, אַךְ בְּעוֹד שֶׁיֶּשְׁנָם מִסְפָּר אַזְכּוּרִים שֶׁל מַלְאָכִים וְסוּגֵי כִּישׁוּף שׁוֹנִים, שֵׁדִים אֵינָם מוּזְכָּרִים כְּלָל.
The Bible does not mention much the existence of supernatural entities <u>in general</u>, but while there are several references to angels and various kinds of spells, devils are <u>not</u> mentioned <u>at all</u>.

(71) בַּעֵת הָעַתִּיקָה הַפּוֹגְרוֹמִים הָיוּ טֶבַח כְּלָלִי שֶׁל אוֹכְלוּסִיּוֹת שׁוֹנוֹת וּבִכְלָל זֶה גַּם יְהוּדִים.
In ancient times, pogroms were general slaughter of various populations, <u>including</u> Jews.

(72) לְפִי תֵּאוּרְיָה זֹאת, גּוֹרְמִים פְּסִיכוֹלוֹגִיִּים (בִּכְלָלָם מַחֲשָׁבוֹת, רְגָשׁוֹת וְהִתְנַהֲגוּיוֹת) מַשְׁפִּיעִים עַל בְּרִיאוּתוֹ שֶׁל הָאָדָם.
According to this theory, psychological causes (<u>including</u> thoughts, feelings and behaviors) influence a person's health.

The suffix refers to the noun גורמים.

(73) הַתַּנָּאִים מַמְשִׁיכִים בַּדֶּרֶךְ זוֹ עַד יְמֵי רַבִּי יְהוּדָה הַנָּשִׂיא וְעַד בִּכְלָל.
The Tannaim continue in this path until – <u>and including</u> – the days the Rabbi Yehuda Ha-Nasi.

3.5 בְּדֶרֶךְ כְּלָל *usually, in general* (sometimes: דרך כלל).
This meaning can also be conveyed with expressions incorporating the word רוב: לָרוֹב, עַל פִּי רוֹב, עַל הָרוֹב.

3.6 לִכְלָל *to, to the point of*
This expression usually collocates (appears together) with the verbs בא, הביא, הגיע. It is interchangeable with לידי.[2] Neither word is quite translatable into English.

(74) לְפִי תּוֹרָתוֹ הַפִּילוֹסוֹפִית, הָאָדָם יָכוֹל לְהַגִּיעַ לִכְלָל הֲבָנַת הָעוֹלָם עַל יְדֵי מַחֲשָׁבָה.
According to his philosophy, man can arrive at an understanding of the world through contemplation.

3.7 כְּלָל- is a semantic prefix before adjectives in the sense of *all of, pan-* (e.g., כלל-אַרְצִי *countrywide*, כלל-אֱנוֹשִׁי *universal*).

3.8 כְּלָלִי/כְּלָלִית/כְּלָלִיִּים/כְּלָלִיּוֹת *general* is an adjective (e.g., הסכמה כללית *general agreement*, בחירות כלליות *general elections*, תובע כללי *attorney general*; example 71 above).

---

[2] See Chapter 8, Confusables, 1(d).

Other adjectives in this root are:

- כּוֹלֵל, כּוֹלֶלֶת, כּוֹלְלִים, כּוֹלְלוֹת *total, inclusive* (e.g., מלחמה כוללת *total war)* and
- כּוֹלְלָנִי, כּוֹלְלָנִית, כּוֹלְלָנִיִּים, כּוֹלְלָנִיּוֹת *general, comprehensive* (e.g., תאוריה כוללנית *general theory).*

3.9 Verbs from the כלל root are: לִכְלוֹל *to include (pa'al),* its *pa'ul* form כָּלוּל *included,* and passive *(nif'al)* counterpart לְהִכָּלֵל *to be included;* in *hif'il* – לְהַכְלִיל *to include; to generalize.*

🏋#6 **4.** בִּפְרָט; פְּרָט ל-; פְּרָט, פְּרִיט; פְּרָטִי

4.1 בפרט *in particular* should be distinguished from פרט ל- *excluding, with the exception of* (example 75).

4.2 The noun פְּרָט has two meanings, *detail* (note the expression פרטי פרטים *minute detail* and the verb לְפָרֵט *to give the details)* and *individual* (e.g., זכויות הפרט *the rights of the individual).* פְּרִיט is *item.*
Note also the expression מן הפרט אל הכלל *from the particular to the general.*

4.3 פְּרָטִי/פְּרָטִית/פְּרָטִיִּים/פְּרָטִיּוֹת is an adjective, *private* (e.g., רכוש פרטי *private property,* but note: שם פרטי *first name* as distinct from שם משפחה *family (last) name).*

> (75) כל המחוזות, <mark>פרט לאחד</mark> היו פעם ערים עצמאיות.
> All the districts <u>except for</u> one were once independent cities.

🏋#2 **5.** אמנם; הַאֻמְנָם

These words are pronounced differently (אמנם /omnan/ and האמנם /ha-umnam/) and have different meanings. The meanings of אמנם are discussed in section 3 above; הַאֻמְנָם is a question word in yes/no questions whose expected answer is "no". It can be ignored in translation or the words *actually, in fact, really* or *indeed* may be used to signal the speaker's doubt.

> (76) <mark>הַאֻמְנָם</mark> נתקיימה עיר בשם תבור בימי הבית הראשון?
> Did a city by the name of Tavor <u>actually</u> exist during the time of the First Temple?

6. בִּלְבַד; לְבַד; לְבַד מִן, מִלְּבַד; וּבִלְבַד שֶׁ-

6.1 בלבד *only, solely,* is a component in לא זאת בלבד . . . אלא גם *not only…but also* or it may stand on its own (e.g., כַּעֲבוֹר חמישה ימים בלבד *after only five days;* example 77).

6.2 לבד (an adverb that may take a pronoun suffix, see Chapter 5, 1.4.1) means *alone, apart, separately* (e.g., Genesis 2.18 "לא טוב הֱיוֹת האדם לְבַדּוֹ" *it is not good that man should be alone,* and example 78).

6.3 מִלְבַד, לְבַד מִן are additive expressions *in addition to* (example 79). When a word of negation is present (e.g., אֵין, לֹא) the translation is *apart from* (example 80).

6.4 וּבִלְבַד שֶ- is translated as *on the condition that, provided that; as long as* (example 81)

---

(77) שִׁחְזוּר הַמְּאוֹרָעוֹת צָרִיךְ לְהֵעָשׂוֹת בְּהִסְתַּמֵּךְ עַל מְקוֹרוֹת חוּץ-מִקְרָאִיִּים **בִּלְבַד**.
The reconstruction of the events should be done <u>only</u> on the basis of extra-biblical sources.

(78) רוֹב הַקַּרְיֶירָה שֶׁלּוֹ עָבַד **לְבַד**.
Most of his career he worked <u>alone.</u>

(79) **מִלְבַד** הַחֲלוּקָה לְסוּגוֹת סִפְרוּתִיּוֹת הַסִּיפּוֹרֶת מְחוּלֶּקֶת לָרוֹב עַל פִּי אוֹרֶךְ הַיְּצִירָה.
<u>In addition to</u> (OR: <u>apart from</u>) the division into literary genres, prose is usually categorized by the length of the work.

(80) מִן הַסֵּפֶר הַשֵּׁנִי לֹא נוֹתַר לָנוּ דָּבָר **לְבַד** מִמַּפְתֵּחַ הָעִנְיָינִים.
From the second book nothing remains (to us) <u>apart from</u> (OR: <u>except for</u>) the subject index.

(81) הָאֲצִילִים יָכְלוּ לַעֲשׂוֹת בְּאֲחוּזוֹתֵיהֶם כָּל הָעוֹלֶה עַל רוּחָם **וּבִלְבַד שֶׁיְּשַׁלְּמוּ** מִיסִים לַמֶּלֶךְ.
The nobles could do in their estates as they wished (literally: whatever came into their mind) <u>provided that</u> they paid taxes to the king.

References

בליבוים, 1995

Muraoka, 1996
Glinert, 1989

Chapter Ten Exercises: Discontinuous Sentence Connectors

exercise #	topic	page
1	לֹא – אֶלָּא	388–389
2	אָמְנָם	390
3	בֵּין	391–392
4	רֵאשִׁית	393
5	כְּלָל	394–395
6	פְּרָט	396
7	לְבַד	397–398

Exercise #1: לא – אלא

> **The rules to go by**: see section 1.
> **What to do**:
> 1. Determine the function of **לא-אלא** in the sentence and enter its number in the appropriate cell in the chart.
> 2. Translate the sentences.
> **Example**:
> מחשבים **אינם** יודעים **אלא** מספרים.
>
> Emphatic function: Computers know only numbers.

addition (both **a** and **b**)	exclusion (not **a** but rather **b**)	emphasis (only **a**; none other than **a**)
		example,

1. הַחַד-קֶרֶן **אינו אלא** חיה דמְיונית.

2. בחג הפורים **אין** היהודים **רק** מזכירים את סיפור המגילה, **אלא גם** מַציגים אותו.

3. **לא** מניעים אידאולוגיים או תיאולוגיים הֵניעו את המאבק, **אלא** מַאבקֵי כוח ושִלטון בקהילה.

4. האדם **אינו** מֵעַל הטֶבַע **כי אם** חֵלֶק ממנו.

5. לפי תְּפִיסת תנועת היידישיסטים, העברית **אינה אלא** שׂפַת העָבָר.

6. השְטיבְּל הוא בית כנסת חסידי, המשַמֵש **לא רק** לתפילה וללימוד תורה, **כי אם גם** לסעודות חסידיות.

Glossary

.1	חד קרן unicorn
	חיה דמיונית an imaginary animal
.2	מזכירים mention
	מציגים perform
.3	מניעים אידאולוגיים או תיאולוגיים ideological or theological motives
	הניעו motivated
	מאבקי כוח ושלטון struggles for power and dominance
.4	טבע nature
	חלק ממנו part of it
.5	תפיסת (תפיסה) understanding, view
	תנועת היידישיסטים The Yiddishist Movement
.6	בית כנסת חסידי Ḥasidic synagogue
	משמש serves for
	סעודות meals

7. הַדַּרְשָׁן (א)**אֵינוֹ** מְפָרֵשׁ מִילִים בּוֹדְדוֹת, **אֶלָּא** רוֹאֶה לְפָנָיו אֶת הָרַעְיוֹן בְּקְבוּצָה שְׁלֵמָה שֶׁל פְּסוּקִים וְהַטֶּקְסְט הַמִּקְרָאִי (ב)**אֵינוֹ** מְשַׁמֵּשׁ לוֹ **אֶלָּא** בָּסִיס לְרַעְיוֹן.

8. הַתַּפְקִיד שֶׁל "שְׁלִיחַ צִיבּוּר" (א)**אֵינוֹ אֶלָּא** תַּפְקִיד טֶכְנִי, לְהַשְׁמִיעַ אֶת תְּפִילַת הַצִּיבּוּר בְּקוֹל רָם; וּ(ב)**אֵין** דְּרוּשִׁים לְכָךְ מוּמְחִים, **אֶלָּא** כָּל אִישׁ מִקֶּרֶב הַצִּיבּוּר רָאוּי לִהְיוֹת שְׁלוּחוֹ.

9. מְגִילַּת אֶסְתֵּר הִיא כּוּלָּהּ אִירוֹנִית וּמִבְּחִינָה זוֹ הִיא **לֹא רַק** יְחִידָה בְּמִינָהּ, **אֶלָּא** נִרְאֵית כְּחוֹרֶגֶת לְגַמְרֵי מִסְגְנוֹן הַמִּקְרָא וַאֲפִילוּ זָרָה לוֹ.

Glossary

7. דרשן	preacher
מפרש מילים בודדות	interprets individual words
רעיון	idea
קבוצה שלמה של פסוקים	an entire group of verses
הטקסט המקראי	the biblical text
משמש לו	serves him
בסיס לרעיון	basis for an idea
8. "שליח ציבור"	"prayer leader"
תפקיד טכני	technical function
דרושים	required
מומחים	experts
מקרב הציבור	from among the community
ראוי להיות שלוחו	fit to be its representative
9. מגילת אסתר	The Book of Esther
אירונית	ironic
מבחינה זו	in this respect
יחידה במינה	unique
נראית כחורגת לגמרי	appears as diverging entirely
סגנון המקרא	the style of the Bible
זרה	foreign

Exercise #2: אמנם

> **The rules to go by**: see section 3 and Confusables section 5.
> **What to do**: determine the meaning of **אמנם** in the sentence and enter its number in the appropriate cell in the chart.

although, yet	*indeed*	**question word expressing doubt**

1. לנשיא יש **אמנם** סַמְכֻיּוֹת אך הן נופלות מאלה שֶׁיֵּשׁ לראש הַמֶּמְשָׁלָה.

2. **אמנם** העיר עלתה והפכה לחזקה ביותר בָּאֵזוֹר.

3. חֵלֶק מהכֵּלִים הללו **אמנם** עשׂוּיים כַּיּוֹם מַמַתֶּכֶת, אך פַּעַם היו עשׂוּיים מֵעֵץ.

4. **הַאמנם** התכוּון האלוהים שֶׁאברהם אָכֵן יַצְיִּית לְצַו נוֹרָא זה של הַקְרָבַת בְּנוֹ או שֶׁמָּא הַהֵפֶךְ?

5. הַטָעֻיּוֹת הפוליטיות גרמו **אמנם** לִפְרוֹץ המלחמה.

Glossary

> 1. סמכֻיּוֹת   powers
>   נופלות מ(ן)   are inferior to
> 2. עלתה והפכה לחזקה ביותר באזור   rose and became the most powerful in the region
> 3. כלים   instruments, tools
>   עשׂוּיים ממתכת   made of metal
>   עץ   wood
> 4. התכוון   meant, intended
>   יציית   will obey
>   צו נורא   terrible command
>   הקרבת בנו   the sacrificing of his son
>   שמא   perhaps
>   ההפך   the opposite
> 5. טעויות פוליטיות   political mistakes
>   גרמו   caused
>   פרוץ המלחמה   the breakout of the war

Exercise #3: בֵּין

> **The rules to go by**: see sections 9 and 11.
> **What to do**: determine the meaning of בֵּין in the sentence (enter its number in the appropriate cell in the chart).

between	among	among other things	whether...or	inter-

1. בדרך כלל מַבחינים **בֵּין** דיקְטָטוּרָה **לְבֵין** מוֹנַרכְיָה.

2. כל סיפור דורש מְסַפֵּר, **בֵּין אִם** הוא מדגיש את קיומו בטֶקְסְט **וּבֵין אִם** לא.

3. הוא מַבְחין **בֵּין** חובה לקהילה, שהוא עניין מוּסָרי, **לְבֵין** החובה לָאֵל, שהיא עניין דתי בִּלְבד.

4. העיר ידועה **בֵּין הֵיתר** בְּשֶׁל הַקַּרנבל הַסַּסגוֹני המתְרַחֵש בה מְדֵי שנה.

5. הַפְּרדה **בֵּין** בנים ובנות מקוּבֶּלֶת במערכות חינוך רבות.

6. הרוֹמָן חוזר לנושאים שבהם עסקה המְחַבֶּרֶת בסְפרים קוֹדְמים, **וּבֵיניהם** – מַעמד האישה.

Glossary

distinguish	מבחינים	.1
dictatorship	דיקטטורה	
monarchy	מונרכיה	
requires	דורש	.2
narrator	מספר	
emphasizes his existence	מדגיש את קיומו	
duty	חובה	.3
a moral matter	עניין מוסרי	
because of	בשל	.4
colorful carnival	קרנבל ססגוני	
takes place each year	מתרחש מדי שנה	
separation	הפרדה	.5
customary	מקובלת	
education systems	מערכות חינוך	
novel	רומן	.6
dealt with	עסקה	
author (f.)	מחברת	
the status of women	מעמד האישה	

7. הַמִשְׂחָק נָפוֹץ בלְפָחוֹת 60 מדינות בַּרְחֲבֵי העולם, **בִּינֵן** ישראל.

8. כְּבִיש **בֵּין**-עירוֹני מחַבֵּר את העיר עם ישׁוּבים אחרים.

Glossary

.7	הַמִשְׂחָק נפוֹץ the game is widespread
	לְפָחוֹת at least
	בְּרַחֲבֵי העולם world-wide
.8	כְּבִיש road
	מחַבֵּר עם יישׁוּבים אחרים connects with other communities

Exercise #4: ראשית

1. כבר **מראשיתה** עסקה הפילוסופיה בשאלות אלה.

2. הוא הקדיש את **ראשית** כְּהוּנתו לחיזוק מַעמדו כנשׂיא.

3. בַּעֲלִילָה **הראשית** מופיעות שלוש דמויות.

4. הסיבה לליקוט המִדרשים בקובץ חדש הייתה כְּפוּלה: **ראשית,** היה חשש כי מִדרשים קטנים עלולים להֵיעָלֵם, שֵׁנית, העוֹרֵך ראה עֵרֶךְ היסטורי ותרבּוּתי בלקיטָתם.

beginning	first(ly)	main

Glossary

dealt with, concerned itself with	עסקה ב- .1
devoted	הקדיש .2
his term of service	כהונתו
strengthening his position as the president	חיזוק מעמדו כנשיא
plot	עלילה .3
appear	מופיעות
characters	דמויות
collecting the Midrashim in a new anthology	ליקוט המדרשים בקובץ חדש .4
fear, worry	חשש
may disappear	עלולים להיעלם
editor	עורך
historical and cultural value	ערך היסטורי ותרבותי
their gathering	לקיטתם

Exercise #5: כלל

> **The rules to go by**: see section 8 and Confusables section 3.
> **What to do**: determine the meaning of **כלל** in the sentence and enter its number in the appropriate cell in the chart.

not at all	including	rule	included (verb)	all, the entire, the totality

to, to the point of	general (adjective)	pan-, -wide, (semantic prefix)	the public, society	generally, usually

1. מִנִּתוּחַ **כלל** הַמֵּידָע עוֹלוֹת סָתִירוֹת וְאִי-הֲבָנוֹת.

2. אֵין מָקוֹם **כלל** לְהַשְׁוָוָאָה בֵּין הַנוֹסָחִים.

3. הַמִתְיַישְׁבִים פִּיתְּחוּ אֶת הַחַוָוה הַחַקְלָאִית לְ**כלל** יִישׁוּב.

4. דִּבְרֵיהֶם אֵינָם מְכֻוָונִים לְ**כלל** הָעָם, אֶלָּא לְתַלְמִידֵי חֲכָמִים בִּלְבַד.

5. הַצֶּוֶות **כלל** חֲמִישָׁה אֲנָשִׁים.

6. הַסוֹפֵר לֹא הִצְלִיחַ לְהָבִיא אֶת הַיְצִירָה לִ**כלל** סִיּוּם.

7. כָּל חֶלְקֵי הַסִּיפּוּר מִשְׁתַּלְבִים בְּמֶסֶר הַ**כְּלָלִי**.

8. הַמַעְיָינוֹת הַחַמִּים נִמְצָאִים **בְּדֶרֶךְ כלל** לְיַד הָרֵי גַעַשׁ.

Glossary

1. ניתוח   analysis
   מידע   information
   סתירות ואי הבנות   contradictions and miscomprehensions
2. השוואה בין הנוסחים   comparison among versions
3. מתיישבים   settlers
   פיתחו את החווה החקלאית   developed the agricultural farm
   יישוב   settlement
4. מכוונים   aimed at
   תלמידי חכמים   scholars (of Torah)
5. צוות   team
6. סופר   author
   יצירה   work
   סיום   conclusion, end
7. משתלבים ב   integrate into
   מסר   message
8. מעיינות חמים   hot springs
   ליד הרי געש   next to volcanoes

9. אָדוֹם, שָׁחוֹר, לָבָן וְיָרוֹק נֶחְשָׁבִים לְצִבְעֵי הַלְּאוּמִיּוּת הַ**כְּלַל**-עֲרָבִית.

10. הוּא תָּמִיד הֶעֱדִיף אֶת הַ**כְּלָל** עַל חַיָּיו הַפְּרָטִיִּים.

11. הַתַּצְפִּיּוֹת מְאַשְּׁרוֹת אֶת הַ**כְּלָל**.

12. הַתְּנוּעָה מְחַנֶּכֶת לְשֵׁירוּת טוֹבַת הַ**כְּלָל**.

13. מֶנְדֶּלְסוֹן הָיָה מוּכָן לְקַבֵּל אֶת הַחֵלֶק הַמּוּסָרִי בְּתוֹרוֹתָיו שֶׁל יֵשׁוּ, אוּלָם **כְּלָל וּכְלָל** אֵין הוּא מְקַבֵּל אֶת הַתְּפִיסוֹת הַדָּתִיּוֹת שֶׁל הַנַּצְרוּת.

14. בִּמְדִינוֹת רַבּוֹת, **בִּכְלָלָן** יִשְׂרָאֵל, נֶחְקְקוּ חֻקִּים הַמַּבְטִיחִים שְׂכַר מִינִימוּם.

15. בְּיַהֲדוּת אַשְׁכְּנַז שֶׁל אוֹתָהּ תְּקוּפָה **כְּלָל**(א) לֹא הָיוּ מְקוּבָּלִים לִימּוּדֵי פִילוֹסוֹפִיָה וּ**בִכְלָלָם**(ב) לִימּוּד הַסֵּפֶר "מוֹרֵה נְבוּכִים".

16. זֶה הָעִיתּוֹן הַ**כְּלָל**-אַרְצִי הַיָּחִידִי הַמּוֹפִיעַ בְּצֶבַע.

Glossary

9.	צבעי הלאומיות	the colors of nationalism
10.	העדיף	preferred
	חייו הפרטיים	his private life
11.	תצפיות	observations
	מאשרות	confirm
12.	תנועה	movement
	מחנכת	educates
	שירות	service
13.	מוכן לקבל את החלק המוסרי	willing to accept the ethical component
	תורותיו של ישו	the teachings of Jesus
	התפיסות הדתיות של הנצרות	the religious views of Christianity
14.	נחקקו חוקים	laws were legislated
	מבטיחים שכר מינימום	ensure minimum wage
15.	יהדות אשכנז	Ashkenaz Jewry
	מקובלים	acceptable, customary
	לימודי פילוסופיה	the study of philosophy
	הספר "מורה נבוכים"	the book "Guide for the Perplexed"
16.	מופיע בצבע	appears in color

Exercise# 6: פרט

The rules to go by: see section 8 and Confusables section 4.
What to do: determine the meaning of **פרט** in the sentence and enter its number in the appropriate cell in the chart.

---

detail(s)	individual(s)	except for	in particular

1. כָּל שִׁירָיו **פֹּרַט** לְאֶחָד הוּלְחֲנוּ.

2. תֵּיאוּר הַדְּמוּיוֹת יוֹרֵד **לִפְרָטֵי פְרָטִים.**

3. זֶהוּ **פְּרָט** קוֹנְקְרֵטִי שֶׁיֵּשׁ לוֹ מַשְׁמָעוֹת סֵמְלִית.

4. יֵשׁ הַמַּצְבִּיעִים עַל הַדְּמְיוֹן בֵּין הַתְּפִילָה הַזֹּו, **בִּפְרָט** בִּשְׁנֵי הַפְּסוּקִים הָרִאשׁוֹנִים שֶׁלָּה, לִתְפִילַת הַקָּדִישׁ בְּיַהֲדוּת.

5. כַּאֲשֶׁר יֶשְׁנוֹ פַּעַר בֵּין רָמַת הַחַיִּים שֶׁל **הַפְּרָט** וּבֵין רָמַת הַחַיִּים לָה הוּא רָאוּי לְדַעְתוֹ, מִתְפַּתְּחִים רְגָשׁוֹת שְׁלִילִיִּים כְּלַפֵּי קְבוּצוֹת אֲחֵרוֹת.

6. אֲסוֹנוֹת טֶבַע פָּגְעוּ בָּאִי בִּכְלָל וּבָעִיר הַבִּירָה שֶׁלּוֹ **בִּפְרָט.**

Glossary

were set to music	הולחנו .1
the description of the characters	תיאור הדמויות .2
here: goes into	יורד ל-
concrete	קונקרטי .3
symbolic significance	משמעות סמלית
there are those who point out to	יש המצביעים על .4
similarity	דמיון
the first two verses	שני הפסוקים הראשונים
the prayer of Kaddish in Judaism	תפילת הקדיש ביהדות
gap	פער .5
standard of living	רמת חיים
deserving	ראוי
negative feelings develop	מתפתחים רגשות שליליים
toward	כלפי
natural disasters	אסונות טבע .6
hit, harmed	פגעו
island	אי
capital city	עיר הבירה

Exercise #7: לבד

> **The rules to go by**: see Confusables section 6.
> **What to do**: Determine the meaning of **לבד** in the sentence and enter its number in the appropriate cell in the chart.

only	apart from	in addition to	as long as, provided that	alone

1. עד שנת 2000 ניתן היה לחצות את הַמֵּצַר בדרך הים **בלבד.**

2. מכל אלה לא שָׂרד דָּבָר **מלבד** מְסְפר רְשימות.

3. **לבד** מסיפוריו הארוכים יותר, הוא כתב גם סיפורים קצרים רבים.

4. הַמְשְׂרָד להֲגָנַת הַסְביבה עוסק, **מלבד** בחוּקֵי הֲגָנַת הסביבה, גם בחינוך סְביבתי.

5. הוא החזיק במְלוכה חודש ימים **בלבד.**

6. בזְמן מִשְׁכן שילֹה לא היה מותר לישראל להַקְריב קרְבָּנות בכל מקום אחֵר **לבד** מן הַמִּזְבֵּח שבמשכן.

7. שַׂר האוצר לא שָׁלַל שוּם שיטה כַּלְכָּלִית **ובלבד** שתְּשָׁרֵת את הַמַטָרָה של בְּנְיַין האומה.

8. הַפָּנְתֵאיזם חוּמְרִי ולכן אינו מזַהה את הָאֵל אלא עם הטֶבַע **בלבד.**

Glossary

.1	מֵצר	strait
.2	שׂרד	survived
	מספר רשימות	a few notes
.4	המשרד להגנת הסביבה	the Ministry for the Protection of the Environment
	חינוך סביבתי	environmental education
.5	החזיק במלוכה	held the throne
.6	משכן שילֹה	the Tabernacle at Shiloh
	לא היה מותר לישראל להקריב קורבנות	the Israelites were not allowed to make sacrifices
	מזבח	altar
.7	שר האוצר	the Minister of the Treasury
	לא שלל שום שיטה כלכלית	did not refuse any economic system
	תשרת את המטרה	serve the goal
	בניין האומה	the building of the nation
.8	פנתיאיזם	Pantheism
	חומרי	material
	מזהה את האלֹ	identifies the deity
	טבע	nature

9.   היא חיה בבְדידוּת וּמֵתה **לבד**.

10. איש, **לבד** מִמשפחתה הקרוֹבה, לֹא ידע את זהוּתה.

Glossary

.9	loneliness בדידוּת
.10	no one איש...לֹא
	her close family משפחתה הקרוֹבה

11. LEXICAL MATTERS

Lexical matters: an overview

The first section of this chapter, called "similar but different," contains information about words and expressions that language learners often confuse with others similar to them in form and/or meaning. The section includes the following:

1.	עָשׂוּי (מ-); עָשׂוּי ל-; עָלוּל
2.	אָמוּר; אָמוּר ל-; כָּאָמוּר; שֶׁנֶּאֱמַר; לֵאמוֹר; כָּזָכוּר, כַּיָּדוּעַ
3.	נִיתָּן; נָתוּן ל-/ב-; נָתוּן
4.	לְבַקֵּשׁ
5.	מֵעֵין
6.	מַעֲבָר (מ-) ... (ל-); מֵעֵבֶר ל-
7.	מִסְגֶּרֶת, בְּמִסְגֶּרֶת-
8.	אֵיפֹה; אֵפוֹא, אֵיפוֹא
9.	כְּדֵי, בִּכְדֵי; תּוֹךְ כְּדֵי; יֵשׁ/אֵין ב-... כְּדֵי; לִכְדֵי, עַד כְּדֵי (כָּךְ); מִכְּדֵי; לֹא בִּכְדֵי
10.	בחן: לבחון, להבחין; מִבְחָנָה, מִבְּחִינַת; בִּבְחִינַת
11.	יחס: יַחַס, יְחָסִים; להתייחס; לְיַחֵס; יַחֵס; בְּיַחַס, יַחֲסִית
12.	הֵחֵל; הֵחֵל ב-; חָל; חל על, הֵחִיל עַל; חוֹלֵל, הִתְחוֹלֵל
13.	מִשּׁוּם שֶׁ, עַל שׁוּם (שֶׁ-); בְּשׁוּם ...; שׁוּם לֹא/אֵין; אֵין ב ... מִשּׁוּם
14.	דָּבָר; דְּבָרִים, לְדִבְרֵי, כְּדִבְרֵי; הַדָּבָר; לֹא ...דָּבָר; בִּדְבַר; מְדוּבָּר ב-/עַל
15.	כֵּן; קוֹדֶם לָכֵן, לִפְנֵי כֵן, לְאַחַר מִכֵּן, אַף עַל פִּי כֵן, עַל כֵּן; כְּשֵׁם שֶׁ-... כֵּן; כְּכָל שֶׁ-... כֵּן; וְכֵן, כְּמוֹ כֵן; לָכֵן; שֶׁכֵּן; וּבְכֵן, אִם כֵּן; אָכֵן
16.	דִּמְיוֹן; דּוֹמֶה ל-, מְדוּמֶּה ל-; בְּדוֹמֶה ל-; וְכַדּוֹמֶה; דְּמוּי-, נִדְמֶה (לְ-) (שֶׁ-), דּוֹמֶה שֶׁ-/כִּי, כִּמְדוּמֶּה; דִּימּוּי; דְּמוּת, תַּדְמִית

The second section of the chapter discusses phrases with an internal object, that is, verb phrases whose verb and object share the same root (e.g., חָלַם חֲלוֹם *dreamt [had] a dream*).

The third section contains examples of binomials, that is, synonymous or identical word pairs used for stylistic and rhetorical purposes (e.g., the greeting שלום וברכה *peace and blessing*).

The last section provides guidance on recognizing and decoding foreign (loan) words.

A. Similar but different

1. עָשׂוּי (מ-)/(ב-); עָשׂוּי לְ; עָלוּל

1.1 עָשׂוּי/עֲשׂוּיָה/עֲשׂוּיִם/עֲשׂוּיוֹת #1

עָשׂוּי, the passive participle form of the *pa'al* verb לַעֲשׂוֹת *to do, to make*, has two (unrelated) meanings:

(a) **עָשׂוּי (מ-/מִן)** *made of/from* is the verb-related meaning (examples 1–4 and 24).

(b) **עָשׂוּי**+**infinitive verb** means *may, might, is likely to* (examples 5 and 47).

Past and future (for either meaning) are indicated with the verb "to be" (example 1).

---

(1) בְּבָתֵי כְנֶסֶת רַבִּים הָיְיתָה הָרִצְפָּה עֲשׂוּיָה פְּסִיפָס נֶהְדָּר.
In many synagogues the floor <u>was made of</u> splendid mosaic.

(2) הַמַּצֵּבָה שֶׁנִּמְצְאָה בְּסוּרְיָה עֲשׂוּיָה מֵאֶבֶן בַּזֶלֶת.
The tombstone that was found in Syria <u>is made of</u> basalt stone.

(3) הַחוֹמֶר שֶׁמִּמֶּנּוּ עָשׂוּי הַקָּמֵעַ יָכוֹל לִהְיוֹת קְלָף אוֹ סוּגִים שׁוֹנִים שֶׁל מַתֶּכֶת.
The material from which the amulet <u>is made</u> may be parchment or various kinds of metal.

(4) לֶחֶם זֶה, הֶעָשׂוּי בְּדֶרֶךְ כְּלָל מִקֶּמַח לָבָן, הֲרֵיהוּ הַחַלָּה.
This bread, which <u>is</u> usually <u>made</u> from white flour, is the challah.

(5) מָוֶות וּלֵידַת גִּיבּוֹר עֲשׂוּיִים לִהְיוֹת מָשָׁל לְהִתְחַלְּפוּת הָעוֹנוֹת.
Death and the birth of a hero <u>may be</u> a parable for the change of seasons.

1.2 עָלוּל can be used instead of עָשׂוּי when unfavorable events are expected. It is translated in the same way as עָשׂוּי – *may* – or, to better convey the original meaning, as *liable to* or *risks*.

---

(6) עִיתוֹנַאי עָלוּל לִגְרוֹם נֵזֶק לִשְׁמָם הַטּוֹב שֶׁל אַנְשֵׁי צִיבּוּר.
A journalist <u>may</u> (OR: is <u>liable to</u>) cause harm to the reputation of public figures.

𝕏#2 .2 אָמוּר; אָמוּר לְ-; כָּאָמוּר; שֶׁנֶּאֱמַר; לְאֵמוֹר

2.1 אָמוּר/אֲמוּרָה/אֲמוּרִים/אֲמוּרוֹת

אָמוּר, the passive participle of the *pa'al* verb אמר *say*, is translated as *said, stated* (example 7). Used as an adjective, אמור is translated *aforesaid, aforementioned* (example 8).

2.1.1 The expression הדבר(ים) אמור(ים) בְּ-[1] can be rendered as *said about, concern,* or *apply to* (example 9); it is synounoymous with -מְדוּבָּר בְּ.

---

(7) אין הוֹכָחוֹת לַאָמוּר בְּמַאֲמָר.
There is no proof for what is <u>stated</u> in the article.

(8) הָרַעְיוֹן הָאָמוּר מוֹפִיעַ שָׁם פְּעָמִים אֲחָדוֹת.
The <u>aforementioned</u> idea appears there several times.

(9) הַדְּבָרִים אֲמוּרִים בִּשְׁנֵי הַשְּׁלִישִׁים הָרִאשׁוֹנִים שֶׁל יְמֵי בַּיִת שֵׁנִי.
These things are <u>said about [OR: concern]</u> the first two-thirds of the period of the Second Temple.

2.2 Before a verb in the infinitive, the meaning of **אָמוּר** is *supposed to*.

---

(10) הָאִם הַמּוּזֵאוֹן אָמוּר לְהַעֲבִיר מֶסֶר אוֹ לְסַפֵּק חֲוָויָה?
Is the museum <u>supposed to</u> deliver a message or provide an experience?

⚠ Note that the verb אמר similarly loses its original meaning of saying and conveys intention when followed by another verb in the infinitive, for example: לא אמר לפגוע בו *did not intend to harm him.*

2.3 כָּאָמוּר *as stated, as mentioned* is a parenthetical comment whose purpose is to remind the reader of a point made earlier in the text. It is usually separated from the rest of the sentence by commas. An alternative expression is כַּנִּזְכָּר (לְעֵיל) *as is mentioned (above).*

---

(11) הַתַּהֲלִיךְ הֵחֵל, כָּאָמוּר, כְּבָר בִּתְקוּפַת הַמַּנְדָט הַבְּרִיטִי.
<u>As previously mentioned</u>, the process began already in the period of the British Mandate.

---

[1] See examples 55–56 in Chapter 1, 5 (b).

2.3.1 כָּאָמוּר should be distinguished from two other parenthetical reminders which allude to the reader's (presumed) recollection or knowledge of some fact <u>not</u> previously mentioned in the text:

(a) **כַּזָּכוּר** *as may be recalled, as you may recall* (literally: *as is remembered*; example 12).

(b) **כַּיָּדוּעַ** (rarely: **בַּיָּדוּעַ**) *as is well known, as everyone knows* (literally: *as is known*; examples 13–14).

---

(12) הספר, **כַּזָּכוּר**, נכתב בשנות החמישים המאוחרות.
The book, <u>as may be recalled</u>, was written in the late 1950's.

(13) **כידוע**, חֵלֶק ניכָּר משמות המשפחה קשור בעיר המוצא.
<u>As is (well) known</u>, a considerable portion of the family names is connected to the hometown (literally: *city of origin*).

(14) החורף **כידוע** מסַמל עַצְבוּת.
Winter, <u>as everyone knows</u>, symbolizes sadness.

2.4 **שֶׁנֶּאֱמַר** is different from כאמור: its function is to introduce a citation (usually from the Bible) in support of a statement made in the text.
But note also the use of שנאמר in the literal sense: *as it is/was said* (e.g., הוא הסכים לְמַה שנאמר *he agreed to what was said*, כפי שנאמר קודם *as it was said before*).

---

(15) ואין הכָּבוד אֶלָא לשמוח לפני ה', **שֶׁנֶּאֱמַר** (שמואל ב ו יד): "וְדָוִד מְכַרְכֵּר בְּכָל עֹז לִפְנֵי ה'."
And the greatest honor is none other than to be joyful before God, <u>according to the verse</u> (OR: <u>as it was said</u>): "David whirled with all his might before the Lord" (Samuel II, 6.14).

2.5 **לֵאמֹר** *that is to say, namely, i.e.,* introduces an explanation; synounomous expressions are כְּלוֹמַר and מַשְׁמַע.
In this sense, לאמור should be distinguished from *to say* (e.g., לא יהיה זה מדויק לֵאמֹר *it would not be accurate to say*); this meaning, however, is more likely to be rendered with the form לוֹמַר (e.g., לא יהיה זה מדויק לומר).

⚠️In unpointed text, make sure to differentiate לֵאמֹר from לָאָמוּר *to that which is said* (e.g., בניגוד לָאָמוּר בהסכם *in contrast to what is said in the agreement*).

---

(16) ברבים מנְאוּמיהם של מַנהיגים פוליטיים יש מְשפטים טאוטולוגיים, **לֵאמֹר**, משפטים החוזרים על עצמם לצורך שכְנוּעַ המַאזינים.
In many of the speeches of political leaders that are tautological sentences, <u>namely</u>, sentences that repeat themselves for the purpose of persuading the audience.

נִיתַן; נָתוּן לְ-/בְּ-; נָתוּן .3

✗#3.1   3.1 נִיתַן *given* is a passive (*nif'al*) form of the verb נָתַן. Like נָתַן, the preposition -לְ links נִיתַן to its (indirect) object. The preposition may appear before or after the verb.

---

(17) **לַבְּעָיָה זו נִיתְנוּ** תְּשׁוּבוֹת שׁוֹנוֹת.

Different answers <u>were given</u> to this problem.

3.2 When followed by a verb in the infinitive, נִיתָן functions as a more formal alternative to אֶפְשָׁר. Unlike נִיתַן in the sense of *given*, which changes to agree with the subject, נִיתָן *it is possible* is impersonal and does not conjugate.

Since in unpointed text the past of נִיתָן is indistinguishable from the present (נִתַּן and נִתָּן, respectively), הָיָה is sometimes used (example 19). In the future, the verb יִהְיֶה is always used (example 20).

⚠ Note that in unpointed text with full spelling, the *pa'al* form נִתֵּן *we will give* and the *nif'al* forms נִתַּן and נִתָּן appear identical (all are spelled נִיתָן) and need to be differentiated from each other on the basis of the surrounding text.

---

(18) **נִיתָן לְדַבֵּר** עַל אֲחִידוּתָה שֶׁל הַלָּשׁוֹן הָעִבְרִית לַמְרוֹת הַהַשְׁפָּעוֹת הַזָּרוֹת עָלֶיהָ.

<u>It is possible to talk</u> about the homogeneity of the Hebrew language despite the foreign influences on it.

(19) מַצָּב זֶה יָצַר חָלָל מִשְׁפָּטִי חָמוּר **שֶׁלֹּא נִיתָן הָיָה לְמַלְּאוֹ.**

This situation created a serious legal vacuum that <u>could not be filled.</u>

(20) כָּךְ **נִיתָן יִהְיֶה לְהָבִין** בְּצוּרָה מַקִּיפָה יוֹתֵר אֶת הַפִילוֹסוֹפְיָה הַיְּהוּדִית בִּימֵי-הַבֵּינַיִם.

In this way <u>it will be possible to understand</u> more comprehensively the Jewish philosophy of the Middle Ages.

3.3 When נִיתָן is followed by a noun (typically, an action noun[2]), it is rendered in English with *can* rather than with *it is possible*.

---

(21) עֲתִידוֹ שֶׁל הַקִּיבּוּץ **אֵינוֹ נִיתָן לְחִיזּוּי.**

The future of the kibbutz <u>cannot be predicted.</u>

---

[2] See Chapter 2, 6.3.

⚠️ Note the potential ambiguity of נִיתָן (*possible* or *given*) in the following sentence:

כל מָדוֹר בָּאנציקלוֹפֶּדיה הוא מַאֲמָר הָעוֹמֵד בִּפְנֵי עַצְמוֹ שֶׁנִּיתָן לִקְרוֹאוֹ בְּנִפְרָד; עִם זֹאת, כל מָדוֹר בָּנוּי כָּךְ שֶׁנִּיתָן לִקְרוֹאוֹ גַּם בָּרֶצֶף.

Each section of the encyclopedia is an independent article <u>that can be read</u> separately; however, each section is structured in such a way that <u>it can be also read</u> consecutively.

NOT: each section in the encyclopedia is an indepedet article <u>that is given to its reader</u> separately; however, each section is structured in such a way that <u>it is given to its reader</u> also in sequence.

The erroneous reading of נִיתָן as *given* is due to the interpetation of the pronoun suffix in לְקוֹרְאוֹ as a possessive suffix after the noun קוֹרֵא *reader* rather than the direct object suffix after the verb לִקְרוֹא *to read* (see Chapter 6, 2.5.2).

While both readings – *given to its reader* and *can be read* – are grammatically possible in the first clause, the reading *given to its reader* in the second clause is grammatically impossible. This is because the new clause after -שׁ כָּךְ would require a subject:

כל מָדוֹר בנוי כך שֶׁהוּא נִיתָן לקוראו בנפרד

Note that had לְקוֹרְאוֹ been spelled according to the rule – לִקְרוֹאוֹ, with a קָמָץ קָטָן – this ambiguity would not have arisen (Chapter 5, 1.2.4(b)).

🏋️#3.2   3.4 -נָתוּן ב; -נָתוּן ל; נָתוּן

3.4.1 נָתוּן *given* (an adjective) is the passive participle form of נתן (e.g., בתקופה נתונה *in a given period*). Note the expressions נתון לחילוקי דעות, נתון במחלוקת, *controversial,* נתון בספק *debatable,* לויכוח *doubtful.*

As a noun, נָתוּן means *datum* (in the plural: נְתוּנִים *data*; e.g., מַאֲגָר נתונים *database*).

---

(22) עַל הַחוֹקֵר לְהַסְבִּיר כל **נָתוּן** וּמִמְצָא.
The researcher should explain each <u>datum</u> and finding.

3.4.2 -נָתוּן ל means *given to* or *prone to* (example 23).

3.4.3 -נָתוּן ב means *found in, placed in*; it is synonymous with נמצא (example 24).

---

(23) הַיְחָסִים בֵּין הַקְּהִילוֹת **הָיוּ נתונים** לִתְנוּדוֹת.
The relationships among the communities <u>were given to</u> fluctuations.

(24) בְּעֵדוֹת הַמִּזְרָח **נתון** סֵפֶר הַתּוֹרָה בְּתוֹךְ נַרְתִּיק מְיוּחָד, עֲשׂוּי כֶּסֶף.
In the oriental communities the Torah <u>is placed in</u> a special pouch made of silver.

4. לבקש

Ordinarily, **לבקש** *to request* involves two "players" (and, therefore, two object complements): one who requests, and another who would carry out the request. However, when followed directly by a verb in the infinitive, לבקש means *to seek, to wish, to want*, signaling the intention or wish of the speaker to perform the specified action himself.
For example:

אני מבקש שתסביר, אני מבקש ממך להסביר *I ask you to explain* (the person addressed will explain)

אני מבקש להסביר *I would like to explain* (the speaker will explain).

---

(25) בספר הנוכחי הוא מבקש לחזק את המֶסֶר שלו.
In the present book, he <u>seeks</u> to strengthen his message.

(26) בפֶּרֶק זה נבקש להתחקות אחר גלגוליו הסמליים של הכַּד באמנות המקומית.
In this chapter, <u>we wish to trace</u> the symbolic metamorphoses of the pitcher in the local art.

The writer uses the "authorial we" to declare his research agenda.

---

5. מעין

Without points, this word could be read in several different ways.

The most likely reading (in academic texts) is מֵעֵין *like, a kind of*, an expression used to hedge or soften an assertion; it is synonymous with כָּעֵין and (כְּ)מִין.

The other possibilities are:

(a) מַעְיָן, *a spring* (if full spelling is used – מעיין),

(b) מֵעַיִן *from an eye* (e.g., נעלם מעין *hidden from sight*), or

(c) מְעַיֵן *[he] reads* (in full spelling – מעיין).

---

(27) היהודים בבָבֶל קיבלו מֵעֵין שלטון עַצְמִי מוניציפַּאלי.
The Jews in Babylon received <u>a kind of</u> municipal self-rule.

(28) בְּקֶרֶב האיסיים הייתה כָּעֵין "קוֹלֶקְטיביוּת רעיוֹנית".
Among the Essenes, there was <u>a kind of</u> "ideological collectivism".

---

6. מַעֲבָר (מ-) (ל-); מֵעֵבֶר ל- #4🏋

In unpointed text, three readings are possible for מעבר.

6.1 מַעֲבָר in the sense of *transition, passage, crossing over* or *move, transfer* is a noun (example 29). As with the related verb לעבור *to pass*, the points of origin and destination can be specified with the prepositions מ-/מן and אל/ל- (example 30).

6.2 The adverb מֵעֵבֶר ל- means *beyond, across, on the other side of*. The preposition ל- is obligatory. Occasionally, the preposition אֶל is placed before מעבר (אל מעבר ל-, example 31). Note also the expression מעל ומֵעֵבֶר ל- *above and beyond* (example 32).

6.3 A third possible reading of מעבר (example 34) is מֵ+עָבָר *from a past* (but note that *from the past* would be: מהֶעבר).

---

(29) הַמַּעֲבָר לְלִינָה בחדרי ההורים הוא מן השינויים החשובים שהתחוללו בחיי הקיבוץ.
The <u>transition</u> to sleeping in the parents' quarters is one of the most important changes that took place in kibbutz life.

(30) מקצועות רבים דורשים מעבר ממקום מגורים אחד לְמקום מגורים אחר בכל כמה שנים.
Many professions require <u>a move from</u> one place of residence <u>to</u> another every few years.

(31) עולם עשיר של רְמזים וסְמָלים המובילים את המִתבונֵן אל מֵעֵבֶר לַנִגלֶה מְאפּיֵין כַּמָה מן הַהֶדפֵּסים.
A world rich in hints and symbols which lead the onlooker <u>beyond</u> the visible characterizes some of the prints.

(32) מַערֶכֶת כַּלכָּלית זו עוֹדְדה גידוּל הוֹצאוֹת על צריכָה מֵעַל וּמֵעֵבֶר לְגידוּל התפוקה.
This economic system encouraged an increase in consumer spending <u>above and beyond</u> the growth in production.

(33) הספרות הזאת תֵיארה את מה שנראָה לה כְּמעבר לְחוֹמְרָנוּת.
This literature described what appeared to it as a <u>transition</u> to materialism.

In unpointed text, the decision to read מַעֲבָר לחומרנות *transition to materialism* rather than מֵעֵבֶר לחומרנות *beyond materialism* depends on the larger context of the discourse.

(34) הקיבוץ מִתרחֵק מֵעֲבָרוֹ הַחַקְלָאִי השיתופי.
The kibbutz is moving away from its collective agricultural <u>past</u>.

The preposition מ- before עברו *its past* is required by the verb מתרחק.

---

7. בְּמִסְגֶרֶת-

While by itself מסגרת means *frame, framework*, במסגרת- (followed by a noun or a pronoun suffix) is translated *as part of, within*.

(35) "הדיאלוג הים תיכוני" הוא שְׁמָה של מסגרת של שיתוף פעולה לְמַעַן השלום שנוצרה
על ידי נאט"ו בשנת 1994.

"The Mediterranean Dialogue" is the name of a <u>framework</u> of cooperation for peace created by NATO in 1994.

(36) תְּחִיַּת הלשון העברית היא תַהֲלִיך שֶׁבְּמסגרתו הפכה העברית מלָשׁון כתובה ללשון
מדוברת.

The revival of the Hebrew language is a process <u>within which</u> Hebrew changed from a written to spoken language.

(37) במסגרת היְחָסים הדיפּלומטיים בין המדינות מתקיימים ביקורים רשמיים של אנשי
מִמְשל.

<u>As part of</u> the diplomatic relations between the states, official visits of state officials take place.

8. אֵיפֹה; אֵפוֹא, אֵיפוֹא

אֵפוֹא (or אֵיפוֹא) *then, therefore, consequently* is a comment adverbial occurring at mid-sentence. Synonyms are: אָם כֵּן, לָכֵן and אֲזַי (a literary version of אָז, *then*).

In contrast, the question word אֵיפֹה *where*, appears at the beginning of the clause.

The two words are spelled and pronounced differently. In אֵיפֹה, the stress falls on first syllable while in אֵפוֹא it falls on the second.

(38) הביטוי מְשַׁמֵּשׁ בעיקר באנגלית ואינו ניתָן אֵפוֹא לתרגום לעברית.

The expression is used mostly in English and <u>therefore</u> cannot be translated into Hebrew.

9. כְּדֵי, בִּכְדֵי; תוֹך כְּדֵי; יֵשׁ/אֵין ב. . . כְּדֵי; לִכְדֵי; עַד כְּדֵי (כָּך); מִכְּדֵי; לֹא בִכְדֵי #5

9.1 The familiar use of **כְּדֵי** (sometimes, **בִּכְדֵי**) is to indicate purpose:

כדי *in order to* is used before an infinitive verb (example 39); **כדי שׁ-** *so that* is used before a clause and the verb is then in the future tense (example 40).

> Make sure to distinguish (in pronunciation as well as meaning) **כדי** from **כְּדַאי** *(it is) worthwhile*.

Note also לְבַל *so as not to, in order not to, lest* (related to the biblical בַּל in the sense of אַל *not*), which similarly requires a future tense verb but is used to indicate an undesirable result. For example: יעל פיתתה את סיסרא לבל יחשוש להיכנס לאוהלה *Yael seduced Sisra so that he would not be afraid to enter her tent.* Synonymous words are פֶּן and לְבִלְתִּי.

(39) כדי לענות על שאלה זאת נֶעֶרכו לָאחרונה כמה מֶחקרים.

<u>In order to</u> answer this question, several studies have been conducted recently.

> (40) בסיפור הַבְּרִיאָה הַבָּבְלִי בּוֹרְאִים הָאֵלִים אֶת בְּנֵי הָאָדָם כדי שיפַרְנְסוּ אוֹתָם.
> In the Babylonian creation story, the gods create humans <u>so that</u> they would provide for them.

9.2 תּוֹךְ כְּדֵי *while, during, at the same time as, in the course of, through* is followed by a noun. The word כדי may be omitted (e.g., תוך דיבור or תוך כדי דיבור *while speaking*).

> (41) תוך כדי הַמִּלְחָמָה נַעֲשׂוּ שְׁגִיאוֹת קָשׁוֹת.
> <u>In the course of</u> the war, serious mistakes were made.

9.3 יֵשׁ בְּ ... כְּדֵי *has some/a measure of, has enough to,* or (with a verb) *can, is able to*
אֵין בְּ ... כְּדֵי *does not have enough, is not sufficient to,* or (with a verb) *cannot, is not able to.*

The word כדי in these expressions softens somewhat the assertion.

> (42) אֵין סָפֵק שֶׁיֵּשׁ בְּכָךְ כדי הֶסְבֵּר לַתּוֹפָעָה, אֲבָל אֵין זוֹ כָּל הָאֱמֶת כּוּלָהּ.
> There is no doubt that <u>there is in this some</u> explanation for the phenomenon, but it is not the whole truth.
>
> (43) אֵין בכך כדי לְשַׁנּוֹת אֶת הַמַּסְקָנָה.
> This <u>cannot (OR: is not sufficient to)</u> change the conclusion.
>
> (44) שְׁלֹמֹה מַרְאֶה לְכוּלָּם כִּי אִם שֶׁחֲפֵצָה בְּמוֹת יַלְדָּהּ אֵינֶנָּה יְכוֹלָה לִהְיוֹת אִימּוֹ, וְכִי יֵשׁ בִּדְבָרֶיהָ כְּדֵי הוֹדָאָה עַל כָּךְ שֶׁהִיא אֵינֶנָּה הָאֵם הָאֲמִיתִית.
> [King] Solomon shows everyone that a mother who wants the death of her child cannot be his mother, and that <u>there is</u> in her words <u>a measure of</u> admission that she is not the real mother.

9.4 לִכְדֵי, עַד כְּדֵי, כְּדֵי *to the extent, to the point of, to*
עַד כְּדֵי כָּךְ *to such an extent*

> (45) הַמַּאֲבָק בַּבְּרִיטִים לָבַשׁ צִבְיוֹן אַלִּים עַד כְּדֵי שִׁימּוּשׁ בְּנֶשֶׁק חַם.
> The struggle against the British took a violent form, <u>to the point of</u> using firearms.
>
> (46) בִּשְׁנוֹת הַמִּלְחָמָה גָּדַל שִׁיעוּר הַמְהַגְּרִים הַיְּהוּדִיִּים מִכְּלָל הַהֲגִירָה לְאַרְצוֹת הַבְּרִית לִכְדֵי 60%.
> During the war, the rate of Jewish immigrants to the United States grew <u>to</u> 60% of the entire immigration.
>
> (47) גִּילָם שֶׁל הָעֵצִים בַּאֲתָרִים מְקוּדָּשִׁים לְמִינֵיהֶם עָשׂוּי לְהַגִּיעַ כְּדֵי מֵאוֹת שָׁנִים.
> The age of trees in holy sites of various kinds may get <u>to</u> (OR: reach) hundreds of years.

(48) לֹא נִמְצְאוּ הַכְּסָפִים שֶׁנִּדְרְשׁוּ לַהֲקָמַת מִבְנֶה גָדוֹל **עַד כְּדֵי כָּךְ**.
The monies required for erecting <u>such</u> a large structure were not found.

9.5 מִכְּדֵי (followed by an infinitive verb) appears after an adjective of quantity or measure (e.g.,
חלש *weak*, גדול *large*, מעט *little*) and is translated as *too*. **מכדי שׁ-** requires a future tense verb.

(49) בֶּעָבָר נִטְעַן כִּי נָשִׁים חֲלָשׁוֹת **מִכְּדֵי** לַעֲסוֹק בְּפוֹלִיטִיקָה.
(אוֹ: בעבר נטען כי נשים חלשות מכדי שׁיעסקו בפוליטיקה)
In the past it was claimed that women were <u>too</u> weak to engage in politics.

9.6 לֹא בִּכְדִי *not in vain, not for nothing, for a good reason* is synonymous with לֹא לַשָּׁווא

(50) **לֹא בִּכְדִי** זָכְתָה הָעִיר לְכִינוּי "הָעִיר הַיְרוּקָה".
<u>Not in vain</u> did the city receive the name "the green city".

🏋 #6 10. בחן

10.1 verbs and action nouns

10.1.1 (אֶת) לִבְחוֹן (*pa'al*) *to examine* (example 51); *to test* (in the passive: לְהִיבָּחֵן *to be
examined, to be tested*; note also the noun נִבְחָן *an examinee*).
The derived noun **בחינה** has two (related) meanings:

(a) *examination, analysis* (examples 52 and 68), and

(b) *test, exam.*

With the preposition (ן)מ added, בחינה becomes *point of view* (10.2 below).

(51) הַמַּפָּה מְאַפְשֶׁרֶת **לִבְחוֹן** אֶת נְתִיבֵי הַמַּסָּע הַמְשׁוֹעָרִים שֶׁל הַצַּלְבָּנִים בְּעֵת מַסְעוֹת הַצְּלָב.
The map makes it possible <u>to examine</u> the hypothesized travel routes of the
Crusaders during the crusades.

(52) לְמַרְאִית עַיִן שְׁנֵי הַחֲפָצִים דוֹמִים, אַךְ **בְּחִינָה** מִקָּרוֹב תַּרְאֶה כִּי הַחֲפָצִים אֵינָם זֵהִים.
At first glance, the two objects are similar, but a close <u>examination</u> will show that
they are not identical.

10.1.2 לְהַבְחִין (*hif'il*) has two distinct meanings, depending on the preposition:

(a) **לְהַבְחִין בֵּין ... וּ(בֵין)** *distinguish between, differentiate* (example 53), and

(b) **לְהַבְחִין בּ-** *observe, notice* (example 54).

In parallel, the noun **הבחנה** is translated either as *distinction, differentiation, discrimination* (example 55) or *observation* (example 56). **אבחנה** is *diagnosis* (hence לְאַבְחֵן, *to diagnose*).

---

(53) הוא איננו **מבחין בין** מָקוֹר מוּקְדָם ומאוחָר.
He does not <u>distinguish</u> between an early and a late source.

(54) החוקרים **הבחינו** בְּהֶבְדֵל שבין שְׁנֵי הנוּסָחים.
The researchers have <u>noticed</u> the difference between the two versions.

(55) מַטרָתָה של תורַת המידות היא לנַסֵחַ את יְסוֹד **ההבחנה בין** התנַהֲגוּת רעה **לבין** התנַהֲגוּת טובה.
The goal of ethics is to formulate the basis of the <u>distinction</u> between bad and good behavior.

(56) הוא היה מְשׁוֹרֵר בַּעַל יְכוֹלֶת **הבחנה** דַקָה.
He was a poet with keen <u>observation</u> ability.

10.1.2.1 The following are derived from להבחין in the sense of *distinguish, differentiate:*

(a) The adjective **חֲסַר הבחנה** *indiscriminate* (e.g., הֶרֶג חסר הבחנה *indiscriminate killing*).

(b) The adverb **לְלֹא הבחנה** *indiscriminately* (e.g., ילדים, נשים ואזרחים נרצחו ללא הבחנה *children, women and civilians were indiscriminately killed*).

(c) The adjective **מוּבְחָן** (a present tense form of *huf'al*) *distinct* (e.g., מיעוט מובחן *a distinct minority*).

10.2 מִבְּחִינָה, מִבְּחִינַת; בִּבְחִינַת

10.2.1 מִבְּחִינָה *from a (specified) point of view, in a (certain) sense* is followed by an adjective to create an adverbial of manner,[3] for example: מבחינה פוליטית *from a political viewpoint, politically.* When followed by a noun, מבחינה takes the construct form **מבחינת**. The translation is then *from the point of view of...*
Note also **מכל הבחינות** *in all respects* (example 61) and מבחינות רבות *in many respects.*

---

(57) אין זה מחוֹבתוֹ של ההיסטוריוֹן להעריך את נוֹשְׂאֵי עבודתו **מבחינות מוּסריוֹת, דתיוֹת או לאוּמיוֹת.**
It is not the duty of the historian to evaluate the subjects of his work <u>from moral, religious, or national viewpoints.</u>

(58) **מבְּחינה מסוּיֶמֶת** סֵפר זה הוא ביטוי למהַפֵּכה כוֹלֶלֶת המתחוֹלֶלֶת כַּיום בתפישׁת העָבָר הישראלי.
<u>From a certain point of view</u>, this book is an expression of the overall revolution taking place today in the understanding of the Israeli past.

---

[3] See Chapter 5, 2.2.

(59) הַסִימְבְּיוֹזָה הַהוּנְגָרִית-יְהוּדִית הָיְיתָה מַשְׁמָעוּתִית – הֵן <mark>מִבְּחִינָתָהּ הַכַּמּוּתִית</mark> וְהֵן <mark>מִבְּחִינַת עוֹמְקָהּ הָאֵיכוּתִי.</mark>

The Hungarian-Jewish symbiosis was significant – both <u>quantitatively</u> and <u>from the point of view of</u> its qualitative depth.

(60) <mark>מִבְּחִינָתֵנוּ</mark>, הַמִּמְצָא הַזֶּה הוּא רַב מַשְׁמָעוּת.

<u>From our point of view</u> (OR: as far as we are concerned), this finding is very significant.

An alternative for מבחינתנו is the Aramaic expression לְדִידֵנוּ (לְדִידוֹ=מבחינתו, מבחינתם=לְדִידָם, מבחינתה=לְדִידָהּ).

(61) סֵפֶר זֶה מוּצְלָח <mark>מִכֹּל הַבְּחִינוֹת.</mark>

This book is successful <u>in all respects</u>.

10.2.2 Expressions with a similar meaning utilize the words נְקוּדָה *point* or זָוִית *angle* in combination with nouns of seeing: מִנְּקוּדַת מַבָּט, מִנְּקוּדַת רְאִייָה, מִנְּקוּדַת רְאוּת, מִזָּוִוית רְאִייָה. A related word is הֶיבֵּט *perspective, aspect* (example 64); תַּצְפִּית *observation point* is another (example 66).

(62) חוֹפֶשׁ הָרָצוֹן נִבְחָן בַּמַּהֲלָךְ הַסֵּפֶר הֵן <mark>מִנְּקוּדַת רְאוּת מַדָּעִית</mark>, פִילוֹסוֹפִית וּתֵאוֹרֶטִית וְהֵן מנקודת רְאוּת דָּתִית.

Free will is examined in the book from a scientific, philosophical and theoretical <u>point of view</u> as well as from a religious <u>point of view</u>.

(63) כָּל מְאוֹרַע מוּצָג <mark>מִזָּוִוית-רְאִייָה</mark> שׁוֹנוֹת.

Each event is presented from different <u>points of view</u>.

(64) אֶת מִשְׁקָל הַהַשְׁפָּעָה הַזָּרָה בָּעִבְרִית הַחֲדָשָׁה אֶפְשָׁר לִבְחוֹן מִשְּׁלוֹשָׁה <mark>הֶיבֵּטִים.</mark>

The importance of foreign influence on modern Hebrew can be examined from three <u>perspectives.</u>

10.2.3 The qualifying בְּבְחִינַת *in the nature of, as, in the status of, in terms of, taken as* (or, occasionally without the preposition, בחינת) can be ignored in translation without much loss of meaning (example 65).

⚠ Make sure to distinguish between (בְּ)בחינת *in the nature of* and the construct form of בחינה *analysis, examination* (example 68).

(65) עֲבוּר הַחֲלוּצִים, הַיְצִירָה הַסִּפְרוּתִית הָיְיתָה <mark>בְּבְחִינַת</mark> מוּצַר לְוַואי בִּלְבַד.

For the pioneers, literary creation was a mere by-product.

(66) הסיפור כָּתוּב מתצפית של מחַבֵּר כל-יודֵע, המַעריך את האֵירוּעים בְּחִינַת נציגוֹ של הָאֵל עלֵי אֲדָמוֹת.
The story is written from the viewpoint of an omniscient author who evaluates the events <u>as</u> God's representative on earth.

(67) מבְּחינַת מַרכּיבָיו ותכָנָיו אין הרומָן שלְפָנֵינו בִּבְחִינַת חידוש.
<u>From the point of</u> view of its components and contents the novel before us is not <u>taken as</u> an innovation.

(68) מוֹקֵד המֶחְקָר היה בחִינת הקֶשֶר בין יַחֲסֵי משפחה ושימור שָׂפה.
The focus of the study was the <u>examination</u> of the connection between family relations and language preservation.

10.2.4. Alternative expressions to בבחינת in the sense of 10.2.3 are בּגֶדֶר and בּחֶזְקַת.

(69) הפעילויות במַדְריך למורה הן בּגֶדֶר הַצָעָה.
The activities in the teacher's guide are <u>in the status of</u> (OR: <u>just</u>) a suggestion.

(70) יוזמות חינוכיות של מורים אינם בְּחֶזְקַת חידוש.
Teachers' educational initiatives are not <u>taken as</u> an innovation.

⚠️ Note the difference between the adverb בחזקת *taken to be, assumed to be, in the state of* and חֶזָקָה *occupation, possession* (a legal term) as well as the meaning of חֲזָקָה within the expression חזקה עליו/עליה שֶ־ *it can be fairly assumed that he/she…*

🏋️#7 11. יחס

This root carries several broadly related meanings: relationship, affiliation, attitude, treatment, reference, attribution and relativity.

11.1 Nouns: יחס, יחסים

11.1.1

- יחס ל-/אֶל/כְּלַפֵּי *attitude to/toward* has one complement (examples 71–72)
- יחס ל-/אֶל/כְּלַפֵּי . . . כְּאֶל *treatment of . . . as*, has two complements (example 73)

With the noun יחס, the (required) prepositions כלפי, אל, ל- are interchangeable.

(71) יַחֲסָם של ההיסטוריוֹנים אֶל האגדוֹת נע בֵּין אמוּן לדְחִייה.
The <u>attitude of</u> the historians to the legends ranges from belief to rejection.

(72) הַיַּחַס שֶׁל הַמִּמְשָׁל כְּלַפֵּי הַיְּהוּדִים לֹא הָיָה מַפְלֶה.
The <u>attitude</u> of the authorities toward the Jews was not discriminatory.

(73) הַמְבַקֶּרֶת מְקַבֶּלֶת אֶת הַהַנָּחָה עַל יַחַס הַסִּפְרוּת הָעִבְרִית אֶל טֶקְסְטִים עִבְרִיִּים כְּאֶל טֶקְסְטִים קְדוֹשִׁים.
The critic accepts the assumption about the <u>treatment</u> of Hebrew texts by Hebrew literature <u>as</u> sacred texts.

- **יַחַס בֵּין . . . וּ(בֵין)** *relationship, connection* (example 74) or, where numbers and quantities are involved, *ratio* (example 75).

(74) הַקּוֹרֵא מַנִּיחַ שֶׁיֵּשׁ הִגָּיוֹן סִיבָּתִי **בְּיַחַס בֵּין** פְּרָטִים.
The reader assumes that there is a causal logic in the <u>relationship</u> among details.

(75) הַדִּיאַגְרָמָה מַבְלִיטָה אֶת הַשִּׁינּוּי שֶׁחָל **בְּיַחַס בֵּין** מִסְפַּר הַסְּטוּדֶנְטִים **לְמִסְפַּר** הַסְּטוּדֶנְטִיּוֹת.
The diagram highlights the change that occurs in the <u>ratio</u> of male and female students.

Note also the grammatical terms מִילַת יַחַס *preposition* and יַחֲסָה *case.*

11.1.2 The plural of יחס – **יְחָסִים** – has several meanings (different from those of the singular noun), including: *relations, relationships, interaction,* and *association.* It entails the use of the preposition עִם *with* or בֵּין *between.*

The noun יחסים often appears in conjunction with the verbs לְקַיֵּים *maintain* and לְנַהֵל *to conduct* as well as within the construct phrase מַעֲרֶכֶת יחסים (example 77).

(76) הַסֵּפֶר עוֹסֵק **בְּיַחַסִים בֵּין** הוֹרִים **וּ**בָנִים.
The book deals with the <u>relationships</u> between parents and children.

(77) רָאוּי לְהִתְמַקֵּד בְּמַעֲרֶכֶת **הַיַּחַסִים בֵּין** כּוֹבְשִׁים **לִ**נְכְבָּשִׁים.
It is worthwhile to focus on the <u>relations between</u> the conquerors and the conquered.

In translation, מערכת *set, system* is ignored.

The following are some expressions with יחסים (by no means an exhaustive list):

יַחַסִים דִּיפְּלוֹמַטִיִּים	*diplomatic relations*
יַחַסִים בֵּינְלְאוּמִיִּים	*international relations*
יַחֲסֵי צִיבּוּר	*public relations*

יַחֲסֵי חֶבְרָה   *social relations*
יַחֲסֵי יְדִידוּת   *friendly relationship*
יַחֲסֵי אֵמוּן   *relationship of trust*
יַחֲסֵי רוֹב וּמִיעוּט   *majority-minority relations*
יַחֲסֵי עֲבוֹדָה   *work relations*

11.2 Verbs and verbal nouns

11.2.1

- **לְהִתְיַיחֵס לְ-/אֶל**
  Several translations are possible, depending on the context: (a) *refer to* (often when the subject is שֵׁם *name*, כִּינוּי *name, title*, מוּשָׂג *concept* or מוּנָח *term*; examples (78–79), (b) *be related to* (example 80), or (c) *deal with, treat* (examples 81–82).

- **לְהִתְיַיחֵס לְ-/אֶל . . . כְּ-(אֶל)** – with two complements, the translation is *treat (someone/ something) as* (examples 83–84).
  An alternative expression (when the subject is animate) is לִנְהוֹג ב-/עם . . . כ-(ב-) (e.g., הֵם נָהֲגוּ בּוֹ כ(ב)אֶחָד מִשֶּׁלָּהֶם *they treated him as one of their own*).

- **לְהִתְיַיחֵס עַל/לְ-** indicates family and ancestral relationship (example 85); hence: אִילָן יוֹחֲסִין *geneological (family) tree*.

---

(78) הַכִּינוּי שֵׁייח' **מִתְיַיחֵס** בְּעִיקָר **לִגְבָרִים**.
The title Sheikh <u>refers</u> mostly to men.

(79) קַיָּימִים חִילּוּקֵי דֵּעוֹת בְּקֶרֶב הַחוֹקְרִים אִם הָהָר הַמּוּכָּר בְּשֵׁם "הַר נְבוֹ" הוּא אָכֵן אוֹתוֹ הָהָר שֶׁאֵלָיו **הִתְיַיחֲסוּ** בַּתּוֹרָה.
There are differences of opinion among the researchers whether the mountain known by the name of "Mount Nebo" is indeed the same mountain that is <u>referred to</u> in the Torah.

(80) סָבִיר לְהַנִּיחַ שֶׁאַף הַשֵּׁם הַמִּקְרָאִי "לֵאָה" **מִתְיַיחֵס לְשׁוֹרֶשׁ** זֶה.
It is reasonable to assume that the biblical name "Leah" is also <u>related to</u> this root.

(81) חֲזוֹן הַנָּבִיא **מִתְיַיחֵס לְאַחֲרִית** הַיָּמִים.
The prophet's vision <u>deals with</u> (OR: <u>treats</u>) the End of Days.

(82) הַמְחַבֵּר לֹא **הִתְיַיחֵס לַהֶיבֵּטִים** כַּלְכָּלִיִּים וַחֲבָרָתִיִּים שֶׁל הַתְּקוּפָה הַנְּדוֹנָה.
The author did not <u>deal with</u> (OR: <u>treat</u>) the economic and social aspects of the period under discussion.

(83) הַמְּדִינָה **מִתְיַיחֶסֶת אֲלֵיהֶם כְּאֶל** תּוֹשָׁבִים זְמַנִּיִּים.
The state <u>treats</u> them <u>as</u> temporary residents.

(84) כָּל הַשְּׁבָטִים הַיּוֹשְׁבִים בִּסְבִיבוֹת הָהָר **הִתְיַיחֲסוּ אֵלָיו כְּאֶל** מָקוֹם מְקוּדָּשׁ.
All the tribes living in the environs of the mountain <u>treated</u> it <u>as</u> a sanctified place.

(85) כַּיּוֹם רוֹב הַיְּהוּדִים **מִתְיַיחֲסִים עַל** שֵׁבֶט יְהוּדָה.
Today most Jews are <u>related to</u> the Tribe of Judah.

Like its source verb, the noun **התייחסות** may take either one or two complements and is rendered in English variably, depending on the context, as *reference to* (example 86), *attitude to* (example 87) or *treatment of* (example 88).

---

(86) אין בגמרא שום **התייחסות לכוס** חמישית.
In the Gemara there is no <u>reference</u> to a fifth cup.

(87) התנועה שָׁאֲפָה לשנות את **התייחסות** הַחֶברה **לנשים**.
The movement sought to change the <u>attitude</u> of society to women (OR: society's <u>treatment</u> of women).

(88) במאמר **התייחסות למעמדו** המיוחד של עץ הזית בתרבות ישראל.
In the article there is a <u>treatment</u> of (OR: the article <u>deals with</u>) the special status of the olive tree in the culture of Israel.

Note the omission of יש[4]: . . . במאמר יש התייחסות ל־

11.2.2 **לְיַחֵס (את) . . . ל־** *attribute to*; in the passive, **יוּחַס ל־** *was attributed to, was ascribed to.*

---

(89) בתרבויות עתיקות נָטוּ **לייחס** גם **לחַיוֹת** נשָׁמָה, רוח וחָכמָה.
In ancient cultures they tended to <u>attribute</u> soul, spirit and wisdom also <u>to</u> animals.

(90) הספר **יוחס לחכמי** המשְׁנָה.
The book <u>was attributed</u> to the sages of the Mishnah.

(91) בחֶברוֹת קְדוּמוֹת **יוחס** עֵרֶך רב **לבֵן זָכָר**.
In early societies a great value <u>was ascribed to</u> a male son.

11.3 Adjective **יַחֲסִי, יַחֲסִית, יַחֲסִיִּים, יַחֲסִיּוּת** *relative*

---

(92) מַעֲרָב ומזרָח הם כיווּנים **יַחֲסִיִּים**, שמַשמעוּתם תלוּיה במָקום שבו נמצא אומְרָם.
West and east are <u>relative</u> directions whose meaning depends on the location of the speaker.

---

[4] See Chapter 9, 1.1.1.

11.4 Adverbs

11.4.1 בְּאוֹפֶן יַחֲסִי, יַחֲסִית, בְּיַחַס *relatively*

---

(93) שְׁמוֹת מִשְׁפָּחָה הוֹפִיעוּ בֵּין הַיְּהוּדִים בְּאַרְצוֹת אֵירוֹפָּה הַשּׁוֹנוֹת כְּבָר בִּתְקוּפָה קְדוּמָה **יַחֲסִית.**

Family names appeared among the Jews in various European countries already at a <u>relatively</u> early period.

(94) יִשְׂרָאֵל נִכְלֶלֶת בִּקְבוּצַת הַמְּדִינוֹת הַנְּדִיבוֹת **יַחֲסִית** בְּיַחַס לִשְׂפוֹת מִיעוּט.

Israel is among the countries that are <u>relatively</u> generous in their attitude to minority languages.

Note in this example the occurrence of the root יחס in different meanings: יחסית *relatively* and (היחס שלהן) יחסן *their attitude.*

(95) הַהֲגִיָּיה הָ'אַשְׁכְּנַזִית', מְאוּחֶרֶת הִיא **בְּיַחַס.**

The "Ashkenazi" pronunciation is <u>relatively</u> late.

11.4.2 בְּיַחַס לְ- *regarding, with regard to* or *relative(ly) to* (example 98). Synonymous expressions are: בְּנוֹגֵעַ לְ-, בְּקֶשֶׁר לְ-, בְּעִנְיָין, לְגַבֵּי.

⚠ Note that in unpointed text it may not be immediately clear whether ביחס ל- should be read as בְּיַחַס לְ- *with regard to* or בַּיַּחַס לְ- *in the attitude to.*
For example: שִׁינוּי בְּיַחַס לַיְּהוּדִים could be read as *a change <u>with regard to</u> the Jews* or *a change <u>in the attitude to</u> the Jews.* The ambiguity can be usually resolved by the context.

---

(96) הַדֵּעוֹת הָיוּ חֲלוּקוֹת **בְּיַחַס** לִיעִילוּת הַמֶּמְשָׁלָה.

Opinions were divided <u>regarding</u> the efficiency of the government.

(97) כַּמָּה מֵהַמְּהַגְרִים נִשְׁאָרִים בִּמְדִינוֹת הַמְּאָרְחוֹת לִפְרְקֵי זְמַן אֲרוּכִּים. זֶה הַמַּצָּב, לְדוּגְמָה, **בְּיַחַס לְרוֹב** הַפָּלֶסְטִינִים שֶׁהִיגְּרוּ לְאַרְצוֹת הַבְּרִית.

Some of the immigrants remain in the host countries for long periods of time. This is the situation, for example, <u>with regard to</u> most of the Palestinians who immigrated to the United States.

(98) שִׁיטַת הַסְּפָרוֹת הָרוֹמִיּוֹת הוּחְלְפָה בְּשִׁיטַת הַסְּפָרוֹת הָעֲרָבִיוֹת בִּשֶׁל נוֹחוּתָה **בְּיַחַס לִסְפָרוֹת הָרוֹמִיּוֹת.**

The system of Roman numerals was replaced by the system of Arabic numerals because of its convenience <u>relative to</u> the Roman numerals.

✗#8 12. הֵחֵל; הָחֵל בְּ-; חָל; חָל עַל, הֵחִיל, הֵחִיל עַל; חוֹלֵל, הִתְחוֹלֵל

Different meanings – *beginning, occurrence* and *application/implementation* – are conveyed by these similar sounding and looking verbs.

The root of הֵחֵל *began* and הָחֵל בְּ- *beginning with* is חלל; this is also the root of חִילֵל *desecrated.*[5] חָל *occurred* (*pa'al*), חוֹלֵל *brought about* (*pi'el*), הִתְחוֹלֵל *happened* (*hitpa'el*) and הֵחִיל *applied, implemented* (*hif'il*) share the same root, חול.

12.1 הֵחֵל, הֵחֵלָה, הֵחֵלוּ *began* are formal variants of התחיל/התחילה/התחילו and may be similarly followed by an infinitive verb (example 99) or an object complement (example 100). In the passive: הוּחַל בְּ- *was begun* (e.g., הוּחַל בבניית המקדש *the building of the Temple was begun*).

---

(99) לא ברור מֵאֵימָתַי <u>הֵחֵל</u> מגן-דָוִד להתקבל כְּסֵמל יהודי.

It is not clear since when the Star of David <u>began</u> to be accepted as a Jewish symbol.

אֵימָתַי is a (Mishnaic) variant for מתי.

(100) תנועת "השומֵר הצעיר" <u>הֵחֵלָה</u> את דַרכָּהּ במזרח אֵירופה בתחילת המאה.

"Ha-Shomer ha-Zair" (The Young Sentinel) movement <u>began</u> (its way) in Eastern Europe at the beginning of the [20th] century.

Note the (same root) adverb בתחילת *at the beginning of.*

12.2 הָחֵל בְּ-/מִ-(וֹ) *beginning with/from, since* is an adverbial; it is often complemented by וכַלֵּה בְּ- *and ending with.*[6]

---

(101) המוזאון מציג מִמצָאים <u>הָחֵל מן</u> התקופה הפְּרֶהיסטורית.

The museum exhibits findings <u>beginning with</u> the prehistoric period.

12.3 לָחוּל (בְּ-) *occur, happen, take place* – this verb is typically used for dates, processes or events and appears in the third person only.

In the present: חָל/חָלָה/חָלִים/חָלוֹת; in the past: חָל/חָלָה/חָלוּ; in the future: יָחוּל/תָחוּל/יָחוּלוּ.[7]

---

[5] חִילֵל *played the flute* is related to the name of the instrument, חליל.
[6] See also Chapter 10, section 13.
[7] תחוֹלנָה (הֵן) is rare.

⚠ Note that when preceded by the subordinator -הַ, the present tense verb forms הַחָל and הַחָלָה *which occurs* appear (in unpointed text) identical to the past tense forms הֵחֵל and הֵחֵלָה *began*.

To further complicate matters, הַחָל *which occurs* is indistinguishable in unpointed text from הָחֵל בְּ-/מִ- *beginning with*.

The distinction among these forms must be made on the basis of the context (as illustrated in examples 102 and 104).

‏(102) שינוי בגישה זו **חל** בעקבות גירוש סְפָרד, **הָחֵל מסוף** המאה ה-15.
A change in this approach <u>occurred</u> after the expulsion from Spain, <u>beginning with</u> the end of the fifteenth century.

Reading החל מסוף המאה ה-15 as **which occurs** *from the end of the 15ᵗʰ century,* where החל is interpreted as הַחָל=שֶׁחָל, a verb whose subject is גירוש ספרד, is not possible because it is contrary to historical fact (the 1492 expulsion was completed by the end of the 15ᵗʰ century). Therefore we read הָחֵל מסוף המאה ה-15 as an adverb of time, *beginning with the 15ᵗʰ century,* that provides the time frame for חל שינוי בגישה זו.

‏(103) חובת בית הדין הייתה לקבוע מתי **יָחוּל** ראש החודש.
The duty of the court was to determine when the beginning of the month <u>would occur</u>.

‏(104) מְאַפְיֵין מֶרְכָּזִי של הפוליטיקה **החל מאמצע** המאה ה-19 הוא הִשְתַתְּפוּת הציבור הָרָחָב בחַיִים הפוליטיים.
A central characteristic of politics <u>beginning with</u> the middle of the 19ᵗʰ century has been the participation of the wider public in political life.

The reading of החל as a verb, הַחָל *which occurs* (i.e., *a central characteristic of politics which occurs from the beginning of the 19ᵗʰ century*) is not possible on semantic grounds: this verb does not co-occur with the noun מאפיין *a characteristic.*

12.4 חל על: the preposition על changes the meaning of the verb from *occur* to *apply to* (example 105).

12.4.1 על ... (את) הֶחִיל *make applicable to,* is a causative of חל על (example 106); in the passive: הוּחַל על *was applied to.*

‏(105) הפֶּרֶק השביעי קובע **על מי חל** החוק ומי הם היוצאים מן הכְּלָל אשר החוק **אינו חל** עליהם.
The seventh chapter determines who the law <u>applies to</u> and who the exceptions are to which the law <u>does not apply</u>.

(106) מדינות שונות החליטו **להחיל** חובה של רישום שמות משפחה **על** התושבים היהודים.
Several countries decided to <u>make applicable</u> the requirement of registering family names to the Jewish residents.

12.5 לחולל means *to create, to bring about*;[8] **להתחולל** *happen, take place* is its intransitive counterpart. These verbs are usually found in conjunction with the nouns שינוי, תמורה *change,* מהפכה *revolution,* סְעָרָה *storm,* מַשְׁבֵּר *crisis,* מִפְנֶה *turning point,* and נס *miracle.*

(107) הַסֵּפֶר **חוֹלֵל** מהפֵּכה עצומה במחשבה המדעית.
The book <u>created</u> an enormous revolution in scientific thinking.

(108) שינוי זה **התחולל** תוך דור אחד.
This change <u>took place</u> within one generation.

13. מִשׁוּם (שֶׁ-), עַל שׁוּם (שֶׁ-); לֹא/אֵין שׁוּם, בְּשׁוּם; יֵשׁ/אֵין ב- . . . מִשׁוּם

13.1 מִשׁוּם (שֶׁ-) and (more formally) **עַל שׁוּם (שֶׁ-)** are causal connectors, translated as *because, as a result of* (example 109).

13.2 שׁוּם *any* or *no* requires a word of negation, אֵין or לֹא, אַל, as does **בְּשׁוּם**, which appears in the expressions בְּשׁוּם פָּנִים וָאוֹפֶן לֹא, בְּשׁוּם פָּנִים לֹא, בְּשׁוּם אוֹפֶן לֹא *(not) at all, (not) under any circumstances* (examples 110–111).

13.3 יֵשׁ ב- . . . מִשׁוּם *have/has something of/have/has a certain measure of* and its opposite **אֵין ב- . . . מִשׁוּם** *do/does not have anything of* are used to minimize an assertion (example 113), similarly to the function of יֵשׁ/אֵין ב . . . כְּדֵי (9.3 above).

(109) שְׁמוֹ של הר הלְּבָנוֹן ניתן לו **עַל שׁוּם** פְּסגוֹתיו המוּשְׁלָגוֹת והלְבָנוֹת.
The name of Mount Lebanon was given to it <u>because</u> of its snowy and white peaks.

(110) **אֵין שׁוּם** מֶרכָּז יהוּדי אחֵר שֶׁבּוֹ היְיתה יצירה כֹּה מְגוּוֶנת וַעֲנֵפָה כמו בְּבֵית מדְרָשׁוֹ של רשִׁ"י.
<u>There is no</u> other Jewish center in which there was such diverse and extensive creation as in the school of Rashi.

(111) חוֹפֶשׁ הדָת הוא זְכוּתוֹ של כל אָדָם לבחוֹר ולקַיֵּים את דתוֹ או **לֹא** לקַיֵּים **שׁוּם** דת.
Freedom of religion is the right of each person to choose to observe his religion or not observe <u>any</u> religion.

---

[8] A different (unrelated) meaning is *to dance.*

> (112) פיתוח כַּלְכָּלִי בְּשׁוֹם פָּנִים וָאוֹפֶן אֵינֶנּוּ מַצְדִּיק וָנְדָלִיזְם סְבִיבָתִי.
> Economic development <u>in no way</u> justified environmental vandalism.
>
> (113) יֵשׁ בַּדְּבָרִים אֵלֶּה מְשׁוּם פִּישׁוּט.
> These words are <u>somewhat</u> simplified (OR: <u>there is some measure of</u> simplification in these words).

14. #9 דָּבָר, דְּבָרִים; לִדְבָרֵי, כִּדְבָרֵי; הַדָּבָר; לֹא . . . דָּבָר; בִּדְבַר; מְדוּבָּר בּ-/עַל

14.1 דָּבָר has several meanings:

(a) *object, thing, item* (examples 114–115),

(b) *matter* (example 120),

(c) *word(s), opinion, message, command* – something that is said or written (examples 116–119).
This meaning is related to the verb לְדַבֵּר. It typically appears in construct phrases, for example: דְּבַר הַמֶּלֶךְ *the word/command of the king*, דִּבְרֵי הַנָּבִיא *the words of the prophet*, דִּבְרֵי שֶׁבַח *words of praise*. Hence כִּדְבָרֵי/לִדְבָרֵי (literally, *in the words of*) – *according to* or *in the opinion of* (example 121).

14.2 הדבר *this (thing)* is a pro-clause, used to refer back to a previous idea.[9]

14.3 לא . . . דבר (שום) With words of negation, דבר is translated as *anything* or *nothing* (example 123); שום may be added for emphasis (e.g., לא נעשה שום דבר *nothing at all was done*). The (colloquial) expression אין דבר means *it does not matter, no matter*.

14.4 בִּדְבַר *regarding, concerning* (sometimes: עַל דְּבַר) appears before a noun (hence its construct form); similar expressions are לגבי, בעניין, בנוגע לְ-, אודות (example 124).
⚠ In unpointed text, בִּדְבַר *regarding, concerning* and בַּדָּבָר or בִּדְבָר *with the/a word/thing* appear identical and the meaning has to be determined from the context (examples 122 and 124).

14.5 מְדוּבָּר בּ-/עַל is translated as *it concerns, it refers to* (NOT: *it is said in*).[10]

14.6 Note the following expressions with דבר, often found in scholarly writing (Rav-Milim, the online dictionary, lists 176 expressions with דבר):

אַחֲרִית דבר, סוֹף דבר	*epilogue, ending*
בָּא בדברים עם	*talked with*
בְּעִיקָרוֹ שֶׁל דָּבָר	*mainly, essentially*

---

[9] See Chapter 3, 2.3.1, examples 37 and 39.
[10] See Chapter 1, 5(b), examples 55–56.

בְּסוֹפוֹ שֶׁל דָּבָר	*in the end, ultimately*
לַאֲמִיתּוֹ שֶׁל דָּבָר	*in fact, truth be said*
דָּבָר אַחֵר	*a different explanation, a different interpretation is…*
דִּבְרֵי הַיָּמִים	*history (e.g.,* דברי ימי רומא *the history of Rome)*
כְּלָלוֹ שֶׁל דָּבָר	*in summary, in conclusion*

---

(114) הַגִּבּוֹר עוֹשֶׂה אֶת הַדָּבָר הָאֶחָד שֶׁאֵינוֹ רוֹצֶה לַעֲשׂוֹת: לוֹמֵד אֶת חֻקֵּי הַמִּשְׂחָק.
The protagonist does the one <u>thing</u> that he does not want to do: he learns the rules of the game.

(115) הַיְּוָנִים הַקַּדְמוֹנִים הִצְטַיְּינוּ כִּמְעַט בְּכָל דָּבָר.
The ancient Greeks excelled almost in <u>everything</u>.

(116) הַנָּבִיא מוּזְהָר מֵרֹאשׁ כִּי הָעָם יִדְחֶה אֶת דְּבָרָיו.
The prophet is warned in advance that the people will reject <u>his words</u>.

(117) הָאִרְגּוּן מֵפִיץ אֶת דְּבָרוֹ בִּמְדִינוֹת רַבּוֹת.
The organization disseminates its <u>message</u> in many countries.

(118) לַמּוֹעֲצָה נִבְחָרִים רַק עוֹשֵׂי דְּבָרוֹ שֶׁל הַמַּנְהִיג.
Only those who do the leader's <u>command</u> are chosen for the council.

(119) בַּסֵּפֶר יֵשׁ דְּבָרִים הַנּוֹגְדִים אֶת דִּבְרֵי חז"ל.
In the book there are <u>things</u> that contradict the <u>words</u> of Ḥazal.

(120) קוֹבֵץ שִׁירִים אַחֵר שֶׁלּוֹ מֻקְדָּשׁ לְדִבְרֵי מוּסָר וְיִרְאַת שָׁמַיִם.
Another collection of poems by him is dedicated to <u>matters</u> of morality and piety.

(121) לְדִבְרֵי יוֹצֵר הָאֲתָר, עֵץ הַזַּיִת מְסַמֵּל חוֹסֶן, פּוֹרִיּוּת וְשָׁלוֹם.
<u>According to</u> the creator of the site, the olive tree symbolizes strength, fertility and peace.

(122) רֵאשִׁית סִיפּוּר הָרָעָב הַגָּדוֹל הִיא בִּדְבַר ה' לְאֵלִיָּהוּ.
The beginning of the story of the great famine is with the <u>word</u> of God to Elijah.

(123) בְּסִפְרוּת חז"ל נְדוֹנָה הַמְּסוֹרֶת הָרִאשׁוֹנָה וְאִילּוּ עַל הַמָּסוֹרֶת הַשְּׁנִיָּה לֹא נֶאֱמַר דָּבָר.
The first tradition was discussed in the rabbinic literature while <u>nothing</u> was said about the second tradition.

(124) מִזְמוֹר ע"ח בַּתְּהִלִּים מְשַׁמֵּר מָסוֹרֶת קַדְמוֹנִית בִּדְבַר מַהוּתוֹ שֶׁל הַמָּן.
Psalm 78 preserves an ancient tradition <u>concerning</u> the nature of the manna.

‏✗#10   15. ‏כֵּן; קוֹדֶם לָכֵן, לִפְנֵי כֵן, לְאַחַר מִכֵּן, אַף עַל פִּי כֵן, עַל כֵּן;
‏כְּשֵׁם שֶׁ- . . . כֵּן; כְּכָל שֶׁ- . . . כֵּן; וְכֵן, כְּמוֹ כֵן; לָכֵן; שֶׁכֵּן, וּבְכֵן, אִם כֵּן; אָכֵן

15.1 In addition to its everyday meaning, *yes*, **כֵּן** is used – usually in conjunction with the verb ‏לעשות – in the sense of *so, thus* (example 125). In this use, ‏כן is stylistically somewhat more elevated than ‏כך and ‏זאת.
To express the opposite, *not so*, ‏לא is employed: ‏לֹא כֵן.

15.2 **כן** appears as a component in a number of adverbial expressions:
‏לְאַחַר *before then, previously;* ‏לִפְנֵי כֵן, קוֹדֶם לָכֵן
‏מִכֵּן *afterward,* ‏אַף עַל פִּי כֵן *however,* ‏עַל כֵּן *there-*
fore, ‏יָתֵר עַל כֵּן *unless,* ‏אֶלָּא אִם כֵּן *moreover.*

> The letter ‏כ in ‏כן is pronounced /k/ at the beginning of the word (e.g., ‏עַל כֵּן), except when the previous word ends with a vowel (e.g., ‏אַף עַל פִּי כֵן, כמו) or after a *sheva* (e.g., ‏וְכֵן).

15.3 ‏כן is also found (interchangeably with ‏כך) in the discontinuous adverbial expressions of comparison – ‏כְּשֵׁם שֶׁ-/כ- . . . כן – *in the same way as . . . so also* (example 126) and extent – ‏כְּכָל שֶׁ . . . כן – *the more . . . the more.*[11]

15.4 **כְּמוֹ כֵן, וְכֵן, גם כֵּן** *also* – these additive expressions replace the colloquial ‏גם (examples 127–128). Note also ‏וְכֵן הָלְאָה *and so on, and so forth* (interchangeable with ‏וְכָךְ הלאה).

15.5 **לָכֵן** *therefore, for this reason* introduces a result clause (example 129); **שֶׁכֵּן** *since, because* introduces the reason for what was stated before (example 130).

15.6 **אִם כֵּן, וּבְכֵן** *if so, so, well then, thus, therefore* rhetorically connect a new statement to a previous one. ‏ובכן usually appears at the beginning of the sentence, followed by a comma. ‏אם כן may appear at the beginning or the middle of the sentence (example 131); it is interchangeable with ‏איפוא (section 8 above).

15.7 **אָכֵן** *indeed, truly* is used to affirm the statement that follows (example 132).

> (125) ‏המלך ציווה להורות למפגינים להתפזר וכאשר לא **עשו כן** הורה לצָבָא להרחיקָם בכוח.
> The king commanded to instruct the demonstrators to disband, and when they did not <u>do so</u> he instructed the army to remove them by force.
>
> ‏כן refers to ‏להתפזר *to disband.*
>
> (126) ‏כְּצֶאֱצָאָיו **כֵּן** המשורר חָשׁ יָתוֹם ועָזוּב על ידי אֱלוֹהָיו.
> Like his descendents, the poet <u>too</u> feels orphaned and abandoned by his God.

---

[11] See Chapter 10, sections 4 and 5.

(127) רָאוּי לִשְׁאוֹל מה מְקוֹרָהּ הַהִיסְטוֹרִי וההלכתי של התפילה **וְכֵן** מָתַי נתחברה.
One should ask what is the historical and halachic origin of the prayer <u>and also</u> when it was composed.

(128) הוא פִּרְסֵם מַאֲמָרִים הָעוֹסְקִים בּרעיונות תנועת העבודה. **כְּמוֹ כֵן** הִיָה צִיר בְּכל הקוֹנְגְרֶסִים הציוניים.
He published articles that deal with the ideas of the labor movement. He was <u>also</u> a delegate in all the Zionist congresses after the First World War.

(129) הַשִּׁמּוּשׁ בְּצֶבַע מְאַפְשֵׁר שִׁינּוּי שֶׁל אֲווִירָה, **וְלָכֵן** הוא נָפוֹץ בְּיוֹתֵר.
The use of color makes a change of atmosphere possible and <u>therefore</u> it is very widespread.

(130) היהודים בקוֹרְסִיקָה נֶחְשָׁבִים כְּחֵלֶק מִיַהֲדוּת צָרְפַת, **שֶׁכֵּן** הָאִי נמצא בשליטת צָרְפַת.
The Jews of Corsica are considered as part of French Jewry <u>since</u> the island is under French rule.

(131) רק בְּמָקוֹם אחד, לִקְרַאת סוֹף הסיפור נשמע קוֹלוֹ של הַמְסַפֵּר. המספר נשאר, **אִם כֵּן, מִשְׁנִי.**
In one place only, toward the end of the story, is the voice of the narrator heard. The narrator remains, <u>then</u>, secondary.

(132) דְּבְרֵי רַבִּי אֶלְעָזָר **אָכֵן** הִתְקַיְּימוּ והנשים יָלְדוּ בָּנִים זְכָרִים.
The words of Rabbi Elazar <u>indeed</u> came true and the women gave birth to sons.

#11 **16.** דִּמְיוֹן; דּוֹמֶה ל, מְדוּמֶה ל; בְּדוֹמֶה ל; וְכַדוֹמֶה; דְּמוּי-; נִדְמֶה (ל-) (שֶׁ-), דּוֹמֶה שֶׁ-/כִּי, כִּמְדוּמֶה; דִּימּוּי; דְּמוּת; תַּדְמִית

The above words share the same root, דמה, and can be roughly grouped into words that express the notion of resemblance and those that express the notion of appearance, or seeming.

> Words derived from דמה should be distinguished from those derived from the root דמם (e.g., דְּמָמָה silence, דּוּמָה, דּוּמָם silently, דּוֹמֵם silent; inanimate).

16.1 The noun **דִּמְיוֹן** carries dual meanings, *similarity* (example 134) and *imagination* (e.g., דמיון עשיר *rich imagination*; example 133). In the first sense – since a comparison is involved – דמיון is usually accompanied by the prepositions -ל, -ב or בֵּין linking the it to another noun (e.g., יש דמיון בֵּין השפות *there is a resemblance between the languages*).

16.1.1 Related to דמיון in the sense of similarity are: **דּוֹמֶה (ל-)** *similar* (the opposite of שונה (מִן)), **בְּדוֹמֶה ל-** *compared to*, **מְדוּמֶה ל-**, *similarly to*, and **וְכַדוֹמֶה** *and the like, similarly* (examples 135–140).

16.1.2 דְּמוּי-, דְמוּיַת-, דְּמוּיֵי-, דְּמוּיוֹת- -*like* appear in construct adjectives[12] (e.g., קָתֶדְרָלָה דמוית-מִבְצָר *a fortress-like cathedral*; example 141).

16.2 In the sense of imagination, דמיון has spawned דמיוני *imaginary* and לְדַמְיֵן *to imagine* (alternatively: להעלות בדמיון), as well as the adjective מְדוּמֶה *imagined, imaginary, fictitious* (example 142).

Several expressions convey the notion of *seeming to be*:

• נדמה (ל-) ש-, דומה ש-/-כי *it appears (to someone) that* are impersonal (example 143); their personalized versions are: נדמה לי ש-/-כי, דומני ש-/-כי[13], דומה עלי ש-/-כי *it appears to me that*

• כְּמְדוּמֶה is a comment adverbial, *seemingly, apparently*, synonymous with כַּנִּרְאֶה.

16.2.1 Like דמיון, דימוי also combines the notions of similarity and appearance: as a literary term it means *a simile* or, more loosely, *an image* (e.g., סרט עשיר בדימויים וסמלים *a movie rich in images and symbols*, דימוי עצמי *self image*; example 144). It is also used as an action noun, *comparing, comparison* followed by -ל (example 145).

16.2.2 The verb לְדַמּוֹת (*pi'el*) may mean either *to compare, to liken* or *to imagine*, while להיָדְמות ל- (*nif'al*) means *to be like, to resemble*.

16.3 The noun דְּמוּת (plural: דְמוּיוֹת) may be translated in several ways depending on the context (examples 134 and 146–149):

(a) A character or personality in a narrative or in history (e.g., דמות היסטורית *historical character, personality*, דמות מקראית *a biblical character*, דמות ראשית *main character, protagonist*).

(b) A figure (e.g., דמות בעלת כנפיים *a winged figure*, דמות נשית *a female figure*).

(c) An image (e.g., בראשית א כו "נַעֲשֶׂה אָדָם בְּצַלְמֵנוּ כִּדְמוּתֵנוּ" *let us make man in our image*, Genesis 1 26).

⚠ Make sure to distinguish the plural noun דמויות from the identical construct adjective -דמויות (e.g., דמויות אדם *human figures* versus מְפְלָצוֹת דמויות-אדם *human-like monsters*).

16.4 Finally, תַּדְמִית refers to perception, or one's image as perceived by others (example 150).

---

(133) הוא משלב ביצירותיו דמיון ומציאות.
In his works he combines <u>imagination</u> and reality.

---

[12] See Chapter 4, 4.4.
[13] See Chapter 3, 1.1.1.

(134) הַדְּמְיוֹן שבין הסיפור החדש לבין מְקוֹרוֹ הוא כַּדְּמְיוֹן שבין דְּמוּת וּבְבוּאָתָהּ בַּמַּרְאָה.
The <u>similarity</u> between the new story and its source is akin to the <u>similarity</u> between a <u>figure</u> and its reflection in a mirror.

(135) כל יצירותיו עוסקות בנושאים דּוֹמִים.
All his works deal with <u>similar</u> topics.

(136) עַמּוּד סֶלַע טבעי מָצוּי על חוֹף האי והוא דוֹמֶה לָאדם.
A natural stone column is found on the shore of the island and it is <u>similar to</u> (looks like) a person.

(137) בתנ"ך שֵׁבֶט דָן בברכַּת יעקב מְדוּמָה לִשְׁפִיפוֹן.
In the Bible, the tribe of Dan <u>is compared to</u> a viper in Jacob's blessing [to his sons].

(138) בדוֹמֶה לַמַּטְבֵּעוֹת אחרים, גם מְקוֹר השם "שֶׁקֶל" הינו במשקל.
<u>Similarly to</u> other coins, the origin of the name "Shekel" is in weight.

(139) הנּוֹדדים נוֹדדים בהֶתְאֵם לזְמינות של מים, מָזוֹן, מרְעֶה, ביטָחוֹן וכדוֹמֶה.
The nomads wander according to the availability of water, food, pasture, security <u>and the like</u>.

(140) דּוֹמֶה שׁגם כאן נָקַט המְחַבּר לָשוֹן מַמְעִיטה.
<u>It appears that</u> here too the author used an understatement.

(141) הָאֲגַם נקרָא כך מִשׁוּם שׁהוא דְּמוּי נָחָש.
The lake is called by this name because it is serpent-<u>like</u>.

(142) הקיסר חיסֵל כל התְנגדות לשׁלְטוֹנוֹ, בֵּין אמיתית ובֵין מדוּמָה.
The emperor did away with any opposition to his rule, whether real or <u>imagined.</u>

(143) היה נדמֶה שׁהמִפְלָגָה תתמוֹך במוּעמדוּתוֹ.
<u>It appeared</u> that the party would support his candidacy.

(144) דִּימוּי הרוֹעֶה הטוב זָכה לפוֹפוּלאריוּת רבה באיקוֹנוֹגְרפיה הנוֹצְרית המוּקְדֶמֶת.
The <u>image</u> of the good shepherd received great popularity in early Christian iconography.

(145) דִּימוּי האָדָם לעֵץ רוֹוֵחַ בשירָתוֹ.
The <u>comparison</u> of man to a tree is common in his poetry.

(146) נָעֲמִי היא דמוּת מְקרָאית ממגילת רות.
Naomi is a biblical <u>character</u> from the Book of Ruth.

(147) על הדֶּגל מצוּיֶּרֶת דמוּת אָדָם.
A human <u>figure</u> is drawn on the flag.

(148) אֶת דמות הַמדינה הַיהודית עִיצֵב הֶרְצֶל בִּשׁנֵי סְפָרָיו.
Herzl formed the <u>image</u> (OR: character) of the Jewish state in his two books.

(149) הַשָׂטָן הוּא דְמוּת מיתולוגית הַמְסַמְלֶת רוֹעַ.
Satan is a mythological <u>personality</u> (OR: figure) that symbolizes evil.

(150) הַמִפְלָגָה הַחֲדָשָׁה ניסתָה לשַׁדֵּר תדמית צעירָה, טֶכְנוֹקְרָטית וְאַקְטיביסטית.
The new party tried to project a young, technocratic and activist <u>image</u>.

B. Internal object (cognate accusative) – מושא פנימי

Some verbs have for their direct object a noun from the same root. The verb-related object is known as an internal object. This stylistic device is already found in classical Hebrew, for example, in the special prayer for Ḥanukkah:

רַבְתָּ אֶת רִיבָם, דַּנְתָּ אֶת דִּינָם, נָקַמְתָּ אֶת נִקְמָתָם
You defended them, vindicated them, and avenged their wrongs.

Since this structure cannot be translated literally without flouting English stylistic norms, in translation either a different verb is utilized or the object is ignored.
For example:

להסיק מסקנה (literally: *to conclude a conclusion*) can be rendered as *draw a conclusion* or *conclude*; לנדור נדר (literally: *to vow a vow*) becomes *take an oath* or *vow*.

Some examples of internal object phrases found in scholarly writing are the following:

לטעות טעות	*make a mistake, err*
להכליל הכללות	*make generalizations, generalize*
לתרום תרומה	*make a contribution, contribute*
לשער השערה	*offer a conjecture, hypothesize*
לפתוח פֶּתַח ל	*give an opening to*
להשיב תשובה	*give an answer, answer*
לחוקק חוק	*legislate a law*
לחטוא חֵטְא	*commit a sin*
לתקן תקנה	*legistlate, introduce an ordinanace*

---

(151) מְסַפְּרוֹת **תָּרְמוּ תְּרוּמָה** לְעִיצוּב הַסִּיפּוּרִי שֶׁל הַהֲוַויי הָאֶרֶצְיִשְׂרְאֵלִי הֶחָדָשׁ.
Women writers <u>made a contribution</u> (OR: <u>contributed</u>) to the narrative shaping of the new life style in the land of Israel.

(152) הַיְּהוּדִים **טָעֲמוּ טַעַם** שֶׁל חֵרוּת מְדִינִית בִּימֵי בֵּית חַשְׁמוֹנַאי.
The Jews <u>had a taste of</u> (OR: <u>tasted</u>) political independence in the days of the Ḥasmoneans.

(153) לְסִפְרֵי הַמִּקְרָא **הִכְתִּיר** הַגָּאוֹן **כּוֹתָרוֹת**, וּכְכָל שֶׁיָּדוּעַ לָנוּ הוּא הָרִאשׁוֹן **שֶׁהִקְדִּים הַקְדָמוֹת** לְפֵירוּשָׁיו.
The Gaon <u>provided titles</u> for the books of the Bible, and as far as we know he is the first to <u>write introductions</u> to his commentaries.

(154) יוֹתֵר **מִשֶּׁצִּיֵּיר צִיּוּר** רֵיאָלִיסְטִי, **צִיֵּיר צִיּוּר** מוּסָרִי-דִידַקְטִי.
More than just <u>drawing</u> (OR: more than he drew) <u>a realistic picture</u>, he <u>drew</u> a moral-didactic one.

When the "verb+internal object" sequence is followed by an adjective, an adverbial of manner is created.[14] In translation, the object can be omitted, and the adjective is then translated as an adverb (e.g., הפתיע אותם הפתעה גדולה *greatly surprised them*).

Two biblical examples and their tranlsation are shown below:

> וַיֶּחֱרַד יִצְחָק חֲרָדָה גְּדֹלָה עַד מְאֹד (בראשית כז לג)
> *And Isaac trembled exceedingly* (Genesis 27.33)

> כִּשְׁמֹעַ עֵשָׂו אֶת דִּבְרֵי אָבִיו וַיִּצְעַק צְעָקָה גְּדֹלָה וּמָרָה עַד מְאֹד (בראשית כז לד)
> *And he cried with an exceedingly great and bitter cry* (Genesis 27.34)

Some examples of internal object phrases with adjectives culled from scholarly articles are the following:

לוותר ויתור מהותי	*make a substantial concession, concede substantially*
להבחין הבחנה חדה	*make a precise distinction, distinguish precisely*
דומה דמיון רב	*has a great resemblance, resembles greatly*
להבין הבנה חדשה	*come to a new understanding, understand anew*
להעריך הערכה עמוקה	*appreciate deeply*
להתרחק מרחק רב מן	*go a great distance from, distance (oneself) greatly from*
להבדיל הבדלה גמורה בין . . ובין	*distinguish completely between..and...*

---

[14] See also Chapter 5, 3.3.

C. Binomials – בינומים אידיומטיים

Binomials are word pairs based on repetition. Two types of binomials are discussed below.

1. "One through two" (Hendiadys)

This term refers to the coordination of two words (usually synonymous and belonging to the same part of speech) to express one concept. Nouns, adjectives, adverbs or verbs can form such word pairs. Some common idiomatic expressions in this pattern are: חָזָק וֶאֱמַץ, חַי וְקַיָּים, אַיִן וָאֶפֶס, רַע וָמָר, שָׂשׂוֹן וְשִׂמְחָה, שלום וּבְרָכָה. This rhetorical device can also be found in English, for example, *safe and sound*.

These expressions cannot always be translated literally or idiomatically into English.

Below are listed by part of speech some examples of binomials culled from academic texts:

Nouns:

אוֹיֵב ושׂוֹנֵא	*an enemy and a foe*
דוגמה ומוֹפֵת	*an example*
הורתה ולֵידָתָה	*her/its origin*
כַּעַס וַחֵימה	*anger and wrath*
לְלֹא הרהור וערעור	*without hesitation*
מִבֶּטֶן וּמלֵידָה	*from birth*
ניסים ונפלָאוֹת	*miracles and wonders*
סִימָן וסֵמֶל	*a symbol*
רוּבּוֹ וּמנְיָינו	*the majority of*
שִׂיג ושִׂיחַ	*exchange of words, contact*
שְׁמוֹ וזִכרוֹ	*his/its name and memory*
שֶׁקֶר וכָזָב	*lie(s)*

Adjectives:

גָלוּי וִידוּע	*well-known*
חַד וחָלָק	*straightforward*
מוּסכָּם וּמקוּבָּל	*agreed upon*
שוֹנים וּמְגוּוָנים	*varied*
שָׂריר וקַיים	*well-established*
תָלוּי ועומד	*pending*
תְקינים ומאוּרגָנים	*well regulated*

Verbs:

גָדַל ונתעצם	*grew and became stronger; increased*
חסם ובלם	*blocked*
נטלו ושָׁאֲלו	*borrowed*
צָף ועלה; קָם וצָץ	*emerged*

<u>Adverbs:</u>

כִּכְתָבוֹ וְכִלְשׁוֹנוֹ   *word for word, exactly the way it is written*

מֵאָז וּמִתָּמִיד, מאז ומעולם   *from time immemorial*

2. Exact or approximate repetition

The function of binomials in this group, like those in the previous one, is to intensify and emphasize.

Some examples are:

בכל דור ודור   *in each and every generation*

בכל עיר ועיר   *in each and every town*

יָשָׁן נוֹשָׁן   *very old*

כל כּוּלוֹ   *all of it*

כל פרטי פרטיו   *all of its details*

כל קהילה וקהילה   *each and every congregation*

מִדֵּי פַּעַם בְּפַעַם   *every once in a while*

לפתע פתאום   *suddenly*

רְבָדִים רבדים   *layers upon layers*

רוֹב רוּבָּם   *most of them*

D. Foreign (loan) words מילים לועזיות

1. The use of foreign words

מלים לועזיות *foreign words* or *loan words* are international terms borrowed by modern Hebrew, recently via English, and adapted to the Hebrew sound system.

> Some loan words are from languages other than English: for example, רומן *a novel*, and אוונגרד *avant-garde* are borrowed from French.

Their use in Hebrew is due to the fact that they do not have a Hebrew equivalent. In some cases, a Hebrew alternative (often minted by the Academy of the Hebrew Language) exists, but has not (yet) become current.

Most loan words are nouns (e.g., שוביניזם *chauvinism*, תאוריה *theory*) or adjectives (שוביניסטי *chauvinist*, תאורטי *theoretical*). Few are verbs (e.g., לְנַטְרֵל *to neutralize*, לְהַפְנֵט *to hypnotize*); these are most often conjugated in *pi'el, pu'al* and *hitpa'el*, the *binyanim* that can accommodate four-consonant roots.

Because of their new guise – Hebrew letters and no vowel points – and their unexpected appearance in the Hebrew text, loan words are often difficult to recognize as such at first glance. However, once recognized, they can be easily understood by English speakers.

The (authentic) sentence below contains seven foreign words, four are nouns and three are adjectives:

המיתוס יחיה רק כמטפורה, לא עוד רק כרמז אסוציאטיבי מקראי, אלא בסיטואציה ריאליסטית אמינה, בקונטקסט פסיכולוגי סביר.

Nouns: מיתוס *myth*, מטפורה *metaphor*, סיטואציה *situation*, קוֹנְטֶקְסט *context*
Adjectives: אסוציאטיבי *associative*, רֵיאָלִיסְטִית *realistic*, פְּסִיכוֹלוֹגִי *psychological*.

#12.1–#12.3 2. Recognizing foreign words

The following clues provide help in recognizing foreign words within a Hebrew text:

1. Most foreign words have four or more consonants, whereas Hebrew words typically have just three or, at most, four (not counting prefixes and suffixes).
   For example: אינְסְטִינְקְט *instinct*, פְּרוֹטוֹקוֹל *protocol*, קוֹרְפּוּס *corpus*, פֶּרְסְפֶּקְטִיבָה *perspective*.

2. Some foreign words are recognizable as such by one or more occurrences of the letter אל"ף (it is used to indicate the /a/ sound).
   For example: מוניציפּאלי *municipal*, פּאראדוֹקסאלי *paradoxical*, פַּרַאפְרַאזָה *paraphrase*.
   However, in recent years there is a tendency (and recommendation) to forgo the אל"ף, thus: מוניציפלי, פרדוקסלי, פרפרזה.

3. There is in foreign words a (relatively) high preponderance of the letters טי"ת and צד"י:
   • טי"ת stands for the letter "t" (e.g., קוֹנְטֶקְסט *context*);
   • צד"י followed by יו"ד represents the English "-ci-" and "-tion" sequences.
   For example: סְפֵּצִיפִי *specific*, אינְטֶרַאקְצְיָה *interaction*, אֶקְסְפּוֹזִיצְיָה *exposition*.

4. The appearance of 'ז, 'צ and 'ג is a sure sign for a foreign name (e.g., צ'רצ'יל Churchill, ג'ורג' George, ז'אן Jean) or loan word (e.g., קולאז' collage, אימאז' image, ז'רגון jargon).

5. Many loan nouns are identifiable by their endings, specifically, the foreign ending -יזְם (e.g., אידאליזְם idealism, סוֹצְיאָליזְם socialism), and also the endings -יָה and -וּת, which are indigenous to Hebrew.

- Nouns with -יה ending are usually adapted to Hebrew from English nouns that end with "-y" or "-ion".
  For example, תֵּאוֹרְיָה theory, אִידֵאוֹלוֹגְיָה ideology, סִיטוּאַצְיָה situation, טֶלֶוִיזְיָה television (and note also אוּטוֹפְּיָה utopia).
- The -וּת suffix may replace "-ism" (e.g., צִיּוֹנוּת Zionism, אַנְטִישֵׁמִיּוּת anti-Semitism) or is used in borrowed nouns whose English endings are "-acy", "-ence", "-ance" and "-ness". For example: אַסֶרְטִיבִיּוּת intimacy, אָמְבִּיוַולֶנְטִיּוּת ambivalence, רֶלֶוַונְטִיּוּת relevance, אִינְטִימִיּוּת assertiveness.

6. Adjectives borrowed from English typically end with -י, and like any other adjective they have four forms (e.g., פַּגָנִי, פגנית, פגניים, פגניות pagan).
   Note that when an English adjective ending with "-c" or "-cal" is adopted by Hebrew, this ending is omitted. For example, epic is rendered as אֶפִּי, theoretical becomes תֵּאוֹרֵטִי and political is פוליטי (NOT: *פוליטיקי).

Once you suspect that an unfamiliar word might be a loan word, try sounding it out until is resembles a familiar English word. Sounding out is also helpful for identifying names of people and places that, in the absence in Hebrew of upper case, are similarly problematic for non-native readers.

The Alcalay Hebrew-English/English-Hebrew dictionary lists some of the more common loan words used in modern Hebrew. Otherwise, a specialized dictionary, מילון לועזי-עברי, can be consulted.

(Be advised that the Alcalay dictionary also contains acronyms and abbreviations. For example: חז"ל=חכמינו זכרונם לברכה our Sages of blessed memory, עמ'=עמוד page).

3. The spelling and pronunciation of foreign words

3.1 Spelling

1. The sequence "th" is spelled with a תי"ו and "t" with a טי"ת: תֵּאַטְרוֹן (also spelled with a יו"ד – תיאטרון, see 3. in 3.2 below) theatre, מַתֵמַטִיקה mathematics.

2. The letter "v" may appear in Hebrew with בי"ת (older and/or established spelling) or with two וו"ים (according to current rules).
   For example: אוניברסיטה university, ציוויליזציה civilization, רלבנטי, רלוונטי relevant, אוניוורסלי, אוניברסלי universal. At the beginning of the word, it is customary to write only one וי"ו. For example: וירוס virus.

3. The letter "w" is also represented with two וו"ים (e.g., וושינגטון Washington, וולט Walt).

4. The letter "s" that is pronounced /z/ in English is currently rendered with the letter זי"ן.
   For example: מוזיקה music, פיזיקה physics; however, מוסיקה and פיסיקה may also be encoutered. (Note the omission of the final "s" in physics, mathematics, ethics and the like – rendered in Hebrew as מתמטיקה, פיזיקה and אֶתִיקה.)

3.2 Pronunciation

1. The letter "g" that in English is pronounced /dž/ (as in *gym*), is pronounced in Hebrew with a /g/ (as in "good").
   For example: in גאוגרפיה *geography* both גימ"ל letters are pronounced in the same way, /ge-o-gra-fia/.

2. The sound produced in English by the letter "j" appearing in mid-word becomes /y/ in Hebrew and is represented with a יו"ד.
   For example: פְּרוֹיֶקְט *project*, אוֹבְּיֶיקְטִיבִי *objective*.

3. The /i/ sound in words such as "archeology", "museum", "theory", "ideological" and the like becomes in Hebrew /e/. The (correct) spelling – to reflect the pronunciation – is without a יו"ד, as follows: אַרְכֵאוֹלוֹגיה, מוּזֵאוֹן, תֵאוֹריה, אִידֵאוֹלוֹגי. However, words in this group may also be spelled (not in accordance with the prescribed rule) with צירה מלֵא *a full tsere*, that is, with a יו"ד after the diacritic (e.g., אַרְכֵיאוֹלוֹגיה, מוּזֵיאוֹן, תֵיאוֹריה, אִידֵיאוֹלוֹגי).

4. The letter "u" – when pronounced /yu/ – becomes in Hebrew וּ, for example: university אוניברסיטה, music מוזיקה.

5. The word "psychology" is rendered in Hebrew as פְּסִיכוֹלוֹגְיָה: the initial "p" is pronounced, "sy" is sounded as /si/, "ch" is pronounced like חי"ת, and the "g" is pronounced /g/.

6. According to the prescribed rule, word stress should fall on the last syllable of the loan word, but in actual use, most speakers stress the next to the last syllable.
   For example: in מיתולוגי *mythological* the stressed syllable would be לו (but גי in normative use).

References

הלוי, 1994
אילני, 2001

Schwarzwald, 2001

Chapter 11: Lexical Matters – Exercises

exercise #	topic	page
1	עשוי	436
2	אמור	437
3.1	ניתן	438
3.2	נתון	439–440
4	מעבר	441
5	כדי	442–443
6	בחן	444–445
7	יחס	446–447
8	חל	448–449
9	דבר	450–451
10	כן	452–453
11	דמה	454–455
12.1, 12.2, 12.3	foreign (loan) words מילים לועזיות	456–458

Exercise #1: עשוי

> **The rules to go by:** see section 1.
> **What to do:** determine the meaning of **עשוי** in each sentence and enter the sentence number in the appropriate cell in the chart. The first one is an example.

may	*made*
1,	

1. בְּנוֹסָף לסִיבּוֹת מִשְׁנִיּוֹת אֵלֶה, **עֲשׂוּיּוֹת** לִהְיוֹת סִיבָּה אוֹ סִיבּוֹת עִיקָרִיּוֹת.

2. בָּאֲגָף הַמִּזְרָחִי שֶׁל הַמּוּזֵאוֹן נִמְצָאִים חֲפָצִים **הָעֲשׂוּיִים** מִמַּתֶּכֶת.

3. שְׁאֵלַת הַיַּחַס לבַעֲלֵי חַיִּים **עֲשׂוּיָה** לְהִיבָּחֵן מִנְּקוּדוֹת מוֹצָא שׁוֹנוֹת.

4. תּוֹךְ כְּדֵי הַחֲפִירָה עָלְתָה הָאֶפְשָׁרוּת כִּי כָּאן **עָשׂוּי** הָיָה לִהְיוֹת מָקוֹם קִבְרוֹ שֶׁל הַמֶּלֶךְ.

5. יַעַר הַגֶּשֶׁם **עָשׂוּי** רְבָדִים רְבָדִים שֶׁל צְמְחִיָּה.

6. הַפְּלַסְטִיק אֵינֶנּוּ חוֹמֶר טִבְעִי, אֶלָּא **עָשׂוּי** בִּידֵי אָדָם.

7. מָוֶות וּלֵידַת גִּיבּוֹר **עֲשׂוּיִים** לִהְיוֹת מָשָׁל לְהִתְחַלְּפוּת הָעוֹנוֹת.

Glossary

1. בנוסף לסיבות משניות   in addition to the secondary reasons
   סיבות עיקריות   main reasons
2. באגף המזרחי   in the East wing
   חפצים   objects
   מתכת   metal
3. יחס   attitude
   בעלי חיים   animals
   להיבחן   be examined
   נקודות מוצא   points of departure
4. חפירה   excavation
   אפשרות   possibility
   קברו של המלך   the king's grave
5. יער הגשם   rain forest
   רבדים רבדים   layers upon layers
   צמחיה   vegetation
6. חומר טבעי   natural material
   בידי אדם   by man
7. מוות ולידת גיבור   death and birth of a hero
   משל   a parable
   התחלפות העונות   change of seasons

Exercise #2: אמור

> **The rules to go by:** see section 2.
> **What to do:** determine the meaning of אמור in each sentence and enter the sentence number in the appropriate cell in the chart. The first one is an example.

said, stated	supposed to	concern, apply to	aforementioned
	1,		

1. הַגְּשָׁמִים הָיוּ **אֲמוּרִים** לְהִתְמַעֵט בָּאָבִיב.

2. דָּת זוֹ קָדְמָה לְהוֹפָעַת שָׁלוֹשׁ הַדָּתוֹת **הָאֲמוּרוֹת**.

3. הַתַּלְמִידִים **אֲמוּרִים** לְפַתֵּחַ חֲשִׁיבָה בִּיקוֹרְתִּית.

4. מִכָּל **הָאָמוּר** לְעֵיל, אֶפְשָׁר לְהַגִּיעַ לִשְׁתֵּי מַסְקָנוֹת.

5. אֵין הַדְּבָרִים **אֲמוּרִים** בָּעִבְרִית בִּלְבַד, אֶלָּא גַם בְּשָׂפוֹת שֵׁמִיּוֹת אֲחֵרוֹת.

6. הַקְדָּמָה **אֲמוּרָה** לִהְיוֹת קְצָרָה.

7. מְדִינִיּוּת קִיבּוּץ הַגָּלוּיוֹת וְכוּר הַהִיתּוּךְ הָיְתָה **אֲמוּרָה** לְגַשֵּׁר עַל פְּעָרִים בֵּין בְּנֵי עֵדוֹת וְתַרְבּוּיוֹת שׁוֹנוֹת.

Glossary

.1	להתמעט	decrease, lessen
.2	קדמה	preceded
	הופעה	appearance
	דתות	religions
.3	לפתח חשיבה ביקורתית	develop critical thinking
.4	לעיל	above
	מסקנות	conclusions
.5	שפות שמיות	Semitic languages
.6	הקדמה	introduction
.7	מדיניות קיבוץ הגלויות	the policy of the gathering of the exiles
	כור ההיתוך	the melting pot
	לגשר על פערים	bridge over gaps
	עדות ותרבויות שונות	different ethnic groups and cultures

Exercise #3.1: נִיתָּן

> **The rules to go by:** see sections 3.1–3.3.
> **What to do:** determine the meaning of נִיתָּן in each sentence and enter the sentence number in the appropriate cell in the chart. The first one is an example.

(not) given	*(not) possible*	*can/could (not)*
1,		

1. בְּסִפְרוּת הַמִּקְרָא **נִיתָן** הַתַּפְקִיד הָרָאשִׁי לַגְּבָרִים.

2. לֹא **נִיתָן** לְבָרֵר זֹאת בַּוַּדָּאוּת.

3. שָׁלוֹשׁ תְּשׁוּבוֹת **נִיתְּנוּ** בַּתַּלְמוּד הַבַּבְלִי לִשְׁאֵלָה זוֹ.

4. אַף אַחַת מִתַּחֲנוֹת הַמִּדְבָּר בְּדַרְכָּם שֶׁל בְּנֵי יִשְׂרָאֵל אֵינֶנָּה **נִיתֶנֶת** לְזִיהוּי וַדָּאִי.

5. **נִיתָן** לְהָבִין אֶת הַמִּילָה מִתּוֹךְ הַהֶקְשֵׁר.

6. הַהַנָּחוֹת אֵלֶּה אֵינָן **נִיתָנוֹת** לְאִימּוּת.

7. לַלּוֹמְדִים **נִיתָנוֹת** מַטְּלוֹת עִיּוּנִיּוֹת וּמַעֲשִׂיּוֹת.

8. שִׁיעוּרֵי בַּיִת **נִיתָנִים** לַתַּלְמִיד כְּאֶמְצָעִי נוֹסָף לַהֲבָנָה וְחַזָרָה עַל הַחוֹמֶר הַנִּלְמָד.

Glossary

1. סִפְרוּת הַמִּקְרָא Bible literature
   תַּפְקִיד רָאשִׁי the principal role
2. לְבָרֵר clarify
   בַּוַּדָּאוּת with certainty
3. תַּלְמוּד בַּבְלִי Babylonian Talmud
4. תַּחֲנוֹת מִדְבָּר desert stops
   זִיהוּי וַדָּאִי certain identification
5. הֶקְשֵׁר context
6. הַנָּחוֹת assumptions
   אִימּוּת verification
7. מַטְּלוֹת tasks
   עִיּוּנִיּוֹת וּמַעֲשִׂיּוֹת theoretical and practical
8. אֶמְצָעִי נוֹסָף an additional means
   חֲזָרָה review

Exercise #3.2: נתון

> **The rules to go by:** see section 3.4.
> **What to do:** determine the meaning of נתון in each sentence and enter the sentence number in the appropriate cell in the chart. The first one is an example.

found in	*given* (adjective)	*prone to*	*datum/data*
		1,	

1. לעיתים קרובות, פוליטיקאים **נתונים** לְלְחָצִים.

2. **נתון** זה מַשְׁמָעוּתי מאוד להבנת הנושא.

3. מֶזֶג האוויר בעונת האָביב **נתון** לשינויים קיצוניים.

4. באותם חודשים היה הנֶגֶב **נתון** במָצוֹר.

5. הספר מתאר את מַעֲרֶכֶת המְתָחים התרבותיים והחברתיים שאנו **נתונים** בה.

6. המסָחָר יחד עם פעילויות כלכליות אחרות **נתון** בשְׁליטת המְמְשָׁלָה.

7. הסָגְנוֹן המוסיקלי של הלַהֲקָה **נתון** לשינויים.

Glossary

1. לעיתים קרובות   often
   פוליטיקאים   politicians
   לחצים   pressures
2. משמעותי   significant
   הבנת הנושא   comprehension of the topic
3. מזג האוויר   weather
   שינויים קיצוניים   extreme changes
4. נגב   Negev
   מצור   siege
5. מערכת מתחים   set of tensions
   תרבותיים וחברתיים   cultural and social
6. מסחר   commerce
   פעילויות כלכליות אחרות   other economic activities
   שליטת הממשלה   government control
7. סגנון מוסיקלי   musical style
   להקה   band
   שינויים   changes

8. לפי **נתונים** היסטוריים וממצאים אַרְכֵאולוגיים, קַיֶּמֶת סְבירוּת שיהודים התְגוררו בּאֵזור העיר.

9. הפוֹנוֹלוֹגיה עוֹסקת בּחֵקֶר היחָסים בּין הֶהֲגָאִים, תְּפקוּדָם וצֵירוּפָם זה לזה בּשפה **נתונה**.

Glossary

ממצאים ארכאולוגיים	archeological findings
קיימת סבירות	there is a likelihood, it is probable that
התגוררו	lived, resided
פונולוגיה	phonology
חקר היחסים בין הגאים	study of the relationship among sounds
תפקודם וצרופם זה לזה	their functioning and [ways of] combining with each other

(8. at top, 9. at פונולוגיה)

Exercise #4: מעבר

> **The rules to go by:** see section 6.
> **What to do:** determine the meaning of **מעבר** in each sentence and enter the sentence number in the appropriate cell in the chart. The first one is an example.

transition	*beyond*
	1,

1. הַמְּצִיאוּת הַמְתוֹאֶרֶת כָּאן נִמְצֵאת בֶּעָבָר הָרָחוֹק שֶׁ**מֵעֵבֶר** לְנִסְיוֹנוֹ הָאִישִׁי שֶׁל הַסּוֹפֵר.

2. רַבּוֹת מִן הַמָּסוֹרֶת מוֹפִיעוֹת בִּתְקוּפוֹת **מַעֲבָר**.

3. הַ**מַּעֲבָר** מֵהָאֹהֶל לְבַיִת כָּרוּךְ בְּשִׁנּוּיִים גְּדוֹלִים בְּכָל אֹרַח הַחַיִּים שֶׁל הַבֶּדוּאִים.

4. מַטְרַת-הַעַל שֶׁל הַמֶּחְקָר הִיא לַעֲמוֹד עַל אֲפְיוֹנֵי הַלְּמִידָה דֶּרֶךְ הָאִינְטֶרְנֶט **מֵעֵבֶר** לַשִּׁעוּרִים הַנִּלְמָדִים בְּבֵית הַסֵּפֶר.

5. הַמַּחְשֵׁב מְאַפְשֵׁר קִיּוּם יְשִׁיבוֹת בֵּין קְבוּצוֹת שֶׁהַמֶּרְחָק הַפִיסִי בֵּינֵיהֶן רַב מְאוֹד, אֲפִילוּ **מֵעֵבֶר** לָאוֹקְיָנוֹס.

6. **מֵעֵבֶר** לְסִיפּוּר הַמְרַתֵּק, מַבַּטָּא הַסֵּפֶר מְתִיחוּת בֵּין עָבָר לַהֹווֶה.

7. נְדוּדֵי הַגִּיבּוֹר כְּרוּכִים בְּ**מַעֲבָר** מֵחֶבְרָה אַחַת לְאַחֶרֶת.

Glossary

.1 מציאות   reality
מתוארת   described
ניסיונו האישי   his personal experience
.2 מסורות   traditions
תקופות   periods
.3 אוהל   tent
כרוך ב   involves, entails
אורח החיים של הבדואים   the Bedouin way of life
.4 מטרת-על   overall purpose
לעמוד על   investigate
אפיוני הלמידה דרך האינטרנט   characteristics of learning via the Internet
.5 מאפשר   enables
קיום ישיבות   holding work meetings
מרחק פיסי   physical distance
אוקינוס   ocean
.6 סיפור מרתק   enthralling, fascinating story
מבטא מתיחות   expresses tension
.7 נדודי הגיבור   the wanderings of the protagonist
כרוכים ב   involve, entail
חברה   society

Exercise #5: כדי

> **The rules to go by:** see section 9.
> **What to do:** determine the meaning of **כדי** in each sentence and enter the sentence number in the appropriate cell in the chart. The first one is an example.

in order to	too (much/little)	to the point of, to	while, during	cannot, not sufficient	not in vain
	1,				

1. הַמָּקוֹם הָיָה מְסוּכָּן **מכדי** שחוקרים יִיכָּנסו לשם.

2. לעיתון יש תְּפוּצָה קטנה עד **כדי** סכנה לקיומו.

3. הספר מתאר את תוֹלְדוֹת היהודים בהונגריה **תוך כדי** רְאִיית קְשָׁרֵי הגוֹמְלִין בין היסטוריה כְּלָלִית להיסטוריה יהודית.

4. אלוהים יוצא ממקום קודשו בהר **כדי** להושיע את עַמּוֹ.

5. העיתון זכה בקהל קוראים רחב עד **כדי** כך שהֵחֵל לצאת מדי יום ביומו.

6. יהוֹדֵי גֶרמניה היו מְעַטִים **מכדי** שמְהַגרים מִקִרְבָּם יוּכְלוּ לשמש גַרעין לקְהִילַת פולין.

7. לא היה בהֶסְבָרִים **כדי** לסַפֵּק את שומעיהם.

Glossary

.1	מסוכן	dangerous
	חוקרים	researchers
.2	תפוצה	distribution
	סכנה לקיומו	danger to its existence
.3	מתאר	describes
	תולדות היהודים בהונגריה	the history of Jews in Hungary
	ראיית קשרי הגומלין	consideration of the reciprocal connections
	היסטוריה כללית	"general" (non-Jewish) history
.4	יוצא ממקום קודשו	comes out from his holy place
	להושיע	save, redeem
.5	זכה בקהל קוראים רחב	gained a wide readership
	החל לצאת	began to be issued
	מדי יום ביומו	(on a) daily (basis)
.6	מהגרים מקרבם	immigrants from among them
	יוכלו לשמש גרעין	would be able to serve as a kernel
.7	לספק את שומעיהם	satisfy those who heard them

8. יֵשׁוּ לֹא הָיָה שׁוֹנֶה מִדְּמֻיּוֹת אֲחֵרוֹת בַּמִּקְרָא, שֶׁ**בִּכְדֵי** לְהָפִיחַ אֱמוּנָה בָּעָם אִפְיְּינוּ אֶת עַצְמָן כְּבַעֲלוֹת תְּכוּנוֹת עַל-טִבְעִיּוֹת.

9. אֵין בְּכָךְ **כְּדֵי** לְהַעֲמִיד תְּשׁוּבָה עַל הַשְּׁאֵלָה שֶׁהִצַּבְנוּ בְּרֹאשׁ דְּבָרֵינוּ.

10. הַמַּשְׁבֵּר הַכַּלְכָּלִי לֹא פָּסַח עַל מוֹסְדוֹת הַצְּדָקָה, שֶׁהַכְנָסוֹתֵיהֶם יָרְדוּ **כְּדֵי** מַחֲצִית.

11. לֹא **בִּכְדֵי** מְכוּנִים יְמֵי הַבֵּינַיִם בְּשֵׁם "עִידָן הָאֱמוּנָה".

Glossary

.8	יֵשׁוּ Jesus
	דְּמֻיּוֹת characters
	לְהָפִיחַ אֱמוּנָה instill faith
	אִפְיְּינוּ אֶת עַצְמָן characterized themselves
	בַּעֲלֵי תְכוּנוֹת עַל-טִבְעִיּוֹת having supernatural qualities
.9	לְהַעֲמִיד תְּשׁוּבָה give an answer
	הִצַּבְנוּ בְּרֹאשׁ דְּבָרֵינוּ we placed at the outset (at the beginning of our words)
.10	מַשְׁבֵּר כַּלְכָּלִי economic crisis
	פָּסַח עַל skipped over
	מוֹסְדוֹת צְדָקָה charitable organizations
	הַכְנָסוֹתֵיהֶם יָרְדוּ their income went down
	מַחֲצִית half
.11	מְכוּנִים called
	יְמֵי הַבֵּינַיִם Middle Ages
	"עִידָן הָאֱמוּנָה" "Era of Faith"

Exercise #6: בחן

> **The rules to go by:** see section 10.
> **What to do:** determine the meaning of **בחן** in each sentence and enter the sentence number in the appropriate cell in the chart. The first one is an example.

distinction	examination, analysis	distinct	as, in the status of	from the point of view	in many respects
	1,				

1. הסיפור עורך **בחינה** מחודשת של עֲרָכים שיתופיים.

2. הַמְחַבֶּרֶת עומדת על התפתחותו של הסיפור תוך **בחינת** נוסח הָאַגָדָה אצל הספרדים לעומת הָאַשְׁכְּנזים.

3. הרצל הדגיש שספרו "אלטנוילנד" אינו **בבחינת** אוטופיה.

4. היו שסברו כי העולם לאחר הגאולה יהיה **בבחינת** מְצִיאוּת חדשה לַחֲלוּטִין.

5. אין קֶשֶׁר לשוני בין שני השמות, **מבחינת** צְלִילָם או מַשְׁמָעוּתם.

6. דור הילדים **מבחינות** רבות מִשְׁתַלֵּב בארץ החדשה בקלות רבה יותר לעומת דור ההורים.

7. הָעַלִייה לארץ הייתה עבורו **בבחינת** הֶלֶם.

Glossary

.1	עורך	conducts
	מחודשת	renewed
	ערכים שיתופיים	values of collectivism
.2	המחברת עומדת על	the author discusses
	התפתחותו של הסיפור	the development of the story
	תוך	through, via
	נוסח	version
	לעומת	in contrast (comparison) to
.3	הדגיש	emphasized
	אלטנוילנד	Altneuland
.4	היו שסברו	there were those who thought
	לאחר הגאולה	after redemption
	מציאות חדשה לחלוטין	a completely different reality
.5	קשר לשוני	linguistic connection
	צלילם ומשמעותם	their sound and their meaning
.6	משתלב בקלות רבה יותר	integrates more easily
.7	עבורו	for him
	הלם	shock

‏8.   בלי **בחינתם** הפילולוגית של המקורות לא ייתכן תֵּיאור תולדותיהם של רַעיונות דתיים.

‏9.   **ההבחנה** בין תוצאות הניסוי למַסְקָנָה המוּסָקת על סָמך התוצאות קשה לתלמידים רבים.

‏10. התנועה מורכֶּבֶת משני זְרָמים **מוּבחנים**.

Glossary

.8	פילולוגית philological
	מקורות sources
	לא ייתכן impossible
	תיאור תולדותיהם של רעיונות דתיים the description of the history of religious ideas
.9	תוצאות הניסוי the result of the experiment
	מסקנה מוסקת על סמך התוצאות conclusion reached on the basis of the results
.10	תנועה movement
	מורכבת משני זרמים made up of two (ideological) currents

Exercise #7: יחס

The rules to go by: see section 11.
What to do: determine the meaning of **יחס** in each sentence and enter the sentence number in the appropriate cell in the chart. The first one is an example.

attitude	relationship	reference	to treat	to refer to	to attribute	be attributed to	with regard to	relatively
1,								

1. הדיון ינסה לבדוק את **יחסם** של המַשׂכּילים אל האישה היהודייה המודרנית.

2. הַשׁפעת החכמים על ענייני בית-הכנסת בתקופה זו הייתה מוּגבלת **יחסית**.

3. כמה מיהודי רוסיה שהיגרו לישראל בסוף העידן הסובייטי **התייחסו** לישראל כמפְלט זְמני.

4. עניינו כאן לחקור מי היה הראשון שהשתמש במימרה זו, וביֶתֶר דיוק, למי היא **מיוחסת**.

5. לַאחרונה נדפסו מוֹנוֹגרפיות אחדות **המתייחסות** לתופָעָה זו גם בעולם היהודי.

6. בראָייה היהודית, אלוהים מקיים עִם עַמו מַעֲרֶכֶת **יחסים** הדומה לזו שבין אָב וּבָנָיו.

7. טְבְעי הוא **לִיחֵס** ל"יד" חוּלְשָׁה או כוח.

Glossary

1. דיון   discussion
   משכילים   Maskilim
2. השפעה   influence
   ענייני בית הכנסת   synagogue affairs
   מוגבלת   limited
3. היגרו   emigrated
   סוף העידן הסובייטי   end of the Soviet era
   מפלט זמני   temporary refuge
4. עניינו   our concern
   לחקור   investigate
   מימרה   saying
   ביתר דיוק   more accurately
5. לאחרונה   recently
   נדפסו מונוגרפיות אחדות   several monographs were published
   תופעה   phenomenon
6. ראייה   view
   מקיים   conducts
   דומה   similar
7. טבעי הוא   it is natural
   חולשה או כוח   weakness or strength

8. עיצוב חינוכי זה הצליח להתְמַמֵּשׁ רק בקבוצה קטנה **ביחס**.

9. **ההתייחסות** לְמְצִיאוּת בדְרָשָׁה בארצות הברית הפכה נְפוֹצָה.

10. סִגְנוֹן המקרא מרוכז וחִסְכָני מאוד, והדבר אמור במְיוחד **ביחס** לתיאוּר חייו הפְּנִימיים של הגיבור.

11. השימוש במונח "קַנָאוּת" **מתייחס** בדֶרֶךְ כְּלָל למִקרים קיצוניים.

12. בחזוֹנוֹ של הֶרְצֵל אין **התייחסות** מפוֹרֶשֶׁת לשפת הדיבור בארץ.

13. **ההתייחסות** של הדְתוֹת להיוָוצְרוּת היקום השתנתה במַהֲלַךְ ההיסטוריה.

14. רעיון זה הינו חדש **יחסית** בהיסטוריה הָאֱנושית.

15. הדֵעוֹת היו חלוקות **ביחס** ליעילוּת הממשָׁלָה.

16. לתַבְלינים שונים **יוחסו** סְגוּלות ריפּוּי, שהעלו את עֶרְכָּם.

17. אני מבקש לברר את **היחס** בין היְסוֹד הדידַקְטי ליסוֹד הָאֶסְתֶטי שבדרשה.

Glossary

educational shaping	עיצוב חינוכי	8.
was realized	התממש	
reality	מציאות	9.
sermon	דרשה	
became widespread	הפכה נפוצה	
the style of the Bible	סגנון המקרא	10.
concentrated and economical	מרוכז וחסכוני	
especially	במיוחד	
the description of the inner life of the protagonist	תיאור חייו הפנימיים של הגיבור	
the use of the term "zealotry"	השימוש במונח "קנאות"	11.
usually	בדרך כלל	
extreme cases	מקרים קיצוניים	
Herzl's vision	חזונו של הרצל	12.
spoken language	שפת הדיבור	
religions	דתות	13.
the formation of the universe	היווצרות היקום	
changed in the course of history	השתנתה במהלך ההיסטוריה	
idea	רעיון	14.
human history	ההיסטוריה האנושית	
opinions were divided	הדעות היו חלוקות	15.
efficiency of the government	יעילות הממשלה	
spices	תבלינים	16.
healing properties	סגולות ריפוי	
raised their value (price)	העלו את ערכם	
didactic element	יסוד דידקטי	17.
esthetic element	יסוד אסתטי	
sermon	דרשה	

Exercise #8: חל

> **The rules to go by:** see section 12.
> **What to do:** determine the meaning of חל in each sentence and enter the sentence number in the appropriate cell in the chart. The first one is an example.

began	occur, happen	bring about, create	apply to	beginning with
1,				

1. הֶרְצֶל **הֵחֵל** בְּאִרְגּוּנָהּ וּבְגִיבּוּשָׁהּ שֶׁל תְּנוּעָה שֶׁתְּיַישֵּׂם אֶת הָאוּטוֹפִיָּה שֶׁלּוֹ.

2. בַּשָּׁנִים הָאַחֲרוֹנוֹת **חָלָה** עֲלִייָּה קְבוּעָה בְּמִסְפַּר הַבִּיקּוּרִים שֶׁל מִשְׁפָּחוֹת בַּמּוּזֵאוֹנִים.

3. הַחִיבּוּר מַקִּיף אֶת הַהָגוּת הַיְּהוּדִית בִּימֵי הַבֵּינַיִים, **הֵחֵל** מִתְּקוּפַת הַגְּאוֹנִים, וְכַלֵּה בִּתְקוּפַת גֵּירוּשׁ סְפָרַד.

4. תְּנוּעַת הַהַשְׂכָּלָה נוֹעֲדָה **לְחוֹלֵל** שִׁינּוּיִים יְסוֹדִיִּים בְּיַהֲדוּת אֵירוֹפָּה.

5. סֵפֶר זֶה הוּא בִּיטּוּי נוֹסָף לַמַּהְפֵּכָה הַכּוֹלֶלֶת **הַמִּתְחוֹלֶלֶת** כַּיּוֹם בִּתְפִישַׂת הֶעָבָר הַיִּשְׂרְאֵלִית.

6. פִּרְסוּם הַדּוּחַ **חוֹלֵל** "רְעִידַת אֲדָמָה" בַּתְּנוּעָה הַצִּיּוֹנִית.

7. הַשֵּׁם "שְׁמִיטָה" **חָל** עַל הַמּוֹסָד הַחוּקִי שֶׁל הַפְסָקַת עִיבּוּד הַקַּרְקַע.

Glossary

.1	its organizing and consolidating ארגונה וגיבושה
	movement תנועה
	will carry out תיישם
	utopia אוטופיה
.2	regular increase עלייה קבועה
	number of visits מספר הביקורים
.3	the work encompasses החיבור מקיף
	philosophy הגות
	Middle Ages ימי הביניים
	the period of the Gaonites תקופת הגאונים
	the expulsion from Spain גירוש ספרד
.4	was destined נועדה
	fundamental changes שינויים יסודיים
.5	an additional expression ביטוי נוסף
	inclusive revolution מהפכה כוללת
	the Israeli understanding of the past תפישת העבר הישראלית
.6	publication of the report פרסום הדוח
	earthquake רעידת אדמה
.7	legal institution מוסד חוקי
	cessation of cultivation of land הפסקת עיבוד הקרקע

8. במעבר מלשון הטֶקְסְט ללשון התרגום **חלו** שְׁני שינויים.

9. בשִׁלְהֵי ימי הביניים **החלו** להופיע ביוֹגְרפיוֹת של מְלכים ואַבירים.

10. **החל** מימי הבית השני נוסף עוד פָּן לדמוּתו של שלמה – יכולְתו לשְׁלוֹט בשֵׁדים.

Glossary

transition מעבר	.8
the language of the translation לְשון התרגום	
changes שינויים	
the end of the Middle Ages שלהי ימי הביניים	.9
appear להופיע	
biographies ביוגרפיות	
kings and knights מלכים ואבירים	
days of the Second Temple ימי הבית השני	.10
another aspect was added נוסף עוד פן	
the figure of (King) Salomon דמותו של שלמה	
his ability to control devils יכולתו לשלוט בשדים	

Exercise #9: דבר

> **The rules to go by:** see section 14.
> **What to do:** determine the meaning of **דבר** in each sentence and enter the sentence number in the appropriate cell in the chart. The first one is an example.

thing(s)	*word(s)*	*this*	*regarding*	*according to, in the opinion of*
1,				

1. בְּמַסֶּכֶת אָבוֹת מְתוֹאָרִים עֲשָׂרָה **דברים** שֶׁנִּבְרְאוּ בָּרֶגַע הָאַחֲרוֹן שֶׁל בְּרִיאַת הָעוֹלָם.

2. קַיָּמוֹת תֵּאוֹרְיוֹת שׁוֹנוֹת **בדבר** מוֹצָאוֹ שֶׁל צְלָב הַקֶּרֶס כְּסֵמֶל פְּרֶהִיסְטוֹרִי.

3. הַפָּסוּק "יְהַלֶּלְךָ זָר וְלֹא פִיךָ" (מִשְׁלֵי כז ב) מַמְלִיץ לָאָדָם לֹא לְפָאֵר אֶת עַצְמוֹ וּלְהַנִּיחַ אֶת **הדבר** לַאֲחֵרִים.

4. **הדבר** הַקָּבוּעַ הַיָּחִיד בַּטֶּבַע הוּא הַתְּנוּעָה וְהַהִשְׁתַּנּוּת.

5. קַיָּמוֹת דֵּעוֹת שׁוֹנוֹת **בדבר** מִיקוּם בֵּית הַמִּקְדָּשׁ.

6. רֵאשִׁית סִיפּוּר הָרָעָב הַגָּדוֹל הִיא **בדבר** ה' לְאֵלִיָּהוּ.

Glossary

.1	מסכת אבות Tractate Avot
	נבראו were created
.2	קיימות תיאוריות שונות there exist different theories
	מוצאו של צלב הקרס the origin of the swastika
	סמל פרהיסטורי prehistoric symbol
.3	פסוק verse
	"יהללך זר ולא פיך" "Let another man praise thee, and not your own mouth"
	משלי כז ב Proverbs 27 2
	ממליץ recommends
	לפאר את עצמו praise himself
	להניח let, allow
	אחרים others
.4	קבוע fixed
	תנועה והשתנות movement and change
.5	קיימות דעות שונות different opinions exist
	מיקום בית המקדש the location of the Temple
.6	סיפור הרעב הגדול the story of the great famine
	אליהו Elijah

7. נָהוּג לחתום את ההקְדָמָה לסֵפר **בדברי** תוֹדָה לִמְסַייעים ביצירָתו.

8. **לדברי** החוקְרים הושפעה המְשוררת עמוקות ביצירתה מן המיסְטיקָה.

Glossary

7. נהוג לחתום	it is customary to conclude
הקדמה	introduction
מסייעים ביצירתו	those who helped write it (literally: in its creation)
8. חוקרים	researchers
משוררת	woman poet
הושפעה עמוקות ביצירתה	was deeply influenced in her work

Exercise #10: כֵּן

> **The rules to go by:** see section 15.
> **What to do:** determine the meaning of כן in each sentence and enter the sentence number in the appropriate cell in the chart. The first one is an example.

(and) also	*since, because*	*then*	*therefore*	*so, thus*
				1,

1. צִיפּוּ מִן הַמְהַגְרִים לשוב לאַרצות מוצאם ורבים עשו **כן**.

2. העיתון לא יכול היה לפַרְסם בגָלוי את אַהֲדָתו למִפְעל הציוני **שכן** הציונוּת הייתה תנועה אסוּרה בּמָרוקו.

3. הָאַרְכֵאוֹלוֹג הימי עוסק, **אם כן**, בחשיפת שְׂרידי העבר בקַרקעית הים וחופיו.

4. מסורות שונות לגַבֵּי מיקום חלקים מהמקדש שָׂרדו במדרָשים, **וכן** בּעֵדֻוּיותיהם של נוסְעים ועולֵי רֶגֶל.

5. השִּׁיטָפוֹן הגדול של 1532–1533 הרס רבים מבּנייניה של העיר. **עַל כן**, רוב המבְנים בעיר הם מהמאה ה-16.

Glossary

1. צִיפּוּ מן המהגרים   the immigrants were expected
   לשוב לארצות מוצאם   to return to their countries of origin
2. לפרסם בגלוי   publicize openly
   אהדתו למפעל הציוני   its sympathy for the Zionist endeavor
   תנועה אסורה   an outlawed movement
3. ארכאולוג ימי   marine archeologist
   עוסק   deals with
   חשיפת שרידי העבר   uncovering the remnants of the past
   קרקעית הים וחופיו   the bottom of the sea and its shores
4. לגבי מיקום חלקים מהמקדש   concerning the location of parts of the Temple
   שרדו   survived
   עדויותיהם של נוסעים ועולי רגל   the testimonies of travelers and pilgrims
5. שיטפון   flood
   הרס   destroyed
   מבנים   structures

‎6. המצרים הקַדְמונים השתמשו בצְבָעים לכְתיבת הירוֹגליפים ולקישוטים, ואחריהם עשו **כן** היוונים והרומָאים.

‎7. ככל שהרְבה האָדָם לקנות דַעַת, **כן** נשתחררה רוחו יותר ויותר מכַּבְלי בַּעֲרות וֶאֱמונות תְּפֵלות.

Glossary

ancient Egyptians	‎6. מצרים קדמונים
used colors	השתמשו בצבעים
writing hieroglyphs	כתיבת הירוגליפים
decorations	קישוטים
the Greek and the Romans	היוונים והרומאים
acquired more knowledge	‎7. הרבה לקנות דעת
	נשתחררה רוחו יותר ויותר מכבלי בערות ואמונות תפלות
his spirit more and more became free from the shackles of ignorance and superstitions	

Exercise #11: דמה

> **The rules to go by:** see section 16.
> **What to do:** determine the meaning of words in the דמה root in each sentence and enter the sentence number in the appropriate cell in the chart. The first one is an example.

it appears/appeared that	*similar*	*similarly to*	*similarity*	*imagination*

character, personality, figure	*image*	*simile*	*-like*	*and the like*
1,				

1. חז"ל ראו ביוסף **דמות** של צדיק, שמתגבר על יְצָרָיו.

2. היה **נדמה** שמקרה זה מבשר את קיצה של האימְפֶּרְיָה הרומית.

3. מַכְשירים וכֵלים רבים מְצוּפים בכֶסֶף על מנת להקנות להם **תדמית** יוקרתית.

4. האֶתיקה של סירת ההצָלָה היא **דימוי** לבעיה המוסרית של חלוקת המַשְׁאַבים בין תושבי כדור הארץ.

5. טַחֲנות מים **בדומה** לטחנות רוח שימשו בעבר לטחינת חיטה לקמח.

Glossary

1. חז"ל   Ḥazal, the sages of the Mishnah and Talmud
   צדיק   righteous person
   מתגבר על יצריו   overcomes his urges
2. מקרה   event
   מבשר את קיצה של האימפריה הרומית   heralds the end of the Roman Empire
3. מכשירים וכלים רבים   many tools and instruments
   מצופים בכסף   are silver plated
   על מנת   in order to
   להקנות   imbue, instill
   יוקרתית   prestigious
4. האתיקה של סירת ההצלה   the ethics of the lifeboat
   בעיה מוסרית   a moral dilemma
   חלוקת משאבים   resource distribution
   תושבי כדור הארץ   the people of the planet
5. טחנות מים   watermills
   טחנות רוח   windmills
   שימשו   were used as
   טחינת חיטה לקמח   grinding wheat into flour

6. רְפָאֵל הוא **דמות** מַלְאָךְ במיתולוגיה היהודית, הנוצרית והמוסלמית.

7. מָגֵן דָּוִיד הוא צורה **דמוית** כוכָב.

8. לְהוֹרְדוֹס יש **דימוי** של שליט אכזר, השולט בניגוד לרצונו של העם.

9. **דמות** שטוחה היא דמות פשוטה שלָרוֹב נבנית סביב תכונה אחת בלבד.

10. סוגות ספרותיות הן שירה, אֶפּוֹס, קוֹמֶדיה, טרגֶדיה **וכדומה.**

11. גיבורת הסיפור חיה חיים מלאי **דמיון.**

12. על פי האַגָדה היה גילגָמֶש שְלִיש אדם ושני שלישים אֵל ולא היה **דומה** לו.

13. יש (א)**דמיון** בין קורותיה של המָשוֹרֶרֶת לבין (ב)**דמותה** בשיר.

14. **דומה** שאין הבְדָלים רבים בין שני הציורים.

Glossary

6.	מלאך angel
	המיתולוגיה היהודית, הנוצרית והמוסלמית the Jewish, Christian and Moslem mythology
7.	צורה shape
	כוכב star
8.	הורדוס King Herod
	שליט אכזר cruel ruler
	שולט בניגוד לרצונו של העם rules against the people's will
9.	שטוחה flat
	פשוטה simple
	לרוב usually
	נבנית סביב תכונה אחת בלבד is constructed around one characteristic only
10.	סוגות ספרותיות literary genres
	שירה, אפוס, קומדיה, טרגדיה poetry, epic, comedy, tragedy
11.	גיבורת הסיפור the protagonist (f.) of the story
	חיה חיים lives a life
12.	על פי האגדה according to the legend
	גילגמש Gilgamesh
	שליש אדם ושני שלישים אל one third man and two thirds god
13.	קורותיה של המשוררת the history of the poet (f.)
14.	הבדלים differences
	ציורים drawings

Exercise #12: Loan words מלים לועזיות

Exercise #12.1

> **The rules to go by:** see section D.
> **What to do:** complete the translation of each phrase by 'translating' the loan word back into English. The loan word may be a noun or an adjective.
> **Example:** ביוגרפיה מפורטת – detailed *biography*

adjective	noun	
social		1. סטירה חברתית
	situation	2. מצב דרמטי
	topics	3. נושאים רלוונטיים
	topic	4. נושא אוניברסלי
	view	5. תפיסה רציונליסטית
	attitude	6. יחס אמביוולנטי
	language	7. לשון פיגורטיבית
	connection	8. קשר אינטימי
	expression	9. ביטוי רטורי
	components	10. מרכיבים תאטרליים
	characteristics	11. מאפיינים אסתטיים
military		12. אסטרטגיה צבאית
main		13. אידאות עיקריות
social		14. אידאולוגיה חברתית
-ethical	question	15. שאלה תאולוגית-מוסרית
	communication	16. תקשורת אפקטיבית
	phenomenon	17. תופעה פונולוגית
	language	18. לשון פורמלית
grammatical		19. ניואנסים דקדוקיים

Exercise #12.2

The rules to go by: see section D.
What to do: translate the phrases; each consists of a noun and an adjective, both loan words.
The first one is an example.

---

1. ארכיטקטורה מודרנית   *modern architecture*

2. אפיזודות דרמטיות

3. אופציה פואטית

4. מוטיבים היסטוריים

5. אנלוגיה תימטית

6. אפקט אירוני

7. אנרגיה פואטית

8. אלמנט אירוטי

9. דיאלוג ראליסטי

10. תאטרון אותנטי

11. אלמנט ויזואלי

12. טקסט ליטורגי

13. נרטיבים היסטוריים

Exercise #12.3

The rules to go by: see section D.
What to do: identify the foreign words in each sentence and give their English equivalents. The number in parenthesis at the end of sentence indicates how many foreign words there are.

1. הסופר אינו מרבה במלים ארכאיות, על מְנת שלא להַגביהַ את המשְׁלב הסְגְנוני. (1)

2. הרומן מתאר את חורְבנה הדיאלקטי של אריסטוקרטיה אידאולוגית. (3)

3. בּמַחצית השנייה של המאה העשרים חל שינוי במעמדו של האתוס האידאולוגי, הלאומי והקולקטיביסטי של האורְיָינות. (3)

4. תְּכוּנה זו מְקרבת את המשל הפתוח אל הספרות הסוראליסטית, שביטלה את הדיכוטומיה בין הראלי לדמְיוני, בחיפושיה אחרי דרכה לפרספקטיבה מורחבת. (4)

5. בחקר תולדות העם היהודי מעלים היסטוריונים וסוֹציולוגים כאחד את הטענה כי הֲבָנת ההיסטוריה היהודית היא במידה רבה לימוד הגאוֹגְרפיה שלהם. (4)

6. המוּשָׂג "מודרניזם" בּמֶחקר זה מוצג לאור הגְדרתו כתפיסה תרבותית כוללת, רְאיית עולם אוניברסלית-כוֹלְלנית, טכנוקרטית ורציונלית. (4)

7. המחקר עוסק ברבים מגורמֵי המַפְתח לתָמורות בחיי היהודים במֵאה הי"ח: המִפְגש עם המדינה הריכוזית ועם המדיניות הרפורמיסטית של המשְׁטר האבסולוטיסטי, אֶתוס התועֶלֶת הכַּלכָּלית למדינה, אקולטורציה, השכלה ורפורמות בחינוך. (5)

8. הפוסטמודרניזם עוסק בשינוי הרדיקלי בּיַחֲסי הייצור ובהתפתחות של טכנולוגיות חדשות, ששינו את תחומֵי הטלקומוניקציה ועיבוד המֵידע, ואת הַפעלת הכוחות הגלובליים. (5)

PART TWO

ANSWERS TO EXERCISES

1. WORD ORDER AND SENTENCE STRUCTURE

Ch. 1 Ex. #1: Locating the subject of a simple sentence

1. נוֹצר 2. כולל 3. נבדקה 4. מסמלת 5. הגבירו 6. פורסם 7. נזכרים 8. עוֹלָה 9. הועלו
10. נמצא 11. אופייני 12. מצא

Ch. 1 Ex. #2: Translating topicalized sentences

1. <u>ישיבה על כיסא האב</u> פירושה לקבל את מקומו במשפחה, את תפקידו ורכושו.
[פירושה של ישיבה על כיסא האב היא לקבל את מקומו במשפחה, את תפקידו ורכושו.]
The meaning of sitting on the father's chair is to receive his place in the family, his role and his property.

2. <u>הלקסיקולוגיה</u> – עיקר עניינה הוא תיעוד אוצר המילים במילון.
[עיקר עניינה של הלקסיקולוגיה הוא תיעוד אוצר המילים במילון.]
The main concern of lexicology is the documentation of the vocabulary of the dictionary.

3. <u>הַמְספר "שבעים"</u> יְסוֹדוֹ בסיפור אַגָּדָה בְּדָבָר שְׁבעים זְקֵנים שהוזמנו על ידי המלך לתַרגם את התורה. [יְסוֹדוֹ של המספר "שבעים" הוא בסיפור אגדה בדבר שבעים זקנים שהוזמנו על ידי המלך לתרגם את התורה.]
The basis for the number "seventy" is a legend concerning seventy elders who were invited by the King to translate the Torah.

4. <u>לשון זו</u> ראשית צמיחתה נעוצה כנראה עוד בימים הראשונים של הבית השני.
[ראשית צמיחתה של לשון זו נעוצה כנראה עוד בימים הראשונים של הבית השני.]
The inception of this language is apparently traceable back (literally: already) to the first days of the Second Temple.

5. <u>גל העלייה הציוני-לאומי הראשון</u> תחילתו בשנת 1882.
[תחילתו של גל העלייה הציוני-לאומי הראשון היתה בשנת 1882.]
The beginning of the first Zionist-nationalist immigration wave was in the year 1882.

6. <u>עדים שהתקשו לענות על השאלות</u> היה נשיא בית-הדין בא לעזרתם.
[נשיא בית-הדין היה בא לעזרתם של עדים שהתקשו לענות על השאלות.]
The president of the court would come to the aid of witnesses who found it difficult to answer the questions.

7. <u>הילד</u> – ברכת "שֶׁעָשָׂני יהודי" ליוּותה בְּשַׁחַר חייו את צְעָדיו הראשונים.
[ברכת "שעשני יהודי" ליוותה את צעדיו הראשונים של הילד בשחר חייו.]
The blessing "who made me Jewish" accompanied the first steps of the child at the dawn of his life.

8. לְדַעַת מְחַבֵּר הספר, <u>דימוי האישה כנחותה</u> מקורו בצְרכים פסיכולוגיים וכלְכָּליים של
האֵלִיטָה הגַבְרִית. [לדעת מחבר הספר, מקור דימוי האישה כנחותה הוא בצרכים פסיכולוגיים
וכלכליים של האליטה הגברית.]

In the opinion of the author, the origin of the image of the woman as inferior is psychological
and economic needs of the male elite.

9. <u>שימוש זה</u> של "הָרים"בהוראת "אֲזורים", האופייני ליחזקאל, האכָּדית היא ברקְעוֹ.
[האכדית היא ברקע של שימוש זה של "הרים" בהוראת "אזורים", האופייני ליחזקאל.]

Akkadian is at the background of this use of "mountains" in the sense of "regions", which is
typical to Ezekiel.

10. <u>היסודות המבדילים</u> בין שני הדיאלֶקטים חותַם העתיקות טָבוּעַ <u>בהם</u>.
[חותם העתיקות טבוע ביסודות המבדילים בין שני הדיאלקטים]

The elements that distinguish the two dialects are marked by the stamp of antiquity.

Ch. 1 Ex. #3: Detecting distant sentence elements

split verb phrase	verb at a distance from its object
1, 2, 4, 5	3

1. בעקבות הנוסע הירושלמי יעקב הלוי ספיר שביקר בגניזה הקהירית והוציא ממנה
מספר דפים <u>החלו</u> אנשים נוספים <u>להוציא</u> חומר מן הגניזה.

2. את רוב החומר אשר מילא את עליית הגג של הגניזה בקהיר <u>הצליח</u> שֶׁכְטֶר <u>להעביר</u>
לקיימברידג'.

3. <u>את הקץ</u> על קהילות היהודים בספרד <u>הביא</u> הניצחון של מלכי ספרד על המוסלמים.

4. ברבות הימים <u>החל</u> תרגום השבעים <u>לשמש</u> בסיס לדרשות האלגוריות של היהדות
ההלניסטית.

5. לעיתים לא הגיעו השליחים בזמן לקהילות המרוחקות שבגולה, ועל-כן <u>נהגו</u>, מתוך
ספק, <u>לחוג</u> שני ימי חג.

Ch. 1 Ex. #4: Identifying impersonal verbs

1. הדפיסו 2. מוצאים 3. היו מקדשים, קובעים 4. סבורים, נהגו לקיים, נראה 5. מכרו
6. אומרים, יכלו

Ch. 1 Ex. #5: Locating the subject of the verb in multi-clause sentences

1. מעידות – **כמויות**; נמצאו – **כלי אוכל**

2. השתמר – **מנהג אלילי קדום**; משקף – **מנהג אלילי קדום**

3. השתרשה – **אמונה באל אחד**; הורגש – **צורך**; נוצר – **מרחק**

4. כולל – **אוסף הגניזה**; משקף – **חומר דוקומנטרי**; מצאה – **הקהילה הארץ-ישראלית
העתיקה**; לא היו אפשריים – **החיים במולדת**

5. ‏נחשפו – **רשימות ספרים**; מגלות – **רשימות ספרים**; אפיינו – **השכלה ותרבות**‏

6. ‏נמצאו – **רבבות קטעים**; נוסד – **מרכז של תצלומים**; מפוזרים – **כתבי יד עבריים**‏

7. ‏מופיעה – **הצהרה מפורשת של הגיבור**; מתקרבים – **חייו**; מורה – **הפתיחה של
הנובלה**; מובילה – **העלילה**‏

8. ‏חזרה ועלתה – **התביעה**; פדו – **אנשים**; התנצרו – **עבדים**; זכו לתהילה – **אנשים**‏

9. ‏זכו – **עבדים**; נזכרים – **עבדים**; ממלאים – **עבדים**‏

10. ‏נתקיימה – **פעילות ספרותית-רוחנית**; משמשות – **עברית וארמית**; יעידו –
טקסטים רבים; באו – **טקסטים רבים**‏

11. ‏השתמש – **רש"י**; חיברו – **חז"ל**; שילב – **רש"י**‏

12. ‏התחיל – **שינוי**; דיברו – **עולי בבל**; חזרו – **עולי בבל**; נוספו – **הלשונות היוונית
והרומית**; קרו – **תהליכי שינוי**; התפתחה – **שפה מדוברת**; היתה שונה – **שפה מדוברת**‏

Ch. 1 Ex. #6: Identifying lexical repetition

‏1. ארץ   2. יסוד   3. יחס   4. ידיעות   5. תופעה‏

Ch. 1 Ex. #7: Identifying appositives

‏1–ז   2–ח   3–ט   4–ה   5–ו   6–ג   7–י   8–יא   9–ד   10–ב   11–א‏

Ch. 1 Ex. #8: Reconstructing elliptical sentences

‏1. התשובה   2. להערכה   3. היה יהודי   4. "על הניסים"   5. הפך‏

Ch. 1 Ex. #9: Differentiating among several functions of an initial ה"א

ה"א השאלה interrogative	part of the word	ה=ש subordinator	definite article before a noun	definite article before an adjective
16	14, 17	3, 5, 11	1, 4, 6, 9, 10, 12, 13, 15	2, 7, 8

Ch. 1 Ex. #10: Determining the meaning of כי

that	because	but also	but rather	although
2	1, 3	5	4	6

2. NOUNS

Ch. 2 Ex. #1: Distinguishing between construct phrases and noun+adjective phrases

construct phrases	noun+adjective phrases
1, 2, 3, 6, 7	4, 5, 8, 9, 10

Ch. 2 Ex. #2: Determining which noun of the construct phrase is modified by the adjective

1. (a)   2. (a)   3. (a)   4. (b)   5. (b)   6. (b)   7. (b)   8. (a)   9. (b)   10. (b)   11. (a)

Ch. 2 Ex. #3: Locating the predicate when the subject is a construct phrase

1. מְאַפְיֵן אחד של יַהֲדות התפוצות (**הוא**/היא/הן) ריבוי הגְוונים שֶׁבָּהּ.

2. הַשְׁפָּעת החכָמים על עִנְיְני בית הכנסת (היה/**הָיְיתה**/היו) קטנה.

3. כמה ימֵי עִיוּן (הוקדש/**הוקדשו**) לעניינים הקשורים במוזאונים.

4. ייחוס תְכונות מַאגִיות לחֲפָצים טבעיים (**ידוע**/ידועות/ידועים) בכל תרבות.

5. שְׁחִיתותו המְנָהָל הרוֹמי (הסעיר/הסעירו/**הסעירה**) את הרוחות.

6. מקורותיו הקדומים של המנהג (אינו ידוע/**אינם ידועים**/אינן ידועות)

7. נְוֵוה מִדְבָּר זה (**היה**/הָיְיתה) מֶרְכז ישיבתם של בני ישראל במדבר
נווה is masculine (see boxed comment, section 1)

8. מַעֲשֵׂהו הראשון של המלך (**היה**/הָיְיתה/היו) בְּנִיָיתה של ירושלים.

9. בְּיִיחוד (**מרכזי**/מרכזית/מרכזיים) מַעֲמָדָם של ירושלים והמקדש בַּהֲלָכָה.
The predicative adjective precedes the subject, מעמד

10. הנחיתות היחסית של מעמדה האישי, הכלכלי והפוליטי של האישה (עומד/ **עומדת**/ עומדות)
במוקד עיסוקן של תיאוריות ופרקטיקות פמיניסטיות.

Ch. 2 Ex. #4: Determining whether nouns with a possessive suffix are singular or plural

their new leaders	מנהיג	שלו שלה **שלהם** שלהן	מנהיגיהם החדש/**החדשים**	.1
their innovative idea	רעיון	שלו שלה **שלהם** שלהן	רעיונם **החדשני**/החדשניים	.2
her rigid positions	עמדה	שלו **שלה** שלהם שלהן	עמדותיה הנוקשה/**הנוקשות**	.3
their possible action	פעולה	שלו שלה **שלהם** שלהן	פעולתם **האפשרית**/האפשריות	.4
his/its rich language	שפה	**שלו** שלה שלהם שלהן	שפתו **העשירה**/העשירות	.5

their spiritual creation	יצירה	שלו שלה **שלהם** שלהן	יצירתם **הרוחנית**/הרוחניות	.6
her difficult struggles	מאבק	שלו **שלה** שלהם שלהן	מאבקיה הקשה/**הקשים**	.7
her personal connections	קשר	שלו **שלה** שלהם שלהן	קשריה האישי/**האישיים**	.8
his early thought/ philosophy	הגות	**שלו** שלה שלהם שלהן	הגותו **המוקדמת**/המוקדמות	.9
her deep isolation/ loneliness	בדידות	שלו שלה שלהם **שלהן**	בדידותן **העמוקה**/העמוקות	.10

Ch. 2 Ex. #5: Determining whether an ‑ות ending is /ut/ or /ot/

‑וּת /ut/	‑וֹת /ot/
1, 3, 4, 5, 7, 10, 11, 12	2, 6, 8, 9

1. מהימנות 2. תעודה 3. עדות 4. אישיות 5. זהות 6. תפוצה 7. נאמנות 8. אמונה
9. מדינה 10. מדיניות 11. מהות 12. תקפות

Ch. 2 Ex. #6: Identifying the reference of the possessive suffix

1. הנאמנות של **ההיסטוריה**; הצרכים של **העם**

2. הייעוד של **מנדלסון**; הבידוד של **היהודים**; האופק של **היהודים**

3. המפעל של **מנדלסון**; העיצוב של **טיפוס יהודי חדש**

4. היצירות של **רש"י**; הפעולה של **תלמידיו**; היצירה של **תלמידיו**; התלמידים של **רש"י**

5. הקוראים של **המספר המקראי**; היצירה של **המספר המקראי**; הדברים של **הדמויות**; האופי של **הדמויות**

6. ההשפעה של **הנצרות**

7. העלייה של **הציונות**; ההתממשות של **הציונות**; ההתבדות של **החזון**

8. ההבנה של **היחס (בין ממצאי קומראן לנצרות הקדומה)**

9. ההשתלטות של **רומא**; ראשיתה של **ההשתלטות**

Ch. 2 Ex. #7: Selecting the possessive suffix in double construct phrases

1. השתלבותם 2. התפתחותו 3. קיומן 4. ייסודו, שקיעתו 5. התפרצותם 6. גורמיהן
7. מניעיה 8. שלביה 9. מקורותיו

Ch. 2 Ex. #8: Differentiating among three noun groups

action nouns	abstract ־וּת nouns	nouns modeled on present tense forms
נתינה, ביסוס, הנחלה, גיבוש, הכרזה, בינוי	ריבונות, זהות, זכות	מייסדים, בונים, מצטרפים, עולים

Translation:

The giving of biblical names to new settlements was an ideological and political tool for consolidating the Jewish sovereignty in the country. The names expressed the spiritual image of the country in the consciousness of its founders and builders, fulfilled a key role in transmitting values and crystallizing the national identity among the new joiners (the new immigrants and the young generation) and constituted a declaration before the nations of the world about the right of the Jewish people to its land. The names were therefore a cornerstone in the construction of the nation.

Ch. 2 Ex. #9: Translating action nouns and identifying their source verbs

.1
צמיחה – לצמוח   *growth*
כתיבה – לכתוב   *writing*
*לימוד – ללמוד   *study*

.2
ידיעה – לדעת   *knowledge*
עלייה – לעלות   *rise*
התפשטות – להתפשט   *spread*
ספיגה – לספוג   *absorption*
השתתפות – להשתתף   *participation*

.3
החייאה – להחיות   *revival*
הוכחה – להוכיח   *proof*
התמודדות – להתמודד   *competing*
מימוש – לממש   *realization*
שיבה – לשוב   *return*
שימוש – לשמש   *use*

.4
*גידול – לגדול   *growth*
ביסוס – לבסס   *consolidation*
קיום – לקיים   *existence*
העסקה – להעסיק   *employment*
ניתוק – לנתק   *dissociation*
המרה – להמיר   *conversion*

3. PRONOUNS

Ch. 3 Ex. #1: Determining the function of third person pronouns

personal pronoun (*he, she, it, they*)	copula (*is, are*)	emphatic copulas	appositive introducer	*its/his/her/their own*	*both*
ב-6	א-4, 7	א-3, 6	Example, 2	1	ב,ג-5, 7

Translation

1. The historian reviews the parallels between the period of the destruction of the First Temple and his own period.
2. Mount Sinai, (that is) Mount Horev, was called "the Mountain of God".
3. Love of life, joy of life, thirst for life – these were the qualities that characterized his paintings and also his personality.
4. There is no one accepted tradition that determines which mountain is the real Mount Sinai.
5. The axe was both a useful work tool and a weapon.
6. It is the event of the fall of Babylon at the hands of Cyrus that was seen (understood) by the prophet as having a theological-historical significance, and in it he sees the fulfillment of the prophecy.
7. Prophecies and poetry, as well as historical documents and compositions that were put in writing after a time (at a later period) are considered "sources" with regard to both the historical facts and their interpretation.

Ch. 3 Ex. #2: Determining the reference of the demonstrative pronoun

1. ב-1950 הושוו זְכוּיוֹתֵיהֶן (וְחוֹבוֹתֵיהֶן) של הנשים לאלו של הגברים.

2. הוא אָמְנָם לִפְעָמִים גֵּירֵשׁ דיבּוּקים, אך פעל זאת בקדושת ספר תורה ובתפילות, ולא בדרכים אחרות.

3. מוטיב זה מופיע בכל הנוּסָחִים המוּכָּרִים, והללו אינם מועטים.

4. יהודים נָשְׂאוּ שֵׁמוֹת זרים, וכאלה נשתמרו אף במִקְרָא.

5. חֲשִׁיבוּתוֹ של המשוֹרֵר עולה על זו של הכְרוֹנִיקוֹן.

6. רש"י מפרש את הפסוק בדרך שונה לַחֲלוּטִין מזו המקובלת כיום.

7. דַרְכָּהּ של התנועה סָטְתָה מִדַּרְכְּכֶם של ראשוני התנועה ואפילו מזאת של מְאוּחָרִים יותר.

8. קשה למצוא לַמְצוא הַקְּבָלָה של מַמָּשׁ בין הפעילות הסְפְרוּתִית שנעשתה בקהילות אַשְׁכְּנַז במאות העשירית והאַחַת-עֶשְׂרֵה ובין זו שנעשתה באותם ימים בסְבִיבָתָן.

9. הסטטיסטיקה מעידה כי חֶלְקָהּ של האישה בסיפור רב מזֶּה של הגבר.

10. בָּבֶל ורוֹמא השתמשו בהַגְלָיָה הָמוֹנִית של עמים שְׁלֵמים כָּעוֹנֶשׁ על מרידוֹת בהן וזאת מתוך הֲנָחָה כי עם המנותק מֵאַרְצוֹ יתפּוֹרֵר וייֵעָלֵם.

‫11. כְּשֶׁהַמַצָּב הַכַּלְכָּלִי היה טוב לא דָרְשׁוּ הַסְפָרַדים מן **הָאַשְׁכְּנַזִים** להשתתף בתשלומי‬
‫הַמַס לַשִׁלְטוֹנוֹת, אך מִשֶׁהוּרַע המצב נֶאֶלְצוּ לתבוע מֵהֶם הִשְׁתַתְּפוּת מְלֵאָה בַנֵטֶל, לְמוֹרַת רוּחָם‬
‫של **הללו**.‬

Translation

1. In 1950, the rights (and obligations) of women were made equal to those of men.
2. Although he sometimes exorcised Dibbuks (demons), he did so through the holiness of the Torah and prayers, and not in other ways.
3. This motif appears in all the known versions, and these are not few.
4. Jews have borne foreign names and such [names] were preserved even in the Bible.
5. The importance of the poet surpasses that of the chronicler of events.
6. Rashi interprets the verse in a way that is completely different from that which is customary today.
7. The path of the movement has deviated from that of its early members and even from that of later ones.
8. It is difficult to find a real parallel between the literary activity that took place in the Ashkenaz communities in the 10th and 11th centuries and that which took place in those days in their surrounding areas.
9. Statistics shows that the woman's role in the story is greater than that of the man.
10. Babylon and Rome used mass deportations of entire peoples as a punishment for rebellions, and this [was] under the assumption that a people disconnected from its country would disintegrate and disappear.
11. When the economic situation was good, the *Sephardim* did not require the *Ashkenazim* to participate in [making] the tax payments to the authorities, but when the situation worsened, they [the *Sephardim*] were forced to demand from them [from the *Ashkenazim*], to their displeasure, full participation in the burden [of taxation].

Ch. 3 Ex. #3: Determining the reference of כך

‫1. השפה מיוחדת בכך שהיא לא השתנתה במידה רבה מאז המאה ה-13.‬

‫2. עם התפתחות האִינְטֶרְנֶט החלו בפרסום מודעות "דרושים" באינטרנט באתרים המיוחדים‬
‫לכך.‬

‫3. כלכלנים רבים הציעו בעבר תֵיאוֹרִיוֹת שונות כיצד הַמַשְׁבֵּרִים הפִינַנְסִיים מתפתחים‬
‫וכיצד ניתן למנוע מִכַך לקרות.‬

‫4. לאזרחי המדינה יש זכות לעזוב את המדינה ואף לחזור אליה בכל עֵת שירצו בכך.‬

‫5. במשך השנים הביא פרוֹיֶקְט "שוֹרָשִׁים" לְכַך שכל בני המשפחה עזרו באיסוף ידע על‬
‫המשפחה.‬

‫6. הסיפוֹרֶת נבדלת מהשירה בעיקר בכך שחוקי הכתיבה שלה דומים יותר לדיבור‬
‫יומיומי ותוֹכְנָה הוא לָרוב סיפורי.‬

‫7. ארגונים פִילַנְתְרוֹפִיים יהודיים בארצות הברית הבדילו את עצמם ממוֹדֵלים מוקדמים‬
‫יותר של צְדָקָה יהודית, בכך שפעלו מחוץ למסגרות של בית הכנסת.‬

8. הפילנתרופיה נעשתה למעין תחליף של השותפות הדתית של היהודים וגם הַחֵלָה
לשקף את ההבדלים המעמדיים והאידאולוגיים הקיימים בתוכם, וּבְכַךְ אפשר לראות בה חלק
מתהליכי המודֶרניזציה והחילוּן של יהודי אמריקה.

Ch. 3 Ex. #4: Distinguishing between אותו as pronoun and as preposition

the preposition את	that, those	the same
3, 6	1, 2, 4, 8	5, 7

Ch. 3 Ex. #5: Distinguishing among אלה/אלו, אֵילוּ, אִילוּ

these	which	if	each other
1, 5, 8-ב, 9, 10	2, 3, 6-א, ב, 8-א	4	7

Translation

1. These findings are certainly encouraging.
2. Which events influenced the character?
3. The law decides which obligations and rights apply to the citizens.
4. If the plan had been executed, it is possible that the state of education would have been better today.
5. These were days of tranquility and purification.
6. The sages decided which books would be included in the Bible and which would not be included in it.
7. The Soviet regime and the nationalistic Right in Poland blamed each other for the pogrom.
8. Which important events took place on these dates?
9. These decisions do not have much influence on determining the character of the state in the century ahead.
10. The machine (industrial) production of matzoth aroused in the beginning bitter controversy among the rabbis with regard to the question whether these matzoth were kosher.

4. ADJECTIVES

Ch. 4 Ex. #1: Translating adjective strings

an original linguistic aspect	1. היבט בלשני מקורי
the first spontaneous reaction	2. התגובה הספונטנית הראשונה
messianic national ideas	3. רעיונות לאומיים משיחיים
a rich archival and literary documentation	4. תיעוד ארכיוני וספרותי עשיר
a distinctive political document	5. תעודה פוליטית מובהקת
a rich and interesting inner world	6. עולם פנימי עשיר ומעניין
a living and breathing urban atmosphere	7. אווירה עירונית חיה ונושמת
a varied social and economic activity	8. פעילות חברתית וכלכלית מגוונת
a great political, economic and military victory	9. ניצחון מדיני, כלכלי וצבאי גדול
old agricultural and industrial installations	10. מתקנים חקלאיים ותעשייתיים ישנים
considerable political and military power	11. כוח פוליטי וצבאי ניכר
a loaded multi-cultural encounter	12. מפגש רב-תרבותי טעון
a non-Jewish intellectual and literary work	13. יצירה ספרותית ואינטלקטואלית לא-
	14. יהודית
an open, tolerant and multicultural social	15. סביבה חברתית פתוחה, סובלנית ורב-
environment	16. תרבותית

Ch. 4 Ex. #2: Identifying adjectives

1. עולה השאלה בדבר היחס בין כוחו המאגי וכוחו הספיריטואלי של הבעל-שם-טוב, וחלקם הפרופורציונלי בפעולת הריפוי.
The question arises regarding the relationship between the magical and spiritual powers of the Ba'al Shem Tov, and their proportional role in the act of healing.

2. בפילוסופיה שלו היה שילוב של שמרנות תרבותית ואסתטית ורדיקליות חברתית ופוליטית.
In his philosophy there was a mix of cultural and aesthetic conservatism and social and political radicalism.

3. ספק אם ישנו בתרבות המערב הוגה דעות שנוי במחלוקת, אמביוולנטי ובעל פנים רבות יותר מפרידריך ניטשה.
It is doubtful whether there exists in Western culture a more controversial, ambivalent and multi-faceted philosopher than Friedrich Nietzsche.

4. אז גם נודעו פרטים רבים נוספים על התגלית אולם מידע זה היה כוללני ובלתי מדויק.
At that time many additional details became known about the discovery, but this information was generalized and inaccurate.
(Note that the first adjective, רבים is translated before the adjective נוספים, even though they are stacked.)

5. צריך לזכור כי הכנעניות – מקורית, מרתקת, או מרגיזה ככל שתהיה – היא רק רכיב אחד בתוך מערכת של מתחים חברתיים ותרבותיים שאנו נתונים בה.

It should be remembered that Canaanism – original, fascinating or irritating as it might be – is only one component in the constellation of social and cultural tensions within which we find ourselves (literally: in which we are found).

6. טקסטים רבים – לא רק הספרותיים אלא גם, ובעיקר, האותנטיים (יומנים, מכתבים וכדומה) – אינם מבטאים חוויה אישית , אלא נכתבים כדי להתאים למודל הדומיננטי.

Many texts – not only the literary but also, and mainly, the authentic ones (diaries, letters, etc.) – do not express a personal experience, but are written in order to fit in with the dominant model.

7. חופש הרצון נבחן בספר הן מנקודת ראות מדעית, פילוסופית ותאורטית, והן מנקודת ראות מסורתית ומוסרית- אישית.

Free will is examined in the book from a scientific, philosophical and theoretical point of view as well as from a traditional and ethical-personal point of view.

8. זהו ספר קריא, בהיר ונגיש, מעניין ושקול, אף שלא נעדרת ממנו נימה אפולוגטית.

This is a readable, clear and accessible book, interesting and level-headed, though not lacking in an apologetic tone.

9. הסיפור מתרחק מפתוס גס ומוגזם מאחר שהוא מאופק, ממותן ומפורט ונע תמיד בין המשלבים – הפתטי, הקומי, הטריוויאלי והנשגב.

The story shies away from crude and exaggerated pathos because it is reserved, toned down and detailed and always shuttles between the registers – the pathetic, comic, trivial and the exalted.

10. בעלייה הראשונה נקבעו הדפוסים התרבותיים של החברה הישראלית בעתיד. כבר אז עוצבה דמות האדם העברי החדש, כבר אז התקיים מפגש בין-עדתי, כבר אז נראו מגמות כנעניות, שמיות ומזרחיות בלאומיות העברית.

During the period of the First Aliya, the cultural patterns of the future Israeli society were determined. Already then, the figure of the new Hebrew person had been formed, an inter-ethnic encounter had already taken place, and Canaanite, Semitic, and oriental tendencies in the Hebrew nationality were already evident.

Ch. 4 Ex. #3: Matching adjectives derived from foreign words with their English equivalent

6	aesthetic	אוניברסלי	.1
4	allegorical	אותנטי	.2
5	ambivalent	אינטלקטואליים	.3
7	apologetic	אלגורית	.4
2	authentic	אמביוולנטי	.5
15	comic	אסתטית	.6
9	dominant	אפולוגטית	.7
8	ethical	אתי	.8

3	*intellectual*	דומיננטי	.9
11	*mystical*	טכנולוגיים	.10
12	*physical*	מיסטיות	.11
14	*pathetic*	פיזיים	.12
13	*proportional*	פרופורציונלי	.13
16	*romantic*	פתטי	.14
10	*technological*	קומיות	.15
17	*theological*	רומנטית	.16
18	*theoretical*	תאולוגי	.17
1	*universal*	תאורטיות	.18

Ch. 4 Ex. #4: Changing the gender or number in adjectives of different patterns

1. שִׁינוי פָּעוֹט עֶרֶךְ

2. תופעות רַבּוֹת חֲשִׁיבוּת

3. מקרים מעוררי גיחוך

4. נשים מַשְׂכִּילוֹת ויודעות סֵפֶר

5. יַהֲדוּת פולין לְמוּדַת הַסֵּבֶל

6. שינויים מַרְחִיקֵי לֶכֶת

7. התפתחות חֲסָרַת תַּקְדִים

8. עיתונאים קַלֵּי הִתְרַשְׁמוּת

9. הקוראת בת הזמן

10. תכניות נְטוּלוֹת אידאולוגיה

11. הַיישוב הלא-קוֹלֶקְטִיבי הראשון

12. בעיות חֶבְרָתִיוֹת-תרבותיות

13. כוח פוליטי-דמוגרפי

14. מְסָרִים בלתי רֶלֶוַונטיים

15. מָקוֹר חוּץ-לְשׁוֹנִי

16. משוררות ברוכות-כישרון

17. מעשים הֲרֵי-אסון

5. ADVERBS

Ch. 5 Ex. #1: Identifying and translating adverbs

1. באופן חופשי *freely*

2. דיים *sufficiently*

3. שוב ושוב *again and again*, ללא ספק *undoubtedly*

4. בעיקר *mostly*, מחדש *anew, newly*

5. באורח פרדוקסלי *paradoxically*, ביעילות ובמהירות *efficiently and quickly*

6. לשונית, חברתית ותרבותית *linguistically, socially and culturally*

7. קשות *severely*, לעתים *sometimes*, כליל *completely*

8. מבחינה כלכלית *economically*, מבחינה דתית *religiously*

9. עודם *[they are] still*, להפליא *incredibly, surprisingly*

10. בהדרגה *gradually*, לרעה *adversely*, בעקיפין *indirectly*, בפועל *in practice*

Ch. 5 Ex. #2: Distinguishing between adjectives and adverbs

adverb	adjective
2 – at length, 6 – generally, 7 – finally, 9 – directly, 11 – much, greatly	1 – long, 3 – personal, 4 – personal, 5 – general, 8 – final, 10 – direct, 12 – many

Ch. 5 Ex. #3: Translating internal object phrases

1. The establishment of local museums is directly linked to the growing importance of the tourist industry. קשורה קשר ישיר

2. He vehemently opposed these ideas. התנגד התנגדות נמרצת

3. The concepts cannot be clearly separated. להפריד הפרדה ברורה

4. The Geniza findings contributed greatly to the study of Judaism. תרמו תרומה עצומה

5. The naval attack failed completely. נכשלה כישלון מוחלט

6. For this sin the brothers were severely punished. נענשו עונש כבד

6. VERBS

Ch. 6 Ex. #1: "Unpacking" infinitive forms with pronoun suffixes

1. הוא ראה 2. הם הוסיפו 3. היא סיפרה 4. הם התקבלו 5. היא הגיעה 6. הוא ניסה
7. הן ידעו 8. הם נעדרו

Ch. 6 Ex. #2: Determining the reference of the pronoun suffix in adverbial time clauses

1. החוקרים הסתמכו 2. הרצל הלך 3. שניהם (המלך והחכם) מחפשים
4. בני האדם צפו 5. היהודים ביקשו, היהודים רצו 6. הבלשנות ההחדישה דנה
7. מאורעות שונים מצטרפים

Translation

1. <u>Relying</u> on the count of the generations in the Bible, the researchers proposed to fix the period of the Patriarchs in the 14th century.
2. Herzl built the institutions of the (Zionist) movement with the awareness that its existence should be taken care of even after <u>his departure</u> OR: <u>after he had left</u>.
3. The king asks questions about the nature of Judaism, the sage replies, and sometimes they argue, <u>searching</u> (OR: in their search) for the truth.
4. <u>When watching</u> (OR: <u>as they watched</u>) the stars, humans noticed changes in their place and position and attributed to this various influences on the earth and the life thereon.
5. <u>When they asked</u> to settle in their towns and <u>when wishing</u> to receive various rights, the Jews were dependent on the good will of various Bishops.
6. <u>When discussing</u> written and dead languages, modern linguistics attempts to penetrate through the written symbols to the spoken language.
7. At the end of the 18th century and the beginning of the 19th, new events took place in the Land of Israel which together (literally: <u>when they join each other</u>) symbolize the beginning of modernity there.

Ch. 6 Ex. #3: Determining the reference of the direct object suffix

1. לתאר אותו – את עולמן הפנימי של הנשים 2. מקיים אותן – את מצוות הדת 3. לקרב אותנו
4. הושיע אותם – את (עם) ישראל 5. שחזרנו אותו – את הנוסח המקורי של הספר
6. התקינו אותן – את התקנות 7. עושה אותו, את נס המן 8. להריח אותו – את האתרוג

Translation

1. Throughout the generations, poets and writers succeeded in entering women's inner world and describing it.
2. He accepts the religious commandments (literally: the commandments of religion) and observes them.
3. Such comparative research may bring us closer to the origin of linguistic forms.

4. According to the prevailing tradition, the Torah was given to the people of Israel in the desert, at Mount Sinai, after God had saved them from enslavement in Egypt. (Note that ישראל is referred to as a collective noun, הם, hence הושיעם, rather than הושיעו).

5. There is an echo for the ancient tradition in the original version of the book as we have reconstructed it above.

6. The ordinances that were in place or that were put in place at the beginning of the 11th century were of three kinds.

7. The Manna was not exceptional among other miracles, and its maker, God, did not create something out of nothing.

8. When the mother wants to take the citron into her hand she is not permitted to touch it, only to smell it.

Ch. 6 Ex. #4: Selecting the direct object suffix

1. בַּעַל כְּתָב-יָד זֶה לֹא הִשְׁמִיט בְּדֶרֶךְ כְּלָל אֶת הַשְּׁאֵלוֹת וְלֹא **קִיצֵר**-וּ, -הָ, -ָם, -ָן, אֶלָּא **הֵבִיא**-וּ, -הָ, -ָם, -ָן בִּשְׁלֵימוּתָן.

2. אֵין זֶה מֵחוֹבָתוֹ שֶׁל הַהִיסְטוֹרְיוֹן לְהַעֲרִיךְ אֶת נוֹשְׂאֵי עֲבוֹדָתוֹ מִבְּחִינוֹת מוּסָרִיּוֹת, דָּתִיּוֹת אוֹ לְאוּמִיּוֹת, אֶלָּא **לְהָבִין**-וּ, -הָ, -ָם, -ָן **וּלְהַסְבִּיר**-וּ, -הָ, -ָם, -ָן.

3. בני ישראל פונים אל אהרון בבקשה כי יעשה להם אלוהים אשר **יוֹבִיל**-וּ, -הָ, -ָם, -ָן במדבר.

4. מֶנְדֶּלְסוֹן תרגם את התנ"ךְ לְגֶרְמָנִית והדפיס את התרגום באותיות עבריות, כדי שכל יהודי יוכל **לִקְרוֹא**-וּ, -הָ, -ָם, -ָן וללמוד מִמֶּנּוּ גרמנית.

5. הַהַנְהָגָה המסורתית נאלצת להיכנע לתכתיבו של יפתח **וְלִמְנוֹת**-וּ, -הָ, -ָם, -ָן למנהיג בימי מלחמה ולשליט עליון אף בימי שלום.

6. כל אחד מן השניים פגש באישה ונתפתה. זה **פָּגַשׁ**-וּ, -הָ, -ָם, -ָן על אם הדרך וזה בשוק.

Ch. 6 Ex. #5: Determining the reference of the pronoun suffix: subject or direct object

1. אברהם בשלחוֹ את הָגָר לַמִּדְבָּר נתן לה לחם ומים. **הוּא/אוֹתוֹ**

2. אביו שׁוֹלְחוֹ לשאול בשלום אחיו שיצאו לקרב. **הוּא/אוֹתוֹ**

3. הפסוק מלמדֵנוּ כי הַלֶּחֶם היה מזון בָּסִיסִי בתקופת הַמִּקְרָא. **אֲנַחְנוּ/אוֹתָנוּ**

4. חז"ל הנהיגו ברכה מיוחֶדֶת שיֵּשׁ לאמרָהּ לפני אכילת לחם. **הִיא/אוֹתָהּ**

5. הם הפרישו קוֹמֶץ מן העיסָה והניחוּהוּ על המִּזְבֵּחַ. **הוּא/אוֹתוֹ**

6. מְקוּבָּל שלא להשליך את פירורי הלחם אלא לאסְפָם בקפידה. **הֵם/אוֹתָם**

7. בהיכָּנְסָם לארץ ישראל הפסיקו בני ישראל לאכול את הַמָּן. **הֵם/אוֹתָם**

8. לֹא ה' מְנַסֶּה את ישראל כי אם הם מְנַסִּים אותו בבקָשָׁם ממנו לחם ובשר. **הֵם/אוֹתָם**

9. בהגיעוֹ לעיר, מבקש הנָּבִיא אלֵיהוּ מן האִישָׁה לכַלְכְּלוֹ. **הוּא/אוֹתוֹ, הוּא/אוֹתוֹ**

Ch. 6, Ex. #6: Distinguishing among possessive, direct object and subject suffixes

1. בעבר הרחוק נתקיימה מסורת שנימקה את אכילת המצות בפסח ברצון לזכור את **עינויים** (שלהם, אותם, הם) של ישראל במצרים ואת המזון שה**אכילום** (שלהם, אותם, הם) **שוביהם** (שלהם, אותם, הם) ב**עבודתם** (שלהם, אותם, הם).

2. רבות עסקו חז"ל בלחם וב**אכילתו** (שלו, אותו, הוא) וזאת בשל **היותו** (שלו, אותו, הוא) המזון המֶרכזי שבחיי האדם.

3. לפי סיפור התורה ירד אברהם עם כל **משפחתו** (שלו, אותו, הוא) למצרים בשל הרעָב הכָבד בארץ כּנַעַן **ביודעו** (שלו, אותו, הוא) כי אשתו היא "יפת תואר", ומֶחֲשָש פֶּן **יהרגוהו** (שלו, אותו, הוא) המצרים ויקחוה (שלה, אותה, היא) ממנו, הוא מבקש ממנה לומר שהיא **אחותו** (שלו, אותו, הוא).

4. ברֶדֶת משה מן ההר וב**ראותו** (שלו, אותו, הוא) את העם החוגג לפני העגל הוא משבר את לוּחות הברית, שורף את העגל, **טוחנו** (שלו, אותו, הוא) וזורה את **אפרו** (שלו, אותו, הוא) על פני המים.

5. הצירוף "לחם עוני" הולם את מאכלם של אסירים, שהרי את אלה מרעיבים כדי להרבות את **סבלם** (שלהם, אותם, הם) אך **לשמרם** (שלהם, אותם, הם) בחיים.

Ch. 6 Ex. #7: Adding an aspectual verb in expanded verb phrases

1. הלכה 2. חוזר/שב 3. הלך 4. מוסיף 5. חזרו 6. חוזר 7. הולך 8. הולכים
9. חוזרת/שבה

Translation

1. The neighborhood grew (expanded) slowly.
2. With the division of the kingdom, the tribe of Ephraim again occupies a most important place.
3. In the 1930's, the economic crisis gradually became more acute.
4. The art garden continues to grow and develop and regularly absorbs new sculptures.
5. The regular annual ceremonies in the schools, that were repeated each year, assumed a uniform character.
6. From the middle of the month to its end the moon gradually diminishes.
7. A lunar eclipse lasts several hours and at its end the moon reappears.
8. In this way, two prophets who are so different from each other – Elijah and Elisha – gradually become similar to each other.
9. In this story is embodied again the ethical and social sensitivity that characterizes Hebrew and Israeli literature.

Ch. 6 Ex. #8: Distinguishing among different uses of היה

habitual	hypothetical	past tense
4, 5, 7	Example, 6, 8, 9, 10	1, 2, 3

Translation

1. This animal was a distinctive Jewish symbol already in antiquity.
2. At the beginning of the 11ᵗʰ century, Rabenu Gershom was a very important participant in the national conventions of the congregations.
3. The general purpose of the Takanot (ordinances) was to correct a serious flaw in the institutional life of the Jews at that period.
4. They would order the laws by kinds and categories, each one according to his way and method.
5. They used to take off their shoes in the yard before entering the prayer hall.
6. It is hard to assume that the Mishnah would have preserved the mention (literally: memory) of his Greek name, had he had a Hebrew name as well.
7. In the various versions of the prayer "On the Miracles", they used to end with words of supplication.
8. It is not clear whether the action would have received the government approval.
9. If most of the revivalists of Hebrew had not been Yiddish speakers, our Hebrew today would have sounded and looked (like) a very different language.
10. It is hard to assume that the exegetic creation would have achieved such great flourishing already in the 11th century without Rashi's explicit encouragement.

Ch. 6 Ex. #9: Identifying the function of the present participle: verb or adjective

verb	adjective
example (א) and (ב), 1, 2, 3, 4-א, 6, 7-א, 9, 11, 12, 15	4-ב, 5, 7-ב, 8, 10, 13, 14

Translation

1. Political-national situations are defined in the books of the prophets in religious terms.
2. The book surveys a number of theories, which are defined by the researchers as innovative.
3. In various discussions about the revival of the Hebrew language the role and influence of Yiddish are emphasized.
4. Ḥasidic gathering often includes marked personal criticism.
5. Earth science uses physics, mathematics, biology and chemistry to allow for a total understanding of the universe.
6. Various legendary traditions advance [the date] of the beginning of the Jewish settlement in Germany to as early as the period of the First Temple.
7. Military operations usually include preliminary planning.
8. Hebrew considerably influenced (OR: had a considerable influence on) Judeo-Spanish in several areas.
9. The influences of Sanskrit are seen in all the languages that developed from it.
10. We will be able to obtain a well-founded answer for questions of this kind only when we have a large and representative electronic corpus of spoken Hebrew.
11. The customary explanation for the custom to dip the bread in salt is based on a verse from Leviticus.

12. In a survey from the 1870's it is indicated that within this period, between 1000 and 1500 Jews arrived to the Land of Israel every year.
13. Shmuel Ben Yehuda Ibn Tibon was known as an excellent translator of the works of the Jewish sages in the Middle Ages.
14. In the book [there is] a comprehensive picture of a central linguistic figure – the metaphor.
15. The work encompasses the Jewish philosophy in the Middle Ages.

Ch. 6 Ex. #10: Identifying the function of an initial נו"ן

אנחנו בעתיד	נפעל	נתפעל
3, 6ב-א, 9, 13, 14, 16ב-א	2-ב, 4, 5, 11, 12, 15	example, 1, 2-א, 7, 8, 10

Translation

1. was formed
2. was accepted; became
3. we will be aided by
4. was eaten
5. is made
6. we will introduce; we will open
7. took place
8. were preserved
9. we will find
10. were commanded
11. were found
12. is found
13. we will focus on
14. we will observe
15. it was argued
16. we will try; we will find it hard

7. COPULAS

Ch. 7 Ex. #1: Selecting the copula that is in agreement with the subject

(The subject is shaded)

1. הקיבוץ הוא/היא/הם/הן צורת חיים מקיפה

2. הדרשה בציבור הוא/היא/הם/הן מנהג קדום.

3. היהדות הוא/היא/הם/הן צירוף ייחודי של דת ואומה.

4. לפי המסורת הבבלית בבל הוא/היא/הם/הן מקום החיבור בין שמים לארץ.
Names of cities and countries are feminine

5. התעמולה והתקשורת הוא/היא/הם/הן האמצעי ולא המטרה.

6. כל הדמויות שברומן הוא/היא/הם/הן קורבנותיו של סדר חברתי המושתת על היררכיה.

7. המוטיבציה של העלייה היהודית לארץ ישראל הוא/היא/הם/הן בעיקר דתית.

8. גידול האוכלוסיה היהודית הוא/היא/הם/הן הגורם הבולט והחשוב ביותר בהתפתחותה של ירושלים בעת החדשה.
The copula agrees with the head noun of the construct phrase, גידול

9. נושאו של ספר זה הוא/היא/הם/הן ספרות ההשכלה.

10. ימות המדבר הוא/היא/הם/הן ימים של כפיות טובה בלתי-פוסקת.
ימות is an alternative construct form for ימי; both are masculine (Ch. 2, 2.1.4)

11. שני המאורעות הגדולים בשחר ההיסטוריה של עם ישראל הוא/היא/הם/הן יציאת מצרים ומעמד הר סיני.
מאורע is masculine

12. השילוב שבין דת ופוליטיקה הוא/היא/הם/הן קרקע פורייה לצמיחתה של קנאות דתית אלימה בעולם כולו.

13. דמות אחרת במקרא שהתאפיינה בקנאות דתית הוא/היא/הם/הן אליהו הנביא.

14. ההתעניינות בתולדות הרפואה בארץ ומאפייניה הוא/היא/הם/הן התפתחות של העת האחרונה.

15. שמה של שפה הוא/היא/הם/הן מוסכמה המעוגנת במסורת היסטורית ובזהות תרבותית.

16. פריחתם של מוזאונים ואתרים המוקדשים להצגת תולדות החלוציות בארץ הוא/היא/הם/הן חלק מנחשול נוסטלגיה השוטף את העולם.

Ch. 7 Ex. #2: Distinguishing between pronouns and copulas

it	*they*	*is*	*are*
5-ב-א, 6-ב, 8-ב	1, 7-ב	Example, 2, 3, 6-א, 8-א	4, 7-א

1. Long before the traditional families in Eastern Europe were influenced by the modernization trends, they were affected by the work of internal factors in Jewish society.
2. The most important source of information about biblical Hebrew is the comparison to other Semitic languages.
3. One characteristic of Diaspora Jewry is its diversity (literally: the multiplicity of shades within it).
4. The number of synagogues and the information that they provide with regard to the Jewish nature of any community are limited.
5. Even though Hebrew was influenced by languages that are not Semitic, and it is still influenced by them, it did not lose its Semitic character.
6. The story *Demise* is a gem; it describes the slow demise of the grandmother.
7. Other possibilities for classifying the stories are according to their theme and also according to the characters that they describe.
8. The main origin of the belief in angels is, apparently, pre-biblical and it appears in different variations in mesopotamic religions.

Ch. 7 Ex. #3: Translating אין

is not	*are not*	*does not*	*do not*
example א, 5-ב-א, 6-א	1, 4	example ב, 2, 3, 6-ב	7

Ch. 7 Ex. #4: Recognizing and translating copulas other than הוא, היא, הם, הן

verbal copula constitute	verbal copula serve as	"becoming" copulas	emphatic copulas
1, 9	example, 6	2, 4, 5, 7	3, 8, 10

Ch. 7 Ex. #5: Distinguishing among different meanings of נעשה

become/became	*made/done*
1, 2, 7	3, 4, 5, 6, 8, 9, 10

1. Philanthropy became a kind of substitute for the religious fellowship of the Jews.
2. "A witness cannot become a judge" is a rule in Jewish law.
3. Many of his movies were made in the tradition of the Italian comedy.
4. The first attempt to reach the top of the mountain was made by an American mission.
5. In the United States, political use was made of censuses (OR: censuses were used for political purposes) since the first days of the Republic in the 17th century.
6. Data processing is done today by means of computer.
7. This instrument became popular lately.
8. Use was first made of chemical weapons (or: chemical weapons were first used) in the First World War by the Germans.
9. In children's literature an extensive use is made of personification of animals.
10. The work was done by (the hands of) a skilled team of builders.

Ch. 7 Ex. #6: Distinguishing between *had* and *became*

became	*had*
1, 4, 7, 8, 9	2, 3, 5, 6

8. PREPOSITIONS

Ch. 8 Ex. #1: Identifying the referent of preposition suffix

1. עם המחבר 2. אודות יעקב 3. כלפי היידיש 4. על עמי אירופה 5. בלי תופעת הלאומיות

Ch. 8 Ex. #2: Choosing the correct form of the inflected preposition

1. בה 2. מהם 3. בה 4. להם 5. בפניו 6. בפניו, לו 7. עמן, אליהן 8. ממנו, להם, בו
9. ממנו, בה, אליה

Ch. 8 Ex. #3: Determining the pronunciation of the prepositions בכ"ל

1. לְתוֹפעה 2. לַתֵיאוֹריָה 3. לְמִבצרן 4. לְעידן 5. בְּהֶמשכו 6. לָעוֹלם, לְמגווֹן, לְתחוֹמי
7. לְמוֹדרניזציה 8. בְּכל, בַּחיים 9. בִּפְעילות, כְּתנאי, לַהתייַשבות

Ch. 8 Ex. #4: Choosing the correct translation of the preposition

preposition	sentence number	preposition	sentence number
0 (no translation)	2	out of	5
according to	3	from among	13
among	4	of itself	14
before	7	of their own	6
by	1	toward	10
by means of, through	9	under	11
for	8	within	12

Ch. 8 Ex. #5: Choosing the correct translation of the preposition -כ

like	*as*	*approximately*
3, 5-ב	1, 2, 5-א, 6	4, 7

Ch. 8 Ex. #6: Choosing the correct translation of the preposition עַל

about	for	with	must	on	no translation
3	4, 7	8	1, 2	6	5

Ch. 8 Ex. #7: Choosing the correct form of the inflected preposition in relative clauses

2. עליה 3. מהן 4. בה 5. להם 6. לו 7. אודותיה

Ch. 8 Ex. #8: Translating עַל יְדֵי and עַל יַד

by	next to	on the hand(s)
2, 5, 6, 7, 9	1, 4, 8	3

9. "BEING" AND "HAVING" SENTENCES

Ch. 9 Ex. #1: Identifying different meanings of יֵשׁ

there is/ there are	*have/ has*	*there are those who …*	*can*	*sometimes*	*should/ must*
2, 8, 13	3, 9, 12, 14	6, 10	7	5	example, 1, 4, 11

1. In order to understand a symbol one must be familiar with the cultural world in which the work was written.
2. There are symbols that are accepted and known to all.
3. Not all symbols have uniform and unambiguous meanings.
4. The direct influence of certain utopian ideas on the building of the State of Israel should be examined.
5. Sometimes two related languages are called by two [different] names.
6. The two languages are so close that there are those who consider them one language.
7. These stories can tell us something about the time of their telling.
8. There are creative elements in every exegetic activity. OR: Every exegetic activity has creative elements.
9. The ties among the communities have great political significance.
10. There are those who exaggerate the influence of Aramaic on the language of Ḥazal, and there are those who minimize it.
11. To the two characteristics a third one should be added.
12. We have examples both from the Bible and from other sources.
13. These stories emphasize the sense of distance between what there is and what was.
14. The costumes and traditions apparently have also a non-Jewish source.

Ch. 9 Ex. #2: Identifying different meanings of אֵין

there is no(t)	*do not have/ does not have*	*cannot/ not possible*	*are not*	*does not*
7-ב, 9-א	1, 4, 5, 6-א, 8-א, 9-ב	example, 2, 3, 6-ב	7-א	8-ב

Translation

1. This description does not have any relation to the main idea.
2. The three examples that I have brought cannot exhaust everything that is found in the Bible.
3. Usually it is not possible to recognize from the shape of the words whether they are new or ancient.

4. This tradition does not have an open expression in the Torah because it has (OR: there is in it) more than a trace (literally: dust) of myth.
5. We do not have enough data to determine where the Midrash was composed (literally: the place of the composition of the Midrash).
6. It cannot be said about a text which does not have its origin in the Siddur that it does not have a defined liturgical role. (Note that the sentence is topicalized; in translation its components were re-ordered.)
7. Most of the languages that are in danger of extinction are not accompanied by writing and there is no written transcript of the pronunciation of their words.
8. We do not have a single book in the Bible that does not contain metaphors.
9. There is no way to quantify these linguistic phenomena as long as we do not have a spoken corpus of Hebrew.

Ch. 9 Ex. #3: Reconstructing sentences with an omitted יש

1. ללשון המשמשת בהתכתבות אלקטרונית **יש** אפיונים משלה; **יש** ללשון המשמשת בהתכתבות אלקטרונית אפיונים משלה.

2. לתפילתם של היהודים **יש** שתי פנים; **יש** שתי פנים לתפילתם של היהודים.

3. לדמותו של שלמה המלך במקרא **יש** פנים רבות; **יש** פנים רבות לדמותו של שלמה המלך במקרא.

4. לכל ההיגדים האלה **יש** מכנה משותף; **יש** מכנה משותף לכל ההיגדים האלה.

5. להשפעה הזרה **יש** שתי סיבות עיקריות; **יש** שתי סיבות עיקריות להשפעה הזרה.

6. ליהודים בספרד המוסלמית בתקופה זו **יש** מקורות פרנסה מגוונים; בתקופה זו **יש** ליהודים בספרד המוסלמית מקורות פרנסה מגוונים.

7. למסורת המשוחזרת בדבר היותו של שמשון ענק בן אלוהים ובת אנוש **יש** מקבילות בעולם התרבותי הסובב את ישראל; **יש** למסורת המשוחזרת בדבר היותו של שמשון ענק בן אלוהים ובת אנוש מקבילות בעולם התרבותי הסובב את ישראל.

8. למספר את סיפורנו **יש** דרכים מגוונות לשכנע את הקורא כי הניצחון אכן מושג בסיוע שמים; **יש** למספר את סיפורנו דרכים מגוונות לשכנע את הקורא כי הניצחון אכן מושג בסיוע שמים.

9. בפירושיו של רש"י לתלמוד נדונים עניינים שלהם **יש** זיקה ליחסי הכפיפות בין רב לתלמיד; בפירושיו של רש"י לתלמוד נדונים עניינים **שיש** להם זיקה ליחסי הכפיפות בין רב לתלמיד.

10. DISCONTINUOUS SENTENCE CONNECTORS – ANSWERS

Ch. 10 Ex. #1: לא – אלא

addition (both **a** and **b**)	exclusion (not **a** but rather **b**)	emphasis (only **a**, none other than **a**)
2, 6, 9	3, 4, 7-א, 8-ב	example, 1, 5, 7-ב, 8-א

1. The unicorn is none other than an imaginary animal.
2. In Purim, the Jews not only mention the story of the Book of Esther, but also perform it.
3. Not ideological or theological motivations prompted the conflict but rather struggles for power and control within the community.
4. Man is not above nature, but rather is part of it.
5. According to the view of the Yiddishists, Hebrew is the language of the past only.
6. The Shtiebel is a Ḥasidic synagogue that is used not only for prayer and Torah study but also for Chassidic meals.
7. The preacher does not interpret individual words, but rather sees in front of him the idea in an entire group of verses, and the biblical text serves him just as a basis for the idea.
8. The function of "prayer leader" is only a technical one, to say out loud the prayer of the community; and experts are not required for this (function), but rather any member of the community is fit to be its representative.
9. The Book of Esther is entirely ironic and in this respect it is not only unique, but (also) appears to diverge entirely from the style of the Bible and is even foreign to it.

Ch. 10 Ex. #2: אמנם

although	*indeed*	**question word expressing doubt**
1, 3	2, 5	4

Ch. 10 Ex. #3: בין

between	*among*	*among other things*	*whether . . . or*	*inter-*
1, 3, 5	6, 7	4	2	8

Ch. 10 Ex. #4: ראשית

beginning	first(ly)	main
1, 2	4	3

Ch. 10 Ex. #5: כלל

not at all	including	rule	included (verb)	all, the entire, the totality
2, 13, 15-א	14, 15-ב	11	5	1, 4

to, to the point of	general (adjective)	pan-, -wide (semantic prefix)	the public, society	generally, usually
3, 6	7	9, 16	10, 12	8

Ch. 10 Ex. #6: פרט

detail(s)	individual(s)	except for	in particular
2, 3	5	1	4, 6

Ch. 10 Ex. #7: לבד

only	in addition to	apart from	as long as, provided	alone
1, 5, 8	3, 4	2, 6, 10	7	9

11. LEXICAL MATTERS

Ch. 11 Ex. #1: עשוי

may	*made*
1, 3, 4, 7	2, 5, 6

Ch. 11 Ex. #2: אמור

said, stated	*supposed to*	*concern, apply to*	*aforementioned*
4	1, 3, 6, 7	5	2

Ch. 11 Ex. #3.1: ניתן

(not) given	*(not) possible*	*can/could (not)*
1, 3, 7, 8	2, 5	4, 6

Ch. 11 Ex. #3.2: נתון

found in	*given* (adjective)	*prone to*	*datum/data*
4, 5, 6	9	1, 3, 7	2, 8

Ch. 11 Ex. #4: מעבר

transition	*beyond*
2, 3, 7	1, 4, 5, 6

Ch. 11 Ex. #5: כדי

in order to	*too (much/ little)*	*to the point of*	*while, during*	*cannot, not sufficient*	*not in vain*
4, 8	1, 6	2, 5, 10	3	7, 9	11

Ch. 11 Ex. #6: בחן

distinction	examination, analysis	distinct	as, in the status of	from the point of view	in many respects
9	1, 2, 8	10	3, 4, 7	5	6

Ch. 11 Ex. #7: יחס

attitude	relationship	reference	to treat	to refer to	to attribute	is attributed to	with regard to	relatively
1, 13	6, 17	9, 12	3	5, 11	7	4, 16	10, 15	2, 8, 14

Ch. 11 Ex. #8: חל

began	occur, happen	bring about, create	apply to	beginning with
1, 9	2, 5, 8	4, 6	7	3, 10

Ch. 11 Ex. #9: דבר

thing(s)	word(s)	this	regarding	according to, in the opinion of
1, 4	6, 7	3	2, 5	8

Ch. 11 Ex. #10: כן

(and) also	since, because	then	therefore	so, thus
4	2	3	5	1, 6, 7

Ch. 11 Ex. 11#: דמה

it appears/ appeared that	similar	similarly to	similarity	imagination
2, 14	12	5	א-13	11

character, personality, figure	image	simile	-like	and the like
ב-13 ,9 ,6 ,1	3, 8	4	7	10

Ch. 11 Ex. #12.1: Loan words מלים לועזיות

adjective	noun		
social	satire	סטירה חברתית	1.
dramatic	situation	מצב דרמטי	2.
relevant	topics	נושאים רלוונטיים	3.
universal	topic	נושא אוניברסלי	4.
rationalistic	view	תפיסה רציונליסטית	5.
ambivalent	attitude	יחס אמביוולנטי	6.
figurative	language	לשון פיגורטיבית	7.
intimate	connection	קשר אינטימי	8.
rhetorical	expression	ביטוי רטורי	9.
theatrical	components	מרכיבים תאטרליים	10.
aesthetic	characteristics	מאפיינים אסתטיים	11.
military	strategy	אסטרטגיה צבאית	12.
main	ideas	אידאות עיקריות	13.
social	ideology	אידאולוגיה חברתית	14.
theological-ethical	question	שאלה תאולוגית-מוסרית	15.
effective	communication	תקשורת אפקטיבית	16.
phonological	phenomenon	תופעה פונולוגית	17.
formal	language	לשון פורמלית	18.
grammatical	nuances	ניואנסים דקדוקיים	19.

Ch. 11 Ex. #12.2

1. modern architecture   2. dramatic episodes   3. poetic option   4. historical motifs
5. thematic analogy   6. ironic effect   7. poetic energy   8. erotic element
9. realistic dialogue   10. authentic theatre   11. visual element   12. liturgical text
13. historical narratives

Ch. 11 Ex. #12.3

1. הסופר אינו מרבה במלים ארכאיות, על מנת שלא להגביה את המשלב הסגנוני. (1)

archaic

2. הרומן מתאר את חורבנה הדיאלקטי של אריסטוקרטיה אידאולוגית. (3)

dialectical, ideological aristocracy

3. במחצית השנייה של המאה העשרים חל שינוי במעמדו של האתוס האידאולוגי, הלאומי
והקולקטיביסטי של האוריינות. (3)

ideological ethos, collectivist

4. תכונה זו מקרבת את המשל הפתוח אל הספרות הסוראליסטית, שביטלה את הדיכוטומיה בין
הראלי לדמיוני, בחיפושיה אחרי דרכה לפרספקטיבה מורחבת. (4)

surrealist, dichotomy, realistic, perspective

5. בחקר תולדות העם היהודי מעלים היסטוריונים וסוציולוגים כאחד את הטענה כי הבנת ההיסטוריה
היהודית היא במידה רבה לימוד הגאוגרפיה שלהם. (4)

historians and sociologists, history, geography

6. המושג "מודרניזם" במחקר זה מוצג לאור הגדרתו כתפיסה תרבותית כוללת, ראיית עולם
אוניברסלית-כוללנית, טכנוקרטית ורציונלית. (4)

modernism, universal, technocratic and rational

7. המחקר עוסק ברבים מגורמי המפתח לתמורות בחיי היהודים במאה הי"ח: המפגש עם המדינה
הריכוזית ועם המדיניות הרפורמיסטית של המשטר האבסולוטיסטי, אתוס התועלת הכלכלית
למדינה, אקולטורציה, השכלה ורפורמות בחינוך. (5)

reformist, absolutist, ethos, acculturation, reforms

8. הפוסטמודרניזם עוסק בשינוי הרדיקלי ביחסי הייצור ובהתפתחות של טכנולוגיות חדשות,
ששינו את תחומי הטלקומוניקציה ועיבוד המידע, ואת הפעלת הכוחות הגלובליים. (5)

postmodernism, radical, technologies, telecommunication, global

PART THREE

TEXTS FOR READING AND TRANSLATION PRACTICE

PRACTICE TEXT #1

העלייה הרביעית: 1924 עד 1928
מאת: יהודה ואלך
מתוך: לא על מגש של כסף: תולדות מדינת ישראל מראשית ההתיישבות עד עידן
השלום, (כרטא ירושלים, 2000), עמי 34

<u>**Terminology specific to the text**</u> (in order of appearance)

the Fourth Aliya (immigration to Israel)	הַעלייה הרביעית
the middle class	המעמד הבֵּינוני
Poland	פּוליָן
Eastern Europe	מזרח אירופה
The United States	ארצות הברית
factories	מִפְעלֵי תַעֲשׂייה
building materials	חומרֵי בִּנייָן
transfer of capital	הַעֲברת הוֹן
those who leave (literally: go down) Israel	יורדים

<u>**Foreign (loan) word**</u>

fiscal (economic)	פיסקָלית

<u>**Miscellaneous**</u> (alphabetical)

in contrast to	בְּניגוד לְ-
mainly, mostly	בְּעיקָר
completely	לְגַמרֵי

<u>**Expressions**</u> (alphabetical)

it is no wonder that	אין פֶּלֶא שֶׁ-
implement a policy	נקטה (לנקוט) מדיניות
a crisis broke out	פרץ משבר

בניגוד לעליות הקודמות, היו רוב אנשי העלייה הרביעית **בני**[1] המעמד הבינוני מפולין ומשאר מדינות מזרח אירופה. **אלה**[2] נפגעו מאוד מן המדיניות הפיסקָלית שנקטה נגדם ממשלת פולין. הם **ביקשו לעזוב**[3] את פולין, ומ**אַחַר ש**[4]שערי ארצות-הברית היו נעולים כמעט לגמרי בפני מהגרים יהודים ממזרח אירופה, פנו לארץ-ישראל. **לפיכך**[5] אין פלא שעלייה זו זרמה **בראש ובראשונה**[6] אל הערים, ובעיקר לתל-אביב, שמספר תושביה גדל מ-16,000 בשנת 1923 ל-40,000 בשנת 1925. קצב ההתיישבות החקלאית **באותה תקופה**[7] היה אטי בהרבה. אנשי העלייה הרביעית הקימו בעיקר בתי-חרושת קטנים (אם כי[8] **באותה עת**[7] נוסדו גם כמה מפעלי תעשייה גדולים), **פתחו ב**[9]פעילות נרחבת של בנייה בערים והקימו תעשייה של חומרי בניין. **אף-על-פי-כן**[10] לא כוננה עלייה זו **בסיס יצרני איתן**[11] לקליטת עלייה גדולה. **זאת ועוד**[12]. **משהגבילה**[13] ממשלת פולין העברת הון אל מחוץ לפולין, פרץ משבר כלכלי חמור בארץ ו**החלה**[14] ירידה ממנה. **הגיעו הדברים לידי כך**[15], שבשנים 1927–1928 גדל מספר היורדים מ[16]מספר העולים.

Clauses whose verb precedes the subject are shaded.

---

(1) בני המעמד הבינוני
members of the middle class (NOT: sons)
Ch.4; 4.8.2

(2) אלה   *these (they)*
demonstrative pronoun used for substitution; Ch.3; 2.2

(3) ביקשו לעזוב   *wished to leave*
Ch.11; 4

(4) מֵאַחַר ש=מפני ש
since, because (NOT: after)

(5) לפיכך=לָכֵן   *therefore*
Ch.8; Confusables 2(d)

(6) בראש ובראשונה
first and foremost, Ch.5; 2.6

(7) באותה תקופה, באותה עת
at that period
Ch.3; 3.2

(8) אם כי   *even though*
Ch.1; Confusables 3.4

(9) פתחו ב-   *began* (NOT: opened)
The preposition changes the meaning of the verb; Ch.8; 2.2

(10) אַף-עַל-פִּי-כֵן   *nevertheless*
Ch.8; Confusables 2(g)

(11) בסיס יצרני איתן
firm productive foundation
stacked adjectives; Ch.4; 3.2

(12) זאת ועוד   *this and more*
pro-clause; זאת refers to the content of the previous clause; Ch.3; 2.3

(13) משהגבילה=כשהגבילה
when it limited; Ch.8; 2.3.4(e)

(14) הֵחֵלה=התחילה   *began*
Ch.11; 12.1

(15) הגיעו הדברים לידי כך ש-
things came to such a point that…
Ch.3; 2.3.1; Ch.8; Confusables 1(d)

(16) גדל מספר היורדים מ*מספר העולים
The number of those leaving Israel exceeded (grew more than) the number of those immigrating to it;
A comparative phrase without יותר;
Ch.4; 2.2.1; Ch.8; 2.3.4(c)

<u>Translation</u>

The Fourth Aliya: 1924 to 1928

In contrast to previous Aliyot (immigrations to Israel), most of the people of the Fourth Aliya were members of the middle class from Poland and the rest of the countries of Eastern Europe. They were greatly harmed by the economic measures (literally: fiscal policy) taken against them by the Polish government. They wished to leave Poland, and since the gates of the United States were almost completely locked before Jewish immigrants from Eastern Europe, they turned to the Land of Israel. There is no wonder, therefore, that this Aliya flowed first and foremost to the towns, and mainly to Tel Aviv, whose number of residents grew from 16,000 in 1923 to 40,000 in 1925. The rate of agricultural settlement at that period was much slower.

The people of the Fourth Aliya established mainly small factories (although at that time several large industrial plants were also founded), began an extensive activity of building in the towns and established an industry of building materials. Nevertheless, this Aliya did not lay a firm productive foundation for the absorption of a large immigration. In addition to this, when the government of Poland limited the transfer of capital outside the country a serious economic crisis broke out in the Land of Israel and things came to such a point that, in the years 1927–28, the number of those leaving the country exceeded the number of those arriving.

PRACTICE TEXT #2

תרגום אונקלוס לתורה

Terminology specific to the text (in order of appearance)

Onkelos the convert   אוּנְקְלוֹס הַגֵּר

Babylon   בָּבֶל

the second century C.E.   הַמֵּאָה ה-2 לַסְפִירה

verse(s)   פָּסוּק, פְּסוּקִים

Babylonian Aramaic   אֲרָמִית בַּבְלִית

Babylonian Talmud   תלמוד בבלי

additions from the Midrash, homiletic additions   תּוֹסָפוֹת מִדְרָשִׁיוֹת

biblical texts   כְּתוּבִים

print edition   מַהֲדוּרַת דְפוּס

margins of the page   שׁוּלֵי העמוד

Foreign (loan) word

equivalent   אֶקְווִיוָלֶנְט

Miscellaneous (alphabetical)

that is to say   כְּלוֹמַר

in its essence, essentially   מֵעִיקָרוֹ

תרגום אונקלוס לתורה הוא המקובל והנפוץ ביותר[1] בתרגומים הארמיים. התרגום מיוחס[2] לאונקלוס הגֵר, שחי בתחילת המאה ה-2 לספירה ועל זהותו אין לנו פרטים. התרגום נכתב בארץ ישראל ונערך בבבל במאות 2–3 לספירה כדי לפרש את התורה ולקרבה[3] אל המוני העם, שלא ידעו עברית. התרגום נאמן למקור ומביע את רוח הפסוקים ותוכנם[4]. תרגום אונקלוס נכתב בארמית בבלית (שָׂבָּה[5] נכתב גם התלמוד הבבלי), והוא מעיקרו[6] תרגום מילולי, כלומר המתרגם משתמש בעקיבות[7] במילה ארמית קבועה (אֶקְוִיוַלֶנְט) לתרגום מילה עברית מסוימת. תרגום אונקלוס הוא גם תרגום פשטני, המביע את רוחו ותוכנו של הפסוק כְּכְתָבו[8], ואינו כולל[9] תוספות מדרשיות בתרגומיו. בתרגום אונקלוס לתורה בולטות כמה[10] מגמות פרשניות, ובהן[11] – הימנעות מתיאורים גשמיים של ה', ומשינוי בכתובים העלול[12] לפגוע בשמם הטוב של גדולי האומה. תרגום אונקלוס היה מקובל על החכמים ועל הציבור הרחב, והדבר[13] מלמד שהסטיות הרבות מן המילוליות[14], המצויות[15] בו, נחשבו כְּשֵׁרות מִבְּחינה תֵאולוגית[16]. בכל מהדורות הדפוס של התורה בימינו מופיע תרגום אונקלוס בשולֵי כל עמוד בצד פסוקי התורה.

Clauses whose verb comes before the subject are shaded.

(1) ביותר -וה...-ה *the most*
superlative; Ch.4; 2.2

(2) מיוחס ל- *is attributed to*
Ch.11; 11.2.2

(3) לקרבה *bring it (Torah) closer*
direct object suffix; Ch.6; 2.3

(4) תוכנם *their content*
The possessive suffix refers to פסוקים;
Ch.2; 5.8

(5) שָׂבָּה *in which*
The inflected preposition in the relative clause refers backward to the feminine singular ארמית בבלית; after the inflected preposition the verb precedes the subject; Ch.8; 3.4, 3.4.1

(6) מעיקרו *essentially*
inflected adverb; Ch.5; 1.4.1

(7) בעקיבות *consistently*
adverb of manner; Ch.5; 2.1

(8) כְּכְתָבו *as it is written*

(9) אינו כולל *does not include*
אין is used for negation before a present tense verb; Ch.9; 4

(10) כמה *several, a few*
(NOT: how many) Ch.3; 5

(11) בהן *among them*
The pronoun suffix refers to מגמות;
Ch.8; 2.3.1(d)

(12) העלול *which might*
This modal indicates an adverse outcome; Ch.11; 1.2

(13) הדבר *this (thing)*
pro-clause; refers to the content of the previous clause; Ch.3; 2.3, Ch.11; 14.2

(14) מילוליות *verbatim sense*
a singular abstract noun (from the adjective מילולי *literal*); Ch.2; 6.1

(15) המְצויות *that exist, that are found*
Ch.9; 1.7.1, Confusables 1.2

(16) כשרות מִבְּחינה תֵאולוגית *theologically acceptable*
adverb of manner; Ch.5; 2.2.1; Ch.11; 10.2.1

Translation

Targum Onkelos for the Torah

The Onkelos translation for the Torah is the most popular and widespread of the Aramaic translations. It is attributed to the convert Unqelos, who lived at the beginning of the second century C.E. and about whose identity we have no information (literally: details). The translation was written in the Land of Israel and edited in Babylon in the second and third centuries C.E. in order to interpret the Torah and bring it closer to the masses, who did not know Hebrew. The translation is faithful to the original and expresses the spirit of the verses and their content. It was written in Babylonian Aramaic (in which language was also written the Babylonian Talmud) and is essentially a verbatim translation, namely, the translator consistently uses a fixed Aramaic equivalent for the translation of a given Hebrew word. It is also a literal rendering that expresses the spirit and content of the verse as it is written, and it does not include *midrashic* (homiletic) additions in its translations. Several exegetic tendencies stand out in the translation, among them the avoidance of corporeal descriptions of God and of changes to the biblical texts that might harm the good name of important national figures. The translation was popular among the sages and the wider public, and this indicates that the many deviations from the verbatim sense that are found in it were considered acceptable from a theological standpoint. In all the contemporary printed editions of the Torah, the Onkelos translation appears at the margins of each page next to the verses of the Torah.

PRACTICE TEXT #3

פילנתרופיה יהודית ומדיניות סוציאלית באמריקה
מאת: רבקה קוברין
מתוך: זמן יהודי חדש, כרך שני, עמי 13–14

Terminology specific to the text (listed in order of appearance)

מְהַגְרִים	immigrants
קְהִילָה	community; congregation
הֲגִירָה הֲמוֹנִית	mass immigration
נִזְקָקִים	(the) needy
קְלִיטה	absorption
"בית הַיְתוֹמִים הָעִבְרִי" שֶׁל בּוֹלְטִימוֹר	Baltimore Jewish Orphanage
צְדָקָה	charity
מַעֲמָד בֵּינוֹנִי	middle class

Foreign (loan) words (alphabetical)

נֵיטְרָלִית	neutral
סִימְבִּיוֹזָה	symbiosis
פִילָנְתְרוֹפִיה	philanthropy
פִילָנְתְרוֹפִיים	philanthropic

Miscellaneous (alphabetical)

בִּשְׁנוֹת ה-	in the decade of (literally: years of)
במְרוּצַת התקופה	in the course of the period

לאלפי המהגרים היהודיים שהגיעו לארצות הברית בין 1820 ל-1880 היתה הפילנתרופיה הַדֶּבֶק הַמְאַחֵד[1] את הקהילה היהודית המתרחבת. אבל בשְׁנות ההגירה ההמונית שלאַחַר מִכֵּן[2], כאשר הֵצִיפוּ מהגרים יהודיים בהמוניהם את הקהילות המבוססות, שגם קוֹדם לכן[2] עסקו בחלוקת סיוע לנזקקים, נזקקו המנהיגים של יהודי אמריקה להקמת ארגונים פילנתרופיים חדשים שיטפלו בצורכיהם המעשׂ-יים של המהגרים החדשים[3] ובד בבד[4] יקלו את קליטתם החברתית [5].

המוסדות הפילנתרופיים היהודיים, בְּעַצְּבָם[6] את העניים היהודיים "לְכְדֵי[7] אזרחים אמריקניים טובים," כְּדִבְרֵי[8] העומדים בראש[9] "בית היתומים העברי" של בוֹלְטימוֹר, בִיקשׁוּ להבטיח[10] שהעוֹנִי והתמוטטות המשפחה בקרב היהודים לא יאפילו על הישׂגיה של הקהילה היהודית[3] הרחבה יותר, אשר השתדלה להתמזג בחברה האמריקנית[11].

---

(1) הדבק **המאחד** את הקהילה
the glue uniting the community
The participle functions as a verb;
Ch.6; 5

(2) לְאַחַר מִכֵּן   *afterward*
קוֹדם לְכֵן   *previously, before*
Ch.11; 15.2

(3) צורכיהם המעשׂיים **של המהגרים החדשים**
the practical needs of the new immigrants
double construct phrase with an adjective; Ch.2; 4.4, 4.5.2

(4) בַּד בְּבַד   *simultaneously*
adverb created through repetition;
Ch.5; 2.6

(5) אבל...את קליטתם החברתית.
a multi-clause sentence with three subordinate clauses, one of them compound. To parse, identify the subject of each verb; Ch.1; 6.4

(6) בְּעַצְּבָם   *by shaping*
The pronoun suffix in the infinitive construct refers to the subject, מוסדות; Ch.6; 1.3, 2.5.1

(7) לְכְדֵי   *into* (NOT: in order to)
Ch.11; 9.4

(8) כדברי   *according to (the words of)*; Ch.11; 14.1(c)

(9) העומדים בראש   *those heading*
Ch.1; 5(d)

(10) ביקשו להבטיח   *sought to ensure*
(NOT: asked to promise); Ch.11; 4

(11) המוסדות...להתמזג בחברה האמריקנית.
The entire paragraph is one sentence consisting of one main and two subordinate clauses. To parse, identify the subject of each of the three finite (conjugated) verbs;
Ch.1; 6.4

ההתפצלות המהירה של הקהילות המאורגנות סביב בתי כנסת במרוצת התקופה הזאת **עשתה**(12) את הצדקה – **כערך**(13) שהוקירו גם המסורת היהודית וגם המעמד הבינוני של אמריקה – **ליוזמה**(12) עממית וניטרלית של יהודים מרקע שונה שאיחדו את כוחותיהם בשאיפה ליצור סימביוזה **בעלת משמעות**(14) בין החיים האמריקניים לחיים היהודיים(15). **בתוך כך**(16) נוצר גם, **למעשה**(17), **מבנה**(18) קהילתי חדש, משותף ליהודים דתיים ושאינם דתיים, **מבנה**(18) ששירת את התערותם של היהודים בחברה האמריקנית.

Sentences whose verb precedes the subject are shaded.

(12) **עשתה** את הצדקה . . . **ליוזמה**
turned charity…into
The parenthetical comment between the dashes separates the components of the verb phrase;
Ch.7; 5.1.1

(13) **כערך**   *as a value*
Ch.8; 2.3.2(b)

(14) סימביוזה **בעלת משמעות**
meaningful symbiosis
Ch.4; 4.5, Ch.9; 2.4.1

(15) **ההתפצלות...לחיים היהודיים.**
a multi-clause sentence;
To parse, identify the subject of each of the three finite (conjugated) verbs;
Ch.1; 6.4

(16) **בתוך כך**
in the meantime, through this
Ch.8; Confusables, 5(a)

(17) **למעשה**   *in effect, practically*
adverb of manner; Ch.5; 1.3, 2.1

(18) **מבנה** קהילתי חדש,..., **מבנה ש** ...
The lexical repetition allows the addition of a subordinate clause;
Ch.1; 7

<u>Translation</u>

Jewish Philanthropy and Social Policy in America

For the thousands of Jewish immigrants who arrived in the United States between 1820 and 1880, philanthropy was the glue uniting the expanding Jewish community. But during the following years of mass immigration, when Jewish immigrants in their multitudes flooded the established communities that had previously engaged in dispensing assistance to the needy, the leaders of American Jews considered [it] necessary to establish new philanthropic organizations that would take care of the practical needs of the new immigrants and at the same time would ease their social absorption.

By shaping the Jewish poor 'into good American citizens,' in the words of those heading the "Hebrew Orphanage" in Baltimore, the Jewish philanthropic institutions sought to ensure that the poverty and collapse of the family among the Jews would not overshadow the achievements of the wider Jewish community, which attempted to blend into American society.

The rapid splintering of the organized communities around synagogues in the course of this period turned charity – as a value cherished by both the Jewish tradition and the middle class of America – into a popular and neutral initiative for Jews from different backgrounds who joined (their) forces aspiring to create a meaningful symbiosis between American and Jewish life. Through this, a new communal structure was in effect created, shared by religious and non-religious Jews, which served to integrate the Jews into American society.

PRACTICE TEXT #4

תקנות שו"ם
Retrieved from:
http://he.wikipedia.org/wiki/תקנות שו"ם

Terminology specific to the text (in order of appearance)

Takkanot, ordinances, regulations	תַּקָנוֹת
Shum, acronym for the towns Speyer, Worms and Mainz	שו"ם
community (public) matters	ענייני ציבור
money (fiscal) matters	ענייני ממונות
community lay leaders	פַּרְנָסִים
Ashkenazi (German) congregations	קהילות אשכנזיות
the Rhine river	נהר ריין
Shulḥan Aruch	שולחן ערוך
Posekim, Deciders (Rabbinic authority on matters of Jewish law)	פוסקים
legal ruling	פסיקה
Responsa	שו"ת=שאלות ותשובות
early commentators/ legal authorities	ראשונים
late commentators/ legal authorities	אחרונים
the Takkana of dowry	תקנת הנדוניה
the Takkana of Ḥalizah	תקנת החליצה

Foreign (loan) word

sanctions	סַנְקְצִיוֹת

Miscellaneous (alphabetical)

because of them	בְּגִינָן (בגין)
among	בְּקֶרֶב
through the ages, for generations	לדורות- (לדורותיה)
because	מִכֵּיוָן שֶ-=מפני שֶ-

תקנות שו"ם הן⁽¹⁾ **תקנות קהילתיות מקיפות**⁽²⁾ בענייני ציבור, בענייני ממונות ובעניינים נוספים, **אשר**⁽³⁾ תוקנו במאה ה-12 ובמאה ה-13 על ידי רבנים ופרנסים מקהילות שו"ם, **הקהילות האשכנזיות הגדולות שעל גדות נהר ריין :שפיירא, וֶרמַיְזָא ומַגֶנצָא**⁽⁴⁾ (כיום: שפייר, וורמס ומיינץ). חלק מהתקנות התקבלו **כמחייבות**⁽⁵⁾ בקרב יהדות אשכנז לדורותיה; **מִקְצָתָן**⁽⁶⁾ אף הובאו בשולחן ערוך ובכתבי פוסקים נוספים, ועד היום הן חלק **בלתי נפרד**⁽⁷⁾ **מהפסיקה היהודית המחייבת**⁽²⁾.

הסיבות שבגינן **תיקנו חכמי שו"ם את התקנות**⁽⁸⁾ הן **שונות ומגוונות**⁽⁹⁾. ביסודן **עמד המצב** המדיני והחברתי ששרר בתקופות **ההן**⁽¹⁰⁾ באזורים **השיי-כים**⁽¹¹⁾ כיום לצרפת ולגרמניה. **חלקן**⁽⁶⁾ תוקנו **כתגובה**⁽⁵⁾ ליחסים **בלתי תקינים**⁽⁷⁾ **בין**⁽¹²⁾ הקהילות היהודיות **לבין**⁽¹²⁾ שלטונות הערים **שבהן**⁽¹³⁾ דרו, **וחלקן**⁽⁶⁾ תוקנו כמענה⁽⁵⁾ לבעיות **פָנִים-קהילתיות**⁽¹⁴⁾.

---

(1) תקנות שו"ם הן   *are*
copula; Ch.7; 1.2

(2) תקנות קהילתיות מקיפות
comprehensive congregational regulations/ordinances
Stacked adjectives are translated backwards; Ch.4; 3.2

(3) אשר=ש   *that*
subordinating particle;
Ch.1; 6.3.1(a)

(4) הקהילות האשכנזיות הגדולות שעל גדות נהר ריין: שפיירא, וורמיזא ומגנצא
appositives signaled with a colon;
Ch.1; 8.1.1

(5) כמחייבות; כמענה
as binding; as a response
Ch.8; 2.3.2(b)

(6) מקצתן; חלקן   *few, part of them*
The possessive suffix in the quantifiers refers back to תקנות; Ch.2; 5.8

(7) חלק בלתי נפרד   *inseparable part*
בלתי is a negating semantic prefix before an adjective; Ch.4; 5.6

(8) תיקנו את התקנות
legislated the regulations
internal object; Ch.11; Part B

(9) שונות ומגוונות   *diverse*
(literally: different and varied);
Ch.11; Binomials, Part C

(10) בתקופות ההן   *in those periods*
remote demonstrative; Ch.3; 3.1

(11) השייכים   *that belong*
-ה is a subordinator; Ch.1; 6.3.1(b)

(12) בין...לבין   *between...and*
Ch.10; 11

(13) שבהן   *in which (refers to the feminine* ערים)
inflected preposition in a relative clause; Ch.8; 3.4

(14) פנים-קהילתיות   *intra-congregational*
semantic prefix; Ch.4; 5

כדי להגשים את **מטרותיהן של התקנות**[15], ~~הִשְׁתַּדְּלוּ הרבנים והפרנסים~~ להשיג להן הסכמה רחבה ככל האפשר, ועל **מֵפֵּרֵיהֶן**[16] ~~הוטלו סנקציות~~ קהילתיות שונות. מכיוון שרוב **התקנות תוקנו**[8] **כמענה**[5] לבעיות מקומיות, **בַּחֲלוֹף הזמן ובחלוֹף הצורך**[17] בהן, **הלכו התקנות ונשתכחו**[18]. לרובן של התקנות ~~לא נמצאו הֵדים~~ בתקופות מאוחרות יותר, וכל הידוע עליהן הוא מִסְפְרֵי השו"ת הסמוכים לתקופתן. **יחד עם זאת**[19], מְסִפּר תקנות תוקנו כמענה לבעיות כלליות **התקֵפות**[11] בכל מקום ובכל תקופה. תקנות אלו **נידונו**[20] **באריכות**[21] בספרות השו"ת לדורותיה, **למִן**[22] תקופת הראשונים **דרך**[22] תקופת האחרונים **ועד**[22] ימינו. עם **אלו**[23] ~~נמנות "תקנת הנדוניה" ו"תקנת החליצה"~~.

Clauses whose verb comes before the subject are shaded.

---

(15) מטרותיהן של התקנות
the goals of the Takkanot
double construct phrase; Ch.2; 4.4

(16) מֵפֵּרֵיהֶן   *those who broke them*
present participle used as a noun;
Ch.2; 6.2
The pronoun suffix —הֶן refers to
תקנות; Ch.2; 5.8

(17) בַּחֲלוֹף הזמן, **בחלוֹף** הצורך
with the passing of time, with the passing of the need
time adverbial: בְּ+infinitive
construct; Ch.6; 1.2

(18) הלכו התקנות **ונשתכחו**
the Takkanot were gradually forgotten
The aspectual verb phrase straddles
the subject; Ch.6; 3.2
נתפעל — נשתכחו form; Ch.6; 6.1

(19) יחד עם זאת
however, nevertheless; Ch.3; 9

(20) נידונו   *were discussed*
(NOT: were judged)

(21) באריכות   *at length*
adverb of manner; Ch.5; 2.1

(22) למִן ... דרך ... ועד
from … through … and until
Ch.10; 13

(23) אלו   *these (ordinances)*
demonstrative pronoun used for
substitution; Ch.3; 2.2

Translation

The Takkanot of Shum

The Takkanot of Shum are comprehensive congregational ordinances concerning public, financial and other matters which were legislated in the 12th and 13th centuries by rabbis and community leaders from the Shum congregations, the large Ashkenazi congregations on the banks of the River Rhine: (today) Speyer, Worms and Mainz. Some of the ordinances were accepted as binding among Ashkenazi Jewry through the generations; a few of them were even included in Shulhan Aruch and the writings of other legal authorities, and to this day are an inseparable part of the binding Jewish ruling.

The reasons for which the sages of Shum legislated the regulations were diverse. At their basis was (literally: stood) the social and political situation that prevailed in those periods in the areas that today belong to France and Germany. Some of them were legislated as a reaction to unsound relations between the Jewish congregations and the authorities of the cities in which they lived, and some were legislated in response to intra-congregational problems.

In order to realize the goals of the ordinances, the rabbis and lay leaders attempted to obtain for them the widest possible consent, and various communal sanctions were imposed on those who breached them. Since most of the ordinances were devised in response to local problems, with the passing of time and the passing of the need for them, they were gradually forgotten. No echoes were found in later periods for most, and all that is known about them is from the books of responsa that (were written) close to their period. However, some ordinances were legislated in response to general problems that are valid in any place and any period. These were discussed at length in the literature of responsa over the generations, from the period of the early legal authorities through the later ones and up to our days. Among them are the ordinances of dowry and Halizah.

PRACTICE TEXT #5

גדליה בן אחיקם: רצח נציב יהודה
מאת: אלי אשד
Retrieved from:
www.e-mago.co.il/Editor/judaism-530.htm (November 22, 2005)

<u>**Terminology specific to the text**</u> (in order of appearance)

commemorative day	יוֹם מוֹעֵד
The Fast of Gedaliah	צוֹם גדליה
Gedaliah son of Aḥikam	גדליה בן אחיקם
the third of the month of Tishrei	ג' תִּשְׁרֵי
the ruler of the people who were left in the land of Judah	מוֹשֵׁל שְׁאֵרִית יהודה
the destruction of the First Temple	חורבן הבית הראשון
the two sons of Aaron	שני בני אהרון
Miriam the sister of Moses	מְרִים אחות משה
Yehoshua (Jeshua) Bin Nun	יהושע בן נון
Eli (the High) Priest	עלי הכהן
the prophet Shmuel (Samuel)	שמואל הנביא
Queen Esther	אסתר המלכה

<u>**Foreign (loan) word**</u>

historical	היסטורית

<u>**Miscellaneous**</u> (alphabetical)

but	אַךְ
however	בכל זאת
particularly, especially	במיוחד
precisely, actually	דַּוְוקָא
etc.	וְעוד
such as	כְּגון
as a result of	כְּתוצאה מ-
throughout the generations	לאורך הדורות
in memory of	לְזֵכר
because	מְשׁוּם שֶ-
again	שׁוּב

<u>**Expression**</u>

called after, given a name	נקרא על שֵׁם

יֶשְׁנוֹ[1] רק יום מועד אחד במסורת העברית **הנקרא**[2] על שמה של אישיות היסטורית **כלשהי**[3], כבוד **שלו**[4] לא זכו גם אישים מפורסמים כמו משה או דוד המלך. זהו "צום גדליה," היום **הַחָל**[5] בג' תשרי. צום זה נקבע לזֵכר **הֵיָרָצחו שֶל**[6] גדליהו בן אחיקם, מושל שארית יהודה, לאחר חורבן ירושלים והבית הראשון בידי הבבלים. גדליהו הוא, **בְּאופן יחסי**[7], אישיות **נטולת חשיבות**[8] בהיסטוריה התנ"כית, ובכל זאת דווקא הוא זכה **לכך שֶ**[9] יום צום ייקרא על שמו. **אמנם**[10] יש במסורת העממית ימי צום לזכר מותם של אישים אחרים, כגון שני בני אהרון, מרים אחות משה, יהושע בן נון, עלי הכהן, שמואל הנביא, אסתר המלכה ועוד, **אבל**[10] אין כל חובה **לקיימם**[11] **ולְמַ־עשה**[12] אינם **בעלי חשיבות מרובה**[13].

---

(1) **יֶשְׁנוֹ**   *there is*
Ch.9; 1.5

(2) **הנקרא=שֶׁנקרא**
ה- is a subordinator before a present tense verb; Ch.1; 6.3.1(b)

(3) **כָּלְשֶׁהִי**   *some*
Ch.3; 4.2.2

(4) **שלו=שֶ+לו**   *that, which*
(NOT: his) -שֶ is a relative clause subordinator before the inflected (untranslatable) preposition required by the verb זכו;
Ch.8; 2.1.1, 3.4.2

(5) **הַחָל**   *that occurs*
Ch.11; 12.3

(6) **הֵיָרָצחו שֶל**   *the murder of*
a verbal noun in a double construct phrase; Ch.6; 1.1.2

(7) **בְּאופן יחסי**   *relatively*
adverb of manner; Ch.5; 2.2; Ch.11; 11.4.1

(8) **אישיות נטולת חשיבות**
unimportant personality
Ch.4; 4.6(c)

(9) **לכך שֶ-**   *that*
refers to content of the next clause; the preposition -ל is required by the verb זכה; Ch. 3; 2.3.1

(10) **אבל...אמנם**   *although*
Ch.10; 3

(11) **לקיימם=לקיים אותם**
to observe them (the fast days)
direct object suffix; Ch.6; 2.3

(12) **למעשה**   *in fact*
comment adverbial; Ch.5; 1.3

(13) **אינם בעלי חשיבות מרובה**
do not have/are not of great importance; Ch.4; 4.5.2; Ch.9; 2.4.1

רק הצום לזכר גדליהו בן אחיקם הוא חשוב **והינו**[(14)]
בגדר[(15)] חובה לכל יהודי.

למרות זאת[(16)], לאורך הדורות זכה גדליהו לתשומת
לב מועטה וסופרו **אודותיו**[(17)] אגדות מועטות ביותר
באופן יחסי[(7)]. אך בעשרות השנים האחרונות
ובמיוחד בעשר השנים האחרונות שוב זכו הוא
והאירועים הקשורים בו לתשומת לב בספרות העב־
רית, גם משום שנראו **בעלי הקשר עכשווי**
ביותר[(18)], כתוצאה מאירועים שונים בהיסטוריה
היהודית והישראלית העכשווית. מאמר זה יסקור
את האופן **בו**[(19)] **מציגות היצירות**[(20)] את הדמות ואת
תקופתה, כמו גם את המקבילות **שהן**[(21)] עורכות **בין**[(22)]
חורבן הבית הראשון והתקופה שלאחריו, **ובכלל זה**[(23)]
הסכסוכים הפנימיים **בין**[(24)] פלגי היהודים השונים,
ובין[(22)] **תקופתנו אנו**[(25)].

Clauses whose verb appears before the subject are shaded.

---

(14) **הינו**   *is*
copula, Ch.7; 3.1

(15) **בְּגֶדֶר** חובה
in the status of, a kind of
Ch.11; 10.2.4

(16) **למרות זאת**   *despite this*
Ch.3; 9

(17) **אודותיו**   *about him*
Ch.8; Appendix, 1

(18) בעלי הקשר עכשווי **ביותר**
with very contemporary context
(NOT: the most contemporary)
Ch.4; 2.2.3, 4.5.3

(19) האופן בו=האופן **שבו**
the manner in which
a relative clause without a
subordinator; Ch.8; 3.4.1

(20) **מציגות היצירות**
the works present
verb before subject in a relative
clause that begins with an inflected
preposition; Ch.1; 1.2.1

(21) **הן** (היצירות)   *they*
Ch.7; 1.4

(22) המקבילות... **בין** חורבן הבית
הראשון והתקופה שלאחריו... **ובין**
תקופתנו אנו
*the parallels **between** the destruction
of the First Temple the period after it
and our own period*
Ch.10; 11

(23) **ובכלל זה**   *including*
Ch.10; Confusables 3.4, example 71

(24) הסכסוכים הפנימיים **בין** פלגי
היהודים השונים
*the internal conflicts **among** the
various Jewish factions*
Ch.10; 11.1

(25) **תקופתנו אנו**   *our own period*
emphatic use of the personal
pronoun; Ch.3; 1.3.1.3

Translation

Gedaliah Ben Aḥikam: The Murder of the Governor of Judea

There is only one commemorative day in the Hebrew tradition that is called after some historical personality, an honor that even famous personages like Moses or King David have not earned. This is the Fast of Gedaliah, the day that occurs on the third day of the month of Tishrei. This fast was set to commemorate (literally: in memory of) the murder of Gedaliah Ben Achikam, the ruler of the people remaining in Judah after the destruction of Jerusalem and the First Temple by the Babylonians. Gedaliah is a relatively unimportant personality in biblical history, and yet he merited that a day of fast would be called after him. Although there are in folk tradition days of fast in commemoration of the death of other personalities, such as the two sons of Aaron, Miriam, the sister of Moses, Yehosha Bin Nun, Eli the Priest, Queen Esther etc., there is no obligation to observe them and in fact they do not have great importance. Only the fast in memory of Gedaliah Ben Aḥikam is important and obligatory for every Jew.

Despite this, through the generations Gedaliah received little attention and relatively few legends were told about him. Yet, in the last few decades, and in particular in the last ten years, he and the events that are linked to him have again received attention in Hebrew literature, also because they are viewed – as a result of various events in contemporary Jewish and Israeli history – as having a very contemporary context. This article will review the way in which these works present the character and its period, as well as the parallels they draw between the destruction of the First Temple and the period following it, including the internal conflicts among the various Jewish factions, and our own period.

PRACTICE TEXT #6

לשון חכמים
Retrieved from:
http://www.safa-ivrit.org/history/hazal.php

Terminology specific to the text (in order of appearance)

Mishnaic Hebrew (literally: language of the sages)	לְשׁוֹן חֲכָמִים
Mishnah	מִשְׁנָה
Talmud	תלמוד
Midrashim	מִדְרָשִׁים
The Second Temple	הבית השֵׁנִי
Babylonian exiles	גּוֹלֵי בָּבֶל
Aramaic	אֲרמית
dialects	לְהגים (לַהַג)
Book of Nehemiah	ספר נְחֶמְיָה
Greek and Roman	יוונית ורומית
spoken language	שפה (לשׁוֹן) מדוּבֶּרֶת
language of the Bible (biblical language)	שפת המִקְרָא
Book of Chronicles	ספר דברי הימים
Book of Ezra	ספר עֶזְרָא
written language	שפה (לשׁוֹן) כתוּבה

Miscellaneous (alphabetical)

by chance, coincidentally	בְּמִקְרֶה
more than	לְמעלה מ-

לשון חכמים, **הקרויה**(1) גם לשון חז"ל, **היא**(2) העברית שאנו מכירים **מן**(3) המשנה, **מן**(3) התלמוד **ומן**(3) המדרשים. לשון זו התפתחה **בהדרגה**(4) מלשון המקרא במשך כמה מאות שנים, והיא נחשבת לתקופה השניה **בתולדות**(5) העברית.

השינוי מלשון המקרא ללשון חכמים **החל**(6) **כנראה**(7) כבר בלשון הדיבור של תחילת ימי הבית השני, כאשר גולי בבל חזרו לארץ. רבים מה**שבים**(8) מבבל דיברו בשפה הארמית, וחלקם דיברו גם שפות ולהגים אחרים (לדוגמה, 'אשדודית' — **על פי**(9) ספר נחמיה). מאוחר יותר, **נוספו** לשפות המדוברות בפיהם גם הלשונות היוונית והרומית. המזיגה של השפות **הללו**(10) ותהליכי שינוי טבעיים שקרו בשפה, הביאו להתפתחות של שפה מדוברת שהיתה שונה משפת המקרא שקדמה לה(11).

---

(1) **הקרויה**=נקראת *that is called*
ל"א-ל"י root alternation
Ch.9; 1.7.1

(2) **היא** *is*
The copula agrees with the head noun of the construct phrase לשון חכמים; Ch.2; 4.6

(3) **מן המשנה, מן התלמוד ומן המדרשים**
repeated identical prepositions before each complement; Ch.8; 3.3

(4) **בהדרגה** *gradually*
adverb of manner; Ch.5; 2.1

(5) **תולדות** *the history of*
Ch.2; 2.2.1(b), 4.5.9

(6) **הֵחֵל**=התחיל *began*
Ch.11; 12.1

(7) **כַּנְרָאֶה** *apparently*
comment adverbial; Ch.5; 1.3, 2.1.1

(8) **שָׁבִים** *returnees*
present participle used as a noun; Ch.2; 6.2

(9) **על פי**=לפי *according to*
Ch. 8; Confusables 2(a)

(10) **הללו** *those*
demonstrative pronoun; Ch.3; 2.1.1

(11) **המזיגה...לה:**
complex sentence comprising a main clause and three dependent clauses. To parse, identify the subject of each verb; Ch.1; 6.4

אם⁽¹²⁾ בספרים שנתחברו⁽¹³⁾ בימי הבית השני,
בספר דברי הימים, בעזרא ובנחמיה⁽¹⁴⁾, מוצאים⁽¹⁵⁾
עקבות מועטים בלבד⁽¹⁶⁾ ללשון החכמים, וסגנונם⁽¹⁷⁾
נוטה עדיין להיות סגנון מקראי, הרי⁽¹²⁾ שבהדרגה,
המשיכה והתגבשה⁽¹⁸⁾ שפת הדיבור של לשון
החכמים עד שהפכה⁽¹⁹⁾ גם ללשון הכתובה, בכתיבת
המשנה.

אוצר המילים של לשון חכמים

מילים רבות שהיו שכיחות ושגורות בלשון המקרא
נעלמו בתקופת חז"ל והוחלפו במילים אחרות.
בעיקר⁽²⁰⁾ מדובר ב⁽²¹⁾מילים הקדומות יותר, אלו שנמצאות בשירה המקראית בלבד. היו גם מילים רבות,
שהשתמשו⁽¹⁵⁾ בהן בזמן המקרא בלשון היומיום,
ושהפסיקו לשמש⁽²²⁾ בלשון חכמים. לעומת זאת⁽²³⁾,
מוצאים⁽¹⁵⁾ בעברית בתקופה זו למעלה משלוש מאות
שורשים חדשים. חלקם שורשים עבריים עתיקים,
אשר⁽²⁴⁾ היו בשימוש⁽²²⁾ גם בזמן המקרא אך⁽²⁵⁾
במקרה לא הופיעו בספרי התנ"ך.

Clauses whose verb precedes the subject are shaded.

---

(12) **אם...הרי ש** *if...then*
Ch.7; Confusables 1.2

(13) **נתחברו** *were composed*
נתפעל; Ch.6; 6.1

(14) **בספרים שנתחברו בימי הבית השני, בספר דברי הימים, בעזרא ובנחמיה**
The second appositive specifies the identity of the books composed at the time of the Second Temple; Ch.1; 8.1.1

(15) **מוצאים**
one finds, we find; are found
impersonal; Ch.1; 5(a)

(16) **בִּלְבַד** *only*
Ch.10; Confusables 6.1

(17) **סגנונם** *their style*
(the style of the books)
possessive suffix; Ch.2; 5.8

(18) **המשיכה והתגבשה**
continued to consolidate
aspectual verb phrase; Ch.6; 3.2

(19) **הפכה ללשון כתובה**
became a written language
Ch.7; 5.1.

(20) **בעיקר** *mainly, mostly*
adverb of manner; Ch.5; 2.1

(21) **מְדוּבָּר ב-**
this concerns, it is a question of
Ch.1; 5(b); Ch.11; 14.5

(22) **לשמש; היו בשימוש**
to be used; were in use
Ch.7; 4.2.1

(23) **לעומת זאת** *in contrast to this*
זאת refers to the content of the previous clause; Ch.3; 2.3

(24) **אשר** *that*
interchangeable with the subordinating particle -ש; Ch.1; 6.3.1(a)

(25) **אך** *but*
connects two coordinate clauses; Ch.1; 6.1

<u>**Translation**</u>

Mishnaic Hebrew

The Language of the Sages, also called Ḥazal Language, is the Hebrew that we know from the Mishnah, the Talmud and the Midrashim. This language developed gradually from the language of the Bible over several hundred years and is considered the second period in the history of Hebrew.

The change from the language of the Bible to the language of the sages apparently began already in the spoken language of the beginning of the Second Temple period, when the Babylonian exiles returned to the land (of Israel). Many of the returnees from Babylonia spoke Aramaic, and some of them spoke also other languages and dialects (for example, Ashdodit – according to the Book of Nehemiah). Later, Greek and Roman were added to the languages that were spoken by the returnees. The fusion of these languages and natural processes of change that occurred in the language brought about the development of a spoken language that was different from the biblical language that had preceded it.

If in the books that were composed during the period of the Second Temple, (namely) the Book of Chronicles, the Book of Ezra and the Book of Nehemiah, are found only few traces of Mishnaic Hebrew and their style still tends to be biblical, spoken Mishnaic Hebrew continued gradually to crystallize until, in the writing of the Mishnah, it became also a written language.

The vocabulary of Mishnaic language

Many words that were common and well-known in the language of the Bible disappeared in the period of Ḥazal and were replaced by other words. This concerns mostly the earliest words, those that are found only in biblical poetry. There were also many words that were used in the time of the Bible in everyday language and which ceased to be used in Mishnaic language. In contrast, one finds in Hebrew during this period more than three hundred new roots. Some of them are ancient Hebrew roots which were in use also at the time of the Bible but, as it happens, did not appear in its books.

PRACTICE TEXT #7

בעקבות המסורת על שלמה המגיקן בספרות חז"ל
מאת: ששון גלעד

Terminology specific to the text (in order of appearance)

מִקְרָא   Bible
בית המקדש   The Temple
גֵּירוּשׁ שֵׁדִים   exorcism (of devils)
הַמֵּאָה הָרִאשׁוֹנָה לִפְנה"ס (לפני הספירה)   the first century B.C.E.
סִפְרוּת חז"ל   the literature of Ḥazal (the sages of the Mishnah and Talmud)
תַּנָּאִים וַאֲמוֹרָאִים   Tannaim (sages of the Mishnah) and Amoraim (Talmudic sages)
מַאֲמָר   article
אבות הכנסיה   The Church Fathers
יֵשׁוּ   Jesus
נָכְרִים   non-Jews

Loan (foreign) words

אַרְכִיטֶקֶט   architect
מגית   magic, supernatural

Miscellaneous (alphabetical)

אַף   also
אַף שֶׁ-   even though
בְּאֶמְצָעוּת   via, through
בִּמְפוֹרָשׁ   explicitly
וְאִילוּ   whereas
לְהַלָּן   the following (Aramaic)

הקדמה

פנים רבות לדמותו של שלמה המלך במקרא[1]:
חכם, עשיר, מכובד **על ידי**[2] מלכי האזור ואף
ארכיטקט מוכשר. **הָחֵל**[3] מימי הבית השני נוֹסַף עוֹד
פֵּן לדמותו של שלמה[4]— יכולתו לשלוט בשדים.
יכולת זו[5] מתבטאת בשתי מסורות עיקריות:
א. מסורת בִּדְבַר[6] השימוש של שלמה בשדים לבניית
המקדש ב. מסורת על **כוחו של שלמה**[4] לרפא
חולים באמצעות גירוש שדים.
שתי המסורות האלה מופיעות החל מהמאה הראשונה
לפנה"ס במקורות רבים, יהודיים ולא יהודיים, במזרח
ובמערב. **מעיון בספרות חז"ל עולה**[7] שהמסורת
הראשונה **בעניין**[8] בניית המקדש **מוזכרת**[9] כמה
פעמים במקורות ארץ-ישראליים ובבליים, ואילו
המסורת השנייה **בדבר**[6] הריפוי[10] באמצעות גירוש
שדים **אינה נזכרת**[11] במפורש, אך יש רמזים שאף
היא הייתה מוכרת לתנאים ולאמוראים.

---

(1) פנים רבות לדמותו של שלמה המלך

The character/figure of King Solomon <u>has</u> many faces
a "have" sentence without יֵשׁ;
Ch.9; 2.2; Ch.11, 16.3

(2) מכובד על ידי

respected by
Ch.8; Confusables, 1(b)

(3) הָחֵל מימי הבית השני

beginning with the days of the Second Temple
Ch.11; 12.2

(4) דמותו של שלמה; כוחו של שלמה

Solomon's figure/character;
Solomon's power
double construct phrase; Ch.2; 4.4

(5) זוֹ=זאת   this

Ch.3; 2.1.1

(6) בדבר=בקשר, בעניין, בנוגע ל

regarding, concerning
Ch.11; 14.4

(7) מעיון בספרות חז"ל עולה ש . . .

a reading of the literature of Ḥazal reveals that…
Ch.1; 5(b)

(8) בעניין   regarding, concerning

Ch.11; 11.4.2, 14.4

(9) מוזכרת=נזכרת   is mentioned

(NOT: is remembered)

(10) ריפוי   healing

an action noun in *pi'el* from לרפא
(ל"א-ל"י root alternation);
Ch.2; 6.3.7.2, 2(d)

(11) אינה נזכרת   is not mentioned

אין replaces לא before a present tense verb; Ch.7; 2.1, 2.2

במאמר שלהלן **אסקור**[12] את המקורות **שמהם**[13] עולות שתי המסורות **ואנסה להסביר** מדוע בספרות חז"ל **נדונה**[14] המסורת הראשונה בלבד, ואילו על המסורת השנייה **לא נאמר דבר**[15].

סיכום

חז"ל ואבות הכנסייה עשו מאמצים רבים לטשטש את הזיקה **בין** שלמה **לישו**[16] – כל קבוצה מטעמיה. חכמים לא רצו לשַווֹת לשלמה דמות **כדמות**[17] **מייסד**[18] הדת היריבה. עמדה זו הביאה את התנאים ובעקבותיהם את האמוראים להוביל מהלך שימוסס את הדמות המגית של שלמה **כמגרש שדים**[18, 19]. התוצאה של מהלך זה הייתה השמטת כל אִזכור **המייחס לשלמה**[20] שליטה בשדים לצורכי רפואה. לכן אף שהמסורת על **כוחו זה של שלמה**[4] הייתה נפוצה בין יהודים ונכרים **בסביבתם ובימיהם של חז"ל**[4], **אין לה**[21] שום מקור בספרות חז"ל.

Clauses in which the verb precedes the subject are shaded.

(12) אסקור, אנסה להסביר
I will review, I will try to explain
The author states his research agenda;
Ch.3; 1.1

(13) המקורות **שמהם** עולות שתי המסורות
the sources from which the two traditions arise
The inflected preposition in the relative clause refers back מקורות; the verb precedes the subject;
Ch.1; 1.2.1; Ch. 8; 3.4.1

(14) נדונה *was discussed*
(NOT: was judged)

(15) לא נאמר דבר *nothing was said*
Ch.11; 14.3

(16) בין שלמה לישו
between Solomon and Jesus
Ch.10; 11

(17) כדמות *like the figure of*
Ch.8; 2.3.2(a)

(18) מייסד *founder*
מגרש *exorcist*
The present participle is used as a noun; Ch.2; 6.2

(19) כמגרש שדים
as an exorcist (of devils)
Ch.8; 2.3.2(b)

(20) המייחס לשלמה
that attributes to Solomon
ליחס ל – Ch.11; 11.2.2
ה- *is a subordinator before a present tense verb*; Ch.1; 6.3.1(b)

(21) אין לה *it does not have*
לה *refers to* מסורת; Ch.9; 2.1

Translation

In the Footsteps of the Tradition about Solomon the Magician in the Literature of Ḥazal

The character of King Solomon in the Bible has many faces: wise, rich, respected by the kings of the region, and even a talented architect. Beginning with the days of the Second Temple, another aspect was added to the character of King Salomon – his ability to rule devils. This ability is expressed in two main traditions:

a. A tradition concerning Salomon's use of devils for the building of the Temple,

b. A tradition about Salomon's power to heal the sick by means of exorcism.

The two traditions appear, beginning with the first century B.C.E. in many sources, Jewish and non-Jewish, in the East and the West. A reading of the literature of Ḥazal reveals (literally: from a reading of the literature of Ḥazal it arises) that the first tradition concerning the building of the Temple is mentioned several times in Israelite and Babylonian sources, whereas the second tradition about the healing by means of exorcism is not mentioned explicitly, but there are hints that it, too, was known to the Tannaim and Amoraim.

In the following article I will review the sources from which the two traditions derive (literally: arise), and will try to explain why only the first tradition was discussed in the literature of Ḥazal while nothing was said (there) about the second one.

Summary

Ḥazal and the Church Fathers made many efforts to blur the association between Solomon and Jesus – each group for its own reasons. The sages did not want to lend to Solomon a character like that of the founder of the rival religion. This position prompted (literally: brought) the Tannaim, and after them the Amoraim, to launch a stratagem that would dissolve the supernatural figure of Solomon as an exorcist of devils. The result of this stratagem was the omission of any reference that attributes to Solomon dominion over devils for medical purposes. Therefore, even though the tradition about this power of Solomon was widespread among Jews and non-Jews in the environment of Ḥazal and in their days, it is not found (literally: it has no source) in the literature of Ḥazal.

PRACTICE TEXT #8

תקופת העליה החמישית
מאת: יוסף גורני
מתוך: מראש-פינה ודגניה ועד דימונה, אוניברסיטה
משודרת, משרד הביטחון ההוצאה לאור 1987, עמ' 77.

Terminology specific to the text (in order of appearance)

restrictions	הַגְבָּלוֹת
the 1920's	שְׁנוֹת ה-20
immigration	הַגִירָה
The United States	אַרְצוֹת הברית (ארה"ב)
Nazi regime	מִשְׁטָר נאצי
Polish Jews	יהודי פולין
Hungarian Jews	יהודי הונגריה
the West	ארצות המערב
the 1930's	שְׁנוֹת ה-30
refugees	פליטים
Second World War	מלחמת העולם השנייה
Fascist powers	מעצמות פאשיסטיות
the rule of the (British) Mandate	שִׁלְטוֹן הַמַּנְדָט
Ha-Yishuv (the pre-State Jewish population in the Land of Israel)	הַיִישׁוּב
the Arab Revolt	הַמֶּרֶד הערבי
revolt, rebellion	התמרדות
lawless bands	"כְּנוּפִיוֹת"

Foreign (loan) words

democratic	דֶמוֹקרטיות
fascist	פאשיסטיות

Miscellaneous (alphabetical)

but	אוּלָם
before	בְּטֶרֶם
at the footsteps of, following; as a result of	בְּעִקְבוֹתֶיהָ (בעקבות)
with at the side of, next to, alongside	בְּצִידָה (בצד)
under (the power, authority of)	בְּתוֹקֶף ה-
as a result of	כְּתוֹצָאָה מִן
without any doubt	לְלֹא כָּל סָפֵק

Expressions

undertake, take upon themselves	ליטול על עצמן
broke out (war, rebellion)	פרצה מלחמה, פרץ מרד

בתוקף ההגבלות על ההגירה שהוטלו בארצות-הברית באמצע שנות ה-20, **חדלה ארץ זו** להיות פתרון לבעית מצוקה יהודית המונית, **ובעקבותיה ובצידה**[1] גם מדינות אחרות לא היו מוכנות ליטול על עצמן את האחריות לטפל בבעיה היהודית ההמונית. הבעיה היתה לא רק של יהודי גרמניה, שנרדפו על ידי המשטר הנאצי, אלא של מיליוני יהודי פולין וגם יהודי הונגריה. ארצות המערב הדֶמוקרטיות חששו, **על כן**[2], לפתוח את גבולותיהן בפני המונֵי הפליטים היהודים מטעמים כלכליים ותרבותיים **כאחד**[3]. באותה תקופה **הפכה**[4] **ארץ-ישראל למקום**[4] ההגירה הגדול ביותר ליהודים. בשנות ה-30 **היגרו** לארץ-ישראל **יותר**[5] יהודים **מאשר**[5] לארה"ב. במספרים מוחלטים, ארץ ישראל תפסה שליש **מכלל**[6] ההגירה היהודית, **ואלמלא**[7] ההגבלות שהוטלו על הגירה יהודית לארץ-ישראל במחצית השנייה של שנות ה-30, **היתה**[7] ארץ-ישראל ללא כל ספק **קולטת**[7] את **רוב רובם**[8] של הפליטים היהודים, אשר יכלו עוד להימלט בטֶרֶם פרצה מלחמת-העולם השנייה.

---

(1) בעקבותיה ובצידה
following it and alongside with it
prepositions with plural and singular
inflections, respectively; the pronoun
suffixes refer to (ארצות הברית) ארץ זו
Ch.8; 1.1.1, Appendix, 4

(2) עַל כֵּן *therefore*
Ch.11; 15.2

(3) כְּאֶחָד *both*
Ch.10; 6.2

(4) הפכה למקום ההגירה *became*
Ch.7; 5.1

(5) יותר מאשר=יותר מ(ן)
more than
מאשר is preferred to מ(ן) before a
preposition; Ch.8; 2.3.4(c)

(6) מכלל ההגירה היהודית שליש
one third of the totality (NOT: *rule*) *of
Jewish immigration*
Ch.10; Confusables 3.2

(7) אלמלא ההגבלות... **היתה ארץ
ישראל קולטת** את רוב רובם של
הפליטים היהודים
*if not for the restrictions..., the Land
of Israel would have absorbed...*
negative hypothetical sentence, the
verb phrase straddles the subject;
Ch.6; 3.3.3.2(c), 3.3.3.3

(8) רוֹב רוּבָּם *most of them, the vast
majority*
Ch.11; Part. C, 2

אולם ההתפתחות היתה **לְרָעָתוֹ שֶׁל הָעָם הַיְהוּדִי**[9]
לֹא רק[10] מחוץ לגבולותיה של **ארץ-ישראל**[9],
אלא גם[10] בארץ-ישראל **עצמה**[11]. כאן, בארץ-
ישראל, **הן**[12] בעקבות ההתערבות של **המעצמות
הפאשיסטיות, גרמניה ואיטליה**[13], באזור **והן**[12]
כתוצאה מהתגברות העלייה היהודית לארץ-ישראל
באמצע שנות ה-30, בשנים 1934- ו-1935 — <mark>פרץ
המרד</mark> הערבי **נגד**[14] שלטון המַנְדָט **ונגד**[14] היישוב
היהודי בארץ-ישראל. מרד זה נשא את כל הסימנים
של התמרדות לאומית **הן**[12] **מבחינת**[15] הארגון,
הן[12] **מבחינת**[15] היכולת לכפות מידה לא מעטה של
מִשְׁמַעַת לאומית **והן**[12] **מבחינת**[15] יכולת הלחימה
ונכונות[16] ההַקְרָבָה של **אנשיו**[17]. בצד **אלה**[18] היו,
כַּמּוּבָן[19], תופעות של שוד ושל רֶצַח, שהיו מעשי
"הכנופיות".

Clauses whose verb precedes the subject are shaded.

---

(9) לְרָעָתוֹ שֶׁל הָעָם הַיְהוּדִי
to the detriment of the Jewish people
double construct phrase; Ch.2; 4.4

(10) לֹא רק...אלא גם
not only...but also
Ch.10; 1.3

(11) בארץ ישראל עצמה
in the Land of Israel itself
emphatic pronoun; Ch.3; 6.2

(12) הן...והן *both* (NOT: they)
Ch.10; 6

(13) המעצמות הפשיסטיות, גרמניה ואיטליה
the Fascist powers, Germany and Italy
appositives separated by a comma;
Ch.1; 8.1.1

(14) נגד שלטון המנדט **ונגד** היישוב היהודי...
against... and (against)...
The identical prepositions are
repeated before each complement;
Ch.8; 3.3

(15) מבחינת ה-
from the point of view of...
Ch. 5; 2.1.1; Ch.11; 10.2.1

(16) נכונות
willingness (NOT: correctness)
The ות- ending is the derivational
suffix -וּת (NOT the plural suffix
-וֹת); Ch.2; 6.1

(17) אנשיו *its people*
(the pronoun suffix refers to מרד);
Ch.2; 5.8

(18) אלה *these (things)*
demonstrative pronoun used for
substitution; Ch.3; 2.2

(19) כמובן *of course*
comment adverb; Ch.5; 1.3

<u>Translation</u>

The Period of the Fifth Aliya

Under (literally: by the power of) the restrictions on immigration that were imposed in the United States in the middle of the 1920's, this country ceased to be a solution to the problem of mass Jewish suffering and in its footsteps, and alongside with it, other countries were also not willing to undertake the responsibility of taking care of the mass Jewish problem. The problem was not just that of German Jews, who were persecuted by the Nazi regime, but [also] of millions of Polish and Hungarian Jews. The democratic West was therefore apprehensive for both economic and cultural reasons of opening its borders to the masses of Jewish refugees.

At that period, the Land of Israel became the largest destination of Jewish immigration. In the 1930's more Jews immigrated to it than to the United States. In absolute numbers, the Land of Israel took in one third of the total Jewish immigration, and if not for the restrictions that were imposed on Jewish immigration in the second part of the 1930's, the Land of Israel would have without any doubt absorbed the vast majority of the Jewish immigrants who could still escape before the Second World War broke out.

But this development was to the detriment of the Jewish people not only outside the borders of the Land of Israel, but also within it. Here, in the Land of Israel, both as a result of the intervention of the fascist powers, Germany and Italy, in the region and the increase in Jewish immigration in the middle of the 1930's, the Arab revolt against the rule of the [British] Mandate and the Yishuv broke out in the years 1934 and 1935. This revolt bore all the signs of a national rebellion, from the point of view of organization and the ability to enforce not a small measure of national discipline, as well as the fighting ability and willingness to sacrifice [on the part of] of its people. Alongside these there were, of course, occurrences of robbery and murder, which were the deeds of lawless bands.

PRACTICE TEXT #9

לשחזור ההיסטוריה הקדומה של עם ישראל: מקרא, ארכאולוגיה וכתיבת היסטוריה

מאת: נדב נאמן
מתוך: זמנים 94, 2006
Retrieved from:
http://www.openu.ac.il/zmanim/zmanim94/94-neeman.html

Terminology specific to the text (in order of appearance)

archeological finding	מִמְצָא אַרְכֵאוֹלוֹגִי
biblical	מְקְרָאִי
Bible	מקרא
historical documents	תעודות היסטוריות
conquest	כיבוש
B.C.E.	לפנה"ס (לפני הספירה)
a military campaign	מַסָע צְבָאִי
desert nomads	נַוְודֵי מדבר
Trans-Jordan	עֵבֶר הַיַרְדֵן
kingdoms	מַמְלָכוֹת
the Book of Joshua	סֵפר יהושע
historical reconstruction	שִׁחְזוּר הִיסְטוֹרִי
destruction of the Canaanite kingdoms	חוּרְבַּן הַמַמְלָכוֹת הַכְּנַעֲניוֹת
archeological digs	חֲפירוֹת אַרְכאוֹלוֹגִיוֹת
external sources	מְקוֹרוֹת חיצוֹנִיים
period of the Judges	תְּקוּפַת הַשׁוֹפְטִים

Foreign (loan) words (alphabetical)

archeological	אַרְכֵאוֹלוֹגִי
archeologists	ארכאולוגים
historians	היסטוריונים
historic	היסטוֹרִית
literary-theological	סְפרוּתית-תֵאוֹלוֹגִית
construction	קוֹנְסְטְרוּקְצִיָה

Miscellaneous (alphabetical)

on the basis of	בהסתמך על
in particular	בייחוד
in the course of	בַּמַהֲלָך
first and foremost	בראש ובראשונה
all the time, constantly	כל העת
like, as	כפי ש-
for the purpose of	לְשֵׁם
to what extent	עַד כמה
at the beginning	תְחילה

Expressions

every other day, frequently	חֲדָשׁוֹת לִבְקָרִים
be careful, take precautions	לִנְקוֹט זהירות

ניתן לסכם[1] ולקבוע, **שהן**[2] הממצא הארכאולוגי **והן**[2] התעודות ההיסטוריות מלמדים עד כמה **זר התיאור המקראי**[3] של **כיבוש הארץ ההיסטורית**[4] במאה השתים-עשרה לפנה"ס. **לתיאור**[5] המקראי **בְּדְבַר**[6] מסע צבאי של נוודי מדבר, **המגיעים**[7] ממזרח, כובשים תחילה את רוב שטחי עבר-הירדן ולאחר מכן מחריבים את כל הממלכות ששכנו ממערב לירדן, **אין כל**[5] יסוד היסטורי. פרשת כיבוש הארץ כפי שהיא מוצגת בספר יהושע היא **בעיקרה**[8] קונְסְטְרוּקְציה ספרותית-תאולוגית, **ואינה יכולה לשמש**[9] בסיס לשחזור היסטורי.

---

(1) ניתן לסכם ולקבוע
it is possible to sum up and state
ניתן (impersonal) before an infinitive verb indicates possibility; Ch.11; 3.2

(2) הן...והן both (NOT: *they*) Ch.10; 6.1

(3) זר התיאור המקראי
the biblical description is alien
The predicative adjective (Ch.4; 1.2.1) precedes the subject after the adverbial עד כמה; Ch.1; 1.1

(4) כיבוש הארץ ההיסטורית
the conquest of the historic land
(NOT: the historic conquest of the land)
construct phrase modified by an adjective; Ch.2; 4.5.1

(5) לתיאור המקראי...אין כל יסוד היסטורי
the biblical description does not have any historical basis
The two parts of the "(not) have" phrase (ל...אין) are far apart; Ch.9; 2.1(a)
כל intensifies the negation; Ch.4; 4.5.2

(6) בְּדְבַר *regarding, concerning*
Ch.11; 14.4

(7) המגיעים *that arrive*
-ה before a present tense verb is a subordinator; Ch.1; 6.3.1(b)

(8) בעיקרה *in the main, mainly*
inflected adverb – the pronoun suffix refers back to פרשה;
Ch.5; 1.4.1

(9) אינה יכולה לשמש *cannot serve*
In the present tense, אין is used to negate (instead of לא); Ch.9, 4

חשוב **לחזור ולהדגיש**[10] **שלא רק**[11] הפרטים, **אלא גם**[11] **התהליך**[12] ההיסטורי של חורבן הממלכות הכנעניות, מראשיתו ועד סופו, **היה שונה**[12] בכל רכיביו ממה שמתואר במקרא. מסיבה זו קבעו היסטוריונים וארכֵאולוגים שלא ניתן להסתמך[1] על מסורת כיבוש הארץ **המופיעה**[7] במקרא לשֵם שחזור המאורעות שהובילו לחורבן הערים הכנעניות, **וכי**[13] שחזור ההשתלשלות ההיסטורית צריך להיעשות בהסתמך על מקורות **חוץ-מקראיים**[14] **בלבד**[15].

אף כי[16] **כמות**[17] הממצאים העומדת לרשותנו לחֵקר שלבי הבראשית של עם ישראל **גְּדֵלָה**[17] כל העת וחפירות ארכאולוגיות נערכות חדשות לבק־רים, התנ"ך נשאר המקור היחיד **המתאר**[7] **באופן שיטתי ורצוף**[18] את תולדות עם ישראל. במהלך הדיון ניסיתי להראות את הבעייתיות הרבה הכרוכה בשימוש בתנ"ך כמקור היסטורי, ובייחוד בסיפורים **המתארים**[7] את התקופות שקדמו **לייסודן והתגב־שותן של ממלכות ישראל ויהודה**[19] במאה התשי־עית לפנה"ס. **את התקופות**[20] שקדמו לכינון שתי הממלכות **יש לשחזר**[21] בראש ובראשונה בהסתמך על מקורות חיצוניים וממצאים ארכאולוגיים, **ויש לנקוט**[21] זהירות רבה בשימוש בפרוזה המקראית **המתארת**[7] את תקופות הכיבוש, השופטים וצמיחת מוסד המלוכה בישראל.

Clauses whose verb precedes the subject are shaded.

---

(10) לחזור ולהדגיש   *re-emphasize*
(NOT: *return*); Ch.6; 3.2

(11) לא רק...אלא גם
not only... but also; Ch.10; 1.3

(12) התהליך ... היה שונה
the *process... was different*
predicate at a distance from the
subject; Ch.1; 3.1

(13) וכי   *and that*
(NOT: *and because*)
כי is a subordinating particle after a
verb of saying (here – קבעו);
Ch.1; 6.3.1(c)

(14) מקורות חוץ-מקראיים
extra-biblical sources
a semantic prefix before an adjective;
Ch.4; 5

(15) בלבד   *only*
Ch.10; Confusables 6.1

(16) אף כי   *even though*
Ch.1; Confusables 3.4

(17) גְּדֵלָה   *grows, is growing*
present tense form in the *pa'el* (פָּעַל)
paradigm; the (distant) subject is
כמות; Ch.1; 3.1

(18) באופן שיטתי ורצוף
systematically and consecutively
coordinated adverbs of manner;
Ch.5; 2.9

(19) ייסודן והתגבשותן של ממלכות ישראל ויהודה
*the establishment and
consolidation of the kingdoms of
Israel and Judah*
double construct phrase, Ch.2; 4.4

(20) את התקופות
direct object at the beginning of the
sentence, Ch.1; 1.2

(21) יש לשחזר
should be reconstructed
יש before an infinitive verb indicates
obligation; Ch.9; 3.2.1

Translation

Toward Reconstructing the Early History of the People of Israel: Bible, Archeology and the Writing of History

It is possible to sum up and state that both the archeological evidence and the historical documents indicate (literally: teach) how alien is the biblical description of the conquest of the historic Land of Israel in the 12th century B.C.E. The biblical description regarding a military campaign of desert nomads who arrive from the east, conquer first most of the areas of Trans-Jordan and afterwards destroy all the kingdoms that inhabited [the areas] west of the Jordan, has no historical basis. The story of the conquest of the Land [of Israel] as it is presented in the book of Joshua is for the most part a literary-theological construction, and cannot serve as the basis for a historical reconstruction.

It is important to re-emphasize that not only the details, but also the [entire] historical process of the destruction of the Canaanite kingdoms, from its beginning to its end, was different in all its components from what is described in the Bible. For this reason historians and archeologists have stated that, for the purpose of reconstructing the events that led to the destruction of the Canaanite cities, it is not possible to rely on the tradition of the conquest of the Land [of Israel] as it appears in the Bible, and that the reconstruction of the historical development should be done solely on the basis of extra-biblical sources.

Although the amount of findings at our disposal for the study of the early stages of the people of Israel is constantly growing and archeological excavations newly take place, the Bible remains the only source that describes systematically and consecutively the history of the people of Israel. In the course of the discussion I tried to show the great difficulty involved in using the Bible as a historical source, and in particular [in using] the stories that describe the periods that preceded the establishment and consolidation of the kingdoms of Israel and Judea in the 9th century B.C.E. The periods that preceded the establishment of the two kingdoms should be reconstructed first and foremost on the basis of external sources and archeological findings, and great caution should be exercised in making use of the biblical prose [sections] describing the periods of the conquest, of the Judges and of the growth of the institution of kingdom in Israel.

**ממפרץ סלוניקי למפרץ עכו: פרק בקורותיהם של דייגים עבריים בין שתי
מלחמות העולם**
מאת: שי סרוגו
מתוך: פעמים 3–122, תש"ע
Retrieved from:
http://www.ybz.org.il/_Uploads/dbsAttachedFiles/122-123_Srogo_009-040-
_13.5.10(1).pdf

<u>**Terminology specific to the text**</u> (in order of appearance)

history	קורות
summary	סיכום
article	מאמר
Salonican fishermen	דייגים סלוניקאים
Salonika	סלוניקי
pioneers	חלוצים
the work of fishing	מלאכת הדָיִיג
the Zionist establishment	המְמְסד הציוני
"Ha-Kovesh" (pioneering) group	קבוצת "הכובש"
Acre	עכו
Zionist directorate	ההנהלה הציונית
longshoremen	פועלי ים
Ḥaifa port	נמל חיפה
Jaffa	יפו
Tel Aviv Port	נמל תל אביב

<u>**Foreign (loan) words**</u> (alphabetical)

historic	היסטורית
Sisyphean	סיזיפית
Zionist	ציונית

<u>**Miscellaneous**</u> (alphabetical)

but	אולָם
there is no point in	אין טעם ב-
generally	בדרך כלל
considering, taking into account	בהתחשב ב-
in the end	בסופו של דָבָר
in the vicinity of	בשְכנות ל-
for the purpose of	לשֵם
from the time that	משעה ש-

<u>**Idiomatic Expressions**</u>

all hope was lost	כָּלוּ כל הקיצין
fulfilled a central role	מילאו תפקיד מרכזי
took shape	קַרַם עור וגידים

<u>סיכום</u>

עמדתי במאמר זה **על**[1] הגורמים **להגירתם של דייגים סלוניקאים**[2] לארץ-ישראל באמצע שנות העשרים של המאה העשרים ועל חבלי קליטתם **בה**[3]. ההחלטה לעזוב את עיר מולדתם ההיסטורית קרמה עור וגידים משעה **שנתערערה**[4] **יציבותם הכלכלית של הדייגים היהודים**[2] בסלוניקי. אפשר שהגירתם לארץ האבות **לא היתה נכשלת**[5,6] **כישלון חרוץ**[6] **לו היו**[5] הממסד המְשַׁלֵח והקולט **נערכים**[5] **כַּהֲלָכָה**[7] לקליטתם בהתחשב במאפייניהם **החברתיים–הכלכל־יים הייחודיים**[8]. הסלוניקאים נבדלו **מבחינות רבות**[9] מקבוצות החלוצים שהיגרו בדרך כְּלָל **באותן שנים**[10] לארץ-ישראל, ובעיקר **במוצאם** הגאוגרפי, **בהרכב** המשפחות וגודלן, **בשפה ובתרבות** חיים[11].

---

(1) עמדתי על   *I discussed* (NOT: I stood on); Ch. 8; 2.2

(2) הגירתם של דייגים סלוניקאים *the immigration of Salonican fishermen* double construct phrase with an adjective; Ch.2; 4.4, 4.5.2

(3) בה   *in it (in the Land of Israel)* Ch.8; 1.1

(4) נתערערה   *was weakened* נתפעל; Ch.6; 6.1

(5) הגירתם לארץ האבות לא היתה נכשלת כישלון חרוץ לו היו הממסד המשלח והקולט **נערכים** *Their immigration to the Land of the Fathers would not have failed completely had the sending and absorbing establishment prepared [for it]* 'unreal' condition; in the second clause, the verb phrase components straddle the subject; Ch.6; 3.3.3.2(a), 3.3.3.3

(6) לֹא היתה נכשלת כישלון חרוץ *(would not have) failed completely* internal object with an adjective – translated as an adverb; Ch.5; 3.3

(7) כהלכה   *properly* Ch.5; 2.1.1

(8) מאפייניהם החברתיים-הכלכליים הייחודיים *their unique socio-economic characteristics* Stacked adjectives are translated backward; the hyphenated adjective is considered one lexical unit; Ch.4; 3.2, 3.3

(9) מבחינות רבות   *in many respects* Ch.11; 10.2.1

(10) באותן השנים   *in those years* Ch.3; 3.2

(11) במוצאם...בהרכב...בשפה ובתרבות החיים *The preposition is repeated before each complement of the verb* נבדלו; Ch.8; 3.3

כְּאוּמָנִים[12] בִּמְלֶאכֶת הַדַּיִג הָיָה לָהֶם יִתְרוֹן מַשְׁמָעוּתִי עַל קְבוּצוֹת מְלָאכָה דּוֹמוֹת, וְאוּלָם **הִתְבָּרֵר כִּי**[13] **מוּמְחִיּוּת זוֹ לֹא הָיָה בָּה דֵּי**[14] לְהִתְמוֹדֵד עִם צָרְכֵי הַזְּמַן. קְשָׁיֵי הַקִּיּוּם, פְּעָרִים תַּרְבּוּתִיִּים **וְאָזְלַת יָדוֹ שֶׁל הַמִּמְסָד הַצִּיּוֹנִי**[2] יָצְרוּ נִיכּוּר **בֵּינוֹ לְדַיָּיגִים**[15] **וּבֵינָם לְ**[16]קְבוּצַת 'הַכּוֹבֵשׁ' שֶׁדָּרָה בִּשְׁכֵנוּת לָהֶם. **מִשֶּׁ**הִתְוֹוסַף[17] עַל שִׁגְרַת הַקִּיּוּם הַסִּיזִיפִית מַצַּב בִּיטְחוֹנִי מְעוֹרְעָר, כָּלוּ כֹּל הַקָּצִין, וְהַמִּפְעָל בַּעַכּוֹ נִתְחַסֵּל[4]. הַצְּרָכִים הַמְרוּבִּים שֶׁל קְבוּצַת הַדַּיָּיגִים, הַמַּחֲלוֹקוֹת בֵּינָם לַמִּמְסָד הַצִּיּוֹנִי וּלְבַסּוֹף כִּישָׁלוֹן הִתְיַישְּׁבוּתָם בְּעַכּוֹ הֵבִיאוּ **כַּנִּרְאָה**[18] אֶת הַהַנְהָלָה הַצִּיּוֹנִית לַמַּסְקָנָה שֶׁאֵין טַעַם **בְּהַעֲלָאָתָם שֶׁל פּוֹעֲלֵי יָם נוֹסָפִים**[2] מִסָּלוֹנִיקִי. קְבוּצָה מִקְצוֹעִית **זוֹ**[19] זָכְתָה לְתְשׂוּמַת לֵב מְחוּדֶּשֶׁת רַק **כְּשָׁלוֹשׁ שָׁנִים**[20] מְאוּחָר יוֹתֵר, בַּקַּיִץ 1933, עֶרֶב פְּתִיחָתוֹ שֶׁל נְמַל חֵיפָה. **מִשֶּׁ**הִתְבָּרֵר[17] כִּי אֵין בְּאֶרֶץ-יִשְׂרָאֵל חֲלוּצִים הַיְכוֹלִים לְבַצֵּעַ כַּהֲלָכָה אֶת הָעֲבוֹדָה הַתּוֹבְעָנִית בַּנְּמָלִים, **חוּדְּשָׁה הַגִּירָתָם שֶׁל עוֹבְדֵי יָם סְלוֹנִיקָאִים**[2] לְשֵׁם הַעֲסָקָתָם בְּנִמְלֵי חֵיפָה וְיָפוֹ. עוֹבְדִים אֵלּוּ **כְּקוֹדְמֵיהֶם**[21] חָווּ **מִצַּד אֶחָד**[22] הַצְלָחָה מִקְצוֹעִית **וּמִצַּד אַחֵר**[22] קְשָׁיִים **חֶבְרָתִיִּים–כַּלְכָּלִיִּים**[23]. וְאוּלָם **שֶׁלֹּא כְ**[24]בַּפֶּרֶק הַיְמֵי שֶׁבְּעַכּוֹ, **הֲרֵי**[25] בִּנְמַל חֵיפָה נִקְלְטוּ הַסָּלוֹנִיקָאִים **בְּסוֹפוֹ שֶׁל דָּבָר**[26] בְּהַצְלָחָה, וְנֶאֶחְזוּ בַּעֲבוֹדוֹת הַנְּמַל, **וּלְאַחַר מִכֵּן**[27] מִילְּאוּ תַּפְקִיד מֶרְכָּזִי בִּבְנִיַּת נְמַל תֵּל-אָבִיב.

Clauses whose verb is before the subject are shaded.

---

(12) **כְּאוּמָנִים**   *as masters*
Ch.8; 2.3.2 (b)

(13) **הִתְבָּרֵר כִּי**   *it became clear that*
(NOT: because); Ch.1; 6.3.1(c)

(14) **מוּמְחִיּוּת זוֹ לֹא הָיָה בָּה דֵּי**
this expertise was not sufficient
topicalized sentence, בה refers to the
topicalized noun מומחיות; Ch.1; 2

(15) **בֵּינוֹ לְדַיָּיגִים**
*between it (the Zionist establishment)
and the fishermen*
Ch.10; 11

(16) **בֵּינָם לְ-**   *between them and...*
Ch.10; 11

(17) **מִשֶּׁ-**   *when*
Ch.8; 2.3.4(e)

(18) **כַּנִּרְאָה**   *apparently*
comment adverbial; Ch.5; 1.3, 2.1.1

(19) **זוֹ=זֹאת**   *this*
demonstrative pronoun; Ch.3; 2.1.1

(20) **כְּשָׁלוֹשׁ שָׁנִים**
approximately three years
Ch.8; 2.3.2 (c)

(21) **כְּקוֹדְמֵיהֶם**
like their predecessors
Ch.8; 2.3.2(a)

(22) **מִצַּד אֶחָד...וּמִצַּד אַחֵר**
on one hand... and on the other hand
discontinuous connector; Ch.10; 7

(23) **חֶבְרָתִיִּים–כַּלְכָּלִיִּים**
socio-economic
hyphenated noun-derived adjectives;
Ch.4; 3.3, 4.2.2

(24) **שֶׁלֹּא כְ-**   *unlike*
Ch.8; 2.3.2(a)

(25) **הֲרֵי**   *then, in fact*
Ch.7; Confusables 2

(26) **בְּסוֹפוֹ שֶׁל דָּבָר**   *in the end*
Ch. 11; 14.6

(27) **לְאַחַר מִכֵּן**   *afterward, later*
Ch.11; 15.2

Translation

From the Bay of Salonika to the Bay of Acre:
A Chapter in the History of Jewish Fisherman between the Two World Wars

I discussed in this article the reasons for the immigration of Salonican fishermen to the Land of Israel in the middle of the 1920's and their difficulties (literally: pains) of absorption there. The decision to leave their historic hometown took shape when the economic stability of the Jewish fisherman in Salonika weakened. It is possible that their immigration of the Land of the Fathers would not have totally failed if the sending and absorbing establishment had properly prepared for their absorption, taking into account their unique socio-economic characteristics. The Salonicans were in many respects different from the groups of pioneers that usually immigrated in those years to the Land of Israel, particularly in their geographic origin, the composition and size of their families, their language and life style.

As master fishermen they had a significant advantage over similar labor groups, but it became clear that this expertise was not enough for coping with the needs of the time. Economic difficulties, cultural gaps and the ineffectiveness of the Zionist establishment created alienation between it and the fishermen and between them and the "Kovesh" group that resided in their vicinity. When unstable security conditions were added to the Sisyphean routine of existence, all hope was lost and the plant in Acre was closed. The manifold needs of the fishermen group, the disagreements between them and the Zionist establishment and, in the end, the failure of their settlement in Acre apparently brought the Zionist administration to the conclusion that there was no point in bringing to Israel additional fishermen from Salonika. This professional group received renewed attention only about three years later, in the summer of 1933, on the eve of the opening of the Ḥaifa port. As it became clear that there were no pioneers in the Land of Israel who could properly perform the demanding work in the ports, the immigration of the Salonican longshoremen (literally: sea workers) was renewed with the objective of employing them in the ports of Ḥaifa and Jaffa. These workers, like their predecessors, experienced on one hand professional success and on the other socio-economic difficulties. But unlike the naval chapter in Acre, in the port of Ḥaifa the Salonicans were ultimately absorbed successfully and held on to the work of the port and later fulfilled a major role in the building of the port in Tel Aviv.

PRACTICE TEXT #11

קליטת עולים מבבל בתקופת המשנה והתלמוד
מאת: יהושע שוורץ
מתוך: קיבוץ גלויות: עלייה לארץ ישראל – מיתוס ומציאות, עורכת דבורה הכהן,
מרכז זלמן שזר לתולדות ישראל, ירושלים, תשנ"ח (1998) , עמ' 51–52

Terminology specific to the text (in order of appearance)

the period of the Mishnah and the Talmud	תקוּפת המִשְׁנה והתלְמוּד
C.E.	סְפירת הנוֹצרים
Babylon	בָּבֶל
sages	חֲכָמים
flow of immigration	זֶרֶם עֲלִייה
immigration	הֲגירה
the land of their fathers	ארץ אבותם
reception	קַבָּלת פָּנים
absorption	קליטה
religious institutions	מוֹסָדות תורָניים

Foreign (loan) words (alphabetical)

autonomous	אוטונומית
elite	אֶליטה
massive	מָסיבית

Miscellaneous (alphabetical)

during	בְּמֶשֶׁךְ
particularly	בִּמְיוּחָד
often	לְעתים קְרובות
sometime	לפְעָמים

<u>הקדמה</u>

במשך תקופת המשנה והתלמוד (70–500 לספירת הנוצרים) היו שני המרכזים הגדולים של עם ישראל בארץ ישראל ובבבל. הראשון בחשיבותו היה המרכז בארץ, והשני לו המרכז בבבל, שהלך **והתחזק**[1] במיוחד בתקופת התלמוד (200–500 לספירת הנוצרים). שני מרכזים אלה, **על**[2] חכמיהם ומוסדותיהם, פעלו לעתים קרובות **בנפרד ובצורה אוטונומית**[3], אך גם **קיימו**[4] לעתים קשרים הדוקים **זה עם זה**[5]. קשרים אלה **הביאו** לפעמים **לידי**[6] שיתוף פעולה ולפעמים **לידי**[6] תחרות קשה. הם גם **הביאו לידי**[6] זרם עלייה מבבל לארץ ישראל.

העולים מבבל באו מחברת החכמים ומשאר חלקי החברה – עשירים ועניים, אנשי מעלה ופשוטי עם. עלייה זו היתה שונה מן העליות וההגירות היהודיות הידועות בתקופות החדשות. היא היתה גדולה, אבל לא מסיבית. העולים מבין פשוטי העם לא היו עניים **ומחוסרי מקצוע**[7]. **מִקְצָת הָעוֹלִים**[8] שהשתייכו לעולמם של חכמים **נמנו עם**[8] אֵליטה תרבותית וחברתית ו**בידוע**[9] שבבל אף **ייחסה**[10] **לעצמה**[11] עֶליוֹנוּת על ארץ ישראל בתחומים שונים ותבעה מעמד שָׁוֶה בעניינים אחרים. גישה זו השפיעה **על**[12] השקפת עולמם ו**על**[12] התנהגותם של עולים אלה, ואפילו **על**[12] אלה **מביניהם**[13] שניסו להתנתק ממסורת ארץ אבותם.

---

(1) הלך והתחזק
grew/became stronger
aspectual verb; Ch.6; 3.2

(2) על חכמיהם ומוסדותיהם
with, including (NOT: about) *their sages and institutions*;
Ch.8; 2.3.5(d)

(3) בנפרד ובצורה אוטונומית
separately and autonomously
coordinated adverbs of manner;
Ch.5; 2.9

(4) קיימו *maintained*
(NOT: established);
Ch.9; Confusables 3(a)

(5) זה עם זה *with each other*
reciprocal pronoun; Ch.3; 7

(6) הביאו לידי *brought about*
Ch.8; Confusables 1(d)

(7) מחוסרי מקצוע
without (lacking) profession
Ch.4; 4.6(b)

(8) מקצת העולים...נמנו עם
some/a small part of the Olim belonged to
The verb agrees with the second noun of the construct phrase when the first one is a quantifier;
Ch.2; 4.6

(9) בְּיָדוּעַ=כַּיָדוּעַ *as is (well) known*
Ch.11; 2.3.1(b)

(10) ייחסה *attributed*
Ch.11; 11.2.2

(11) לעצמה *to itself*
reflexive pronoun; Ch.3; 6

(12) השפיעה על...ועל...ואפילו על...
influenced
The (repeated) preposition required by the verb is not translated;
Ch.8; 2.1.1.1, 3.3

(13) מביניהם *from among them, of them;* Ch.10; 11.1

גורמים אלה גם עיצבו את קבלת הפנים **שזכו לה**[14] העולים **בהגיעם**[15] **ארצה**[16].

נבדוק[17] במאמר זה במסגרת של **חֵקֶר**[18] הגירה וקליטה את קבלת הפנים הזו ואת מידת הקליטה של העולים מבבל בארץ ישראל בתקופת המשנה והתלמוד. **כמו כן**[19] **נעמוד על**[20] השפעת קליטה זו – **על**[2] הצלחותיה וכישלונותיה – **על**[21] **תולדות**[22] היישוב בארץ ישראל בתקופה זו.

סיכום

בתקופת המשנה והתלמוד נקלטו עולי בבל בארץ ומצאו בה פרנסה, אבל קליטתם החברתית לא היתה מלאה בגלל התנהגותם. התנהגות זו גרמה מתיחות **בינם לבין**[23] תושבי הארץ, אבל לא שנאה של ממש, ואף פעם לא רדיפות או הפליה קשה. המתח החברתי חיזק עוד יותר את הזהות הבבלית בארץ ישראל, **ובכך**[24] ליכד וחיזק גם את החברה הארץ ישראלית. המתיחות תרמה לביסוס המוסדות **התורניים**[25] בארץ ישראליים ולחיזוקם והבטיחה לארץ ישראל שמירה על עליונותה **הרוחנית**[25] בעם ישראל בתקופת המשנה והתלמוד.

Clauses whose verbs precede the subject are shaded.

---

(14) **שזכו לה**   *that they received*
The (inflected) preposition required by the verb is not translated; the verb in the relative clause precedes the subject; Ch.8; 2.1.1, 3.4.1

(15) כשהגיעו=**בהגיעם**
when they arrived, upon their arrival
The pronoun suffix attached to the infinitive construct form refers to the subject, עולים; Ch.6; 1.3

(16) **ארצה**=לארץ (ישראל)
directional ה"א; Ch.5; 1.2

(17) **נבדוק**   *we will examine*
The "authorial we" is used to state the research agenda; Ch.3; 1.1

(18) **חֵקֶר**   *the study of*
Ch.2; 4.3.9; Ch. 8; 2.2

(19) **כמו כן**   *also*
Ch.11; 15.4

(20) **נעמוד על**   *we will discuss*
(NOT: we will stand); Ch.8; 2.2

(21) השפעת קליטה זו – **על** הצלחותיה וכישלונותיה – **על** תולדות היישוב בארץ ישראל
the influence of this absorption – with its successes and failures – on the history of the settlement
The second על is required by the noun (as it is by the related verb); Ch.8; 2.1.1.1, 2.3.5(d)

(22) **תולדות**   *the history of*
Ch.2; 2.2.2(b), 4.3.9

(23) **בינם לבין**   *between them and…*
Ch.10; 11

(24) **ובכך**   *and by this*
כך refers to the previous idea;
Ch.3; 2.3.1

(25) **תורניים**   *religious*
רוחנית   *spiritual*
noun-derived adjectives ending with נִי—; Ch. 4; 4.2.3

The absorption of immigrants from Babylon in the period of the Mishnah and the Talmud

Introduction

During the period of the Mishnah and Talmud (70–500 C.E.) the two large Jewish centers were in the Land of Israel and in Babylon. The most important (literally: the first in its importance) was the center in the Land (of Israel) and second to it was the center in Babylon, which grew stronger particularly in the period of the Talmud (200–500 C.E.). These two centers, with their sages and institutions, often acted separately and autonomously, but also sometimes maintained close ties with each other. These ties sometimes brought about cooperation and at times harsh competition. They also brought about a flow of immigration from Babylon to the Land of Israel.

The immigrants from Babylon came from the circle (literally: society) of sages and other parts of society – rich and poor, higher and lower class (literally: simple) people. This immigration was different from the Jewish immigrations known in modern eras. It was large, but not massive. The lower class immigrants were not poor or without profession. Some of the immigrants who belonged to the world of the sages were part of a cultural and social elite, and it is well known that Babylon also attributed to itself superiority over the Land of Israel in various areas and demanded equal status in other matters. This attitude influenced the world view and behavior of these immigrants, and even those among them who tried to detach themselves from the tradition of their fatherland. These factors also shaped the reception of these immigrants when they arrived in the Land of Israel.

In this article, we will examine within the research framework of immigration and absorption this reception and the extent to which the immigrants from Babylon were absorbed in the Land of Israel in the period of the Mishnah and Talmud. We will also discuss the influence of this absorption – with its successes and failures – on the history of the settlement in the Land of Israel in that period.

Summary

In the period of the Mishnah and Talmud, the immigrants from Babylon were absorbed in the Land of Israel and found [their] livelihood in it, but their social absorption was not complete because of their behavior. This behavior caused tension between them and the inhabitants of the land, but not real hatred, and never persecutions or severe discrimination. The social tension strengthened even more the Babylonian identity in the Land of Israel, and in this way also united and strengthened the local society. The tension contributed to the consolidation and strengthening of the religious institutions in the Land of Israel and secured for it the preservation of its spiritual superiority within the Jewish people in the period of the Mishnah and Talmud.

קברי צדיקים
Retrieved from:
http://he.wikipedia.org/wiki/קברי_צדיקים

Terminology specific to the text (in order of appearance)

graves of Zaddikim (holy/righteous men)	קִבְרֵי צַדִּיקִים
place of burial	מקום קְבוּרה
exemplary figures	דְּמוּיוֹת מוֹפֵת
pilgrimage	עלייה לְרֶגֶל
Mircea Eliade	מירצ'ה אליאדה
a site of holiness	אֲתר קְדוּשׁה
institutionalized religion	דת מִמְסְדית
The Temple Mount	הר הבית
The Foundation Stone (in the Temple)	אֶבֶן הַשְׁתִייָה
The Holy of Holies	קודש הקוֹדָשִׁים
Victor Turner	ויקטור טרנר
rite of passage	טֶקֶס מַעֲבר

Alphabetical list of foreign (loan) words appearing in the text
(consult Ch. 11 to determine the English source word)

אנרגיות, אפקט, אקסצנטרי, לימינליות, מודל, מונותיאיסטיות, סולידריות, סטטוסים, פורמ־
ליים, קונצנטרי, קרניבלייים

Miscellaneous (alphabetical)

particularly	בְּמיוּחָד
and so on	וכָך הָלְאָה
sometimes	לְעָתים
usually, generally	לָרוֹב

ביהדות קברי צדיקים הם מקום קבורתם, לעתים המשוער, של **אישים**(1) **הנחשבים**(2) דמויות מופת. סביב ציון הקבר של צדיקים מתפתח לעתים פולחן הערצה. לתופעה זו של קברי קדושים **יש**(3) מקבילות בתרבויות רבות, והיא חזקה במיוחד בדתות המונותיאיסטיות,**שבהן**(4) קיים צורך קיים חזק בישות **מתווכת**(5) **בין**(6) **המאמין**(7) **לבין**(6) האל.

לפולחן קברי הצדיקים **יש**(3) שני מרכיבים: המקום הקדוש **עצמו**(8), והמסע אליו. הקדושה **המיוחסת לאתר**(9) הקדוש, מתבטאת בשתי משמעויות עיקריות: **ראשית**(10), המקום הקדוש **מהווה**(11) זירה מתווכת, משופעת בסמליות, **המקשרת**(2) **בין** המאמין **ובין**(7) העולם האלוהי, הנצחי, הנשגב. **שנית**(10), המקום נתפס כמשופע באנרגיות פלאיות, **המייצגות**(2) את ברכת האל ושפע חסדו למאמיניו. **מבחינה חברתית**(12), **למפגש המשותף**(5) של המאמינים במקום הקדוש **יש**(3) אפקט **מלכד**(5) **התורם**(2) לסולידריות החברתית, **בין אם**(13) **זו**(14) המקומית, במקרה של צדיק מקומי, **ובין אם**(13) **כלל-דתית**(15), במקרה של צדיק כלל-דתי.

(1) **אישים** *personalities*
Ch.2; 2.1.2(b)

(2) **שנחשבים**=**הנחשבים** *who are considered*
-ה is a subordinator before a present tense verb; Ch.1; 6.3.1(b)

(3) **יש** . . . זו **לתופעה** *this phenomenon has*
Ch.9; 2.1

(4) **שבהן** *in which*
The inflected preposition at the beginning of a relative clause refers to the previous noun (here – דתות); the verb in the clause precedes the subject; Ch.1; 1.2.1; Ch.8; 3.4.1

(5) **מתווכת** *mediating*
משותף *shared, common*
מלכד *unifying*
The present participle functions as an adjective; Ch.4; 4.1

(6) **לבין...בין** *between…and*
Ch.10; 11

(7) **מאמין** *believer*
The present participle functions as a noun; Ch.2; 6.2

(8) **עצמו** המקום הקדוש *the holy place itself*
emphatic pronoun; Ch.3; 6.2

(9) **ל מיוחסת** *attributed to*
Ch.11; 11.2.2

(10) **שנית** ,...,**ראשית** *first,… second*
discontinuous connector; Ch.10; 14

(11) **מהווה** *constitutes*
verbal copula; Ch.7; 4.1

(12) **מבחינה חברתית** *from a social standpoint, socially*
adverb of manner; Ch.5; 2.2.1; Ch.11; 10.2.1

(13) **ובין אם...בין אם** *whether…or*
discontinuous connector; Ch. 10; 9

(14) **זו** *this (solidarity)*
demonstrative pronoun used for substitution; Ch.3; 2.2

(15) **כלל-דתית** *pan-religious*
semantic prefix before an adjective; Ch.4; 5

פולחן קברי צדיקים **הוא**[16] מקרה פרטי של עלייה
לרגל, **אם כי**[17] ביהדות מונח זה **מזוהה**[18] בעיקר
עם[18] עלייה לבית המקדש. **ישנם**[19] שני מודלים
מרכזיים של עליות לרגל. על פי המודל הקונצנטרי
של מירצ'ה אליאדה, המאמין נע מהשוליים אל המרכז
הקדוש. מודל זה תואם **לרוב**[20] את אתרי הקדושה
של הדת הממסדית. כך למשל, ביהדות ארץ ישראל
היא[21] מרכז העולם, ירושלים **היא**[21] מרכז ישראל,
הר הבית הוא מרכזה של ירושלים, וכך הלאה עד
אבן השתייה שבקודש הקודשים. ויקטור טרנר הציע
מודל אקסצנטרי, **במסגרתו**[22] המאמין נע מהמרכז
אל השוליים. המאמין **נפרד מחיי** השגרה[23], **מלב**
החברה[23], ומתחיל מסע אל אתר מקודש **הנמצא**[2]
במה שהוא מכנה "Centre out there", שהוא מקום
מחוץ למסגרת החברתית היומיומית. לטענת טרנר,
המסע אל הקבר והחוויה בקבר **עצמו**[8], **הם**[24] חוויות
לימינליות, **במסגרתן**[22] המאמינים חווים תחושת
התעלות, אחווה, השלתם של סטטוסים חברתיים
ומחיצות חברתיות. מצב זה, שהוא השלב השני
בטקס מעבר, מייצר רגשות עזים שהם **בבחינת**[25]
קרקע פורייה לשינויים אישיים וחברתיים. המודל
של טרנר מתאים יותר לפולחן סביב קברי הצדיקים,
הנמצאים[2] לרוב במקומות רחוקים וקשים להגעה,
ומעצם[26] הֶיוֹתם מקושרים לדת העממית **אֲזַי**[27] גם
בלתי פורמליים וקרנבליים **באופיים**[27].

<u>Clauses whose verb comes before the subject are shaded.</u>

---

(16) פולחן קברי צדיקים הוא　*is*
The copula agrees with the head
noun of the construct phrase, פולחן;
Ch.2; 4.6

(17) אם כי　*even though*
(NOT: if because);
Ch.1; Confusables, 3.4

(18) מזוהה עם　*identified with*
The preposition עם (required by
the verb) does not follow it directly;
Ch.8; 3.2

(19) יֶשְׁנָם　*there are*
The pronoun suffix refers to the
following noun; Ch.9; 1.5

(20) לרוב　*in most cases*
Ch.5; 1.3; Ch. 10; Confusables, 3.5

(21) היא　*is*
Cities and countries are considered
feminine; Ch.7; 1.2

(22) במסגרתו, במסגרתן
within which
Ch. 11; 7; a relative clause without a
subordinator; Ch.8; 3.4.1

(23) נפרד מחיי השגרה, מלב החברה
takes leave of
The preposition required by the verb
is repeated before each complement;
Ch.8; 3.3

(24) הם　*are*
The copula agrees with the masculine
subject (מסע) even though the
second (coordinate) subject (חוויה) is
feminine; Ch.7; 1.2

(25) בבחינת　*like, in the status of*
Ch.11; 10.2.3

(26) מעצם היותם מקושרים
*from the very [fact of] their being
linked*
Ch.3; Confusables, 3.1

(27) אזי　*then*
Ch.11; 8

(28) באופיים　*in their character*
The possessive suffix refers back to
קברי צדיקים; Ch. 2; 5.8

Translation

Graves of Zaddikim

In Judaism, the graves of Zaddikim (holy men) are the sometimes conjectural place of burial of personalities who are considered exemplary figures. Around the grave marking of these men a ritual of reverence sometimes develops. This phenomenon (of holy men's graves) has parallels in many cultures and it is particularly strong in monotheistic religions, where there exists a strong need for a mediating entity between the believer and God.

The ritual has two components: the holy place itself and the voyage to it. The holiness that is attributed to the holy site is expressed in two main senses: first, the holy place constitutes a mediating arena, abundant in symbolism, which links the believer with the divine, eternal, and sublime world. Secondly, the place is viewed as overflowing with wondrous energies that represent God's blessing and plenitude of grace to his believers. From a social viewpoint, the communal gathering of the believers in the holy place has a unifying effect that contributes to social solidarity, whether local, in the case of a local Zaddik, or pan-religious, in the case of a pan-religious holy man.

The ritual of holy men's graves is a special (literally: private) case of pilgrimage, although in Judaism this term is identified mainly with pilgrimage to the Temple. There are two central models of pilgrimages. According to the concentric model of Mircea Eliade, the believer moves from the margins to the holy center. This model is usually suitable to the sites of holiness of institutional religion. Thus, for example, in Judaism, the Land of Israel is the center of the world, Jerusalem is the center of Israel, Temple Mount is the center of Jerusalem and so on until the Foundation Stone in the Holy of Holies. Victor Turner suggests an excentric model within which the believer moves from the center to the margins. He takes leave of humdrum life, of the center (literally: heart) of society, and begins a voyage to a sanctified site that is found in what Turner calls "centre out there," a place that is outside of the everyday social framework. As Turner claims, the voyage to the grave site and the experience in the grave (site) itself are liminal experiences, within which the believers experience a feeling of elation, solidarity and the shedding of social positions and social barriers. This condition, which is the second stage in a rite of passage, produces strong feelings that are fertile ground for personal and social changes. Turner's model fits better the ritual around graves that are usually found in distant and hard to reach places and [that] by the very [fact] of their being linked to popular religion are, then, also informal and possess a carnival-like quality.

PRACTICE TEXT #13

ניקול, דניאל ומה שביניהם: מגמות באוריינטציה התרבותית של עולי שנות התשעים כפי שהיא משתקפת בשמות שהם בוחרים לילדיהם
מאת: אביאל קרנצלר
Retrieved from:
http://www.cbs.gov.il/publications/int_name.pdf (November 2004)

<u>**Terminology specific to the text**</u> (in order of appearance)

abstract	תַּקְצִיר
the Olim (immigrants to Israel) of the 90's	עוֹלֵי שְׁנוֹת ה-90
the former USSR	בריה"מ לְשֶׁעָבַר
Aliya, immigration to Israel	עלייה
immigration	הגירה
the early 90's	שְׁנוֹת ה-90 המוקדמות
emigrating from Israel; emigration	לרדת מן הארץ; ירידה
here: footnote	הערה
summary	סיכום
a decade	עֲשׂוֹר שנים

<u>**Foreign (loan) words**</u> (alphabetical)

orientation	אוֹרְיֶינְטַצְיָה
indicator	אִינְדִיקָטוֹר
graphic	גְרָפִית
homogeneous	הוֹמוֹגֶנִיוֹת
perspective	פֶּרְסְפֶּקְטִיבה

<u>**Miscellaneous**</u> (alphabetical)

through	בָּאֶמְצָעוּת
among	בְּקֶרֶב
that is to say	דְּהַיְינוּ
in fact	לְמַעֲשֶׂה
in contrast to	לְעוּמַת
formerly; ex-	לְשֶׁעָבַר
immediately	מִיָּד

<u>תקציר</u>

באמצעות ניתוח השמות שנתנו עולי שנות התשעים
מבריה"מ לשעבר לילדיהם, <mark>נבחנת האוריינטציה
התרבותית</mark> של עולים אלו בפרספקטיבה רחבה ושונה
מהמקובל. **תהליך השינוי** באוריינטציה התרבותית
של העולים **מתואר**[1] **בצורה גרפית**[2] שנה אחרי
שנה, מהתקופה שלפני העלייה עד שנת 2002. מִיָד
לאַחַר ההגירה לארץ, <mark>משתנה האוריינטציה</mark> של
העולים **והופכת להיות**[3] יותר ישראלית ופחות רוסית.
ישנם[4] הבדלים משמעותיים **בין**[5] עולים יהודים
לעולים[5] שאינם יהודים, **ובין**[5] עולי שנות התשעים
המוקדמות **לעולי**[5] השנים המאוחרות יותר. **בְּכְלָל**[6],
ככל שהעולים[7] היגרו מאוחר יותר, הם נטו **פחות**[7]
לתת שמות ישראליים לילדיהם, דְהַיְינוּ, הָאוֹרְיֶינְטַצְיָה
הישראלית שלהם פְּחוּתָה יותר. מִמְצָא נוסָף: העולים
שנתנו שמות זרים נטו יותר לרדת מהארץ **מאֵלו**[8]
שבחרו בשמות ישראליים. כלומר, יש קשר שלילי
בֵּין[5] הָאוֹרְיֶינְטַצְיָה הישראלית של העולים לירידתם[5]
בְּפוֹעַל[9] מהארץ.

---

(1) תהליך השינוי…מתואר
the process… is described
verb at a distance from the subject;
Ch.1; 3.1

(2) בצורה גרפית *graphically*
Ch.5; 2.2

(3) הופכת להיות *turns into, becomes*
Ch.7; 5.1

(4) יֶשְׁנָם *there are*
The pronoun suffix refers to
following noun – הבדלים; Ch.9; 1.5

(5) בֵּין…לְ *between…and*
Ch.10; 11

(6) בְּכְלָל *as a rule*
Ch.10; Confusables 3.1

(7) כְּכָל שֶׁ-…פָּחוּת
the more… (the) less…
Ch.10; 5

(8) אֵלּוּ *those*
demonstrative pronoun used for
substitution; Ch.3; 2.2

(9) בְּפוֹעַל *in actual fact*
adverb of manner;
Ch.5; 2.1.1, 2.1.2, example 16;
Ch.10; 2.1

<u>הערה</u>

בעבודה זו **נעשה שימוש**(10) במושג "אוריינטציה"
כמושג חליפי ל"זהות," **כאשר**(11) **מושג-העל**(12) **הַנּוֹ**(13)
אוריינטציה תרבותית. השימוש במושג "אוריינטציה"
נעשה(10) משום שלדעתי הוא מתאר טוב יותר את
מהות בחירת השמות. ההנחה **היא**(14) שבחירת שם
הַנָּה(13) אינדיקטור לנטייה(15) **ולזיקה**(15) תרבותית
יותר **מאשר**(16) לתחושת(15) שַׁיָּכוּת, שהמושג "זהות"
מדגיש.

---

(10) נעשה שימוש במושג
"אוריינטציה," השימוש במושג
"אוריינטציה" נעשה
The term "orientation" is/was used
(literally: *use is/was made of the term*
"orientation")
NOT: we will make use of the term;
Ch.7; 5.2.1, 5.2.2

(11) כאשר *with* (NOT: *when*)
Ch.1; Confusables, 1.5

(12) מושג-העל
the superordinate term
semantic suffix; Ch.4; 5.9, footnote 9

(13) הוא=הַנּוֹ *is*
copula; Ch.7; 3.1

(14) ההנחה היא *the assumption is*
obligatory copula before a clause;
Ch.7; 1.2.1

(15) לנטיה ולזיקה...לתחושת שייכות
The preposition is repeated before
each complement; Ch.8; 3.3

(16) יותר מן=יותר מאשר *more than*
before a preposition, מאשר is
preferred to מן; Ch.1; Confusables,
1.3; Ch.8; 2.3.4(c)

סיכום

כשנתיים[17] לפני הגירת העולים מבריה"מ לשעבר לארץ מסתמן אצלם גידול בהענקת שמות ישראליים. לאחר העלייה לארץ יש בקרבם גידול משמעותי במַתַן שמות ישראליים, **המֵעיד**[18] על שינוי משמעותי באוריינטציה שלהם. בשנים הראשונות שלאחר העלייה אין כמעט ירידה ברמת האוריינטציה הרוסית אך יש עלייה באוריינטציה הישראלית וירידה **בזו**[19] היהודית. גם לאחר יותר מעשׂור שנים בארץ האוריינטציה של העולים החדשים שונה **מזו**[19] של ילידֵי ישראל, והם עדיין נוטים **יותר**[20] לתת שמות רוסיים, שמות זרים ושמות ישראליים-בינלאומיים **מילידי הארץ**[20]. אפשר לראות **בכך**[21] אינדיקציה שנוצרה "תרבות שלישית". העולים מבריה"מ לשעבר אינם נטמעים בחברה הישראלית וכך **נוצרה קהילה חדשה**. למעשׂה, אפשר לזהות הִתבדלות בקֶרֶב העולים הרשומים כלא-יהודים, משום שבנוסף **לכך שֶ**[22]הם נתנו פחות שמות ישראליים מהעולים היהודים יש מְגמה שלילית של בחירה פחותה בשמות ישראליים **ככל שֶ**[7]השהייה בארץ מתארכת; **זאת**[23], לעומת מגמה הפוכה בקרב העולים היהודים. בולטת גם ההומוֹגֵניות בבחירת השמות שלהם **יחסית**[24] לעולים היהודים, כך **שֶניתן לומר**[25] שהם נוטים להתבדלות לעומת העולים היהודים שמגלים נטייה להשתלבות.

Clauses whose verb comes before the subject are shaded.

---

(17) כשנתיים לפני הגירת העולים
about two years before the immigration
Ch.8; 2.3.2(c)

(18) המֵעיד על
that testifies to, points to
ה- is a subordinator before a present tense verb; Ch.1; 6.3.1(b)
The (remote) subject of the verb is גידול; Ch.1; 3.1

(19) זאת=זו *that*
demonstrative pronoun used for substitution: refers to אוריינטציה; Ch.3; 2.2

(20) יותר . . . מילידי הארץ
more than native born Israelis
The components of the comparative phrase are at a distance; Ch.8; 2.3.4(c)

(21) אפשר לראות בכך
it can be seen in this
בכך refers to the content of the previous clause; Ch.3; 2.3.1

(22) בנוסף לכך שֶ . . . .
in addition to [the fact] that
שֶ כך- refers to the content of the coming clause; Ch.3; 2.3.1

(23) זאת *this*
pro-clause; Ch.3; 2.3

(24) יחסית ל- *relatively to*
adverb of manner; Ch. 5; 2.3.3; Ch.11; 11.4.1

(25) ניתן לומר=אפשר לומר
it is possible to say
When followed by an infinitive verb, ניתן indicates possibility; Ch.11; 3.2

Translation

Nicole, Daniel and What Lies behind Them:
Trends in the Cultural Orientation of the 1990's Immigrants to Israel as Reflected in the Names They Give to Their Children

Abstract

Through the analysis of the names that immigrants to Israel from the former USSR in the 1990's gave to their children, these immigrants' cultural orientation is examined from a broad and unique perspective. The process of change in the cultural orientation of the immigrants is described graphically, year by year, from the period before the immigration until 2002. Immediately after the immigration to Israel, the immigrants' orientation changes and becomes more Israeli and less Russian. There are significant differences between Jewish and non-Jewish immigrants, and between immigrants of the early 90's and those of later years. As a rule, the later they came, the less inclined they were to give their children Israeli names, that is, their Israeli orientation was lower. Another finding: the immigrants who gave foreign names had a greater tendency to leave the country than those who chose Israeli names, that is, there is a negative correlation between the Israeli orientation of the immigrants and their actual emigration from Israel.

Footnote

This study makes use (literally: use is made in this study) of the concept "orientation" as an alternative concept to "identity," with "cultural identity" being the super-ordinate term. The term "orientation" is used because, in my opinion, it describes better the nature of the choice of names. The assumption is that the selection of a name is an indicator for an inclination and a cultural connection more than it is [an indicator] for a sense of belonging, which the term "identity" underscores.

Summary

About two years before the arrival to Israel of immigrants from the former USSR, a rise in the giving of Israeli names begins to become apparent. After the immigration, there is among them a considerable increase in giving of Israeli names, testifying to a significant change in [their] orientation. In the first years after the immigration, there is almost no decrease in the level of Russian orientation but there is an increase in the Israeli one and a decrease in the Jewish orientation. Even after more than a decade in Israel, the orientation of the new immigrants is different from that of native Israelis and they are still more inclined than native Israelis to choose Russian names, foreign names and Israeli-international names. This can be seen as an indication of a creation of a "third culture". The immigrants from the former USSR have not assimilated in Israeli society and so a new community has been created within it. In fact, it is possible to notice (literally: identify) insularity among the immigrants who are registered as non-Jews, because in addition to the fact that they gave fewer Israeli names than the Jewish immigrants, there is a negative trend of a lesser selection of Israeli names as their stay in the country becomes longer; this, in contrast to an opposite trend among the Jewish immigrants. The homogeneity – relatively to the Jewish immigrants – of name choices also stands out, such that it can be said that the non-Jewish immigrants are predisposed to insularity whereas the Jewish immigrants display a disposition toward integration.

PRACTICE TEXT #14

תחיית הלשון העברית

Retrieved from:
http://he.wikipedia.org/wiki/תחיית_הלשון העברית

Terminology specific to the text (listed in order of appearance)

revival of the Hebrew language	תְּחִיַּת הַלָשׁוֹן הָעברית
the Zionist Revolution	הַמַהְפֵּכָה הַצִיוּנית
the new Jewish settlement (in the Land of Israel)	הַיִישׁוּב הָעִברי הֶחדש
the founding of the State of Israel	הֲקָמת מדינת ישראל
modern linguistics	הַבַּלְשָׁנות הַמודֶרְנית
native speakers	דוֹבְרִים יְלִידיים
Yiddish	ייִדיש
Chaim Nachman Bialik (the poet)	חיים נחמן בִּיאליק

Foreign (loan) words (alphabetical)

ideologies	אידֵאולוגיות
dialog	דיאלוג
liturgical	ליטורגית
modern	מודרנית
narrative	נַרָטיב

Miscellaneous (alphabetical)

but	אוּלָם
in the end	בסופו שֶל דָבָר
first and foremost	בָּרֹאש ובראשׁוֹנָה
at the beginning of	בִּתְחילת-
unique	יָחיד בְּמינוֹ
a time period	פֶּרֶק זמן

תחיית הלשון העברית היא תהליך שהתחולל[1] באירופה ובארץ ישראל בסוף המאה התשע עשרה ובתחילת המאה העשרים, ובמסגרתו[2] הפכה השפה העברית מלשון[3] כתובה וליטורגית המשמשת[4] לצרכים דתיים או ספרותיים בעיקר, ללשון[3] מדוברת, רב-מערכתית[5] ולאומית. תהליך זה לא[6] היה תהליך לשוני גְרֵידָא[7], אלא[6] הוא השתבץ במערכת רחבה של תהליכים שחלו[8] בעם ישראל באותה תקופה[9], ובעיקר המהפכה הציונית והתפתחות היישוב העברי החדש בארץ ישראל. תהליכים אלה הביאו, בסופו של דבר, להקמת מדינת ישראל כמדינה לאומית עברית.

השם "תחייה" אינו[10] שם מדויק לתהליך זה, משום שלפי רוב ההגדרות לא הייתה העברית לשון מתה לפני התהליך; נעשה בה שימוש[11] נרחב וניכרו בה תהליכים של התפתחות והשתנות גם לפני תחילת התהליך. עם זאת, התהליך נחשב לתהליך יחיד במינו, והבלשנות המודרנית איננה מכירה[12] מקרה נוסף שבו[13] לשון שכלל לא[14] הייתה מדוברת בפי דוברים ילידיים הפכה ל[15]לשון לאומית המשמשת[4] באופן רב-מערכתי[16], וכל זאת[17] בתוך פרק זמן של כמה עשרות שנים בלבד[18]. (מוכרים כמה תהליכים שבהם[13] לשון שהייתה מדוברת בפי מיעוט הפכה ללשון כללית.)

---

(1) התחולל *took place*
Ch.11; 12.5

(2) במסגרתו *within it, as part of it*
Ch.11; 7

(3) הפכה השפה העברית מלשון...ללשון
changed from... to Ch.7; 5.1

(4) משמשת ל- *is used for, serves*
Ch.7; 4.2.1

(5) רב-מערכתית *multi-system*
semantic prefix before an adjective;
Ch.4; 4.6, 5, Confusables 1(a)

(6) לא...אלא *not... but rather*
adverb of manner (Aramaic);
Ch.5; 2.5

(7) גרידא *only, merely*
Ch.10; 1.2

(8) חלו *occurred*
Ch.11; 12.3

(9) באותה תקופה *at that period*
Ch.3; 3.2

(10) אינו שם מדויק
is not an accurate name
negative copula; Ch.7; 2

(11) נעשה בה שימוש נרחב
an extensive use was made of it, it was used extensively Ch.7; 5.2.2

(12) איננה מכירה=לא מכירה
does not know
אין instead of לא before a present tense verb; Ch.7; 2.2

(13) שבו, שבהם *in which*
inflected preposition in a relative clause; Ch.8; 3.4

(14) כלל לא *not at all*
Ch.10; Confusables, 3.3

(15) הפכה ל- *became*
Ch.7; 5.1

(16) באופן רב-מערכתי
in a multi-system way
adverb of manner; Ch.5; 2.2

(17) וכל זאת *and all this*
pro-clause; Ch.3; 2.3

(18) בלבד *only*
Ch.10; Confusables, 6.1

התהליך הביא גם לשינויים לשוניים בשפה. **אַף שֶׁ**(19) בתודעתם של מחוללי התהליך הם רק המשיכו את השימוש בשפה "מהמקום שבו נפסקה חיותה," **הֲרֵי**(19) לאמיתו של דבר הם יצרו מצב לשוני חדש, שמאפייניו שאובים גם מן השפה העברית **עַל**(20) כל תקופותיה וגם מן השפות האירופיות שעל רקען התחולל התהליך, בראש ובראשונה היידיש. הלשון החדשה שנוצרה היא העברית הישראלית **בת זמננו**(21).

התהליך של תחיית העברית נע **לְמַעֲשֶׂה**(22) בשני קווים מקבילים: תחיית העברית הכתובה-הספרותית ותחיית העברית המדוברת. בעשרות השנים הרא־שונות התהליכים האלה היו מנותקים **זה מזה**(23) ואף התרחשו במקומות שונים: העברית הספרותית התחדשה בערי אירופה, **וְאִילוּ**(24) העברית המדוברת התפתחה בעיקר בארץ ישראל (היו ניסיונות לדיבור עברי גם באירופה, אולם הם נבלעו במִגְוון העצום של תנועות אידאולוגיות שפעלו ביהדות אירופה בתחילת המאה ה-20). המפגש בין התהליכים התחיל רק בתוך המאה העשרים, ונקודת ציון חשובה בעניין זה **הִיא**(25) עלייתו של חיים נחמן ביאליק לארץ ישראל ב-1924. גם לאַחַר המַעֲבָר(26) של העברית הספרותית לארץ נשאר הבדל נִיכר(27) בין מאפייני העברית הספרותית והמדוברת, וההבדל הזה **קיים**(28) גם היום; מאפיינים של דיבור עברי חדרו ללשון הדיאלוג בספרות רק **הָחֵל בשנות הארבעים**(29) וללשון הנרטיב בספרות רק **בשנות התשעים**(30).

---

(19) **אַף שֶׁ-...הֲרֵי**   *even though...*
After an expression of concession הֲרֵי is ignored in translation;
Ch.7; Confusables, 1.2(d)

(20) **עַל כל תקופותיה**
with/including all its periods
Ch.8; 2.3.5(d)

(21) **בת זמננו**   *contemporary*
Ch.4; 4.8.2

(22) **לְמעשה**   *in fact*
comment adverbial; Ch.5; 1.3

(23) **זה מזה**   *from each other*
reciprocal pronoun; Ch.3; 7

(24) **וְאילו**   *whereas*
connects two coordinate clauses;
Ch.1; 6.1; Ch.6; Confusables, 2.1

(25) **הִיא**   *is*
The copula agrees with the head noun of the construct phrase נקודת ציון; Ch.2; 4.6

(26) **מַעֲבָר**   *transition*
Ch.11; 6

(27) **הבדל נִיכר**
considerable difference
Distinguish between ניכר as an adjective (*considerable*) and as a verb (2nd paragraph above: ניכרו תהליכים *processes were seen*); Ch.4; 4.1.3

(28) **קיים**   *exists*
Ch.9; 1.2, 1.7.2, Confusables, 3

(29) **הָחֵל בשנות הארבעים**
beginning with the 1940's
(NOT: that occurs); Ch.11; 12.2

(30) **וללשון הנרטיב בספרות רק בשנות השבעים** = וללשון הנרטיב בספרות **חדרו** רק בשנות התשעים
Ellipsis – the verb is not repeated and can be reconstructed; Ch.1; 9

Clauses whose verb precedes the subject are shaded.

Translation

The Revival of the Hebrew Language

The revival of the Hebrew language is a process that took place in Europe and the Land of Israel at the end of the 19th century and the beginning of the twentieth, and within it Hebrew changed from a written and liturgical language used mainly for religious or literary purposes into a spoken, multi-system and national language. This process was not merely a linguistic one, but rather it fit into a wide array of processes that occurred within the Jewish people at that period, primarily the Zionist revolution and the development of the new Jewish settlement in the Land of Israel. These processes eventually led to the establishment of the State of Israel as a Jewish national state.

The name "revival" is not an accurate one for this process, because according to most definitions Hebrew was not a dead language before [the beginning of] the process; it [Hebrew] was used extensively and forces of evolution and change were visible within it even before the beginning of the process. Nevertheless, the revival is considered unique, and modern linguistics does not know of another case in which a language that was not spoken at all by native speakers became a national language that is used multi-systematically, and all this within a period of only a few decades (processes by which a language that was spoken by a minority and became generalized are known).

The process of linguistic revival also brought about linguistic changes in Hebrew. Even though in the mind (literally: consciousness) of the revivalists all they did was to continue the use of the language "from the place where its vitality had ceased," in truth, they created a new linguistic situation whose features were drawn from all the periods of the language as well as from the European languages against whose background the process took place, principally Yiddish. The new language that was created is contemporary Israeli Hebrew.

The process of revival moved, in fact, in two parallel lines: the revival of the written-literary language and the revival of spoken Hebrew. In the first decades, these processes were disconnected from each other and even took place in different places: literary Hebrew was renewed in European cities, whereas spoken Hebrew developed mainly in the Land of Israel. (There were attempts to speak Hebrew also in Europe, but they were lost in the tremendous variety of ideological movements that operated in European Jewry at the beginning of the century.) The meeting point between the two processes began only in the twentieth century and an important signpost in this matter is the immigration to Israel of Chaim Nachman Bialik in 1924. Even after the move of literary Hebrew to Israel there remained a considerable difference between the characteristics of literary and spoken Hebrew, and this difference exists also today; features of spoken Hebrew penetrated the language of dialogue in literature only since the beginning of the 1940's, and the language of narrative in literature only in the 1990's.

PRACTICE TEXT #15

מאפייני המשיחיות היהודית דתית: המשיחיות כסוג של מנהיגות
מאת: יוסף דן
מתוך: המשיחיות היהודית המודרנית, אוניברסיטה המשודרת, הוצאת משרד הבטחון
ואוניברסיטת תל אביב, תל אביב תשנ"ט, עמ' 11–12.

Terminology specific to the text (in order of appearance)

שָׂדֶה סֶמַנְטִי	semantic field
מְשִׁיחִיּוּת	Messianism
מַנְהִיגוּת	leadership
מְשִׁיחָה בַּשֶׁמֶן הַמִּשְׁחָה	Anointing with the oil of anointment
הַכְתָּרָה	coronation
נַצְרוּת	Christianity
מָשִׁיחַ	Messiah
אִיסְלַם	Islam
מַנְהִיג	leader
"מהדי"	Mahdi/Mehdi (in Shia belief, the messiah)
מַדָּע הַמְּדִינָה	political science
מוֹקֵד	focus, center
בְּשׂוֹרָה	message, Gospel
מַעֲרֶכֶת	system
"הִלְכוֹת מְלָכִים"	"Laws of Kings"
רמב"ם	Maimonides
מִשְׁנֶה תּוֹרָה	Mishneh Torah
מחשבה מְדִינִית	political thought
קְהַל יַעַד	target audience
חקיקה דתית	religious legislation

Foreign (loan) words (alphabetical)

בְּיוּרוֹקְרָטִית	bureaucratic
דִיסְצִיפְלִנָרִית	disciplinary
הִיסְטוֹרִית-פּוֹלִיטִית	historical-political
הִיסְטְרִיוֹגְרַפִיָה	historiography
נוֹרְמָטִיבִית	normative
סֶמַנְטִי	semantic
רַדִיקָלִיִּים	radical

Miscellaneous (alphabetical)

בְּרֹאשׁ וּבְרִאשׁוֹנָה	first and foremost
בְּרֹאשָׁם	primarily
וְכַיּוֹצֵא בָּאֵלֶּה	etc., and others
לְעִתִּים קְרוֹבוֹת	often
לִפְרָקִים	sometimes
מִכָּאן	hence
עַד כֹּה	till now

Expressions

the same applies to	הוא הדין ב
takes part in, participate	נוֹטֵל חֵלֶק ב

מבחינת(1) השדה הסמנטי, המשיחיות שייכת לתחום התופעות **שניתן לכלול**(2) תחת הכותרת – מנהיגות. התופעות המשיחיות **הנן**(3) תופעות של מנהיגות דתית: **משיחת אדם**(4) בשמן המשחה, בהקשר המקראי, **מבטאת**(4) את הכתרתו למנהיג. הנצרות אימצה מושג זה כדי לאפיין את מנהיגה הרוחני, והשתמשה בתרגום היווני של המושג העברי משיח – כריסטוס. **מבחינה**(1) לשונית, המושגים "משיחיות" ו"נצרות" הם מושגים זהים, ושניהם **מתייחסים**(5) **בבירור**(6) **לדמות**(7) של מנהיג דתי. הוא הדין באיסלם – תופעות רבות **המקבילות**(8) למשיחיות **מצויינות**(9) בו **על ידי**(9) המושג "מהדי," שהקשרו הוא מנהיגותי **בצורה ברורה**(6).

תופעות של מנהיגות שייכות, בחלוקה הדיסציפלינרית המקובלת, לתחום מדע המדינה. משיחיות היא, **אם כן**(10), תופעה פוליטית **המעוגנת**(8) בתחום הדתי. **ניתן לומר**(2) **כי**(11) המשיחיות היא אחד הביטויים הרדי־קליים של "תרגום" האמונה הדתית והחיים הדתיים לפעילות היסטורית־פוליטית.

---

(1) מבחינת השדה הסמנטי
from the point of view of the semantic field, semantically
Ch. 5; 2.2.1; Ch.11; 10.2.1

(2) ניתן לכלול
it is possible to include
ניתן followed by an infinitive indicates possibility; Ch.11; 3.2

(3) הנן *are*
copula, Ch.7; 3.1

(4) משיחת אדם...מבטאת
verb at a distance from the subject; Ch.1; 3.1

(5) מתייחסים ל- *refer to*
Ch.11; 11.2.1

(6) בבירור, בצורה ברורה *clearly*
two alternative forms for the same adverb, Ch.5; 2.8

(7) דמות של מנהיג דתי
figure of a religious leader
Ch.11; 16.3

(8) המקבילות *that are parallel to*
ה- is a subordinator before a present tense verb; Ch.1; 6.3.1(b)

(9) מצויינות על ידי *are marked by*
(NOT: excellent)
Present participle used as a verb; Ch.6; 6; Ch.8; Confusables, 1(b)

(10) אם כן *therefore*
Ch.11; 15.6

(11) כי *that* (NOT: because)
introduces a content clause after a verb of saying; Ch.1; 6.3.1(c)

לשונה של המשיחיות(12) היא, אפוא(13), בראש ובראשונה, לשון פוליטית. במוקדה(14) ניצבת דמותו של מנהיג דתי(15), המביא(8) בכוח(16) פעילותו לשינוי ערכים בתוך המציאות ההיסטורית. הוא מהווה(17) מוקד למעבר ממציאות של עבר-הווה למציאות עתידה ולמישור היסטורי חדש, המסמל(8) לעיתים קרובות, את קץ ההיסטוריה שהיכרנו עד כֹּה. המשיחיות מעורה בתוך המרקם ההיסטורי ומבקשת(18) לשנותו(19) באמצעים היסטוריים, שעיקרם(20) – פעילות של המנהיג, המשיח.

במקרים רבים, המשיח מהווה(17) באישיותו ובבשורתו מוקד לפעילות היסטורית חברתית מקיפה(21), שנוטלים בה חלק אנשים רבים(22). במקרים אלה מצטרפים ל"מילון המשיחי" המושגים הקשורים להאצלת סמכויות(23), לארגון חברתי(23), להקמת(23) מערכת מנהיגותית משנית ומערכת ביורוקרטית, ומכאן, לפרקים, גם להקמת(23) מערכת חינוכית ומוסדות חברתיים אחרים.

---

(12) לשונה של המשיחיות
the language of Messianism
double construct phrase; Ch.2; 4.4

(13) אפוא   *therefore, then*
Ch.11; 8

(14) במוקדה   *in its center*
The possessive suffix refers back to
משיחיות (fem.); Ch.2; 5.8

(15) דמותו של מנהיג דתי
the figure of a religious leader
double construct phrase with an
adjective; Ch.2; 4.5.2

(16) בכוח פעילותו
through the power of his action (NOT: forcefully)
Ch.5; 2.1.2, example 19

(17) מהווה   *constitutes*
verbal copula, Ch.7; 4.1

(18) מבקשת   *wishes, seeks*
Ch.11; 4

(19) לשנותו=לשנות אותו   *change it*
The direct object suffix refers to
מרקם; Ch.6; 2.3

(20) שעיקרם   *whose essence*
The possessive suffix refers back to
אמצעים; Ch.2; 5.8

(21) פעילות היסטורית חברתית מקיפה
comprehensive social historical activity;
Stacked adjectives are translated
backwards, Ch.4; 3.2

(22) שנוטלים בה חלק אנשים רבים
in which many people take part
The inflected preposition in the
clause refers to פעילות;
the verb phrase נוטלים חלק precedes
the subject; Ch. 8; 3.4.1

(23) הקשורים ל...ל...ל...גם ל...
that are connected to..., (to)...,(to)...
The preposition required by the
adjective is repeated before each
complement; Ch.8; 3.3

הדוגמה העברית המובהקת ביותר לתופעות אלה **היא**[24] "הִלְכוֹת מְלָכִים" בסוף **מִשְנֵה תורה לרמב"ם — אחת התעודות המשיחיות החשובות ביותר בתולדות המחשבה היהודית**[25]. מסמך זה הנו[3] **תעודה פוליטית מובהקת**[21], **שכל לשונה וכל ענייניה**[26] נעוצים במסגרת המחשבה המדינית.

לטקסטים משיחיים רבים אופייני השימוש במושגים השאובים[8] מן השדה הסמנטי של צבא ומלחמה — נצחונות ותבוסות, קרבות וכלי נשק, מצביאים ומפקדים וכיוצא באלה.

המסרים הפוליטיים, החברתיים, החינוכיים והצבאיים[27] של הטקסט המשיחי מבוססים, **מעצם טבעם**[28], על אמונה ב**כוחה של הלשון**[12] להעביר לקוראיה ולשומעיה משמעות נורמטיבית. **לשונו של הטקסט המשיחי**[15] היא לשון סמנטית – **המביעה**[8] משמעות ואמונה **כי**[11] משמעות זו יכולה וצריכה להיקלט על ידי קהל היעד **המתבקש**[8] לפעול **על פיה**[29]. **מבחינה**[1] זו, הטקסט המשיחי שייך לרובד הלשוני **המאפיין**[8] תחומים רבים מאוד בהבעה הדתית, ובראשם – החקיקה הדתית, ההיסטוריוגרפיה הדתית ואף הנבואה.

the example is **הַדוּגמה...היא** (24)
copula, Ch.7; 1.2

מִשְנֵה תורה לרמב"ם – אחת (25) **התעודות המשיחיות החשובות ביותר בתולדות המחשבה היהודית**
Mishneh Torah by Maimonides – one of the most important messianic documents in the history of Jewish thought
The appositives are signaled with a dash; Ch.1; 8.1.1

שכל לשונה וכל ענייניה (26)
all whose language and concerns
The possessive suffixes refer back to תעודה; Ch.2; 5.8

המסרים הפוליטיים, החברתיים, החינוכיים והצבאיים (27)
the political, social, educational and military messages
coordinated adjectives, all belonging to the -י group;
Ch.4; 3.1, 4.2

מעצם טבעם (28)
by their very nature
Ch.3; Confusables, 3.1

על פיה (29) *according to it*
The preposition merges with the pronoun; the pronoun suffix refers backward to משמעות; Ch.8; 1.1

Clauses whose verb comes before the subject are shaded.

Translation

The characteristics of Jewish Messianism: Messianism as a type of religious leadership

From the viewpoint of the semantic field, Messianism belongs to the domain phenomena that can be included under the heading – leadership. Messianic phenomena are phenomena of religious leadership: the anointing of a person (with the oil of anointment) expresses, in the biblical context, his coronation as a leader. Christianity adopted this concept in order to characterize its spiritual leader, and used the Greek translation for the Hebrew concept "messiah" – Christos. Linguistically, the concepts "Messianism" and "Christianity" are identical, and both clearly refer to a figure of a religious leader. This applies also to Islam – many phenomena that are parallel to Messianism are marked in it by the concept "Mahdi," whose context is clearly one of leadership.

Phenomena of leadership belong, according to the customary disciplinary distribution, to the area of political science. Messianism is therefore a political phenomenon that is anchored in the religious arena. It is possible to say that Messianism is one of the (most) radical expressions of "translating" religious faith and religious life into historical-political activity.

The language of Messianism is, then, first and foremost, a political language. In its center stands the figure of a religious leader who by the power of his activity brings about change of values within the historical reality. He constitutes a focus for a transition from a reality of past-present to a future reality and a new historical plane, which often symbolizes the end of history as we have known it till now. Messianism is an integral part of the historical texture and it seeks to change it with historical means whose essence is the activity of the leader, the messiah.

In many cases, the messiah constitutes in his personality and his message a focus for a comprehensive social historical activity in which many people take part. In these cases, to the "messianic dictionary" are added concepts that are associated with delegation of authority, with social organization, with establishment of a secondary leadership system and hence – sometimes – also with the establishment of an educational system and other social institutions.

The most distinctive Jewish example for these phenomena is the "Laws of Kings" at the end of Mishneh Torah by Maimonides – one of the most important messianic documents in the history of Jewish thought. This document is a distinctive political document whose entire language and interests are rooted within the framework of political thought.

Many messianic texts are typified by the use of terms drawn from the semantic field of army and war – victories and defeats, battles and weaponry, generals and commanders etc.

The political, social, educational and military messages of the messianic text are based by their very nature on belief in the power of language to transmit to its readers and listeners a normative meaning. The language of the messianic text is a semantic language that expresses meaning and belief that this meaning can and should be absorbed by the target audience that is being asked to act according to it. From this point of view, the messianic text belongs to the linguistic stratum that characterizes very many areas of religious expression and primarily – religious legislation, religious historiography and even prophecy.

Practice texts glossary[1]: nouns and adjectives

Nouns[2] שמות

character	אוֹפִי
area, region	אֵזוֹר
mention, reference	אִזְכּוּר
citizen	אֶזְרָח
responsibility	אַחְרָיוּת
event	אֵירוּעַ
personality	אִישִׁיוּת
personalities, personages	אִישִׁים[3]
belief	אֱמוּנָה
means	אֶמְצָעִי
organization, organizing	אִרְגּוּן
choice	בחירה
expression	בּיטוּי
consolidation	בּיסוּס
building	בְּנִיָּיה
basis	בָּסִיס
difficulty, problematicalness	בְּעָיָיתִיּוּת
border(s)	גְּבוּל (גבולות)
cause	גּוֹרֵם
increase, growth	גִידוּל
approach, attitude	גִישָׁה
discussion	דִיוּן
character(s), figure(s); image	דְּמוּת (דמויות)
religion(s)	דָת (דתות)
difference	הֶבְדֵל
expression	הַבָּעָה
definition	הַגְדָּרָה
avoidance	הִימָנְעוּת מִן
achievement	הֶישֵׂג
the masses (of the people)	הֲמוֹנֵי העם
assumption	הַנָחָה
consent	הַסְכָּמָה
bringing up	הַעֲלָאָה
giving	הַעֲנָקָה
employment	הַעֲסָקָה
discrimination	הַפְלָיָה
success	הַצְלָחָה
founding, establishment	הֲקָמָה

---

[1] The translation gives the meaning of the word in the given text; full spelling and partial vocalization were used. For verbs, see Appendix II.
[2] Some (unpredictable) plural forms are given in parentheses.
[3] The singular form has a different meaning: אִישׁ man, person (Ch. 2, 2.2.2(b)).

sacrificing   הַקְרָבָה
context   הֶקְשֵׁר
composition   הֶרְכֵּב
removal, shedding   הַשָׁלָה
omission   הַשְׁמָטה
influence   הַשְׁפָּעה
worldview   הַשְׁקָפת עולם
integration   הִשְׁתַלְבוּת
progression, development   הִשְׁתַלְשְׁלוּת
changing   הִשְׁתַּנוּת
self-separation   הִתבַּדְלוּת
increase   הִתגַּבְּרוּת
consolidation   הִתגַבְּשוּת
settlement   הִתְיַישְׁבוּת
coping with   הִתְמוֹדְדוּת עם
collapse   הִתמוֹטְטוּת
behavior   הִתְנַהֲגוּת
intervention   הִתְעָרְבוּת
assimilation, integration into   הִתְעָרוּת ב
splitting up   הִתפַּצְלוּת
development   הִתפַּתחוּת
identity   זֶהוּת
connection   זיקה
society   חֶבְרָה
obligation   חוֹבה
strengthening   חיזוּק
division, distribution   חֲלוּקה
part, some   חֵלֶק
importance   חֲשׁיבוּת
reason   טַעַם
claim, argument   טַעֲנָה
initiative   יוֹזְמה
relations, relationship   יְחָסים
founding   יִיסוּד
ability   יְכוֹלֶת
basis, foundation   יְסוֹד
stability   יַצִיבוּת
work (of art); creation   יְצירה
emigration from Israel; decrease   יְרידה
entity   יֵשׁוּת
advantage   יִתְרון
heading   כּוֹתֶרֶת
establishment   כינוּן
failure(s)   כִּישָׁלוֹן (כישלונות)
quantity   כַּמוּת
fighting   לְחימה
event(s)   מָאוֹרע (מאורעות)

effort	מַאֲמָץ
characteristic	מְאַפְיֵין
structure	מִבְנֶה
variety	מִגְוָון
trend, tendency	מְגַמָּה
policy	מְדִינִיּוּת
nature, entity	מַהוּת
move	מַהֲלָךְ
expertise	מוּמְחִיּוּת
term	מוּנָח
origin	מוֹצָא
concept	מוּשָׂג
blend	מְזִיגָה
goal	מַטָּרָה
measure, extent	מִידָה
minority	מִיעוּט
level, plane	מִישׁוֹר
establishment	מִמְסָד
finding	מִמְצָא
framework, frame	מִסְגֶּרֶת
tradition	מָסוֹרֶת
document	מִסְמָךְ
voyage	מַסָּע
conclusion	מַסְקָנָה
message	מֶסֶר
status	מַעֲמָד
answer, response	מַעֲנֶה
system, constellation	מַעֲרֶכֶת
gathering, meeting	מִפְגָּשׁ
situation	מַצָּב
distress, suffering	מְצוּקָה
reality	מְצִיאוּת
parallel	מַקְבִּילָה
origin(s), source(s); the original	מָקוֹר (מקורות)
few (of)	מִקְצָת
case	מִקְרֶה
centre	מֶרְכָּז
component	מַרְכִּיב
discipline	מִשְׁמַעַת
tension	מֶתַח
tension	מְתִיחוּת
giving	מַתָּן
prophecy	נְבוּאָה
tendency, inclination	נְטִיָּיה
alienation	ניכּוּר
attempt(s)	ניסיון (ניסיונות)
analysis	ניתוּח

signpost נְקוּדַת צִיּוּן

style סִגְנוֹן

type, kind סוּג

deviation from סְטִיָּה מִן-

reason סִיבָּה

aid, assistance סִיּוּעַ

sign סִימָן

conflict, dispute סִכְסוּךְ

symbolism סֵמְלִיּוּת

poverty עוֹנִי

study, reading עִיּוּן בְּ-

superiority עֶלְיוֹנוּת

immigration; going up; increase עֲלִייָּה

position עֶמְדָּה

the poor עֲנִיִּים

matter, interest עִנְיָין

value עֶרֶךְ (עֲרָכִים)

faction(s) פֶּלֶג (פְּלָגִים)

aspect(s) פַּן, פָּנִים

activity פְּעִילוּת

detail פְּרָט

affair, story פָּרָשָׁה

livelihood פַּרְנָסָה

need(s) צוֹרֶךְ (צְרָכִים)

community קְהִילָה

line קַו

absorption קְלִיטה

end קֵץ

tempo, rate קֶצֶב

economic difficulties (literally: difficulties of survival) קְשָׁיֵי קִיּוּם

connection קֶשֶׁר

feeling(s) רֶגֶשׁ (רְגָשׁוֹת)

persecution(s), oppression רְדִיפוֹת

layer, stratum רוֹבֶד

component רְכִיב

level רָמָה

hint(s) רֶמֶז (רְמָזִים)

background רֶקַע

aspiration שְׁאִיפה

the rest of שְׁאָר הַ-

routine of existence שִׁגְרַת הקיום

stay שְׁהִייָה

belonging שַׁייָכוּת

use שִׁימוּשׁ

change שִׁינּוּי

cooperation שִׁיתּוּף פְעוּלה

stage שָׁלָב

authorities שִׁלְטוֹנוֹת
hatred שִׂנְאָה
plenitude שֶׁפַע
reaction תְּגוּבָה
process תַּהֲלִיךְ
consciousness תּוֹדָעָה
content תּוֹכֶן
phenomenon תּוֹפָעָה
result תּוֹצָאָה
resident תּוֹשָׁב
area, domain תְּחוּם
feeling, sensation תְּחוּשָׁה
competition תַּחֲרוּת
description תֵּיאוּר
document תְּעוּדה
industry תַּעֲשִׂייה
period תְּקוּפָה
culture תַּרְבּוּת (תרבויות)
attention תְּשׂוּמֶת לֵב

Adjectives[4] תארים

characteristic אוֹפְייני
personal אִישִׁיים (אישי)
divine אֱלוֹהי
international בֵּין-לְאוּמִיים (בין-לאומי)
tight, close הָדוּק
reverse הֲפוּכה (הפוך)
identical זֵהים (זֵהֶה)
strange, foreign, alien זר, זרים
social חֶבְרָתִיים (חברתי)
educational חִינוּכי
alternative חֲלִיפִי
agricultural חַקְלָאִית (חקלאי)
natural טִבְעִיים (טבעי)
only יחיד
unique ייחוּדיים (יחודי)
economic כַּלְכָּלִית, כַּלְכָּליים (כלכלי)
general כְּלָלִיוֹת (כללי)
national לְאוּמִית (לאומי)
linguistic לְשׁוֹנִית (לשוני)
established מְבוּסָסוֹת (מבוסס)
varied מְגֻוָּוֹנוֹת (מגוון)
rapid מְהִירה (מהיר)

---

[4] The adjectives are presented in the form(s) in which they appear in the text; the singular masculine (if different) is given in parentheses.

distinctive מוּבְהֶקֶת (מובהק)

absolute מוּחְלָטִים (מוחלט)

talented מוּכְשָׁר

small, scanty, few מוּעָטִים (מועט)

binding מְחַיֶּיבֶת (מחייב)

disconnected מְנוּתָקִים (מנותק)

certain, specific מְסוּיָם

anchored מְעוּגָּן

integrated מְעוֹרָה

unstable מְעוּרְעָר

parallel מַקְבִּילִים (מקביל)

accepted, popular, common, usual מְקוּבָּל

local מְקוֹמִיּוֹת (מקומי)

linked, connected מְקוּשָּׁרִים לְ- (מקושר)

comprehensive מַקִּיפָה, מַקִּיפוֹת (מקיף)

professional מִקְצוֹעִיִּים (מקצועי)

biblical מִקְרָאִי

conjectured מְשׁוֹעָר

common, shared מְשׁוּתָּף

significant מַשְׁמָעוּתִי, משמעותיים

secondary מִשְׁנִי

expanding מִתְרַחֶבֶת (מתרחב)

faithful נֶאֱמָן

additional נוֹסָף, נוֹסָפִים

widespread נָפוֹץ, נפוצה

eternal נִצְחִי

extensive נִרְחֶבֶת (נרחב)

sublime נִשְׂגָּב

in proximity to, close to סְמוּכִים לְ- (סמוך)

main, principle עִיקָרִיִּים, עִיקָרִיּוֹת (עיקרי)

contemporary עַכְשָׁווִי

popular, folk- עֲמָמִית (עממי)

less than פְּחוּתָה (פָּחוּת)

internal פְּנִימִיִּים (פנימי)

literal, simplistic פְּשָׁטָנִי

holy קָדוֹשׁ

previous קוֹדְמוֹת (קודם)

great רַבָּה (רב)

well-known, usual שְׁגוּרוֹת (שגור)

equal שָׁווֶה

different שׁוֹנָה, שׁוֹנִים

common שְׁכִיחוֹת (שכיח)

negative שְׁלִילִי

demanding תּוֹבְעָנִי

valid תְּקֵפוֹת (תָּקֵף)

cultural תַּרְבּוּתִיִּים (תרבותי)

APPENDIXES

NUMERICAL VALUES OF THE LETTERS OF THE ALPHABET
AND
THE CONVERSION OF A HEBREW DATE (YEARS) TO A GREGORIAN
CALENDAR DATE

The use of the letters of the alphabet as numerals in Hebrew is ancient and predates the use of Arabic numerals. Nowadays, letters are used instead of numerals to mark pages and chapters in religious texts and to indicate the Hebrew date.

1. Converting letters into numerical values

As seen in the chart below, the numbers 1–9 are represented by the first nine letters, from א to ט, the numbers 10–90 are represented by the next nine letters, י to צ, and 100–400 are represented by ק to ת.

9=ט	8=ח	7=ז	6=ו	5=ה	4=ד	3=ג	2=ב	1=א
90=צ	80=פ	70=ע	60=ס	50=נ	40=מ	30=ל	20=כ	10=י
					400=ת	300=ש	200=ר	100=ק

1.1 Written from high to low, the letters combine to create numbers up to 999, which would be represented by the sequence תתקצט: ת=400 + ת=400 + ק=100 + צ=90 + ט=9.

1.2 Note that the numbers 15 and 16 are written as 9+6 (ט"ו) and 9+7 (ט"ז), respectively, to avoid creating letter sequences that signify God's name.

1.3 To indicate thousands (as might be needed for dates), letters followed by inverted commas are used. For example, the year 5,708 to the creation of the world according to Jewish tradition is ה'תש"ח.

2. Converting Hebrew calendar dates into Gregorian calendar dates

To convert a date specified in Hebrew letters to its Gregorian calendar equivalent, two steps are necessary:

(a) In dates beginning with 'ה (five thousands count to the creation of the world according to Jewish tradition), the thousands are ignored and each of the remaining letters are added up according to their numerical value.

---

[1] The appendix was researched and drafted by Ms. Orna Goldman.

(b) 1240 is added to the sum total (for dates before 1,000 C.E. only 240 is added).

For example: ה׳תש"ח adds up to 400 + 300 + 8 = 708 + 1240 = 1948.

2.1 Note that the Jewish year begins about four months before the non-Jewish year. For example: a Hebrew date in September 2010 is marked as תשע"א, that is, 2011. The calendar years overlap beginning January 1st.

3. Writing and pronunciation conventions of letters used as numerals

3.1 When page and chapter numbers are shown as letters, those letters are read in full. For example, page 3 is shown as ג and read *gimmel*. Psalm 116 is shown as קטז and read *kof* (or *kuf*) *tet zain* (as per the rule for 16 in 1.2 above).

3.2 When the letter is part of a phrase, it is marked with an inverted comma and the name of the letter is read in full. For example: ג׳ יום *yom gimmel* (Tuesday). When more than one letter is involved, inverted commas appear before the last letter and all letters are read out from high to low. For example: ל"ו צדיקים *lamed vav zaddikim (36 righteous men)*, י"א באדר *yod aleph be'Adar* (eleventh day of [the month of] Adar).

3.3 Years are sometimes read as words. For example, תש"ח may be read either *taf shin xet* or *tashax*; the Cossack massacres of 1648–49 are referred to as גזירות ת"ח ות"ט *g'zerot tax ve tat* (rather than *taf xet ve taf tet*). Some dates lend themselves to word play; thus the Aliya of Yemenite Jews in 1881 – תרמ"ב – was called "עֲלִיַּית אֲעֶלֶה בְתָמָר," the word בתמר *in a palm tree* deriving from a reordering of the date letters תרמ"ב → בתמר.[2]

---

[2] wikipedia.org/wiki/הלוח_העברי.

APPENDIX II
GLOSSARY OF VERBS COMMONLY FOUND IN ACADEMIC TEXTS[1]
מילון פעלים נפוצים בכתיבה אקדמית

אָזְכֵּר refer to
אוזכר

איחד unite
אוחד

אימץ adopt
אומץ

איפשר make possible
התאפשר

אישש confirm
אוشש

איתר locate
אותר

אָפְיֵּן characterize
אופיין, התאפיין

בדק check, examine
נבדק

בחן examine
נבחן

בחר choose
נבחר

בֵּיאֵר interpret, explain
בואר, התבאר

ביטא express
בוטא, התבטא

ביסס על base on
בוסס, התבסס

ביצע carry out, execute
בוצע, התבצע

בֵּירר look into, inquire

ביקש demand; wish, seek

בלט stand out

ברא create
נברא

גוֹלֵל unfold

גילה discover
התגלה

---

[1] The verbs are shown in the past tense singular masculine form (full spelling and partial pointing are used); the English equivalent is given in the present tense. The passive form – if in general use – appears (indented) below the active form of the verb.

גילם embody
גולם, התגלם
גרם ל- cause
נגרם
גרס be of the opinion, maintain
גרש expel
גורש
דחה reject
נדחה
דן ב discuss
נדון
הֶאֱפִיל על overshadow
הִבְהִיר clarify
הובהר
הִבְחִין distinguish; notice
הִבִּיע express
הובע
הִבְלִיט stress, emphasize, make conspicuous
הובלט
הִגְבִּיל limit
הוגבל
הִגְדִּיר define
הוגדר
הִגִּישׁ present, submit, deliver
הוגש
הִגְשִׁים realize, carry out, execute
הוגשם, התגשם
הִדְגִּים illustrate, demonstrate
הודגם
הִדְגִּישׁ emphasize, stress
הודגש
הוֹבִיל lead
הובל
הוֹכִיחַ prove
הוכח
הוֹפִיע appear
הוֹקִיר respect, hold dear
הִזְדַּהָה עם identify oneself with
הִזְכִּיר mention
הוזכר
הֶחֱזִיק ב- hold; maintain, belive
הֶחֱלִיף change, exchange
הוחלף
הֶחֱרִיב destroy
הוחרב
הֵטִיל impose
הוטל

stress, emphasize הִטְעִים
הוטעם

know, recognize הִכִּיר
ניכר

determine, decide הִכְרִיעַ
הוכרע

deny, contradict הכחיש
הוכחש

demonstrate, make concrete הִמְחִישׁ
הומחש

guide הִנְחָה
הונחה

place; suppose, assume הִנִּיחַ
conclude הִסִּיק (מסקנה)
begin to show signs, become apparent הִסְתַּמֵּן
rely on הִסְתַּמֵּךְ עַל
testify to, affirm הֵעִיד עַל
comment on הֵעִיר עַל
raise הֶעֱלָה
הועלה

inform about הֶעֱמִיד עַל
grant, endow, give הֶעֱנִיק
הוענק

intensify הֶעֱצִים
הועצם

produce הֵפִיק
הופק

become, turn into הָפַךְ לְ-
internalize הִפְנִים
הופנם

activate הִפְעִיל
הופעל

point at הִצְבִּיעַ עַל
justify הִצְדִּיק
הוצדק

join הִצְטָרֵף
place, pose הִצִּיב
הוצב

present הִצִּיג
הוצג

propose, suggest הִצִּיעַ
הוצע

dedicate, devote הִקְדִּישׁ
הוקדש

establish, found הֵקִים
הוקם

make easy, facilitate	הֵקֵל
	הוּקַל
provide, impart, instill	הִקְנָה
	הוּקְנָה
excel in; be distinguished by	הִצְטַיֵּן בּ-
compare	הִשְׁוָוה
	הוּשְׁוָוה
achieve, obtain	הִשִּׂיג
	הוּשַּׂג
succeed	הִשְׂכִּיל (לַעֲשׂוֹת)
influence	הִשְׁפִּיעַ עַל
	הוּשְׁפַּע מִן
invest	הִשְׁקִיעַ
	הוּשְׁקַע
fit in	הִשְׁתַּבֵּץ בּ-
try hard, make an effort	הִשְׁתַּדֵּל
belong to	הִשְׁתַּיֵּיךְ לְ-
integrate	הִשְׁתַּלֵּב בּ-
be implied	הִשְׁתַּמַּע מִן
be reflected in	הִשְׁתַּקֵּף בּ-
base, found on	הִשְׁתִּית עַל
	הוּשְׁתַּת עַל
contemplate, consider	הִתְבּוֹנֵן בּ-
stand out	הִתְבַּלֵּט
become clear that	הִתְבָּרֵר שׁ-/כִּי
consolidate, crystalize	הִתְגַּבֵּשׁ
come into being, form	הִתְהַוָּוה
be added	הִתְוַוסֵף
take place, occur; break out	הִתְחוֹלֵל
blend into	הִתְמַזֵּג בּ-
trace, examine closely	הִתְחַקָּה עַל/אַחֲרֵי
refer to, relate to	הִתְיַיחֵס לְ-/אֶל
grapple with, cope; compete	הִתְמוֹדֵד עִם
focus on	הִתְמַקֵּד בּ-
proceed, be conducted	הִתְנַהֵל
experience	הִתְנַסָּה
disengage, severe oneself from	הִתְנַתֵּק מִן
ignore	הִתְעַלֵּם מִן
be weakened	הִתְעַרְעֵר
develop	הִתְפַּתַּח
be accepted	הִתְקַבֵּל
take place	הִתְרַחֵשׁ
focus on	הִתְרַכֵּז בּ-
take shape	הִתְרַקֵּם
ascertain, confirm	וִויִדֵּא
identify	זִיהָה
	זוּהָה

receive, merit, win, achieve   זָכָה בְּ-/לְ-

cease   חָדַל

enter, penetrate   חָדַר

experience   חָוָוה
נֶחֱווה

connect; compose   חִיבֵּר
חובר

strengthen   חִיזֵק
חוזק

research, study   חָקַר
נחקר

expose, uncover   חָשַׂף
נחשף

be apprehensive of   חָשַׁשׁ מִן

take care of, treat   טִיפֵּל בְּ-
טופל

argue, claim   טָעַן
נטען

attribute, ascribe   יִיחֵס לְ-
יוחס לְ-

represent   יִיצֵג
יוצג

manufacture, produce   יִיצֵר
יוצר

apply   יִישֵׂם
יושם

establish, found   יָסַד
נוסד

create   יָצַר
נוצר

conquer   כָּבַשׁ
נכבש

establish, found   כּוֹנֵן

call a name   כִּינָה
כונה

include   כָּלַל
נכלל

enforce   כָּפָה
נכפה

clarify   לִיבֵּן
לובן

unite   לִיכֵּד
לוכד

be aware of   (היה) מוּדָע לְ-

dissolve   מוֹסֵס
התמוסס

classify   מִיֵּן
מוין

map out   מִיפָּה
מופה

focus on   מִיקֵד
התמקד ב-

locate   מִיקֵם
מוקם

exhaust   מִיצָה
מוצה, התמצה

realize, make come true   מִימֵשׁ
מומש

prevent   מָנַע

hand over, transmit   מָסַר
נמסר

originate, derive from   נָבַע מִן

turn into   נֶהְפַּךְ לְ-

be added   נוֹסַף

remain   נוֹתַר

mention   נִזְכַּר

refer to, discuss, treat (a matter, an issue, an argument)   נִזְקַק לְ(עניין, סוגיה, טענה)

be considered as   נֶחְשַׁב לְ-/כְ-

tend to   נָטָה לְ-

assimilate   נִטְמַע בְּ-

be present in   נָכַח בְּ-

be endowed with   נֵיחַן

give a reason, substantiate   נִימֵק
נומק

try   נִיסָה
נוסה

stand   נִיצָב

analyze   נִיתַח
נותח

fail   נִכְשַׁל

escape   נִמְלַט

be counted among, belong   נִמְנָה עִם

avoid, refrain from   נִמְנַע (מִן)

move   נָע

disappear   נֶעֱלַם

become   נַעֲשָׂה לְ-

it appears that   נִרְאָה שֶׁ-

bear, carry; marry   נָשָׂא

remain   נִשְׁאַר

classify   סִיוֵוג
סווג

summarize   סִיכֵּם
סוכם

symbolize סִימֵל
סומל

mark, signal סִימֵן
סומן

survey סָקַר
נסקר

contradict סָתַר
נסתר

read, study; consider, weigh -עִיֵּן ב
form, shape עִיצֵב
עוצב

mix; involve -עִירֵב ב
-עורב ב

discuss; point out עמד על
engage in, deal with, practice (a profession) -עָסַק ב
set, arrange, hold (an event); edit עָרַךְ
נֶעֱרַךְ

prepare for -נערך ל
object, disagree, doubt, refute עִרְעֵר על
interpret, explain פֵּירֵשׁ
פורש, התפרש

harm, injure -פָּגַע ב
נפגע

act פָּעַל

doubt -פִּקְפֵּק ב
detail פֵּירֵט
פורט

develop פיתח
פותח

quote, cite צִיטֵט
צוטט

indicate צִיֵּן
צוין

draw צִייֵר
צויר

expect צִיפָּה
state, determine; fix קָבַע
נקבע

come before, precede -קָדַם ל
fulfill; hold (an event); maintain קִייֵם
קוים

bring close קֵירֵב
קורב

absorb, take in; comprehend קָלַט
נקלט

happen קָרָה

tie, connect   קָשַׁר
נקשר
heal   רִפֵּא
רופא, התרפא
allude to, hint   רָמַז על\ל
נרמז
write down   רָשַׁם
set, place, lend   שִׁיוָּה ל-
attribute, ascribe   שִׁיֵּיךְ
שוייך
integrate   שִׁילֵּב
שולב
serve as   (כ) שִׁימֵּשׁ
surmise, hypothesize   שִׁיעֵר
שוער
serve   שֵׁירֵת
dwell   שָׁכַן
rule   שָׁלַט
נשלט
negate, deny, contradict   שָׁלַל
נשלל
reflect   שִׁיקֵּף
השתקף
sketch   שִׂרְטֵט
שורטט
prevail, exist   שָׂרַר
demand, require; sue   תָּבַע
נתבע
document   תִּיעֵד
תועד
describe   תֵּיאֵר
תואר
date (a document, an archeological finding)   תִּאְרֵךְ
תוארך
correct; pass/institute an ordinance   תִּיקֵּן
תוקן
distill, summarize   תִּמְצֵת
תומצת
grasp, understand, comprehend, view   תָּפַס/תפש
נתפס/נתפש
contribute   תָּרַם
נתרם

REFERENCES

אבינרי, יצחק. "תואר הפועל בעברית." *לשוננו לעם,* יג, קונטרס ד קכ"ו. תשכ"ב. 97–123.

אורנן, עוזי. "ניתוח מכני והוראת התחביר." *לשוננו,* כג, ד. תשי"ט-9–1958. 243–257.

—— "האנגלית מבעד לעברית." *הארץ.* "תרבות וספרות." ל' בניסן תש"ס. 5.5.2000.

אילני, נגה. "זיהוי והגדרתו של המושא הפנימי בעברית החדשה." *ספר בן ציון פישלר: מחקרים בלשון העברית ובהוראתה.* עורכים: אורה (רודריג) שורצולד ורפאל ניר. אבן יהודה: הוצאת רכס. 2001. 153–162.

אלון, עמנואל. "פסוקיות זיקה ופסוקיות תוכן בעברית הישראלית." תמסיר להרצאה Austin, Texas: NAPH. 2004.

בליבום ריקי. *תחביר +.* ירושלים: אקדמון. תשנ"ה-1995.

בן-אשר, מרדכי. *עיונים בתחביר העברית החדשה.* תל אביב: הוצאת הקיבוץ המאוחד. תשל"ג-1972.

בן-חיים, זאב. "לשון עתיקה במציאות חדשה." *במלחמתה של לשון.* ירושלים: האקדמיה ללשון העברית, המכון לטיפוח העברית. תשנ"ב-1992. 36–85.

ברי, נמרוד. "שם-תואר מועצם ושם-עצם מותאר בעברית חדשה דיבורית." *העברית בת-זמננו.* עורך: שלמה מורג. ירושלים: אקדמון. תשמ"ח-1988. 445–465.

גלינרט, אליעזר. "התנאי הבטל בעברית החדשה." *דברי הקונגרס העולמי השמיני למדעי היהדות* ירושלים. חטיבה ד. תשמ"ב. פרסומי האיגוד העולמי למדעי היהדות. תשמ"ב-1981. 51–55.

דורון, עידית. "לסוגיית כינוי הגוף הכפול." *בלשנות עברית, 36.* 3–1991. 65–70.

הלוי, רבקה. *עברי בדגש לקסיקלי.* ירושלים: אקדמון. תשנ"ד-1984.

—— "הרכבים בעלי תחיליות או סופיות סמנטיות." (תמסיר הרצאה), השתלמות מורי אוניברסיטאות מחו"ל, ירושלים: האוניברסיטה העברית. (7.1.2003).

ורטהיימר, עדה. "עיונים נוספים במשפטים מבוקעים." *בלשנות עברית. 49.* תשס"א. 21–34.

חרל"פ, לובה. "הלכה ומציאות בפיסוק העברי." *Journal of Hebrew Higher Education,* 10. 2002. pp. 151–159.

טרומר, פנינה. "הפועל האוגדי במשפטים שמניים." *בלשנות עברית, 44.* תשנ"ט. 33–46.

מוצ'ניק, מלכה. "המושא החבור בעיתונות." *העברית שפה חיה: קובץ מחקרים על הלשון בהקשריה החברתיים-תרבותיים.* עורכים: עוזי אורנן, רינה בן-שחר וגדעון טורי. חיפה: הוצאת הספרים של אוניברסיטת חיפה. תשנ"ג-1992. 119–128.

עבאדי, עדינה. *תחביר השיח של העברית החדשה.* ירושלים: מאגנס, האוניברסיטה העברית. תשמ"ח.

צדקה, יצחק. *מחקרים בתחביר ובסמנטיקה.* באר שבע: הוצאת הספרים של אוניברסיטת בן-גוריון בנגב. תשנ"ח-1997.

—— "מילות יחס מצורכות: בחינה מחודשת." *דברי הקונגרס האחד עשר למדעי היהדות* . חטיבה ד, כרך ראשון: הלשון העברית, לשונות היהודים ירושלים. האיגוד העולמי למדעי היהדות. תשנ"ד-1993. 109–116.

—— *תחביר העברית בימינו.* ירושלים: קרית ספר. תשמ"א-1981.

קדרי, צבי. "תואר הפועל בעברית המודרנית." *הוראה, אקדמית של העברית בת-זמננו: דברי הסדנה א.* עורך: רפאל ניר. ירושלים : המרכז הבין-ארצי להוראת תרבות ישראל באוניברסיטאות. 79–65. תשמ"ה-1985.

רודריג (שורצולד), אורה. "הערות אחדות על נטיות "יש" ו"אין" קיומיות בעברית המדוברת." *העברית בת זמננו.* עורך: שלמה מורג. ירושלים: אקדמון. תשמ"ח. 480–491.

—— "לשימושי המקור המוחלט בעברית החדשה" *לשוננו,* נ"ג, חוברות 1–2, תשמ"ט. 107–112.

—— *פרקים בתולדות הלשון העברית, יחידות 9–10,* תל אביב: האוניברסיטה הפתוחה. תשנ"ד-1994. 101–104.

רודריג-שוורצולד אורה ומיכאל סוקולוף. *מילון למונחי בלשנות ודקדוק.* אבן יהודה: רכס. תשנ"ב.

רוזן, חיים. "אספקטים בחקר סדרי חלקי המשפט בעברית הישראלית הכתובה." *דברי הקונגרס השמיני למדעי היהדות.* חטיבה ד. האיגוד העולמי למדעי היהדות. ירושלים תשמ"ב. 39–43.

שלזינגר, יצחק. *לשונות העיתון,* באר שבע: אוניברסיטת בן-גוריון בנגב. 2000.

—— *פרקים בתולדות הלשון העברית, יחידה 11,* תל אביב: האוניברסיטה הפתוחה. 1994.

Adler, Rutie. *Zeh Lo Nora: Reference book for students of Hebrew.* Eugene, Oregon: Wisp & Stock Publishers. 2006.

Berman, A. R. "The case of an (s)vo language: Subject less constructions in modern Hebrew." *Language,* 56(4). 1980. pp. 759–776.

Celce-Murcia, M. & Larsen-Freeman, D. *The Grammar Book* (second edition). NY: Heinle & Heinle. 1999.

Coffin E. A. & Bolozky, S. A. *Reference Grammar of Modern Hebrew.* Cambridge: Cambridge University Press. 2005.

Glinert, L. *The Grammar of Modern Hebrew.* Cambridge: Cambridge University Press. 1989.

Muraoka, T. *Modern Hebrew for Biblical Scholars.* Wiesbaden. Harrassowitz Verlag. 1996.

Ornan. Uzzi. "Hebrew Grammar." *Encyclopedia Judaica.* Second edition, volume 8. Detroit: Thomson Gale, 2007. pp. 654–618.

Quirk, R. & S. Greenbaum. *A Concise Grammar of Contemporary English.* NY: Harcourt Brace Jovanovich. 1975.

Rav Milim. Online dictionary. Melingo Ltd. <www.ravmilim.co.il>.

Richards, C. J., Platt, J. & Platt, H. *Dictionary of Language Teaching and Applied Linguistics.* Singapore: Longman Singapore Publishers. 1992.

Rosen, Ḥaiim B. *A Textbook of Israeli Hebrew.* Second edition. Chicago: University of Chicago Press. 1966.

Schwarzwald, R. O. Modern Hebrew. *Lincom Europa: Languages of the World/ Materials* 127. 2001.

Weingreen. *A Practical Grammar for classical Hebrew.* Second edition. Oxford University Press 1959.

SUBJECT INDEX

INDEX OF HEBREW WORDS

The entries are shown (and alphabetized) by their full spelling, the form in which they are likely to appear in modern academic texts. As an aid to pronunciation, partial pointing was added.

Item location in the book is indicated by chapter and section, as follows: (a) the chapter number is bolded and separated by a comma from the section number; (b) section numbers within the same chapter are separated by commas; (c) a semicolon separates chapter numbers.

Example: אַךְ **1**, 6.1, Confusables, 4; **10**, 2.1, 3

Explanation: אַךְ is discussed twice in Chapter 1 (in section 6.1 and in section 4 of the Confusables) and twice in Chapter 10 (in sections 2.1 and 3).

Grammatical information (when provided) appears in brackets.